Personality:
A Systems Approach

Edition 1.8

John D. Mayer

This book was previously published by *Pearson Education, Inc.*

RUBBER DUCK PUBLISHING

Durham, New Hampshire

Personality: A Systems Approach

Edition 1.8

John D. Mayer

This book was previously published by *Pearson Education, Inc.*

ISBN-13: 9780990667827

To my family...
JDM

PERSONALITY PSYCHOLOGY:
A SYSTEMS APPROACH

Table of Contents in Brief

Table of Contents in Detail

About Editions 1.5 and 1.8

Dear Students and Instructors,

Editions 1.5 and 1.8 of *Personality: A Systems Approach* represent key updates relative to the first edition of the textbook. With each edition, I made substantial changes to the book, rewriting sections to improve the reading experience, and adding in more contemporary research.

I have been able to provide updates to the book in a more flexible fashion than has been possible in the past owing to the advantages provided by online publishing. To reflect that flexibility, I have numbered the editions "software style," designating each release with its own increment number.

I introduced Edition 1.5 in the summer of 2014 to provide an alternative to the original 1st edition. The original publisher had run low in stock of the 1st Edition; Edition 1.5 provided not only a much-needed update of the material, but allowed for the printing of a new edition.

Edition 1.8 is a substantial update of Edition 1.5, picking up with further rewriting, reformatting, and updates.

I hope you enjoy these editions.

Best,

Jack

John (Jack) D. Mayer

Preface for Students

Personality: A Systems Approach (Editions 1.5 and 1.8)

Dear Students,

I wrote this book in order to provide you with the very best textbook in personality psychology that I could imagine. The book has been motivated by my own lifelong curiosity about—and deep caring for—the field of personality psychology, as well as my optimism regarding the future of the field.

The most typical way to teach personality psychology today is by covering a series of theoretical perspectives on personality first laid out in the early to mid-20th century by figures such as Sigmund Freud, Carl Jung, Carl Rogers, and others. With such books, a student learns the psychodynamic approach, the trait approach, and other theoretical approaches covered in Chapter 3 of this book. The problem with such an approach, to me, is that it relies on a somewhat outmoded, early 20th century way of thinking about psychology.

The present textbook employs a new scientific framework that uses all the above theories together to focus on a single, integrated picture of personality. The textbook and the new scientific framework were developed together. As I developed this book, I wrote a series of journal articles addressed to my colleagues about how the field should be reorganized, and why. That new outline, which I called the *Personality Systems Framework* for the field, divides the study of personality into four major topics:

What (and where) is personality? Personality is in the person somewhere, perhaps, but where more precisely?

What are personality's parts? Shyness? Sociability? Emotionality?

How are those parts organized into a whole? How is personality structured, and what sorts of dynamics take place within it?

Finally, how do the parts and the whole develop and change over time?

These four topics: Defining personality, learning about its parts, its organization, and its development, can provide an overview of the whole field of personality psychology, and the four parts of this textbook mirror those four topics.

In the process of publishing the theoretical articles that developed these topics, I received a great deal of peer review—colleagues commenting on my articles, sometimes positively, and sometimes negatively. That peer review allowed me to rethink areas of the outline that needed rethinking, revise my ideas, and, in a couple of cases, publish new articles that the field needed before a book such as this could be written.

As you read and study personality psychology with this book, you can be confident that you will enjoy:

The Liberal Use of Case Examples. Wherever possible, examples of personality are drawn from real people's lives.

A Variety of Study Aids, Including:

An Advanced List of Key Points for Each Chapter

A Carefully Developed Glossary

Study Questions at the Conclusion of Each Chapter

In addition to my own ideas, this textbook reflects the comments, needs, and hopes of students who have taken the personality course with me in past years. I hope you will find this book interesting, inspiring, and to those who continue to study in the area, an ongoing resource in understanding the field!

~John (Jack) D. Mayer, June 21st, 2015

Preface for Instructors

Personality: A Systems Approach (Editions 1.5 and 1.8)

A Vision

When the discipline of psychology was founded in the 1880s, Wilhelm Wundt, who established the first laboratory in the field, conducted experiments on human perception and memory—but he had a vision of the future. Wundt foresaw that one day personality psychologists would integrate findings about psychology into a broad picture of an individual's mental life (Wundt, 1897). As a group, psychology's founders hoped that, from the study of our mental lives, an integrated picture of personality would emerge that would begin to answer important questions such as: "Who am I?" and "How should I live my life?" (Alexander, 1941; Allport, 1937; Greebie, 1932; Wundt, 1897).

Maintaining that vision throughout the field's history has been challenging. The advent of the grand theories of personality during the early part of the 20th century—those of Sigmund Freud, Carl Jung, and Henry Murray—captured the imagination of many scholars. Yet as enticing as those grand theories were, they diverted attention from the painstaking, gradual accumulation of research findings in the field. Many courses on personality psychology became courses about the personality theories of Freud, Jung, Maslow, and others (e.g., Hall & Lindzey, 1978). Each theory used a different terminology and many of them denied the validity of the other theories. Moreover, a sense of how to reintegrate the accumulating research in the field—and how to teach it—was lost (e.g., Mendelsohn, 1993).

With so many competing theories, a return to a unified picture of personality and to the original vision of the field became increasingly difficult and for various reasons it would take the greater part of the 20th century to resolve.

To be sure, there were attempts to reintegrate the field: Robert Sears (1950) laid out the topics he believed one should study when looking at a whole system like personality: "Structure, Dynamics, and Development." Unfortunately, the terms he employed went undefined, and even those psychologists who wanted to use his approach were confused as to how to apply his vision (e.g., Messick, 1961).

In the over half-century since Sears' simple formula, several advances occurred that eased the way toward a new integration of the field.

The first advance was the recognition that the grand theories of personality are not as contradictory as they first seemed. In fact, many of the theories have been translated into one another's terminology: as examples, Freudian "transference" has been translated into the social-cognitive idea of significant-other schemas, and Jungian extraversion paved the way for today's dimensions of the broad trait of extraversion (e.g., Dollard & Miller, 1950; Erdelyi, 1980; Mayer, 1993-1994; 1995a; 1995b; 1998; 2001; 2004; Westen, 1991; 1998).

A second advance was the emergence of a new and sizeable research base so that when people describe what is known about personality apart from the earlier grand theories, there is now a fair amount to say.

A third change has been the development of unifying frameworks for the field. My development of the personality framework used in this book is one of those key approaches. The framework allows for personality to be discussed as a system without the constraints of general systems theory, cybernetics, and similar approaches. Rather, talking about personality as a system can be done simply and directly according to four topics: personality's definition, parts, organization, and development (Mayer, 1993-1994; Mayer & Allen, 2013). Other psychologists have kindly reviewed the framework, sometimes expressing reservations, but always helpfully, strengthening it along the way (e.g., Craik, 1998; Emmons, 1998; Funder, 1998; 2002; Hogan, 1998; McAdams, 1998; Singer, 1998; Tennen & Affleck, 1998; Sheldon, 2011).

In 2007, when the first edition of this text was published by Allyn & Bacon (Pearson Education), I wrote that it was my hope that the textbook would become a touchstone in the reorganization—and revitalization—of the field of personality psychology. Changing the discipline from a theories-based to a more integrated approach has taken longer than I had hoped, but it is plainly taking place. Over the past several years, I have gratefully responded to a number of invitations to write further about the framework (Mayer & Korogodsky, 2012; Mayer & Allen, 2013; Mayer & Lang, 2011; Mayer, 2014). Other personality psychologists have offered alternative integrated approaches independent of the personality systems framework, but I continue to believe that personality framework used here provides a well-thought-out and key approach to the discipline.

Organization of the Book and the Course

Personality psychology is often taught today by examining a number of theoretical perspectives on the system such as the psychodynamic, behavioral, trait, and so on. This leads to a fragmented approach—and one that becomes strained when attempting to fit in current research.

PERSONALITY: A SYSTEMS APPROACH evolved from an intentional re-focusing on the central mission of personality psychology: To describe directly the personality system and its major psychological subsystems. The framework that organizes this textbook divides the study of personality into four areas. These proceed from: (a) describing personality and the discipline of personality psychology, to (b) examining personality's parts, (c) personality's organization, and (d) personality's development. The framework's four topics, and the chapters that accompany each, appear in Table PF-1.

Table PF-1: The Four Topics of This Book and the Organization of Chapters Within Them			
Introductory Issues	*Parts of Personality*	*Personality Organization*	*Personality Development*
1. What Is Personality? 2. Research in Personality Psychology 3. Perspectives on Personality	4. Motivation and Emotion 5. Interior Selves; Interior Worlds 6. Mental Abilities and Navigating the World 7. The Conscious Self	8. How the Parts of Personality Fit Together 9. Dynamics of Action 10. Dynamics of Self-Control	11. Personality Development in Childhood and Adolescence 12. Personality Development in Adulthood

Using the Book

One natural concern for an instructor is: How much time will it take to use this new book, and how easy is it to convert to this new organization? Two qualities make it relatively easy to convert to this new approach. First, the book represents change primarily in the organization rather than content of the course. This means that instructors can use many materials from their existing course—just in a new order. Second, a variety of materials are available to assist instruction with the course that make the switch as easy as possible—including a complete set of lecture outlines in PowerPoint.

"The counterpoint of specialization is always organization—organization is what brings specialists…into a working relationship with other specialists for a complete and useful result." – John Kenneth Galbraith (1908-2006)

Using Current Lectures in a New Order

The first aspect of the book that makes a switch convenient is that most lectures commonly employed in a theories approach can be used with this new book. Examples of some common lectures from personality psychology that can be employed with only modest modification are shown in Table PF-2. Topics as lectures on Freudian defense mechanisms, Murray's Thematic Apperception Test, Jung's archetypes, and Costa and McCrae's Big Five fit into Chapters 10, 4, 5, and 8, respectively.

Table PF-2: How Perspectives-Oriented Lectures (e.g., Psychodynamic, Trait, Humanistic, etc.) Can Be Used With This Book	
Common Perspectives-Oriented Lecture Topic(s) in Personality Psychology	*The Lecture Topic Can Be Used in Chapter:*
Defining personality and describing the field	1: What Is Personality?
Reliability and validity	2: Research in Personality Psychology
Introduction to psychodynamic, trait, humanistic, socio-cognitive, and other perspectives	3: Perspectives on Personality
Murray's TAT; Eysenck's model of neuroticism and extroversion	4: Motivation and Emotions
Kelly's personal constructs; Jung's archetypes; Markus' possible selves; Higgins' ideal and actual selves	5: Interior Selves; Interior Worlds
Adler's creative personality; standard lecture on intelligence	6: Mental Abilities and Navigating the World
Freud's ego; Jung's ego; free will versus determinism	7: The Conscious Self
The Big Five traits; Mischel's model of person-situation interactions; MacLean's Triune brain; the conscious versus unconscious	8: How the Parts of Personality Fit Together
Mood-congruent phenomenon; Interaction of motives; personal strivings; personal projects; latent versus manifest content of behavior	9: Dynamics of Action
Freud's mechanisms of defense; hypnotic phenomena; feedback loops; auto-suggestion	10: Dynamics of Self-Control
Erikson's eight stages of development; attachment theory; birth order; the identity crisis	11: Personality Development in Childhood and Adolescence
Levinson's stages of adult development; adult relationships and marriage; Maslow's self-actualized person; Erikson's generativity versus despair	12: Personality Development in Adulthood

Advantages of the Organization

The new outline employed here permits a rational progression of study that focuses on the best elements of the field, while employing a clear, organized pedagogy. The resulting advantages include holding student interest, coping with students from different majors, and focusing on the best of the field. Examples of how the text addresses the challenges of teaching the personality course are outlined in Table PF-3.

Table PF-3: Some Advantages of the Systems Approach in the Classroom		
The issue in brief	*How it plays out in the course*	*How this text addresses the issue*
Raising the interest level...	Students become bored with coverage of one theorist after another, or one experimental research topic after another.	This book shifts the focus from theory and research to the personality system itself. The book's organization covers favorite student topics from emotions to hypnosis to the unconscious. It also includes the liberal use of case examples to illustrate material.
Different student interests...	Some students want to understand theories of personality. Others, with more science background, want to learn about research studies.	Both the theory and empirical research of personality are integrated and applied to the topics of personality.
Improving the presentation of the field...	Students feel let down by contradictions among theories.	The book selects the most plausible and best-supported theoretical work in the discipline and the research relevant to it.
Addressing commonly used statistics in the field...	A lot of personality psychology nowadays involves discussion of advanced mathematics such as factor analysis.	The book teaches students how to read mathematical techniques such as factor analysis. The "reading research" treatments are carefully worked over to ensure their clarity, and are presented at a level accessible to most students.
Students want to learn something about their lives...	Students face the developmental task of fitting into the world occupationally, and of creating bonds with others. They look to this course for answers...	Students learn about how personality relates to life throughout the book. They learn about relationship themes, attachment theory, and more. They learn about traits, and then about the trait profiles of individuals in many different careers.

Outstanding Features

The most outstanding feature of this book is how its cumulative approach integrates theory and research in the field. This is best appreciated by carefully examining actual selections from the book itself. That said, a few central advantages also can be summarized here.

A Cumulative Approach. Each part of the book lays the groundwork for the next. The study of the field's scope, methods, and theories (Part 1) lays the groundwork for the study of the parts of personality (Part 2). The study of personality's parts prepares students to understand structural divisions and dynamic processes of personality (Part 3). Finally, students are prepared to appreciate how personality's parts and its organization develop and grow over time (Part 4).

A Balanced, Considered Use of Theories. Personality perspectives are introduced in Chapter 3, as part of the book's first section. Thereafter, the book draws upon parts of those theories on an as-needed basis to explain how a part of personality functions, rather than the theories being covered as whole topics in and of themselves. Relevant portions of different theories often appear together where their complementary perspectives often enrich discussion of a given topic. For example, the discussion of models of the self draws on the concepts of Freud's ego-ideal, Higgins' actual, ideal, and ought selves, and Markus' possible selves, and integrates such ideas with contemporary research.

Personality theories that are no longer making important research contributions to the field are de-emphasized. If a theory is of some historical interest but no longer motivates contemporary research, it is mentioned along with the new research that now carries along its tradition or addresses the same questions. Portions of older theories that are of continued research interest are dealt with fully; this includes studies of defense mechanisms as well as the study of transference. The narrative guides students through the complexities and contradictions of the field, commenting freely on them. This eases the students' way and enhances the learning experience.

Contemporary Research Coverage. The personality systems organization makes it easy to fully integrate contemporary research in personality. Nearly 1,300 original sources of theory and research are cited across the 12 chapters of the book. This is competitive with that of any other textbook of its length. Moreover, a large portion of those sources date from 1980 forward, with many articles from the past several years. Contemporary research is carefully matched to the appropriate areas of coverage of personality's parts, its dynamics, or its development. The textbook covers personality research that has not often appeared in personality texts before despite its obvious relevance to the field, including research on hypnosis, cognition and affect, intelligence, creativity, and self-regulation.

The Liberal Use of Case Examples. Wherever possible, the discussion of personality is clarified and enlivened by the use of examples from real people's (and occasionally, fictional people's) lives. Some of these are historical and some are contemporary. For example, intelligence in the context of personality is illustrated with real-life selections from an autobiography of an individual suffering from *trisomy-21*, as well as by the writings of individuals who have been judged to possess high intelligence.

Addressing Contemporary Issues. The book is sensitive to such current issues of concern as personal versus social responsibility, group and ethnic diversity, cross-cultural psychology, and evolutionary psychology.

Pedagogical Features

There are many good ways for faculty to teach and for students to learn. This book supports different ways of teaching and learning favored by faculty and their diverse students (Benassi & Fernald, 1993). Each chapter contains:

An advanced organizer for the chapter. Each chapter begins with a Chapter Preview that presents a brief sketch of what the chapter will cover.

A glossary at the end of each chapter. Key terms are defined in a glossary at the conclusion of each chapter.

Quotations. Relevant quotations are arranged in the text to stimulate thinking about a topic.

A chapter summary. The narrative of each chapter concludes with a Chapter Summary that briefly reviews its coverage and poses questions with which students can test their knowledge.

Tables and Figures. The book makes liberal use of diagrams and tables so as to support visual presentation of the material in the text.

Acknowledgements

This book is as good as it is because of the contributions of dozens of individuals.

Some of the contributions were relatively indirect, but of importance to me because they concerned my own education. These include the contributions of my parents, Edna and Arthur C. Mayer, and the teachers of the Ardsley, NY public school system, including especially Arthur Rosenberg, Vincent Carravaglio, John Conroy, Robert Clancey, Brian. O'Toole, and Cynthia Blanchard. At the University of Michigan, I'm especially grateful to Peter Ferran, Warren Hecht, and Bert Hornback. At Case Western Reserve University, Sandra Russ, Irving Weiner, Fred Zimring, Herbert Rie, Jane Kessler, Douglas Schultz, and Douglas Detterman all shaped my views of psychology, as did Gordon H. Bower, who sponsored me as a post-doctoral scholar at Stanford University. I am grateful as well to my colleagues at the University of New Hampshire and beyond, including Victor Bennassi, Peter Fernald, Michelle Leichtman, Kathleen McCartney, Edward O'Brien, and Rebecca Warner. Peter Salovey and David R. Caruso, both of Yale University, have also helped to educate me, and have been close friends and collaborators.

A number of graduate students worked with me at the University of New Hampshire, many of whom are now my colleagues, and have commented on the book or taught classes using it, including Jayne Allen, Bonnie Barlow, Mike Faber, Glenn Geher, Kevin Carlsmith, Heather Chabot, Dennis Mitchell, Alex Stevens, Marc Brackett, and Zorana Ivcevic.

Representatives from several publishers encouraged and guided this book. Joseph Jansen III of Norton Publishers first took an interest in my writing a textbook. From 1987 forward he guided me as I converted my notes to textbook form. In 1998, Marianne Tafflinger, the acquisitions editor for personality (and other areas of psychology) at Wadsworth Publishing (now Brooks/Cole), provided a publisher's perspective and guided it in important ways. In 1998, the book had still not reached fruition and we both gave up on it for a while. Then, Nancy Forsyth, President of Allyn & Bacon, expressed interest in the book in the fall of 2001 and renewed my own pursuit of the project. With her encouragement, Carolyn Merrill, the acquisitions editor at Allyn & Bacon, contracted the book in the spring of 2002. Mary Connell served as the first Development Editor for the book. Thanks also to Karon Bowers, of Allyn & Bacon, Richard Wilcox, and Christine Poolin. During the development of the book, three "Classroom Test Editions" were printed by Pearson Custom Publishing; these were guided by Tanja Eise, Kim Brugger and my (then) Pearson representative, Grace Sullivan. Elise Cantor's original watercolors introduced each of the four sections of the Pearson custom book. Elise Cantor, Nicole Frechette, and Kate Edwards assisted in the formatting of the Pearson editions.

Marc Brackett, Robert Eckstein, Zorana Ivcevic, and Dubravka Vidmar all used the "Classroom Test Editions" in their own courses, sharing the vision of a new approach to personality psychology and providing me with invaluable feedback during the final stages of the development of the book.

My undergraduate students at Case Western Reserve, the State University of New York at Purchase, and at the University of New Hampshire, have helped shape every lecture—you might say—every sentence of this book.

Jayne Allen, Bonnie Barlow, Mike Faber, Jill Kaplan, and Kateryna Sylaska, listed as members of the book's advisory board, have provided guidance to me through the development of these interim editions.

I'm very grateful to Deborah Hirsch and Brendan C. Lortie, for their contributions to the book's editing and production over the summer of 2014. They were instrumental in getting Edition 1.5 off the ground and paving the way for future editions. Deborah Hirsch and Angie Joachim provided additional extensive assistance with the editing of Edition 1.8 in 2015.

Finally, an extra special thanks to my wife, Deborah, and daughter, Sarah, for helping me find the time to write this book and for their patience while I worked on it. They have taught me that when I take time to enjoy life with them, the book I write is the better for it.

This book cannot possibly reflect the quality of all the wonderful teaching and guidance I have received, for I am an imperfect student. Whatever quality the book does possess has been immeasurably strengthened by what others have offered me.

~ *John (Jack) D. Mayer*, 6/12/2015

PERSONALITY PSYCHOLOGY: PART 1

PART 1: EXAMINING PERSONALITY introduces the personality system and the field that studies it. The personality system is defined and located in relation to other biological and social systems with which it interacts. Many people think about their own and others' personalities, of course. Psychologists, though, bring special methods to their studies of personality that build a scientific basis for their findings. In addition, they have developed important theories that help us focus our understanding of personality.

The watercolors introducing each of the book's four parts are by Elise Cantor, and are used with permission of the artist.

Chapter 1: What Is Personality?

What is personality? How did the field of personality psychology start and how did it develop? What can be learned from a course in personality psychology? These questions provide a departure point for studying the field. Understanding personality can help us understand ourselves and others.

Previewing the Chapter's Central Questions

•**What Are the Fundamental Questions Addressed by Personality Psychology?** "Who am I?" and "What is my future?" are just two of the questions from antiquity that still motivate the field today. These questions can be used to trace some of the intellectual history of the field—and to help identify some of its current concerns.

•**What Is Personality?** Psychologists have defined personality in different ways throughout the field's history, but most psychologists now agree that personality is a system. Specifically, personality is the system that organizes the many psychological parts of our minds—our perceptions, memories, and emotions.

•**What Is the Field of Personality Psychology?** The field of personality psychology is the area of psychology relating to the study of personality. We'll examine how someone becomes a personality psychologist, what such individuals do, and how other people use findings from the discipline.

•**Why Study Personality Psychology?** By studying personality, we learn about ourselves and other people with whom we interact. We will read research that informs us of the scientific basis for our evaluations of other people.

•**How Is This Book Organized—And What Will You Learn?** We'll preview the organization of topics covered in this book: Personality's definition, its parts, its organization, and its development.

What Are the Fundamental Questions Addressed by Personality Psychology?

Big Questions and Science

Who am I? What is my future? People have asked these questions since the beginning of written history. They have asked other big questions as well: How did the universe begin? What is life? Over time, many of our greatest scholars turned to the sciences to address these questions. Astronomers examined the universe, biologists examined life, and psychologists examined the mind. As each science took on its modern form, it became a sophisticated field dealing with hundreds of topics. But many of the sciences also retained branches that connected back to the basic questions of philosophy. For example, the area of astronomy called cosmology addresses how the universe began and certain areas of biology deal with the origins of life (Rosenberg, 2000).

Psychology, too, addresses big, fundamental questions. **Psychology** is the scientific discipline concerned with how a person's mind works. Psychologists study such questions as how a neuron works, how the eyes see, the structure of the brain, and how people understand language. **Personality psychology** is a discipline within psychology that asks how our major mental systems—our motives, emotions, and thoughts—work together as a whole, and what that overall functioning means for a person's life. The personality psychologist's specialty, in other words, is looking at the person comprehensively (e.g., Hall & Lindzey, 1978; Funder, 2004; Little, 2005).

Because personality psychologists take a big-picture perspective when they view the individual, they provide a crucial connection between the science of psychology, on the one hand, and the philosophical questions about who we are and how we live, on the other. Personality psychologists are particularly responsible for addressing fundamental questions such as "Who am I?"

Developmentally speaking, the "Who am I?" question often arises for people as they enter young adulthood (Erikson, 1963; Marcia et al., 1993). Questions such as "Who am I?" also often emerge out of conflicts felt by the individuals who ask them (Alexander, 1942; Woodhouse, 1984, p. 4). Here are some versions of the "Who am I?" question from students who wrote into an advice column called, "*Big Questions Real Answers*,"

> "My school has kids of all different races, but I'm afraid to make friends with them. Am I a racist?"

> "I daydream a lot. Does that mean I'm lazy?"

> "My older brother is always calling me stupid, a moron, a loser. I try to ignore it, but sometimes it gets to me and I think I am stupid. What can I do?" (Perry, 2001a; 2001b; 2001c).

These questions also reflect an important concern with "Who am I" in the eyes of others?" The answer may vary depending who the others are (Jopling, 2000, p. 166).

Questions and Inquiry

We can regard questions such as "Who am I?" as generating an intellectual path from antiquity to the present that can help us understand the history behind personality psychology. There are a number of big questions about identity and mental life that personality psychologists have addressed in their research. Three questions in particular help direct the field's investigations (though others are possible): "Who am I?" (and "Why is it so hard to know myself?"), "Why are people different?", and "What is my future?" (Mayer, 2007). Asking and wondering about such questions can organize our learning (Bonwell & Eison, 1991, pp. 7-31; Hamilton, 1985). These questions sensitize us to the personal and intellectual quests that helped establish the foundations of personality (Roback, 1928; Winter & Barenbaum, 1999).

Who Am I?

Knowing Ourselves

> "One rediscovers oneself in others." – Goethe (1749-1832)

Consider: "Who am I?" During the years from 800 to 200 BCE, a temple stood at Delphi, in ancient Greece, erected to the god Apollo (La Coste-Messelière, 1950). At its entrance was the command "Know thyself," carved into a column by Chiron of Sparta (Diodurus, 1935/1960, Book IX, 9. 10). The great philosopher Socrates agreed with the command; he said he was interested in self-knowledge above all other values (Griswold, 1986, p. 68). Asking "Who am I?" for Socrates was a moral necessity, because self-knowledge was key to understanding how to treat others well (Griswold, 1986, p. 2, 7; Jopling, 2000, p. 1).

Why Is it so Hard to Know Ourselves?

Although at first it seemed that knowing oneself was simply a matter of desiring to do so, later thinkers regarded self-understanding as more tenuous and challenging. By the time of the Middle Ages, an individual's personality seemed driven by all sorts of mysterious forces—even at times by a spirit or devil. In 1775, Father Johann Gassner, an exorcist of the time, claimed that he could cure many illnesses by expelling the devil from people he believed to be possessed. He mounted a number of public demonstrations in which he cured people suffering from tremors, tics, and fatigue (Ellenberger, 1981, pp. 53-57).

As the biological and social sciences grew, however, scientific explanations supplanted the idea that people were possessed. For example, Anton Mesmer discovered "animal magnetism" or "animal gravity"—a means of influencing other people that today we refer to as hypnosis. Mesmer was able to perform cures similar to those of Gassner using animal magnetism. Although Mesmer's animal magnetism was only poorly understood at the time, his attempt to put such cures on a scientific footing opened the door to empirical examinations of suggestibility and the unconscious.

A century later, the philosopher Schopenhauer (1819/1966) portrayed individuals as driven by blind instincts and deluded by their own wills. Furthermore, he said, the will blocks out what is unpleasant to it, and this may be responsible for mental illness. Soon after, Eduard Von Hartmann (1869) published the "Philosophy of the Unconscious," in which he collected together examples of how people deceive themselves, surprise themselves, and otherwise pit non-conscious ideas against the conscious (Ellenberger, 1981, pp. 208-210). Just two decades later, Freud would create an even more comprehensive theory of the unconscious. Still today, contemporary research makes clear that the problem of self-knowing is considerable (e.g., Dunning, 2005; Vogt & Colvin, 2005; Wilson & Dunn, 2004).

Implicit Personality Theory

As we develop an understanding of ourselves, we construct our own informal and sometimes unstated theory of how people behave. Bruner and Tagiuri (1954) introduced the term **implicit personality theory** to describe our unstated assumptions and ideas about how people feel, think, and behave. Implicit personality theories are often a research topic themselves.

Understanding others is often crucial to our social well-being. Most people recognize different types of people around them—the warm fuzzy type, the nerd, the jock, and so forth—and act differently depending upon whom they are with. Knowing another person closely invites predictions of how the individual will react or behave. "That should make her happy!" we think, just before we tell our jealous friend about her ex-boyfriend's misfortune. Most people's judgments are intuitive—a kind of casual collection of information drawn from personal experience, observation, and the ideas of others.

To help us identify our own implicit theories of personality, Anderson and colleagues suggested answering, "What questions do you sometimes ask yourself when meeting a new acquaintance?" (Anderson, Rosenfeld, & Cruikshank, 1994). The answer to that question—what you consider important to know about someone—may indicate what you think motivates others, or simply what you like and enjoy in others.

In a survey of personality psychology students, Wang (1997) found that students' assumptions about personality varied in a number of important ways. About 53% of the students surveyed believed in the importance of watching actions, rather than listening to what a person says; the remaining 47% was more interested in listening. About 27% of the students thought that people (and their personalities) existed on earth for a higher purpose. Only 12% of the students thought personality was heavily influenced by genetics. Eighty-five percent believed in unconscious influences before starting Wang's course and about the same percent also believed people were very complex to study. Only about 25% thought personality could easily change.

Even trained psychologists' theories often start with their own implicit ideas (Monte, 1999, p. 26; Wegner & Vallacher, 1977, p. 21). By bringing more formal personality theories to light and studying them using the scientific method, we can improve our theories of people and use our knowledge with greater confidence.

How and Why Are People Different?

People often ask not only "Who am I?" but also "Who are you?" The answers are different because people differ. The Ancient Greek Theophrastus wondered: "Why it is that while all Greece lies under the same sky and all the Greeks are educated alike, it has befallen us to have characters variously constituted?" (cited in Roback, p. 9). From Theophrastus' question first emerged **characterology**, a literary endeavor to describe the different sorts of individuals who existed. An example of a character description from Theophrastus concerned the flatterer. The flatterer, as Theophrastus defined him, was someone who engaged in a degrading form of companionship that might, however, bring him or her profit.

> The flatterer is a person who will say as he walks with another, "Do you observe how people are looking at you? This happens to no man in Athens but you. A compliment was paid to you yesterday...More than thirty persons were sitting there; the question was started, 'Who is our foremost man?' Everyone mentioned you first, and ended by coming back to your name..." (Cited in Roback, 1928, p. 10)

As writers outlined the different characters, early physicians tried to explain how those differences came about. One early scientific approach to this question involved the study of **temperament**. **Temperament** refers to the physiologically based motivational and emotional styles people exhibit. In the fourth century BCE, the great Greek physician Hippocrates, and later, Galen, developed a four-fold classification of personality, dividing people into **cholerics**, **melancholics**, **phlegmatics**, and the **sanguine**.

In the four-fold system, the choleric type was described as tall, thin, and easily irritated. Such a person easily became enraged and tended to hold grudges as well; this was all a consequence of too much yellow bile. The melancholic type was contemplative in a sad, resigned way; he or she lacked energy and expected the worst in everything; this was a consequence of too much black bile. The best personality type was thought to be the sanguine type. This even-tempered individual was generally cheerful and hopeful and displayed a ruddy complexion. He or she could be assertive but not angry or vindictive. The sanguine type's pleasant disposition was a consequence of more blood than the other types. The phlegmatic type slept too much and was perceived to be dull, cowardly, sluggish, and overweight. This individual suffered from an excess amount of phlegm (think about how you feel when you have a cold!).

Although starting out as purely as a literary endeavor, philosophers carefully examined such works and drew out their implications. For example, Francis Bacon (1561-1626) suggested that some peoples' minds would be better suited to certain occupations than others. Some people, he said, excel at thinking about many matters at once, whereas others' minds are suited to focusing on just a few matters; some people do things very quickly, whereas others are more suited to work on projects that take a great deal of time (Bacon, 1861/2001; Book VII, Chapter 3).

Today, many areas of personality psychology concern individual differences; just these sorts of variations from person to person—and the implications they hold for a person's life.

What Will My Future Be?

> "Personality can never develop unless the individual chooses his own way, consciously and with moral deliberation." – Carl G. Jung (1875-1961)

Finally, consider, "What will my future be?" Throughout history, philosophers have asked how we can lead our lives to the fullest and act in the best ways possible. In the 5ᵗʰ century BCE China, Confucius worked out a system—the Analects—for instructing people on how to bring about harmony in a socially chaotic world. Aspects of Confucianism involve the importance of learning and education, and overcoming the self (Stevenson & Haberman, 1998, pp. 32-38). There are many other such systems developed throughout the world.

Ancient Athenians and Spartans traveled to the temple at Delphi to have their future foretold. Within the shrine, an oracle—a young woman from the town—sat amidst vapors in a cave-like area. She spoke in tongues, probably under the influence of ethylene, a volcanic gas with hallucinogenic effects (Spiller, Hale & DeBoer, 2002).

Government officials in ancient China were already using mental tests in the 2ⁿᵈ century BCE—using civil service examinations to place people in government positions; a more limited use of mental tests arose in ancient Greece (Bowman, 1989; Doyle, 1974).

In the Middle Ages, newly established European universities awarded degrees and honors to their students on the basis of formal examinations. Psychological testing continued to focus on mental ability through the beginning of the 20ᵗʰ century (Goodenough, 1949). Then, it broadened into tests of attitudes, temperament styles, and personality more generally as the 20ᵗʰ century progressed. Contemporary personality psychologists employ a variety of assessments including mental tests to address these questions of how to live.

People who take personality inventories may receive partial answers to "Who am I?" from their test results. Their test results also speak to "How are people different?"—because scores vary from person to person. Psychologists have also learned to make predictions from test results to a person's future—using the scores to predict the jobs that an individual might thrive at (Lubinski, 2000).

Together, the questions "Who am I?" and "What will my future be?" can also be interpreted as reflecting a more personal desire to be more than one is, to ask, "How shall I make myself more of a person?" (Greenbie, 1932, pp. 1, 21).

Different Kinds of Answers

The exact answer to the question "Who am I (or are you)?" or "How should you live your life?" or any other question will be dependent upon the circumstances in which it is asked and the person who is asked (Gasking, 1946; Hamblin, 1967, p. 49). A friend might tell us that we are kind or caring, or have more strengths than we know. During an argument, however, that same friend may tell us that we are stubborn and thick-headed. Over time, comments from parents, friends, and others lead us to build up a particular view of ourselves. Seeing ourselves as others see us is sometimes referred to as the "looking glass self"—we begin to see ourselves as others see us (Cooley, 1902; Mead, 1934; Tice, 1992).

Researchers such as David Funder (1995; 1999) have found that observers are fairly accurate in perceiving readily noticeable traits such as how talkative, lively, and sociable a person is. For more internal sorts of qualities, such as intelligence, however, observers are less accurate.

Interest in Personality

Psychologists label an interest in who we are and why we do what we do as psychological mindedness. **Psychological mindedness** refers to an interest in understanding relationships among psychological processes and how they influence a person's life (Shill & Lumley, 2000).

Personality psychologists rank high in psychological mindedness—at least that's a fair guess—no one has tested us as a group. Certainly other people view us as contemplating mental life. "One of the downsides of attending dinner parties," my colleague, Dan McAdams, wrote, "is telling people I am a psychologist and then hearing them say things such as, 'I bet you're trying to figure me out,' or 'Oh, good, maybe you can tell me what makes my husband (wife, son, daughter, friend, etc.) tick'" (McAdams, 1995, p. 368).

Personality psychologists including Dan McAdams, myself, and others refrain from analyzing our friends, relatives, and coworkers—that kind of analysis isn't very helpful to day-to-day relationships, nor could we be adequately impartial about what we're thinking.

At the same time, our psychological mindedness can emerge in other ways. Dan McAdams related how his wife and he had met an intriguing woman at a party—she was smart, held an enviable job, traveled a lot, and seemed very confident. On their drive home, McAdams and his wife discussed how they were initially intimidated by their new acquaintance and then reviewed what else they learned about her during the evening, and speculated about how her personality operated. This is similar to our professional pursuits; as McAdams put it: "In the professional enterprise of personality psychology…making sense of persons is or should be the very raison d'être of the discipline." (McAdams, 1995, p. 368). Given that focus, it isn't surprising that many of us want to make sense of people in all the contexts of our lives, not just in professional contexts. Of course, personality psychologists do not have a monopoly on psychological mindedness. People in all walks of life are often psychologically minded and observe, think, and draw conclusions about the people around them much of the time.

If the questions in this chapter—and the types of answers provided by personality psychology—piqued your interest, then the next step is to consider what personality is.

What Is Personality?

A System of Systems

In 1887, Wilhelm Wundt founded the first psychological laboratory in Leipzig, and that is often taken as the date modern psychology began. Experimental psychologists of the time addressed such issues as, "What is sensation?", "What is perception?", and "What is learning?" Wundt saw that smaller psychological systems—to which those questions were addressed—built into larger ones in a hierarchy of complexity. For example, at the middle level of complexity were systems such as motivation, emotion, and intelligence. At the global, highest level, for Wundt (1887, p. 26), was the "total development of a psychical personality." For Wundt and others the level of psychical personality was where the answers to the larger personal and social questions would be found.

"Observe all men; thy self most." – Benjamin Franklin (1706-1790)

Scientists often employ a **molecular-molar continuum** to organize what is being studied within a given field, and across fields, as well. The molecular-molar continuum is one that divides smaller objects of study from larger ones. **Molecular** things are relatively small. Examples of smaller, molecular psychological processes include sensing the color orange, feeling a momentary pang of envy, or thinking that an apricot is a fruit (see Figure 1, bottom row). These mental processes or events are small because they involve individual sensations (e.g., of orange), emotions (e.g., envy), and cognitions (e.g., of an apricot). More **molar** psychological processes are larger and combine smaller processes. For example, feeling envious of a friend who owns a beautiful painting of a bright orange apricot combines the smaller psychological processes just discussed into a larger whole (see Figure 1-1, row 2). The larger whole is molar relative to the individual parts.

Even feeling envious over a painting is still fairly modest in size compared to some larger psychological processes. Consider that the person might momentarily think of taking the envied painting and at the same time experience a moral correction and decide to leave the painting where it is. Together, such a reaction represents the collective action of many psychological subsystems: perception, emotion, motivation, morality, and a sense of self.

For Wundt and those who came after, understanding the combined operation of all the major psychological systems together—the most molar level of psychology—involved the study of personality psychology (Wundt, 1897, pp. 25-26). Figure 1-1 shows how Wundt saw the more molecular psychological processes building into personality psychology. Wundt's definition was a systems definition at a time during which scientists had become increasingly interested in systems (cf. Whitehead, 1929; Laszlo, 1973). And, Wundt concluded that it was the study of personality that would best allow psychology to address the big questions about identity and how to live.

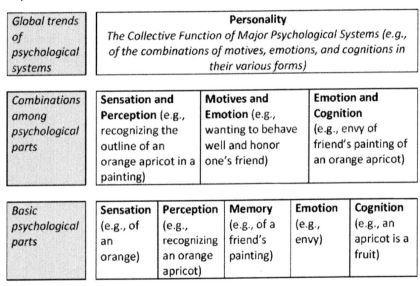

Figure 1-1 *Wilhelm Wundt's Personality Psychology*
Wilhelm Wundt, one of the founders of modern psychology, saw personality as the global system that integrated other major psychological subsystems.

What Is a System?

Simply put, a system is any set of interrelated parts. As applied to personality, the parts might be mental mechanisms such as short-term memory, mental models including one's view of oneself, or a trait, such as whether one is sociable. These parts are interrelated: If you are sociable, you'll learn things about yourself—that you're talkative and like parties, for example—that differ from what you'd learn if you were introverted and preferred solitary activities.

Systems can be simple or complex, rational, or haphazard-seeming. An example of a visible, readily comprehensible physical system is the solar system. The solar system follows many rules—rules that make it possible to construct star charts, to predict such things as eclipses, and to calculate the possibilities for space travel. Other examples of systems include computers, cars, and an electric fan.

Defining Personality

Wundt's definition of personality as a system that organized psychological systems was the first of a number of similar versions. For example, the psychoanalyst Prince (1921, p. 532) referred to personality as: "...the sum-total of all the biological innate dispositions...and the acquired dispositions and tendencies...." (cf. Allport, 1937, p. 48; Lewin, 1935).

Although the systems definition had the widest currency in personality psychology, there was a loyal opposition of psychologists who wanted to define personality as the study of individual differences. The **individual differences** definition emphasizes that the proper study of personality is the analysis of how people differ from one another. According to this perspective, the personality psychologist should (a) measure differences among people, (b) classify people according to these differences, and (c) predict how these differences will influence a person's behavior at a particular time. This definition has the advantage of describing accurately what a great number of personality psychologists do; it does, however, have certain disadvantages.

One of the drawbacks of this definition is that it reduces personality psychology to a single focus— the study of individual differences. Some personality psychologists, however, are interested in describing consistencies in personality across all individuals (for example, Freud believed most everyone had an ego). In a widely repeated passage, Kluckhohn and Murray (1953, p. 53) noted that each individual is in certain ways:

> ...like all other people
>
> ...like some other people, and
>
> ...like no other people. (Kluckhohn & Murray, 1953, p. 53)

Personality research addresses all three of these possibilities at one time or another. That is one reason that the individual differences approach is incomplete.

Pervin (1990) noted that, in his own textbook, he struggled between using an individual differences approach and a more general systems approach:

> ...it is my sense that...[the study of an organization of parts] is what is truly distinctive about the field, and that recognizing this would lead to a greater emphasis in research on the system aspects of personality functioning. (Pervin, 1990, p. 12)

Following this line of thought, let's define **personality** in this way:

> Personality is the organized, developing system within the individual that represents the collective action of that individual's major psychological subsystems.

A more light-hearted definition of personality comes from the mid-century physician and psychiatrist, Karl Menninger, who said that:

> ...it means the individual as a whole, his height and weight and loves and hates and blood pressure and reflexes; his smiles and hopes and bowed legs and enlarged tonsils... (Menninger, 1930, p. 21)

Menninger's description is delightful, but should definitions of personality psychology really include bowed legs and enlarged tonsils? To find out we need to consider more carefully where the personality system is located.

Locating the Personality System

The Molecular-Molar Dimension

Scientists connect their system of study—a particle in physics, a chemical, the brain, or personality—to other systems of study along organizing dimensions. Wundt used the molecular-molar dimension to describe how personality was a global system made up of smaller psychological subsystems. Let's now extend that molecular-molar dimension to more completely connect personality to other scientific areas of study.

In Figure 1-2, the molecular-molar continuum first shown in Figure 1-1 is extended to include more systems. The lowest level begins with biological processes, which include neurons communicating, the function of brain areas and the like. The middle level shows personality psychology—the study of larger psychological systems. Specific details of individual psychological processes—individual sensations, emotions, and cognitions—are omitted to keep the picture simple. The dimension is also extended upward past personality to larger systems that involve groups of personalities—as would be found in a family, in other small groups, or in a larger community. The larger social groups of which the person is a member are depicted at the top of Figure 1-2.

Personality's location on the molecular-molar dimension tells us that it will be influenced by systems "underneath" or "underpinning" it, including the brain and influences on the brain. It will also be influenced by organizations "above" or "including" it—social systems such as the family and society.

The Internal-External Dimension

Many sciences also make use of an **inner-outer (or internal-external) dimension** to further distinguish their objects of study (Henriques, 2003; Mayer, 1995a; Singer, 1984). The personality system is internal to the person, inside the skin, with perhaps the innermost part of personality being consciousness itself. The internal personality is joined to the outside world through the sensory-motor boundary. Most signals traveling from personality to the outside world are communicated by the person's motor systems through speech, posture, and actions. Conversely, information from the outside environment must be sensed and converted into symbols before they can reach personality.

Personality's location on the internal-external dimension means that a separate, private internal personality exists within the individual's skin. Outside observers can typically see only our external experiences. Only an individual has access to his or her interior self. Personality operates internally, but it also operates by expressing itself in the external, ongoing social situations in which it finds itself. This internal-external dimension is represented by the horizontal dimension of Figure 1-2.

The Time Dimension

A third dimension is that of time. Personality develops; it changes over time, from infancy to childhood, from adulthood to maturity. Personality is different during each life epoch, and this too is important in locating the system. This volume will mostly address adult personality, but it also will refer to how personality develops during childhood.

To sum up, personality is a global system of smaller psychological systems. It is inside the person but expressed outwardly in the situation, and it develops from infancy to maturity.

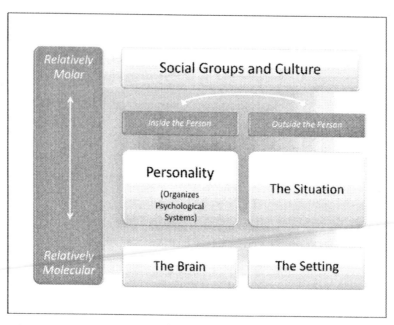

Figure 1-2 *Personality's Location*

Personality can be viewed amidst its neighboring systems of scientific study. In this diagram, personality is related to those systems according to a molecular-molar dimension (vertical) and an internal-external dimension (horizontal). Biology is molecular relative to personality, the social situation is external, and larger social systems incorporate both personality and the external situation.

What Is the Field of Personality Psychology?

What Is a Field of Science?

A field of science consists of an organized group of individuals who study a common topic, and who add to what we know about it. The scientists are recognized as belonging to the field, and educate students about the field. Their students then go on to become the next generation of scientists.

These people are organized and represented within institutions such as colleges and universities, and other research bodies. Most colleges and universities include in their psychology departments one or more psychologists who study personality psychology. Similarly, granting agencies often designate funds for the study of personality. Moreover, professional associations provide a community for such individuals.

Using a variety of scientific methods, these scientists formulate hypotheses and test them, discover relationships, and publish their results in peer-reviewed journals, in chapters in edited books, and in full-length books. Sometimes they translate their findings for the public in magazines and newspapers as well. The next sections describe the emergence of modern psychology to provide a context for the discipline and what the study of personality is all about.

The Emergence of Modern Personality Psychology (1890 to 1949)

Recall that at the close of the 19th century, Wilhelm Wundt had envisioned personality as the study of a person's major psychological subsystems. In the years immediately following Wundt's vision, the first personality psychologists arose. Many of them, like Sigmund Freud, Carl Jung, Alfred Adler, and others, attempted to synthesize all that was known at the time into a single, grand theory of personality (Wundt's term "personality" was not yet regularly employed, and Freud and his colleagues employed a number of terms alternative to personality for their studies).

Freud was pre-eminent among those who designed such comprehensive theories. In the late 19th and early 20th centuries, he synthesized many of the early writings on hypnotism, psychopathology, and case analyses of his patients to arrive at a novel understanding of how personality operated called psychodynamic psychology—how one part of the mind influenced another. Other theorists at work at that time included Carl Jung, who wrote about psychoanalytical psychology and Alfred Adler, who wrote about "individual psychology." These various "psychologies"—views of personality, really—were sometimes published alongside studies of sensation, memory, and other topics without many editorial distinctions among them (e.g., Murchison, 1930).

Among those who helped review and consolidate the field, perhaps the foremost early contributor was Abraham Roback. Roback (1927) noted that by the mid-1920s, in the Boston area, courses in personality psychology were underway on a regular basis. His book, *The Psychology of Character*, became an early textbook in personality psychology (Roback, 1927). To write it, Roback conducted an exhaustive historical review of studies in character, temperament, and mental conflict, and ending in the Freudian era. Another key figure, Gordon Allport, taught a similar personality survey course in 1924 and 1925 at Harvard (Winter & Berenbaum, 1999, p. 10).

Twelve years later, Allport and others published a cluster of new textbooks in the field—Gordon Allport's (1937) *Personality Psychology*, Henry Murray's (1938) *Explorations in Personality*, and Ross Stagner's (1937) *Psychology of Personality*, and with that, the discipline of personality psychology officially began (Craik, 1993). For his volume, Allport collected together dozens of meanings of the term "personality," and took considerable care in explaining why it was a good term for the discipline. Murray's *Explorations* focused on motives—both conscious and unconscious—and Stagner's book focused a bit more on systems and behavior.

Each of these textbooks employed its own language and terminology, and Allport and Murray introduced their own theories as well: Allport introduced a theory of traits, Murray a theory of needs. By the end of World War II, still more new theories emerged. Humanistic psychologists such as Abraham Maslow and Carl Rogers emphasized the human potential for growth and positive mental health, and described how people could attain it. Social cognitive psychologists examined learning about the world as a part of personality.

The action in the field was taking place at a theoretical level rather than at a level of trying to understand personality through research. This wasn't necessarily a bad thing: there was great intellectual excitement in these diverse, exciting theories.

This and the further background of the field are depicted in the timeline of personality psychology shown in Figure 1-3.

Evolving Viewpoints on the Field (1950 to the Present)

Throughout the latter part of the 20th century, as more and more students were attracted to the area, research blossomed, and the field was rich with both theory and empirical findings. Today, typing the word "personality" into *PsycINFO*—the database for psychological literature—returns over a quarter-million responses. Hence, a central problem for the field was to develop a good approach to organizing and teaching its expanding understanding.

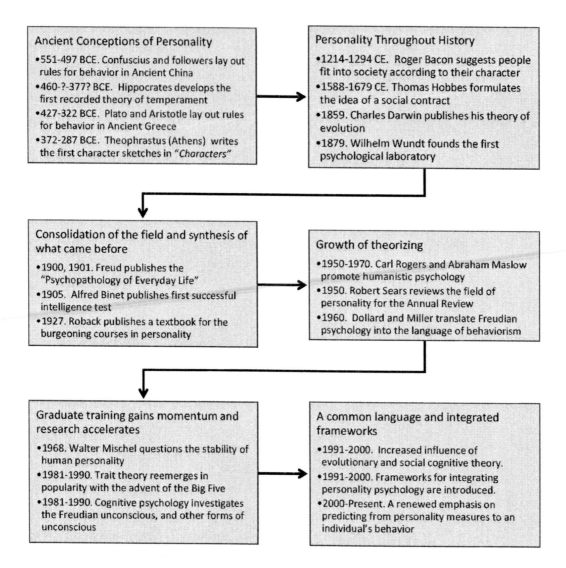

Figure 1-3 *A Timeline of the Development of Personality Psychology*

The way a field of science understands itself—the lens through which it understands its own work—can be referred to as a discipline's fieldwide framework. The framework of a field is important because it is employed to understand what the field ought to be studying and explains and organizes the research in the field. Of considerable importance to those taking a course in personality psychology, the framework also is used to organize textbooks in the area. In a sense, the framework represents a field's identity (Mayer, 1993-1994; 1998).

During the middle of the 20th century, the major framework for the field was a theory-by-theory approach. Calvin Hall and Gardner Lindzey (1957) introduced a personality textbook that presented, in historical order, a balanced coverage of the global psychological theories of Sigmund Freud, Carl Jung, Alfred Adler, Carl Rogers, Abraham Maslow, and many other theorists. Each chapter focused on presenting a theory, and then concluded with an evaluation of the theory, and any research evidence for it. Several generations of students were exposed to this approach to personality psychology and it is still used today. Descriptions of prominent early members of the discipline appear in Table 1-1.

A new major framework for the field—the one used here—has emerged to address such issues. It is called the personality systems framework for personality psychology (Mayer, 2005; 2015). The systems framework for personality is a new outline for the field that focuses directly on the personality system itself (as opposed to theories). Its four major topics of study are: (1) The identification and location of personality; (2) the parts of personality; (3) personality organization; and (4) personality development.

Table 1-1: Examples of Important Personality Psychologists of the 20th Century	
Theorist	*Description*
Sigmund Freud (Major works 1890-1939).	Freud was a Viennese physician who developed the first modern, comprehensive personality theory. He provided descriptions of the unconscious aspects of mental life, and integrated ideas of the unconscious both with brain functions (as understood then) and a sophisticated view of social and cultural influences.
Carl Rogers (Major works 1940-1979).	Rogers was a clinical psychologist whose first professional job was at a Rochester, NY, guidance clinic. There, he outlined some of the basic processes of personality change in therapy. His work contrasted with Freud's in emphasizing more positive aspects of personality and the potential to develop an authentic self.
Albert Bandura (Major works 1960-2000s).	This Stanford psychologist first gained prominence for a study that demonstrated how children learned aggressive behavior from watching a video of other children interacting aggressively with a life-size doll. Later in his career, Bandura developed broader theories of social learning and motivation.
B. F. Skinner (Major works 1930-1989).	Skinner was raised on the East Coast, studied in the Mid-West, and then moved to Harvard University where he spent much of his career understanding how reinforcements could control an organism's behavior (chiefly, rats and pigeons). A colorful and provocative writer, he argued that people's behaviors could be understood in the context of the patterns of reinforcement around them, and that it was unnecessary to delve into any inner workings of a person's mind.
Gordon Allport (Major works 1930-1959).	This psychologist began his career at Dartmouth and later moved to Harvard and wrote an early influential textbook on personality. He transplanted much European thinking about traits to the United States and discussed how personality traits such as generosity, honesty, and aggression influenced human behavior.
Karen Horney (Major works 1930-1969).	This Berlin physician was a follower of Freud's. Ultimately settling in New York, Horney practiced psychoanalysis and then set about revising Freud's theory. Compared to Freud, Horney emphasized the critical nature of interpersonal relationships and interpersonal strategies to a person's mental health. She also introduced what she referred to as feminine psychology into the psychoanalytic establishment, criticizing earlier characterizations of women and constructing a new and more constructive view of women's mental lives.

*Key figures identified in Mayer & Carlsmith (1998).

Each major topic of the framework has been carefully defined over a series of reviews, and subsidiary divisions under each topic also have been developed. This new approach is one among several that have been developed to integrate the study of personality psychology (Cervone, 2004; Henriques, 2003; Pervin, 1990; Sternberg & Grigorenko, 2001). It is this new framework that, in part, makes this new textbook possible (Mayer, 1993-1994; 1995a; 1995b; 1998; 2005). As new as this framework is, its mission is still to address, in part, the questions that began this chapter: "Who am I?", "How are people different?", and "What is my future?"

Although this framework is new, it draws on a long intellectual tradition in the discipline, beginning with Wundt's founding vision of personality as organizing a person's psychology (e.g., Pervin, 1990; Sears, 1950; Mayer, 2005). It also owes its existence to a small but intrepid group of psychologists who translated the terminology of one major theoretical perspective to another—thus building unity into the contemporary discipline. Such psychologists translated Freudian dynamics into behavioral terms (e.g., Dollard & Miller, 1950), or cognitive terms (Erdelyi, 1982), with many variations (Mayer, 1995; Westen, 1990). Many others experimented with alternative frameworks of note (e.g., Maddi, 1972; McAdams, 1996).

Training and Research in Personality Psychology

By the 1960s, graduate study in psychology had become popular. Government agencies such as the National Institutes of Mental Health and private foundations such as the Ford Foundation funded research in psychology. Graduate students were trained, and then hired as new professors—or went to work in business, education, and government.

The first several decades of training in personality psychology, from the 1940s to the 1970s, were often allied with clinical programs (programs that train psychotherapists), which made sense because many personality theories of the time had important implications for how to assess an individual, and how to conduct psychotherapy. Over the years, however, graduate training programs in personality have become more closely allied with social psychology (e.g., Swann & Seyle, 2005). Both personality and social psychology address normal personality, use similar research methods, and are concerned with how people behave in social situations. Social psychology, however, studies people's attitudes toward the world, and the world's influence on the individual and social groups. Personality, as we have seen, is concerned with how the personality system operates and its implications for a person's life.

Professors of personality psychology taught undergraduates and trained graduate students, some of whom became the next generation of professors. This training and research cycle has resulted in an explosion of research in personality psychology and related disciplines. Each year, hundreds of studies are carried out in the discipline and more data is collected related to how personality operates. Figure 1-4 shows the number of articles mentioning the term "personality" by decade, as indicated by a search of PsycINFO—one of the field's central databases. There were 192 such articles between 1901 and 1910, and a gradual rise over the decades of the 20th century, to near 100,000 such articles in the first decade of the 21st century.

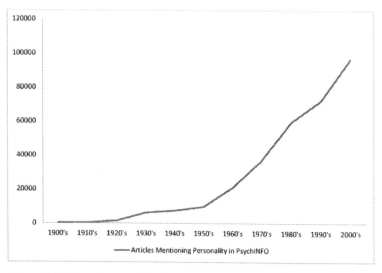

Figure 1-4 *Rising Research Levels in Personality Psychology*

Today, every fall and early spring, undergraduates apply to graduate programs in psychology or related fields throughout the world. In the United States and Canada, about 55 graduate programs train students specifically in personality psychology (American Psychological Association, 1996).

If you are interested in a career in psychology—and perhaps in personality psychology—you can visit the American Psychological Association's website at www.apa.org, or the American Psychological Society's at www.psychologicalscience.org. Both sites contain a great deal of information for students who are thinking about becoming psychologists. The American Psychological Association also publishes regularly updated books such as *Careers in Psychology* and *Graduate Study in Psychology*. More specific information about the field of personality psychology can be found at the website for the *Society for Personality and Social Psychology*: www.spsp.org, and the *Association for Research in Personality*: www.personality-arp.org. Some of the career options are shown in Table 1-2.

Table 1-2: Career Paths of People Who Study Personality Psychology	
Career Path	*Description*
A professor of personality psychology	Most professors who teach personality psychology began by earning an undergraduate degree in psychology or a related field. They then go on to obtain a graduate degree (Ph.D.) concentrating in personality or personality and social psychology. As faculty members, these individuals teach a variety of courses, and conduct research in personality psychology and areas related to it.
A clinical psychologist who studies personality psychology	Some clinical psychologists also work in the area of personality psychology. Most began by earning an undergraduate degree in psychology or a related field. They then obtain a professional degree related to conducting psychological assessment and psychotherapy (a Ph.D. or Psy. D.). They may work solely in private practice, hold an appointment at a college or university, or both. Such individuals draw on their clinical experience with patients to inform their theorizing and research in personality psychology.
A psychiatrist who studies personality psychology	Psychiatrists receive medical training and after obtaining their MDs may go on for further training in psychotherapy. Psychiatrists often bring insight into healthy and unhealthy personality functioning to the field, from their experience treating people with mental disorders and from observing their patients in therapy.
A human resources officer who studies personality psychology in an organization	Human resource officers typically work in larger business, governmental, or educational settings. Although those in human resources deal with a variety of issues, some focus on selection and development of personnel. Such individuals have typically earned a bachelor's degree, and possibly an MBA in organizational behavior, or they have psychological training at the undergraduate or graduate level. They are often certified to give psychological tests measuring personality. Such individuals may select tests for the purposes of hiring or development of staff, administer tests, and conduct institutional and sometimes more basic research, related to such activities. They also engage in coaching employees to make them more effective.

Why Study Personality Psychology?

The discipline of personality psychology's task is to catalog, unify, and organize information from the rest of psychology and to apply it to questions of individual uniqueness and human nature. Whereas many sub-disciplines of psychology concern one psychological system—emotions or cognition—personality psychology is devoted to providing an overview of them all. As one of the broadest of the sub-disciplines of psychology, personality provides a bridge from psychology to philosophy, and between personality and other sciences such as the brain sciences, education, robotics, and sociology.

The "Who Am I?" Question—A Part of Scientific Inquiry

Returning to the question, "Who am I?"—some have argued that understanding one's self and others is a value in and of itself—knowledge for knowledge's sake (Jopling, 2000, p. 3). Personality psychology as a science provides us with tools to analyze ourselves: methods for measuring our mental features, a sophisticated language for the parts of personality and their organization, and procedures for studying our lives over time. Rather than just describing ourselves as shy and intelligent, we may develop a richer way of thinking about who we are. For example, we might learn we are "introverted" rather than shy. There is a subtle difference between the two: Shy people want to be with others but are socially avoidant; introverts often prefer being alone. We might realize that, along with other introverts, we love to read and watch videos, and seem somewhat more sober than our more sociable friends. Our more precise language about ourselves can improve our self-knowledge (Christiansen et al., 2005; Mayer, 2014).

The "How and Why Are People Different?" Question—Asked in Personality Assessment

The question "How and why are people different?"—particularly *how we differ*— is a central question addressed by clinical psychologists who carry out **personality assessment**. Personality assessment refers to the "sizing up" people—something clinicians do to help their clients (Kleinmuntz, 1982, p. 1). We all "assess" the people in our lives for the purpose of relating with them sensibly: we notice a new friend values her privacy and we don't pry too much into her life; we respect our supervisor's talkativeness. In a clinical setting, a trained psychologist adds to this art of sizing up people by employing techniques of observation, conducting interviews, and administering and interpreting psychological tests.

The assessment setting may be a medical complex, a psychologist's office, or an assessment center—a specially constructed environment (typically, offices) in which a person is asked to perform various tasks and sometimes interact with others in simulations of on-the-job behavior. Children are sometimes assessed at school. Personality psychologists help develop assessment procedures in university laboratory settings.

Using data from the observations, interviews, and tests, the psychologist composes a narrative description of the personality under study, discussing personality's parts, organization, and development and, typically, answering specific questions about the individual. The questions about the person typically depend on the setting. In a legal setting, the tests may indicate something about whether the person had moral capacity at the time of committing a crime. In an organizational setting, the assessment may deal with the strengths that an individual can bring to a job. In a clinical setting, psychological assessments may deal with why a person is experiencing life difficulties, and the areas in which a person can improve (Butcher, 1995).

The "What Is My Future?" Question—Prediction, Selection, and Change

Prediction and Selection

Personality psychology also serves a predictive or forecasting purpose. When we ask a personality psychologist, "What's my future?" we're asking about the likely path someone like us will follow. Personality psychologists can, in fact, learn about our traits and, from those traits, make statistical forecasts of what's more likely for us relative to others. A person higher in extraversion is likely to be less bothered by health concerns (although she may have a similar number of health issues as her introverted friend); a person who is higher in intelligence is more likely to escape poverty, and so forth (Mayer, 2014).

People have probably been making decisions about the people around them from the time human beings first evolved (Buss, 1991; Haselton & Funder, 2006). Our ancient ancestor's choice of a good hunting partner was probably a life or death decision in some instances (Buss, 1991).

Admissions officers at colleges and human resource professionals at businesses often employ personality tests to assess applicants for positions. Using those measures, they're able to make statistical predictions about who is most likely to perform well at a school or on the job.

Consider the selection and training of police officers. Dayan, Kasten, and Fox (2002) examined candidates for the police force in an assessment center setting. In the assessment center, the police candidates went through simulations of on-the-job encounters—everything from handing out a traffic citation to searching a suspect. The candidates' performance was observed and assessed by their peers and by trained evaluators. The observers' evaluations turned out to be highly valid for predicting the candidates' subsequent on-the-job performance (Dayan et al., 2002). In addition, part of the candidates' assessments involved taking psychological tests, which are known to predict on-the-job performance. People who earn higher scores on tests of general cognitive ability and on tests of conscientiousness generally perform better on the job (Black, 2000; Cortina et al., 1992; Dayan et al., 2000). In one study, candidates for the police force who scored low on scales of maturity, low on commitment to values, and low on self-control were found to be at greater risk for serious breaches of trust on the job such as the use of undue force, and likelihood of corruption (Hargrave & Hiatt, 1989). When organizations use psychological assessments, they can meaningfully increase the quality of their workforce. These tests can also identify members of the workforce who can benefit from training so as to raise their skills in particular areas such as understanding emotion—or understanding personality itself. The widespread use of psychological assessment, careful selection, and targeted training can help members of occupations function in a more competent and professional manner.

Applications to Personality Change

A final reason to study personality is to gain knowledge so as to change oneself, others, or one's relationships. Personality psychology highlights areas a person might want to change, whether because a part of one's own personality is causing the person problems, or because personality psychologists hold out models of optimal functioning, and some people aspire to make themselves better if they can.

After studying the constructive and destructive patterns of couples over many years, Gottman and Silver (1999) made a number of recommendations to help people better handle their interactions in relationships, modeling their recommendations on what successful couples did. Simple routines such asking your partner about her day, and reminding your partner that you notice his positive qualities were important to maintain a good relationship. The researchers' other recommendations included doing things together during good times, and being sure to talk to one another during bad times. They recommended focusing on the relationship itself—"What is good for us?"—separately from focusing on each other as individuals. When couples argue, Gottman and Silver explained, they should proceed gently, repair hurt feelings, and not let emotion take over. And if you can't do all this? Well, personality psychology has also contributed to the methods we use to improve ourselves. None of us are perfect, after all.

These are some of the applications and contributions that personality psychology has made within the discipline.

How Is This Book Organized—And What Will You Learn?

Some Cautions, and a Beginning

"Who am I?" "What is my future?"—We now have an idea of some of the questions that emerged in our distant intellectual past—and that the field of personality psychology addresses. Personality psychology is not the only discipline that addresses these questions, of course. If you ask a biologist "Who am I?" you're likely to hear about how human beings are both similar and different from other primates, and of our evolutionary development. If you ask "Who am I?" of a theologian, you may hear about the relationship between an individual and a spiritual force or supreme being (e.g., Heschel, 1965, pp. 91-92). Ask an ethicist "How shall I live?" and she'll tell you about what is good and right to do (Marinoff, 1999).

Personality Psychology's Answers

To a personality psychologist, "Who am I?" opens an inquiry into our mental qualities—including our traits and identity. Asking "Who am I?" gets into issues of "How does a mind work?" (Marinoff, 1999). If we ask a personality psychologist "How should I lead my life?" she may answer in part by saying, "Well, you're an extravert—talkative, sociable and lively," and then tell us the strengths and weaknesses of extraverts, the occupations they like, and how they do over time (both extraverts and introverts do well, by the way). Most centrally, personality psychology addresses: "How does a person's psychology work—and what implications does it have for the individual's life?"

To address those questions, this book is organized into four topics: What (and where) is personality? What are the system's parts? How is personality organized? And, how does personality develop? These topics are known as the general outline of the **personality systems framework**—one contemporary model for organizing the study of the field (Mayer, 2015). To provide you with a sense of how these four topics will work, let's take a look at the coverage of the book in brief.

Identifying Personality

Part 1 of this book—and the first part of the systems framework—concerns defining and identifying personality. In this chapter, we've already defined personality and examined its location amid other systems of study (the brain and body, the setting, situation, and social groups).

We'll learn in Chapter 2 that we can study personality in a variety of ways. We can use a case study method, examine multiple people in a method referred to as "observationism," use correlational studies or experimental techniques.

Chapter 3 examines theories of personality. Theories direct our attention to particular aspects of a person's psychology. Trait theories, for example, focus us on a person's psychological and behavioral consistencies such as his happiness or sociability. Humanistic theories draw our attention to how individuals grow and attain their potential.

Overall, the first part of the book provides you with a foundation to understanding personality, its study, and some of the major theories in the field.

Parts of Personality

The second part of the book focuses on the parts of peoples' personalities: their motives, emotions, relationships, and other qualities. A **personality part** or **component** is a discrete mental quality or area of mental function within a person (Mayer, 1995b, p. 828).

Some parts of personality concern motivations—such as the need to achieve or to be with people. Other parts of personality concern mental abilities. Cognitive intelligence is crucially related to a person's occupational and marital status. Other parts of personality concern self-control and a sense of personal choice or agency.

Chapter 4 examines the motivational and emotional parts of personality. Chapter 5 examines a person's mental models (e.g., how people form representations of themselves and the people around them). Chapter 6 examines intelligences and other mental abilities. Finally, Chapter 7 examines consciousness, will, agency, and related parts of personality.

The second part of the book provides you with knowledge about many varied parts of personality. You'll be able to recognize and label many different aspects of your own personality and the personalities of others in ways you haven't been able to before.

Personality Organization

The third part of this book considers how the parts of personality are organized. Are there sensible ways to divide up personality so we can ensure we have an overview of its most important functions? Beyond that, how do the parts function and act together to bring about personality dynamics?

Chapter 8 examines the structural organization of personality—the ways that psychologists "divide up the mind" to make sense of it. **Structural organization** refers to the long-term basically stable divisions of the personality system. Knowing these makes it easier to think about the personality system piece by piece. **Dynamic organization** refers to the major causal pathways that bring about important consequences of mental functioning. Chapter 9 covers the dynamics of action: How a person moves from being motivated, to acting on a motive. Chapter 10 examines the dynamics of self-control: How a person manages her own mental life and what forms of self-control may be particularly effective.

At this stage of the text, you will have learned powerful ways of putting personality together—that is, by looking at personality through the lens of its structure and by examining personality dynamics. These concepts allow us to integrate what we know about a person's specific parts of personality—and to understand something of how they may act.

Personality Development

The fourth part of the book examines how personality develops. **Personality development** concerns how the personality system grows and changes over the course of a lifetime. Chapter 11 surveys life-span development, with a focus on children and adolescence. Chapter 12 considers areas of emerging adulthood, adult development, and maturity, examining what is stable and what changes over a person's life span.

At the conclusion of the book, you should have a complete overview of how to envision a personality—from its location, to its parts, to its organization, through its development.

The personality course provides students with the opportunity for increased self-understanding, the potential for predicting our own and other people's thoughts and feelings, and some tools for changing ourselves. It's fair to ask whether the questions personality psychology addresses are worth understanding, whether the field has applications of importance, and whether we can better understand ourselves and each other through a study of the discipline. We personality psychologists believe, and I hope this book will show, that the answer is yes.

Reviewing Chapter 1

The primary goal of this chapter is to introduce you to the field of personality psychology. It covers contemporary issues such as how people become personality psychologists, and it is designed to help you understand a bit of the field's history. Finally, the chapter is aimed at providing you with an overview of what will come next in the book. To help ensure that you have learned the more important points of the chapter, please review the following questions, which are arranged according to the major sections of the chapter:

Questions About "What Are the Fundamental Questions Addressed by Personality Psychology?"

1. Questions Addressed by Personality Psychology: One way to get the big picture of a field is to understand the sorts of questions that motivated its creation. "Who am I?" is a basic question that in part organizes and motivates personality psychology. What are some related questions?

2. An Early Typology of Human Personality: The early temperament theory of personality—the four-fold classification of humours worked out by Hippocrates—is important to our contemporary understanding of personality (as we will see later). Can you describe each of the four personality types: sanguine, choleric, melancholic, and phlegmatic?

3. Understanding of Unconscious Processes: Before Sigmund Freud and modern psychology came on the scene, a number of individuals had studied phenomena related to the unconscious. These included studies of animal magnetism (mesmerism). What has become of the research today?

Questions About "What Is Personality?"

4. Definition(s) of Personality: Definitions of personality tend to stress the fact that it is an organized system of parts. Who was the first to suggest such a definition? How could personality psychology contribute specifically to the field of personality? Note how personality is defined specifically in this textbook. There exist other definitions of personality as well, including those that stress individual differences, and those that stress behavioral consistency. What are some of the drawbacks (if any) of these alternative definitions? What are some of their advantages?

5. Locating Personality: The personality system does not exist in isolation. Rather, it is embedded in other surrounding systems. Personality is "located and identified" amidst other systems of scientific study in this chapter. It is distinguished from its biological bases and from more complex systems such as social groups. Two of these dimensions are the molecular-molar dimension and the internal-external dimension. Can you explain what these are? What is yet another dimension?

6. Personality's Neighboring Systems: Using some of the dimensions to arrange personality amidst its neighbors, what are the various systems that can be arranged around personality, and where can they be placed in a dimensional system?

Questions About "What Is the Field of Personality Psychology?"

7. The Establishment of Modern Personality Psychology: In 1890, Wilhelm Wundt recommended the establishment of the discipline. Between that time and the 1920s, two trends occurred: consolidation and synthesis. Consolidation involved collecting what was then known about personality psychology. Synthesis concerned integrating what was known into grand theories. Do you know the roles of Sigmund Freud, Arthur Roback, and Gordon Allport in such activities?

8. Views of the Field: How was personality psychology taught in the mid-20th century? Gradually, the field has become more integrated across theories. This has depended upon several lines of work including translating the language of one theory into another, increasing research, and better defining the central topics of personality psychology. Do you know the first major translation of one theory into another?

9. Increased Research: After World War II, more Americans than ever decided on obtaining a college education. Psychology became an important major on campus. A number of foundations began funding psychological research in general and personality research in particular. Today, graduate students often apply to psychology departments to study personality psychology. Do you know to what area(s) of specialization they apply? Also, what happened to theorizing during this time of increased research?

10. Training in the Field: The training of personality psychologists varies; early personality psychologists came from a variety of disciplines, but personality training programs are increasing in importance. What are some characteristic career paths of personality psychologists today?

Questions About "Why Study Personality Psychology?"

11. Reasons for Studying Personality Psychology: Anyone can study personality psychology simply to seek knowledge for its own sake. In addition, personality psychology has a number of applied uses: for personality assessment, selection, and prediction. Can you give an example of how personality assessment works? What about selection and prediction?

Questions About "How Is This Book Organized—And What Will You Learn?"

12. Limits of Personality Psychology: Can personality psychology really answer questions such as "What is the best way to live?" or "Who am I?" Even if those questions could be answered, what are the limits involved in studying a complex system? Although these limits exist, studying personality can still be a rewarding, exciting experience, and personality psychology has important practical applications.

13. Personality Components: How are personality components defined? The section on personality parts will examine motives and emotions; mental models of the self, world, and relationships; thinking with those models; and the more mysterious parts of personality including free will and consciousness.

14. Personality Organization: Personality organization refers to how the parts of personality are related to each other. Organization can be divided into two parts. Structural organization refers to the stable, long-term arrangement of personality's parts. Can you define dynamic organization?

15. Personality Development: Personality development refers to how the parts of personality and their organization change over time. Personality development is often divided between personality origins and growth in childhood and development in adulthood.

Chapter 1 Glossary

Terms in Order of Appearance:

Psychology: A scientific discipline that studies how the mind works.

Personality Psychology: A scientific discipline that addresses the questions, "Who am I?" and "Who are others?" Personality psychology involves the study of a person's mental system, with a focus on its largest, most important parts, how those parts are organized, and how they develop over time.

Implicit Personality Theory: The informal, often unnoticed or unconscious system of beliefs an individual holds about how his or her own personality operates, and how the personalities of other people operate.

Characterology: A literary tradition in which an author writes a series of short descriptions about the different character types he or she has recognized. Each description of a type is designed to bring forth a definite feeling of recognition in the reader that he or she has seen an example of that type of person as well.

Temperament: The study of people's innate, motivational and emotional styles.

Choleric: One of four ancient personality types. The choleric type is quick to action, has a short temper, and is lean.

Melancholic: One of four ancient personality types. The melancholic type is slow to move, self-preoccupied, and most distinctly, unhappy and depressed.

Phlegmatic: One of four ancient personality types. The phlegmatic type has little energy, is prone to eating too much, and is somewhat indifferent in disposition.

Sanguine: One of four ancient personality types. The sanguine type is cheerful, lively, and easygoing.

Psychological Mindedness: A person's trait or predisposition to analyze one's own and others mental characteristics, and how those mental characteristics lead to a person's behaviors.

Molecular-Molar Continuum (or Dimension): A dimension or continuum along which various scientific systems of study can be located, from those that are smallest to those that are largest.

Molecular Systems: Systems of scientific study that are relatively small, such as atoms and molecules.

Molar Systems: Systems of scientific study that are relatively large, such as the economy or the ecosphere.

Individual Differences: A topic of scientific study that addresses the questions of how one person differs from another. Some people use this as an alternative definition of personality psychology.

Personality: Personality is the organized, developing, psychological system within the individual that represents the collective action of that individual's major psychological subsystems.

Inner-Outer (Internal-External) Dimension: As applied to personality psychology, a dimension or continuum that separates the internal parts of personality ("beneath the skin") from the external aspects of personality (behavior, environment).

Personality Systems Framework: The systems framework is an outline of the field of personality psychology that divides it into the study of (a) the definition and location of personality, (b) personality parts, (c) personality organization, and (d) personality development.

Personality Components (or Parts): Individual instances of personality function, content, or processes are known as personality's parts or components. These components or parts may be biological mechanisms such as a *need for water* in the case of thirst, or learned contents such as the *multiplication tables*, or thematic ways of feeling, thinking, and acting, such as *shyness*, among others.

Structural Organization: This aspect of personality organization refers to the relatively long-term, stable positioning of one part of personality in relationship to another.

Dynamic Organization: Personality dynamics involve trends of causality across multiple parts of personality; in other words, how the parts of personality influence one another. For example, dynamics of action describe how a person's urges end up being expressed in the individual's actions.

Personality Development: Personality development concerns how the personality system develops over the individual's life span.

Chapter 2: Research in Personality Psychology

Now that we have defined personality, let's take a look at how psychologists study personality: in specific, the methods they use to do so. Psychologists use research designs that range from case studies to experiments; they focus in particular on how best to measure personality's many features, how to manage multiple measurements together, and how to use those measurements to predict important outcomes.

Previewing the Chapter's Central Questions

•**Where Do the Data Come From?** No matter what we research, we start with information about the personality system itself. But, where does our data come from? It can come from external sources, such as institutional records or observer reports, or from personal reports—data emanating from inside the individual him- or herself.

•**What Research Designs Are Used in Personality Psychology?** As we notice the personalities around us, we develop ideas—hypotheses—about what people are like. Psychologists develop ideas about what people are like and then test their hypotheses using different research approaches. Each research approach contributes in a different way to the knowledge of the field.

•**What Does It Mean to Measure Personality?** No matter what research design is used, at some point psychologists will need to measure a person's mental traits and other qualities. But what, exactly, is measurement and how do psychologists evaluate an individual's mental functioning? The field of psychometrics addresses such questions.

•**How Do Personality Psychologists Manage the Study of so Many Variables?** Personality psychologists like to take a broad view of personal functioning, so they often want or need to collect many different measurements on a person. The problem then becomes how to organize the variables that have been collected. Several mathematical techniques are available for that purpose, notably factor analysis and structural equation modeling.

Where Do the Data Come From?

Olympian Issues

The Olympic Games bring together some of the best athletes in the world in a highly demanding sports competition. The best athletic performances are rewarded with bronze, silver, and—best of all—gold medals. The idea of ranking athletes on a scale of bronze, silver, and gold arose in ancient Greece, with Plato's idea expressed in *The Republic*, that people in a society differed from one another, with some "of bronze," some "of silver," and some "of gold."

In psychological research, as in the Olympics, data about people are collected and evaluated to make important decisions. Psychologists pay attention to the different kinds of data they collect; Olympic judges collect different kinds of data about the athletes as well. Data reflecting the timed duration of a performance are different in nature, for example, from expert judges' more subjective evaluations of the performance of athletes in a skating routine. In a skating routine the music played can influence the judges independent of the athletic merit of the performance. Other extraneous factors may enter in as well. In the 2002 Olympic figure skating competition, one judge's objectivity was compromised by political considerations; the accuracy of judges' ratings is subject to many factors (Swift, 2002).

Data concerning an individual's personality, like data concerning athletic performance, comes in different forms, and each kind of data must be evaluated on its own merits. Psychologists need to understand the merits and drawbacks of different kinds of data. The data can then be used in a variety of research designs, and through it, we can begin to understand the personality system.

Observer Data

"There are no perfect indicators of personality; there are only clues, and clues are always ambiguous. …When you try to learn about or measure personality, you cannot base this endeavor on just one kind of information. You need many kinds." – David Funder

In the Olympics, the judges observe and report on the athletes, thereby providing us with a kind of data known generally as "**observer**" or "**informant data**." In our own lives, our friends, roommates, parents, and colleagues observe us. If a psychologist collected data about us from any of these people, they would be collecting observer data.

Observer data tends to be particularly useful when the trait being measured is readily visible like athletic performance in the Olympics. In the psychological realm, some mental qualities that involve clear outward behavior such as extraversion can be fairly readily detected. Extraverts often behave in sociable, outgoing ways, seeking social contact, whereas shy people may tend to look nervous, or to look away from others. Not all mental traits, however, are quite so obvious to observers. Observers are notoriously bad judges of people's less visible qualities such as their intelligence.

Under ideal circumstances, the observer is under little pressure to perceive things one way or another. Under some circumstances, such as social pressure, observers can be biased in small or not-so-small ways. For example, in competitive figure skating championships, some judges brought their rankings of final events closer to the rankings of the other judges after seeing the posted results in earlier competitions (Wanderer, 1987). Judges also appear to favor athletes from their own countries or from countries that are politically aligned with their own (Seltzer & Glass, 1991).

The relation a person has to the person being judged may also affect the perceived facts about an individual. For example, one supervisor may perceive an employee differently than another supervisor, even though both are observing the same individual. Phillip Tetlock and colleagues studied managers who were high on tests of integrative complexity—the capacity to see things from different perspectives. This complexity is crucial to the success of creative architects, scientists, and writers, but individuals with this capacity may be challenging to have as colleagues. Although supervisors rated these cognitively complex managers as comparatively high in initiative and as objective about themselves compared to those who were lower in such complexity, the managers' coworkers were decidedly cooler about working with them: The coworkers saw these managers as narcissistic and antagonistic compared to others. Observer ratings are often said to reflect a person's reputation, and plainly, these managers had different reputations among their supervisors and co-workers (Tetlock, Peterson, and Berry, 1993).

The Life Sphere and External (Life) Data

Observer ratings are just one type of data about an individual. There are many such sources of data. These sources of data can be organized first according to where they come from. In Chapter 1, we saw that personality is surrounded by such neighboring systems as its neurobiological environment including the brain, and its underlying situational setting, including the person's location and nearby objects and people. The surrounding systems further include the interactive situation, whether it is reading a book or being with friends, as well as the larger groups in which the person is a member. Personality and those surrounding systems are shown in Figure 2-1, much as they were in Figure 1-2 of Chapter 1.

The systems surrounding personality make up what has been referred to as the person's life space (Lewin, 1935, pp. 172-173; Cattell, 1965, p. 60; Mayer, Carlsmith, & Chabot, 1998). Data related to that life space (and to personality) have been superimposed on Figure 2-1, arranged according to where they come from.

More Molar Level Systems such as the family, culture, society, and the environment.	**Institutional data** drawn from groups including or interacting with personality	
More Molar Level Systems such as the family, culture, society, and the environment.		
Level of the Individual Systems such as mental life, psychological processes, and the psychological situation.	**Self-report, ability, and projective data** from the internal personality	**Observer or Informant data** from the external situation
More Molecular Level Systems such as the brain and its parts, other bodily organs, local settings, possessions.	**Biological data** drawn from the underlying nervous system and brain	**Setting data** concerning the situational elements in the person's life

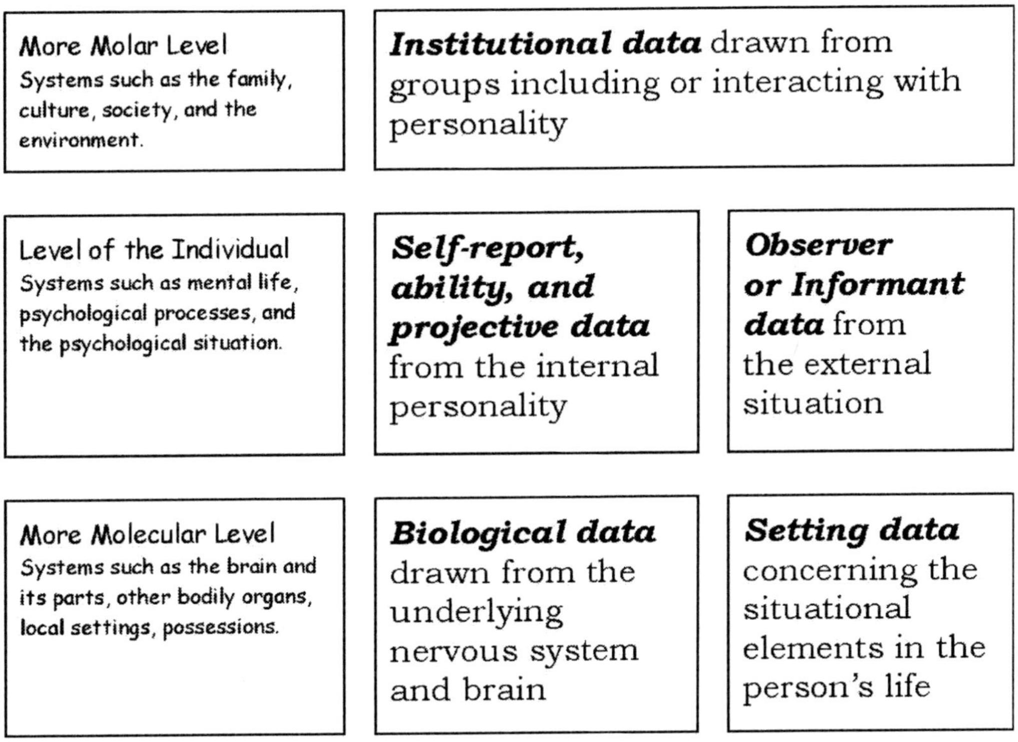

Figure 2-1 *Data Sources Drawn from Personality and Its Surrounding Systems*
Data that pertain to personality can come from the personality system itself (e.g., self-report data) or from the systems surrounding it, such as institutional and observer data.

Data that arise external to personality—from biology, settings, interactions, and institutions—are referred to as **external-source**. Such **external-source data** include any data that emerge from the systems that surround us. For example, say researchers ask someone we know about what we are like. In this case, we're the "target person" being evaluated and our friend is the observer. The observer's data about us comes from outside us—it's one kind of external data. External-source data might also include information about our medical status and history, the grades that are kept by the registrar's office at our college, and whether we keep a neat or disorderly room (Cattell, 1965, p. 60; Mayer, 2004).

Samuel Gosling of the University of Texas and colleagues collected data about a person's setting. They found that people with clean, comfortable, and organized bedrooms score higher in the trait of conscientiousness than people with messier bedrooms. People with decorated, distinctive bedrooms with many different kinds of books, on the other hand, were higher in cultural openness, as assessed by an independent test. Thus, a person's living space and other surroundings provide important data that reflect on their personalities (Gosling, Ko, Mannarelli, & Morris; 2002, p. 391).

Personal-Report Data: Self-Judgment, Criterion-Report, and Thematic-Report

Whereas external-source data comes from the areas surrounding personality, **personal-report data** come from the individual him or herself. Personal report data are data that the individual communicates, discloses, or otherwise reports to a psychological investigator. Interviews and questionnaires yield personal-report data, as do more elaborate psychological tests. We can briefly introduce a few main categories of such data (e.g., Mayer, 2004; 2005).

Self-judgment (or self-report) data arise when the individual is asked to describe or explain something about herself. For example, a person might go through a series of statements such as "I like mechanics magazines" or "Most people think of me as shy" and indicate how much each one applies to his or her personality. This kind of data directly measures an individual's self-concept. Tests of self-concept and tests of personality traits such as extraversion and neuroticism are of this type.

A variation of self-judgment data is **process-report data**. Process-report data involves the individual's report of an ongoing mental process, such as an emotion or a thought. For example, people generate process-report data when they answer test items such as, "Are you happy right now?" and "Are you trying to avoid how you feel right now?" Process-report data is often of value because it tracks ongoing mental states, and therefore does not depend on an individual's memories as much as some self-judgment data.

Criterion-report (or mental ability) data arise when the individual answers a test question with a response that will be judged against a criterion of correctness. Criterion-report items ask questions such as, "If 4 people begin work at 9AM, at what time would they complete a 16-hour job?" and "What does 'ocean' mean?" Educational achievement tests, memory tests, and tests of intelligence often employ criterion-report data.

A third kind of data, **thematic-report data (or projective-report data)** arise when the individual responds to an ambiguous stimulus, such as an inkblot, and is asked to say what it looks like or to tell a story about it. The responses may be scored according to a given theme—such as how well the person constructs reality, or to what degree an individual expresses a specific motivation, such as acquisitiveness, in response to the ambiguous stimulus.

Any or all of these sources of data may be drawn upon when considering a research design to study a problem. Some interesting research issues arise concerning which data are best to collect for a given purpose. For example, some researchers have asked whether self- or observer-judgments are more accurate in assessing personality. Most people can report their inner feelings with reasonable accuracy—particularly when it comes to our emotions and certain attitudes. In other instances the people who observe us are far more accurate—as when it comes to evaluating our mental abilities such as our ability to solve problems in logic (e.g., Dunning, 2005).

"There are only two kinds of data. The first kind is Terrible Data: data that are ambiguous, potentially misleading, incomplete and imprecise. The second kind is No Data. Unfortunately, there is no third kind, anywhere in the world." – David Funder

What Research Designs Are Used in Personality Psychology?

Types of Research Designs

The exact data we choose to collect is in part a function of the research design we're using. Research designs are often divided into three broad areas: case studies and observationism, correlational research, and experimental research. Loosely speaking, case studies involve observing a person. The correlational approach involves quantifying the relationship between two or more variables. The experimental method involves manipulating a variable to determine its influence on another variable. These research designs will be described in greater detail, and ideas about them will be refined over the next sections.

The Case Study Method

Case Studies and the Scientific Method

A **case study design** involves the intensive examination of a single person—the "case"—over some period of time. Whenever we consider a given individual and his life, we are potentially employing a case study design. Case studies serve three functions (McAdams & West, 1987; Sears, 1959). The first is *exemplification*, meaning that the case can be used to illustrate, display, and provide examples of a particular psychological phenomenon. Case studies are often easily understandable, requiring of the reader little or no knowledge of methodology or statistics. Therefore, they communicate well. Moreover, the best case studies can be colorful and interesting in making their points. The description of a person's life, the obstacles he or she contends with, and the ultimate success or failure she faces can often bring to life a concept in a way a table of statistical results cannot.

A second function is the *evaluation of explanations* of personality by testing hypotheses according to whether they are plausible. For example, if we wanted to evaluate a theory that social support contributes to good performance at the Olympic Games, we could test our hypothesis by examining the situation of a medalist at an Olympic competition. We could examine the support from her family, coach, and community to see whether that contributed to the athlete's performance (Swift, 2004, p. 48). Of course, one case example is not enough to decide whether a theory is sound, but it can help illustrate the value of a theory in certain instances.

A third function of case studies is *discovery*. This involves learning about new problems that scientists may not have encountered before. Because case studies include a great deal of rich, "unfiltered" information, they can be a great source for hypothesis generation. Small details included in the case may trigger new ways of thinking about a problem and may suggest new causes of behavior.

The disadvantages of case studies, however, are also quite important to recognize. The individual in a case study is not a randomly selected representative of a group. Quite the contrary, the individual may have become the object of study precisely because she or he is a colorful character, faces unusual circumstances, or is otherwise unrepresentative. That limits one's confidence in generalizing from the individual case to a more general group. Second, the observer(s) of the case are subject to individual biases and social pressures. A related point is that some connections in human nature are so subtle that an honest observer might miss them. Still, case studies are of considerable use to the personality psychologist.

Using Case Studies to Study Personality Psychology

A recent case study was conducted of Dodge Morgan, a wealthy man who sought—successfully—to circumnavigate the globe on a sailboat by himself. As a boy, Morgan had worked in a boatyard owned by his uncle and had accumulated a remarkable 25,000 miles of sailing experience by the time he was a young man. After sailing from Maine to Ketchikan, Alaska (through the Bahamas) he returned to his native Massachusetts to work at a high tech firm. Some years later, he bought a company that was spun off from it, called Worcester Controls Corporation (WCC). As owner of WCC, he amassed a small fortune.

Then, at age 54, although in a successful marriage, and raising a son and daughter, Morgan decided to sail around the world in an easterly direction, on a solo, nonstop voyage to be completed in 180 to 220 days (Morgan, 1989, p. 191; Nasby & Read, 1997, p. 827). In June of 1984, he had completed a 17-page description of the project. A portion of it provided a self-assessment of his own mental and emotional factors:

> My mental faculties are more than adequate. My emotional status is sound. I have a strong will and singular determination to succeed. I do not easily give up. I can concentrate well over long periods of time and can focus a natural impatience on realistic objectives, satisfied with inches of progress if that is the order of the day or task. I know how to sort priorities and do not become confused by too many details. I know well the power of planning and time to reach an objective. I am very happy in my own company and can find loneliness a rather delicious feeling. And I don't suffer from seasickness. (Morgan, 1989, p. 200)

He was driven, he said, to find out, "How much more is there?" to life, and the irresistible sense that "It is time to try again to find out. There is so little time left." (Morgan, 1984, cited in Nasby & Read, 1997, p. 827). Against the advice of his wife and friends, he commissioned a boat to be built in record time and departed shortly after its completion. In a letter to the psychologists, he wrote that voyage was an opportunity to bring about profound personal change (Nasby & Read, 1997, p. 884).

Although Morgan completed his voyage successfully in 150 days, the psychological transformation he had sought hadn't arrived. Instead, the journey left him somewhat unsettled, confused, and worried: "If anything," he wrote, "I feel more isolated than ever. I feel I have less in common with others than ever…I understand the need for compassion in people more than I did but find myself less able to practice it…" (Nasby & Read, 1997, p. 1040).

Recall that cases are useful for exemplification, evaluation, and discovery. Some have used Morgan's personality as an example of independence, aggression, and rejection of other people, noting that he provides a nearly heroic example of achievement to many (Wiggins, 1997, pp. 1076-1079).

The case can also be used for evaluation of theories. One theory of psychology is that peoples' lives reenact the lives of recurring characters in myths, such as heroes. Nasby and Read (1997) suspected that Morgan identified with the myth of the hero. They describe Morgan's voyage as reenacting a myth in which the hero must separate from others, face an arduous task, and understand its meanings upon his return. Their interpretation predicted that although Morgan had not yet discovered his truth at the conclusion of his seafaring, he would discover it in the future (Nasby & Read, 1997). Other theories, beyond the scope of this methodological review, have also examined the case. Does this short case study suggest any areas of research that might be worth further study? If so, the case fulfilled its role in encouraging discovery.

The Method of Observationism

Observationism is an outgrowth of the case study method. Instead of one case examined in depth, this method involves repeated examinations of many different cases (Mayer & Bower, 1986). Observationism can be defined as the intensive investigation of multiple cases with the intention of drawing generalizations from them that can be applied to a general population. The early personality psychologists were often physicians or clinical psychologists by training, and their observations went hand-in-hand with their attempts at treatment (Mayer & Bower, 1986; Mayer & Carlsmith, 1998).

Sigmund Freud was a physician by training and argued persuasively for the use of observationism as he examined his patients and first began to define the use of the method (Gay, 1988, pp. 295-305). First, Freud believed that a high frequency and duration of observation created a kind of magnifying lens for the quality of personality data. He observed his patients for an hour a day, four, five, or six days a week. Where possible, he continued these observations for from six months to two years. It seems plausible that observing and listening to anyone with such frequency and duration can yield considerable information (Gay, 1988, pp. 295-305).

Second, for Freud, observationism was helped by employing a consistent environment in which to observe the individual. Freud was quick to realize that an individual will react sensitively to various environments. When observing his patients, therefore, he retreated to the background—literally sitting behind a couch (which a patient reclined on while speaking) out of sight—and keeping his own remarks to a minimum. The combination of being (relatively) unseen and unheard was intended to create the sense of a blank slate on which the patient could record his or her thoughts with minimal interference. We know today that by creating such an ambiguous situation, in which the patient could say anything, Freud also maximized the variety of individual differences he observed (Caspi & Moffitt, 1992).

A third aspect of observationism, for Freud, was more unique to his own research and involved the technique of **free association**. Free association is a method by which patients are instructed to tell the therapist/observer whatever comes into their minds, no matter how personal, nonsensical, or even embarrassing the thoughts are. The idea was that people were to associate freely from one thought to the next. In doing so, they would reveal (we would say today) the structure of their memories and their mental models of the world. The result would allow a therapist such as Freud to track down the causes of certain thoughts by following their associations from present concerns back to an earlier time in their lives. Although other psychologists shared with Freud a belief in using repeated observation and keeping the observational setting a constant, they did not all use free association. For example, Carl Rogers employed a technique that involved empathic listening in which the counselor repeated key feeling statements made by the individual to help clarify them (Rogers, 1951, pp. 27-30).

Freud believed that observationism represented a potential pinnacle of the scientific method for personality psychology. The natural sciences had made great strides by enhancing observational techniques. Modern biology had employed the microscope to discover the first one-celled organisms. Modern astronomy had developed the telescope to discover craters on the moon and spots on the sun. Freud believed that the repeated observation of the same individual could be psychology's lens on the person—a new instrument with which to study personality in detail.

The Observational Method and the Development of the Discipline

> "The revolution which the experimental method has affected in the sciences is this: It has put a scientific criterion in the place of personal authority." – Claude Bernard (1813-1878)

In many respects, the method of observationism and the early discipline of personality psychology grew together. Throughout his life, Freud continued to claim that observationism was the best of all psychological research methods. In fact, when an American psychologist wrote to Freud to tell him he had gathered experimental evidence to support the concept of "repression" (the forgetting of unpleasant material), Freud wrote back that although he appreciated the gesture, it was really unnecessary: His own observational studies had already confirmed the concept's existence and any further experimental evidence was superfluous (Rosenzwieg, 1941).

The Limits of Observationism

Freud's claim that observationism is a secure, useful method was based in part on the idea that any two therapists listening to a patient would agree with what the other observed. Not only did Freud suppose that different observers would agree, but also that the patient would verify certain conclusions about her condition as well. Adolph Grunbaum (1986) referred to that as the tally argument: the points on which the patient and therapist agreed were considered to be true and the remainder were discarded as false.

The tally argument, however, wasn't as persuasive to others as Freud had hoped. Critics pointed out that therapists who shared Freud's theoretical perspective might agree with him and therapists who believed otherwise might disagree. At first, Freud's claim for the consistency of observational data received some support. He trained a number of colleagues and students who reported seeing much the same phenomena as he did. After a while, however, some of Freud's colleagues developed alternative theories and observed different phenomena than he had. Carl Jung notably said he was unable to trace conflicts to the same sexual motivations as Freud had, even though he used the same free-association technique. Similarly, Otto Rank traced neurotic conflicts to conflicts between wanting to live and wanting to die. These defections seemed to argue against the use of observationism by itself.

A disagreement doesn't mean a method is all bad. After all, astronomers disagreed for centuries over whether the lines they saw on Mars were natural structures or canals built by Martians—but they didn't throw out their telescopes simply because they couldn't settle the issue. Rather, they admitted the limitations of their research tools and sought new ones to settle the debate. In 1958, Erik Erikson, a renowned child psychoanalyst, described some of the virtues and limits of the observational approach in a detailed description of his use of the procedure in a response to critics of the method (Erikson, 1958). By that point in the history of the field, observationism had contributed a good deal to our understanding—but its limits were apparent and additional research methods were needed.

A number of researchers began to ask, "Exactly how good are we at understanding other people by observing them?" and they carried out laboratory studies to find out. Their findings suggested that people are accurate observers in some ways—when they look at readily detectable behavior and other clues—but not in others (Funder, 1999). Meanwhile, psychologists of Freud's time, and those of today, have gone on to establish other research methods with complementary powers and drawbacks.

"The great tragedy of Science—the slaying of a beautiful hypothesis by an ugly fact." — T. H. Huxley (1825-1895).

The Correlational Research Design

The Nature of Correlational Research Design

The purpose of a correlational design is to find the relation between two or more personality variables. A **variable** is a characteristic that changes across a group of people, such as their degree of shyness or friendliness.

Extroversion and creativity are both personality variables, as is the number of parties a person goes to in a week. Correlational studies connect two or more variables: the relation between extroversion and the number of parties a person attended in a month. Once we know the interrelation between the two variables, we can predict the level of one variable from another. The central part of the correlational design is to assess the relationship between two variables (in more advanced applications, correlations are examined among multiple variables).

For example, Totterdell (1999) examined the moods and the performances of professional male cricket players. Cricket is one of most popular sports in England. It is played by two teams of 11 players, with balls, bats, and wickets. Totterdell hypothesized that a player's mood would change as a function of his performance in the game. In this case, the two variables that Totterdell measured were mood and performance on the field and he found that happier players generally played better. The **correlation coefficient** is a statistic that represents the degree of association between two variables, such as mood and performance. By itself, the correlation doesn't tell us whether better playing caused a positive mood, or whether a positive mood caused better playing. Correlations speak of relationships, not causation.

Relating Two Measurements: A Review

Let's briefly review the concept of the correlation coefficients. (You have probably encountered it already in other courses.) A correlation refers to the "co-relation" between two variables; for example, between two sets of scores on tests. Look at the scores obtained by the five people who took tests X and Y shown in Table 2-1.

Table 2-1: Scores of 5 Participants on Tests X, Y, and Z			
Test-Taker	Test X	Test Y	Test Z
Erin	0	2	4
Abigail	2	0	6
Max	3	3	3
Sarah	4	6	0
Glenn	6	4	2

You can see that as people scored higher on Test X, they generally scored higher on Test Y as well. Let's say these were tests of confidence and mental toughness among athletes (Gould, Dieffenbach, & Moffett, 2002). Mental toughness is defined as a tenacious motivation to meet one's goals. Table 2-1 indicates that Erin and Abigail scored lowest on both tests, Max scored in the middle, and Sarah and Glenn scored highest on both tests. In this sample of athletes, as scores on test X (confidence) go up, they also go up on test Y (mental toughness). The relation is not perfect, but it is plainly present. When this occurs, scores are said to be positively correlated.

Now compare tests X and Z. Let's say Test Z measures non-conformity. It is negatively correlated because, in this sample, as scores on test X go up, scores on test Z go down. Erin and Abigail scored lowest on test X (confidence) but highest on test Z (non-conformity), Max scored in the middle, and Sarah and Glenn scored highest on test X (confidence), but lowest on test Z (non-conformity). From results like these we could say that confidence and non-conformity are negatively correlated among samples of athletes.

The degree of correlation is typically represented by a product-moment correlation coefficient, or Pearson's *r*. The correlation, *r*, varies between -1.00 and +1.00. When $r = -1.00$, a perfect, negative relationship exists. For example, an $r = -1.0$ exists between tests T and U in Table 2-2. A positive $r = 1.00$ exists between tests T and V.

The $r = -1.0$ relation reflects that the higher the test T score, the lower the test U score. (The scores on Test U are a bit higher than those on Test T, but what matters is that each time Test T goes up by 1, Test U goes down by 1). Similarly, the $r = 1.0$ between tests T and V exists because the higher the test T score, the higher the test V score. The relation between tests T and V is said to be perfect (and therefore $r = 1.0$) because an increase of one in test T equals an increase of the same interval in test V.

Now consider the same set of scores, but with an added test: Test W (Table 2-2). Notice that a perfect relation also exists between tests T and W even though the scores on Test W are larger than the scores on Test T. Despite the difference in the size of the scores, the two tests change in a predictable way: As test T goes up 1, test W goes up 5. An increase of 1 in T always predicts an increase of 5 in W. Because the prediction from one to the other is always perfect and linear (would graph as a straight line), Tests T and W are considered perfectly correlated, $r = 1.0$.

Table 2-2: Scores of 5 Participants on Tests T, U, V, and W

Test-Taker	Test T	Test U	Test V	Test W
Erin	1	8	2	10
Abigail	2	7	3	15
Max	3	6	4	20
Sarah	4	5	5	25
Glenn	5	4	6	30

Correlations and Scatterplots

A correlation between two variables is sometimes represented as a **scatterplot**, a diagram representing pairs of measurements on two variables, X and Y. The plots are displayed in a two dimensional space in which by convention the horizontal dimension represents the X variable; the vertical dimension, Y. For example, we set up an X and a Y axis and plot the points as illustrated in Figure 2-2. The X axis represents scores on test T, the Y axis represents scores on test V. Each point in the plot represents a pair of scores that one person received on two tests.

For example, Figure 2-2 has a "dot" at the pair of points (1,2), representing the fact that Erin received a '1' on Test T, and a '2' on Test V. Plotting the two tests for the participants in Table 2-2, along with a few more test-takers, makes clear the perfect relation between the two tests. That is, one test can be predicted perfectly from the other. The same is true when $r = -1.0$, as it does in Figure 2-3, where Tests T and U are plotted for the test-takers in Table 2-2 (several additional data points have been added).

Figure 2-2 *A Correlation of +1*

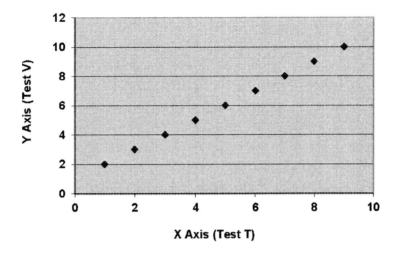

X Axis (Test T)

Figure 2-3 *A Correlation of -1*

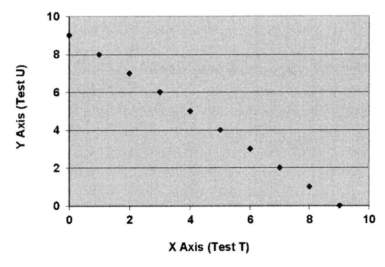

X Axis (Test T)

If the tests were imperfectly related (which is most often the case), the points would no longer form a straight line, but rather would hover around a hypothetical straight line. That was the case with the $r = .75$ correlation between tests X (confidence) and Y (mental toughness) in the earlier table, which is graphed in Figure 2-4 along with a few more test-takers. If the two scales were entirely unrelated, then the correlation between them would be $r = 0$, and the points would form a random, haphazard pattern, as in Figure 2-5.

Correlational designs stress the relationship between variables without necessarily revealing whether one variable might be causing another. One way to examine the question of causation is to manipulate one variable and assess its influence (if any) on another variable. Variables are manipulated in experimental designs.

Natural Experiments

Experimental designs in personality research take two general forms: **Natural experiments** (also known as quasi-experiments), and true experiments. In experiments, two or more groups are examined. The experimental group or groups have received a **treatment** or "manipulation"; the control group has not. The two groups are then compared on a dependent (outcome) variable. In natural experiments, people pursue their lives—find jobs, get married—all without experimental controls and randomization. Later, personality psychologists divide people into groups after the fact, such as employed or unemployed—and regard employment as the treatment. They then try to identify the factors that led the people to arrive at a particular destination in life.

Figure 2-4 *A Correlation of +.75*

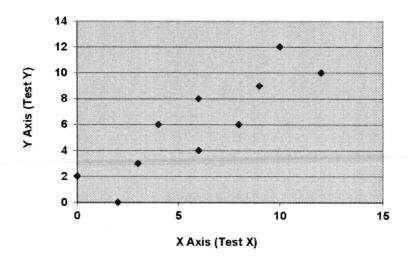

Figure 2-5 *A Correlation Close to .00*

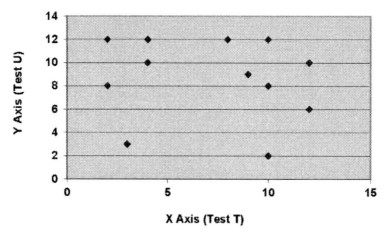

The "natural" part of a natural experiment refers to the fact that the group(s) who received the treatment were not randomly assigned. Rather, uncontrolled, and perhaps unknown, circumstances led to their group membership. For example, Carter (1998) employed a natural experimental design to examine the use of anabolic steroids—synthetic versions of the male sex hormone, testosterone—among athletes. Athletes who use steroids increase their muscle strength, but do so illegally and can incur serious medical complications.

Carter recruited 96 male bodybuilders from several health clubs, then she classified them into three groups: current steroid users, former steroid users, and bodybuilders who had never used steroids. The treatment "administered" by the researcher in this case was anabolic steroid use. Remember, though, that this was a natural experiment, so although Carter divided the bodybuilders into different groups, she never actually administered any steroids—that was done by the bodybuilders themselves. The control group consisted of those who did not receive the treatment, i.e., the 36 who had never used steroids. The dependent measure of interest was a set of personality traits. All the participants were asked to take psychological tests to measure those traits. Carter was interested in personality differences between drug users and non-users. Carter found that body builders who used steroids in the past were lower in conscientiousness, more anxious, and more resentful relative to the control group. The bodybuilders actually on steroids at the time of the study were also relatively depressed, obsessive-compulsive, and hostile.

The value of natural experiments is that they tell us about the personality differences among real groups of people—in this case, people who do or do not use steroids to improve their athletic performance. The drawback is that differences across groups may not be caused by the treatment studied. For example, some participants in Carter's control group might actually have taken steroids but preferred not to say they had. Carter might therefore have observed differences between steroid users who were candid and open about their drug use *and* their negative traits. Or, the admitted steroid users might have been included a few criminals whose psychopathology accounted for the differences. To avoid such issues of interpretation, psychologists use true experimental designs.

True Experimental Designs

True experimental designs involve the random assignment of people to groups including one or more experimental groups and one control group. The experimental groups are administered a treatment decided upon by the experimenter and the control group receives no treatment. After the intervention, the people are assessed to see if there is a change in the dependent variable—the variable the experimenter hopes to change.

Life would be a bit easier for personality psychologists if they could employ experimental treatments that convincingly altered an individual's personality for short periods of time. Imagine fostering parental conflict in members of an experimental group in order to study how family discord affects personality! Researchers in the 1930s actually tried to do this: They hypnotized experimental participants and implanted memories of disturbing conflicts with their mothers while they were under trance. After the memories were induced, the participants behaved in a more pathological fashion (Kubie, 1939; Luria, 1932). (After they took their measurements, the researchers removed the participants' implanted memories and then woke them from their trances.)

Aside from the possible ethical issues involved, experiments such as these raise concerns of **ecological validity**. Ecological validity refers to the degree to which an experimental treatment approximates real life. It seems unlikely that a hypnotically suggested memory of a parental conflict can closely approximate a real-life conflict. People who have real, disturbing conflicts with parents are probably different from those who have hypnotically induced conflicts. Real conflict arises from something in an individual in interaction with his or her parent. Conflicts with parents also evolve over decades, reinforcing certain feelings, memories, and behavioral patterns throughout the personality system. This is likely to have a more extensive impact than an experimental induction of a personal conflict that lasts for only an hour or so.

Certain parts of personality, however—including mood and learning—can be convincingly manipulated. Twenty-seven members of the United States Figure Skating Association participated in an experiment to see if their skating ability could be improved. Skaters in the experimental group were assigned a mental rehearsal treatment. They imagined a skating competition, seeing themselves on the ice and visualizing their coach waiting for them at the entrance to the rink and the panel of judges sitting on the side. As they imagined this, music for their skating routine was played, and they drew their movements on a page. The skaters in the control group were assigned stretching exercises for the same period of time. Results showed that in a subsequent competition, the skaters in the mental rehearsal group improved their performance relative to the control group for jumping, spins, and connecting moves (Garza & Feltz, 1998).

There are many other opportunities for research that employs experimental changes in personality. For example, considerable experimental work has been devoted to changing peoples' moods through mood manipulations and seeing what influence that has on their thoughts (e.g., Forgas, 2001). Other research has instructed people to control their thoughts in various ways so as to examine what is most effective in blocking out unwanted ideas (e.g., Wegner, 1989). Still other research has involved experimentally inducing fear (by telling participants they are about to receive painful electrical shocks) to try and determine what distinguishes people who recognize they are afraid from those who don't (Weinberger, Schwartz, & Davidson, 1979). The results from such experiments tell us a good deal about how personality operates—as we'll see in upcoming chapters.

What Does It Mean to Measure Personality?

The Psychometric Approach

What Is Measurement?

Whether the research design employed is a case study, a correlational design or a true experiment with random assignment, some measure of human attributes plays a role in the investigation. But what is measurement? We never actually measure an object itself, but rather a property of an object. For example, we don't measure tables, diamonds, or horse races. Rather, we measure the *length* of a table, the *weight* of a diamond, or the *duration* of a horse's run around a track. In the same way, we don't measure personality, but rather the *intelligence*, *extroversion*, or *emotionality* of a personality.

Personality measurement is the assignment of numerals to the various features or properties of personalities according to some orderly system. By a property or attribute of a person we mean any characteristic that can vary. The properties that vary are referred to as variables.

At the outset of the 20th century many psychologists doubted that the measurement of abstract qualities such as intelligence, extroversion, or emotion was possible. Only after the 1920s did experts come to agree that such measurement could be carried out adequately. Some milestones in the first 100 years of testing are shown in Table 2-3. The evolution of psychological measurement is typical of many disciplines in that progress required many innovations and considerable time.

Fundamentals of Measurement

Psychometrics is a field devoted to developing measurement techniques for the assessment of a person's mental qualities. Psychometricians develop theories of test scores and what those scores tell us about the people who take tests. Their psychometric theories enable us to evaluate a test so that we can decide how good or bad it is.

A psychological **test** can be defined as a systematic procedure in which individuals are presented with a set of constructed stimuli called "items" to which they respond in some way. Test items come in a variety of forms from "Do you like broccoli?—Yes/No" to "How many uses can you think of for a teaspoon?" The term **scale** is used interchangeably with the word test.

Table 2-3: Selected Milestones in a Century of Personality Testing

Year	Milestone
1904	An important early textbook on tests and measurement, *Introduction to the Theory of Mental and Social Measurement,* is published by E. L. Thorndike.
1905	The first intelligence test is published by Binet and Simon.
1910	The first word-association test designed to study the mental complexes of psychiatric patients is published by Carl Jung.
1917	The first group intelligence tests are used to place enlistees by the U.S. Army in World War I.
1921	Herman Rorschach introduces the world to the inkblot test with the publication of *Psychodiagnostics: A diagnostic test based on perception,* in German.
1927	The first career-interest tests are published by Edward K. Strong.
1936	The Graduate Record Exam is first used to screen graduate school applicants.
1938	Henry Murray and his colleagues introduce the Thematic Apperception Test—a projective test, often used for measuring motives.
1942	The Minnesota Multiphasic Personality Inventory—a test of abnormal personality—is introduced.
1952	The APA's Committee on Test Standards publishes the first technical recommendations for psychological measures.
1956	In "Wanted – A good cookbook," Paul Meehl argues that test evaluations outperform clinical judgment in assessments of people.
1961	In a U. S. Air Force technical report Tupes & Christal publish the first consistent findings of what became known as the Big Five personality traits.
1966	The first *Standards for Educational and Psychological Tests and Manuals* is published jointly by the *American Psychological Association* and the *American Educational Research Association.*
1968	Walter Mischel publishes "Personality and Assessment," in which he finds that many tests (excluding intelligence tests) have an upper limit of around $r = .30$ in predicting single behaviors. The figure was later revised upward to $r = .40$ or .45.
1980	Seymour Epstein publishes "The Stability of Behavior: II. Implications for Psychological Research" in which he shows that tests predict trends of behavior over multiple situations and times.
1994	By 1994, over 3,009 mental tests are in print, a sizeable number of which measure personality attributes from achievement motivation to xenophobia.

Key Sources: 1904-1939: Intelligence and Occupational testing Aiken (2003, p. 5); through 1938: Murray (1938); to 1994: C. A. Peterson (1997); also Meyer et al. (2001)

Classical Test Theory (CTT)

Most of the standard procedures for creating and evaluating tests are based on a set of assumptions and mathematical derivations that has come to be called **classical test theory**. While there have been some more contemporary developments of psychometric theory, classical test theory provides a good introduction to the field (Allen & Yen, 1973; Bechger et al., 2003; Cronbach et al, 1965; Murphy & DeShon, 2000; Novick, 1966). The fundamental hypothesis of classical test theory is that a person's **obtained score** on a test is a function of their *true* **score** and an *error* **score**. A true score reflects the person's actual level on a characteristic. An error score reflects extraneous factors that influence a person's answer independent of their true level. If Michael receives a score of 60 on a test of extraversion, that score reflects some portion of his true level of sociability and some error. In terms of an equation, the fundamental assumption of classical test theory is:

X = T + E, where

X = an obtained score on a test.

T = a person's true score on a test.

E = a person's error score on a test.

Michael's true level of extraversion might be T = 50. Given that his obtained score, X, was 60, his score included an error score, E, of 10, meaning that he scored 10 points too high. How could that happen? Right before walking into the test, he might have had an enjoyable, lively conversation with several friends. Recalling that conversation might cause him to inflate his response to the question "Do you like being with groups of people?" relative to what he might otherwise have answered. If instead, he had recalled an unpleasant relationship as he answered that test item, he might have lowered his score to 40, in which case his error score would have been E = -10.

Criteria for Good Measurement

One of the purposes of psychometric theory is to permit us to decide whether a test is an adequate measure of a concept. Psychometrics has two primary criteria of whether a test works: Whether the test is reliable, and whether it is valid.

Reliability

What Is Reliability?

A commonsense understanding of **reliability** equates it to stability, predictability, dependability, and consistency. For example, a bathroom scale that gives you the same weight when you step on it two or three times in a row is reliable. A reliable test yields the same score for people with the same level of a given attribute each time it is given. A reliable test measures whatever it measures with consistency.

Further insight into reliability is offered by recalling the concepts of obtained, true, and error scores from classical test theory. Recall that the obtained score equals the true score plus the error score, or, X = T + E. In classical test theory, tests are more reliable when the error is small. When the obtained score equals the true score, there is no error (X = T), and the test has perfect reliability. Test reliability is in fact defined as the correlation between the test's obtained score and true score. When X = T, the correlation between them—and the test reliability—is 1.0. Of course, it is unusual for the obtained score to equal the true score exactly. There is usually some error (E). When the error is small the correlation between the obtained score and true score may be $r = .80$ or more. If the error is large, however, the reliability may approach zero. When the obtained scores on the test equal only error (X = E), the test is said to possess no reliability at all, $r = 0$. (Reliability coefficients typically range from zero to 1.0; they do not commonly fall into negative territory).

Estimating Reliability

There is no way to directly calculate reliability by, say, correlating obtained scores with true scores. The reason? True scores are theoretical entities and cannot be known directly. It is relatively easy, however, to *estimate* reliability using any of several methods. Derivations from classical test theory indicate that these methods provide closely equivalent estimates of reliability under many conditions.

Types of Reliability

Parallel Forms Reliability

Perhaps the most straightforward way to judge a test's reliability is to write two strictly parallel tests and correlate them. Parallel tests have comparable items. For example, an item on one test might ask, "Are you moody?" whereas the corresponding item on the parallel test might ask, "Does your mood go up and down?" Other items would be similarly parallel across forms. In such an instance, the reliability of either test is equal to the correlation between the two tests. This is known as **parallel forms reliability**. Although this method is sometimes used, it is labor intensive because the psychologists need to produce two tests when often only one is needed.

Internal Consistency Reliability

Another way to determine a test's reliability is to estimate its internal consistency. **Internal consistency reliability** refers to the degree that different parts of a test "agree" with one another in their measurement. The simplest form of internal consistency is a *split half reliability*. The split half method involves first dividing a test into parallel halves. For example, the test might be divided into its odd-numbered items and even-numbered items. We consider the two halves as representing parallel forms of one larger test (see parallel forms reliability, above). The correlation of the two halves is a direct estimate of the reliability of half the test. It must be corrected upward to get a reliability of the whole test, and this can be done by employing a special correction.

One limitation of split-half reliability is that there is usually more than one way to split a test in half. It could be divided into odd and even halves, into first and second halves, or by selecting random halves. Each different split yields a somewhat different estimate of reliability. To get around this problem, most psychologists employ coefficient alpha, which is roughly equivalent to the average of all the split-half reliabilities. It is the most commonly employed reliability estimate today.

Test-Retest Reliability

A final way to calculate reliability is **test-retest reliability**. To calculate test-retest reliability, psychologists administer the same test at two different points in time to find out whether the test-taker's scores stay the same over time. The reliability estimate is equal to the correlation of the people's test scores at two different points in time. The test-retest estimate works well for tests that measure characteristics such as intelligences or attitudes that are relatively constant over a period of months or years. The method is inappropriate for variables that change quickly, such as hunger levels, because the changes in test levels might result from actual shifts in the person's hunger rather than from any inconsistency in the test's measurement.

Note that test-retest reliability tells us something more than just about the test itself. It tells us both that the test is consistent and that the quality being measured is stable over time. In essence, the reliability coefficient is telling us the score indicates something stable over time.

Evaluating Reliabilities

For basic research, a reliability of $r = .50$-60 is not uncommon, but $r = .70$ or higher is considered desirable. For other personality assessments where the test may be used to help determine someone's future, reliabilities of at least $r = .85$ are considered necessary, because reliability influences how accurately one's predictions about the individual will be.

Recall that reliability assesses whether a test measures *something* with consistency. Reliability is a necessary attribute of a good test. For a test to truly work, however, it must also measure what it is intended to measure. This aspect of a test's performance is called validity.

Validity

Validity refers to whether a test measures what it is intended to measure. The validity of a test is based on many types of evidence. Some evidence for a test's validity may be based on logical argument; other evidence may come from how the test correlates with other similar tests. A test-maker needs to find supporting evidence of many kinds to build confidence that a test measures what it claims to measure (Landy, 1986). A joint committee of the *American Psychological Association*, the *Educational Research Association*, and the *National Council on Measurement* publishes standards that tests should meet. Those standards direct psychologists and educators to collect evidence of the most important kinds to establish a test's validity (Joint Committee, 1999).

Validity Evidence from Test Content (Content Validity)

Validity evidence from test content refers to whether the given test measures the content that it is supposed to measure. For instance, if a test-maker wants the test to measure "hostility," then the test should contain items that ask about hostility and the specific expressions that make it up. Buss and Durkee (1957) defined hostility as including: (a) assaults on others, (b) indirect hostility (e.g., not helping a person who would otherwise be harmed), (c) irritability, (d) negativism, (e) resentment, (f) suspicion, and (g) verbal hostility. They then wrote a scale that carefully included items to measure each of these seven areas. That process helped ensure that their scale had validity evidence based on its content.

Validity Evidence from Test Structure

Validity evidence from test structure refers to whether there is a match between the scales and subscales of a psychological test and the way the actual items on the test behave empirically. Test structure in specific refers to the correlations among a test's parts—the correlations among its subscales, if it has subscales, and the correlations among its items. By looking at the correlations among the parts of a test, researchers determine whether a test measures one thing, two things, or more things, even without knowing what those things are. When you measure the height of a window and the temperature outside, you know that you are measuring two different things in part because height and temperature vary separately. When people take a well-designed test that has two subscale scores, the scores on the subscales should be partly independent of one another, indicating that the two subscales are measuring separate mental qualities.

To provide evidence from test structure, researchers try to determine whether a test actually measures the number of things it says it does (Loevinger, 1967). If a test author says a test measures two things and it does, then it is structurally valid. If the test measures only one variable or four variables, however, it would lack evidence for its validity in this area because the test would fail to match the theory on which it is based. In practice, a test-maker might claim his or her test measured only extroversion. A structural analysis of the test, however, might indicate that it measured three different scores—none of which were related to the other. In such a case, the test would lack structural validity. Structural validity is determined by using factor analysis, a mathematical technique that is described later in this chapter.

Validity Evidence from Criterion Correlations (Criterion Validity)

Validity evidence from criterion relationships refers to the fact that a test correlates with various criteria the way we would expect if the test measures what it is supposed to. A criterion is a standard of performance or an outcome such as grades, behaviors, or good health. Because intelligence tests correlate with school grades, they are said to exhibit evidence for their validity because intelligence ought to predict school grades. When intelligence tests correlate with students' current grades they are said to have *concurrent* predictions because they are predicting a criterion that is occurring at (roughly) the same time as the testing. When intelligence tests correlate with future school performance they are said to have *predictive* relations because they are correlating with an outcome that occurred well after the testing. Tests with criterion validity are used to assess psychiatric symptoms, to select people for jobs for which their skills and aptitudes are a good fit, and to help people understand themselves. A woman's high score on a test of sociability might help her decide to go into sales, because sociable people enjoy working in sales relative to those who prefer solitude.

Evaluating Validity

There is no single way to evaluate validity. Some tests have good evidence for their validity in certain areas, but fail to measure what they are supposed to measure. A test might ask all about a person's willingness to lie, but liars might lie on the test and say they are trustworthy! Most good tests are valid for some purposes but not for others. Intelligence tests, for example, are valid for measuring a person's ability to solve intellectual problems, but not for judging whether they are usually in a good mood. Some tests are valid in some settings, but not in others. A self-report test of honesty might work when it is filled out anonymously, but almost everyone might claim to be honest if they were applying for a job and had to put their name on the test. To pick the right test for the right purpose requires understanding concepts of validity and how a specific test will perform in a particular context.

How Do Psychologists Manage the Study of so Many Variables?

Multiple Variables and Multivariate Techniques

Personality is multifaceted and for that reason researchers often prefer to measure many of the variables that reflect its functioning. Let's say a group of researchers wants to predict employees' performance on the job. In a lab meeting they decide to measure achievement motivation, people's emotional styles, intellectual competence, and coping styles. They go on to select scales in each area: For coping styles, they select measures of persistence, adaptability, emotional self-management, stress-management, and the use of meditation. In this way, variables multiply.

To deal with so many variables, psychologists have developed **multivariate statistical techniques.** These techniques are extensions of simpler statistics such as a correlation for use with larger numbers of variables. Knowing how to interpret a multivariate statistical technique is typically the subject of an advanced undergraduate or graduate level statistics course. If you develop a basic understanding of one widely used technique right now—**factor analysis**—you might find it very helpful. Our present-day understanding of the parts of personality relies heavily on this technique and many examples of factor analysis will appear in forthcoming chapters.

The Logic of Factor Analysis

Factor analysis is the oldest and best-developed technique for organizing many variables. It can be used to group traits according to their similarities. For example, it tells us that thrill seeking, liveliness, and sociability are all part of extraversion. As an introduction to the technique, we will focus on the factor analysis of a single test and its items. Recall from the earlier section on test validity that the structure of a test (technically, its covariance structure) refers to how many things the test measures. Factor analysis is the mathematical technique helps describe that determines test structure.

The logic of factor analysis is straightforward. If two test items, A and B, are typically answered the same way, then they are said to measure the same thing. For example, if one group of people describe how they cope by endorsing a test item that says they "Increased efforts to make things work" and they also agreed that they "Changed what [they] did to improve the situation," they are answering the two items the same way. Further evidence that people answer items A and B comes if another group of people agree that when facing a challenging situation, they never "Increased [their] efforts" and never "Changed what [they] did."

Table 2-4: A Brief Coping Test

Test Instructions. Please answer the following questions using this scale:
1: strongly disagree; 2: disagree; 3 neutral; 4: agree; 5: strongly agree

A. ___	Increased my efforts to make things work.
B. ___	Changed what I did to improve the situation.
C. ___	Found kindness and compassion from someone.
D. ___	Talked about my feelings with a friend or advisor.

For a similar full-length scale see Folkman et al. (1986, Table 3).

In a study of people's coping styles, participants were asked to recall a recent stressful event: losing the affection of someone important, appearing uncaring or unethical to other people, or coping with harm to a loved one (see Anshel, Williams, & Williams, 2000; Folkman et al., 1986). The participants then described their typical coping response by answering the questions like those in Table 2-4. For example, for item A, a respondent might agree or disagree with the idea that he had, "Increased my efforts to make things work," or for item B, "Changed what I did to improve the situation." Both of these items seem to describe a proactive, effortful response to stress and it seems likely people who would use one strategy would use the other. A person who would respond to A with a "4" (agree) might also respond to B with a "4." A person who used some other coping strategy, such as doing nothing, would tend to disagree with both items (responding with a "1" or "2," to disagree). Therefore, items A and B would be answered in much the same way. According to the logic of factor analysis, they would be measuring the same thing. When two or more items are said to measure the same thing, that thing is referred to as a factor. Thus, in the terminology of factor analysis, we would say that items A and B—"Increased efforts" and "Changed what I did"—are two items that measure one factor.

Now consider items C: "Found kindness and compassion from someone," and D, "Talked about my feelings and concerns with a friend or advisor." These items both reflect seeking support from others. It also seems likely that people would answer these two items in similar ways. After all, a person who likes to get help from others would both accept compassion from others (item C) and talk about his feelings (item D), so he would mark 4 (agree) or 5 (strongly agree) for both items. If items C and D are answered in the same way, they also would be measuring the same thing according to the logic of factor analysis. Again, one would conclude that items C and D are two items that measure one factor.

Finally, compare items A and B with items C and D. Some proactive copers (who endorse items A and B) might also seek support from others (endorse items C and D). Other proactive copers, however, might cherish their independence and avoid seeking help from others (disagree with C and D). Answers to items A and B tell us little or nothing about answers to items C and D. For that reason, items A and B would measure something different from items C and D. The four items measure two "things" (called factors). That's what our logical analysis leads us to conclude—but is it accurate?

Table 2-5: Raw Data Matrix for the Coping Test

Test-Taker	Item A: Increased efforts	Item B: Changed actions	Item C: Found kindness	Item D: Talked feelings
Person 1	5	5	1	1
Person 2	5	4	4	5
Person 3	1	2	3	3
Person 4	5	5	5	4
...	...	...	...	...
Person 100	1	1	1	1

Factor analysis involves an empirical check of such logic. The first step of a factor analysis involves taking a set of test items such as those in Table 2-4, administering them to a group of people, and then finding the correlations among the items. For example, our four-item test might be given to 100 people. We'd then collect the participants' responses and arrange them as shown in Table 2-5.

Table 2-5 suggests that people tend to give answers to items A and B that are similar to one another; they also tend to give the answers to items C and D that are similar to each other. On the other hand, their answers to items A and B seem unrelated to their answers on items C and D.

The exact degree to which people give the same answers to various item pairs can be described with a correlation coefficient. The more people who tend to give the same answers on two items, the higher the correlation. The correlations among items A, B, C, and D are shown in the correlation matrix in Table 2-6. A correlation matrix is a table that has a set of variables across the top and the same set of variables down the side. A given correlation coefficient—say, between items A and B—can be found where column A intersects with row B.

Like any correlation matrix, only one half of the matrix is shown (in this case, the lower triangle of correlations) because the other half would be identical. The diagonal (the diagonal line of numbers that slopes across the table) is all 1.00s, indicating that each variable correlates with itself perfectly. The remaining correlation coefficients indicate the relationships among the variables we have just discussed. The (A) "Increased efforts" item correlates substantially with the (B) "Changed actions" item ($r = .40$). The (C) "Found kindness" and (D) "Talked feelings" items correlate highly as well ($r = .39$). But neither the (A) "Increased efforts" nor the (B) "Changed actions" items correlate with the (C) "Found kindness" item ($r = .10$ and .10, respectively) or the (D) "Talked feelings" item ($r = -.13$ and -.01).

Why don't the items that we thought might measure the same thing correlate with each other more highly, close to $r = 1.0$? They seem to correlate closer to $r = .40$. This occurs because each test item alone is very unreliable. Individual items can be thought of as the shortest possible test one can construct—and they are also the least reliable. Because the items are so unreliable by themselves—they contain so much error variance—their correlations with other similar items are relatively low.

Table 2-6: Correlations Among the Coping Items

Test Items	Item A: Increased efforts	Item B: Changed actions	Item C: Found kindness	Item D: Talked feelings
A. Increased efforts	1.00			
B. Changed actions	.40	1.00		
C. Found kindness	.10	.10	1.00	
D. Talked feelings	-.13	-.01	.39	1.00

Even though these correlations of around $r = .40$ are low, they are still relatively higher than the remainder of the correlations which seem very close to zero—between $-.15$ and $+.15$, in fact. The correlation matrix is another way of showing what we have already discussed. Items A and B seem to measure one thing, and items C and D measure a second, different thing. Note that we have now collected data that support our guess: Factor analysis will sort the items based on these empirical relationships into separate groups: "Increased efforts" and "Changed actions" on the one hand, and "Found kindness" and "Talked feelings" on the other.

Reading the Results of a Factor Analysis

If all the results were as clear as those in the correlation matrix above, the analysis could stop here. But when a researcher is dealing with dozens of items rather than four, and when the correlations are closer together, the second step of factor analysis becomes very important. This step is called "extracting factors" or "estimating parameters." The mathematics employed are complex and outside the scope of this course, but we can read the results. Factor analysis rearranges mathematical information so that the relations between each of the original test items and the factors that now group the test items are clear.

In this instance, statistical software would create a table in which the original test items are listed down a column on the left-hand side with the factors numbered across the top. This arrangement is shown in Table 2-7. Table 2-7 is referred to as a "factor-loading table." It provides: (a) the original items, (b) the number of factors (things) the test measures, and (c) the correlation of the original variables with the factors, which are called **factor loadings**.

In Table 2-7, the four coping test items can be divided into 2 factors (designated by Roman numerals). The original items measuring "Increased efforts" and "Changed actions" are highly correlated with the first factor, and the second group of original items "Found kindness" and "Talked feelings" are highly correlated with the second factor. The factor names are given by the researchers based on their judgment of the group of items that load on the factor. (We say the items "load" on the factors when the correlations between the item and the factor are high; recall those correlations are called "factor loadings"). Based on these results, we can name the first factor "Planful Problem-Solving" and the second factor "Seeking Social Support."

Today, many factor analyses are carried out as part of a broader mathematical technique called Structural Equation Modeling. In the context of that newer technique, this second step of factor extraction is called parameter-estimation, and is often represented in a figure as well as a table. Such a diagram is shown in Figure 2-6. There, the original test items are represented in boxes and the factors are represented as ovals. The variables are connected to the factors by lines and the factor loadings appear next to each line. That is, the factor loadings that had been found in the table are instead transferred next to the line in the figure connecting the given item to the factor. For example, the factor loading of $r = .71$, which represented the relation between "Increased efforts" and the Planful Problem-Solving factor in Table 2-7, is found in Figure 2-6 on the line connecting the original item (in the square) and the factor (in the oval).

Table 2-7: Factor Results for the Coping Scale

Test Items	Factor	
	I	II
A. Increased my efforts to make things work.	.71	-.05
B. Changed what I did to improve the situation.	.59	.13
C. Found kindness and compassion from someone.	.15	.57
D. Talked about my feelings and concerns with a friend or advisor.	-.08	.56

Researchers often prefer this newer approach to factor analysis because it makes it easier to compare different theoretical models by adding or altering lines between items and factors—and to test which models are better than others (e.g., Bentler, 2000; Gorsuch, 1983; Maruyama, 1998; Raykov & Marcoulides, 2000; Jöoreskog & Sörbum, 1999).

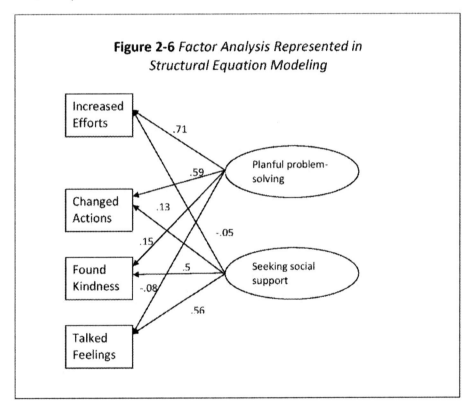

Figure 2-6 *Factor Analysis Represented in Structural Equation Modeling*

High vs. Low Correlations in the Correlation Matrix versus in the Factor Table

A few additional clarifications can complete this picture of factor analysis. Recall that the initial correlations among test items often include a fair number of low correlations in the correlation matrix. These correlations had resulted because the individual test items are often unreliable. You might wonder, then, why the individual items have far higher loadings on factors. The reason that the correlations between items and factors are so much higher in the factor-loading table (or diagram) is that this phase of factor analysis corrects for the unreliability of items. Typically, those items with loadings of $r = .40$ to .90 are considered good indicators of the factor; those items with loadings below $r = .30$ are considered relatively independent of the factor.

Bipolar Factors and Negative Correlations

What about negative correlations among items? To find out, let's return to the coping scale we first examined and add a negatively correlating item: Test Item E, "Couldn't figure out anything to do and so didn't do anything," as illustrated in Table 2-8.

Table 2-8: The Generic Coping Test With an Added Item

Test Instructions. Please answer the following questions using this scale:
1: strongly disagree; 2: disagree; 3 neutral; 4: agree; 5: strongly agree

A. ___	Increased my efforts to make things work.
B. ___	Changed what I did to improve the situation.
C. ___	Found kindness and compassion from someone.
D. ___	Talked about my feelings and concerns with a friend or advisor.
E. ___	Couldn't figure out anything to do and so didn't do anything.

Let's suppose that planful problem solvers (who agree with items A and B) will tend to disagree with item E. Conversely, people who endorse item E "Couldn't figure" don't cope well and will disagree with A and B. If that's so, then item E will correlate *negatively* with items A and B, because as E goes up, A and B will go down, and vice versa. If we test this empirically, it will turn out to be the case. We would obtain a correlation matrix such as the one in Table 2-9.

Table 2-9: Item Correlations Among the Extended Coping Test

Test Items	Item A: Increased efforts	Item B: Changed actions	Item C: Found kindness	Item D: Talked feelings	Item E: Couldn't figure
A. Increased efforts	1.00				
B. Changed actions	.40	1.00			
C. Found kindness	.10	.10	1.00		
D. Talked feelings	-.13	-.01	.39	1.00	
E. Couldn't figure	-.49	-.40	.07	-.03	1.00

Table 2-9 still indicates that only two factors are being measured: planful problem-solving and seeking social support. The high negative correlations between E, and A and B (i.e., $r = -.49, -.40$) mean that there is a strong negative relationship between actively problem solving, on the one hand and not doing anything on the other. They're opposite sides of the same coin. Moving on to the second step of the factor analysis, the factor table would look like that shown in Table 2-10. The planful problem-solving factor is represented as the set of factor loadings under the Roman numeral "I." The "Couldn't figure" item appears—with a fairly high negative correlation—on the planful problem-solving factor.

Table 2-10 indicates that whenever planful problem-solving is present, action is present, inaction is missing, and vice versa. Seeing the performance of the "Couldn't Figure" item, the analyst might want to rename the first factor "Planful Problem-Solving versus Inaction," to reflect the fact that it has variables that define both extremes of coping. Sometimes a factor that displays this double-sided quality is referred to as a **bipolar factor**. Otherwise, the factor is referred to as a **unipolar factor**.

Table 2-10: Factor Results for the Extended Coping Scale

Test Items	Factor	
	I	II
A. Increased my efforts to make things work.	.71	-.05
B. Changed what I did to improve the situation.	.61	.03
C. Found kindness and compassion from someone.	.15	.57
D. Talked about my feelings and concerns with a friend or advisor.	-.08	.56
E. Couldn't figure out anything to do and so didn't do anything.	-.65	-.12

"Mathematics, rightly viewed, possesses not only truth, but supreme beauty—a beauty cold and austere, like that of sculpture, without appeal to any part of our weaker nature, without the gorgeous trappings of painting or music, yet sublimely pure, and capable of a stern perfection such as only the greatest art can show." – Bertrand Russell (1872-1970)

A Critique of Factor Analysis

Factor analysis is a useful technique for grouping variables according to their similarities. But factor analysis cannot substitute for good theories and careful thought about what the variables that we employ mean. The technique may sometimes group together items that, although highly correlated, are clearly theoretically distinct (Mayer, Salovey, Gomberg-Kaufman, & Blainey, 1991). For example, height and weight are highly correlated—the taller someone is, the more they weigh. Together height and weight describe a person's overall size. Yet physicians would be foolish to overlook the differences between the two variables. They would miss that short height and high weight co-occur in obesity or that tallness and low weight is a sign of Marfan syndrome. Factor analysis more or less mindlessly clusters together correlated variables. For some purposes that is the right thing to do; for other purposes, as with height and weight in medicine, it may well be the wrong thing to do. Only a good theoretical analysis can make a final determination of when it is right and when it is wrong to combine variables.

There are many opportunities for data collection and studying the relations among variables. Psychological tests ask many good questions. Factor analysis is an invaluable tool for organizing similar items together into factors so as to simplify the research task.

Reviewing Chapter 2

This chapter seeks to introduce you to how research is conducted in personality psychology. After examining the sorts of data available to the psychologist, several research approaches to personality psychology were discussed, including case studies and correlational designs. Whatever design a psychologist uses, some measurement must be taken of the individual and/or her surroundings. Some elements of psychological measurement were covered, particularly the fundamental ideas of psychometrics, including reliability and validity. Personality psychologists like to examine a number of personality variables together. The last section examined the multivariate technique of factor analysis. Can you answer the following questions, arranged by the major sections of the chapter?

Questions About "Where Do the Data Come From?"

1. <u>Data come from a variety of sources:</u> Data about the person can come from the person's life sphere or life space. That data is often called Life data, or L data. Data from the person's life sphere may include institutional information from school records, biological information from medical tests, and observer-ratings. Data can also come from within the person, for example, from personal reports including self-reports. What kinds of data come from the person him- or herself?

Questions About "What Research Designs Are Used in Personality Psychology?"

2. <u>Case studies:</u> Probably the earliest method used in personality psychology is the case study approach. When describing a single person, one is using a case study method. What can case studies accomplish that other methods can't do as well? What are some of the drawbacks of case studies?

3. <u>Observationism:</u> How is observationism similar to the case study? How is it different? What historical events led to a de-emphasis on observation?

4. <u>Correlational Research Designs:</u> What does correlational design involve? What does the method tell us? A correlation coefficient indicates the relationship between two variables. It is of central importance to conducting studies using correlational designs. These coefficients have a range from –1 to 1. Can you say what a coefficient of 1.0 mean? What about 0.0 and –1.0?

5. <u>Natural Experiments and Full Experimental Designs:</u> In an experiment, two groups are compared, and hypothesized to be different in relation to an outcome, called the dependent variable. Typically, the two groups are called the experimental and the control groups. The experimental group has been changed through a treatment. The treatment is a manipulation of some sort that is expected to make the experimental group different from the control group. In a full experimental design, people are randomly assigned to the control and experimental groups, and then the treatment is applied in the experimental group. In a natural experiment, however, two groups that are naturally different are selected, such as two different occupational groups. What is the advantage of a full experimental design relative to a natural experiment? Given that superiority, why are natural experiments considered so useful in the study of personality?

Questions About "What Does It Mean to Measure Personality?"

6. <u>The Psychometric Approach:</u> The field of psychometrics is concerned with creating workable mathematical models for measuring people's qualities. One doesn't measure a person, but rather, one measures the attributes or features of a person. The fundamental theorem of psychometrics is that $X = T + E$, or, in words, that any observed score (X) reflects both a person's true quality (T) on the attribute, and some degree of error (E). What happens if an error positive, or if it is negative?

7. <u>Test Reliability:</u> Reliability is a property of all adequate measurement and concerns the degree to which tests measure with consistency. There are several different ways of assessing reliability, including the parallel test, internal consistency, and test-retest methods. Can you define each of these?

8. <u>Test Validity.</u> Validity refers to whether a test measures what it claims to measure. There are a number of kinds of evidence that are relevant to a test's validity. Can you define each of them?

Questions About "How Do Personality Psychologists Manage the Study of so Many Variables?"

9. <u>Psychologists Study Multiple Variables:</u> Personality is a comprehensive system, including many individual parts, their organization, and their development. Measuring enough aspects of personality to make sense of it (and enough aspects of the life sphere to make sense of that) requires large numbers of individual observations. What is it about how we think of personality that encourages measuring so many different variables?

10. <u>Approaches to Multiple Variables:</u> Statistical techniques that examine many different variables are called multivariate techniques. A widely used method of looking at multiple variables is called factor analysis. When multiple variables are used, one often begins by calculating a simple index of relationship between each pair of variables. What statistic tells us about how two variables are related?

11. <u>Factor Analysis:</u> Factor analysis concerns studying how many things a test measures. It can be used to reduce the number of variables of a test, and also to demonstrate a type of validity. Do you know which sort of validity it helps determine? If you were presented a test that claimed to measure five things, and a factor analysis said it only measured three things, would you be able to conclude anything about the test's structural validity?

12. <u>Reading a Factor Analysis:</u> Basically, findings from a factor analysis are presented as follows: A list of original variables forms a left hand column. To the right are columns representing factors, each labeled with a Roman numeral. The columns themselves contain a correlation between an original variable and its factor. Do you know what the correlation between a test item and a factor is called?

13. <u>Factor Analysis and Dimensions:</u> Factors with only positive (or negative) loadings are considered unipolar and are designated with one name (e.g., Extraversion). Factors with both positive and negative loadings are called bipolar and are designated with two opposing names: (e.g., Extraversion-Introversion). Seeing a factor table, would you be able to read a factor analysis and name the factors?

Chapter 2 Glossary

Terms in Order of Appearance:

Observer or Informant Data: A type of data about the person that comes from observers of the person such as specially trained raters, acquaintances, or friends.

External-Source Data (or Life Data): A type of data about a person that comes from the person's surrounding life; for example, from institutional records and the observations of others.

Personal-Report Data: A type of data of that the person generates him- or herself. This kind of data is often generated in interviews, while taking a test, or in similar activities.

Self-Judgment (or Self-Report) Data: A type of data about the person that the person generates him- or herself, and that typically involves some judgment of his or her own qualities and features.

Criterion-Report (or Mental Ability) Data: A type of test data in which the person must solve problems or engage in tasks, and then his or her performance is judged against a standard.

Thematic-Report (or Projective) Data: A type of test data in which a person constructs a response to an ambiguous stimulus, and that is often thought to reflect important motivational, affective, and cognitive processes in personality.

Case Study Design: A scientific research design in which one person ("the case") is studied in depth.

Observationism: A scientific approach in which multiple case studies are studied, and principles are deduced and tested from examining what has gone across the cases, and what is similar or different across them.

Free Association: A method of case-study observation in which a person is asked to talk aloud about anything that enters his or her stream of consciousness, however trivial or even embarrassing it might seem.

Variable: A feature of a person, situation, or other entity, which can take on more than one value. For example, level of creativity, number of siblings, and height are all variables.

Correlation Coefficient: A statistic, ranging from –1 to +1, that describes the relation between two variables.

Scatterplot: A graphical depiction of points, in which each point represents a pair of observations, such as the achievement-motivation score on a test, and the earned income of that individual. The magnitude of one variable is represented on the horizontal, X axis; the magnitude of the other variable is represented on the vertical, Y axis.

Natural Experiments: An experimental design in which the treatment of the experimental group (also known as the experimental manipulation), has already occurred naturally, rather than being randomly assigned. For example, in a comparison of airline pilots with middle managers, "career" is manipulated, but the individuals have already chosen their profession, and so profession has not been randomly assigned.

Treatment: In regard to experiments, the specific procedure employed to manipulate the independent variable.

True Experimental Design: A formal plan for carrying out an experiment, usually by comparing control and experimental groups on a dependent variable. Members of the experimental group receive a treatment, which is hypothesized to alter their level on the dependent variable, relative to the control group.

Ecological Validity: In regard to personality experiments, the degree to which the treatment brings about a change in personality that is similar to the actual personality phenomenon being studied in the real world. For example, the degree to which experimentally introducing a mental conflict approximates an actual mental conflict.

Personality Measurement: A research procedure in which numerals are assigned to features of a personality in a systematic fashion.

Psychometrics: A branch of psychology concerned with measuring mental and behavioral attributes.

Test (or Scale): In psychometrics, a defined group of questions or tasks (called items), to which a person can respond, that is intended to measure one or more attributes of the person.

Classical Test Theory: A theory underlying much psychological measurement, classical test theory is notable for its clarity and powerful predictions. Also known as classical true-score theory and classical reliability theory.

Obtained Score: In psychometrics, the score a person obtains on a test.

True Score: In psychometrics, a hypothetical score a person would obtain on a test that has measured the person perfectly; that is, the score that reflects the real level of the attribute in the person who is being measured.

Error Score: In psychometrics, a hypothetical score that reflects mistakes in measurement that are either positive or negative. Positive error scores reflect testing that gives the respondent too much credit; negative error scores reflect testing that has not given the respondent enough credit.

Reliability: In psychometrics, the consistency with a test measures. More technically, the correlation between people's obtained scores on a test and their corresponding true scores.

Parallel Forms Reliability: A reliability coefficient calculated by developing two parallel forms of the same test and correlating them.

Internal Consistency Reliability: A type of reliability estimated by examining the correlations of items on a test. Examples include split-half and coefficient alpha reliability coefficients.

Test-Retest Reliability: A type of reliability that is estimated by giving the same test to a group of people at two points in time, typically a few weeks apart, and then correlating the scores across test administrations.

Validity: In psychological measurement, the fact that a test measures what it claims to measure.

Validity Evidence from Test Content: A type of validity a test exhibits when its items are systematically selected from the areas the test claims to measure. For example, if the test measures U.S. history from 1900 to 1950, and its items sample history questions from the five decades in question, that would reflect content validity.

Validity Evidence from Test Structure: A type of validity a test exhibits when its items form a number of groups (as determined empirically by a technique such as factor analysis) that correspond to the number of things the test as a whole claims to measure. For example, if research indicates a test has three distinct groups of items, and those groups correspond to three scales that claim to measure three things, the test has structural validity.

Validity Evidence from Criterion Relationships: A type of validity a test exhibits when it correlates with a criterion of interest.

Multivariate Statistical Technique: A statistical technique designed especially to answer questions about more than two variables at a time.

Factor Analysis: A mathematical technique for grouping variables together based on their inter-correlations. Factor analysis is used to reduce large numbers of variables to smaller sets, and also for determining structural validity; that is, how many things a test measures.

Factor Loading: The correlation between an observed variable and a hypothetical variable called the factor (representing a group of variables).

Bipolar Factor: In factor analysis, a factor that has both positive and negative variable loadings.

Unipolar Factor: In factor analysis, a factor that has only negative, or only positive variable loadings.

Chapter 3: Perspectives on Personality

Previewing the Chapter's Central Questions

• **What Are Perspectives on Personality?** Questions about personality often stem from a particular point of view—such as: that personality is influenced by biology or by the social world. Such outlooks are called perspectives on personality.

• **What Is the Biological Perspective?** The idea that personality is closely connected to the brain and other biological influences is known as the biological perspective. This perspective highlights the brain's contribution to personality and how some personality mechanisms may have evolved.

• **What Is the Intrapsychic Perspective?** An intrapsychic perspective emphasizes how one psychological part of personality influences another. For example, trait theorists may be interested in understanding which psychological qualities contribute to extraversion. Psychodynamic theorists are interested in how parts interact—and often conflict—with one another.

• **What Is the Sociocultural Perspective?** A key part of the sociocultural perspective is the idea that people are who they are because of the situations they face and their culture.

• **What Is the Developmental Perspective?** The developmental perspective takes the long view of an individual—considering what he or she is like as an infant, a child, an adolescent, and then an adult.

• **How Do We Reconcile Multiple Theories?** Each of these perspectives has been responsible for focusing research efforts on a particular question about personality. The research hypotheses generated by such theories can be organized according to whether they address the parts, organization, or development of the personality system.

What Are Perspectives on Personality?

Frameworks, Perspectives, Theories

Personalities come in a startling variety of forms and types. One example of an unusual personality is Paul Erdős, a mathematician who, in the latter decades of his life, traveled to and from the homes of different colleagues, living out of a suitcase and relying on a network of relatives and trusted colleagues and their students. Erdős supported himself through academic lectures and gave away most of his money to various charities, while encouraging young mathematicians and trying to keep up the spirits of those who were aging. Erdős and his more than 485 coauthors published 1,475 academic papers in mathematics, some of monumental importance. Of Erdős, it was said that he could pose just the right problem for a fellow mathematician—just far enough ahead of his or her thinking to be challenging, just near enough to his or her abilities to be solved (Hoffman, 1998, pp. 7-10, 13, 42).

Why did Erdős devote his life to mathematics? Have you ever imagined yourself devoting yourself to a single project or aim in your life? Recall that a **field-wide framework** for a discipline divides personality into topics of study. The personality systems framework used in this book divides personality into a description of the system, it parts, organization, and development. Frameworks, however, don't directly explain why people behave as they do.

Psychologists draw on explanatory approaches to explain why people behave as they do. These explanatory approaches range from the very general to quite specific viewpoints. At the most general level are global perspectives, such as that biological, intrapsychic, or social events cause behavior. At a middle level a psychologist might draw on a theory of human behavior, such as one stemming from evolutionary psychology or the psychodynamic theory formulated by Sigmund Freud. At a still more specific level would be a micro-theory, which consists of a set of specific hypotheses. We will examine all these levels in this chapter.

Perspectives on Personality

At the broadest explanatory level are perspectives on the field. Concretely, the term "perspective" refers to the fact that, if you stand in a particular place, you can see some things and not others. In theoretical terms, a perspective provides us with a particular view of personality in which some things can be seen well, and other things are, perhaps, a bit more obscured. A perspective involves "a place from which to view" certain parts of personality.

Formally, a **personality perspective** is based on a set of assumptions or beliefs about what the most important influences on personality are. Psychologists often favor studying one or another influence on personality that they believe to be most important, be it knowledge of personality itself or one of its neighboring systems—biology, situations, or social groups—that surround and influence it (Larsen & Buss, 2002, pp. 15-16). The major perspectives basically parallel personality and its surrounding systems: biological, psychological, and sociocultural influences. In addition, there is a developmental perspective (cf. Larsen & Buss, 2002; Funder, 2001; Mischel, 1998). The perspectives are shown in the top row in Table 3-1.

The perspectives give us a hint as to where to look in understanding personality—to biology, or culture, for example—but they are not explicit in telling us how personality operates or how it came to be. For example, the biological perspective directs us toward examining the relationship between the brain and how it influences personality. The perspective is too broad in itself to generate specific hypotheses for scientific testing. For that reason, psychologists think at a level that's more specific than the perspective—at a theoretical level as well.

Personality Theories

Each general perspective encompasses a number of specific theories. In this chapter, I'll illustrate each perspective with two well-known theories that employ its point of view. A **theory of personality** contains a set of statements or assumptions about how personality operates. It develops this series of assumptions into a picture of the individual. A good theory also will contain rules for relating those assumptions and definitions to real, observable, empirical events. Examples of personality theories are in the second row of Table 3-1.

Psychologists use theories to make predictions about how personality operates in the real world; their educated guesses are called hypotheses. Researchers then test these hypotheses by employing empirical research, which in turn may bear out the entire theory, portions of it, or none of it (Hall & Lindsey, 1978, p. 17-18). Thereafter, the theory may be modified to make it more accurate. The better the theory operates, the more weight it will be given.

Some personality theories are expressed in a logical organized fashion. For example, the social-cognitive theorist George Kelly (1955a) began his personality theory with a central postulate that a person is like a scientist trying to discover and predict the world. He then set forth additional assumptions that systematically elaborated his views. Most larger personality theories, however, are developed over a series of publications. Freud's 20-plus volumes of writings about psychodynamic theory represent his original theory and its growth and changes over a 40-year period. To some extent, Freud left it to his followers to systematize his work (Rappaport, 1960).

Conceptual level	Description	Examples
Table 3-1: Explanatory Approaches to Personality: Perspectives, Theories, Micro-theories, and Findings from Research		
Perspective Level	Perspectives provide a general way of looking at the field. The systems framework identifies areas such as biology, psychology, sociology, and time (development) as common perspectives on personality (Mayer, 1995). These areas are commonly associated with scientific areas of training and expertise related to personality (Larsen & Buss, pp. 15-16).	Biological Intrapsychic Social Developmental
Theoretical Approach	"Big" or "Grand" theoretical approaches begin with a perspective and add to it specific assumptions, descriptions, and explanations of how personality operates (Larsen & Buss, pp. 15-16; tradeoffs, Funder, 2000, p. 5).	Evolutionary Psychology Biopsychology Trait perspective Psychodynamic Social-cognitive Cross-cultural Psychosocial Development Humanistic
Micro-theories	Micro-theories are smaller, more precisely defined hypotheses that may be inspired by theoretical approaches, but are not necessarily uniquely related to those theories. They are most often the subject of empirical research.	Specific gene behavior connections Frustration causes aggression Changing a thought pattern will change an emotion The perception of emotions changes slightly across cultures
Findings about personality	Empirical findings in the field tell us directly about personality. The systems framework sorts the findings into those that pertain to personality's parts, organization, and development.	General empirical findings

Each theory makes predictions about people. For example, George Kelly supposed that if you asked a person to reconsider what they are thinking at the right time, it should bring about desired change in therapy (Kelly, 1995b, p. 1090). If Kelly's predictions seem fairly general, they weren't alone in that respect, particularly among theories of the early-to-mid-20th century. The predictions of Freud, Jung, and Rogers were also often ill-specified by contemporary standards. The descriptions of behavior used by these and other theorists were so general that they weren't useful in motivating direct scientific investigations. Often, the general personality theories were too large, diffuse, and sometimes self-contradictory to be accessible to scientific test (e.g., Hall & Lindzey, 1978; Larsen & Buss, 2002; Mendelsohn, 1993). Some psychologists now prefer to talk about "approaches" rather than theories, believing that the original personality theories were so general that calling them theories was misleading (e.g., Funder, 2001). Whether or not that is the case, a better bridge between theories and research was needed than what personality theories provided. Micro-theories created this bridge.

Micro-Theories and Research

Micro-theories connect theories (or approaches) to actual research. They represent a more particular level of theorizing—a level that addresses specific, relatively narrow problems in personality rather than trying to explain the whole personality (Johnson et al., 1980). The bottom right of Table 3-1 contains a description of these specific formulations (which elsewhere have also gone by the names of "mid-level theory" and "limited-domain theory" (e.g., Maddi, 1973, p. 89; Schulz & Schulz, 2001, p. 445).

Micro-theories often arose in the research laboratory: Personality psychologists who conducted high quality research often formulated clearly stated but narrow theories that could be reasonably tested. Some micro-theories reframed a part of a grand theory of personality—for example, drawing on Freud's theory of repression, researchers predicted that threatening words would be forgotten more quickly than other kinds of words (which turns out not to be the case). Other researchers proposed micro-theories that tested new questions, for example, about the consistency of personality traits. The micro-theory level is crucial, because that is the theoretical level at which most personality research takes place.

Each micro-theory is empirically tested, and then results are obtained and interpreted. Typically, these results have implications for an understanding of personality's parts, organization, and development, as shown at the very bottom row of Table 3-1. It is these findings, drawn from various theories, that we'll employ to describe each of the remaining topics of this book: the parts of personality, personality organization, and personality development.

First, however, it is worth learning something of the broader theories that have guided thinking in the field. Only the briefest sketch of each perspective and its theories can be presented in a single book chapter, but we'll return to the theories and the ideas behind them in the later chapters of the book. The sketches provided here provide sufficient information to introduce these important theoretical influences on the field. If you're interested in learning more about the theories, you can read the original theoretical writings or examine one of the textbooks that accurately summarize a good deal of those early theories of the field (e.g., Hall & Lindzey, 1978; Monte, 1999).

What Is the Biological Perspective?

The biological perspective emphasizes the influence of genetics, neurology, and the brain on an individual's mental and social functioning. Among the most influential biological approaches are theories of evolutionary psychology and of biopsychology. Evolutionary psychology emphasizes that much of the way an individual feels, thinks, and behaves is due to longstanding evolutionary processes. This theory supposes that we have emotions and memories because they assisted our survival. The biopsychological perspective investigates the direct influences of the brain on mental life. The two approaches are complementary to one another. As people evolved, so did the direct influences exerted by the nervous system and brain on behavior.

Evolutionary Psychology Views the Person

From an evolutionary perspective, each of us is the product of a very long line of ancestors. If any one of our ancestors in that long chain had failed to survive and reproduce, we would not be here. Long before evolutionary theory was developed, it was understood that animal species—including the human species—changed over time. The fossil record was full of organisms, most notably dinosaurs that had become extinct. The same fossil record showed that other organisms that are with us today have changed gradually over time.

Evolutionary theory helps explain why some organisms survive and reproduce and others do not. Charles Darwin was the first to propose a theory of natural selection that described the process by which this occurs. In Darwin's original formulation, the evolution of species took place according to two processes: natural selection and sexual selection.

Natural and Sexual Selection

Natural selection describes how organisms with certain characteristics are better able to adapt to hostile forces of nature than are others. Because they are better adapted, they are most apt to survive and to reproduce. For example, at one time, the giraffe's ancestors had shorter necks. Over generations, competitor species began eating the lower growing leaves of the trees on which giraffes fed. Because the giraffes with longer necks were able to eat the high-growing leaves that the other animals could not reach, they were more likely to survive and reproduce. In each generation, giraffes with longer necks fared better; as a consequence, the species gradually developed the long neck as an adaptation to the environmental change imposed by its competitor species.

Adaptive responses to challenging environments, however, appear insufficient to explain all evolutionary phenomena. It is not enough for organisms to merely survive. In order to perpetuate a species, organisms also must attract mates and reproduce. Consequently, some adaptations evolve for the purposes of sexual selection. The peacock's extensive and colorful feathers are not adaptive in the context of natural selection. In fact, they create a problem for the peacock because they are very noticeable to predators. They are adaptive, however, in terms of mate selection. The plumage attracts peahens and thus increases the likelihood of a peacock's sexual reproduction.

This simple model is the one that Darwin proposed in 1850. Since that time, Darwin's basic ideas have been modified in certain important ways. Modern evolutionary theory is called "inclusive fitness theory" (Hamilton, 1964). It is concerned not solely with the individual and his or her genes, but also with the broader gene pool to which the individual belongs. Modern evolutionary theory better takes into account the way that an organism can benefit from helping a relative to survive and to mate. Brothers, for example, share 50% of their genes in common. For that reason, if one brother helps another survive (say, by protecting him against bullies), then that brother has enhanced the survival of his own genes as well. Psychoevolutionary theorists describe the existence of certain mental mechanisms—such as preferences for helping relatives—as a consequence of natural and sexual selection.

A Micro-Theory about Jealousy and Evolution

The evolutionary perspective is sometimes used to explain the mating and reproductive behavior of men and women. For example, one of the central issues driving relationships between men and women from an evolutionary perspective concerns the certainty of parenthood. The condition of men and women in this regard is quite different. Mothers have an essentially 100% likelihood of knowing who their biological children are because they give birth to them. For fathers, however, the chances that they know their biological offspring are somewhat less than 100%: a newborn might be the offspring of another man. Many fathers voluntarily raise other men's children in cases of step-parenting and adoption. From the strict standpoint of evolutionary psychology, however, raising another man's child while believing it to be one's own has disastrous consequences because it means the father's genes failed to survive in the next generation.

Therefore, evolutionary psychologists believe that men have evolved mental mechanisms to make them very wary of possible threats to the sexual fidelity of their mates.

The woman knows that her genes have been passed along to the next generation. Yet in the era of human evolutionary adaptation—perhaps half-a-million years ago—she was dependent upon her partner for material resources when raising her children. Evolutionary psychologists believed it was most adaptive for women to prevent the loss of resources from her mate should he become interested in another woman. A given woman knew her children were biologically her own even if her mate had other sexual partners, but if the man became emotionally committed to another woman, he might leave and withdraw his help with children, food gathering, and protection.

Evolutionary psychologists used this reasoning to conclude that men and women evolved different mental mechanisms to monitor infidelity in a relationship. Men should have developed mechanisms for monitoring their partners' other sexual liaisons; women should have developed mechanisms aimed at preventing men from straying from their emotional commitments. In short, men should jealously guard their mate's sexual fidelity; women should jealously guard their mate's emotional fidelity.

In a series of studies on sexual versus emotional jealousy, men and women were asked to imagine a strong, committed, romantic relationship they had had in the past. Then they were asked to rate how distressed they would feel if their partner had "formed a deep emotional attachment" to someone else, or if their partner had "enjoyed passionate sexual intercourse" with someone else. In keeping with the evolutionary hypothesis, 60% of all men reported more sexual than emotional jealousy. On the other hand, 80% of all women reported more emotional than sexual jealousy. This pattern is consistent across several Western cultures (Buss, Larsen, Westen, and Semmelroth; 1992; Buunk et al., 1996).

In this case, evolutionary psychology appears to offer a compelling and straightforward explanation for an otherwise difficult-to-explain difference in the psychological makeup of women and men. The limitation of this perspective is that it is sometimes difficult to prove that evolution is at work rather than other causal mechanisms such as cultural learning. In addition, evolutionary psychology seems focused on universal adaptive and reproductive differences. It can predict the existence of individual differences (diversity increases survival), but it focuses less on telling us what those specific individual differences are, who has them, and how one should behave under the circumstances. For answers to these questions, other perspectives are helpful.

Biopsychology Views the Person

The biopsychological approach to personality views the individual's mental phenomena through the lens of how the nervous system and its surrounding biology influence a person's mental life. The nervous system is divided into two parts: the peripheral nervous system, which extends throughout the body, and the brain.

The brain itself has sometimes been described as composed of three layers representing three phases of its evolution. The innermost part is called the reptilian brain because its central structures are shared by most reptiles. The layer surrounding the reptilian brain is the old- or paleo-mammalian brain, so-called because its central structures are found in all mammals. Finally, the outside layer is called the neo-mammalian brain because it is found only in the most complex mammals, reaching its fullest development in human beings. From the perspective of biopsychology, much or everything a person wants, feels, and thinks, is a product of the functioning of the central nervous system. Some of the key features of the biopsychological approach can be seen in Table 3-2, where it is compared to the evolutionary approach.

Table 3-2: A Comparison of Evolutionary Psychology and Biopsychological Theories

	Evolutionary Psychology	Biopsychological Theories
View of Personality	*Personality is the result of a long genetic line of ancestors, each of whom successfully met the challenges of survival and reproduction. *Personality is made up of many mental mechanisms that enhance survival.	*Personality is the direct result of neural structure, activity, and associated chemical influences. *The individual's motives, feelings, and thoughts are formed by the action of their underlying biological systems.
Central Issues	*How have evolutionary pressures shaped human nature? *What mental mechanisms have evolved?	*How does the brain bring about personality? *What biological changes will affect personality?
Typical Research Approach	*Comparisons across species; survey approaches with human beings to identify universal preferences.	*Studies of patients with neurological disorders, brain scans; studies of the effects of psychoactive drugs, experimental brain studies in animals.

The Nervous System and Its Influences on Psychology

The nervous system and brain influence mental experience and psychological action through four means: a person's brain structure, neurotransmitters, hormones, and the immune system.

Brain Structure

The link between brain structure and personality was first made in the 1790s, but early connections were mostly speculative and research after that was slow (Allport, 1937, p. 79). Today, information about brain structure has become dramatically more accessible due to modern brain-imaging techniques. For example, Magnetic Resonance Imaging (MRI) is an extremely sensitive technique that scans the brain for magnetic fields surrounding the atoms of its tissues. This and other techniques provide a view of the brain's structure and can uncover interesting individual differences in anatomy.

As one instance, scientists have observed that species with larger brain size relative to their bodies exhibit more intelligent behavior compared to species with smaller brains relative to their bodies. This has led some scientists to ask whether among human beings' brain size is related to intelligence. Numerous studies do point to a relationship between head size and IQ. Critics have pointed out, however, that most studies estimated brain size from head circumference—and it's difficult to estimate brain size from measures made of the outside of a person's head. In addition, these scientists could have been influenced by a desire to see a relationship that is not there (e.g., Gould, 1981). More recently, MRI brain-scanning techniques have permitted direct measures of brain size independent of the skull. Measures made with these new methods add to the evidence that brain size is consistently, if modestly, related to intelligence (e.g., Andreasen et al., 1993; Bigler, Johnson & Blatter, 1999; Pennington et al., 2000).

Brain Neurochemistry

A second way that the brain influences personality is through its neurochemistry. Neurons are information-processing cells that operate according to principles of both electrical and chemical transmission. The neuron is made up in part of a series of branches, called dendrites that lead into the cell body. It is also made up of an axon that leads away from the cell body toward the dendrites of other neurons. The neuron's axon ends at a synapse, where it meets the dendrite of the next neuron. The space between the end of the axon and the beginning of the next neuron's dendrite is called the synaptic cleft. This area is important because chemicals called **neurotransmitters** are transmitted across the synapse.

Neurotransmitters are chemicals that transmit neural impulses from one neuron to the next. Many chemicals manufactured in the brain and body, including neurotransmitters, hormones, and immune system chemicals influence certain areas of the brain's function. The amount of such chemicals present in the body is influenced both by genetic and environmental factors (Grigorienko, 2002; Zuckerman, 1991, pp. 200-201). Although hundreds of such chemicals are active in the brain, there exist a small "classical group" of neurotransmitters and hormones, so called because they were discovered decades ago, that have been more intensively studied than others. This classical group includes serotonin, which is involved in stress reactions and depression, and dopamine, which is implicated in attention and other cognitive functions. Also included are glutamate and acetylcholine, which have been found to play a role in memory. Another member of the classical group is endorphins, which are natural opiates that modulate pain and are often studied in relation to drug addictions.

Neurotransmitters are secreted by the neurons of the brain, but they are not the only chemicals that influence neural transmission. Many **hormones** act as neurotransmitters as well (McEwan, 1991). Hormones are secreted by endocrine organs and from there enter the bloodstream. Hormones primarily influence specific target cells in certain organs, including the heart, the liver, the pancreas, and also certain regions of the brain. Hormones that influence personality include sex hormones such as estrogen and androgen. Estrogen is secreted by a woman's ovaries and activates the reproductive system by stimulating the uterus, enlarging the breasts and by stimulating the brain to increase interest in sexual activity. In men, androgens stimulate the maturation of sperm and increase both a male's motivation for sexual activity and his aggressiveness. Both men and women produce estrogen and androgens, however the concentration of estrogen is relatively higher in women and that of androgen is relatively higher in men. Hormones influence behavior in many positive ways. One thought-provoking finding, however, is that, among men imprisoned for crimes, individuals convicted of violent or coercive sexual crimes such as rape and child molestation have higher testosterone levels than others (Dabbs et al., 1995).

The Immune System

The latest research on psychopharmacology is now paying particular attention to the immune system. Originally, the brain and the immune system were viewed as fairly independent of one another. More recently, the connection between psychological stress and illness has become clearer (Dunn, 1989). For example, Cohen (1991; 1998) has conducted an impressive series of studies indicating that psychological stress alters the immune system—making it more likely, for example, to catch a cold.

Beyond such research, many biological factors appear unrelated to personality. For example, no connections have been found between blood type and personality, despite several large studies of the relationship (Wu, Lindsted, & Lee, 2005).

A Micro-Theory That Traits Are Inherited

One link between evolutionary psychology and biopsychological perspectives is the study of genetics and its influence on behavior. One type of research study that emerges from the biopsychological perspective is the "twin study" approach to demonstrating the heredity of certain psychological attributes. **Twin studies** examine pairs of people with high genetic similarity and compare them to pairs of people with less genetic similarity, such as cousins or strangers, to see whether those with higher genetic similarity are more similar in a given trait. If pairs of people who are genetically similar are also similar in a given trait, then that provides evidence that a genetic influence may underlie the similarity.

At one end of genetic similarity are identical or **monozygotic twins**. Identical twins share 100% of their genes in common because they are born from one egg that divides early in reproduction. Such individuals can be contrasted with fraternal or **dizygotic twins**, who develop from two different (but simultaneously fertilized) eggs, and share only 50% of their genes in common. Siblings also share 50% of their genes in common. First cousins share 25% of their genes in common, and strangers share 0% of their genes in common. According to the logic of twin studies, the degree to which identical twins exceed fraternal twins in similarity indicates the degree to which genetic material is controlling development. Some understanding of the role environment plays in personality can also be gained this way. For example, researchers can examine adopted siblings—children who, like strangers, have no genes in common, but who, unlike strangers, are raised in the same family environment, and see the degree to which they are similar.

Table 3-3 shows an example of the correlations of several personality traits across pairs of people according to their genetic similarity. The correlation for intelligence across identical twins is $r = .86$, far higher than it is for siblings of the same parents, at $r = .47$. This relationship would be expected if genes contributed to intelligence, because it indicates that people with 100% overlap (identical twins) are more similar in intelligence than siblings, who share only 50% overlap. In turn, intelligence between siblings is more related, at $r = .47$, than intelligence between cousins ($r = .15$) or between other individuals, for whom the correlation drops to about zero.

Table 3-3: Correlations Between Pairs of Individuals with Different Degrees of Relatedness for Several Traits[a]

Trait	Monozygotic Twins Raised Together	Monozygotic Twins Raised Apart	Siblings Raised Together	Siblings Raised Apart	Cousins	Unrelated Pairs (Expected value)[b]
Intelligence	.86	.72	.47	.24	.15	.00
Extroversion	.54	.30	.06	.04	–	.00
Neuroticism	.41	.25	.24	.28	–	.00
Openness	.51	.43	.14	.23	–	.00

a. Intelligence figures are from Bouchard and McGue (1981), Extraversion figures are from Pedersen, Plomin, McClearn, and Friberg (1988), and Openness figures are from Bergeman et al. (1994).
b. Unrelated pairs have been tested in a few studies, and do, in fact correlate about $r = 00$ with one another. Given the obviousness of the prediction, and the expense of data collection, this group is often omitted.

Some people have argued that identical twins might have more family resemblance simply because twins are probably treated more alike than other family members. Furthermore, twins experience the same family history (not to mention societal history), usually attend the same schools simultaneously, and are more likely to take part in the same activities than their non-twin siblings. There is a way to examine the influence of family environment on the similarity between twins: We can examine sets of twins who were raised together and compare them to twins raised apart—where (for example) one or both twins were adopted. These values are shown in the two "monozygotic twin" columns in Table 3-3. We see that the relation for intelligence between identical twins drops from $r = .84$ for those raised together to $r = .72$ for those raised apart. That is, the relationship remains high and is only slightly higher when the twins are raised in the same environment (Bouchard & McGue, 1981).

Other traits seem heritable as well—but at levels somewhat lower than intelligence. For example, neuroticism (emotional anxiety and mood swings) correlates $r = .41$ between identical twins and $r = .24$ between siblings. Although this plainly indicates a genetic component for neuroticism, environmental factors appear to affect such emotionality more dramatically than they do general intelligence (Pendersen et al., 1988).

From such analyses it is possible to generate a heritability quotient that indicates within a population how much variation in a trait is due to genetic influence and how much is due to other influences. Different researchers use different data and methods for making the estimates that produce different results. The range of heritability estimates (h) for IQ is from $h = .30$ to $.70$, meaning that about 30% to 70% of the individual differences in IQ is determined genetically—a broad range for a heavily studied topic (Plomin, 1990, 70-71). It is worth noting that there isn't one gene for IQ or emotionality, or probably for most other traits. Rather, these traits are likely the products of many genes and their interactions.

Paul Erdős and the Biological Perspective

Perspectives also can be applied to the analysis of an individual's personality. Applications of the biological perspective to a person's life typically can't develop a full sense of the person, but it can illuminate important specifics in a person's life. Consider the eminent mathematician Paul Erdős. He published widely and traveled the world to help other mathematicians develop their own work. He was quite unusual in having no home during the latter part of his life, traveling instead from one mathematician's home to another, and relying on others to manage his affairs.

Psycho-evolutionary theory has interesting things to say about traveling behavior in general. Perhaps Erdős constant movement was an inheritance from our hunter-gatherer days, when changing locations was important to maintain one's livelihood. In addition, Erdős was renowned for visiting young mathematicians and posing challenging problems to them to encourage their thinking. The teaching component of Erdős' life may fit into the altruism that many of us inherit and that promotes the survival of our species.

Finally, toward the latter part of his life, Erdős consumed huge quantities of coffee and amphetamines, at the same time publishing a large number of papers. The biopsychological theories would explain (as did Erdős himself) that the caffeine he ingested kept him awake and operating at a feverish pitch of productivity. In fact, Erdős often remarked that, "A mathematician is a machine for turning coffee into theorems." The intrapsychic and socio-cultural perspectives will yield more ideas concerning Erdős' life.

What Is the Intrapsychic Perspective?

The biological bases of human behavior indicate that human beings are uniquely evolved to learn from and to modify their behavior depending upon the surrounding social environment. Intrapsychic perspectives examine in particular how the psychological parts and organization of the mental system create personality. Psychologists who study intrapsychic features of mental life freely acknowledge that both biological and social systems influence what goes on inside the individual. They recognize the joint action of biology and learning in much of the action of the personality system, but these psychologists are focused on the operation of personality at the psychological level itself.

The first category of these theorists I'll introduce are trait psychologists. Trait psychologists examine the relatively consistent patterns in inner personality and their expressions (e.g., Allport, 1937; Costa & McCrae, 1995). Today, many trait theorists view traits as the defining feature of a person's behavior. I'll compare trait psychologists to psychodynamic psychologists. Psychodynamic psychologists look at the ever-changing dynamics that take place in the context of personality structure.

The Trait Psychologist Views the Person

Trait theorists view personality as consisting of relatively consistent long-term patterns called **traits**. Traits involve an individual's most persistent styles of feeling, thinking, and responding to situations. Traits are not all there is, to be sure, but when a trait psychologist hears a person say, "I don't enjoy large parties," she views the statement as a potential indicator of the trait of introversion. Upon hearing a series of similar comments—"I like to be alone," "I like to read"—the trait theorist would conclude that the person is "introverted" and prefers to be alone rather than extraverted and wanting to be with other people. Other examples of traits include high intelligence and emotional stability. Trait theory and research addresses such questions as what a trait is, the best way to measure traits, and how traits can be used to predict life outcomes.

The Nature of Traits and Their Role in Personality

One early advocate of trait research was Gordon Allport. For Allport, a trait existed when an observer could identify, "by some acceptable method the *consistency* in a person's behavior" (Allport, 1961, p. 343). Allport wrote:

> Suppose you say that a certain friend of yours is <u>generous</u>.... And suppose I ask, "How do you know he is?" Your reply would surely be, "Well, I've known him quite a long time and in situations where other people's interest and welfare are concerned he usually does the big-hearted thing…" (Allport, 1961, p. 340)

Allport believed some traits were innate—such as an infant's love for its mother—and other traits were learned. He described a man who "decorates his room in blue, is also unusually fond of blue in clothes, and plants many blue flowers in his garden." Where might this preference for blue have come from? One possible contribution to the trait of blue preference is from **classical conditioning** (Allport, 1937, p. 152).

Classical conditioning addresses how an organism's innate responses to stimuli in the environment can become paired with other originally neutral stimuli. Allport suggested his readers think back to when the man was an infant. At that time, like most infants, he would have had an innate, strong, positive reaction to his mother. The color blue, in contrast, would have been initially neutral for him.

If the man's mother liked blue and kept many blue things around her, including blue pictures, flowers, glasses, and clothes, then blue, which was originally neutral for him, would become paired with the pleasure of seeing his mother. Innate (or pre-learned) responses to stimuli are called "unconditioned." In the terminology of conditioning, the man's mother was an **unconditioned stimulus** and his positive emotions in response to her were an **unconditioned response**. As he experienced the color blue being paired with his mother, he'd exhibit a positive response to blue. Blue became a **conditioned stimulus** for him; that is, a new stimulus paired to mother. His pleasure in response to the color blue (which would likely be less than the pleasure in reponse to his mother) is referred to as the **conditioned response**. The conditioned response is the response that is elicited in reaction to the conditioned stimulus after learning (Pavlov, 1906). This relationship is outlined in Figure 3-1.

Another possible way a personality trait might arise is through **operant conditioning**. Operant conditioning, in contrast to classical conditioning, emphasizes the consequences of behavior. It presupposes that many behaviors are learned and maintained because they are rewarded or punished at certain intervals. For example, a gambler gambles because every so often, he or she wins. A person considering a life of crime might be persuaded to lead a law-abiding life, if she were convinced that at some time or another she would get caught. The rate at which one's behavior is reinforced positively (i.e., attaining a winning in gambling), or negatively (i.e., removing an unpleasant stimulus, such as reducing a debt owed), is referred to as a reinforcement schedule.

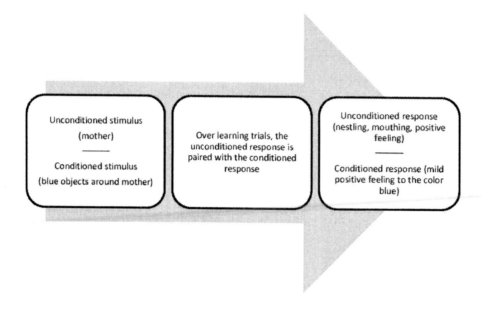

Figure 3-1 *Classical Conditioning: The Color Blue Takes on a Special Meaning*

A person who exhibits the trait of extroversion—lively sociability—may begin with certain basic biological tendencies including a desire for excitement, high energy, and a tendency to feel lively. She may find that attending nearly every single party to which she is invited is positively reinforced by the greetings and smiles of the people she encounters there. This in turn will encourage her to attend even more parties. Her tendencies may then promote more complex learning. She'll learn how to talk effectively to people at parties, and learn about the different kinds of parties that exist. She'll become a more competent partygoer, and someone who enjoys them more than she otherwise might, in part because she understands parties so well. Thus, biology and learning weave together intrapsychically to support consistency of traits (Mayer, 1995b; 1998).

In terms of development, traits are considered to be relatively consistent over long periods of time (e.g., years or decades of a person's life). It is important to note, however, that although a person's trait may be consistent throughout his life, the particular expression of the trait is likely to change as the person develops. For example, the expression of aggression will change considerably over the life span. Table 3-4 shows some different ways that aggression expresses itself at different ages. Whereas an aggressive 1-year-old is apt to bite, a 30-year-old who bites other people would be quite unusual. Aggressive 30-year-olds are more prone to arguments or road rage, or to have successfully channeled their aggression into sports or occupational competition.

A Micro-Theory about Central Personality Traits

One major question in trait research concerns identifying the most important traits in personality and how they interact with one another. Today, many researchers believe that a good picture of personality traits can be developed using five "super" or "big" traits (Goldberg. 1993). The existence of super or big traits— global traits, each of which is made up of smaller traits—was suggested by the English psychologist Hans

Eysenck (1972). The idea that there are five such traits is based on careful examinations of the English language (and now other languages) and collections of the language's major trait terms.

Table 3-4: Hypothetical Changes in the Trait of Aggression Over the Life Span

Age	Age-Typical Expression of Trait
1 year old	Pouting, biting, and screaming
2 year old	Temper tantrums
7 year old	Bullying others
18 year old	Participating in more violent sports (e.g., wrestling, football)
25 year old	Seeking occupations with aggressive aspects (e.g., criminal, butcher, courtroom lawyer)
30 year old	Arguing vehemently at home and at work
35 year old	Teaching one's own children to fight
45 year old	Promoting violent solutions to problems for family members

In this work, the trait adjectives that describe personality are carefully collected and placed on personality tests. One kind of this test employs a list of trait words or brief phrases as items, and test-takers are asked to endorse whether or not they possess that quality: "punctual" or "likes artwork." The other kind asks test-takers to endorse more extended phrases such as "I am usually on time wherever I go." Tens of thousands of people have answered such survey items. Through factor analysis, researchers find that the individual traits on such surveys fall into five groups (i.e., factors) corresponding to the five big traits. These traits, often called the Big Five (e.g., Goldberg, 1993), include extraversion-introversion, neuroticism-emotional stability, openness-closedness (sometimes called cultured-uncultured), friendliness-hostility, and conscientiousness-carelessness (which is measured by such qualities as punctuality, dutifulness, and reliability).

Each big factor, in turn, can be divided into more specific subcomponents. Extraversion can be divided into the more specific traits of impulsiveness, liveliness, and sociability. In one approach, each of the five big traits at the "top level" is broken down into six more specific traits (Costa & McCrae, 1985).

Critics have argued that the Big Five omit many important traits and that there is much more to personality than traits alone (Block, 1995; Buss & Craik, 1985; Loevinger, 1994; Mayer, 2003). Still, there is considerable consensus that these five traits provide an excellent way to describe personality. I'll discuss some of the issues surrounding the Big Five in my discussion of Personality Structure in Chapter 8.

Psychodynamic Theory Views the Person

The trait approach is a highly regarded approach to understanding the internal parts of the mind and how the mind's consistencies are expressed. In some ways, it's surprising to find that it is possible to describe the internal workings of personality in a way that is utterly different from that of examining traits. This other way, called the psychodynamic approach, is not so much interested in the consistencies of behavior as it is in emphasizing the tensions, conflicts, and interactions among personality parts—often caused by conflicts between biological needs and the cultural demands that may prevent them from being met.

Psychodynamic research began with the case studies and observational methods employed by Sigmund Freud. He developed the idea that many psychiatric symptoms were formed as a consequence of early conflicts between the individual and parents, who represented society, or through early traumas such as child sexual abuse or other traumatic events caused by uncontrolled social forces. A number of colleagues were drawn to Freud's theorizing and developed theories of their own, including the theories of Alfred Adler, Carl Jung, Karen Horney, and others whose work stemmed from the psychodynamic tradition.

Psychodynamic theories view personality as caught between a desire to satisfy basic biological yearnings—often sexual or aggressive—and social pressures to civilize those natural yearnings. From the psychodynamic perspective, a central part of the human condition is that people are animals—immensely bright and talented animals, to be sure—who experience lust and greed and the need to defend themselves, and who behave aggressively at times. At the same time, individual humans are weak relative to the world in which they function and would not survive without the protections and institutions of human civilization. As a consequence, individuals must make compromises between their biological needs and the requirements of living in an organized society.

A chief way people compromise with civilization is by trying to suppress internal sexual and aggressive feelings and needs when they violate social norms. Because people are rewarded for doing so, they often lose touch with their own instinctual drives. Thus, self-knowledge is limited for most people, who lose track of their own motivations and reasons for doing things. According to psychodynamic theory, a split occurs between what is retained in an individual's conscious and what is actively blocked out of our consciousness. That which is "blocked out" is ultimately forgotten and blocked from consciousness. A comparison of the trait and psychodynamic perspectives is shown in Table 3-5.

Defenses, Mental Models, and the Role of Dynamics

Perhaps the most influential depiction of the mind Freud developed was his **topographic model**. Topography most commonly refers to the drawing of maps and charts in order to describe the areas of a region. Freud's first map of the mind divided it into the conscious, preconscious, and unconscious.

For Freud, consciousness was an internal sense organ—a sort of inner eye that watched over the rest of the mind. This innermost observing self was also the seat of rationality. The preconscious consisted of relatively neutral information that could become conscious at a given point, but that existed outside of awareness much of the time because of the limitations of what consciousness can attend to at any moment in time. Examples of preconscious contents include the meanings of words, the multiplication tables, and who is related to whom in one's family. The unconscious, by contrast, was characterized as a seething cauldron of urges, fantasies, and their associated memories. Freud was influenced by evolutionary theory and he depicted the unconscious as a less evolved part of the human being representing animal desires. Some mental contents were said to come from instincts that originated from biological level processes. Some of these contents were so threatening that the person avoided thinking about them. This avoidance allowed worrisome thoughts to recede into the background until they were no longer conscious.

Freud sometimes used the analogy of an office with a receptionist and troublesome urges in a waiting room to describe consciousness and its defense against threat. Consciousness was in the position of an executive in an innermost office. If an idea or feeling wanted to become conscious, it would need to get into the innermost office to visit consciousness. To do so, however, the idea or feeling would need to get by a receptionist—a group of mental defenses whose job it was to block out the most troublesome and painful thoughts so that consciousness wouldn't be disturbed. The receptionist was willing to let in many mental contents, such as relatively neutral thoughts in the preconscious. The receptionist was often strict, however, and other ideas and feelings would be blocked: Especially unwanted, for example, were forbidden sexual attractions—such as those toward relatives. These would be blocked out and sent back to the unconscious. At the same time, they would not necessarily go away altogether. Rather, they might influence behavior by subtly sexualizing a relationship the individual wished to keep neutral. Watching cousins at a party, one might momentarily notice the sexualized way one of them begins to treat the other and even feel uncomfortable noticing. This was the sort of hidden sexual motive that Freud thought provided a common undercurrent to daily life, and sometimes became visible to others, even as the person involved was unaware of the feelings he or she expressed.

	Psychodynamic Theories	Trait Theories
Table 3-5: A Comparison of the Psychodynamic and Trait Approaches		
View of Personality	*Personality must compromise between biological urges and the pressures of society to be civilized. *Consciousness is limited and much of mental life takes place in the unconscious.	*Personality is a collection of long-term consistencies in behavior called traits. Traits arise due to biological and/or social influences. *Traits change only gradually, although their expression may vary.
Central Issues	*How do compromises between biological needs and social order affect the individuals? *Why is it so difficult to understand ourselves?	*How do people differ from one another? What are the central traits of personality?
Typical Research Approach	*Early work was based entirely on case studies and observationism. *Since mid-century, correlational and experimental tests of hypotheses related to mental defense and other concepts have been employed.	*Develops tests and testing methodology; typically, large samples are collected and measured on various tests. The tests, in turn measure one or more personality states or traits.

In the early 1900s Freud lived and worked as a neurologist in Vienna. In 1902, he founded the Psychological Wednesday Society, which consisted of a group of interested colleagues who met at his house each week to discuss the psychoanalytic method. Six years later the group became the Vienna Psychoanalytic Society. Over time, society members emerged as a new generation of eminent personality theorists, including Carl Jung and Alfred Adler, who were influenced by the psychodynamic tradition. The weekly Society meetings (and Freud's writings more generally) provided fertile ground for a number of psychodynamic perspectives that branched out from Freud's seminal work. These perspectives changed over time and new theories were introduced, many under the banner of "object relations theory." A number of key figures have succeeded in translating the original theories and their descendants into contemporary psychological thought and research (Baumeister, 1998; Elliott, 1994; Erdelyi, 1984; Westen, 1990).

A Micro-Theory of Hidden Sexual Desire

Part of psychodynamic theory concerns how certain mental contents are kept out of consciousness. This has fascinated the fans of the theory including numerous research investigators. Wegner and colleagues (Wegner, Shortt, Blake, & Page, 1990) became interested in the process of blocking out thoughts: whether it can be done, how it is done, and what happens when it is done. They studied the suppression of sexual thoughts. **Thought suppression** involves the attempt to stop thinking about something. Some participants in their studies were instructed not to think about sex, others to not think about a variety of other topics, such as dancing. The participants who were told to suppress sexual thoughts had elevated skin conductance levels—a measure of physiological stress—compared to those who were instructed not to think about various other topics. The successful sexual suppressors often showed stronger skin conductance levels—increased sweating relative to others—when sexual material was brought up later. This suggested that blocking out thoughts creates greater responsiveness to them later on.

Along the same lines, Morokoff (1985) studied sexual guilt among women. Consistent with psychoanalytic theory, she viewed guilt as a powerful means of social control and wondered whether a person who felt guilty about sex might try to suppress certain thoughts about it. In her study, women subjects were first administered a psychological test to assess their levels of sexual guilt and then divided them into high- and low-guilt groups. Next, both groups watched erotic videos while their sexual arousal was monitored via blood flow in the genital area. The high-sexual-guilt group self reported feeling less sexual arousal while watching erotic videos relative to the low-sexual-guilt group. At the same time, however, blood-flow monitoring indicated that the high-sexual-guilt group was actually experiencing more sexual arousal than the low-guilt group.

These findings seem broadly consistent with Freud's idea that sexual thoughts blocked from consciousness continue to be active in the mind. The avoidance of sexual thoughts led to more responsiveness to sexual ideas in Wegner's study and to greater sexual arousal in Morokoff's.

It is worth noting that psychoanalytic theory has elaborated many parts of personality. Freud was the first to suggest that a person did not interact with actual others, but rather with mental models of others. His ideas came about as he noticed that his patients repeatedly misperceived him, apparently viewing him as they had viewed their parents—searching for clues that he would behave as their parents did. From this, he suggested that individuals carried about stereotyped views of their parents or significant others that they mistakenly transferred to others (Freud, 1917, Chapter 27). These models of significant others can be very powerful and today are frequently studied in social-cognitive theory under the name of "schemas" and "prototypes" (Westen, 1991; 1998).

The Intrapsychic Approach to Paul Erdős' Personality

How would the intrapsychic perspectives on personality approach the case of Paul Erdős, the mathematician? Trait theorists would look for consistencies in his personality: his creativity, his industriousness, his love of learning and teaching, his concerns with death, and his bleak outlook on life. If we tried to translate these impressions into the Big Five approach, we might say that Erdős was high on Openness/Culture and appeared to be somewhat neurotic.

A psychodynamic analysis might focus on Erdős' single-minded pursuit of mathematics, and interpret it, in part, as an attempt by Erdős to block out or avoid other thoughts. Certainly, Erdős' hard work as a mathematician and his constant traveling reduced many distractions. Erdős' work began in earnest after his mother's death, and it may have been a defense against the loss of a person who was both a beloved parent and his first mathematics teacher. The psychodynamic tradition also examines the symbolic meaning of a behavior. Erdős' father was sent to a Russian prisoner-of-war camp for six years, and later perished in the Holocaust. Perhaps Erdős' traveling was a means to see if he could withstand the arrest and exile his father experienced, as well as a means to be free of any single government's power, so as to avoid his father's fate.

What Is the Sociocultural Perspective?

Sociocultural perspectives highlight how the environment shapes personality and its functioning. We will examine two theoretical approaches that use a sociocultural perspective: the social-cognitive view and the cross-cultural approach.

The Social-Cognitive View of the Person

As the social-cognitive theorist sees it, each of us is constantly adjusting to external situations around us, both responding to society's demands and looking for personal advantage where we can find it. Social cognitive theory is concerned with how society influences the person and how the person's behavior arises as consequence of those influences. As such, it views the individual as a sort of scientist himself, forming theories of the world, testing them out in various situations, and attempting to meet his needs as efficiently as possible in an uncertain world.

The Person and Environment in Interaction

"Learn from others what to pursue and what to avoid, and let your teachers be the lives of others." – Dionysius Cato (C.E. 4th century)

Some of the richest theorizing in the social-cognitive theory emerged from the counseling center at Ohio State University in the years between 1935 and 1955. Julian Rotter was one of the pioneers who worked there. In a 1954 book entitled "Social Learning and Clinical Psychology," Rotter laid out a series of principles that would define the burgeoning social-cognitive perspective. His first principle boldly proclaimed that, "The unit of investigation for the study of personality is the interaction of the individual and his meaningful environment." (Rotter, 1954, p. 85). Rotter believed that the individual's behavior could be understood as a function of the individual's goals. The seventh principle of his theory stated that people's actions were a function of what they expected from the environment surrounding them.

In the late 1960s, Walter Mischel reviewed studies of the consistency of personality and concluded human behavior was not terribly consistent and that most of the individual variation was due to social influences. Mischel acknowledged high levels of consistency for some traits, such as IQ. He also noted, however, that although the study of broad stable dispositions was historically justified, there turned out to be upper bounds to what such traits could predict, because people's behaviors are so influenced by situations. Today, reviews of the literature suggest an upper bound of about $r = .40$ for the predictions of individual behaviors—although the figure can rise higher under certain conditions (Mischel, 1968, p. 147-148; Nisbett, 1980).

To explain why we see so much consistency in behavior, Mischel and others suggested that much of the consistency is a cognitive illusion. For example, Shweder and D'Andrade suggested that the reason people perceive a consistent "factor" of extroversion is because terms such as "outgoing" and "sociable" are near-synonyms to one another, and that creates a cognitive illusion in people's minds of relatedness among behaviors—relatedness that doesn't really exist. That is, consistency is "caused" by the language rather than by any consistency in a person's behavior (Schweder, 1975; Schweder & D'Andrade, 1979).

Schweder and D'Andrade's arguments about cognitive illusions are contradicted by the fact that traits predict both simultaneous and future life actions and outcomes for individuals. Moreover, we now know that predictions can be enhanced well over the $r = .30$ boundary Mischel set in the 1960s. This can be done, for example, by averaging a person's specific behavior, such as how on-time he is over a series of situations rather than employing just one observation (Epstein & O'Brien, 1985). Such approaches were unknown at the time Mischel wrote. In fact, they were developed in response to his critique.

The still-valid part of Mischel's point is that situations do determine a great deal of an individual's moment-to-moment behavior. The emphasis of the social-cognitive perspective remains on the interaction between the individual and the social environment. For example, the social-cognitive concept of reciprocal determinism refers to the idea that the environment, behavior, and the person all influence one another.

Social-cognitive psychologists acknowledge that traits influence behavior: Tradition-minded people are more apt to follow traditions than others. But these psychologists also believe that behavior is guided by the environment. A young man returning to his family's annual Thanksgiving dinner would behave more according to tradition than if he were celebrating Thanksgiving by eating out with friends in a new city. Finally, people influence their environment, which in turn can increase their level of a trait. For example, a tradition-minded person will likely attend more observances such as marriages and funerals where there are other tradition-minded people, and this will reinforce her traditional outlook on life (Bandura, 1978; 1984).

Social-cognitive theorists also discuss internal parts of personality—particularly learned beliefs about society. George Kelly (1955) depicts the individual as flexibly behaving so as to understand and react to the outside world. For Kelly, the individual, like a scientist, is always trying to learn about the people around her so as to anticipate and control what people will do (Kelly, 1955a, p. 4). To do so, the individual developed a number of theories about the surrounding world that governed his or her behavior. A person's collective theories were contained in a **personal construct system**, a collection of beliefs and predictions that ultimately channeled behavior (Kelly, 1955a, p. 56).

Today, social-cognitive theories recognize many internal cognitive mechanisms for representing and interacting with the outside world. These include expectancies and beliefs about what may happen in the future, emotional reactions to outside events, personal goals, as well as plans for self-regulation to ensure those goals are met (Cervone, 2005; Mischel & Shoda, 1995, p. 253).

A Micro-Theory of Conditional Aggression

Social-cognitive research attempts to understand how a person's behavior changes from one situation to another. Mischel and his colleagues developed the idea of **if-then (conditional) traits**—the idea that a person would express a trait-related behavior in some situations but not in others (Mischel, 1973, p. 258; Shoda & Leetiernan, 2002). If-then traits describe a sort of behavioral signature of an individual; understanding them can enhance our predictions of how a person will behave. These conditional traits can be illustrated with some data collected by Yuichi Shoda and his colleagues at a summer camp for children (Shoda, Mischel, & Wright, 1994).

At Camp Wediko, children participated in activities such as woodworking, playground time, and cabin meetings. Shoda and his colleagues first divided the campers' interpersonal interactions into those with peers and those with adult counselors. They further divided the situations into those that were positive, such as those that involved receiving praise from a peer or counselor, and those that were negative, such as those that involved teasing from peers or warnings and punishments from counselors.

Observers recorded the campers' behaviors in these various activities. For the purposes of the research report, the observers focused on aggressive verbal behavior (making threats, name-calling, and the like). The researchers predicted that the campers' verbal aggression would vary conditionally—according to the situation. For example, Figures 3-2 and 3-3 refer to two campers in the study. The zero point on the "Y" (vertical) axis represents the average level of verbal aggression and the numbers above and below it represent standard deviations from the mean.

Camper 1 was usually not verbally aggressive—except when he was punished by an adult; then he made angry comments at well above average levels (Figure 3-2). Camper 2, by contrast, scored well above average in verbal aggression when around his peers—even when peers were merely approaching him. On the other hand, he was roughly average in aggression when in the presence of an adult (Figure 3-3). Note that each child's graph has two lines. These lines represent two independent times of assessment. The profiles are highly similar (Child 1's two measurements correlate $r = .96$; Child 2's profile was less consistent, but still $r =$

.48). These children's aggression was conditional: for example, Child 1 was more likely to talk back to a counselor than to a fellow camper.

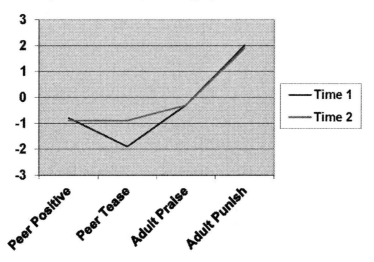

Figure 3-2 *Child 1's Level of Verbal Aggression (cf. Shoda et al., 1994, Fig. 1)*

Such studies indicate that psychologists may be able to go beyond traits in understanding the stability of behavior. A person also behaves in a stable way in "micro situations"—according to his or her psychological perceptions of the situation, and dependent upon his or her goals and plans in each situation.

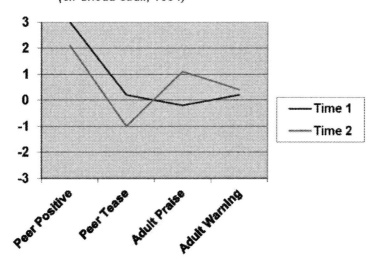

Figure 3-3 *Child 2's Level of Verbal Aggression (cf. Shoda et.al., 1994)*

The Cross-Cultural View of the Person

The cross-cultural approach to personality goes further than the social-cognitive approach in emphasizing that an individual is a product of his culture. From this perspective, an individual is a carrier of cultural knowledge. His personality is evaluated according to the expectations of others who share the same culture.

Western scientific observers may perceive differences in a culture—say Japan's—that are quite different from how Japanese scientists perceive it as insiders. A certain caution about the inherent biases of the Western scientific viewpoint is worthwhile (Marsella, Dubanoski, Hamada, & Morse, 2000). The recognition that personalities vary over cultures is critical to understanding the various forms that personality may take. A comparison of the socio-cultural and cross-cultural perspectives can be found in Table 3-6.

Psychologists pay particular attention to the differences in personality that arise in **collectivist** and **individualistic** cultures. People who live in collectivist societies and who follow a relatively collectivistic philosophy are known as **allocentrics**. Allocentrics tend to define themselves in relation to other people (e.g., "Other people think of me as nice."). These individuals focus on their relationships with others and the good of the groups to which they belong.

Table 3-6: A Comparison of the Social Cognitive and Cross-Cultural Approaches

	Social Cognitive	Cross-Cultural
View of Personality	*The individual is involved in a constant interaction with the environment. *The person attempts to anticipate and control the surrounding environment.	*The person is the way he or she is because of the culture in which the individual was raised. *The culture, from its language to practices, to current events, shapes personality.
Central Issues	*How does the person see the world? *How do mental models influence behavior?	*How can cultures be classified? *How do cultures influence their members?
Typical Research Approach	*Experimental examinations of behavior change depending upon the situation. *Survey approaches to how traits vary in different situations.	*Anthropological research and cultural studies are employed to examine cultures. *Cross-cultural survey research is often employed to detect differences in people across cultures.

People who live in individualist societies and learn a relatively individualistic philosophy are known as **idiocentrics**. Idiocentrics define themselves in relation to themselves (e.g., "I am nice."). These individuals emphasize their own goals and find social rules confining and restrictive. They view their progress in life as dependent upon their own individual characteristics such as their motives and traits. Although idiocentrics are more common in individualistic societies, some can be found in collectivist societies. Similarly, some allocentric people can be found in individualistic societies (Triandis, 2001, p. 910).

These outlooks have different influences on personality. Whereas allocentrics feel more social support, their self-esteem may be lower; idiocentrics may feel more self-esteem, but often feel lonelier (Markus & Kitayama, 1991). In other words, the collectivism or idiocentrism of the culture is also reflected in the individual—and there exist important variations among individuals in a given culture.

Applying Social Approaches to Understanding Paul Erdős' Personality

The socio-cultural perspective directs us to aspects of Erdős' personality that are different than those of the earlier approaches. For example, Erdős exhibited many conditional traits. People who knew him often remarked that he changed his behavior around children. He was especially kind to children and often spontaneously gave them gifts, but he nearly never behaved that way with adults. Erdős also hid many of his outspoken views in the presence of children and spoke to them in a loving, more conventional way. By contrast, when he was with adults, he was quite frank about his concerns about death and a hostile universe. The Cross-Cultural viewpoint might direct our attention to Erdős' concern with death and dying. These were common preoccupations in Hungary at the time Erdős was coming of age. A Hungarian expression of the time could be loosely translated as "Burying people; that is something we understand well." In this sense, at least, Erdős' personality appears to have absorbed the outlook of his culture.

What Is the Developmental Perspective?

Psychologists interested in personality development view the personality system over the life span. Psychosocial theorists examine how our mental life develops over the life span and how our development is supported by social institutions such as our family and schools. Humanistic and positive psychologists are interested in what healthy development looks like and how we can become better versions of ourselves. Psychosocial theorists and humanistic and positive psychologists are focused on how personality develops over the life span—optimally, if possible.

A Psychosocial Stage Theory and Development

According to psychosocial theorists, as an individual grows, he progresses through a sequence of psychological stages of life: infancy, toddlerhood, early and later childhood, adolescence, young and mid-adulthood, through to old age. These developmental stages are marked by social activities, rituals, observances, and institutions, which are tailored to each phase of life and are designed to support and guide the person as he grows. For example, as a child becomes ready to read, he enters kindergarten and first grade where such skills are taught; as a young adult seeks independence, he enters an institution such as a college or trade school, the armed forces or the peace corps, where considerable independence is possible and yet there still exists the opportunity for adult guidance and supervision.

Erik Erikson developed an influential theory of psychosocial growth. According to Erikson, people progress through eight stages of development throughout the life span. To get a flavor of the theory, consider Erikson's first stage, trust versus mistrust. (In chapters 11 and 12, we will explore these stages further.)

The trust versus mistrust stage corresponds roughly to the first year or two of life. During this time, the infant is thrust into a social world of interaction with agents of society—parents! When the social environment is well constructed, the parents accept and love the infant, are attentive, understand his developing needs, and can satisfy most of them. They are responsive to him, encourage him to explore the world and provide a secure environment. The infant develops a sense of basic trust in his environment. But sometimes the social environment is less welcoming: the parents create an untrustworthy environment for the infant in which he is not attended to and his actions are thwarted and discouraged, either deliberately or out of ignorance.

Next, according to Erikson's theory, the child learns autonomy versus shame and then moves through further stages. By adolescence, the individual must develop an identity or else be confused by what role to play in life. In adulthood, the person addresses issues such as how to be intimate (versus isolated). By the final stage, if all has gone well, a person has developed a sense of integrity.

A great deal of compatible theorizing has developed stemming from Erikson's framework of developmental stages. Attachment models examine the early interaction between infant and parent and how those patterns of attachment persevere through youth and into adulthood (Ainsworth, et al, 1978; Bowlby,

1988; Meyer & Pilkonis, 2001). The Soviet psychologist Lev Vygotsky viewed the child as a social apprentice to older peers, learning how to operate among others in the older world (Emihovich & Lima, 1995). What ties each of these theoretical approaches together is a willingness to consider the interaction between the individual's psychological development and his social milieu.

A Micro-Theory of the Emergence of Traits

Rothbart and her colleagues have found that new psychological capacities emerge in the transition from infancy to toddlerhood. For example, both infants and toddlers' temperament can be described fairly well by two emotion-related factors: surgency (positive feelings) and negative affect (negative feelings). A third infant dimension involves how soothable, cuddly, and desirous of contact infants are. This is an important dimension because cuddlier infants probably attract more positive attention from parents on average (Gartstein & Rothbart, 2003).

As their infant reaches toddlerhood, parents become less concerned with their blossoming toddler's cuddliness and pay more attention instead to his ability to control himself. By two or three years of age, children are perceived according to their ability to exert self-control (Rothbart & Putnam, 2002). Perhaps this change reflects Erikson's idea that the infants and parents have made a transition to a new stage of interaction that emphasizes autonomy: a key developmental task for the toddler is to control her social interactions. Toddlers with superior effortful control may accrue a number of advantages later on, including being able to express more empathy and altruism to other children, and therefore enter later stages of development with greater peer respect (Kochanska et al., 2000).

The Humanistic and Positive Psychology Views of the Person

A second theoretical perspective that has important developmental implications in regard to personality concerns the positive psychology perspective and the humanistic tradition from which it emerged. Humanistic psychologists view the person as a holistic, growing organism that strives toward fulfillment. These theorists have elaborated a number of motives and traits that lead to the most positive developmental outcomes possible. Many theories stress a concept called "actualization," which means that the individual personality becomes everything it is capable of being. Positive psychology represents a more recent approach that emphasizes cataloging important human strengths. The psychosocial development approach is compared with these humanistic, positive approaches in Table 3-7.

Humanism takes many of its ideas from "A Humanist Manifesto," a 1933 article which appeared in the philosophical magazine *The New Humanist* (Wilson, 1995, Chapter 13). The creators of the humanist manifesto viewed themselves as creating a new religion that considered "the complete realization of human personality to be the end of man's life and seeks its development and fulfillment in the here and now." It also aims to "foster the creative in man and to encourage achievements that add to the satisfactions of life." These ideas appear over and over in humanistic psychology's vision of the healthy personality (Wilson, 1995, Chapter 13; quotes from propositions 8 and 12).

In psychology, the humanistic movement emerged in the 1950s and 1960s under the joint influence of Carl Rogers and Abraham Maslow. Rogers, then a young psychotherapist at the Rochester Guidance Clinic, employed a radically new therapeutic technique that asked therapists to adopt a warm empathic tone with a client, in order to create a safe environment in which that person could grow. Rogers' idea was that by supporting a client with compassion and openness, the therapist could encourage him to gradually discover the right path toward optimal psychological health. Using the therapist as a model, the client could cast off false selves—qualities that didn't really fit his innermost motives and feelings—and gradually progress to a healthier state.

Meanwhile, Abraham Maslow studied a number of individuals he identified as extremely healthy so as to characterize what such healthy individuals were like. His aim was to capture a sense of what was best in human nature (Maslow, 1970). In the past few years, Seligman and Csikszentmihalyi (2000), among others, have renewed and updated the call for the study of the positive aspects of human nature.

Today's positive psychologists have created a project to catalogue the positive traits they find in individuals. Members of the positive psychology movement distinguish themselves from humanists in their emphasis on empirical research into positive traits, into how those traits can be developed and what those traits lead to (Seligman et al., 2005).

> "I found in myself, and still find, an instinct toward a higher or, if it is named, spiritual life, as do most men, and another toward a primitive rank and savage one, and I reverence them both." – Henry David Thoreau (1817-1862)

A Micro-Theory of Empathy and Psychotherapy

The humanistic tradition encouraged and fostered research both in traits and in change processes (e.g., Hattie & Cooksey, 1984; Shostrom, 1964). Carl Rogers was one of the first therapists to openly encourage the recording of psychotherapy sessions. He also conducted some of the first therapy-outcome studies on the client-centered approach he pioneered. Remember that the humanistic tradition stresses the importance of a human-centered, encouraging environment in which people can grow and actualize themselves. If this viewpoint holds true, then individuals in such a positive environment should grow best. Rogers (1959) attempted to state his theory of psychotherapy in a way that was clear enough to be studied empirically. He hypothesized that a therapist's empathy, genuineness, and positive regard toward the client were the most important factors in the client's personal growth. Of these three characteristics, empathy is perhaps most studied.

Results from many studies support the importance of empathy to good outcomes in psychotherapy. For example, William Miller developed a system of "Motivational Interviewing," which is a brief, directive, client-centered approach to helping patients resolve conflicts over drinking. Rather than telling patients, "You must stop drinking!," the interviewer elicits the client's own thoughts about the behavior, and reinforces his or her concerns about drinking and desires for change. Miller's belief is that such a process highlights a developmental goal: for the client to move forward by adopting the practice of abstinence. In one study by Miller and Taylor (1980), the empathy ratings of the counselors conducting the therapy predicted a considerable degree of positive client outcomes at half-year, year, and two-year post-treatment intervals at significant levels ($r = .50$ to $.85$; Miller & Taylor, 1980). Another general study of the therapeutic process found that, among a group of psychotherapy trainees divided according to those who were more and less effective, the more effective ones scored higher in empathy (Lafferty, Beutler, and Crago, 1989). In general, empathy and related characteristics such as warmth and genuineness do not by themselves guarantee good therapeutic outcomes. When coupled with sound psychotherapeutic approaches, however, they appear to lead to a greater likelihood of positive change (Beutler, Crago, & Arezmendi, 1986, p. 279).

Table 3-7: Comparison of the Psychosocial and Humanistic/ Positive Psychology Approaches

	Psychosocial Theories	*Humanistic/Positive Theories*
View of Personality	*As the person develops, he or she faces a sequence of new social tasks; society creates practices and institutions relevant to each task.	*In humanistic approaches, the individual is viewed as a developing organism that attempts to maximize (actualize) its potential. *In positive psychology approaches, the individual is viewed as possessing many potential strengths and positive qualities.
Central Issues	*What are the major tasks of development and how do they unfold? *What are the possible variations of the developmental sequence and what implications do they have for the individual?	*What are a person's potential strengths? *How can a person actualize those strengths?
Typical Research Approach	*Case study and observationism. *Cross-sectional and longitudinal studies of peoples' growth.	*Humanists employed case study and observational methods; they also conducted therapy-outcome studies. *Both humanistic and positive psychologists emphasize trait measures and correlational studies of positive human attributes.

Developmental Perspectives on Paul Erdős

Erdős' amazing productivity and his ability to draw out the best in his fellow mathematicians reflect both his enormous gifts and his actualization of those gifts in the practice of mathematics. According to contemporary positive psychologists, his life and work expressed a number of positive qualities worth emphasizing in a person's life. These included a sense of conscious involvement in his work termed "flow," humor, and the pursuit of meaningfulness in life through his work in mathematics.

> "The living self has one purpose only: to come into its own fullness of being." – D. H. Lawrence (1885-1930)

How Do We Reconcile Multiple Theories?

Which Theory Is Right?

We have considered the biological, socio-cultural, intra-psychic, and developmental perspectives on personality. We examined some representative theoretical approaches of each perspective and some research that each one inspired. This treatment is a condensed version of what you might experience in a semester-long course on personality perspectives or theories. If you are like most people, you found at least one or two of these theories provided intriguing insight into the people around you—and perhaps you found one you agreed with in particular. If you are like most people, you are now also wondering: "Which theory is best?" It is traditional to attempt some kind of answer to that question at the conclusion of most theory-focused courses.

The problem is that there is no easy answer to the question. Hall and Lindzey (1978), who first organized theories according to perspectives, concluded pessimistically that all the theories were wrong and that learning them was a path toward finding better future theories. Salvatore Maddi (1993, p. 100) tended to agree. By teaching the theories and comparing them, however, he hoped that the better theories could be distinguished from the worse ones, and that the better ones would form a basis for future generations of theory writers. Maddi's comparison of theories was largely theoretical at the time, though he considered some limited research.

One empirical test pits the theories against one another: testing their power as treatments for people suffering from mental disorders. The more important theories have given rise to their own forms of psychotherapy: Psychodynamic theory is associated with psychodynamic therapy. Social-cognitive theory is closely allied to cognitive-behavioral treatments. To compare the theories, perhaps we could compare the therapies that developed from them. Smith and Glass examined which approaches to therapy worked best and concluded that many of the theories had merit, particularly the social-cognitive and psychodynamic approaches.

One problem with this approach is that there are perfectly good theories, such as trait theory, that lack a therapeutic approach associated with them. It is also possible to have a good theory linked to a less good therapy. So Smith and Glass's work doesn't answer the question of which theory is best. Moreover, newer approaches such as the biopsychological and psycho-evolutionary approaches were not included in their assessment.

One alternative to multiple theories is the One Big Theory that explains everything and solves all the problems. Unfortunately, there is no One Big Theory today and, although I'd like to be mistaken in this instance, I don't see one just around the corner. So, although the one big theory approach is appealing, it doesn't appear possible at present (Hall & Lindzey, 1978; Funder, 2001, p. 5).

The Systems Approach

Another idea is that the multiple theories are complementary to one another because each one addresses a somewhat different set of research questions (Funder, 2001, pp. *xxi*, 509). I use that approach in this book. Fortunately, forward-looking theorists within personality psychology have spent considerable effort to develop a common terminology across theoretical perspectives. This allows me to use a common language in this book.

Starting with the next chapter, personality's parts will be examined in sequence (and later, personality's organization and development). As a given topic is examined—say, emotion—the discussion will draw on the most powerful or promising theoretical and research ideas related to the topic.

For example, the four theoretical perspectives we just covered are listed down the first column of Table 3-8. Personality's parts, organization, and development are listed across the top. The table provides examples of how a given section of the book draws on the perspectives. The "Personality Parts" section of the book (column 2) will draw on micro-theories from evolutionary psychology to understand emotions and from the trait perspective to understand the motives people experience. "Personality Organization" will draw on biopsychological theories to understand how the mind is divided into different processes such as motivation, emotion, and cognition, and it will draw on social-cognitive theories to understand how people seek feedback to direct their lives (column 3). Further examples are provided for personality development (column 4). Thus, personality theories are an integral part of this book, because this book draws on the most relevant theories—and the micro-theories they have given rise to—in order to explain its topics. Although I'll discuss the theories in the next chapters, the focus of this book is using the theories to gain a better understanding of the personality system itself.

Table 3-8: Theoretical Perspectives Examine Personality's Parts, Organization, and Development			
Perspectives on Personality	*Examining Personality Parts*	*Examining Personality Organization*	*Examining Personality Development*
Biological	Evolutionary theories examine the role of mental mechanisms in feelings such as jealousy in sexual relationships	Psychobiological theories inquire about whether separate structures within the brain coincide with different areas of personality function such as motivation, emotion, and cognition	Psychobiological theories examine how sexual maturation contributes to some of the issues of identity formation
Intrapsychic	Trait theory helps describe the different motives human beings experience	Psychodynamic theory examines how conscious attention may be diverted from unpleasant thoughts about oneself	Attachment theory (an extension of psychodynamic theory) examines the forms of infant-caregiver bonds
Sociocultural	Social-cognitive theories examine how people form "schemas"—mental models of themselves and the world, and the consequences of such models	Social-cognitive theories help explain how and why people seek feedback to direct their behavior	Cross-cultural research examines whether personalities develop differently, on average, in individualistic and collectivist cultures
Developmental	The humanistic perspective is employed to describe a developmental hierarchy of motives	Theories of personality development examine whether mental defenses such as denial and sublimation can be arranged in a hierarchy of maturity, with some mental defenses immature, and others more mature	Psychosocial theory examines the ways in which people form or fail to form identities and fit into society; positive psychology examines how personality leads to good outcomes in living.

Reviewing Chapter 3

The purpose of this chapter was to acquaint you with the idea of personality perspectives, theories and micro-theories. Four major perspectives are covered including the biological, intrapsychic, socio-cultural, and developmental. The chapter also examines the problem of conflicting perspectives, and alternatives to studying personality in that way. Can you answer the following questions, organized according to the major sections of the chapter?

Questions About "What Are Perspectives in Personality?"

1. <u>Frameworks and Perspectives</u>: A field-wide framework provides an overall organization of a discipline. How does that differ from a theoretical perspective?

2. <u>Perspectives on Personality</u>: The biological and intrapsychic represent two perspectives on personality. What are the two others described in this textbook?

3. <u>Perspectives and theories</u>: A perspective provides a broad viewpoint on a field. How would you distinguish a theory from a perspective?

Questions About "What Is the Biological Perspective?"

4. <u>The Evolutionary Perspective</u>: The evolutionary perspective tries to understand the mental mechanisms that have evolved within personality to promote survival and reproduction. The pressures surrounding a person are divided into the forces of natural selection and sexual selection. Can you define those two terms?

5. <u>Studies of Brain Structure and Function</u>: Different brain structures influence personality. There are sometimes said to be three evolutionary "layers" of brain development: the reptilian brain, the old (paleo-) mammalian brain, and the new mammalian brain. Can you characterize the functions of each?

6. <u>Similarities and Differences Among Neurotransmitters, Hormones, and the Chemistry of Immunity</u>: As anyone who has ever tried an alcoholic beverage or taken a painkiller knows, chemicals influence brain function. Several classes of chemicals are often studied in relation to the brain, including neurotransmitters, hormones, and chemicals of the immune system. Can you describe the differences among these classes? What important relationships have been found between the neurotransmitter serotonin and behavior? What about dopamine and behavior?

7. <u>Twin Studies</u>: Genes—units of heritability—are thought to underlie at least some psychological function. Studies of the inheritance of psychological traits have focused on examining people with different degrees of relatedness. Do you understand how monozygotic twins and other groups differ in their degrees of relatedness? What is the logic behind studying the inheritance of psychological traits across groups of people with differing degrees of relatedness?

Questions About "What Is the Intrapsychic Perspective?"

8. <u>The Ways that People Learn</u>: One thing biology makes clear is that human beings are learning organisms. People learn according to a variety of principles. At a behavioral level, these include classical conditioning, operant conditioning, and modeling. Can you explain the basics of each of these three principles?

9. <u>Traits and Trait Psychologists</u>: The trait perspective emphasizes the identification of consistencies in mental and behavioral life called traits. It is probably one of the oldest perspectives on character and personality. Some psychologists believe traits are mostly biological; others view them as primarily behavioral; there is also an integrated position. Can you describe the biological and learned portions of a trait such as extraversion? More recently, trait theorists have conceived of traits as arranged in a hierarchy. "Super" or "Big" traits are composed of smaller, fine-grained traits.

10. <u>The Big Five</u>: Today, personality is often said to be studied according to the Big Five, five big traits thought to encompass much of personality. Do you know what the Big Five traits are?

11. <u>Psychodynamic Theory and Psychodynamic Psychologists:</u> The psychodynamic perspective views the individual's mental life as working out compromises between biological needs and sociocultural expectations and requirements. The conflict set up by these two forces causes the individual to suppress and defend against certain mental contents, which become unconscious. What two fundamental areas of threatening mental contents did Freud propose? Freud's topographic model suggested a division of the mind into three areas related to levels of awareness. Can you list and define them?

12. <u>Mental Defense:</u> Mental defense involves the blocking out of certain ideas that are painful or threatening to think about. One form of mental defense is thought suppression. Can you define suppression and describe a study in suppression that represents some research from the area? Society exerts social control inducing guilt. How do women who experience higher levels of sex guilt react to erotic pictures? How do their reactions compare to those of women who experience lower levels of sexual guilt?

Questions About "What Is the Sociocultural Perspective?"

13. <u>The Social-Cognitive Perspective:</u> The social-cognitive perspective views the person as a thinking, analyzing being who behaves in interaction with the environment. One of the founding principles of social-cognition is that the individual exists in interaction with the environment. Can you identify the author of that principle? A contemporary view of this relationship between the person and the environment is called "reciprocal determinism." Do you know who described "reciprocal determinism" and can you describe how it operates?

14. <u>Person-Environment Interactions:</u> Walter Mischel noted that traits can only go so far in predicting behavior. In fact, across situations, there appear to be upper bounds on consistency. A person's trait will generally correlate only $r = .40$ with their behavior in given situation (this is revised upward from Mischel's initial claim and excludes intellectual traits, which are more predictive). This relationship is a modest one, and doesn't seem to reflect the consistency we perceive in others. How did Mischel and others explain the consistency we see in other people? What has the response been to Mischel's concern?

15. <u>The Social-Cognitive Perspective:</u> The social-cognitive view emphasizes stable parts of personality such as expectations and personal constructs. Can you define both the personal construct system and expectancies?

16. <u>Conditional Traits:</u> One idea of social-cognitive theory is that some aspects of traits are "if-then," or conditional: that is, they are expressed under certain circumstances but not others. Can you describe a research study that examined conditional traits?

17. <u>Culture Influences Personality:</u> There are many ways that culture influences personality and many different dimensions along which culture varies. One way culture varies is according to how much a culture emphasizes community and the commonality among people (communal cultures) and how much the individual is emphasized (individualistic cultures). Can you describe the difference? What differences are found in people in the two sorts of cultures?

Questions About "What Is the Developmental Perspective?"

18. <u>Psychosocial Theory:</u> Psychosocial theory views the individual's development as working in synchrony with practices and institutions provided by society. As a person matures, he or she engages with a sequence of practices and institutions that are appropriate to their age level. Can you provide an example of this? What is an example of a trait that toddlers have that is not present in infants?

19. <u>Humanistic and Positive Psychology:</u> The humanistic perspective emerged in the mid-20th century and applied principles of humanistic philosophy specifically to psychology. Can you identify some of those humanistic principles?

20. <u>Positive Psychology:</u> Abraham Maslow focused on the study of psychological health and the needs individuals face. Carl Rogers was a clinician who focused on the therapeutic conditions his clients needed to grow mentally healthy. More recently, since the mid-1990s positive psychologists have been active elaborating positive human qualities. What are some of those qualities?

21. <u>Research in Empathy:</u> In the 1950s, Carl Rogers suggested that psychotherapists should adopt certain characteristics to facilitate their clients' growth. Can you name those characteristics? He and others researched the psychotherapeutic process and found that empathy was a contributor to positive client outcomes. How is empathy defined?

Questions About "How Do We Reconcile Multiple Theories?"

22. <u>Integrating Theories:</u> Each of the above theories has attractive points, but which one is right? The question cannot be answered. Those who advocate learning about the theories often view the decision as to which one is best as an individual choice. Another alternative looks to developing one big theory that combines all the theories covered here. Has this been done? How does the systems framework approach the question of integrating the theories?

Chapter 3 Glossary

Terms in Order of Appearance:

Field-wide Framework: An outline of that field's most important topics.

Personality Perspective: A manner of looking at personality that is made up of a number of related theories that emphasize certain influences on personality and share certain assumptions. Examples include the psychodynamic perspective and the trait perspective.

Theory of Personality: A set of statements or assumptions about human mental life or behavior that explains why people are the way they are.

Neurotransmitters: Chemicals secreted by neurons at the pre-synaptic sac that influence neighboring neurons.

Hormones: Chemicals secreted by the endocrine organs and sent into the bloodstream that can influence brain function.

Twin Studies: A type of study in which people with different genetic overlap (e.g., identical and fraternal twins, siblings, cousins, and unrelated people) are compared with regards to their similarity on a given trait.

Monozygotic (Identical) Twins: Twins who develop from a single fertilized egg and thus share all their genetic material in common.

Dizygotic (Fraternal) Twins: Twins who develop from two different eggs and thus share 50% of their genetic material in common.

Traits: Thematic regularities in personality—a person's most common styles of and capacities for feeling, thinking, and responding to situations.

Classical Conditioning: Learning based on the pairing of a stimulus to a natural, reflexive (unconditioned) response.

Unconditioned Stimulus: A person, object, or symbol that naturally and automatically triggers a response.

Unconditioned Response: An innate response to an unlearned stimulus, such as salivating in response to food.

Conditioned Stimulus: An originally neutral stimulus that, having been paired with an unconditioned stimulus, now produces a response.

Conditioned Response: The learned response to an originally neutral stimulus.

Operant Conditioning: Learning as a consequence of the various rewards and punishments surrounding an individual.

Topographic Model: Freud's division of the mind into the conscious, preconscious, and unconscious.

Thought Suppression: The conscious blocking out of threatening material.

Personal Construct System: A system of beliefs and predictions that help direct behavior.

If-Then or Conditional Traits: Traits that only occur when very specific situational cues are present.

Collectivistic Cultures: Cultures that emphasize the interdependencies among people, families, and groups.

Individualist Cultures: Cultures that emphasize the personal goals and needs of individuals.

Allocentrics: People with collectivistic outlooks.

Idiocentrics: People with individualist outlooks.

Empathy: The capacity to understand and feel what another person is experiencing.

PERSONALITY PSYCHOLOGY: PART 2

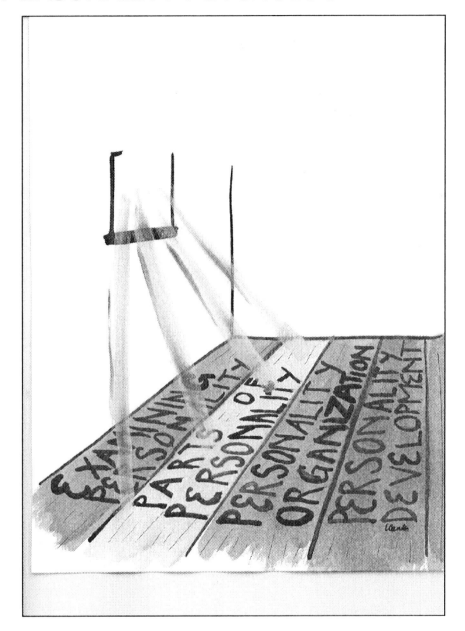

PART 2: PARTS OF PERSONALITY continues the exploration of the personality system. Through the past century, psychologists have been developing and refining their understanding of the most important parts of the personality system. Parts of Personality brings us through an examination of many of those parts: of motives and emotions, of mental models of the self and the world, of intelligence and other mental abilities, and finally, of fascinating—though less well understood—parts such as the conscious, the innermost self, and free will. The definitions and measures of these parts will be discussed, as well as how people differ from one another in the personality parts they possess.

Chapter 4: Motivation and Emotion

Guided by theory, and using research tools such as psychological measurement and experimental design, psychologists have gradually sorted and begun to understand the specific parts of personality. This chapter begins our exploration of the parts of personality with a look at an individual's motives and emotions. Motives help direct our behavior—they guide us toward some aims and away from others. Emotions interact with motives, amplifying or subduing them. Emotions also tell us about our relationships with others and how to achieve our aims in a social context.

Previewing the Chapter's Central Questions

•**What Are Motives and How Can They Be Measured?** Motives, goals, and plans propel us to do the things we do. Researchers use psychological tests to help them understand which motives and goals are fundamental.

•**How Are Motives Expressed?** Our motives aren't just something we feel internally—they have real-life impact on the choices we make. For example, a person who values achievement will behave differently from someone who values power.

•**What Are Emotions and Why Are They Important?** Of course, we don't just follow our motives wherever they lead. Motives are expressed—or not—depending in part on how we (and others) feel about them. If we like a motive, our emotions can amplify the behavior; if we feel guilty or ashamed about a motive, our emotions can subdue the motive. Emotions also signal us about our relationships with others.

•**What Are Emotional Traits and How Are They Expressed?** Many different emotions exist—happiness, sadness, anger—and we often perceive these feeling states along pleasant-unpleasant and other dimensions of feeling. People also vary in their emotional traits—the emotions they have a tendency to feel over time. Most noticeably, some people are sadder than others; some happier; some angrier.

•**What Are Happy People Like?** If people vary in how emotional they are, then what are the characteristics of the very happiest people?

What Are Motives and How Can They Be Measured?

Motives, Instincts, and Needs

What possible motive could a person have for climbing Mount Everest? On March 10, 1996, Jon Krakauer, a reporter for *Outside* magazine, was riding aboard a Russian-built helicopter with other members of an expedition that would climb Mount Everest, on the border between Tibet and Nepal in the Himalayan Mountains. The other members of his team had paid steep fees to be guided to the top by an experienced mountaineer—$65,000 a head. At the start of the expedition, Krakauer had wondered about his fellow climbers: Who were they and why were they there? Krakauer questioned their **motivation**. In this instance, motivation refers to the reason people do things; it also can refer to a person's desire to accomplish a goal. Krakauer's life would depend upon these expedition members during the climb: How willing would they be to help one another and to balance their dream of reaching the summit with the danger of the mountain

(Krakauer, 1998, pp. 37-38)? Why *did* Krakauer and his fellow climbers spend two months away from their homes and families and strain themselves to the breaking point in order to climb the mountain?

"Because it is there" was the famous reason George Leigh Mallory gave for climbing Mount Everest. Mallory had become irritated by the repeated questioning of a reporter when he provided that response. Was Everest's "there-ness" the real reason that Mallory, and later, many others, such as Krakauer, would risk their lives to climb it? Were there other aspects of their personalities that entered into the equation as well? The ascent is unquestionably dangerous; Mallory died while attempting it on June 8, 1924, as have one in four climbers since (Krakauer, 1998, p. 18, 28). Krakauer's self-described motives included his childhood idolization of mountaineers. A number of mountaineering teams ascended the peak on the same day as Krakauer's team. An unexpected storm, along with other mishaps, took the lives of a number of people. Although Krakauer survived, many of those he climbed with did not, including the leader of the expedition.

A person can be motivated by a situation "because it is there," in the case of Mount Everest, or by identification with a hero. People also vary in the amount of excitement they seek. Krakauer reported that the brochure for the guided ascent he went on, appealed to people's desire for thrills. It began by declaring, "So you have a thirst for adventure!" (Krakauer, 1996, p. 37). Psychologists regard individuals who thrive on excitement as "sensation seekers." These individuals often engage in potentially dangerous activities such as parachuting, hang-gliding, and extreme skiing so as satisfy their need for thrills and adventure. There are many motives other than sensation-seeking: to eat, to engage in sex, to affiliate with friends, and to seek power over people, to mention a few. Each motive may have a different origin in the brain, and bring to mind a different goal.

Instincts, Motives, and Goals

Those who study motivation often distinguish between basic motives or needs, on the one hand, and goals that are learned or acquired from the social environment, on the other. Among basic motives and needs are a variety of biologically based desires including hunger, thirst, varieties of sexual behavior, and tendencies toward different sorts of social behavior. These basic motivations are often innate although they can be modified through learning. In contrast, more specific goals might be to learn Spanish or to play World of Warcraft. The next sections of the chapter outline some of the basic motives that serve as a foundation for a person's learned goals and strivings.

Historically, many human motives were viewed as arising from an **instinct** (William James, 1890). Instinct refers to a biologically based urge that could be satisfied by a specific action. In the early twentieth century, for example, William James saw expressions of sympathy, modesty, sociability, and love as involving innate qualities. Freud described motives by tracing them from their biological origins in the brain to their psychological manifestations. For Freud, instincts were:

> ...a borderland concept between the mental and the physical, being...the mental representative of the stimuli emanating from within the organism and penetrating to the mind. (Freud, 1915/1963a, p. 87)

For Freud, humans' chief instincts were sexual and aggressive. Freud viewed sexuality broadly—as synonymous with seeking pleasure from living—an instinct that ultimately included many feelings of friendship and love. In the infant, this sexual instinct involved nearly any bodily pleasure; touching, eating, and even defecating were all considered part of the sex, or pleasure, drive. Any impulse to join others was part of this broadly defined instinct. Freud even viewed curiosity as beginning with the sexual instinct because sexuality encourages people to explore the physical sensations of their own bodies alone and with other people. Toward the end of his career, Freud (1937) defined a second class of human of instincts related to aggression and death.

Other scientists criticized these early formulations of motives. Anthropologists' work suggested that wide cultural variations in people's behavior undercut any simple idea of inherited instincts (e.g., Benedict, 1959; Mead, 1939). Their observations indicated that a given motive might be expressed in different ways depending upon the culture. Psychologists gradually gave up speaking of universal instincts expressed in fixed ways and began to speak in terms of **motives.** Motives are defined as biologically based and environmentally shaped urges or tendencies to behave in a particular manner.

The term "motive" is often used interchangeably with the terms "need," "urge," and "desire." Whichever term is preferred, a motive directs us toward certain aims or goals that will satisfy it (Winter, John, Stewart, Klohnen, & Duncan, 1998). A motive such as thirst can be satisfied in a simple fashion by drinking some water, or in a more elaborate manner by sipping an *espresso Italia*. Different motives emerge from different areas of the brain, activate different plans, and work in different ways.

Take the comparison between hunger and sex, for example. Hunger arises from a combination of short-term neurophysiological processes, such as the detection of sugar in the bloodstream, and fat molecules in the blood, and also from environmental stimuli such as the presence of a good-smelling, attractive meal. Hunger aims to help a person maintain his or her energy level (Mook, 1996, pp. 72-73). When a person is prevented from eating, he or she fantasizes about food more frequently (Keys et al., 1950).

Sex with another person is regulated in part by the rhythms of our sex hormones, including especially testosterone for men and estrogen for women, which vary according to monthly and annual patterns. Desires for sex bear little immediate relation to sugar or fats in the blood (Mook, 1996, p. 111). In addition, sex is socially complex. Adults with fewer sexual encounters fantasize about sex *less* frequently than do those with more sexual experience (Knafo & Jaffe, 1984). These examples serve to make the point that each motive is individually complex and may vary dramatically from the others.

Each of us is motivated in diverse ways. We may know some of our motives, whereas others of our needs may be unobserved, unnoticed, and outside of our awareness. Motives interact with one another dynamically—a point that will be covered in Chapters 9 and 10, which deal with personality dynamics. Some psychologists have even proposed the existence of a "master motive" called self-actualization: a need to become all that we can be. That motive for growth will be examined in the chapters on personality development.

Types of Motives

In the late 1930s, a psychologist named Henry Murray headed up of a team of researchers at the Harvard Psychological Clinic and published *Explorations of Personality,* a book that produced a long and seemingly exhaustive list of human needs. One version of the list appears in Table 4-1. The list ranges from needs having to do with objects, such as acquiring possessions, to those concerned with affection, such as the need to nurture others. Murray and his colleagues identified these needs by using a special form of psychological testing known at the time as projective testing, and also referred to today as thematic testing. Murray's group employed thematic testing because they weren't at all sure that people would—or could—accurately describe their own needs.

Table 4-1: Henry Murray's Overview of Human Needs[a,b]

I. Needs having to do with inanimate objects

n Acquisition	To gain possessions and property; to grasp, snatch, or steal things.
n Conservance	To collect, repair, clean, and preserve things.
n Order	To arrange, organize, and put away objects.
n Retention	To possess things, to refuse to give or lend, to be frugal.
n Construction	To organize and build.

II. Needs for ambition, will-to-power, accomplishment and prestige

n Superiority	To seek power over things, people, and attainments; to gain status and approval, including needs for achievement and recognition.
n Achievement	To overcome obstacles and do something difficult and well quickly.
n Recognition	To seek praise and commendation, to demand respect, to boast and exhibit one's accomplishments.

III. Needs complementary to superiority, involving the defense of status

n Inviolacy	To seek self-respect and a "good name"; to defend against criticism.
n Infavoidance	To avoid failure, shame, humiliation, and ridicule.
n Defendance	To defend against blame or belittlement; to justify one's actions.
n Counteraction	To proudly overcome defeat by re-striving and retaliating.

IV. Needs concerned with human power

n Dominance	To influence or control others; to persuade, lead, and dictate.
n Deference	To admire and willingly follow a superior allied other.
n Similance	To empathize, to imitate or emulate and to identify with others.
n Autonomy	To resist authority and coercion and to seek independence.
n Contrariance	To act differently from others; to hold unconventional views.

V. Needs reflecting sado-masochistic desires

n Aggression	To assault, injure, or to belittle, harm, blame, accuse, or maliciously ridicule a person.
n Abasement	To surrender, confess, and accept punishment; to apologize and atone.

VI. Needs concerned with human affection

n Affiliation	To form friendships and associations; to greet, join, and live with others; to co-operate and converse sociably with others.
n Rejection	To snub, ignore, or exclude others.
n Nurturance	To nourish, aid, or protect a helpless other.
n Succorance	To seek aid, protection, or sympathy.
n Play	To relax, amuse oneself; to seek diversion and entertainment.

[a]Note: Murray preceded each of his needs with an "*n*" to indicate he was measuring the need as expressed in personality – not as a self-report).
[b]Quoted from the text with some summarization, from Murray, 1938, pp. 80-83).

Projective Measures of Motives

"A man always has two reasons for the things he does—a good one and the real one." – J. P. Morgan (1837-1913)

Do you like to dominate and control other people? If you do, would you admit it on a psychological test? People may not only hide such motives from others, they may hide the urges from themselves, or even be unaware of them. The idea that many basic psychological motives are caused by biological mechanisms suggests that they may arise somewhat automatically and never reach consciousness. Moreover, even if the motives were momentarily conscious, people may avoid thinking about them to the extent that their urges conflict with social ideals. People, in other words, may often not know or accept their own motives. Based on such logic, psychologists sought ways to measure people's non-conscious motives.

Projective Testing and the Projective Hypothesis

The key element that defines a **thematic test (or projective test)** is the presence of an ambiguous stimulus to which an individual responds (Frank, 1939). The hope is that by examining the overall themes of a person's responses, their motives and other qualities may be understood (McClelland, Koestner, & Weinberger, 1992).

Researchers use the **Thematic Apperception Test** or **TAT** (Murray, 1938; Morgan, 1995) and newer variations of picture-story exercises to identify hidden motives. The original TAT consists of a group of cards, each one with a drawing or picture on it, mostly of people alone or in interaction with one another. Probably the best-known card shows a boy who is gazing into space, sitting at a desk on which rests a violin. The examiner presents a card of the TAT to the participant and says, "Tell me a story about this picture. Tell me how it began, what is going on now, and what will happen in the end?" The test-taker then composes a story, weaving together elements of the picture as the examiner dutifully records what the respondent says.

The content of the test-taker's stories are then evaluated according to the themes and ideas the individual has expressed. Note that the test-taker answers nothing directly about him- or herself, yet using the themes, the examiner makes hypotheses as to what concerns, or even preoccupations, are important to the individual. For example, a person who describes the boy with the violin as dreaming of a concert at Carnegie Hall might be judged to have a need to achieve. A person who discusses love and romance in various stories would be judged as needing other people.

Contemporary evidence suggests that picture-story exercises (PSEs) such as the Thematic Apperception Test and new measures using updated images are both valid and reliable, indicating that the technique is well worth further research (Lang, 2014; Schultheiss et al., 2009; Slabbinck et al., 2013).

What Motives Are Found with Projective Measures?

Many of the needs measured by the TAT seem immediately recognizable—but though the list that Murray and his team created is long, there are other motives of importance recognized today that go beyond Murray's list. Xu and colleagues (2013) found evidence for such needs as health, self-improvement, honesty, and efficiency.

To simplify the long list of human needs, some researchers have focused on a three-fold division of Murray and colleagues' findings representing **needs for achievement**, for **power**, and for **affiliation**. The needs are often abbreviated as ***n* achievement**, ***n* power**, and ***n* affiliation**. The "*n*" refers to the fact that the need is assessed as a theme on the TAT or similar instrument, rather than depending upon self-judgments. The three broad groups of needs can be viewed as a somewhat loose confederation of more specific needs. For example, *n* achievement includes a need to meet standards of excellence which is specifically called the *n* for achievement, as well as a need to be superior to others, known as *n* superiority, and the need to develop an independent perspective on the world, known as *n* autonomy. Similarly, *n* affiliation includes other needs such as the need to play, the need to seek aid and protection, collectively known as *n* succorance, and the need to seek others who can care for oneself, known as *n* nurturance. One benefit of using the three broad motives rather than the more specific ones is that it is easier to develop a scoring system that accurately identify one of the three needs, rather than trying to code for 20-plus needs.

Self-Report of Motives: Standard Self-Judgment

Not all psychologists use projective methods to study motives; some prefer a more direct approach of asking people about their needs. These psychologists have developed tests of motivation that employ **self-judgment (or self-report) items**. Psychologists who use these tests understand that people sometimes conceal undesirable motives and may lack self-knowledge. The researchers are nonetheless interested in what people will answer about their motives when they are asked directly.

For example, the self-report-based Motivation Analysis Test includes items such as, "I want to lie in bed in the mornings and have a very easy time in life," and "I want to enjoy fine foods, fine drinks, candies, and delicacies," to which people agree or disagree (Cattell, Horn, & Butcher, 1962). Jackson's (1974) Personality Research Form (PRF) includes questions for each of 20 needs identified by Murray. Jackson's test has been subjected to a number of factor analyses.

Lei & Skinner (1982) examined the Personality Research Form, a psychological test that measured 21 needs from Murray's list—using 21 subscales to do so. Using factor analysis, they concluded that the 21 subscales could be described by five dimensions. The first represented a need for order and achievement; the second involved dominance and exhibitionism; the third, autonomy; the fourth, aggression; and the fifth, a need for achievement and endurance.

At first glance, Lei and Skinner's results seem quite different than the needs for achievement, power, and affiliation used with the TAT. Some experts, however, see at least a loose correspondence between these results and the three broad motives studied with the TAT. For example, the first factor may correspond to *n* Achievement. The second factor, "Outgoing, Social Leadership," could be related to *n* affiliation, and the third, "Self-Protective Versus Submissive Orientation," might correlate with *n* power. That still leaves, however, two new clusters of motivations not addressed by projective testers. Other experts have wondered whether what looks like "Outgoing, Social Leadership," might simply measure a more general trait such as extroversion (e.g., Ashton, et al., 1998).

Aside from the similarity (or lack of it) in measuring motives across methods, some researchers have expressed skepticism over whether self-judgment items can assess a person's true motives. Consider the test item, "I want to see violent movies where many people are injured or slain." If a young man enjoyed watching such mayhem, would he really admit to it? Many young men might be concerned that others would question their values if they made such an admission. For such reasons, modified self-judgment methods have been introduced.

Modified Self-Judgment (Self-Report): The Case of Forced-Choice Responding

The willingness of a person to endorse a test item has to do in part with the **social desirability** of the test item. Social desirability concerns the value society places on a particular way of thinking or feeling. For example, the thought "For me, family comes first," represents a socially desirable attitude, whereas, "I care more about fine wine and fast cars than family," does not. Although there are people who care more about fast cars than family, at least some people who hold such attitudes may be cautious about letting others know how they feel.

To control for the impact of social desirability on test responding, psychologists have developed a form of self-report item called the **forced-choice item** (Edwards, 1957). Test-takers respond to a forced-choice item by choosing between two alternatives of roughly equal social desirability. In the Edwards Personal Preference Inventory, test items were developed to measure 15 of Murray's needs by using forced choice methodology. A test-taker might see a test item that asks, "Which would you prefer?" followed by two alternatives:

(a) To watch a sexy movie

(b) To watch a violent movie.

Notice that the two alternatives measure different needs—and that they are both low in social desirability compared to other possible preferences ("To help other people"). The 225-item scale seems to circumvent a person's possible hope to appear desirable to others and it has been employed in a great deal of research and correlates well with other tests that use self-judged needs (e.g., Edwards & Abbott, 1973; Edwards, Abbott, & Klockars, 1972). The forced choice method does have some drawbacks, however. For example, to equalize the social desirability of items measuring the need for aggression and the need for autonomy, the aggressive-need item might have to be phrased mildly to match the undesirability of an autonomy item, given that autonomy is valued by many. In theory, at least, one could end up with a relatively mild aggression item such as "I don't mind it when children play with toy guns," paired with a relatively negative autonomy item such as "I think a person's independence takes precedence over other people's needs."

Self-Judgment and Thematic Measures Compared

In cases when thematic and self-judgment tests measure the same need, such as n achievement, they often don't correlate very highly. Conscious self-reports and thematically expressed motivations seem to reflect two different motivational qualities. McClelland (1992, p. 52) has argued that self-reported motivation indicates what a person thinks guides her behavior at a given moment in time whereas thematic measures reflect a person's actual long-term needs. So, if a person judges herself as feeling motivated by achievement, she may choose to engage in an achievement-oriented activity such as studying rather than an affiliative activity like going to a party. The thematically measured trait, the "implicit motive," however, is more likely to guide the individual's long-term goals. Put another way, a person's conscious motivational preferences— preferring to study rather than to go to a party—can predict one's immediate behavior, but it is the deeper, longer-term, more automatic ways of organizing the world—revealed by thematic tests—that determine where one will go in life. Of course, tests such as the TAT have both their critics and defenders and the debate continues as to their validity for use in individual cases. Most critics acknowledge that research with such tests indicates validity for some purposes (Garb, Wood, Lilienfeld, & Nezworski, 2002; Hibbard, 2003). Research from such scales tell us about how people express their motives over the life span.

How Are Motives Expressed?

The Achievement Motive and Its Relation to Personality

A person's life is fundamentally guided by her motives. Achievement-oriented people are motivated to compete against standards of excellence, attain unique accomplishments, and commit themselves to pursue a goal over the long term (McClelland, Atkinson, Clark, & Lowell, 1992). One picture-card on the TAT shows young people watching a surgeon in an operating room. A person high in achievement motivation told the following story in reaction to it:

A group of medical students are watching their instructor perform a simple operation
on a cadaver…. In the last few months they have worked and studied. The skillful
hands of the surgeon perform their work. The instructor tells his class *they must be able to*

work with speed and cannot make many mistakes. When the operation is over, a smile comes over the group. Soon they will be leading men and women in the field (McClelland, et al., 1992, p. 160).

In a review of the literature on *n* Achievement, McClelland (1992) concluded that people high in achievement set challenging goals that keep them learning, improving, and approaching their standards of excellence. They avoid goals that are so easy as to be boring or that are impossibly difficult. In addition, they are more persistent than are others when their progress at various tasks is frustrated, and they are more future-oriented.

Students high in *n* Achievement obtain their chief satisfactions primarily from tasks they perceive as relevant to their goals. Interestingly, *n* Achievement does not predict overall school achievement (McClelland, 1992). Rather, students with high achievement motivation will get higher grades only in those courses they perceive to be relevant to their future goals. In work settings, high *n* Achievement people are more interested and involved in their occupations and are more upwardly mobile. They tend to be highly entrepreneurial and enterprising and better at finding jobs when they are unemployed (McClelland, 1992).

Achievement Imagery in Society

When a person tells a story in response to a picture from the Thematic Apperception Test, the story is coded for motivational themes. But the coding systems developed for the TAT can be applied to other texts as well—for example, to the literature people in a given country prefer to read. David McClelland (1958) reported the results from a senior honors thesis by Berlew in which the achievement theme was gauged for ancient Greece from 900-100 BCE. Central pieces of Greek literature from that ancient time were coded for achievement imagery. If an Athenian poet rhapsodized about the beauty of a runner who excelled and won a race, *n* Achievement would be scored, whereas if the poet ruminated on love, an affiliative motive would be applied. Berlew found that achievement imagery declined over the 800-year period studied, along with a decline in the number of nations with which Greece traded. This suggested a connection between the Greeks' cultural emphasis on achievement and their economic prosperity. These results were replicated for Spain during its economic decline (1200-1730; Cortés, 1960).

But does the achievement motive *cause* economic development? Bradburn & Berlew (1961) found that, from the 1400s to the 1830s in England, there were two waves of achievement imagery. There were flashpoints of such imagery in the late 1500s and the late 1700s, as measured in popular English plays, songs, and accounts of sea voyages. Each of these bursts of achievement imagery preceded periods of rapid economic expansion, arguing for a possible causal connection.

McClelland went on to analyze second- through fourth-grade school readers in 23 countries from 1920 to 1929 and in 140 countries from 1946 to 1950. The amount of achievement imagery in those readers was unrelated to previous economic growth but strongly predicted national economic growth for the years afterward. The correlation between achievement imagery and later economic growth was $r = .45$! This prediction held for the following 15 years of economic growth as well ($r = .40$; Winter, 1992, p. 112).

The Power Motive and Personality

The power motive involves direct and legitimate control over other people's behavior—that is, interpersonal power (Winter, 1992a, p. 301). People exhibit a focus on power when they monitor and heighten their influence, impact, and control over others (Winter, 1992b, p. 312). For example, a high-power person might tell TAT stories in which characters directly express their power (e.g., "They plan to attack the enemy."), try to influence, impress, or control other people (e.g., "She told him she went to Harvard."), or try to protect them. A test-taker exhibited these power themes in response to a TAT picture of an older man and a younger man:

> These two men are planning a break from the political party to which they both belong. The elder man is the instigator. Noticing the disapproval the young man has shown with the party policy, *he is convincing him to join with him. The elder man was pushed into the party.* At first, he thought it was a good idea. As he saw the workings of it he became more against it...*The two will start a new opposition party.* (Veroff, 1992, p. 290)

Power-motivated people tend to enter professions in which they direct the behavior of other individuals and in which they can reward or punish others within the legitimate policies and procedures of organizations (Winter, 1992b). Such occupations include business executives and managers, psychologists, and mental health workers, teachers, journalists, and members of the clergy. Occupations in which the use of power is arguably more indirect, such as in law, science, or medicine, are less likely to attract those high in *n* Power. Although people might guess that politicians are all high in *n* Power, many politicians run for office because of their need to achieve or to be loved instead. Those politicians who are higher in *n* Power are distinguished by being more likely to initiate their own candidacies for office. Among presidents of the United States, those highest in *n* Power are, relative to other presidents, judged as greater figures by historians, but they are also more likely to enter the country into war (Winter, 2005).

How do power-seeking individuals attain power? They seek visibility, sometimes by taking extreme positions or gambles. Student leaders high in *n* Power may write letters with extreme opinions to campus newspapers. Other students high *n* Power may acquire possessions that others may not be able to afford (such as big-screen TVs, cars, and nicer apartments). In addition, high *n* Power students in general build alliances with others, particularly with those of lower status, and encourage them to participate in the organizations in which they are trying to attain power. People high in *n* Power are not necessarily well liked, nor are they perceived as working hard or creating the best solutions for problems. In addition, such individuals may seek power to compensate for a fear of being controlled by others (Veroff, 1992).

The Affiliation Motive and Personality

The third broad area of motivation studied by Murray's intellectual descendants was the need for affiliation. People who need affiliation tell stories that include companionship, mutual interest, and sympathetic understanding. A person needs to exhibit more than a relationship theme alone, however. Affiliative imagery is centered on maintaining or restoring a positive emotional relationship with a person (Heyns, Veroff, & Atkinson (1992, p. 213). For example, the following test-taker expressed affiliative needs to the same picture of two men used in the earlier *n* Power example:

> A younger man is approaching a man older than himself for help or advice on a problem. The younger man is *worried about his lack of acceptance in the new social group* he just became acquainted with. The young man seeks restoration of his confidence. He knows his problem. A short conversation will ensue in which the older man will restore the younger man's confidence (Heyns et al., 1992, p. 221).

People with higher affiliation needs spend more time with others, visit their friends more often, talk on the phone more frequently, and write more letters. In addition, these individuals appear more sympathetic and accommodating toward others, are interested in people-oriented careers, and have heightened desires to live in a peaceful world. Interestingly, these people end up being less popular than others. That result has led to the concern that affiliation imagery may indicate a more dependent, anxious social motivation than originally thought (Koestner & McClelland, 1992, p. 208). Among presidents of the United States, those who were high in affiliation were more likely to enter into relationships that resulted in scandals in their administrations (Winter, 2005).

Some psychologists believe that a somewhat different motive, the **need for intimacy,** might be more important in predicting success in relationships. Intimacy is defined as "the sharing of one's thoughts, feelings, and inner life with other human beings" (McAdams, 1992). Scoring intimacy themes on a thematic measure emphasizes the exchange of personal information between characters: "They enjoyed talking to each other." or "She had fun telling him a secret." or even, "They had a friendly argument about which movie was better." The measure of n Intimacy correlates only modestly with n Affiliation (r = .30 or so, Koestner & McClelland, 1992, p. 209).

Intimacy motivation (but not affiliation) does predict general psychosocial adjustment, including better job satisfaction and marital satisfaction, as much as 15 years after original measures were administered. (McAdams, 1992a).

The Sex Drive and Related Motives

Motives beyond those studied by Murray and his students also are worth studying. Freud viewed the sex drive (or instinct) as exerting important influences over a person's life and most of us would likely agree. The first widespread surveys of sexual behavior in the United States were conducted by Alfred Kinsey in the 1940s and William Masters and Virginia Johnson in the 1960s (Kinsey, Pomeroy & Martin, 1948; Kinsey, Pomeroy, Martin, & Gebhard, 1953; Masters & Johnson, 1966). Since that time, the techniques used to survey people about sex have been refined to promote better sampling and more accurate answers, and to ensure the ethical treatment of respondents.

For example, Laumann, Gagnon, Michael, & Michaels (1994) used a stratified random sample that was representative of the United States population. Once the researchers identified potential participants, they did whatever they could to persuade them to participate. The interviewers were trained to clarify their questions so as to make sure that people understood the questions being asked. If participants were embarrassed about answering certain questions, they could answer the questions anonymously by placing written responses in a sealed envelope. The survey wasn't perfect—the question of subjects' sexual orientation was asked face-to-face only. Consequently, some people might have been reluctant to acknowledge any homosexual experimentation or a homosexual orientation directly, so it's possible, if not likely, that the survey underestimated the number of homosexuals in the population.

This survey found that the average rate of sexual activity in the United States was rather conservative, with most married adults engaging in sex about once a week. One third of married couples reported experiencing little or no sexual activity over the prior year. In addition, most participants reported few sexual partners over the course of their lives. The survey painted a picture of considerable difference in sexual activity among people, with wide variations in sexual frequency, number of partners, and sexual orientation.

Shafer (2001) developed a sexuality scale on which people describe how alluring, sexy, seductive, ravenous, and lusty they are. College students who score high on the sexuality scale are more likely to be single, have higher interest in dating, date for longer periods of time, get over their last relationship more quickly and start dating again than low scorers. Higher levels of sexuality also predict having more partners and a more active dating life in early adulthood (Shafer, 2001). Getting married is another story—one covered in adult development in Chapter 12.

Development of Needs and Personal Strivings

Maslow (1943) argued that needs unfold in a hierarchy, according to their personal urgency (cf. Aldefer, 1967; Murray, 1938). In Maslow's scheme, people begin by ensuring their physiological needs are met—that they have enough air to breathe, food to eat, and water to drink. Empirical studies indicate that physiological needs do come first for people (Wicker et al., 1993). According to Maslow's theory, they next seek to fulfill their safety needs by finding safe havens from violence, crime, and other threats to their physical selves. People who experience trauma are particularly focused on safety needs (Aronoff, 1967). After ensuring their safety, people try to meet their love and belongingness needs—to find others to be with and to share with. Fourth, people hope that others will respect who they are: Maslow called this group our "esteem needs." Once a person meets all these needs, according to Maslow, she can focus on further developing who she is herself—a process called self-actualization (see Hagerty, 1999), discussed in greater length in Chapter 12, which focuses on Adult Development.

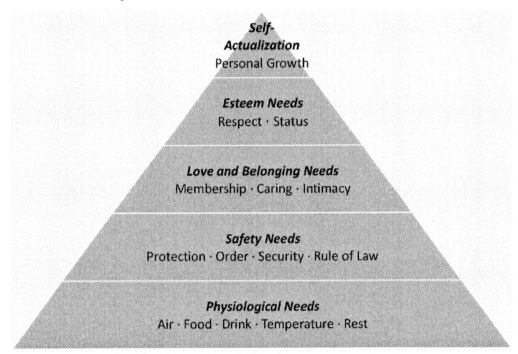

Figure 4-1 *Maslow's Hierarchy of Needs.* Maslow thought of needs as forming a hierarchy in which some needs—physiological and safety needs—were more urgent and required satisfaction before tending to higher level needs such as seeking love and respect.

People meet their needs through **personal strivings.** Personal strivings describe the class of things that a person does to attain his or her goals (Emmons, 1985). Emmons writes:

> For instance, a person with a striving to be physically attractive may have separate goals about exercising, ways of dressing, or wearing his or her hair in a certain way. Thus, a striving may be satisfied via any one of a number of different concrete goals.

Emmons found that people can reliably report the things for which they strive (e.g., staying in shape, doing well in school). How a person strives affects how a person feels. People who set realistic goals that require great effort tend to generate positive feelings and emotions for themselves. Holding goals that are unlikely to be met, however, leads to negative feelings. A person who holds a goal such as being charitable, which causes little conflict with another goal to make friends, is also likely to feel greater well-being than someone who holds two goals that conflict. (We'll examine the interaction of goals in Chapter 9: Dynamics of Action.) Next in this chapter, we turn to the relationship between motives and emotions.

What Are Emotions and Why Are They Important?

The Motivation-Emotion Connection

If you're like most people, you've been motivated to do something because of the way you've felt. For example, you might have been angry and that might have made you feel like becoming aggressive: shaming or yelling at someone. Certain motives appear to be accompanied by specific emotions.

Plutchik (1984) identified eight basic motives that are common to many animals and that are important to successful adaptation. These motives (which he referred to as functions) include self-protection, destruction, reproduction, and exploration. Plutchik paired each motivational function with a subjective experience—that is, an emotion that frequently accompanies it. For example, he paired self-protection with fear because responding to a threat with fear—and escape behaviors—can help preserve us. Other pairings include reproduction and joy, rejecting others, and disgust (cf. Plutchik, 1991, Table 2.1, p. 54).

Are there really relationships between motives and emotions like those Plutchik proposed? Izard and his colleagues (1993) studied the relations between various motives (as measured by the Jackson Personality Research Form) and emotions. The list of motives was a bit different than that proposed by Plutchik, but Izard found results consistent with such thinking. For example, aggressive motives were moderately related to anger. But most of the motives were related to several different emotions rather than to a single emotion: Affiliation motives were related to interest and joy; aggression related not only to anger, but equally to disgust and even more to contempt.

Emotions can even more generally amplify or diminish motives (Murray, 1938, pp. 90-91). Consider a person who is very depressed—devoid of feeling except for extreme sadness and hostility toward the self. In Table 4-4, moderate levels of sadness, shame, and guilt reduce all motives but aggression. At extreme levels, depression acts as a global motivation dampener, reducing desires and needs until very little seems pleasurable and worth doing. Severely depressed individuals feel unmotivated and even useless (American Psychiatric Association, 2013).

The Neuropsychology of Emotion-Directed Behavior

Today, biopsychologists and evolutionary psychologists have suggested the existence of two brain areas that relate to negative and positive emotional feelings. The **behavioral inhibition system (BIS)** has been described as a "stop, look, and listen" system to emphasize that it reduces behavior and increases attention (Gray, 1987). It helps the organism monitor surroundings, anticipate fear-provoking stimuli, and behave cautiously. This system is associated with negative emotions, particularly anxiety and sadness (Cray, 1987; Fowles, 1987; 1994).

By contrast, the **behavioral facilitation system (BFS)** encourages the organism to engage with its outside surroundings, to explore, and to investigate (Depue et al., 1984; Watson, Wiese, Vaidya, & Tellegen, 1999). It is highly associated with positive emotions such as happiness and joy, although anger may also play a part in this behavioral system. There is some evidence for hemispheric differences in these two behavioral systems as well. Davidson, Tomarken, and their colleagues have found that happy, positive people have greater neural electrical activity in their left prefrontal cortex when resting. Dissatisfied, negative people show greater electrical activity in their right prefrontal cortex when resting (Davidson & Tomarken, 1989; Tomarken & Keener, 1998).

Why are there two largely independent systems—behavioral inhibition and behavioral facilitation—rather than one? Cacioppo, Gardner, & Berntson (1999, p. 847) have suggested that two systems permit the organism to be shaped through learning in more subtle ways than would be possible with one system. As a person experiences various events, the two systems learn to respond in partial independence of one another. Sometimes a person may be rewarded for inhibiting certain behaviors, sometimes for facilitating behaviors, and sometimes for both. Because there are two partially independent systems acquiring experience from the environment, more emotional configurations are possible—such as being both inhibited and facilitated or being neither inhibited nor facilitated at the same time—in reaction to a given situation.

Emotions as an Evolved Signal System

From Motives and Emotions to Cognitive Signals?

Emotions also signal meanings about situations. Our emotional system recognizes the situations around us and responds to them. The Renaissance thinker Baruch Spinoza, for example, described how threat can make a person fearful, how being denied justice often makes a person angry, and how being cared for and loved by another makes a person happy—relations confirmed by present-day research (DeRivera, 1977; Mayer, Salovey, Gomberg-Kaufman, & Blainey, 1991; Roseman & Smith, 2001; Scherer, Schorr, & Johnstone, 2001; Plutchik, 1980). These connections between situations and emotions make sense and they suggest that human beings may show some universal understandings of emotion. To better understand these possibilities we turn to the study of emotional expressions in the face.

Facial Manifestations

If each specific emotion arises in response to a certain kind of situation, we can think of emotions as specific signals about the situation we face. Could this language of emotions be universal, and if so, could it be the same the world-around? Charles Darwin argued that facial expressions of emotion had evolved to function as a signal system (Darwin, 1873/1965). Particular expressions that are especially important to purposes of survival, such as anger, are especially similar across species. For example, the arched back of the cat, the way it bares its teeth, and its snarl and spit, are all readily recognizable and seem comparable to the growl of the dog and the snarl of an angry person.

Darwin argued that human facial expressions were universal, and conducted some studies on the matter, soliciting observations on the facial expressions of indigenous peoples from biologists and other acquaintances from around the world. "Mr. J. Scott of the Botanic Gardens, Calcutta," wrote Darwin:

> …observed during some time, himself unseen, a very young Dhangar woman from Nagpore, the wife of one of the gardeners, nursing her baby who was at the point of death; and he distinctly saw the eyebrows raised at the inner corners, the eyelids drooping, the forehead wrinkled in the middle, the mouth slightly open, with the corners much depressed. He then came from behind a screen of plants and spoke to the poor woman, who startled, burst into a bitter flood of tears, and besought him to cure her baby. (Darwin, 1965, pp. 185, 186)

By the early 1970s, various researchers had come to demonstrate that much of what Darwin said about the universality of emotional expression was correct.

Cross-Cultural Issues

Modern Studies of Cross-Cultural Facial Expression

Paul Ekman and colleagues developed the **Facial Affect Coding System (FACS)** to create a language of the face and its expressions. The FACS is a method of coding the muscular system of the face as it enters into various emotional expressions. Ekman and colleagues collected 3,000 photographs of people's facial expressions and then selected those that were particularly pure representatives of the basic emotions of happiness, anger, fear, sadness, disgust/contempt, and surprise (see Figures 4-3 to 4-5). This work led to the identification of representative examples of basic emotional facial expressions.

Ekman and his colleagues then showed these representative photographs to individuals in five literate but diverse cultures in Japan, Brazil, and elsewhere. Individuals were asked to identify which emotion each face displayed. Across cultures, individuals agreed that a given face showed a particular emotion more than 80% of the time.

Next, Ekman and his colleagues wanted to see whether people in preliterate cultures would understand the faces in the same way as people in literature cultures. The researchers set off to Borneo, New Guinea, to test their hypothesis. Although members of the preliterate societies correctly identified many faces, they performed at levels far below those who participated from more developed nations. The Borneo participants were at a disadvantage however. Having no written language, they were unable to refer to the written list of emotion alternatives that those in literate societies had used. The Ekman team returned to the United States with the idea of revisiting Borneo with a new approach—which they did soon thereafter.

Once back in New Guinea, they employed a new procedure: Each participant was told a story (developed with help from people familiar with Borneo) designed to elicit an emotion (e.g., happiness, anger, fear, etc.). At the same time, the examiners laid out the six face photographs. At the end of the story they asked the individual to choose the face that went with the story. The happiness story was simple, "Her friends have come and she is happy." The fear story was a bit more complex:

> She is sitting in her house all alone and there is no one else in the village; and there is no knife, ax, or bow and arrow in the house. A wild pig is standing in the door of the house and the woman is looking at the pig and is very afraid of it. The pig has been standing in the doorway for a few minutes and the person is looking at it very afraid and the pig won't move away from the door and she is afraid the pig will bite her. (Ekman, 1973, p. 211)

Using this procedure, agreement about which emotion was expressed in a face rose to the mid-80%—about the same as that for literate societies.

Initial Skepticism about Ekman's Results

Karl Heider, an anthropologist who had conducted extensive research among the Dani people, also of Papua, New Guinea (now Indonesia) was initially skeptical about Ekman's findings. He and a psychologist colleague, Eleanor Rosch, collaborated in a research project designed to check what Ekman had found. Heider had been studying the Dani people of West Irian for many years. The Dani people were among the most isolated on earth. Heider knew that they lacked words for some of the six emotions Ekman had studied (i.e., happiness, sadness, anger, fear, surprise, and disgust). When Heider heard about Ekman's findings in Papua, New Guinea, he visited Ekman, learned his research techniques, and then traveled back to West Irian to test Ekman and his team's findings (Ekman, 1999, pp. 308-310; Heider, 1991, p. 88).

To their surprise, Heider and his colleagues were able to replicate Ekman's work with the Dani. They tested two Dani subcultures, one known for their placidness and peacefulness, the other known for their emotionality, and found results supporting Ekman's work in both cases. As a consequence of this study and more recent studies of the brain physiology of the Minangkabau culture of West Sumatra (e.g., Levenson, Ekman, Heider, & Freisen, 1991), the universality of central aspects of emotional expressions has become widely accepted.

Why then, had anthropologists observed some differences in facial expressions across cultures? Ekman suggested that there were **cultural display rules**—rules by which people in a particular culture are taught to express their feelings. For example, men may be taught not to express fear and women may be taught not to express anger. For some of Ekman's Borneo studies, for example, only women's faces were used as stimuli because men denied ever feeling fear.

Since Ekman's groundbreaking work, researchers have concluded that although emotion recognition is universal, people do exhibit a slight advantage when they look at faces from their own country. Elfeinbein & Ambady referred to this difference in emotion recognition as reflecting an "emotion dialect"—an analogy to the idea that people in a given country may all speak the same language, but they may speak it using different dialects in different regions. Although the language is the same, the accent many change slightly (Elfenbein, 2013).

Acknowledging such differences, what Ekman (1973, p. 219) wrote remains the case: "One hundred years after Darwin wrote his book on emotional expression, a conclusion is possible. There are some facial expressions of emotion that are universally characteristic of the human species." (Ekman, 1973, p. 219).

Emotional States, Moods, and Emotion-Related Traits

So, the emotions system is a universally evolved signal system. It is extensive in its scope. It amplifies motives and responds to specific situations. Certain emotions are universal in their meaning.

At the same time, the emotions system is very personal in regard to how it works in an individual. Some people are sad, some glad, and many in between. To better understand this idea, it helps to distinguish discrete emotions from moods and from emotion-related traits.

The emotion system responds to a situation in the short-term with emotions. Emotions can be considered transitory states—moments when the organism shifts into a particular configuration: afraid, sad, or happy. Those states, however, are different from an individual's longer-term emotional qualities, which are described by **emotion-related traits**. Emotion-related traits are long-term characteristics describing the individual's tendency to be fearful, sad, happy, or in another state.

Charles Spielberger first drew attention to the distinction between a momentary feeling, an emotional **state**, and a long-term likelihood of feeling a certain way, an emotion-related **trait**. He and his colleagues developed a set of scales called the **state-trait scales** of anxiety (e.g., Spielberger & DeNike, 1966). These psychologists pointed out that a person could be in an anxious state—waiting for a medical test result—without being an anxious person. A generally anxious person—called a *trait-anxious* person—was more likely to be anxious in more situations more often than others, but might not be anxious at a given time. Some people use the term "mood" to indicate a mental state somewhere between a relatively quick emotional reaction and a long-term trait. If emotional states occur in seconds and minutes, moods are more on the order of hours and days, and traits reflect personality tendencies that extend for months, years, and decades.

What Are Emotional Traits and How Are They Expressed?

As we begin to examine peoples' emotions and emotion-related traits, a key question is how many emotions there are. Recall that Ekman studied six. Strong cases have been made for as many as 16 or as few as five. A few researchers continue to express doubt as to whether it is useful to label emotions as basic at all (e.g., Averill, Ekman, Panksepp, et al., 1994; Izard, 1992; Ortony & Turner, 1990).

Individual Differences in Emotionality

People vary along a number of emotional traits depending upon how happy or sad they usually are and how variable their mood is, among other characteristics. In daily life we rely on people's statements about their emotional experiences to assess how they feel. Because those feelings are internal and hidden, a person's self-statements are the best and most obvious ways we have of knowing what emotional reactions a person is having. For those reasons, self-judgment techniques have been the measures of choice when examining emotions.

The 1960s saw the introduction by drug companies of the first mood-altering pharmaceuticals. To understand how a drug affected a mood, pharmaceutical researchers needed good measures of how a person was feeling. To address this question, researchers such as Vincent Nowlis (1965) asked people to describe their present moods by checking off how much they felt each of a series of feelings. A sample version of such a scale is shown in Table 4-2.

The test-taker was instructed to read through each mood-adjective and check off how he or she felt at the moment. When Nowlis first factor-analyzed a mood scale, he obtained a large number of factors, but they didn't seem very elegant. He concluded there were perhaps eight factors, beginning with "surgency," (a blend of liveliness and dominance) and proceeding through other moods such as aggression, joy, and anxiety.

Table 4-2: Example of Items From a Mood Adjective Checklist

Instructions: How much do you feel each emotion?				
Emotion terms:	Definitely Don't Feel	Somewhat Don't Feel	Somewhat Feel	Definitely Feel
Happy	YY	Y	X	XX
Sad	YY	Y	X	XX
Angry	YY	Y	X	XX
Afraid	YY	Y	X	XX
...	...	...	...	...

The Two-Factor Approach to Measuring Emotion

About 15 years later, using newer approaches to factor analysis, James Russell (1979) found a very elegant two-factor depiction of mood. The first factor represented a **Pleasant-Unpleasant Mood (or Affect) Factor**. The term **affect** is often used in a slightly broader sense than mood, to include along with mood such states as alertness and tiredness. Russell's second factor reflected an **Activated-Deactivated Mood (or Affect) Factor**. Sometimes Activation-Deactivation is simply referred to as "Aroused-Calm." A schematic overview of this solution is shown in Figure 4-1.

Research by Deiner and Emmons (1984) and others (e.g., Zevon and Tellegen, 1982) generally supported Russell's findings and expanded them by considering two alternative dimensions to explain the same phenomena. This well-known alternative solution re-divides aspects of mood to yield two alternative dimensions of affect: **Positive Mood (or Affect) versus Tiredness**, and **Negative Mood (or Affect) versus Relaxed**. These two alternative sets of dimensions are all part of the same picture—literally! These dimensions can also be found in Figure 4-2: they are oriented at 45 degree angles from the Pleasant-Unpleasant and Aroused-Calm dimensions.

In Figure 4-2, the Pleasant-Unpleasant and Aroused-Calm dimensions run vertically and horizontally. The Positive-Tired and Negative-Relaxed dimensions run at 45 degree angles to them. The specific, individual emotions such as fear, sadness, happiness, surprise, and so forth, are arranged within the sets of axes. The two sets of axes represent directions like North-South, and East-West. In this case, however, there are no agreed-upon poles. Today both pairs of dimensions, Pleasant-Unpleasant/Aroused-Calm, and Positive-Tired/Negative-Relaxed, are commonly employed to organize specific emotional reactions and there is an ongoing debate as to which is best (e.g., Green, Salovey, & Truax, 1999; Russell, 1999; Russell & Barrett, 1999; Watson, Wiese, Vaidya, & Tellegen, 1999).

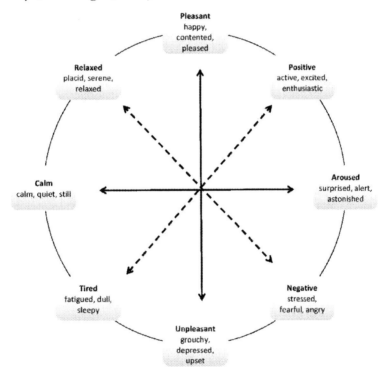

Figure 4-2 *A Two-Dimensional Model of Mood with Rotated Axes.* For at least a century, psychologists believed that many feeling terms could be represented according to two dimensions. In this specific example, the vertical and horizontal dimensions are labeled pleasant-unpleasant and arousal-calm mood *(after Barrett & Russell, 1999; Watson & Tellegen, 1985).* Two additional axes are depicted by the dotted lines: Positive and Negative affect (these dimensions are typically referred to by one name each).

There are, of course, more dimensions of mood. For example, there is a Fear-Anger (or Submission-Dominance) sub-dimension that is of some importance. Still, these two dimensions of positive and negative affect serve as a good first approximation of the dimensions along which specific emotions can be described.

"Dimensions" Are More Than Just Drawings: Advanced Ideas

Depictions of dimensions of mood such as those in Figure 4-2 are more than just clever drawings; they follow mathematical rules. Recall from Chapter 2 that every test item (an emotion term, such as "happy," in these analyses) has a factor coefficient associated with it that represents the correlation between a test item and a dimension (factor). These coefficients vary from -1.0 (a perfect negative relationship) to +1.0 (a perfect positive relationship) with a correlation of 0 indicating no relationship.

These factor loadings have a second interpretation as well in geometry. The correlations between items on a test and the factor-dimensions can be interpreted as the *cosines of angles* (e.g., Gorsuch, 1983, p. 63). The two factors of a factor analysis are often modeled so that the correlation between them is zero. A correlation of zero can be translated geometrically into a cosine of zero—and that corresponds to an angle of 90 degrees. This is the case with the Pleasant-Unpleasant Mood factor and the Arousal-Calm Mood factor, and is why the researchers place the dimensions at right angles (90 degrees) to one another.

If researchers find that a Pleasant-Unpleasant Mood dimension correlates with an alternative dimension of Positive-Tired $r = .707$, the cosine also would be .707, which corresponds to an angle of 45 degrees. That is why a Positive Affect dimension is placed at a 45 degree angle relative to Pleasant-Unpleasant. In a good deal of mood research, Pleasant-Unpleasant and Arousal-Calm Mood dimensions are the dimensions of choice and are arranged North-South, East-West, to create a diagram in which specific moods can be fit. Many researchers, however, prefer the Positive Affect and Negative Affect dimensions. These correlate about .707 with the original mood dimensions. For that reason, they can be placed in the same two-dimensional space, but rotated 45 degrees from the originals. That is how psychologists develop the sort of diagram illustrated in Figure 4-1: In addition to the Pleasant-Unpleasant, Arousal-Calm dimensions, they add in a second set of dimensions rotated 45 degrees to the right, to obtain the Positive-Tired and Negative-Relaxed dimensions. This is referred to as "factor rotation." Individual moods like "happy" or "calm" are placed in the diagram depending upon their factor loadings (cosine) in relation to the axes. The axes, in turn, represent the factors.

From Emotional States to Emotion-Related Traits

The Work of Hans Eysenck

A powerful psychological system such as our emotions is likely to have long-term effects on other parts of personality. Our tendency to experience emotions, in fact, influences a key group of socioemotional traits. In the 1930s, Hans Eysenck, a British psychologist, was among the first to study personality traits using factor analysis. Eysenck was studying a scale that later became known as the Eysenck Personality Inventory that included about 120 items similar to the following:

(1) Do you enjoy going to parties on weekends? YES / NO

(2) Do you often worry? YES / NO

(3) Are you often happy or often sad for no obvious reason? YES / NO

Eysenck's factor analysis indicated that his test actually measured two uncorrelated factors. The first factor, **Neuroticism-Stability** (or more tactfully, **Emotionality-Stability**) was represented at the emotional end by negative emotions, mood swings, anxiety, and uncertainty. Asked, "Do you worry?"—the test-takers high on this dimension answered "Yes." People at the stable end were calm and secure. The second factor was **Introversion-Extraversion**. When asked, "Do you enjoy parties?" people high on the extroversion dimension would answer "yes," whereas more introverted individuals answered "yes" more often to the question "Do you enjoy reading?"

Eysenck could describe personalities by positioning them within the two-dimensional space of trait terms in Figure 4-3. For example, a person high in emotional stability and extraversion would be located in the upper right of the two-dimensional space, and be described by such terms as "lively" and "easygoing," whereas an introverted, neurotic individual would be located in the lower left and be described as "pessimistic" and "sober." Stable introverts (upper left) represented "peaceful and thoughtful" individuals, whereas extroverted neurotics (lower right) were "changeable and excitable." Eysenck was able to arrange a great number of personality trait terms according to this framework.

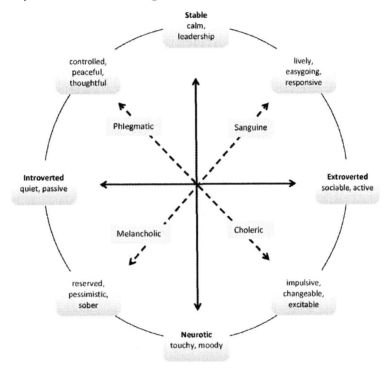

Figure 4-3 *Eysenck's 2 Dimensions of Personality* Hans Eysenck proposed that many personality traits could be described along the dimensions of Introversion-Extraversion, and Neuroticism-Stability. Here, many different personality traits are organized together in a circle described by those dimensions (see also Eysenck & Eysenck, 1963, Figure 1).

In fact, Eysenck believed that his two dimensions created four quadrants that closely corresponded to Hippocrates' ancient division of personality into four humours. Notice the four terms, "phlegmatic," "sanguine," "melancholic," and "choleric," in the inner portion of the diagram. Remember from Chapter 1 that the physician Hippocrates had earlier classified personalities that way, as described in the section "Personality before personality." Eysenck saw evidence that his factor analysis integrated the ancient observations of Hippocrates with modern research measurements.

By 1980, there existed a two-dimensional model of mood and a two-dimensional model of personality. A number of personality researchers were intrigued by the similarity between these two models and wondered if they might be related in some way. Costa and McCrae (1980) suggested that a person described by an Eysenckian trait could be described by a parallel tendency to experience a particular type of mood. For example, highly neurotic people might typically feel negative moods, whereas extroverts might typically feel positive moods. If correct, then the two-dimensional personality trait structure would correspond to the two-dimensional mood structure, and they could be superimposed on one another in the same diagram. This has been done here in Figure 4-4; the major personality trait dimensions (e.g., Introverted, bolded) and mood dimensions (also bolded) are combined to form the main circle. Inside the circle is the four-fold system of antiquity (e.g., Phlegmatic). Conceptually, the personality and mood terms appear to correspond. Subsequent research supported Costa & McCrae's empirical findings that there were also day-to-day relations between mood and personality: Introverted neurotics experienced more negative affect, and stable extroverts experienced more positive affect (Gross, Sutton, & Ketalaar, 1998; De Raad & Kokkonen, 2000).

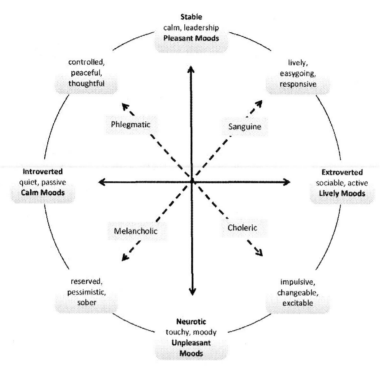

Figure 4-4 *Combining the 2 Dimensions of Mood and Personality.*
Beginning in the early 1980s, researchers began to identify similarities in the 2-dimensional representations of mood and personality. They wondered whether personality traits could, at a broad level, be a function of moods. Here, Eysenck's 2 dimensions of personality are shown with the moods that correspond to them.

Biological models of Introversion-Extraversion and Neuroticism-Stability exist as well. Eysenck, for example, has suggested that introverts have higher physiological responsiveness to stimuli and a higher resting level of activation than do extraverts. For example, if you place a drop of lemon juice in the mouths of an introvert and an extrovert, introverts will salivate more than extroverts will (Von Knorring, Moernstad, & Forsgren, 1986). Introverts, in essence, strive to minimize the stimulation they experience so as to keep their activation level from rising even higher than its already high set point. Extroverts, on the other hand, go out and find stimulation so as to raise their initially too-low level of excitement (Eysenck, 1967; 1990, p. 248). All such explanations are at present little more than hypotheses, and their specific nature will be modified with more research (Zuckerman, 1991, p. 135-137).

Emotional Learning and Culture

Although emotional meanings are universally understood, the experiences that elicit a given emotion and the way the emotions are expressed vary from person to person. For example, a toddler who receives a shot from a doctor may learn to associate the white coats of doctors with pain, and future doctors in white coats may elicit fear automatically as a conditioned reaction (Lewis, 2000). The child at 8 months may exhibit only relatively simple fears such as those in response to being alone or loud noises. By 2 years of age, however, a child may perceive more complex social relations—and feel apprehensive, for example, upon breaking her parents' favorite lamp (Lewis, 2000). Emotional learning proceeds based on early exposure to objects and people. A child who brushes his teeth with Willard's of Vermont Toothpaste while standing next to his mother may connect the brand to his mother and develop a basic positive reaction to it (Parkinson & Manstead, 1992).

Cultural factors come into play to shape emotional learning: Consider the case of anger and aggression. Among the !Kung bushmen of northwestern Botswana, if a small child has a tantrum, he or she is typically allowed to frown, grimace, and cry, and also to throw objects at the mother and to hit her. Mothers behave in a serene fashion during such tantrums, brushing off the tiny blows, and laughing and talking to other adults while they take place. As the children grow older, their aggression is directed toward animals: They are free to kill small animals, and to chase and hit dogs and cows, in preparation for hunting. The !Kung children fight among themselves relatively infrequently.

In a community in the Baltimore area of the United States, by comparison, mothers often teased their children and encouraged them to fight in order to learn to defend themselves against others. One mother described wrestling matches in which she encouraged her daughter to make a fist and hit her. When her daughter gave her a surprise punch, the mother reacted with pride and feelings of confidence that her daughter would be able to defend herself against others (Saarni, 2000, pp. 306-307). Such differences in emotional environment will certainly affect how a person feels anger and aggression, its psychological meaning, and how it is expressed. Thus, both biological and sociocultural influences act upon the emotion system.

How Are Emotional Traits Expressed?

Wessman & Ricks (1966, p. 195) described an extremely emotionally stable college student they studied—dubbed "Shield"—like this:

> …Shield manifests no apparent nervous mannerisms and few expressive gestures. His features are regular and good-looking, though not striking. He is inconspicuously well groomed. His speech is quiet, soft, low, and gentle. He gives a sense of calm reserve and aloofness—polite but detached. No zest, no enthusiasms, no spontaneity ripples his urbane composure. He provides little warmth and appears to ask for none in return..." (Wessman & Ricks, 1996, p. 195)

They also described a more emotional student—dubbed "Swallow":

> …Usually laughing and smiling, Swallow readily tosses puns and jokes into conversation, however inappropriate they may be. What he says is often colorful, spontaneous, and unguarded. On occasion there will be a slowness, or a plaintive clutch or sob in his voice that belies his humorous banter…He has periods of soaring enthusiasm when all the world is bright and promising and he is supremely self confident. At other times he is despondent, melancholy, hopeless. (Wessman & Ricks, 1966, pp. 214-215)

Both Shield and Swallow grew up in families with divorced parents and it is interesting to compare their autobiographies in that regard. In Shield's case, "The entire sequence of the family disruption, mother's death, and father's remarriage is recounted in barest outlines, entirely devoid of any account of Shield's personal emotions." (Wessman & Ricks, 1966, p. 200). Shield says of his parent's divorce that, after his father fell ill, the "relations between my mother and father deteriorated and finally they were separated…" (Wessman & Ricks, 1966, p. 200).

Swallow's narration, in contrast, was highly emotional: "When my parents were divorced, my mother, sister, and I came to live with my grandmother in the house that she owns. It's a real madhouse, everybody fighting with everybody else, really yelling and really violent tempered house…" (Wessman & Ricks, p. 219).

The emotion-related traits of emotionality-stability, and extraversion-introversion, can also reflect the career path an individual chooses later in life. For example, salespeople are very extroverted and are in between emotional neurotic and stable extremes. Office assistants and administrators, students, and managers tend to be more emotionally stable. These relationships seem to agree in part with our intuitions about what people in those groups are really like (from Eysenck & Eysenck, 1968).

More Emotion-Related Traits

Today, Eysenck's two-dimensions are still studied both on their own and in the broader context of the Big Five personality traits, of which they are part. In Chapter 3 we discussed the Big Five traits in some detail; they include Extraversion, Neuroticism, Openness, Agreeableness, and Conscientiousness. From model to model, the exact nature of a trait may change. For example, Neuroticism as measured in some of the Big Five models, emphasizes self-consciousness and emotional vulnerability rather than Eysenck's mood instability (e.g., Costa & McCrae, 1985). Others have suggested adding one of the Big Five traits— Agreeableness-Disagreeableness—to Eysenck's model to form a three-dimensional model "socio-emotional sphere" (Saucier, 1992). These dimensions form a group that can be used to define and locate an even larger number of more specific traits than Eysenck first organized.

What Are Happy People Like?

"Too much of a good thing is wonderful." – Mae West (1893-1980)

Natural Happiness

Many people's emotional styles involve soberness or negativity; only a few possess the exact traits in precisely the right amount to experience happiness. What are such happy people like? In trait terms, happiness involves being low in neuroticism, somewhat high in extraversion, and having a general sense of well-being.

A first point to make about happiness is that some people seem to feel it rather naturally, whereas others do not (e.g., Watson, 2002). The great 20th century psycho-diagnostician Paul Meehl (1975) wrote that some people seem to have more "happiness juice" than others, whereas others, according to one Wild West maxim, are born "three drinks behind" (Meehl, 1975, p. 299). Meehl (1975) describes those who lacked the ability to experience pleasure as often experiencing life as a struggle:

> Well, you know, I have to get up in the morning when I hear the alarm clock ring and
> go out and shovel the walk [Meehl worked in snowy Minnesota] and all that kind of
> junk, and what do I really get out of it? I mean, it strikes me that life is often pretty
> much a big pain in the neck—it just isn't worth it. (Meehl, 1975, p. 300)

Reading the above description from today's perspective brings to mind the fact that seasonal decreases in sunlight (as in Minnesota winters) can also lead to a rise in negative feelings.

The happy person, by contrast, is "born three drinks ahead" (Meehl, 1975, p. 300). Such individuals are fun-loving and cherish their experiences. Indeed, research indicates a fair degree of heritability of positive emotions, with estimates at about $r = .40$ for both positive and negative emotions (measured on the Neuroticism-Extroversion-Openness (NEO) scale (Jang et al., 1998).

Demographic Influences

Neither age nor sex is correlated with happiness; income is only weakly related to it. Between 1960 and 2000 in the United States, inflation-adjusted income more than doubled from roughly $7,000 to $16,000. Yet, over the same years, the percentage of people saying they were very happy remained surprisingly constant, hovering around 30% (Myers & Diener, 1995, Figure 4). Today in the United States the correlation between income and happiness is only $r = .13$. Extreme poverty does impact happiness negatively. For example, in a survey of 43 nations completed in 1993, the then-poor nations of India and the Dominican Republic rated below average in happiness (Diener & Diener, 1996; Veenhooven, 1993; for reviews, see Argyle, 1987; Myers & Diener, 1995; and Watson, 2002).

The Happiest Students

Returning to happy people: Diener and Seligman (2002) examined 222 college students' emotions reported on a day-by-day basis over 51 days, including their positive and negative thoughts, their general life satisfaction, and other similar measures. They then selected the 24 happiest students, as judged by all the criteria. In certain respects, the happiest students were much like everyone else. They were identical to the depressed and normal students in their perception of how much money they had, their grades, how conscientious they were, their objective physical appearance (rated from photographs), and their time spent doing anything from watching TV to participating in religious observances.

The happy students were different from the other groups in some significant ways. They were highly satisfied with their lives, they nearly never thought about suicide, they could recall many more positive events than negative ones, and, almost every day, they reported many more happy emotions than unhappy ones (Diener & Seligman, p. 82). These individuals had good relationships with both family and friends. On the Minnesota Multiphasic Personality Inventory (MMPI)—a scale measuring various psychopathologies—they scored within the normal range in every category, with one exception—6 of the 24 scored a bit high on a scale measuring mania (the happy part of bipolar disorder).

Only 10% of us qualify for that most happy group. Is there anything the person born without a tendency toward happiness can do? Paul Meehl (1975) foresaw advances in psychopharmacology when he wrote in the mid-1970s that psychoactive drugs would someday offer the less happy individual important support. In addition to such biological interventions, he believed that less happy individuals might improve by paying more attention to their emotional bookkeeping. To do so, individuals needed to "purchase" activities most carefully. He wrote that, "…it matters more to someone cursed with an inborn hedonic defect whether he is efficient and sagacious in selecting friends, jobs, cities, tasks, hobbies, and activities in general." (Meehl, 1975, p. 305). A second issue for such individuals was to free themselves somewhat from cultural pressures to interact and go to parties, given that that was not what they generally enjoy. As Meehl put it, "I have a strong clinical impression that, at least in American culture, many people develop a kind of secondary guilt or shame about it….not everybody gets a big "kick" out of social interaction—there is no compelling reason why everybody has to be the same in this respect…" (Meehl, 1975, p. 305).

Subsequent research has obtained some encouraging findings concerning positive and negative affect. As a person ages, his or her happiness tends to increase—at least through age 70 (Mroczek, 2001). For men, being both extroverted and married further reinforces this trend (Mroczek & Kolarz, 1998). A variety of psychotherapies exist that are effective in teaching a person how to employ a more positive perspective on life. Such therapies are as effective as many drug therapies in improving a person's sense of well-being (Wampold, Minami, Baskin, & Tierney, 2002; Westen & Morrison, 2001). Additional benefits come from developing a sense of personal meaning (Mascaro & Rosen, 2005).

Members of the positive psychology research movement have identified a number of means by which people can improve their moods. Sonja Lyubomirsky (2008) observed that people can raise their happiness levels by practicing positive thinking—framing what happens in realistic but reassuring fashions, and avoiding rumination and overthinking. She further argues that practicing gratitude—for example, by realizing how much other people do for us and thanking them for it can make people feel better. She and others are also advocates of taking care of oneself physically and of improving the connections we maintain with other people.

These learned positive ways of thinking can make a person happier over the long term. The creation and influence of mental models of oneself, the world, and one's relationships is the topic of the next chapter, "Interior Selves; Interior Worlds."

Reviewing Chapter 4

The goals of this chapter were to introduce you to the motivational and emotional systems, and to discuss the role those systems play in allowing personality to function. In addition, the chapter examined key attributes of those systems, how they are measured, and how they are expressed. The chapter prepares you for the discussion in upcoming chapters of other parts of personality, the personality system's organization and its development.

Questions About "What Are Motives and How Can They Be Measured?"

1. Motives, Needs, and Goals: The motivational system is made up of basic urges that drive the individual, motives, and needs. Can you define these terms?

2. Projective Measures of Motives: Projective measures of motives, such as the Thematic Apperception Test, were developed because researchers assumed that many people might not understand their own motives or might be reluctant to speak openly about them. Can you describe how a projective test works and how it is scored?

3. People's Central Motives: People are motivated by different desires and goals. Freud emphasized sex and aggression. Early in the century, Henry Murray laid out a list of between 20 and 30 motives. Can you recognize examples of Murray's motives? Since then, three larger areas of motivation–achievement, affiliation, and power have been examined, along with sexual motivation. Can you describe each of these?

4. Self-Report Motives: Some psychologists believe that if you ask people to report their own motivations directly, you will obtain some useful answers. Sometimes to get such answers it is helpful to use "forced choice" formats. Can you describe the forced choice method and any differences in findings between self-report and projective measures?

Questions About "How Are Motives Expressed?"

5. <u>Personal Strivings and Goals:</u> Personal striving refers to some of the paths people take to achieve their goals. Personal projects are the routes by which people hope to achieve those goals. Striving toward some goals will make a person feel better; other kinds of goals, however, may damage psychological health. Can you distinguish between the sorts of goals that will help and the ones that will not?

6. <u>The Achievement Motive and Personality:</u> People with strong achievement motives often compare themselves to standards of excellence. They do well in entrepreneurial situations and on tasks they view as relevant to their performance. What else can be said about people high in this motive?

7. <u>The Power Motive and Personality:</u> People with a high need for power tend to engage in power-motivated behavior, such as attempting to impress others. They may also be drawn to careers such as medicine, psychotherapy, or teaching. Can you say what attracts these people to such occupations?

8. <u>The Affiliation Motive and Personality:</u> People with high needs for affiliation place greater value on— and more frequently engage in—relationships with others. They are not, however, necessarily well-liked in their relationships. This has led psychologists to examine the need for intimacy. Do you know the difference between affiliation and intimacy? How are these two needs expressed?

9. <u>The Sex Drive:</u> Very little is known about the sex drive in relation to personality beyond the facts that people vary substantially in their sexual interests and that women and men show different mating patterns. For example, men prefer women younger than themselves and women prefer men of higher occupational status. Evolutionary psychologists have tried to account for some of those differences; can you explain how?

Questions About "What Are Emotions and Why Are They Important?"

10. <u>The Motive-Emotion Connection:</u> Motives and emotions are intertwined with one another. For example, some emotions can be paired directly with corresponding motives: anger and aggression, fear and escape, love and altruism. Beyond such direct pairing, it appears that some emotions have amplifying effects on motives, whereas others dampen motives. Can you give an example of an emotion that amplifies motives and an emotion that would dampen them?

11. <u>Emotions as an Evolved Signal System:</u> Emotions appear to have evolved in mammals to communicate social relations and intentions Do you know who first proposed this idea?

12. <u>Cross-Cultural Issues:</u> The idea that emotions are universal communications about relationships requires testing across cultures. Paul Ekman provided such tests, first among Westernized nations, and then among relatively isolated communities in New Guinea and elsewhere. Do you know the general level of agreement across cultures about basic emotion expressions?

Questions About "What Are Emotional Traits and How Are They Expressed?"

13. <u>The Two-Factor Approach to Measuring Emotions:</u> Mood-adjective checklists are scales in which a person indicates how much of each of a number of feelings he or she is experiencing (e.g., happy, sad, angry, peaceful, etc.). Factor analysis can provide ways of summarizing these large numbers of feelings. One good solution from factor analysis indicates that mood can be represented according to two dimensions. There are, actually, two sets of two dimensions, depending upon how one wishes to label

moods. One set describes mood as falling along Pleasant-Unpleasant and Arousal-Calm dimensions. Can you describe the other set?

14. <u>From Emotional States to Emotional Traits:</u> There is a two-dimensional representation of emotion suggested by several research teams, and Hans Eysenck earlier found a two-dimensional representation for personality that spanned Emotional-Stable and Extraversion-Introversion axes. This led to the idea that there might be a relation between the two dimensions. Do you know what it is?

15. <u>How Emotional Traits Are Expressed:</u> Whatever one's emotional style, it has consequences in a number of areas, from how people appear to others to one's choice of occupation. Can you relate some of the more important consequences of emotion-related traits to everyday life?

Questions About "What Are Happy People Like?"

16. <u>Natural Happiness:</u> Some people may be born happier than others; others are "three drinks behind." Can you name the eminent 20th century psycho-diagnostician who proposed this notion?

17. <u>Demographic Influences:</u> Happiness has been studied in relation to nationality, socio-economic status, and other variables. Mostly there is no relationship between happiness and these factors. Do you remember the one exception?

18. <u>The Happiest Students:</u> A recent study examined extremely happy students, selecting them according to a variety of different criteria. Can you say how they differed from the less happy students?

Chapter 4 Glossary

Terms in Order of Appearance:

Motivation: Motivation can refer to the reason why a person does something, or to the level of a person's desire to accomplish a goal (for example, a certain person's motivation to get married is high).

Instinct: A biologically pre-programmed, fixed set of behaviors that, when triggered, is meant to accomplish a particular goal under certain circumstances.

Motive or Need: Basic motives and urges involve a mostly innate part of personality that directs the individual toward a specific source of satisfaction.

Thematic (or Projective) Test: A test that uses ambiguous stimuli as its items. The test-taker must respond to each item by completing a sentence, telling a story, or otherwise supplying a response.

Thematic Apperception Test (TAT): A projective test developed by Henry Murray and Christiana Morgan consisting of pictures. The respondent must tell a story with a beginning, a middle, and an end in response to a picture she is shown.

Need for Achievement: A broad need characterized by the desire to meet standards of excellence.

Need for Power: A broad need characterized by the desire to exert control over others.

Need for Affiliation: A broad need characterized by the desire to be friendly and cordial with other people.

Self-Judgment (or Self-Report) Items: Test items in which a person is asked a direct question about himself, e.g., "Do you like parties?"

Factor (in factor analysis): A factor is a hypothetical variable that can be used to summarize two or more specific, observed variables. Sometimes the factor is said to "underlie" the observed variables.

Social Desirability (of a test item): The social desirability of a test item concerns the degree to which endorsing the item would be viewed as good by society.

Forced-Choice Items: Test items in which a person is forced to choose between two items that are paired such that they are equivalent in social desirability. The two items might both be highly desirable or highly undesirable. The item type is believed to force the participant to express a motive or preference, independent of social pressure.

Need for Intimacy: The need to share inner urges, feelings, and thoughts with others.

Personal Strivings: Activities people engage in so as to meet their goals. Many types of striving may be necessary in order to meet a single goal.

Behavioral Inhibition System (BIS): A brain system that interrupts and suppresses behavior so that the individual can think and examine a situation.

Behavioral Facilitation System (BFS): A brain system that encourages and facilitates behaviors such as fighting or joining with others.

Facial Affect Coding System (FACS): A method developed for coding emotions in the face according to the position of muscles in the face and facial features.

Cultural Display Rules: The rules that people in a culture employ when expressing emotions, e.g., in some Western cultures, men are taught that they should not show fear.

Emotion-Related Traits: A type of personality trait (e.g., long-term psychological quality) that describes a person's overall emotional quality (e.g., happy-go-lucky, sad).

States: Momentary feelings or internal qualities or activities.

Traits: Relatively long-term characteristics of the person, typically composed of thematically related features.

State-Trait Scales: Scales that measure parts of personality, such as anxiety, in two different ways—once as a momentary state and once as a trait.

Pleasant-Unpleasant Mood (or Affect) Factor: One member of a pair of two basic dimensions for describing the interrelation of specific emotions. The other pair member is Activation-Deactivation. This dimension is obtained through factor analysis of mood scales. Other factor solutions yield a second pair of dimensions.

Affect: A term used to encompass both moods and other related states such as alertness and tiredness.

Activated-Deactivated Mood (or Affect) Factor: One of a pair of two basic dimensions for describing the interrelation of specific emotions, based on how much the emotion conveys energy or action. The other pair member is Pleasant-Unpleasant Mood. This dimension is obtained through factor analysis of mood scales. Other factor solutions yield a second pair of dimensions.

Positive Mood (or Affect) versus Tired Mood (or Affect) Factor: One member of a pair of two basic dimensions for describing the interrelation of specific emotions. The other pair member is Negative-Relaxed Affect. This dimension is obtained through factor analysis of mood scales. Other factor solutions yield a second pair of dimensions.

Negative Mood (or Affect) versus Relaxed Mood (or Affect) Factor: One of a pair of two basic dimensions for describing the interrelation of specific emotions, based on how much the emotion conveys energy or action. The other pair member is Positive-Tired Affect. This dimension is obtained through factor analysis of mood scales. Other factor solutions yield a second pair of dimensions.

Neuroticism-Stability or Emotionality-Stability: A personality dimension (obtained through factor analysis) describing highly emotional individuals on the neurotic/emotional side, and people who are relatively emotionally stable on the stable end.

Introversion-Extraversion: A personality dimension (obtained through factor analysis as well as simple observation) describing people who like to keep to themselves on the introverted end, and those who prefer sociability, on the extroverted end.

Chapter 5: Interior Selves; Interior Worlds

In the previous chapter, we examined how motives direct behavior and how emotions assist in their expression. We now move to mental models—records in memory of what we—and the world—are like. We create mental models as we strive to understand ourselves and the world. These models address the questions: Who am I? How does the world around me operate? What is my path in life?

No one has perfectly accurate models of themselves or the world, but people must have some way of thinking about who they are and how the world functions. Some people develop models that are very helpful to them; others find this more challenging.

Previewing the Chapter's Central Questions

•**What Are Mental Models?** Mental models are structures in memory that describe the self, the world, and the self in the world. Beyond that, mental models take on different forms from archetypes to scripts. Several of these forms are explored in this chapter.

•**What Are Our Models of Ourselves?** Each of us develops mental models of ourselves, including a model of our actual self and of the possible selves we might become. We also develop life stories about ourselves.

•**What Are Our Models of the World?** Models of the world concern how we look at and represent the world around us. They include the formal learning we acquire at school as well as more casual scripts we pick up for navigating social situations. Some of our more important models concern how we understand other people.

•**What Are Our Models of Relationships?** Each of us must learn how to relate to others. This learning begins with models of how to relate to our parents and other significant caretakers. As we mature, we develop models for how to carry out more sophisticated social roles.

•**How Good Are Our Mental Models?** Some people are able to develop very accurate and constructive mental models of the world; other people are less able to do that. This section examines what makes for a constructive model and what people are like who hold such constructive models.

What Are Mental Models?

Several weeks into the semester, a professor asked a student in his class to come see him. He told the young woman that he had been distracted over the last few class periods by her behavior toward him. During the lectures, he said, she had begun rolling her eyes, and then looked alternately smug or disgusted. Her expressions had made him increasingly uncomfortable, and he asked her if she would stop. The student explained she was unaware of behaving in the way he described, although she couldn't deny that she had an expressive face and was reacting a lot to the lectures. She told him, though, that mostly she had been enjoying the class. (Seymour Epstein, 1998, p. 73, provides the original account from which I have drawn).

The professor believed the student—but he also believed his own eyes. He wondered whether something occurring in the lecture was triggering her feelings without her being fully aware of it. A mental model is an organized structure in memory that depicts the self, the world, or the self in the world. Such mental models often can trigger strong emotions. This student's memory was likely triggering feelings of anger and insecurity that, in turn, were leading her to express her disgust and superiority (as represented by her eye-rolling and smirking).

To help the student understand her mental model—and to reduce his own discomfort—the professor suggested that she monitor her feelings during his next few lectures and check when unpleasant feelings arose. Then, he asked her to check if those feelings reminded her of something in her past that she felt particularly strongly about.

During the next few classes, the student mostly paid attention to the lectures, but she gradually turned her attention to her reaction to them as well, charting her feelings and responses to what the professor said. She found that her reactions were fairly positive during some of the class, but she began to feel uncomfortable and hostile whenever the professor spoke about his research. The professor's behavior reminded her of her father, a professional who also had been very wrapped up in his work. She had resented her father, who, she felt, had never had enough time for her.

She returned to the professor's office two weeks later, excited about the connection she had made. She described how the image of her father—and her hurt feelings over his neglect of her—had come up in class. In her mental model, she wanted the attention of her father, and yet he would often hurt her by paying more attention to his work. Over time, she grew to resent her father's attention to his work. Once the student recognized the source of her feelings, she realized that her sense of anger in class didn't fit the current situation, and she changed her behavior (Epstein, 1998, p. 73).

The mental models we use are essential to our understanding of the world around us. They guide us in how we deal with the people and situations we encounter and help us to make sense of our world. Our mental models provide us with clues about when something is about to happen and how to deal with our ongoing circumstances. We need to be careful about how we view the world, because our predictions and reactions are only as good as the mental models on which they depend. These mental models can take a variety of forms.

Mental Models and Their Structure

A **mental model** (also called a **schema**) is a group of organized information about a topic in a person's thoughts. It is usually learned and can serve as a preconceived way of fitting information together— the schema represents a reality that a person expects to encounter. For example, a woman may think in terms of traditional sex roles, believing that all men are supposed to act strong and all women are supposed to be caring. She will categorize people according to their gender, and many observations she makes will be based on whether she is dealing with a woman or a man, and whether the person fits the mental schema she has. Such a simple schema may work a good deal of the time, but it is a simplistic view and will fail to capture the actual diversity of gender roles. For that, better models—more sophisticated schema—are required.

Mental models can be distinguished according to the specific memory structures involved: prototypes, scripts, and life stories that are relevant to how we view the world. Table 5-1 provides an overview of some mental models.

Schemas can take the form of a **prototype.** A prototype is a model of an object based on a list of its most typical or common features (Anderson, 1980, p. 133). If you are asked about your mental model of nearly anything, you are apt to recall its most prototypical features first. For example, if you are asked to describe a moral person, you are more likely to begin with highly defining attributes such as *honest, genuine, loving,* and *respectful,* and only later retrieve less typical qualities such as *does not gossip* and *diligent* (Lapsley & Lasky, 2001).

Table 5-1: Mental Models and Their Corresponding Mental Structures (as Applied to Personalities)

Knowledge Structure or Schema	General Definition and Relevance to Personality	Specific Examples
Schema	A general term for a memory structure that organizes knowledge about a given topic. Self-schemas consist of a group of characteristics that describe the self.	• An *actual self* is list of defining qualities a person uses to describe herself
Prototype	A list of features that collectively describe a type of person, typically emphasizing the most common, defining qualities first.	• *Talkative, sociable, lively, energetic*, to describe an extroverted person
Script	Scripts are memory structures that consist of a sequence of stereotyped actions that help us navigate the world.	• *Feel hungry, find a restaurant, walk in...*for the start of a restaurant script
Life Story	A specific sequence of events that tells a story of something that has happened to a person. We create a life story to explain ourselves to others.	• A high point in our life • A turning point in our life
Relationship Style	A motivational and emotional quality of attachment used to relate to others.	• Secure attachment • Avoidant attachment
Roles	A socially defined part that one plays in society.	• Being a masculine man • Acting like a professional

Mental models can refer to the self, the world, or the part one plays in the world. Mental models of the self are our internal representations of who we are. For example, a person may say, "I am generous, thrifty, and kind." Another person may say, "I am often tired and sad, and have little energy." These self-descriptions are sometimes referred to as one's **self-concept**, or a **self-schema**. A self-concept is a mental model of the self. The positivity or negativity of the self-schema is referred to as an individual's **self-esteem**. Models of the world, on the other hand, are representations of the outside world by which we navigate our surroundings. They tell us the rules by which the world operates. For example, some of us believe that "love makes the world go 'round," whereas others among us believe that "everyone is out for himself."

Another type of mental model is the script. **Scripts** are stereotyped sequences of events and actions ordered in time (Schank & Abelson, 1977; Tomkins, 1984). For example, most people who live in the world today know the script for a fast-food restaurant: You walk in, get in line (if there is one), and while in line, look at an overhead menu that is typically displayed behind the counter. You then wait for a staff member to make eye contact with you, place your order, and then pay the cashier. A foreknowledge of such scripts helps an individual navigate the outside world in an efficient manner.

The script concept can be applied to more open-ended interpersonal interactions as well. For example, a person in a relationship might envision him- or herself as playing a particular character in a script, repeating the same interactions over and again. Marriage partners often realize they repeat the same argument over and over and seek to change it. Eric Berne (1957) said that each of us chooses among the roles of a parent, a child, or an adult as we interact with others. When we play the role of a parent, we are full of rules: "Chew with your mouth closed," "Be sure to get enough sleep." If we *are* a parent with a young child, playing a parent can be just right. Sometimes, however, if we "behave" as the parent with a roommate, friend or co-worker, they are unlikely to appreciate it.

Another kind of mental model, the **life story**, is a narrative description of our life events, often formulated to make a point. When we ask people about themselves, they often respond with a part of a life story calculated to make an impression on us. For example, a biographer of Robert Hughes (a mid-20th century art critic) helped established his authority for describing his subject by mentioning he met Hughes at the University of Sydney in 1956. He continued, "I am certain of one thing: a sense of something that could only be described as *style* was unmistakable even before he had spoken," (italics added; Riemer, 2001, pp. 1-2). The biographer tells us this part of his story to communicate that he had met Hughes early on and had recognized his style.

The story a person chooses to tell us will highlight some aspects of their life—in this case, acquaintance with another figure, and de-emphasize other aspects that might not fit into a particular purpose. Such stories are the means, in part, by which we define our identity for ourselves and for others.

A fourth sort of mental model concerns relationships. **Relationship structures** contain not only knowledge about the world, but also "procedural knowledge"—the procedures for how to do something. For example, in his best-selling book, "How to Win Friends and Influence People," Dale Carnegie (1936) taught millions of people how to make friends by following simple rules such as becoming genuinely interested in other people, smiling, and remembering and using the other person's name. Models of relationships also include the roles we know how to carry out and play—the role of a student, a party-goer, a friend. We will examine these models of the self and world in this chapter.

Mental Models are (Usually) Learned and Applied

Where Do Mental Models Come From?

Let us start with the observation that although mental models are typically learned, at least a few of these memory structures have specific biological underpinnings. Chapter 4 outlined how human beings recognize basic emotional facial expressions such as those of anger, fear, and happiness. Evidence for a genetic contribution to such perceptual skills come from cross species comparisons: Domesticated dogs can read human emotional facial expressions—but the wolves from which they are descended are unable to distinguish a happy from a sad expression (Bekoff, & Goodall, 2003; Hare & Wrangham, 2002; Hecht, 2002).

Another kind of innate mental model involves "prepared fears." Human beings and their evolutionary cousins, chimpanzees, very readily develop phobias for spiders, lightning, and snakes—consistent dangers that were present over thousands of years of our species' evolutionary development. Human beings are far less likely to develop phobias of more recent present-day objects such as bicycles, cars, and knives—that are far more injurious. Relative to the threats persistently faced by our ancestors, there has been relatively little evolutionary time to evolve caution in respect to those newer objects. (de Silva et al., 1977; de Silva, Mineka, et al., 1984; Rachman, & Seligman, 1977; Poulton et al., 2001).

We human beings also have evolved a capacity to learn that allows us to grasp many novel aspects of our environments. Much of what children accomplish each day is to acquire knowledge structures that directly help them understand the situations they face. With the help of their parents and teachers, they add these new concepts and use them to better comprehend and navigate the challenges they face. People can learn mental models very quickly (Hess, Pullen, & McGee, 1996; Haslam, 1994; Mayer & Bower, 1986).

Implicit Mental Models

We often model our world without knowing we are doing so. Our mental models are so much a part of us that we fail to notice how they influence our vision of the world; they become intrinsic, unnoticed, and unseen. **Implicit knowledge** goes unnoticed in that way: It is information we have acquired, often without realizing we have done so; knowledge we have gained while doing other things. We are like fish that don't know they are swimming through water because they are totally surrounded by water. Only rarely (if at all) do we intentionally sit down and say, "Now I am going to create a model with which to understand people." Rather, most of our models are learned gradually through observation and through listening to others talk.

The Generalization and Overgeneralization of Models

We often use our models without knowing we have them. We grow accustomed and fond of the familiar ways we use to see the world, and we are so comfortable with our own viewpoint that we will tolerate it even if it misleads us to a degree, so long as it is "accurate enough." Our cognition takes the form of a beloved habit we engage in and we may at times overuse our knowledge, applying our beliefs and attitudes too broadly—resulting in what I think of as "model creep." One of the critical aspects of our mental models is that they can be applied correctly and judiciously, but they can also be over-applied and over-generalized. We will examine some examples of this as we continue.

Differences in Models Across People

Another characteristic of mental models is that they differ markedly from individual to individual. These differences determine, in part, the richly different ways human beings have of understanding and reacting to the same phenomenon. Consider Robert, a student in an advanced undergraduate seminar in which the members were exploring how mental models affect our personalities.

The professor asked Robert to describe a recent encounter with a family member. Robert's parents were getting divorced, and blamed each other for the breakup. Robert described coming home from school to pick up his winter clothes. When he arrived, he discovered that his mother had locked all the doors and changed the locks, so he couldn't enter. She yelled at him through an open window that he "didn't deserve to come in because…[he had] sided with his father" in their marital battles. Frustrated and very angry, Robert called the police, who, on arrival, escorted him into his home to collect his clothes (Epstein, 1996, pp. 27-29).

About two thirds of the seminar students told Robert they would have reacted as he had. But he was surprised to discover that a third of the students said they would have reacted differently. One young woman said she would have been afraid that she had done something very bad for her mother to treat her that way. Another woman expressed fear that her mother might be going crazy. Yet another student said he'd be coolly detached, finding it amusing how a parent could behave so ridiculously. The seminar members' reactions vividly illustrate how people's varied mental models often lead to markedly different reactions to situations (Epstein, 1996, pp. 27-29).

What Are Our Models of Ourselves?

The Self and Self-Models

Perhaps our most personal mental model is the model each of us has of our self. We can think of our self as composed of two parts, wrote William James, a founder of American psychology. The self that is most relevant here is our mental representation of ourselves—our "me" according to James. James' "me" corresponds to the self-schema—our model of who we are. The self-schema often includes a list of the key attributes that we possess: We may realize we are honest, humble, introverted, and a bit sad (or something else entirely). The second aspect of the self is the part that is aware and watches. James refers to this as the "I"; he said that, "The I watches the me." In later chapters, I will refer to that aware component of the self as the conscious executive or conscious self.

Returning to the "me" self, or self-schema, here is a description given by a fifth-grade girl in response to the question, "Tell us about yourself":

> Well, I am not very smart in some areas. I am not very pretty. I like almost all kinds of activities, especially summer sports. I like to have a good time at parties and get-togethers. I like dogs very much and horses. I do not have very many friends but the ones I have I like and get along with very well. I like to play my records while I am doing my homework and in my spare time I have a baby-sitting job. I am 14 and I have my problems too. (McGuire, 1984, p. 90)

At its simplest level, a model of the self can be interpreted as list of traits or features one notices and assigns to oneself. For example, Ivcevic and colleagues (2003) asked college students to write a brief essay describing their personalities. The descriptions were then coded into a number of content categories, from traits to childhood experiences. The participants' self-descriptions included such areas as preferences (e.g., "I like good conversation") to descriptions of spontaneity ("I am flexible, impulsive, random…"), to coping styles ("I can laugh at myself"), and relationships ("My parents trust me").

People process self-related information faster and more efficiently than other information (e.g., Lewicki, 1984; Markus, 1977). In one study, 48 undergraduate women were divided into two groups: those who thought of themselves as dependent on others and those who viewed themselves as more independent. The participants were asked to rate descriptive trait words as applying to themselves ("me" or "not me"), including trait words related to dependency, such as "conforming," and "submissive." Those participants who thought of themselves as dependent endorsed the dependence-related items far more quickly than the independence-related adjectives; the independent participants were relatively faster endorsing adjectives like "individualistic" and "assertive" (Markus, 1977).

Possible, Actual, and Perhaps Unconscious Selves

Most of us employ more than one model of who we are. Our **actual self** is a model of what we think we are like in reality. Our actual self may be a very accurate representation of who we are or it may be quite different from the facts. The more accurate our actual self, the better we can navigate the situations we face (Mayer, 2014). In addition to our actual self, we think about **possible selves**, a broad class of alternative selves we anticipate we could become, given a particular set of life circumstances (Markus, 1986).

Hazel Markus, a pioneer in research on the self, made the point that the actual self is often distinctly different from the possible self. She and her colleague, Paula Nurius, asked 210 college students questions such as "Do you have a lot of friends?" For each attribute, the researchers asked whether the statement described the respondent now and whether it might describe their possible future self. The students distinguished between who they were now and who they might be in the future in several ways. Whereas 44% of the students said traveling widely described them now, 94% said it would describe them in the future. Although only 52% of the sample thought they were physically sexy, 74% hoped to be sexy in the future. On the downside, although only 11% said they could be described as having had a nervous breakdown, 43% believed it was possible that they might in the future. Back to the bright side: Although 88% said they were happy at the time of the survey, *everyone* in the sample thought it could describe them in the future (Markus & Nurius, 1986, p. 959).

One possible self is the **ideal self**—Freud's label for the self that one would like to become (Freud, 1923/1960). When we imagine how we would like to be ideally, we set forth a road map for how we would like to change. If our actual and ideal selves are very different, we may feel humility as we recognize how much we need to change to attain our desired qualities. Alternatively, the actual-ideal discrepancy can cause some of us emotional distress (Dewey, 1887/1967; Freud, 1923/1960, p. 27; Higgins, 1987, p. 322; Rogers, 1951, pp. 510-513). When the actual and ideal self are more similar, it can reflect several possibilities: a failure to recognize who we really are, flexible standards regarding our ideal, or, in more positive instances, our considerable psychological health.

Ideal and Ought Selves

Our ideal self represents our personal goals and ambitions, and promotes our motivations to grow in the way we believe is best (Higgins, Shah, & Friedman, 1997). Theorists have also distinguished an **ought self** from the ideal self. This ought self represents the standards of behavior we believe other people expect of us. The ought self helps us steer clear of what others might find objectionable so as to protect us against feared negative outcomes imposed by people around us.

To understand these selves, Higgins (1987) asked research participants to list ten characteristics of their actual selves and ten characteristics that define their ideal selves. A participant might have described her ideal self as: (1) always kind to others, (2) creative, (3) open-minded, and continued through to (10) living a purposeful life. Next, Higgins asked participants to list qualities of their ought selves (the way others expected the person to be). The same participant might answer (1) being a good daughter, (2) doing well in school, (3) being more responsible through to (10) going out to bars less frequently.

Higgins then compared a person's various selves by calculating a discrepancy score between selves. An actual-ideal discrepancy of zero indicated that all ten characteristics of a person's actual self also appeared on their list for their ideal self. As you can imagine, discrepancies of zero are fairly rare. More commonly, peoples' actual selves only partially overlap with their ideal and ought selves.

It makes a difference whether you are farther from your ideal or from your ought self. People with large discrepancies between their actual and ought selves often imagine themselves failing to do what society says they should and are prone to feel anxious and distressed as a consequence. In contrast, people with big discrepancies between their actual and ideal selves feel as if they aren't who they want to be. These individuals tend to feel sad and depressed as a consequence (Higgins, 1987).

Feared and Desired Selves

Markus and Nurius (1986) focused on another classification of possible selves: into those we fear versus those we desire. **Desired selves** are similar to ideal selves: extremely positive selves we hope we will become. A young person might imagine herself as an intelligent, warm lawyer, who is physically fit and who can accurately "read" other people. **Feared selves** are extreme negative selves. The same woman might imagine that if things went wrong in her life, she might end up as an alcoholic and lose her job.

We often vividly imagine our feared possible self. In her memoir *The Broke Diaries*, Angela Nissel described how during her senior year at college in Philadelphia she was unable to pay a bank penalty. As a consequence, she was unable to open any further bank accounts anywhere in the metropolitan area. She wrote in her diary at the time: "I am really teetering on the edge of this temporarily broke/permanently poor dividing line because of this whole…episode. All I need is one push…and I might trip over that line and land smack-dab on Poor." (Nissel, 2001, p. 38).

Different groups exhibit powerfully different possible selves. Oyserman and Markus (1990) examined three groups: Non-delinquent youth who were wards of the state due to general family problems; delinquent youth who were wards of the state due to criminal justice issues, and college students. The non-delinquent youth, who resided in a group home, had possible selves that included "on Aid to Dependent Children (ADC), no job, poor housing, cannot pay bills" (see also Oyserman & Saltz, 1993). By contrast, 35% to 40% of the delinquent group had feared possible selves that involved legal violations including "criminal, murderer, pusher, junkie, physical abuser of spouse or child." These possible selves existed within the delinquent group despite their reports of high levels of self-esteem.

College students differed from the two youth groups in having generally positive possible selves. Writing about the college participants in the mid-1980s, Markus noted:

> Virtually all respondents thought it was possible for them to be rich, admired, successful, secure, important, a good parent, in good shape, and to travel the world. In contrast, almost none of our respondents thought it was possible that they could be a welfare recipient, a spouse or child abuser, a janitor, or a prison guard. (Markus & Nurius, p. 958)

Possible selves also reflect a person's confidence about their future. Markus examined people shortly after they had experienced a life crisis such as the loss of a long-standing relationship or the death of a spouse. She divided the group into those who believed they were adjusting poorly to the tragedy and those who believed they were adjusting well. Immediately after the loss, people in both groups felt equally sad, lost, and helpless in the wake of their life crisis—but their possible selves differed: people who believed they were recovering well had future selves that were optimistic, helpful, and confident; people who felt more poorly adjusted had future selves that were less popular, unimportant, and unable to fit in (Markus & Nurius, 1986, p. 962).

Are there selves that are more integrated than these feared or desired possible selves? Showers (2002) researched people who have "compartmentalized" selves—they view themselves as all good or all bad under many conditions, versus those who have selves that are more integrated. A person with a compartmentalized self, for example, might view himself as hardworking, mature, capable at work, but tense, insecure and isolated in "bad situations." A more integrated person would view himself as both hardworking and capable at work, but also sometimes irritable, sad, and blue (Ditzfeld & Showers, 2014). People with integrated, positive selves who are able to add small doses of negative attributes to how they view themselves—"I perform differently in my various courses depending upon how much I like them," appear most healthy and able to adapt to change and have fewer emotionally extreme mood changes (Showers, 2002, p. 284; Showers, 2014).

Unconscious Selves

Is it possible that a negative or threatening self-concept could be unconscious altogether? Carl Jung, a prominent early 20th-century theorist, suggested that most people possessed both a conscious self and an opposite, unconscious **shadow**. The shadow represented information about the self that the person could not recognize—often because the secret information made the person feel so uncomfortable that it was blocked from consciousness (Jung, 1968, pp. 21-24). For example, a religious and upright person might harbor a shadow replete with vengeful feelings towards others.

Jung suggested that men and women each contain within them aspects of the opposite sex that are often unrecognized. He referred to a man's female side as his **anima** and a woman's male side as her **animus**. Jung was writing at a time when sex roles were more restrictive than they are today. Thus, people may have been more likely to block out opposite-sex characteristics than they do today and to relegate them to the shadow.

Federico Fellini's semi-autobiographical movie of 1963, titled *8 ½*, depicts a film director who has repressed his feminine self. The director behaves in a macho sexist fashion and is also creatively blocked and cannot figure out what movie to make. The shadow is not entirely negative for Jung. Rather, the shadow is a resource full of animal energy and, if it can be integrated with the conscious part of the individual, can often contribute to life energy. For Jung, a person entirely cut off from his or her shadow would appear two-dimensional and lifeless (Jung, 1968, p. 23). In the middle of Fellini's film a mindreader extracts a thought from the director's mind: "Asa nisi masa"—a magical phrase from his childhood (that contains "anima" within it). By recollecting the magic words, the director breaks through a mental block caused by his over-identification with his male qualities (Bonadanella, 1998, pp. 102-104). When the director finally accepts his feminine self, he is able to bring the movie to completion. (This Fellini film is consistently ranked among the greatest films of all time.) Filming a movie isn't on the horizon for most of us, yet, Jung might say, we all have the opportunity to discover something new about who we are. What we have learned comes from the shadow portion of our self-conception—that part that normally lies in darkness (Jung, 1968, pp. 21-24).

It is clear that many people have imperfect self-knowledge and hidden sides—some of them shocking and even unspeakable—though most of them fall into the more everyday variety of undesirable wishes and urges. Although the shadow has not been regularly studied, there exists considerable research on mechanisms people use to avoid unpleasant parts of themselves. These will be covered in Chapter 10 on Dynamics of the Self.

Self-Esteem and Self-Efficacy

Are you pretty confident about yourself? Do you think you are easy to like? **Self-esteem** refers to the overall positive or negative evaluation one makes of oneself. People who like and value themselves are said to have high self-esteem; those who devalue and dislike themselves are said to have low self-esteem. Self-esteem is generally measured by asking people to endorse statements such as "I can usually take care of myself," which reflects high self-esteem, versus "I often feel as if I'm not good enough," which reflects low self-esteem (e.g., Rosenberg, 1965; Coopersmith, 1967; 1975; Robinson, Shaver, & Wrightsman, 1991; Wylie, 1974).

Beginning in 1986, a California task force spent three years and three-quarters of a million dollars to study self-esteem. Did high self-esteem enhance students' learning or reduce their violence or drug use? The task force found little evidence of any such promising relationships. Despite the lack of evidence, self-esteem programs continued to flood the public school systems—and continued to be judged as failures (Joachim, 1996; Leo, 1990). Self-esteem, in fact, has a dark side: Some people with very high self-esteem possess a sense of entitlement and a willingness to exploit others, including violent and discriminatory behavior (e.g., Baumeister, 1997). For example, juvenile delinquents and similar groups have self-esteem equal to or higher than college students and others. The exact value of high self-esteem has remained elusive (McCrae & Costa, 1990).

A second dimension of self-evaluation is that of self-efficacy. **Self-efficacy** refers to one's self-judged ability to perform a certain task in life. For example, some students generally feel confident about taking an exam, but are worried about writing a paper; other students feel the reverse. Albert Bandura (1977, p. 79;

1999) introduced the concept of self-efficacy to describe such feelings vis-a-vis particular tasks in life. Bandura and others have found that when a person feels able to handle a specific task, he or she is more likely to carry it out well (Bandura, 1977; 1999). For example, to examine a person's self-efficacy for learning to speak a foreign language, one specifically asks questions on the order of, "How good are you at learning a foreign language?" (e.g., Bong, 1999; Pajares, 1996). Despite the apparent better focus of self-efficacy research, some have suggested that it is, in the end, best considered part of a broader concept of self-esteem (e.g., Judge, 2001).

Stories of the Self

"Always remember that you are unique. Just like everyone else." – Unknown

The final model of the self we will examine is the person's self-constructed life story (Bruner, 1990; Cohler, 1982; Josselson, 1995; McAdams, 2001; Singer, 2001; Singer & Salovey, 1993). Storytelling is a fundamental way people communicate information about themselves and their worlds. Life stories stress some events while they de-emphasize or omit many others. Alfred Adler, an early 20th-century psychologist with both psychodynamic and humanistic interests, was especially interested in studying people's earliest memories. He felt that because they were the beginning of an individual's story, these earliest memories had particular significance (Adler, 1931/1958), but little has come from such research (Watkins, 1992).

Contemporary perspectives take a more comprehensive approach to life stories. For example, Dan McAdams elicits life stories through structured interviews in which he asks research participants to divide their lives into parts like the chapters of a book, with chapters covering earliest memories, childhood, and adolescence, as well as chapters on low points, high points, and turning points (McAdams, 1993). Diana C. was a 49-year-old teacher and mother who participated in one such study. In the early chapters of her life, she described herself as "the first baby ever born" in a Methodist parsonage founded by her father, a minister. She enjoyed an exalted social status as a child, and later, when her family moved to a wealthier congregation in Chicago, associated with many famous people. Tragedy struck when she was 8 and her younger brother was hit by a car and died. At the same time, she had a second-grade teacher who was institutionalized. But after that, she remarked, "things picked up." (McAdams et al., 1997, pp. 688-689). Although she could not become the son her father lost, she married a young man who became like a son to her father. Together, they raised a family. She reported that she feels inspired by her job as a teacher.

McAdams and his colleagues coded this and other stories according to the number of **redemptive** or **contamination sequences** they contain. Redemptive sequences involve segments of life stories in which a person is able to redeem the value of a difficult or traumatic experience. For example, a woman might recognize how the death of a family member drew her family closer together; in another instance, a youth might appreciate how his bad year at school led to his success at a new and better school. By contrast, McAdams and colleagues identify a contamination sequence when a person emphasizes the injurious, harmful features of an unfortunate life event. For example, a woman who tells a story of herself by skipping over her wonderful marriage of 20 years, during which time she and her husband raised several healthy and happy children, and instead focused almost exclusively on her divorce, would be reporting a contamination sequence (McAdams & Bowman, 2001). Those who describe relatively more redemption sequences in their lives are higher in well-being and lower in depression than individuals whose stories contain more contamination responses (McAdams, Reynolds, Lewis, Patten, & Bowman, 2001).

What Are Our Models of the World?

Formal Models and Implicit Models

Formal Knowledge

Our models of ourselves determine how we think and feel about who we are. Our models of the world account for how we interpret and act within the world. Formal models of the world are carefully thought-out, learned ideas about how the world works. These models draw on reasoned analysis, logical proofs, and empirical demonstrations. Formal education assists people to create carefully worked-out, valid mental models of the world around them. Every course one takes and every degree one earns is valued precisely because it reflects the creation of more accurate models of the world. Our society handsomely rewards such increases in accuracy of world models. Figure 5-1 shows that the higher the educational degree a person earns, the higher their income (Cheeseman, Day & Neuberger, 2002).

Figure 5-1 *Average Earnings as a Function of Educational Attainment.* Our information-oriented societies increasingly reward people for their level of education. We can think of education as a proxy for the accuracy of the mental models a person has constructed.

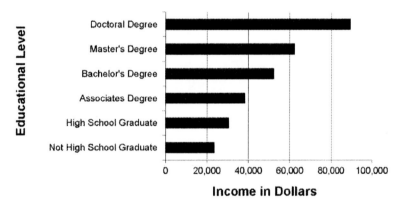

The formal education carried out in schools, colleges, and universities is not, however, the only one way of learning. There is also less formal learning that takes place in day-to-day observations of our situations—learning that depends on our street smarts and that is obtained in the "university of life." Psychologists distinguish between the formal learning one receives in school and the more "vibe-driven," less formal learning that occurs throughout our daily lives.

Implicit Knowledge

Tacit Knowledge

Learning about everyday life has been referred to variously as implicit, practical, and experiential as well as by other terms. **Implicit models** are gradually learned through living and watching what goes on rather than learned on purpose as, say, part of school curriculum (Epstein, 1998; Sternberg & Horvath, 1999). Other terms for this kind of learning include "episodic" (Tulving, 1972; 2000) and "narrative" (Bruner 1986; 1990).

Robert Sternberg, Richard K. Wagner, and their colleagues call this **practical** or **tacit knowledge.** Tacit knowledge is focused on how things work in various social and institutional settings. Practical knowledge often goes unstated or remains obscure in its statement. If your mother told you when you were a child to behave well at the house of someone you (and she) did not like, you may have realized that she attached some importance to the individual. Your sense that the person you visited was important in some way was tacit in that it was never explained (Sternberg & Horvath, 1999; Wagner, 1987; 2000).

Every organization has stated rules for how things happen, but there are also the unstated rules that "everyone" knows (Sternberg et al., 2000). In the legal profession, savvy beginning lawyers apprentice themselves to more experienced colleagues to learn the ropes of the profession and how to operate in their chosen area of practice. Lawyers who fail to absorb accepted social practices may derail their careers (Spaeth, 1999).

Scripts for Navigating the World

Another example of practical everyday knowledge is the development of scripts. Scripts are relatively stereotyped sequences of actions that we follow in order to accomplish goals (e.g., Anderson, 1983; Tomkins, 1979). If you were to read that John went into a restaurant and ordered lasagna, and that he later came out with a full stomach, you would know exactly what had happened inside the restaurant. That understanding comes from a long developmental sequence in which you have learned the restaurant script very well.

For example, here is a 3-year-old's script for a restaurant as quoted from the work of Shank and Abelson:

> Interviewer: Tell me a story—what happens in a restaurant? What happens—you go
> inside the restaurant...
>
> Hannah: You sit down, and you uh, eat food.
>
> Interviewer: How do you get the food?
>
> Hannah: From the waitress.
>
> Interviewer: How does the waitress know what to give you?
>
> Hannah: If you ask for a hamburger, then she gives you a hamburger.
>
> Interviewer: What happens if you ask for hotdog, do you get hamburger?
>
> Hannah: No you get hot dog.
>
> Interviewer: And then what happens after she gives you the food?
>
> Hannah: She gives you dessert.
>
> Interviewer: And then what happens?
>
> Hannah: And then you leave.
>
> Interviewer: And then you leave? Just like that?
>
> Hannah: No, the waitress gives you some money and you pass some money to her and
> she gives you some money back to you and then you leave. (Schank & Abelson,
> 1977, p. 223)

Hannah's restaurant script is fairly impressive at three years of age, but it isn't completely developed. By a year later, it is much more comprehensive:

> Interviewer: Now, I want you to tell me what happens when you go to a restaurant.
>
> Hannah: OK.
>
> Interviewer: What happens in a restaurant? Start at the beginning.

> Hannah: You come in and you sit down at the table. And then the waitress comes. And
> she gives you a menu. And, then she takes it back and writes down your order.
> And, then you eat what she gave you. And, then you get up from the table. And
> you pay the money and then you walk out of the store. (Schank & Abelson, 1977,
> p. 224)

Most people in our society have a similar restaurant script, although it may vary somewhat from region to region. Computers have been taught such restaurant scripts and use them to create better understanding of stories. Some people may have only a limited number of scripts, for example, they may perceive every encounter as a competitive situation. Other more sophisticated people may employ a variety of social scripts. If you know a person who is able to handle every social situation comfortably and always knows how to do the right thing, that individual likely has a number of carefully learned scripts for how to engage in social situations.

Learning Personality Types

To understand our world, we form models about other people and how they operate. People are exquisitely sensitive in discriminating among personality "types." In one laboratory study, researchers "invented" a new type of person who was characterized by sixteen randomly selected features. The purpose of creating the new personality type was to avoid any influence from real-life types the research participants might have been familiar with. Each characteristic of the new personality type was fairly unrelated to the others—as you would guess, given that they were chosen randomly. The prototype of one new type created this way is given below; the sixteen randomly varying features are underlined:

> VJ was a thoughtful child, raised in a close family by caring parents. He was brought up
> in a poor Midwestern suburb, and is now married. He is clumsy, unimaginative, and
> frivolous. Those who know him describe him as cold. He believes in gaining other's
> respect and also in being a leader. Physically, he is thin and good-looking. (Mayer &
> Bower, 1986)

After creating the prototype, the researchers generated 60 variations on it by changing the initials and systematically altering the underlined descriptive features. For example, M. L. might be an "active" child as opposed to a "thoughtful" one, and physically "tall" rather than "thin." If M. L. (or any other such "person") possessed at least nine of the prototype's 16 features, the person was a member of the group. Non-members possessed seven or fewer overlapping features. There were several billion possible members and non-members. The researchers wondered: Could people learn to identify the type of person?

The study procedure began with the experimenter instructing participants that they would read descriptions of people and then decide whether each person was a member of the group. The participant then read the first of the 60 descriptions of people they would see. After reading the first description, the participant was asked, "Is R.L. a member of the group?" The typical participant then asked, "What group?" and was told that, since they knew nothing about the group at the outset of the experiment, they would have to guess for the first description. After their guess, the experimenter told the participant whether or not R.L. had been a member (based on the 9-matches-or-more rule for membership). The participant then moved on to the second description, with only the knowledge that R.L. was (or was not) a member of the group. The process was then repeated for the third and fourth descriptions—of A.R., P. B., and so on. Remarkably, after reading through 20 descriptions and receiving feedback about them, people began to discriminate members of the group (that is, the personality type) from non-members.

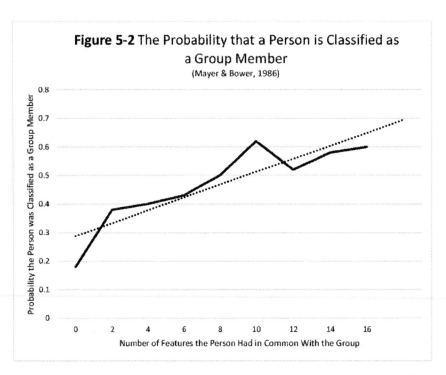

Figure 5-2 shows the average performance of participants after they had seen 60 descriptions with feedback. People were able to classify instances that had 16 features as belonging to the group nearly 60% of the time. People also correctly classified individuals with no overlapping features as not belonging to the group 80% of the time. People were also fairly accurate for person-descriptions with an in-between number of features.

Accurate and Inaccurate Perceptions of Others

Once a person identifies someone else as being a certain type—a random type as above, or an extrovert, an angry person or a saint, people may remember the person's characteristics as corresponding to the type more closely than the person conforms in reality. That is, when we type someone as extroverted, we fill in information about her from our mental model: we may "remember" our extroverted friend talking constantly at a party, even though she may have been sitting quietly for much of the time when we weren't paying attention.

To demonstrate this phenomenon, Cantor and Mischel (1978) identified traits that were unrelated, moderately, or highly related to extraversion. Their study participants learned about Jane, a character they identified as an extrovert, because she was described by a number of traits moderately related to extraversion, such as "energetic," "entertaining," "impulsive," and "ambitious." Jane was also described by traits unrelated to extraversion, such as "punctual" and "neat." Figure 5-3 provides an overview of their experimental procedure.

After learning the traits that described Jane, the participants were shown descriptors and asked whether or not they had seen each one before. The unseen items included some that were moderately or highly related to extraversion, and those that were unrelated to extraversion. Among the terms not seen before, participants more readily believed that they had seen terms highly descriptive of extraversion, such as "spirited" and "exuberant," than that they had seen unrelated terms such as "thrifty." That is, they showed a bias toward remembering the features that were associated with the extroverted type.

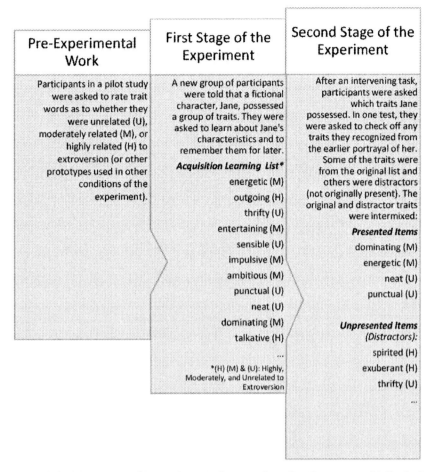

Figure 5-3 *Overview of Experimental Procedure for Cantor and Mischel, (1978)*

The results are shown in Table 5-2. The same bias was found in test results when Jane was described as an introvert: Participants attributed more introverted qualities to her. The results from laboratory research indicate that people learn and use personality prototypes to understand others.

Do the results from these experimental studies generalize to real-life situations? David Funder and his colleagues' research indicates that observers are likely to perceive people as types, at least initially. Observers—also called "judges"—who encounter a person initially agree with one another as to what a target person is like—but aren't necessarily very accurate. As judgment time increases and more information is provided, these same judges increasingly focus on the information provided and, as they do so, they agree less with one another because some judges abandon the original stereotype and others do not. At the same time, the judges' overall accuracy about the person increases (Blackman & Funder, 1998; cf. Sap, Funder, & Colvin, 1996).

Funder and colleagues also find that people are more accurate in observing plainly visible traits such as extraversion and assertiveness, which can be inferred from a person's talking, smiling, and other overt behavior. Other traits such as emotionality and intelligence remain more hidden, and observers are less good at assessing those (Funder & Dobroth, 1987; Funder & Colvin, 1988).

Table 5-2: Summary of Key Findings From Cantor and Mischel (1978)		
	Trait Was in the Acquisition List	*Trait Was Not in the Acquisition List*
Trait was Related to Prototype	Moderately endorsed these (e.g., energetic) *(Reflects accurate memory)*	Moderately endorsed these (e.g., spirited) *(Inaccurate when endorsed)*
Trait was Unrelated to Prototype	Moderately endorsed these (e.g., neat) *(Reflects accurate memory)*	Did not endorse these often (e.g., neat) *(Inaccurate when endorsed)*

Implicit Theories of Personality

Sometimes our beliefs about people are centered on human nature in general rather than on perceiving a person as a type. One central belief many of us hold is how much people can change. Dweck, Chiu, & Hong (1995) observed that if they ask a group of individuals, "Can people change?" everyone will agree—but to varying degrees. **Entity theorists** are everyday people who believe that individuals are mostly stable, although they can sometimes change a bit. Entity theorists agree with test items such as "A person's moral character is something very basic and it can't be changed very much." Or "Whether or not a person is responsible or sincere is deeply ingrained in his or her personality." By contrast, **incremental theorists** believe almost everyone is capable of adaptive, flexible, changing qualities (Dweck et al, 1995). Incremental theorists perform better in response to challenges such as difficult courses because they have a greater belief in their own flexible responses to problems and capacity to learn (Dweck, Chiu, & Hong, 1995, p. 269).

> "We don't see things as they are, we see things as we are." – Anais Nin (1903-1977)

The Concept of the Archetype

As we have seen, people classify one another into types of personality such as extroverts and introverts. People may also sometimes use an **archetype**, a special type of schema, to represent another person. An archetype can be understood as a universal embodiment of an imaginative cultural icon (Jung, 1968). Archetypes include heroes and heroines, witches and devils, kings and queens, medicine healers, magicians and tricksters. According to Carl Jung, the concept's originator, we encounter these universal images of key personality types in story characters, artworks, and our dreams. The same small group of archetypes appears across cultures. For example, the healer archetypes may be a medicinal healer in Africa, an acupuncturist in China, an attending physician in a Western-style hospital, or a saint who helps the sick in her community. When a healer plays his part, he enters into a caring relationship with us, and we respond with respect, gratitude, and maybe some awe: If all goes well, we experience a cure to what ails us. Evidence for the existence of archetypes comes from literary and cultural analyses that find the same sorts of characters arise in mythic stories across diverse regions and cultures of the world (Campbell, 1949; 1972; Faber & Mayer, 2009). For examples of archetypes, see Table 5-3.

Certain symbols may also represent archetypes. For example, Jung claimed people associate femininity with the moon, and health with the snake. Evidence supports this claim, suggesting that people make these associations more or less automatically (Huston, Rosen, & Smith, 1999; Pietikainen, 1998; Rosen et al., 1991; Stevens, 2000).

Because most people have similar associations to these symbols regardless of their education or cultural background, Jung believed that human beings shared a **collective unconscious**, a non-conscious part of our minds that contains material that is largely the same from one person to another. Jung speculated that people exhibit individual differences in the archetypes to which they respond: Certain people respond emotionally to certain archetypes more than others. Research indicates that there are groups of people, for example, who resonate most to a "hero" archetype, whereas others resonate to the "everyperson"—see Table 5-3 for more examples (Faber & Mayer, 2009).

Table 5-3: Commonly Discussed Archetypes*

Class of Archetype	Specific Examples	Description
Knower	magician, sage, creator	An expert or teacher who values enlightenment and knowledge
Carer	caregiver, innocent	A protective, devoted, nurturing and sacrificing figure; often parental
Hero	hero, ruler	A courageous and often noble person who hopes to prove worth to others
Conflictor	shadow, outlaw	A rebellious misfit, often vengeful, disruptive, angry and wild
Everyperson	everyday person, explorer, lover	A common person, a neighbor or underdog, often wholesome

*After Faber & Mayer, 2009

George Lucas, director of the *Star Wars* films, consciously employed Jungian ideas in the construction of his films (Seabrook, 1999, p. 205). Lucas introduced his main characters very early in the original *Star Wars* movie (Episode 4): the young hero, Luke Skywalker; the dark father, Darth Vader. Because they were based on archetypes, he expected that the audience would recognize and respond emotionally to them very quickly—and it did. Many other archetypes exist in the *Star Wars* movies as well. The two robots R2D2 and C-3PO exemplify the clown archetype.

What Are Our Models of Relationships?

Significant Other Models

The final class of mental models we'll explore in this chapter is models of relationships. Relationship models found their origins in psychodynamic theory in what are now called models of **significant others**. Significant others are parents and caretakers to whom we are entrusted as children, or other adults who are very important to our lives and with whom we have spent appreciable time. Significant-other models are the models we construct of those people and how they behave.

Sigmund Freud first observed the importance of significant-other schemes in his attempt to explain a strange-seeming occurrence he observed in his early practice of psychodynamic therapy. (Later, he realized the phenomenon was common.) His patients typically entered therapy in good spirits, but then, some sessions later, the patient would often fall in love with or grow demanding and angry with the therapist.

Where did these strong feelings come from? Freud believed that his patients' perceptions of their therapist emerged from earlier learning about their parents and other significant people. Freud hypothesized that the patients were generalizing the feelings they had felt toward their parents to their image of the therapist. Freud called this process **transference**.

In Freud's words:

> …the cause of the disturbance is that the patient has transferred on to the doctor intense feelings of affection which are justified neither by the doctor's behaviour nor by the situation that has developed during the treatment… (Freud, 1920/1966, lecture XXVII; pp. 440-441)

Transference involves the reemergence of a feeling pattern that had originally been directed toward a significant person in one's life, and is now redirected—automatically and irrationally—to a new person. Even a small overlap between the new person and the significant other can trigger this transference of emotional patterns to the new relationship.

In one experimental study of transference, Andersen and Cole (1990) asked participants to describe a significant other person from their life. Later, the same participants read descriptions of people who were new to them, some of whom possessed a few features that had been customized to overlap with the qualities of their significant other. When the research participants learned about the people who shared features of their significant others, they perceived them to be more like those individuals from their past than they actually were, and had stronger emotional reactions to them than they did to dissimilar people (Andersen and Cole, 1990). Freud believed that such early mental models set the tone for our later relationships and that, in many circumstances, the individual would repeat these learned patterns of interaction over and over again. Freud referred to such patterns as "repetition compulsions."

Core Conflictual Relationship Themes

Relationship Models in Therapy

The specific relationship patterns that a person employs can be identified in a more certain fashion than unaided clinical observation. Luborsky, Crits-Cristoph, and colleagues got permission from research participants to obtain recordings of their actual psychotherapy sessions. The researchers then divided each client's therapy transcript into segments called "relationship episodes."

The following examples of relationship episodes come from a patient who underwent psychotherapy in the early 1980s (Gill & Hoffman, 1982a; 1982b, reprinted in Luborsky et al., 1986). In the first episode, the young man is narrating what happened when a new acquaintance dropped by for a beer:

> …I pretended to be enjoying it, enjoying him, you know, in the spirit of good fellowship and shit and stuff, but…[he] was keeping me from reading and that hassled me. I really fucking resented it a lot. You know among my friends, they're respecting and always have really respected my wanting to do my own thing...But you know, with a guy like this [clear throat], he's just in another world totally from that. And, you know, he wouldn't understand if I said that, you know, he would be insulted and that kind of shit. You know it was kind of a hassle. (Gill & Hoffman, 1982b, p. 151)

Recordings like these can then judged by additional therapists who are not involved in the treatment. Lubosky and Crits-Christoph trained clinicians to look at the episodes for expressions of the client's relationship models—models they called "core conflictual relationship themes" (CCRT; Luborsky, Crits-Christoph, & Mellon, 1986; Luborsky, & Crits-Christoph, 1988). The researchers then assessed the extent of agreement among the clinicians as to what mental models they noted. Based on Freud's theory of transference, the researchers expected that the same themes would recur across the client's various relationships episodes.

The same young man quoted above recounted a second relationship episode that involved his reaction to his psychotherapy session and his relationship with the therapist:

> This morning I like didn't particularly feel like coming here, you know. Because like, I don't know, I felt some kind of, you know, I felt like I didn't need it. I guess I was just, you know, my spirits were a little raised. If only now I could get out of the bag of feeling that I have to... (Gill & Hoffman, 1982b, p. 152)

In a third episode, the young man revealed his perception of the therapist's reaction to him:

> Well, now I'm getting that same feeling that, you know, I'm sort of talking about worthless shit. Because, and you know, my basis for thinking that is the fact that you haven't said anything. Jeez, we go through this same nonsense every session, it's just amazing to me. I'm sort of ashamed that my mind isn't a little more creative, to think of different hassles. You know, it's sort of boring going through the same hassle four times a week, for what at this point seems like a timeless period. (Gill & Hoffman, 1982b, p. 154)

In the first episode, the young man wants to get away from his drop-in visitor and resents the intrusion. In the second episode, he doesn't want to see the therapist, and in the third he imagines that the therapist feels bored by his "nonsense," with the implication that the therapist feels intruded upon. In each of the relationship episodes, the young man is describing someone who wants to be free of someone else but feels resentful because it is difficult to get away. Indeed, therapist-judges listening to the three episodes agreed at levels far above chance that the central theme the young man presented was one of wanting to be free of someone, but feeling resentful and compelled to suffer the other's presence. In one study, 16 graduate student-judges individually scored the above instances and obtained an agreement level of $r = .88$.

The raters agreed about the transcripts, and they also indicated that the young man was reporting the same concern over and over again—to be free of obligation and imposition. Not only does the young man himself wish to be free of these burdens, but he attributes this desire to be free of others to other people he knows (e.g., the therapist). Here is the young man's relationship model again in an episode in which he is trying to make a date with a telephone operator:

> When I finally got through to her roommate yesterday and found out that she wasn't going to be in, like all the woman obligations just went off me. I knew that there was nothing I could do to find a woman and, you know, there was a kind of relief. (Gill & Hoffman, 1982b, p. 153)

Raters again agreed that the young man feels obligated to date women and finds it a relief to be free of them.

Attachment Styles as Relationship Models

Some adults develop secure attachment styles; others are more worried about their relations. These styles can be measured by scales such as the Adult Attachment Interview (AAI) (Hesse, 1999; cf. Bowlby,

1988, p. 129). The **secure attachment** relationship pattern represents other people as caring, reliable, and providing security. **Insecure/dismissing attachment** refers to a model of relationships that involves others rejecting and thwarting one's identity. **Insecure/preoccupied attachment** refers to a confused mixture of love and hate that involves giving love but taking away respect, or giving respect without love.

Crowell et al. (2002) observed 157 engaged couples as they discussed a point of concern in their relationship for 15 minutes. Each statement by the couples was coded for support, hostility, withdrawal, and similar qualities. Secure couples, as measured by the AAI, differed from those with insecure attachment models. The secure couples showed more direct, proactive communication. They made straightforward communications that assumed the relationship could and should involve trust. For example, "Our relationship is supposed to help us each be better than we can be on our own..." or direct requests for help such as "It would help me if you could..." (Crowell et al., 2002, p. 7). Couples with more secure attachment styles reflected greater happiness, less verbal aggression, and fewer threats to abandon one another. The development of attachment models has been studied extensively and will be covered in greater depth in Chapter 11, Child Development.

Roles and Role Playing

The Persona

We have been talking about models of the everyday people around us. One important aspect of our lives, however, is that we don't always act how we feel. Rather, society sometimes demands that we behave not as we are, but according to a culturally defined role. Carl Jung viewed people as taking on a **persona** in the real world so as to inhabit such a role. The persona, a term which comes from the Greek word for mask, is a model that we "put on" in order to make a specific social impression (Jung, 1934/1953, Chapter 3).

For example, students in a lecture class often wear a "responsible student" persona, which consists of looking attentively toward the instructor, appearing to pay attention, and taking notes. But on certain days, even the best of students don't feel like doing this. Their minds are a million miles away on thoughts of romance, family issues, or what to eat for lunch. Meanwhile, they maintain the student persona: pen in hand, eyes on the professor, and the rest. The mask hides their daydreams and mental meanderings. Of course, professors sometimes employ a persona as well. They may be distracted by a personal concern or simply want to be someplace else; still, they act out interest in their topic—so as to appear professional and to maintain their students' interest. Certain personas have clear developmental origins. In the United States, a cheery-person persona develops in response to our parents' requests of us to "Please try to be pleasant!"

Role Structure Theory

Robert Hogan's (1983) *socio-analytic* theory of personality argues that individuals engage in a series of social roles to portray themselves in positive ways. Even very young children play roles. Peekaboo games are one such example—in which a young child alternately hides and reintroduces his face to make a baby laugh. By three years of age, children left in a playroom will initiate role-playing as a way to structure their play together:

> ...Nothing much happens [among young children] until at some point one child...says something like, "Pretend you were Batman and I was Robin." At that point, both children begin talking to one another, moving around, and gesticulating in a synchronous fashion—in short, interacting. (Hogan, 1983, p. 75)

By three or four years of age we have a pretty good idea about social roles, and can act them out and manipulate them. A four-year-old girl often plays with her father by urging, "Daddy, you pretend you're the teacher." If he agrees, she then points to stuffed animals and dolls, assigning each the role of a different member of her preschool class. Once the roles are assigned, a lengthy, imaginative drama can take place.

Hogan believes that relationship models are apt to fail unless they assign clear roles to the interacting people. Hogan points to his personal experience of encountering a famed philosopher at college without an adequate social role to play:

> I was walking to the computer center when I saw, coming down the sidewalk toward me, a man whom I thought was probably Ryle. Without thinking, I said, "Pardon me, sir, but aren't you Gilbert Ryle?" Ryle peered at me in the befuddled and mildly incompetent manner of an Oxford don and then allowed that he was indeed himself. Not knowing what to do next, I said, "Gee, it's just like meeting Robin Hood," and walked away. (Hogan, 1983, p. 74)

For Hogan, this story illustrates how, when appropriate roles are not available, a person may feel sort of foolish.

According to Hogan, we carry out roles in order to maintain our reputations. We try to measure up among our relatives or teachers, and to earn the respect of our friends and acquaintances. It is not always possible to please all groups at once. For example, a person who tries to satisfy one group of his peers may be very popular but perceived as overly trendy by another peer group. Hogan recommends we maintain a balance among such roles (Hogan, 1983, p. 79).

A Case Study: Playing a Role While Playing Basketball?

Sometimes playing a new role can be liberating. Madeleine Blais is a journalist who wrote about "Kathleen," a high school basketball player who was transformed when she envisioned herself in a new role among her teammates. Kathleen had been playing with a tightly knit group of friends on her high school basketball team for several years. She was a starter on the team, but as one observer put it, "the only thing she was fierce about was being gentle...She constantly backed away from her opponents, she ran around screens; she played in an unconfident way" (Blais, 1995, p. 127). When she bumped into other players, she said, "I'm sorry." She didn't like to hurt animals and she was a vegetarian.

Her coach, Ron Moyer, had warned her several times never to use the words "I'm sorry" on the court again. After Kathleen slipped up—again saying she was sorry to one of her teammates—Moyer announced she was to go home immediately—Kathleen was no longer wanted on the team. The other team members stopped in mid-dribble to hear what was going on. Moyer said he wanted a new person on the team, and improvising (and drawing on the name of an evil comic-strip character who popped into his mind), he stared at Kathleen and said, "...the new Hurricane is ... named Skippy."

Moyer looked at Kathleen and said, "Okay, Skippy, put on your game face...Let's see Skippy take the ball to the basket." After Kathleen realized she was being asked to try on a new identity, the idea appealed to her:

> She grabbed the ball. She stormed forward, her face a seamless mask of concentration.

> She bashed the ball in.

[Coach Moyer yelled:] "Skippy, I like that mean look. If there's a pick there, knock it over. Let's stay in that frame of mind. Hold that."

This is great, he thought: *I can yell at Skippy*... (Blais, 1995, pp. 127-128)

Kathleen's behavior also changed off the court. In the locker room, "Skippy" freely told jokes that would have been far too vulgar for Kathleen (Blais, 1995, p. 201). The team made it to the state championships and in the final championship game, Kathleen (Skippy?) made a daring shot from the foul line that "was nothing but net," and helped to win the state championship for the team. (Blais, 1995, p. 254).

When Kathleen first became Skippy, perhaps she was merely playing a role—but that role enlarged her understanding of her possible selves. Roles and selves can interact in potentially powerful ways.

Morals and Values

Recall that "ideal" and "ought" selves describe people's possible selves and what they should be like. Relationship models elaborate on those ideas and expand them into ethical, moral, and ideological spheres. Each of us must learn ethical and moral rules and develop a philosophy by which to live. Freud believed the conscience was developed in response to the child's fear of receiving punishment from the parent (Freud, 1923/1960). He recognized, however, that mature men and women maintain their ethical or moral structure in part because of a voluntary social contract. Adults realize that only when people follow ethical and moral rules—giving up some personal freedoms—can civilization meet the requirements of its citizens. A society in which people refused to work together or to respect those with legitimate authority could not create efficient organizations by which to feed, nourish, protect, and educate its people (Freud, 1930/1961).

Some people employ moral structures that seem relatively simplistic: all black-and-white, with few areas of grey. Others employ more complex sorts of moral reasoning. To investigate this, Kohlberg (1981) described a series of ethical/moral stages. At an early stage of development, a child behaves morally out of a fear of receiving punishment from parents (as Freud proposed). As young people develop, they begin to tell right from wrong according to their own analyses. Still later, our ethical and moral standards may become relativistic, as we appreciate that other people hold different sets of standards from us. Finally, we may become recommitted to a particular moral/ethical standard even though we appreciate others' points of view.

People also develop different types of values (e.g., Allport & Vernon, 1931; Rokeach, 1973). Some people believe that a deity has set the rules for human conduct. They believe there exists a moral reality apart from human beings and that humans must strive to meet the objective standards of that outside reality. Individuals who hold these beliefs emphasize politeness and courtesy in human behavior and de-emphasize imaginativeness.

Other people believe in the intrinsic value and autonomy of human beings and believe that any supreme being exists within each of us. People who hold this perspective tend to set their own standards according to an inner authority and to favor humanistic values that emphasize broadmindedness and love (de St. Aubin, 1996; Stone & Schaffner, 1988; Tomkins, 1963). Other research looks at extensions of such models to people's perceptions of justice; the standards of justice are remarkably similar across cultures, but vary from person to person (Cohn, White, & Sanders, 2000).

Table 5-4: People With Mental Models That Needed Revision*

Models of the Self	"The thought of being President frightens me. I do not think I want the job." —Ronald Reagan in 1973, then the Governor of California.
	"It doesn't appear that the FBI is going to catch us anytime soon. The FBI is a joke."—the "Unabomber" (domestic terrorist) less than a year before being captured by the FBI.
	"And yet I told your Holiness that I was no painter." —Michelangelo, in a remark to Pope Julius II, who was complaining about the progress of the Sistine Chapel ceiling, 1508.
Models of the World	"The world was created on 22nd October, 4004 B.C. at 6 o'clock in the evening." – James Ussher, Archbishop of Armagh, 1581-1656 (C&F, p. 3). "Heaven and earth…were created…on the twenty-third of October, 4004 B.C., at nine o'clock in the morning."—Dr. John Lightfoot, 1859, Vice Chancellor of the University of Cambridge.
	"X-rays are a hoax." — Lord Kelvin, British physicist and former President of the British Royal Society, c. 1900.
	Benjamin Franklin "…has very moderate abilities. He knows nothing of philosophy but his few experiments in electricity." —John Adams, diary entry, 1779.
	On Fred Astaire: "Can't act. Can't sing. Can dance a little." —MGM executive, reacting to Fred Astaire's screen test in 1928.
Models of Relationships	"We'll make it work. You can take it to the bank."—CBS News Anchor Dan Rather assuring skeptical reporters that he and his co-anchor Connie Chung would work well together. Two years later, with ratings at their lowest ever, the anchors split.
	"I will never marry again." —Barbara Hutton, in 1941, after divorcing her second husband. "I will never marry again. You can't go on being a fool forever."—Barbara Hutton, after divorcing her third husband, Cary Grant, in 1945. "This is positively my final marriage." —Barbara Hutton, in 1955, remarking on the sixth of her seven husbands.

*Quotes drawn from Cerf and Navasky (1998): Reagan, p. 111; Unabomber, p. 314; Michelangelo, p. 310; Ussher, p. 3; Lightfoot, p. 3; Kelvin, p. 334; Adams, p. 307; MGM exec, p. 191; Rather, p. 111; Hutton, p. 21.

How Good Are Our Mental Models?

Developing Constructive Models

People often develop mental models that are inaccurate and need revision—some examples of expert ideas gone awry can be found in Table 5-4. Is there a global way to assess how good or accurate a person's mental models really are? Probably not, but Epstein and his colleagues have developed a model of **constructive thinking** that helps provide some insight into the question (Epstein & Meier, 1989). Constructive thinking is defined as the degree to which a person's implicitly learned mental models facilitate solving problems in everyday life at a minimum cost in stress (Epstein, 1998, p. 26). Epstein focuses on certain signs indicating that a person's models will be constructive rather than off base. These signs include positive indicators of good coping, and negative indicators of irrational and destructive lines of thought. Table 5-5 provides an overview.

Table 5-5: Key Elements of Constructive Thinking

Area of Constructive Thinking	Description
	Positive Indicators
Emotional Coping	Managing emotions effectively, such as (mostly) avoiding worry about things you can't control.
Behavioral Coping	Acting to control those things one can, such as taking action to change situations for the better.
	Negative Indicators
Categorical Thinking	Thinking in stark, stereotyped categories, such as thinking some people are all good or all bad.
Personal Superstitious Thinking	Holding cultural beliefs for which there is little evidence, for example, believing in good and bad omens.
Esoteric Thinking	Paying attention to good-luck charms or other unusual beliefs.
Naïve Optimism	Maintaining attitudes that are so positive as to be unrealistic and out-of-touch with everyday experience, such as believing that everyone should always love their parents.

Positive Indicators of Constructive Thinking

People who think constructively are able to cope with setbacks. A salesperson who copes poorly in the emotional realm might conclude, "I failed to put across this deal, so I guess I'll never amount to anything." Someone better at coping would have a more realistic model, concluding that he lost only a single sale and that he can learn from the experience (Epstein, 1998, p. 43). Similarly, behavioral coping involves a successful action-oriented approach. Behavioral coping involves replacing a worry about a deadline with taking action to actually meet it. Epstein views coping as taking place when it can assist the mind "…to obtain pleasure and avoid pain…to make sense of our experience…to have satisfying relationships with others; and…to think well of yourself" (Epstein, 1998, pp. 83-84).

Negative Indicators of Constructive Thinking

In addition to building mental models that facilitate active coping, constructive thinkers avoid models that are inaccurate. Epstein's model includes four common ways models go awry: categorical thinking, esoteric thinking, superstitions, and naïve optimism. People who are good at coping see the nuances of situations rather than dividing the world into dichotomies such as right and wrong, or into winning and losing sides. They also avoid models that involve esoteric beliefs, beliefs in the paranormal, good luck charms, bad luck omens, and the like.

People good at coping also avoid mental models that employ **naïve optimism.** Naïve optimism refers to unrealistic beliefs that things will turn out well. Such beliefs, although reassuring to the person who holds them, can sometimes be counterproductive. For example, a student who is a naïve optimist may fail to prepare for a test because he expects to do well without trying.

Expressing Better Mental Models

Do people who hold mental models that help them cope and that discourage irrational thinking do better in school and careers than others? Epstein studied constructive thinking among students in the classroom and on the job—most of his students worked 10 to 20 hours a week in part-time jobs. Constructive thinking was related to job performance and success in student politics, although not to performance in the classroom. Students with high constructive thinking scores held more offices in clubs and organizations than did those with lower scores (Atwater, 1993; Epstein, 1998, pp. 108-109). Those who scored lower in constructive thinking also exhibited a greater incidence of drug abuse (Ammerman, Lynch, Donovan, Martin, & Maisto, 2001; Giancola, Shoal, & Mezzich, 2001). In one study, Epstein compared 50 million-dollar-earning salespeople with a group of 200 successful sales and marketing executives who exhibited high but less than exceptional performance in their occupations. Although the two groups worked equal numbers of hours, the super-achievers had advanced more rapidly at work and reported higher job satisfaction. On the personal side, the super-achievers were more satisfied with their family lives and spent more time at home. They were happier and experienced less anxiety, depression, and uncontrolled anger. Finally, the super-achievers exhibited more constructive thinking on virtually every dimension measured. In emotional coping, their mental models revealed that they were relatively unconcerned with others' disapproval and were very action-oriented. They were also much less superstitious than members of their comparison group, avoided esoteric thinking more easily, and were less prone to naive optimism (Epstein, 1998, pp. 102-105).

Constructive thinking measures provide a general "temperature" of peoples' models of the self and the world. Another way to do this is to examine a person's intellectual capacity—what their intelligences are and how they are applied to the individual's life. That approach will be examined in the next chapter, which focuses on mental abilities.

Reviewing Chapter 5

This chapter introduced you to the nature of mental models of the self, the world, and relationships. Now that you have read it, you will know what these models are, how they can be assessed and how they are expressed in a person's life. Review questions follow.

Questions About "What Are Mental Models?"

1. Models of the Self, World, and Relationships: Models are often divided according to the contents they describe: the self, the world, and relationships. Do you remember another term for "models of relationships"?

2. Mental Models are Structured: Mental models are memory "structures"—that is, they are stored in memory in specific ways. For example, the most important attributes of a model are recalled first. Different kinds of mental models possess different structures. Can you describe the difference between a schema and a script?

3. Mental Models are Learned and Applied: Mental models are learned. We recall them when they seem useful in our attempts to interpret the world. There is room for error in our use of mental models. Can you identify one way mental models are often misapplied?

4. Differences in Models across People: Mental models differ from one person to the next. How do those models affect our emotional and other reactions to events?

Questions About "What Are Our Models of Ourselves?"

5. Possible, Actual, and Unconscious Selves: Models of the self can be as simple as a list of traits, or as evocative as an imagined self—as an alcoholic or as demented—that one is afraid to become. The starting point among all these selves is the actual self—how one thinks one actually is. Then, there are

ought selves and ideal selves, feared and desired selves, and even an unconscious self, called the shadow. Can you define these different selves?

6. Self-Esteem and Self-Efficacy: People feel better or worse about themselves depending upon their self-esteem. Self-efficacy is more specific and action-oriented than self-esteem; it refers to the confidence people have in approaching a task. Research with self-efficacy has turned up some fairly reliable findings. Can you say what they are?

7. The Storied Self: Arguably, the broadest mental model we create of ourselves is our life story. Life stories are not simply ordered accounts of every life event a person has faced. Rather, each of us weaves together the elements of our lives that strike us as most important to who we are (and how we would like to communicate our identity to others). What is one way that psychologists categorize the episodes of these stories?

Questions About "What Are Our Models of the World?"

8. Formal Models and Implicit Knowledge: Formal knowledge is the sort of knowledge we acquire in settings such as schools and universities. Implicit knowledge, by comparison, is picked up informally by observing the events, objects, and people, around us. Can you think of a way that formal knowledge affects a person's life?

9. Scripts for Navigating the World: Scripts are important both to artificial intelligence and to human beings in understanding how the world works. As children grow, for example, they need to learn many scripts, such as what happens at a restaurant and how to go to a birthday party. Can you describe what a script is?

10. Implicit Theories of Personality: Each of us creates models of the people around us and how they behave. For example, people can be described as entity theorists or as incremental theorists. Can you define entity and incremental theories?

11. Learning Personality Types: Beyond general theories of personality, people create models of particular personality types: e.g., the shy person, the extrovert, and the "significant others" in their lives. Can you describe some research in this area and what it tells us?

12. The Concept of the Archetype: One special kind of personality type is the archetype: a model of an iconic or mythic figure such as a magician, hero, or queen. Can you name the theorist who proposed the theory of archetypes? What profession makes some use of the archetype concept?

Questions About "What Are Our Models of Relationships?"

13. General Attachment Models: Attachment theory specifies two or three types of attachment patterns. Can you name them and describe them?

14. Core Conflict Relationship Themes: Do people really repeat patterns of relationship over and over again? To examine this question, Luborksy, Crits-Cristoph, and others recorded psychotherapy transcripts and then coded them for their relationship themes. What were their major findings?

15. Adult Roles and Relationships: Robert Hogan developed a socio-analytic theory of roles: What was its central idea? Can you name a few of the roles? Can you define Jung's concept of the persona?

16. Moral and Values: Another kind of relationship model concerns the rules one lives by. What are some stages of the development of morality? What are some of the differences in values and morals that people exhibit?

Questions About "How Good Are Our Mental Models?"

17. <u>Developing Constructive Models:</u> Constructive thinking is a way of creating positive, constructive models of the world about us. What are some characteristics of constructive models?

18. <u>Avoiding Irrational Models:</u> Constructive thinking involves avoiding irrational models of one type or another. Can you list several kinds of irrational models people often hold of the world around them?

Chapter 5 Glossary

Terms in Order of Appearance:

Mental Model or **Schema:** Information (knowledge) in memory related to a particular area of knowledge, that possesses organization that can be determined through cognitive research; a cognitive structure for organizing information about a specific topic or topic(s) such as "the self concept," or (the idea of) "elephants."

Prototype: A type of schema consisting of a list of features that collectively define a concept or object. Typically, the most defining or common features are listed first, with progressively less-defining qualities following later in the list.

Self-Concept: A mental model one constructs of oneself (often used interchangeably with self-schema).

Self-Schema: A memory structure that holds information about the self (often used interchangeably with self-concept).

Self-Esteem: How positive or negative one feels toward oneself.

Scripts: Stereotyped sequences of events and actions that describe how to do something.

Life Stories: Narrative descriptions of the highlights of a person's life that a person uses to describe him or herself.

Relationship Structures: Structures that contain procedural knowledge—knowledge about how to do something. Relationship structures contain information about how to act in a relationship.

Implicit Knowledge: Knowledge that is acquired unintentionally, in the course of doing or thinking about other things.

Actual Self: How a person thinks of his or her qualities, life experience, and interactions.

Possible Self: A mental model of what our self might be like in the future if it were to change (or in the past, if we had been different).

Ideal Self: A model of oneself that one would like to become.

Ought Self: A self that sets a standard for what one should live up to.

Desired Self: An extremely attractive positive vision of oneself that an individual desires to become.

Feared Self: An extreme negative version of the self that an individual fears he or she will become.

Shadow: An unconscious model of the self that contains the attributes and qualities that a person actually possesses, but rejects at the conscious level.

Anima: Proposed by Jung, a self that includes the female qualities of a man.

Animus: Proposed by Jung, a self that includes the male qualities of a woman.

Self-Esteem: The overall positive or negative feeling one experiences toward one's self.

Self-Efficacy: One's self-estimated ability to perform a specific task.

Redemptive Sequence: A portion of a life story in which a person encounters a challenge or trauma and is then able to redeem the value of the experience.

Contamination Sequence: A portion of a life story in which a person encounters an ambivalent or negative event that is seen as negatively defining one's life.

Implicit Models: Models of the world that are learned incidental to, or as a consequence of living, rather than learned in a formal, purposive way.

Practical or Tacit Knowledge: A type of knowledge concerned with how the world actually works, as opposed to how it is said to work, or how teachers, instructors, and other experts say it works.

Entity Theorists: Those who believe there are relatively fixed parts of personality. Almost everyone is an entity theorist in part.

Incremental Theorists: Those who believe that personality can change over time.

Archetype: A schema that represents an imagined cultural icon, such as a hero or magician, which people from many backgrounds and cultures recognize and respond to emotionally.

Collective Unconscious: A part of unconscious that contains material that is more-or-less universal across people, such as emotional images of parents, kings, queens, and magicians.

Significant Others: Internal representations of others, including parents and important relatives, friends, and teachers, who have played important roles in their lives.

Transference: The idea that one will transfer what one has learned about a significant other to new people that one meets. This term developed originally in the psychodynamic tradition, but is now more generally used.

Secure Attachment Pattern: The healthiest of three relationship patterns commonly studied in attachment literature, in which the person feels unambivalent security with loved others.

Insecure/Dismissing Attachment Pattern: One of the three relationship patterns commonly studied in the attachment literature in which a child or adult feels frustrated or even rejected by others.

Insecure/Preoccupied Attachment Pattern: One of the three relationship patterns commonly studied in the attachment literature in which a child or adult feels ambivalent toward being intimate with others.

Persona: A mask or social role that an individual uses to uphold social standards while carrying out tasks. Examples include "the concerned doctor," "the strict professor," and so forth.

Constructive Thinking: Thinking that is productive for an individual, and is based on the person's having accumulated accurate positive mental models and having avoided irrational, superstitious mental models.

Naïve Optimism: A set of especially unrealistic beliefs that emphasize that things will turn out well, and that an individual may hold so as to excuse him or herself taking responsibility for contributing to a given goal.

Chapter 6: Mental Abilities and Navigating the World

An individual uses mental abilities, including intelligences, cognitive styles, and creativity to analyze what the outside world is like, to establish accurate mental models, and to invent new and better models. People with higher levels of these mental abilities create more accurate maps of the world and function more effectively as a consequence.

Previewing the Chapter's Central Questions

• **What Is a Mental Ability?** Why is it that some people seem to be able to solve problems that others cannot answer? What mental abilities do successful problem-solvers possess?

• **Which Intelligences Were Studied First?** Psychologists seek to investigate and identify people's key mental capacities. Among the first of the abilities they identified was verbal-propositional intelligence.

How Does Intelligence Develop? To effectively measure the first intelligences, psychologists developed an age-based concept of how intelligences develop: People possess a mental age as well as a chronological age.

• **What Is g and What Are Broad Intelligences?** General intelligence, often denoted as g, is a person's overall capacity to reason and solve problems. An individual's general intelligence is made up of broad intelligences, which include verbal-propositional and perceptual-organizational intelligences, as well as perhaps six or seven more, including possibly personal intelligence (an intelligence about personality).

• **What Is the Relationship Between Personality and Intelligence?** Although personality draws on many mental abilities, most of our non-intellectual personal qualities—including our motives and emotions—are independent of our mental abilities.

• **How Are Mental Abilities Expressed?** People's success in school, on the job, and at home in some ways, depends on our personalities and on the mental abilities that are available to us.

What Is a Mental Ability?

Questions About Mental Ability

Personality could not function without a varied and extensive set of mental abilities. An ability refers to the capacity to carry out a task: to lift 25 kilograms, to run a five kilometer race, or to add a column of numbers. A **mental ability** refers specifically to the capacity to work with information to obtain a desired answer. One type of mental ability is an **intelligence**. An intelligence is a specific kind of mental ability that involves the capacity to carry out abstract reasoning about a problem so as to find a correct solution. There are, however, other kinds of mental abilities. For example, creativity is a mental ability that involves coming up with new, unexpected and useful answers to problems. (Some psychologists regard creativity as an intelligence; others do not). The better a person's mental abilities, the more accurate are his models of the surrounding world, and the more in tune he will be with the world and the better able to cope with it.

Intelligence involves heightened capacities to problem solve in many areas of our lives. Marilyn vos Savant wanted to be a writer but she didn't want to be poor. Finding college unchallenging, she left after just two years to enter the worlds of finance and real estate. After five years, she had earned enough money to achieve financial security for the remainder of her life. She was now prepared to realize her dream of becoming a writer.

Before she made much progress toward her dream, however, *The Guinness Book of World Records* revealed her IQ score, which it had obtained from a group of the roughly 30 highest-IQ individuals in the world, who called themselves the Mega Society. Whereas the average IQ is about 100, and one in a hundred people score above 145, vos Savant's IQ was an extraordinary 228.

Vos Savant was an outgoing, fun-loving individual. She enjoyed the fame that her IQ score brought her, appeared on television talk shows, moved to New York City, and married Robert K. Jarvik, a celebrated heart surgeon who had developed one of the first artificial hearts (Gale Research, 1988).

Vos Savant began writing a column for the *Sunday Parade Magazine* in which her readers sent questions for her to answer. In 1991, she addressed a challenging statistical problem that concerned a television game show named "Let's Make a Deal." In the game show there is a fabulous prize—say, a trip to Hawaii—behind one of three doors. If you pick the right door, you win it.

After a you pick a door the host, Monty Hall, opens one of the *other* two doors, and there is a novelty prize behind it (a year's worth of cat food). Hall asks if you want to change from your original pick of a door to the remaining door. The question is: "Does it make sense to change your choice at this point?"—after Hall has opened one door.

Vos Savant said you should change your choice to the other unopened door. For her troubles, professors of statistics resoundingly criticized her because they believed she got the answer wrong and misled her readers. Wrote one, "Our math department had a good, self-righteous laugh at your expense." Vos Savant stood her ground, however, and further explained her position. John Tierney, an enterprising *New York Times* journalist, then consulted with the nation's best statisticians (and, for fun, with the game show host, Monty Hall, himself): The experts declared her correct (see Tierney, 1991, for a discussion of why). Vos Savant's example suggests that being high in intelligence allows a person to accomplish her goals more readily and to make many judgments better than other people can.

What part do mental abilities such as intelligence and creativity play in vos Savant—or anyone's—life? Every individual requires intelligence to think about how to conduct his or her life. Both intelligence researchers and personality psychologists, from Cattell to Wechsler, agree that the intelligences form an inseparable part of personality (e.g., Cattell, 1966; Guilford, 1967; Gardner, 1993; Sternberg & Ruzgis, 1994; Wechsler, 1950). People with high intelligence tend to be good all-around problem solvers—and our society values such skills.

Mental Abilities and Society

The English scientist, Sir Francis Galton (1822-1911) was a cousin of Sir Charles Darwin, and was fascinated by his cousin's theory of evolution. Galton wondered whether good mental abilities—especially intelligence—would increase a person's evolutionary fitness and enhance her chances of survival. Looking at social success in England, he suggested that the English upper classes—those educated in the best schools— had higher intelligence than those found elsewhere. He also believed that people of great genius came from certain families in the upper classes more commonly than they came from the poor.

Some reformers of the time argued that there were also many people in the lower and middle classes with high mental ability that should be elevated across the class barriers of inherited wealth and aristocracy. The debate became more important as public education became widespread across Europe.

By the late 1800s, the French government wanted to place nearly every child in school. The officials recognized that at least a few children wouldn't be able to learn well in a regular school environment. The decision as to who was able to learn was crucial: If a teacher mislabeled a student as intellectually disabled, the child's future could be severely compromised. Would teachers judge the children of the aristocracy more favorably than children from the lower classes? The officials were sufficiently concerned that they sought an impartial way of making the decision as to which students were competent. In 1904 the French government appointed a commission to examine the state of mental subnormality in France. Alfred Binet (1857-1911), a founding member of the commission, developed the first successful intelligence tests in response. The French government employed his tests to assess students' mental ability—providing a key supplement to teachers' judgments.

Which Intelligences Were Studied First?

Verbal Intelligence and the Binet Scales

A teacher assigned his students an essay: They were to evaluate the merits of establishing a human colony on Mars by 2040. For their assignment, the students needed to read several essays—both pro and con—about the goal, evaluate the logic of the arguments, and write an opinion as to whether colonization on our neighboring planet was a good idea. To do this, the students needed to understand the words, sentences, and arguments of the essays and to form their own opinions based on which arguments they believed to be best.

A student's ability to perform the above tasks will draw heavily on a kind of intelligence called **verbal-propositional intelligence**. Verbal-propositional intelligence includes memory for word meanings (as in vocabulary tests) and the understanding of the logic of propositions.

Verbal-propositional intelligence is the first of a number of intelligences we examine here. By the early 1900s, Alfred Binet had constructed his first intelligence scales for testing the capacity to learn in schools and it was largely focused on verbal reasoning. Binet's tests evaluated how well students could remember short sentences, understand vocabulary, and recognize meanings. Understanding aspects of mathematical reasoning is also considered verbal-propositional, in that formulae make propositional statements about the relations among numbers. Binet's early intelligence tests measured mostly verbal intelligence. Today's revised version of the original test—the Stanford Binet—is a thoroughly modern intelligence test that measures problem solving outside the verbal realm, but continues to assess the verbal reasoning area that grew out of Binet's original work (Thorndike, Hagen, & Sattler, 1986).

Perceptual-Organizational Intelligence and the Wechsler Scales

Almost from the start of intelligence testing, some theorists believed that more intelligences existed than just verbal-propositional intelligence. For example, L. L. Thurstone (1924; 1938) argued for the existence of eight mental abilities, including word fluency, memory, and reasoning. Verbal-propositional intelligence did such a good job of predicting school performance, however, that there was little motivation to pursue other intelligences.

That changed when a practical problem arose in the United States in the 1930s: assessing the mental abilities of new immigrants to the country. Some immigrants appeared to have difficulty adjusting to their new country, and it was unclear why. Many could not take a traditional IQ test because they were unfamiliar with English, and the intelligence tests had only been translated into a few other languages at that time.

In those days, David Wechsler was a staff member at New York's Bellevue Hospital (he later became Director of Psychology). Wechsler himself had immigrated to the United States from Romania, as a child, along with his parents. Many new immigrants who had difficulties finding housing or holding a job, were brought to New York City's Bellevue Hospital for psychological testing. Sensitive to their challenges, Wechsler addressed the language problems by creating a new intelligence test, initially called the Wechsler-Bellevue. Like earlier tests, it measured verbal-propositional intelligence. To do so, it employed six tasks. For the *vocabulary* task, people were asked to define words. For the *similarities* task, they identified what was similar about two concepts, such as light bulbs and fire. In the *comprehension* task, people were asked questions concerning their understanding of the everyday world, such as, "What could you do if you became lost in a city?"

The second portion of the test used measures that were relatively language-free. This second part consisted of new scales that today are considered measures of **perceptual-organizational intelligence.** Perceptual-organizational intelligence is used when people perceive visual patterns, organize the perceptual information in them, and are able to divide the patterns into parts and reconstruct them. This intelligence is important for many crucial tasks, such as creating patterns with fabric, creating mechanical designs by drawing, putting together pieces of a puzzle, or assembling mechanical objects such as a bicycle or engine (e.g., Kamphaus, Benson, Hutchinson, & Platt, 1994; Sattler, 1992; Tulsky, Zhu, & Ledbetter, 1997; Tulsky & Ledbetter, 2000).

A key measure of this intelligence is *block design.* In the block design task, a person examines blocks the sides of which are colored red, white, or both. Next the person is shown a geometrical design and asked to recreate it by using four blocks (or nine, in harder problems). In another task, *picture completion*, the individual's job is to see what part of a drawing is missing. For example, a car might be missing one of its tires. In *object assembly*, test takers are asked to assemble puzzle pieces, and in *picture arrangement*, people arrange pictures so that they tell a coherent story. These tasks provided an alternative way to assess intelligence among people who were relatively unfamiliar with English. Test results revealed that although perceptual-organizational and verbal-propositional intelligence were partially related, they were also somewhat different from each other.

How Does Intelligence Develop?

Verbal-Propositional Intelligence and Mental Development

Binet's Critical Insight

Verbal-propositional intelligence exhibits a key hallmark of intelligences more generally: the capacity to reason in the area increases with age. As children grow, they are increasingly able to reason about word meanings and literature through about 20 years of age. Intellectual power in the area plateaus thereafter, although people can continue to learn and to develop their language skills. The same holds true for perceptual-organizational intelligence: Mental ability in the area grows through childhood and adolescence until it plateaus around 20 years of age. People of the early 20th century recognized that children knew less than adults, of course, but they attributed a child's intellectual limits to the fact that their few years of experience were insufficient to teach them what they needed to know.

As long as age was neglected as a factor in intelligence, early attempts to measure it yielded confusing findings. For example, Alfred Binet, the French psychologist, developed his first tests of intelligence without age in mind. His tests assessed a child's memory, imagination, attention, and comprehension. Binet gave his tests to students of different ages, some of whom were intellectually disabled and some not. He discovered that normally developing students outperformed the intellectually disabled groups on average, but there were always a few intellectually disabled students who outperformed the normally developing children. At first, these results undermined Binet's hope to develop a workable intelligence test (Fancher, 1985, p. 71). Then Binet realized that the age of children might affect their mental abilities. If he were right, it would be necessary to take age into consideration when comparing children who were intellectually disabled with those who were not. He then began to build scales of mental abilities tailored to different age groups.

Binet determined the sorts of mental tasks that children of each age could accomplish. For example, the average five-year-old is able to repeat a sentence of ten syllables, count four pennies, and copy a square. The average twelve-year-old can repeat a sentence of 26 syllables, repeat seven figures, and interpret the meaning of a complex picture. Binet constructed scales for children of each chronological age.

Some children could do much more than average for their age; other children, far less. The level at which they performed was said to be their **mental age** or **MA**. Mental age refers to the highest age level at which a student could pass all the relevant mental ability items. Someone with a mental age of 13 would think and solve problems at the level of the average 13-year-old. Binet found that people who did well at school had higher mental ages relative to their chronological ages; people who did poorly at school had lower mental ages relative to their chronological ages. The first successful intelligence tests worked by comparing each child's mental ability to the norm for their age. The child's rate of mental development successfully discriminated among students who could readily learn and those who had difficulty learning in school (Fancher, 1985).

Intellectual Development

The **rate Intelligence Quotient**, or **rate IQ**, reflects how quickly a child's intellect grows (Stern, 1914). The **rate IQ** involves a ratio of mental age (MA) to chronological age (CA), which is then multiplied by 100 to yield the IQ; that is (MA/CA) x 100. The formula for the rate IQ is also in Table 6-1.

Table 6-1: Comparison of Rate and Deviation IQs		
Type of IQ	Rate IQ	Deviation IQ
Components	MA = Mental Age CA = Chronological Age	X = Raw Score (e.g., number correct) M = Mean of the X Scores in the Sample S = Standard Deviation of the Raw Scores
Formulae	$IQ = \frac{MA}{CA} \times 100$	$IQ = \left\{ \left(\frac{X-M}{S} \right) * 15 \right\} + 100$
The Concept in Words	The rate IQ is simply the ratio of mental age to chronological age, multiplied by 100.	The deviation IQ begins (in the innermost parentheses) with the participant's deviation from average, divided by the standard deviation. This is known as a "z-score." That z-score quantity is then multiplied by 15 and added to 100.

When a child's mental age exceeds his chronological age, the intelligence quotient is greater than 100 and the child is considered mentally advanced. When the child's mental age is less than his chronological age, the quotient is less than 100 and indicates that the child is developing mental skills more slowly.

A child with a mental age of five and a chronological age of five would be developing at an average rate, and have an IQ of five divided by five times 100, or 100. A five-year-old with a mental age of four would have an intelligence quotient of 80 (4 years / 5 years) x 100). A rate IQ of above 100 means that a child's mental growth is progressing faster than the norm. A five-year-old who can do what the average seven-year-old can would obtain an IQ of 140 (7 years/5 years) x 100).

The Deviation IQ Concept

Rate IQ was essential to understanding the developmental nature of intelligences. It is, however, not in general use today because of two drawbacks. First, intelligence slows its dramatic increase at about age 20. Therefore the calculation of a rate IQ in this way after age 18 is problematic. An average 36-year-old would score at about the same mental age of an 18-year-old. Using the rate IQ formula for an older adult (i.e., 36/18 x 100 = 50) would provide a gross underestimate of the average older adult's capacity, which in reality would seem average, not what a rate IQ of 50 would suggest. Second, the same mental age may mean very different things for two different people. A five-year-old and a 20-year-old, both with a mental age of 10, are quite different individuals. The five-year-old will be seen as extremely clever and intellectually advanced, whereas the 20-year-old's intellect will seem plodding and over-taxed.

The **deviation IQ** provides an alternative to the rate IQ (Wechsler, 1958). The deviation IQ is based on a person's standing compared to other people of the same age. A person at the mean (average) of the intelligence-score range would be given an IQ of 100 as with the rate IQ. Scores are then assigned above or below the mean depending upon how far a person's mental abilities are above or below the average of those

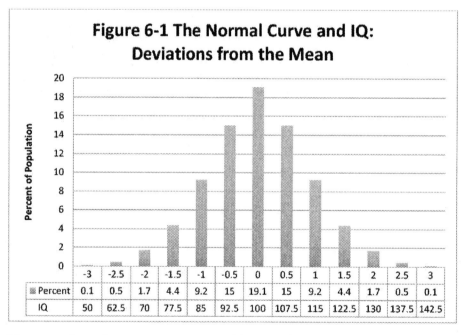

Figure 6-1 The Normal Curve and IQ: Deviations from the Mean

	-3	-2.5	-2	-1.5	-1	-0.5	0	0.5	1	1.5	2	2.5	3
Percent	0.1	0.5	1.7	4.4	9.2	15	19.1	15	9.2	4.4	1.7	0.5	0.1
IQ	50	62.5	70	77.5	85	92.5	100	107.5	115	122.5	130	137.5	142.5

of the same age. Distances from the mean are measured in **standard deviations (SD)**, which are set at 15 points. A standard deviation is a statistic that indicates the dispersion of an individual's scores around the mean (these are the numbers from -3 to 3 in the first row below the bars in Table 6-1). A person scoring one standard deviation above the mean, relative to his or her peers, would be given an IQ of 115. An IQ of 70 would indicate that an individual scored two standard deviations below the mean relative to his or her age peers (see Figure 6-1).

IQ scores are normally distributed (roughly speaking). For that reason it is possible to translate the scores into percentiles. When scores are normally distributed, 68% of the people will score plus-or-minus 1

SD from 100 (85-115), 95% plus-or-minus 2 SD (70-130), and 99.7% plus-or-minus 3 SD (55-145). In addition, a person with an IQ of 115 will have scored above 84% of other people, or at the 84th percentile. An IQ of 70 places the individual at the 5th percentile. These conversions are shown in Figure 6-1. (They are obtained by formulae taught in an introductory statistics course.)

IQs calculated this way are very similar to those calculated using rate IQs. Because so little was lost in the conversion, psychologists rapidly adopted the deviation IQ, and today it is the more frequently employed measure of IQ.

What Is *g* and What Are Broad Intelligences?

g Theory

Early intelligence tests assigned a single score to describe a person's intelligence level. Even the Wechsler intelligence scales, which measured separate verbal-propositional and perceptual-organizational intelligences and provided stand-alone IQs for each one, also reported an overall IQ score that combined the two. Many psychologists regarded that single IQ as an adequate summary of all a person's problem-solving abilities. They had a powerful theoretical reason to think this way: their belief in a **general intelligence**, or simply, *g*.

Charles Spearman (1927) first suggested the existence of general intelligence. This *g*, he believed, was a general index of a person's overall intellectual functioning. Spearman's hypothesis was based on the idea that there existed a hierarchy of intelligences, with specific mental abilities at the bottom and a single general intelligence at the top. Although everyone acknowledges that separate mental abilities exist, Spearman's theory included the idea that all measured mental abilities correlate together: If a person does well on one test, he tends to do well on others; if a person does poorly on one test, he tends to do poorly on them all. Hence the average skill level, or more technically, the person's level on the first general factor of intelligence (from factor analysis), takes on a special significance.

Table 6-2: Characteristic Correlations Among Selected Subscales of Intelligence*

Generic Intelligence Test Subscales	Sentence Under-standing	Arith-metic	Vocabu-lary	What's Missing	Designs	Puzzle Assem-bly
Sentence Understanding	1.00					
Arithmetic	.54	1.00				
Vocabulary	.72	.58	1.00			
What's Missing?	.54	.46	.57	1.00		
Designs	.45	.48	.46	.61	1.00	
Puzzle Assembly	.38	.37	.40	.51	.59	1.00

*The nature of the scales and the findings are modeled after Birrin & Morrison, 1961.

This idea works fairly well for many intelligence measures. For example, Table 6-2 contains correlations among intelligence subscales like those found on the Wechsler Adult Intelligence Scale including arithmetic, vocabulary, and the ability to put together a puzzle quickly. Notice that ability at all the tasks are positively correlated. When researchers factor-analyze the mental abilities involved, a first general factor arises on which all the subtests "load" (that is, all the subtests correlate with this first factor; see the section on factor analysis in Chapter 2).

Table 6-3 illustrates a typical result (cf. Morrison, 1967, p. 318). When you look at this first factor, you are looking straight at *g*. This is the mathematical evidence that Charles Spearman first saw for general intelligence. (Incidentally, for this data set, the second factor might be a perceptual-organizational intelligence and the third factor might represent a verbal factor—although the results are not very clear in this example.

Table 6-3: An Example of Factor Loadings on a Generic Intelligence Test*

Problem Solving Test	Factor		
	I	II	III
Sentence Understanding	**.84**	-.20	-.15
Arithmetic	**.75**	-.22	-.09
Vocabulary	**.70**	.03	**.43**
What's Missing?	**.69**	**.62**	-.10
Designs	**.86**	**.27**	-.22
Puzzle Assembly	**.63**	.05	- .22

*Values with an absolute value of greater than .25 are bolded. Cf. Morrison (1976, p. 318).

The Three-Stratum Theory of Intelligences

John Carroll (1993) reanalyzed 450 studies of mental abilities to create an updated view of the data on mental abilities. A portion of his "three-strata" model is depicted in Figure 6-2. To make sense of the relationships among the mental abilities, Carroll modeled them at three levels. The most general level, at the top, is Spearman's overarching general intelligence or *g*. The most specific mental abilities are represented at the lowest level. Here, you find measures of highly specific mental abilities, such as those measured by individual tests of vocabulary, block design, or picture arrangement (puzzles), and many others.

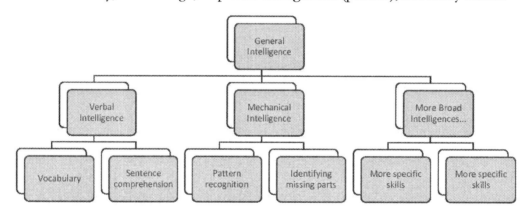

Figure 6-2 *A Partial Overview of a Hierarchy of Intelligences*

The middle level is particularly intriguing, because it depicts a number of **broad intelligences**. A broad intelligence involves the ability to solve problems in a set of related but diverse tasks. Verbal intelligence, for example, includes not only vocabulary knowledge, but also comprehending sentence meanings and paragraph structure. Carroll's complete model has approximately 70 specific abilities at the bottom level and eight broad intelligences in the middle.

Carroll's model provided a contemporary way to talk about a number of new kinds of mental skills that researchers were investigating at the time, from spatial intelligence to emotional intelligence to creativity.

Broad Intelligences

Each of us has a particular level of general intelligence. Beyond that general level of performance, we each also excel in certain areas of thinking, such as holding items in memory or recognizing musical melodies and rhythms. The broad intelligences describe many such areas and include working memory capacity, verbal-propositional intelligence, spatial intelligence, auditory intelligence, and even an intelligence for understanding personality called "personal intelligence." Psychologists have examined many of these broad intelligences and their impact on people's lives (Schneider & Newman, 2015). Next, we will look at a few examples of broad intelligences to get a sense of what they entail. Some of the intelligences below such as spatial, creative, and emotional intelligences fairly clearly belong to the set of broad intelligences. Others are too new to have been considered for the set, but are likely candidates to be added.

Spatial Intelligence

Have you ever tried to create a mental image of the roads on which you were traveling and how they fit together? Did you check it against Google maps, perhaps rotating the map so that the roads were facing in the same direction that you were visualizing? If so, you were using **spatial intelligence.** Spatial intelligence refers to the capacity to reason about the movements of objects in space. The term "spatial intelligence" was used early in the 20th century, but the skill was not well measured until the work of Roger Shepard and his colleagues in the 1970s (Brigham, 1930; Coetsee, 1933; Kyllonen, Lohman, & Woltz, 1984; Lohman, 2001, p. 319).

Shepard and his colleagues developed tasks in which people see a three-dimensional object. They are then asked to rotate the object in their minds, to see if they can identify which of several alternatives the rotated object might look like (e.g., Cooper & Shepard, 1984; Shepard & Metzler, 1971). Answering the question "Is that an accurate picture of the rotated object?" required the test taker to rotate the object in his mind 45 degrees, 90 degrees, or 135 degrees, in two or three dimensions. Shepard and his colleagues showed that people took longer to answer the question the further an object needed to be rotated mentally: For example, longer if they had to rotate it 90% than by 45%. Talk about "turning something over" in your mind! The intelligence to rotate such figures is measured by the spatial aptitude subscale of the Differential Aptitude Test and is somewhat distinct from perceptual-organizational intelligence (Bennett, Seashore, & Wesman, 1989). Individuals highest in this intelligence gravitate toward occupations that require spatial knowledge: architecture, engineering, mathematics, and certain computer sciences (Shea, Lubinski, & Benbow, 2001).

Social Intelligence

Intelligences such as the verbal, perceptual-organizational, and spatial can be considered "cool" intelligences as they concern matters of general reasoning that often can be independent of one's personal concerns. Such cool intelligences can be contrasted with the "hot" intelligences. **Hot intelligences** are so-called because they operate on information that is of more immediate social and emotional relevance to the person's well-being—whether her feelings, *or* her personal or social status. Hot intelligences include the social and practical, personal, emotional intelligences and others (Mayer, Salovey & Caruso, 2004).

E. L. Thorndike (1920) first proposed the existence of a **social intelligence**, and defined it as "the ability to understand and manage men and women, boys and girls—to act wisely in human relations" (Thorndike, 1920, p. 228). He had concluded that the "cooler," academic sorts of intelligence were insufficient to fully describe how human beings thought. For college students, social information processing and social intelligence are required to figure out which friends to make, which dormitories or apartments to choose, and what activities to join (e.g., Cantor & Kihlstrom, 1987; Kihlstrom & Cantor, 2000).

One defining task of social intelligence involves describing a social situation and asking why it unfolds as it does (Moss & Hunt, 1927; Thorndike & Stein, 1937). For example, participants taking the *Social Insight Test* learned about a character named Mr. Asher. Mr. Asher criticized a neighbor for buying too expensive a car, but then obtained a loan so as to purchase an equivalently expensive car. Why would Mr. Asher do such a thing? A test-taker could choose as an alternative that Mr. Asher criticized his neighbor because he felt envy at first, and later satisfied his envy by buying a similar car himself (Chapin, 1968).

Although social intelligence was at first difficult to distinguish from verbal-propositional intelligence (e.g., Cronbach, 1960), more recent studies indicate that it is more independent of verbal-propositional intelligence than was once thought—research about social intelligence continues at a modest rate (Lee et al., 2000; O'Sullivan & Guilford, 1976; Jones & Day, 1997; Lee, Wong, Day, Maxwell, & Thorpe, 2000).

Practical Intelligence

Sternberg and Wagner proposed a **practical intelligence** that seems closely related to social success (Sternberg, Wagner, and colleagues, 2000). Practical intelligence focuses on the capacity to identify and think about unstated, tacit knowledge, including social rules and obligations, related to obtaining one's goals. Have you heard the expression, "It's not *what* you know, it's *who* you know"? Well, even "who you know," requires a form of mental ability (as well as family contacts and networking). Making contacts, knowing people, and the ways those connections can be used fall within the realm of practical intelligence. Practical problems are characterized by having multiple solutions, each with different advantages and drawbacks, and there are multiple methods of obtaining a given solution. Practical intelligence includes knowing such things as "…what to say to whom, knowing when to say it, and knowing how to say it for maximum effect" (Sternberg et al., 2000, p. xi, 204).

Richard Moran wrote a book entitled *Never Confuse a Memo With Reality*, in which he pointed out how the realities in a workplace were often very different from "official statements." A few of his choice pieces of advice are illustrated in Table 6-4.

Table 6-4: Examples of Using Practical Intelligence at Work*

- Never take a problem to your boss without some solutions. You are getting paid to think, not to whine.
- Never confuse a memo with reality…most memos from the top are political fantasy.
- Remember that the purpose of business is to make or do something and sell it. The closer you can get to those activities, the better.
- Learn to remember people's names. If your memory is poor, develop a system.
- Don't hang your diplomas in your office unless you're an M.D.
- Learn what finished work looks like and then deliver your own work only when it looks the same way.

*Richard Moran's 1993 book, *Never Confuse a Memo with Reality* pointed out how everyday on-the-job knowledge relates to practical intelligence. Above are his items 6, 25, 32, 58, 61 and 216.

One of the first practical knowledge tests was conducted with newbie faculty members at a research university in the 1980s to see how well they understood how to become successful in their careers (Wagner, 1987; 2000, p. 381). The professors who participated in the study were asked to imagine it was their second year as an assistant professor, that they had average teaching evaluations, had one graduate student in a lab, and hoped to get tenure. They were asked to read through some activities and indicate which alternatives would most help them attain their goal of becoming tenured. The alternatives ranged from serving on a departmental committee to writing a grant proposal to recruiting more graduate students. Their practical knowledge scores were evaluated against the judgments of a sample of expert "judges" (highly competent, tenured professors). Some of the hopeful professors recognized that writing a grant proposal and recruiting graduate students were good choices for their careers, but a few of the test-takers missed those central truths.

As it turned out, the closer the assistant professors' ratings converged with the expert judges' selection of the correct answers, the better the assistant professors' performance on jobs at that time, as evaluated by departmental performance ratings and how much their research was cited by others.

Emotional Intelligence

Just as we reason about verbal information or practical information, so we reason about emotional information (Mayer, Caruso & Salovey, 2015; Salovey & Mayer, 1990). Emotions are evolved signals about relationships (see Chapter 4). For example, happiness indicates the desire to join others; fear signals the need to escape, and anger signals the presence of threat. **Emotional intelligence** concerns the capacity to reason about these emotional signals and the capacity of emotion to facilitate reasoning (Mayer, Salovey, & Caruso, 2000). More specifically, emotional intelligence is said to involve four branches of skills: accuracy at emotional perception, understanding emotional meanings and concepts, self-management of emotion, and the capacity of emotion to facilitate thought (Mayer & Salovey, 1997). This four-part model is illustrated in Figure 6-3.

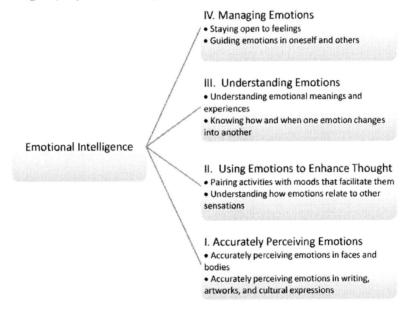

Figure 6-3 *The Four-Branch Model of Emotional Intelligence*
People solve problems about emotions in four areas, according to the Four-Branch model of emotional intelligence. They accurately perceive emotions, use them to facilitate thinking, understand emotional meanings, and manage emotions in themselves and others. (Mayer & Salovey, 1997).

What if some of your friends wanted to play a practical joke and you thought it was a bad idea? One high school student who scored highly on an emotional intelligence scale faced just such a situation. Her friends wanted to paint someone they knew while he was asleep. One of them dared another to do it. The student carefully monitored how, as her friends' dares escalated, their excitement escalated. Instead of going along with the prank, she asked her friends to think about how the sleeping person would feel when he woke up—painting a vivid picture of his embarrassment and loss of control. By doing so, she put an end to the prank before it started (Mayer, Perkins, et al., 2000). Adolescents lower in emotional intelligence are more likely to act on dares from their friends despite the negative consequences.

Scales of emotional intelligence present people with emotional problems and ask them to provide the correct answer. Sample test items ask people to recognize emotions in faces, understand emotional vocabulary, and recognize the outcomes of different types of emotional communication between people (Mayer, Salovey, & Caruso, 2002). People who score high on such scales are more empathic and connected with others. There are also self-report scales of emotional intelligence that largely measure how emotionally perceptive people think they are, but not their actual ability in the area (see Mayer, Salovey, & Caruso, 2008).

Personal Intelligence

Researchers have recently begun to study **personal intelligence**—an intelligence about understanding personality itself. Personal intelligence is defined as the capacity to understand and reason about personality and personality-related information. It involves the capacity to identify and read the clues people give off about their personalities, to form accurate models of oneself and other people, to guide one's choices by taking into account personality-related information, and to systematize one's life's goals and plans so that they form a part of a coherent story (Mayer, 2014). The *Test of Personal Intelligence* (TOPI) measures personal intelligence. An item like those on the test asks:

Which of the following characteristics usually go together as a group?

  a. religious, cold, comical
  b. orderly, sociable, moody
  c. sensitive to slights, negative mood, sociable
  d. lively, sociable, risk-taking

If you've read Chapter 4, you might have answered "d," lively, sociable, and risk-taking. You may have recalled that extroverted people tend to have high energy, like to be with others, and are prone to impulsive behavior. Of course, there are more than a few extroverted people who are prone to moodiness, but they are relatively less common. People who take the test exhibit reliable individual differences in reasoning across a broad range of problems related to our personalities (Mayer, Panter & Caruso, 2012).

Personal intelligence can be viewed as a key part of personality's guidance system in that it consists of a representation of our self and representations of other people, and based on that information it guides our personal and social behavior. From one standpoint, personal intelligence can be thought of as a broadening of emotional intelligence to include the capacity to reason about motives, traits, the self and self-management, and to understand how to apply that knowledge to guide our lives (Mayer, 2014).

Creative Intelligence

Creativity involves the ability to come up with new and novel solutions to problems (Brown, 1989; Sternberg & O'Hara, 2000). Creative people are often known for their unusual and unexpected solutions to important problems. They work in a broad range of fields from the arts to the sciences. Among the many people known for their creativity are Albert Einstein, Pablo Picasso, Johann Sebastian Bach, Ludwig van Beethoven, and Michelangelo.

A variety of mental measures tap creativity. For example, **verbal fluency** is both a part of verbal intelligence and an example of a creativity measure. (Verbal fluency and other specific mental skills sometimes reflect more than one broad intelligence). Verbal fluency is the capacity to generate a large number of relevant words or concepts in response to a problem. Sample verbal fluency test items ask a participant to come up with all the words that rhyme with "bend," or all the names that rhyme with "Harry" (Cattell, 1971).

Another measure of creative skills is the **alternate uses** problem (Getzels & Jackson, 1962; Wallach & Kogan, 1965). Participants who take an alternate uses measure try to think of as many uses of an object as possible. In response to "book," a creative individual might respond, "It is useful for reading…You could use it for a paper weight. You could hollow it out and hide something in it…You could flatten a leaf inside it… You could balance it on your head to improve your posture." The thinking exhibited by answering such questions is often referred to as **divergent thinking** because it involves coming up with answers to questions that diverge from the common way of looking at matters (Guilford, 1967).

Another task that reflects creativity is the **Remote Associates Task** (Mednick, 1962). A typical remote associates test problem would present you with three words and ask you to come up with another that links them. For example, you might be instructed as follows:

Find a fourth word that is related to all three of the given words: *light, movie, fish*

After some time, you might answer "star," because there is starlight, and there are movie stars and starfish.

Just as there are multiple intelligences so there may be multiple creativities. Averill and Thomas-Knowles (1991) developed an emotional creativity task called emotional triads. In emotional triads, the test-taker must create a story in which a person feels three different emotions. For example, in response to the triad "lonely/angry/joyful," one emotionally creative participant related the following:

> Driving on never to return—I wish. Another family fight, my typical reaction, get in the car and take off. Riding into the summer night air, mild and damp, makes me glad to be in motion. The breeze coming through the windows produces sensations of joy—I'm angry as I was chased out of my own home…And I'm lonely as I drive alone with my broodings…that it is I who must go into the night… It's a lonely feeling yet so peaceful it brings its own joy—and so I run [until]… I yield to my weariness and head for home. (Averill & Thomas-Knowles, 1991, p. 292)

Creativity tasks correlate among themselves at moderate levels. This suggests that they define a distinct domain of mental ability. In addition, different types of creativity have been distinguished from one another; i.e., emotional creativity differs from cognitive creativity. The creativities tend to be relatively independent of general intelligence (Wallach & Kogan, 1965; Ivcevic, Brackett, & Mayer, 2007). Nonetheless, they are mental abilities and some psychologists consider them intelligences as well. For example, they have been included in recent hierarchical models of intelligence (e.g., Carroll, 1993; Sternberg, 2003).

What Is the Relationship Between Personality and Intelligence?

"You don't realize that you're intelligent until it gets you into trouble." – James Baldwin (1924-1987).

Psychologists have explored a number of relationships between personality and intelligence. Three key ideas are that (1) intelligences are parts of personality, and are particularly well-developed in human beings, (2) personality draws on mental abilities and (3) mental abilities operate with considerable independence from other features of personality.

Intelligences Are a Part of Personality

Personality's Definition and Intelligence

Personality has been defined as the organization of a person's major mental systems (see Chapter 1). These major mental systems include the intelligences with which we solve mental problems. As personality is defined, in other words, intelligences are clearly a part of personality. Many psychologists throughout the history of the field agree: Raymond Cattell included an intelligence dimension in the central personality test he worked on throughout his life (the 16 PF).

The Unique Aspects of Human Intelligence

Although all animals possess intelligence, human beings are particularly well-endowed in their problem-solving capacities. Not only do humans learn more rapidly than most other animals, they are also capable of creating complex models of the world, and of engaging in abstract reasoning and future planning.

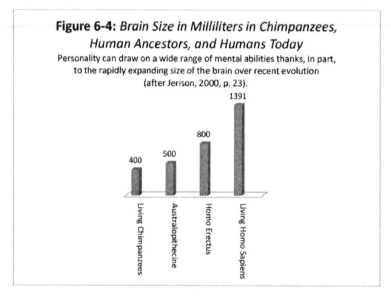

Figure 6-4: *Brain Size in Milliliters in Chimpanzees, Human Ancestors, and Humans Today*
Personality can draw on a wide range of mental abilities thanks, in part, to the rapidly expanding size of the brain over recent evolution (after Jerison, 2000, p. 23).

Generally speaking, intelligence-like behavior increases over animal species according to the size of the brain relative to the body (Jerison, 2000). Figure 6-4 indicates the relative sizes of chimpanzee and human brains (estimated from the size of their skull cases), with some human ancestors added for purposes of comparison. Chimpanzees and human beings have the largest brain-body ratio of any animals, with the exception of dolphins. A human being's larger brain and its greater processing capacity accounts, in part, for our greater range of intellectual performance when compared to other living organisms (Jerison, 2000). Recent research using MRIs has revived the idea that individual differences in brain size within human beings also relates to a person's intelligence—although the relationship is far from perfect (Flashman, Andreasen, Flaum, & Swayze, 1998; Jensen & Johnson, 1994; Gould, 1981; Pennington et al., 2000; Rushton & Ankney, 1996 Schretlen et al., 2000; Wickett, Vernon, & Lee, 2000).

Human beings may have evolved an increased speed of mental processing due to the particular form of connections between neurons—and this may also account for a portion of our intellectual functioning (e.g., Bates & Eysenck, 1993; Jensen, 1987). Unsurprisingly given these biological bases, genetics makes a substantial contribution to an individual's potential range of mental performance, with estimates that as much as 50-70% of the variance of general intelligence may be due to genetic factors (McGue et al., 1993, p. 353).

Personality Draws on Abilities

Mental Abilities and Learning

Each of us has at our command many mental abilities. Personality development involves drawing on our mental abilities to enhance our knowledge—particularly in regard to solving problems that matter to us. When we use our abilities well—and when our abilities are highly developed—we can attain awe-inspiring reasoning and creativity.

Public education enhances personality and its abilities as well: Societies worldwide devote extensive time and effort to schooling their youth; they recognize how crucial formal teaching practices are. Each year of schooling during junior high school and high school may raise an individual's IQ as much as 2 points (Gustafsson, 2001). From one perspective, the fact that it requires full-time academic study for a year to create a 2-point IQ difference seems a modest outcome. On the other hand, it adds up to a substantial effect over several years.

We can see the rise in IQ at work at a social level among immigrant groups. As groups from poorer countries come to wealthier nations they may at first score lower on their chosen country's intelligence tests (Eysenck & Kamin, 1984). These same groups often show rises in intelligence to the average or to levels above average as they assimilate in the general culture (Ceci, 1996; Loehlin, 2000). One factor contributing to the rise includes learning the new country's language, others may involve improved pre- and post-natal medical care and better nutrition. One caution: If immigrants—or members of any group—are stereotyped as less intellectually adequate, the stereotype itself can temporarily reduce the group-members' test performance (Aronson, Lustina, & Good, 1999; Steele, 1998; Steele & Aronson, 1995).

Crystallized Intelligence and Mental Models

A key to our personalities is the mental models we construct of ourselves, our relationships and the world (see Chapter 5). We draw on our intelligence to create such models, to evaluate them and to improve them when they are off the mark. Intelligence researchers sometimes refer to the mental understandings we have acquired as our **crystallized intelligence.** Crystallized intelligence involves well-learned mental models of key aspects of the world around us. It includes our understanding and mastery of vocabulary, arithmetic, and more advanced aspects of mathematics, and our understanding of social relationships such as our family relationships, relationships with teachers, and with authority figures more generally (Cattell, 1963; Carroll, 1993, p. 626). For example, our cousin might exhibit her crystallized intelligence as she discusses the plays of William Shakespeare, and the different forms such literature takes: dramas, comedies, episodic accounts and more experimental structures.

Crystallized intelligence contrasts with **fluid intelligence.** Fluid intelligence refers to the active, immediately occurring problem-solving we engage in when we solve novel problems for the first time—for example, identifying a theme in a book or solving a logical problem. That same cousin might employ her fluid intelligence to try to assess a newly posed question about Shakespeare's *Macbeth*: "What are the key lessons Shakespeare imparts about what a person can and cannot control?" Although she knows the play, the question of control is new to her and she must puzzle over whether Shakespeare's message is that supernatural forces are genuine or whether suggestible people respond to them as self-fulfilling prophecies, or whether the issue can be decided at all. Fluid and crystallized intelligence operate together, of course: As our cousin uses her fluid intelligence to identify new meanings in Shakespeare's play, she draws on her crystallized knowledge of word meanings, sentences, and relationships. To return to the central point here: We draw on our intelligences to form our mental models; the more accurate our models are, the better we are able to solve problems and navigate the world.

The Relationship Between Mental Ability Traits and Other Traits

Perhaps the most striking aspect of personality is how distinctly independent its parts can be: Extroverts can be conscientious or careless; narcissists can be neurotic or stable. And similarly, a person of high intelligence may exhibit any of a number of personality characteristics. Put another way, intelligence and most other personality traits are at best only moderately correlated. The Big Five trait of openness correlates about $r = .30$ with general intelligence; neuroticism exhibits a relationship of $r = -.15$; extraversion a mere $r = .05$, agreeableness and conscientiousness hardly at all. An exception to the rule is that both personal and emotional intelligences correlate with agreeableness at about the $r = .18$ level, and personal intelligence correlates with conscientiousness at the same level (DeYoung, 2011; Mayer, Panter & Caruso, 2012). Returning to general intelligence, there appear to be a few traits more specific than those found in the Big Five that do relate to intelligence.

Intelligence and Absorption

Intellectual absorption is the capacity to become absorbed in intellectual problems to the point of forgetting what is going on around you. Geniuses such as Isaac Newton and Michelangelo seemed to possess an absorbed, flowing involvement in their intellectual work. Newton's absorption in his work was so intense and complete that no one got to know him well enough to record the rest of his life.

More recently, the mathematical physicist Mitchell Jay Feigenbaum immersed himself in modeling irregular objects as he was developing a key portion of chaos theory. He became so involved in his pursuits that he took more plane trips than strictly necessary, because he wanted to see the chaotic aspects of cloud patterns up close. This so frustrated his supervisors at Los Alamos Laboratories that they had to suspend his scientific travel privileges (Gleick, 1987, pp. 1-2; Mayer et al., 1989, p. 121). Even young people demonstrate this quality: A study of highly intellectually gifted 14-year-olds indicated that they were higher in intellectual absorption than incoming first-year college students of the same mental age, and also higher in intellectual absorption than a same-age control group of other 14-year-olds of average intelligence (Mayer et al., 1989).

Broad Intelligences and Their Correlates

Certain broad intelligences correlate more highly with other personality traits than does general intelligence. Emotional intelligence correlates with self-reported empathic feelings at a level of about $r = .35$. (cf. Geher, Warner, & Brown, 2001). Personal intelligence correlates with psychological mindedness—an interest in understanding one's own and others' thought processes—also at about $r = .35$ (Mayer, Panter & Caruso, 2012). Creativity is related to the Big Five trait of openness to experience. Openness to experience involves the willingness to appreciate and to try new things. People who score high on scales of openness endorse such statements as, "I like to taste new foods I haven't tried before."

Creative Intelligence and Psychopathology

Although creativity is a healthy psychological strength for many people, it seems related to at least two areas of psychopathology: schizophrenia and bipolar disorder. Some creative individuals experience alterations in conscious experience that are similar to those found in the milder forms of the schizophrenic-spectrum disorders. Both those who are creative and those with a **schizotypal style** of thinking endorse test items that indicate unusual mental experiences, such as, "It has seemed at times as if my body was melting into my surroundings," and "I have felt there were messages for me in the way things were arranged, like in a store window" (Fisher et al, 2004, pp. 25-26). Such manifestations of a schizotypal mind-set have been associated with better performance on divergent thinking tasks. Moreover, the first-degree relatives of people with schizophrenia can be found in more creative occupations than others (Brod, 1997; Karlsson, 1984). The creative thinking style, however, can be found in otherwise healthy personalities and does not mean a person has or will develop a mental disorder.

High levels of creativity may also be related to **bipolar disorder**. Bipolar disorder is a mental disorder marked by severe mood swings, often alternating between paralyzing depressions and out-of-control excited states called mania. People without bipolar disorder but who nonetheless experience relatively strong variations in mood appear to be more creative, perhaps benefiting from seeing problems from alternating optimistic and pessimistic perspectives (Jamison, 1993; 1996; Mayer et al., 1995). This variation in mood exists in many normal people, but appears stronger in first degree-relatives of those with bipolar disorder, who also are found in more creative occupations than others (Richards et al., 1988).

How Are Mental Abilities Expressed?

Intelligence in the Expression of Thought

Concrete and Abstract Reasoning

People express themselves differently depending upon their intellectual level. Nearly everyone exhibits **concrete thinking**. Concrete thinking involves observing, labeling, and remembering events and occurrences. Nigel Hunt suffered from an intellectual disability due to Trisomy-21, a genetic abnormality also known as Down Syndrome. Tutored extensively by his parents, who were both teachers, Nigel learned to read and write, and in his late teens produced a complete autobiography with only minimal help from others. "I am Nigel Hunt," he began:

> …and I live at 26 Church Avenue, Pinner, England with my parents. They are very nice indeed. I was born at Edgware in 1947. I have never been to America yet. The lady who advised me to write this was Mrs. Eileen J. Garrett and she says that I shall be very busy.
>
> So it's hallo! Welcome to my first good attempt in making this book and Douglas Hunt [his father] is assisting me… (Hunt, 1967, p. 46)

Nigel's autobiography is full of descriptions of his warm family life, his interests, and activities. Here, he describes his education at the Atholl School:

> Since my father was Headmaster I had joined the school at the age of eleven. I was very proud of my school. I had very good teachers, such as: Mrs. C. Parry, Mr. Warrington, and the school's old Headmaster, Mr. J. H. Hale…
>
> The first time I went to school my father had left something behind; it was his handkerchief, and my mother told me to take it to him. When I got to school one of the boys came up to me and said, "Would you like to play cricket?" and do you know who the boy was? Michael Killick, who played well in the athletics match at Harrow Town.

> One day I was taught good English from Mr. Hunt and then came the periods. Periods 1, 2, 3, 4, and so on; when I went there I became independent and polite to all the boys. Then we had two French teachers. One French master was Mr. Piper. He was a very good person... (Hunt, 1967, pp. 105-106)

This passage contains a variety of accurate individual observations, facts, and feelings that characterize concrete thought. Although it is easy to appreciate the points as they are brought up, they can seem disorganized as a whole.

Researchers have observed that more intelligent-appearing expression reflects **abstract reasoning**. Abstract thinking extends beyond the concrete to include the relationships among individual observations and perceptions: Such abstract reasoning reflects the ability to hold concepts in mind, to evaluate their similarities and differences, to organize them, to generalize across concepts, and to synthesize ideas.

In 1921, a number of eminent psychologists participated in a symposium in which they were invited to submit definitions of intelligence (Thorndike, 1921). Abstract reasoning featured prominently: the "ability to carry on abstract thinking" (Louis Terman); the "ability to judge, understand, and reason well" (Alfred Binet), and the "...apprehension of relevant relationships" (cited in Wyatt).

Abstract thinking is expressed in the communications of people with high levels of intelligence. For example, Alexander Hamilton (1757-1804) was a close confidant of George Washington and an author of the Federalist Papers, which recommended ratification of the new United States constitution. As a young man, just before the U.S. War for Independence, he wrote a letter to a schoolmate in which he neatly balanced several concerns for his own future:

> ...To confess my weakness, Ned, my ambition is prevalent, so that I contemn the groveling condition of a clerk or the like, to which my fortune, etc., condemns me, and would willingly risk my life, though not my character, to exalt my station. I am confident, Ned, that my youth excludes me from any hopes of immediate preferment; nor do I desire it; but I mean to preface the way for futurity. I'm no philosopher, you see, and may justly be said to build castles in the air; my folly makes me ashamed, and I beg you'll conceal it; yet Neddy, we have seen such schemes successful when the projector is constant... (Cited in Terman, 1926, p. 785)

Hamilton draws a careful distinction between taking risks in general, versus risking one's character, and he has noticed, as well, how plans can succeed for those who are constant. Such abstract reasoning is a hallmark of intelligence. Hamilton composed and sent the letter when he was 12 years old.

Rapid Development

The personality of an individual with high intelligence is characterized not only by abstract thinking but also by fast-developing mental capacities. An extreme example makes the point: John Stuart Mill (1806-1873) learned Greek at 3 and read Plato with understanding at 7. At 8 he studied Latin. Also at 8 (2nd or 3rd grade), he covered geometry and algebra. At age 9, he was familiar with the conic sections and spherics of geometry, and had begun studying calculus. As he learned math, his tutors remarked that, "He performed all problems without the book and most of them without any help from the book" (Cox, 1926, p. 707).

He began a history of Rome, the first paragraph of which was as follows:

Alban Government: Roman conquest in Italy. We know not any part, says Dionysius of Halicarnassus, of the History of Rome till the Sicilian invasions. Before that time, the country had not been entered by any foreign invader. After the expulsion of Sicilians… Aeneas, son of Venus and Anchises… succeeded Latinus in the government, and engaged in the wars of Italy. The Rutuli, a people living near the sea, and extending along the Numicius up to the Lavinium, opposed him. However, Turnus their king was defeated and killed by Aeneas. Aeneas was killed soon after this. The war continued to be carried on chiefly against the Rutuli, to the time of Romulus, the first king of Rome. By him it was that Rome was built. (quoted in Terman, 1926, p. 795)

Mill wrote the above at age 6 ½, by which time he had already developed a quite mature writing style (note the flair in the last sentence). The writing shows a good ability to communicate complex concepts, as well as careful qualifications of generalizations—for example, he characterized Aeneas' war as directed *chiefly* against the Rutuli. Although only a few individuals will have mental development this rapid, the example serves to indicate just how fast intellectual development can be. Mill's IQ has been estimated to be 200.

Adaptation

Some people argue that intelligence also involves successful adaptation to life (Gardner, 1983; 1993; Sternberg, 1997). Wechsler, for example, described intelligence as involving the understanding of how to deal effectively with the environment, and providing the "resourcefulness to cope with its challenges" (Wechsler, 1975, p. 139).

Others are less sure about intelligence and adjustment, noting that well adapted creatures—moths and ants, for example—don't require much individual intelligence. People with extremely high levels of intelligence may become frustrated with those around them. John Stuart Mill, despite his estimated IQ of 200, suffered a nervous breakdown as a young man, perhaps because his intellect made him so different from others (e.g., Mayer et al., 2001).

The Stability of IQ

A person's intelligence tends to be stable over his or her lifetime. When IQ is measured in a group of children at age 3, for example it generally correlates r = .83 with those same children's scores at age 4 (Sontag, Baker, & Nelson). After a 10-year period, it correlates between $r = .72$ to .78 with the same children's scores, and still exhibits a relationships of about $r = .60$ level after as long as 25 years (Bradway, Tompson, & Cravens, 1958; Harnqvist, 1968; Husen, 1951).

Intelligences at School

IQ and Educational Performance

Binet's original intelligence tests were designed to predict school learning. Both his original tests, as well as the intelligence tests of today, make successful predictions of education attainment. The left-hand side of Table 6-5 lists school level beginning with the elementary/middle-school grades and rising through junior high, high school, college, and college graduates (cf. Reynolds, Chastain, Kaufman, & McLean, 1987). The average IQ of students at each level rises gradually from an IQ of 82 for elementary- and middle-school children, to an IQ of 116 for college graduates. IQ rises with level of education because people with lower IQs drop out of the educational system over time. For example, high school students with IQs less than 84 have only a 14% chance of graduating; those with IQs between 84-94 have a 54% chance, and those with IQs above 115 have nearly a 90% chance (Matarrazzo, 1972). Additionally education will gradually raise a person's IQ. Altogether, the correlation between IQ and years of schooling is $r = .61$ (Bajema, 1968).

The right-most column of Table 6-5 shows the prediction from IQ to grades in the form of a correlation coefficient. In primary and second school, the correlation between IQ and grades is roughly $r = .45$ to .50. In high school, it rises to $r = .60$ as the material becomes more advanced (Matarrazzo, 1972).

Table 6-5: Average IQ at Different Grade Levels, and Correlations Between IQ and Grades*

Educational Level	Average IQ at Educational Level	Correlation Between IQ and Grades
Elementary/middle	82	.65
Junior high**	90	.61
Some high school	96	.60
High school	100	.58
Some college	108	.44
College graduate	116	.50

*Average values are reported where multiple sources were available; **prorated from elementary and high school values. Sources: Cattell & Butcher, 1968, Chapter 3; Conry & Plant, 1965; Matarazzo, 1972, Chapter 12; Matarazzo & Herman, 1984; Reynolds, Chastain, Kaufman & McLean, 1987.

In the first year of college, the correlation between IQ and grades declines somewhat to $r = .44$ (Matarazzo, 1972, p. 284; Jensen, 1980, p. 329). Researchers believe the prediction drops because the range of intelligence levels decreases among evermore highly selected groups of students. As only the better students continue with their education, prediction becomes more difficult. In graduate and professional schools, only the highest IQ individuals are left and there is less difference in IQ among them. Nonetheless, the overall prediction from IQ to attending graduate or professional school is $r = .50$.

Does Emotional Intelligence Matter in School?

Emotional intelligence does correlate with academic performance, but its predictions mostly duplicate predictions already possible from the SATs and other measures of intelligence (Boyce, 2002; Lam & Kirby, 2002). Emotional intelligence may predict unique performance that is particularly germane to understanding oneself and others: Marsland and Likavec (2003) studied graduate students who were training to become clinical psychologists. The new psychotherapists were evaluated for their promise by their supervisors. Their capacity to be empathic—but not their academic performance—was predicted by ability scales of emotional intelligence. Others have found that higher emotional intelligence leads to better communication and smoother relationships on the job (Lopes, Salovey, Coté, Beers, & Petty, 2005).

On-Task Behavior

People with higher mental abilities often take longer to begin certain tasks. Laboratory studies of high IQ individuals suggest that they spend more time understanding a problem than comparison groups with lower IQs, but then take a shorter period of time in actually executing a plan. A brighter student might take longer choosing a topic for a class paper, researching the topic, and in outlining her remarks. Once writing gets underway, however, she may work faster than others (e.g., Sternberg, 1981; Larkin, McDermott, Simon, & Simon, 1980).

Intelligences and Other Mental Abilities at Work

Intelligence tests also predict some degree of occupational success. In one study, 18,000 soldiers' IQ scores were examined in relation to the 48 civilian occupations they occupied. The results replicated studies done in World War I (see, for example, Tyler, 1965, pp. 330-364). On average, people who possess higher intelligence are found in occupations requiring high education and possessing high prestige.

The correlation between the rated prestige of an occupation and the average IQ of the individual within the occupation is about $r = .80$ (Matarrazzo, 1972, pp. 178-180; Morris & Levinson, 1995). Three of the most prestigious occupations studied were accounting, law, and engineering. People in those occupations had average IQs of 128, 128 and 127, respectively. By comparison, three occupations with relatively low prestige ratings included mining, farming, and cooking. People in those occupations had average IQs of 91, 91, and 92, respectively (Harrell & Harrell, 1945; Stewart, 1947).

The above correlations granted, there are high-IQ individuals in all occupations. Even very bright people may not have the opportunity to use their mental gifts—and some high-IQ individuals choose to use them in less prestigious but otherwise appealing occupations. In the large-sample studies above, a few miners had IQs that rivaled those of engineers and accountants. But low-IQ individuals are not found in all occupations. Intellectually demanding occupations such as the law and journalism require above-average IQs to perform at a minimally adequate level, and people in those occupations with the lowest IQs still tested at 95 or higher.

General and Broad Cognitive Intelligences

General intelligence is important in predicting occupational success, with predictions of $r = .23$ for cognitive simple jobs to $r = .58$ for the most cognitively demanding jobs (Ree & Earles, 1992; Schmidt & Hunter, 2004). Beyond general intelligence, broad intelligences also exhibit predictive powers. For example, people high in spatial intelligence choose (and succeed at) certain occupations, including architecture and engineering, more than those with lower skill levels, who are unable to perform as well in such roles (Shea, Lubinski, and Benbow, 2001; Lubinski, Webb, & Morelock, 2001).

Practical Intelligence at Work

With regard to practical intelligence, studies suggest that those highest in this mental ability are more likely to be employed in a company with greater prestige and to have higher salaries. Within an organization, those higher in practical intelligence also are likely to attain higher positions and higher salaries (after taking into account age and longevity in the organization). Salespeople who are high in practical intelligence sell more than those who are not (Wagner, 2000). The incremental prediction of practical intelligence above general intelligence is uncertain; demonstrations of incremental predictions often require larger samples in order to reach conclusions (Gottfredson, 2003; Sternberg, 2003).

Creativity at Work

Creative intelligence also influences people's lives. High school students who scored high on a battery of creative abilities had distinctive life patterns 12 years later according to research by Torrance (1972; see also Runco, 1986). Highly creative people experienced more relevant but unusual detours in their training and occupational paths when compared to others. The more creative participants also experienced a tendency to have their careers delayed by relevant work or educational experiences. Once settled on a path, they ended up in innovative, distinctive occupations. These individuals became writers, entertainers, and artists, also dog trainers, centerfielders on baseball teams, and similar less usual pursuits. Sometimes the creativity was reflected in an unusual combination of training. For example, one creative individual had obtained advanced degrees in law, economics, and history, and had life experience in social action. The study participant ended up teaching American Public Policy and Constitutional Law (Torrance, 1972, p. 79). Creative individuals also produced more creative output that received public recognition than less creative people: more poems, dances, musical pieces and scientific publications as adults—even when the follow up was more than 23 years after the time of testing (Torrance, 1988, p. 61).

Intelligence and Creativity Interacting at Work

Biographical studies of scientists' and artists' works indicate that the higher their overall output, the more likely they will be regarded as creative. Often, highly creative individuals don't seem to be creative if you examine just one of their works at a time. They innovate, rather, by producing so much more than other people, that they generate creative works as an apparent byproduct of their myriad outputs. The highly productive individuals in these studies were identified because they met very high standards for the quality of their work, so overall quality of work also contributes to creativity. Happily, creative output can occur any time in life, and there is no period of life in which creativity is most likely (Simonton, 2004).

Intelligences in Relationships

People with high emotional intelligence have more harmonious relationships than others. Such individuals engage in fewer problem behaviors: They have a lower risk of excessive use of alcohol and drugs, keep fewer alcoholic beverages and drugs in their homes, are less likely to smoke cigarettes, and are less likely to engage in recreational drug use with their parents. They also exhibit a lower tendency to get into fights with others (Brackett & Mayer, 2003; Brackett, Mayer, & Warner, 2004; Formica, 1999; Rubin, 1999). People higher in emotional intelligence have closer social networks and can rely on more assistance from others. More generally, they possess the ability to regulate their own and others' emotions to make relationships smoother, and in the workplace, perform better in certain on-the-job situations (Lopes, Brackett, Nezlek, Schutz, Sellin, & Salovey, 2004).

General mental ability also affects relationships. **Assortative mating** refers to the tendency of people to pick marriage partners who are similar to themselves on certain observable features. The correlation between IQs in spouses is $r = .50$ (Jencks, 1972, p. 272). This indicates that people with high intelligence tend to marry one another, and people of lower intelligence tend to marry one another as well. Marriages between one person high and one person low in intelligence are fewer than would be expected by chance.

Personality and Mental Abilities: The Big Picture

> "I not only use all the brains I have, but all I can borrow." – Woodrow Wilson (1856-1924)

Intelligence, Education, and Training

A fine education can often compensate for a less-than-fine intellect. No matter how smart a person is, he or she benefits from learning what others know. This is true not only for academic skills such as learning algebra or how to parse a sentence grammatically, but also for social and emotional skills. For example, people can be taught how to be liked—up to a point. When meeting someone new, for instance, is it best to be ingratiating or to be self-promoting?

It pays to be ingratiating. This is true not only of social situations but even of job interviews (e.g., Godfrey, Jones, & Lord, 1986; Higgins & Judge, 2004). How to be ingratiating? One skill that might help is called partner attention. Partner attention involves partner references, questions, and continuations of topics started by the other person. There is some belief that partner attention can reduce the loneliness experienced by those with few friends, although the available research findings are not accepted by everyone (Bell, 1985; Vandeputte, et al., 1999).

Moral education, too, can enhance a person's effectiveness. For example, the educational program, "Facing History and Ourselves," involves studying historical racial, ethnic, and religious conflicts so as to enhance understanding across groups. A recent outcome study of the program studying 346 learners in 14 classes, along with a comparison group, indicated that the program reduced school fights for all participants, reduced racist attitudes (for women only) and promoted maturity (Schultz, Barr, & Selman, 2001).

A Broader Approach to Mental Abilities

There is little question that creativity, intelligence, and other mental abilities predict a number of criteria of importance. At the same time, the measures now in use may not work for everyone. For example, the predictions between intelligence and various criteria are excellent, but such relationships might come about even if the tests worked for only, say, 75% of the population. The tests might be less valid for some types of individuals who have a different approach to thinking not readily tapped by tests currently in use, perhaps for those people who are especially creative, come from a different culture, or possess other idiosyncratic or as- yet unknown qualities.

Consistent with the above idea, there has been a gradual broadening of the types of mental abilities studied. Whereas work early in the 20th century focused mostly on verbal intelligence, attention has since turned to broad mental abilities including spatial, emotional, and personal intelligences, as well as to creativity. It seems likely that a better understanding of less-understood talents, as well as the discovery of further mental abilities, will continue into the future. What is known already, is that the personality system can draw on many mental abilities to achieve its goals.

Reviewing Chapter 6

Intelligences and mental abilities are important to personality. They contribute to planning, to understanding one's mental models of the self, world, and relationships, and to other areas of personality. Society values and rewards those who have certain mental abilities.

The aim of this chapter was to help you understand what mental abilities are, what kinds of mental abilities there are, how they are related, and what they predict. Kinds of intelligence vary from verbal-propositional intelligence to personal intelligence. The concept of general intelligence, or g, serves as a summation of at least some of these abilities. Personality calls on those mental abilities to perform its tasks. Each intelligence predicts important life outcomes, from school performance and occupational prestige to better social relations.

Questions About "What Is a Mental Ability?"

1. <u>Mental Ability:</u> What is a mental ability and how does it differ from a motivational or emotional trait?

2. <u>Mental Ability and Society:</u> Sir Frances Galton, in England, and Alfred Binet, in France, were both interested in studying intelligence. How were their approaches similar and how were they different? What social pressures lead to the study of mental abilities?

Questions About "Which Intelligences Were Studied First?"

3. <u>The First Intelligence Tests:</u> The early Binet scale asked questions that depended upon a good understanding of language, and it often asked about words and language. What intelligence was it said to measure as a consequence?

4. <u>A New Intelligence:</u> Wechsler was faced with a population of immigrants in New York, not all of whom were fluent in English. What intelligence did he measure to correct for such difficulties in language?

Questions About "How Does Intelligence Develop?"

5. <u>Mental Development and the IQ Score:</u> One of the key aspects of mental capacity is that it develops with age, at least through childhood. Which intelligence researcher developed that insight? How does rate IQ capture the idea of mental development?

6. <u>The Deviation IQ:</u> Deviation IQs are not calculated according to rate of development. Do they reflect rate of development anyway? If so, how?

Questions About g and "What Are Broad Intelligences?"

7. <u>The Theory of "*g*":</u> Charles Spearman suggested that there existed one general intelligence that contributed to all the other intelligences. His theory of "*g*" was based on what observation about the correlation among mental abilities?

8. <u>Spatial Intelligence:</u> Researchers in the mid-20th century first proposed that a spatial intelligence might exist. How did Roger Shepard and his colleagues measure it?

9. <u>Social Abilities:</u> In the 1920s, some psychologists began to study social intelligence. Unfortunately, it was difficult to distinguish from verbal intelligence, and was so heavily criticized, that work in the area languished. What is the present status of this intelligence?

10. <u>Practical Intelligence:</u> Another kind of intelligence is practical intelligence. What does it measure? It is based on implicit-tacit knowledge: Can you define what sort of knowledge that is?

11. <u>Emotional Intelligence:</u> In the 1990s, some psychologists studied emotional intelligence. At this time, considerable evidence has been obtained reflecting the existence of the ability. What are some sample tasks that measure emotional intelligence?

12. <u>Personal Intelligence:</u> Personal intelligence is a recently proposed intelligence. How would you define personal intelligence?

13. <u>Measuring Creativity:</u> Creativity involves the capacity to come up with novel solutions to problems. One mental ability related to creativity involves verbal fluency—the ability to come up with words to fit a given requirement, such as rhymes to a word like "clang." What other ways are there of measuring creativity?

Questions About "What Is the Relationship Between Personality and Intelligence?"

14. <u>Personality Draws on Mental Abilities:</u> Personality draws on mental abilities to get its work done. Mental abilities seem to be greater in human beings than in other animals. Intellectual capacity seems to rise across animal species, as brain size increases. This has led researchers to try to connect brain size and

intelligence. What new neural imaging techniques have researchers employed to connect brain size to intelligence? Are there any genetic bases for intelligence?

15. Relationships between Mental Ability Traits and Other Traits: Most motivational and emotional traits—such as extraversion and neuroticism—are unrelated to intellect-related traits. There are some exceptions; for example, empathy is related to emotional intelligence. Which traits relate to creativity and which to cognitive intelligences? Creativity is associated with alterations of consciousness and mood swings; though creativity is itself a healthy process. What mental disorders are characterized by unusual conscious experiences and mood swings?

16. Personality, Mental Abilities, and the Construction of Mental Models: There is evidence for environmental influences on intelligence. What happened to immigrant groups after a few generations in the United States? Schooling influences intelligence as well. How does a year in school affect IQ? Fluid intelligence involves pure, abstract reasoning. What is crystallized intelligence and how does it relate to mental models?

Questions About "How Are Mental Abilities Expressed?"

17. Intelligence and the Expression of Thought: Nearly everyone carries out concrete thinking, recording times, objects, and events. A central characteristic of higher intelligence is abstract reasoning. Can you say what abstract reasoning involves? What other characteristics of intelligence were commonly mentioned in this chapter?

18. Intelligences at School: Cognitive intelligences are highly predictive of school performance. The relationships are expressed as correlations between intelligence tests and various criteria. What are some of the educational outcomes that intelligence predicts, and what are the general levels of those predictions?

19. Intelligences and Mental Abilities at Work: Although intelligence tests were not developed to measure occupational performance, research has shown that there are correlations between IQ and occupational choice and success. One of the most striking findings concerns the relationship between the average IQ of people in a given occupation and the prestige of the occupation. Do you know what this relationship is? What are some other relationships between IQ and occupational status? How does practical intelligence relate to work performance? People with higher creativity produce more creative products—books, poems, and scientific studies. Creativity alters an individual's career path—can you say how?

20. Intelligences and Mental Abilities in Relationships: Emotional intelligence predicts academic success, but often not much better than cognitive intelligence. When it comes to relationships, however, emotional intelligence appears to predict a variety of outcomes. What is the relationship between emotional intelligence and connectedness? What does emotional intelligence predict about problem behaviors?

21. The Scope of Intelligence: As the measures of intelligence broaden, it is more likely that more of people's abilities will be accurately measured, and that the intelligence tests will become fairer. What are some of the other limitations or strengths of intelligence measurement?

Chapter 6 Glossary

Terms in Order of Appearance:

Mental Ability: The capacity to perform mental tasks such as recognizing and solving problems.

Intelligence: A specific type of mental ability involving the capacity to reason abstractly so as to arrive at the proper solution to a problem.

Verbal-Propositional Intelligence: An intelligence that involves the capacity to reason validly with words and language, and to understand the meaning of words and language.

Perceptual-Organization Intelligence: A type of intelligence that involves perceiving visual patterns, organizing the perceptual information in them, being able to divide the patterns into parts, and to reconstruct them.

Mental Age: The age that a person's mental functioning most closely resembles. For example, if a child can solve problems that most six-year-olds can solve, but fails most problems seven-year-olds can solve, the child is said to have a mental age of six.

Intelligence Quotient: A score originally proposed as an index of a person's rate of mental (versus chronological) growth. The Intelligence Quotient, or IQ, has come to mean any score that reflects an individual's level of general intelligence.

Rate IQ: A measure of intelligence. The rate intelligence quotient (IQ) is calculated by taking a person's mental age, dividing it by their chronological age, and multiplying by 100 (compare to Deviation IQ).

Deviation IQ: A measure of intelligence. The deviation IQ is calculated by examining a person's distance or deviation from the average performance of all other people his or her age (compare to Rate IQ).

Standard Deviations: A measure of distance from a group mean. The standard deviation is a unit of measure. It is calculated by first summing the squared deviations from the mean of each person, second, obtaining the average of the summed squared deviations (referred to as the variance), and finally, taking its square root.

General Intelligence (g): A person's general ability to reason abstractly with information; a "first" or general factor of intelligence. General intelligence reflects a person's overall ability to solve problems accurately and quickly across all areas of symbolic reasoning—language, perceptual organization, spatial rotations, and others.

Broad Intelligence: An intelligence that relates to a particular mode or area of thinking, such as auditory intelligence or verbal intelligence.

Spatial Intelligence: A type of intelligence pertaining to understanding how objects move in space. Spatial intelligence is often measured by examining people's capacity to accurately rotate objects in their minds and identify what the rotated object would look like.

Hot Intelligences: A group of intelligences concerned with understanding and reasoning about information of direct personal significance to the individual (for example, emotional intelligence).

Social Intelligence: A type of intelligence concerned with understanding social relations and how to carry out social tasks.

Personal Intelligence: A proposed intelligence that involves accuracy of self-understanding; research on the intelligence has just begun.

Practical Intelligence: A type of social intelligence involving the capacity to understand problems in everyday life that are often left undefined or poorly defined. Practical intelligence requires the problem solver to formulate the social problem him- or herself, under conditions in which information necessary to a solution may be lacking. It is said to operate on tacit knowledge—that is, knowledge not often explicitly stated.

Emotional Intelligence: The ability to reason with emotions, and to use emotions to enhance thought. Emotional intelligence involves the capacity to accurately perceive emotions, to use them in thinking, to understand emotions, and to manage emotional experience.

Personal Intelligence: The ability to reason about personality, including identifying information relevant to personality, forming models of people, guiding choices with information relevant to personality and systematizing one's plans, goals, and life story.

Creativity: The capacity to come up with multiple, novel solutions to problems.

Verbal Fluency: The capacity to come up with a large number of appropriate words that fit a specified category, e.g., words that rhyme with "smell."

Alternate Uses: A task in which a participant tries to think of as many uses as possible for an everyday object, such as a desk or a pen.

Divergent Thinking: The capacity to generate many alternative solutions to a specified problem, e.g., "What are all the things you can do with a water bottle?"

Remote Associates Task: A measure of divergent thinking in which a person identifies an association that several words share in common, for example: "water, cream, cold": *ice*.

Fluid Intelligence: A type of ongoing mental capacity or ability to deal with novel, new problems.

Intellectual Absorption: A trait related to intelligence that concerns the capacity to become involved in intellectual problems to the point of losing track of other activities.

Schizotypal Style: A cognitive style associated with a mental disorder involving very odd forms of thinking and perceiving, and behavioral eccentricities.

Bipolar Disorder: A mental disorder marked by severe swings in mood.

Crystallized Intelligence: Knowledge stored about the world that can be applied to the solutions of mental problems.

Concrete Thinking: Thinking that correctly holds symbols, ideas, and thoughts in memory, but without any comparisons or generalizations about those ideas.

Abstract Reasoning: The capacity to manipulate symbols, see relationships among concepts, and to integrate ideas in thought.

Assortative Mating: The tendency for people to marry or otherwise mate with those people who are similar to themselves on particular dimensions or traits. People exhibit assortative mating based on intelligence.

Chapter 7: The Conscious Self

The conscious self is one of the most mysterious parts of personality. Sometimes equated with a soul or a "ghost in the machine," it is a considerable challenge to scientists. What is consciousness? Can a person exercise free will? Might there exist other, hidden, parts of personality that temporarily exert control over an individual? What does it mean to have an authentic conscious self?

Previewing the Chapter's Central Questions

•**What Is the Conscious Self?** What does it mean to say that a person is a conscious, willful being? What is the individual's innermost "I"? These ideas refer to a self that has both subjective awareness and the power to influence events.

•**What Does It Mean for the Self To Be Conscious?** What is the nature of consciousness? How is consciousness explained—and how do scientists try to deal with something they cannot fully explain?

•**Does the Self Possess Free Will?** Can a person decide to act entirely on her own, apart from prior influences and events? If so, does that contradict the basic tenets of science? What is the difference between a person's voluntary and involuntary action (if any) and how is that related to free will?

•**Are There Alternatives to the Conscious Self?** The conscious self can be considered part of a broader collection of personality "agencies." Agencies are "sub-personalities" that are hypothesized to act in place of the conscious self—such as the id and superego. But do such agencies as these really exist?

•**How Is the Conscious Self Expressed?** We will examine some individual differences in conscious selves regarding how consciousness is structured and individual differences in levels of awareness.

What Is the Conscious Self?

The Appearance of the Conscious Self

The French artist Paul Gauguin (1848-1903) was highly self-conscious and valued his independence (Rapetti, 1996, p. 187). He purposively cultivated an image as an "untamed" artist, and attributed his character to his mother's influence; she traveled ceaselessly and others often perceived her as egotistic.

Gauguin's family fled France for South America during political turmoil in 1848. His father died during the voyage, and the young painter's early years were spent in relative luxury at an uncle's estate in Lima, Peru. His mother and he then returned to France, where he took a job as a stockbroker. In 1873 he married Mette-Sophje Gad, a young Danish woman, and they had five children together.

During this time, Gauguin was increasingly attracted to the art world and began to paint, earning some initial praise for his works from art critics. When the stock market crashed in 1882, he lost his job in the brokerage. In a period of conscious personal reflection, he committed himself to "paint every day" (Gauguin, 1998, p. 147). He moved his family to Copenhagen but neither he nor his paintings were well received in Denmark. Struggles with his in-laws contributed to strains with his wife, and his marriage deteriorated. He returned to France alone except for one son. He now escalated his commitments, self-consciously determining to sacrifice everything for his art.

During the autumn of 1890, despite poor health, Gauguin made a dramatic decision: He would set sail for Tahiti so as to learn from and to be inspired by the art forms there. True to his guiding lights, he left friends and remaining family contacts behind. He sold off his paintings to raise money for the voyage, and arrived in Tahiti in 1891. This was followed by a second, longer visit during which his favorite daughter died and he broke off communication decisively with his wife (Gowing, 1995, p. 236). Tahiti had proven to be a bit of a disappointment in terms of its nature and art, and so he had brought some native art forms from China, Japan, and elsewhere, to fill in the gaps. His paintings matured during this time. They became more colorful and more representative of an island paradise—a paradise, perhaps, more of his imagination than reality. These later paintings firmly established his international reputation as an artist through to the present. He died of illness at the age of 55.

Reflecting the outline of Gauguin's life, we might wonder about the deliberate and conscious series of decisions he made about his art: How and why did he decide, in young adulthood, to paint every day? We might further contemplate his similar decisions to leave his wife and several children in Copenhagen so as to return first to France, and most famously, to travel to Tahiti to paint.

As psychologists interested in the self, some of the striking facets of Gauguin's life included his acute awareness of his own life and of the role art played within it. His life decisions about painting illustrate what people often mean when they speak of free will. Here, it seems, is a person making his own decisions, almost regardless of the consequences. Moreover, Gauguin's decisions seem, at least, to be related to his growth as a person and an artist.

Philosophers have wondered whether Gauguin's life decisions made sense—and whether they were moral in the sense of creating the greater good for the greatest number of people (Williams, 1993; Statman, 1993). Did Gaugan commit himself to art simply because he was convinced he was a great artist? If so, how did he know? Could any egotistical person with an inflated self-image feel entitled to decide similarly? Perhaps Gauguin should have consulted professors of art to see if his decision was warranted (Williams, 1993, p. 39). Part of what the philosophers conclude is that Gauguin could not know how matters would turn out. In essence, he was rather lucky.

In this chapter we will examine the aware self, its consciousness, and its self-control. We will inquire as to the role that the conscious self plays in an individual's personality and broader life.

James' Self-as-Knower

The seat of conscious awareness in personality has been variously referred to simply as consciousness, or as the ego, or as a **self-as-knower**. The self-as-knower, according to William James, was that part of you that observed and had awareness of what was going on in the mind (James, 1892). To fully imagine it, James suggested a thought experiment. Imagine losing parts of your body, he said: your legs, your trunk, arms, and neck; and then imagine losing your hearing, your sight, and your sense of touch. These are all parts of you that you could lose and still be yourself. Now imagine losing some memories, such as what you ate for breakfast this morning. The part that was left after everything else had been taken away was the self-as-knower. It is the conscious, aware sense of yourself James regarded as the essence of "you."

Our conscious self consists of our personal sense of observing and awareness. It is the innermost citadel of a person (James, 1892). For each of us, our self-as-knower possesses a special, personal, familiar quality that no one else's consciousness has. The conscious self can be distinguished from the kinds of models of the self we discussed in Chapter 5. Whereas a person's self-model might contain a list of attributes including strong-willed, obstinate, introverted, and conscientious, the conscious self is something inside that looks at that mental model with awareness of what is going on inside. We might change our model of our self, deciding that we are more careless than conscientious on a day we feel troubled, but our innermost awareness is always our own.

James' self-as-knower had two central, internal qualities: consciousness and will. Both are challenging topics to study. What, after all, can we say about consciousness? How much of it can we understand?

Freud's Concept of the Ego

Freud, too, had an idea of a conscious self—although only partially conscious. Freud's name for it was the **ego**. The ego begins development near the body homunculus, a brain area in the precentral gyrus of the cerebral cortex that controls the fingers, the legs, the arms, and so forth. Neural pathways project from this primary motor cortex to the rest of the body. Freud imagined his self as growing out of this motor representation of the outside, acting self—a not terribly far-fetched idea, from an evolutionary standpoint. This is also why Freud saw the ego as managing access to the outside world: It did so by controlling the movement of the physical body.

The ego's primary function is to judge and reason. It learns rationality and reasoning from its trial-and-error experience with the outside world. One element of the ego is consciousness, which Freud defined as a sense organ for the inside of the mind:

> We have formed the idea that in each individual there is a coherent organization of mental processes; and we call this his *ego*. It is to this ego that consciousness is attached; the ego controls the approaches to motility—that is, to the discharge of excitations into the external world; it is the mental agency which supervises all its own constituent processes, and which goes to sleep at night, though even then it exercises the censorship on dreams. (Freud, 1923/1960, p. 7)

Although the ego contains this conscious, acting self, some of its rationality and planning is also unconscious. Indeed, the ego helps enlarge the unconscious by repressing material that is unpleasant to it (Freud, 1923/1960, p. 7).

The Dialogical Self

A rather different perspective on the conscious self is Hermans and colleagues' **dialogical self**. This is a version of a normal person's self-as-agency, but instead of one stable, organized self, the dialogical self shifts around the person, inhabiting and breathing action and perspective into other fictional entities (Hermans, Kempen, & van Loon, 1992). For example, if you have an imaginary conversation with your father, the dialogical self is first you, then your father, and then you again, and so on. This self-model provides a more flexible view of the traditional self-as-knower. The knower not only knows himself, but also the imagined character of many others. In some ways, the dialogical self occupies a kind of gray area between the traditional self-as-knower and non-conscious parts of oneself that may also participate in controlling the mind.

To the modern theorist concerned with the self-as-knower, the exciting thing about the self is that it is the part of the person that can exert control over the rest of the person to change it according to its hopes and dreams. It is the part of personality that decides among careers of doctor, lawyer, or chief. Should some people be cast by disposition and environment into the dark boundary between mental health and madness, or between goodness and evil, it is the self that can at some point marshal itself to choose between the two (e.g., Epstein, 1972; James, 1892).

What Does It Mean for the Self To Be Conscious?

What Is Consciousness?

What Does the Word "Consciousness" Mean?

What does it mean for the self to be conscious? The origins of the word "consciousness" can provide some insight into what the term means. The term consciousness originates from the Latin *conscientia*, which refers to the mutual understanding or joint knowledge of a number of people who are engaged in a common goal or plan. For example, two people plotting a coup-d'état would share *conscientia*, as would two people plotting a surprise birthday party (Baruss, 1986-7; Natsoulis, 1986-7).

It is only a short jump from shared knowledge between people to shared knowledge within a person. Perhaps the idea of sharing knowledge with yourself seems odd, but what about when you talk to yourself? In such an instance, one part of the individual is sharing information with the other. Who is doing the talking? …the listening? This interaction between two parts of the self seems quite a bit closer to the idea of consciousness because the listener must be aware of what the talker is saying, and such awareness seems close to consciousness (Hilgard, 1977).

What Is Consciousness?

Many philosophers of mind divide what we mean today by consciousness into three aspects: self-awareness, access to information, and subjective experience (Block, 1995; Jackendoff, 1987; Pinker, 1997, pp. 134-148). **Self-awareness** means reflective awareness rather than simple awareness—that is, awareness that reflects on itself. One psychologist describes self-awareness as involving a realization such as: "Not only can I feel pain and see red, I can think to myself, 'Hey, here I am, Steve Pinker, feeling pain and seeing red!'" (Pinker, 1997, p. 134).

A second sense of consciousness is to have **access to information**. For example, if you tell someone what is on your mind right now, it might include your current worries, your delights, and your plans for the day. It would not include the internal flows of your neurotransmitters, the patterns of neural firings in your brain, or even the relative activation of various concepts in memory. You have access to some material of the mind, but no access to neural-level activities (Dennett, 1978, pp. 150-160).

One aspect of this access to information is that consciousness puts some ideas under the spotlight of attention. Consciousness may be adaptive precisely because it focuses attention on important matters. Think of the mind as perpetually engaged in trade-offs in taking in and attending to the world. It can either do a lot of things poorly, or a few things very well. Consciousness provides a working area in which a few things can be thought about well—or at least as well as possible.

Consciousness seems critical to providing comprehensive information processing. When something is in our consciousness, we can think relatively clearly about it, define it in detail, and give it the thought it deserves. Matters outside consciousness, by contrast, will be unglued, floating, and in the periphery. It is peripheral processing that leads to common cognitive errors—seeing "World's Worst Coffee" on a sign, when in fact it reads, "World's Best Coffee," or seeing "Brothel Hotel," instead of "Brother's Hotel" (Pinker, 1997, p. 142). When we are surprised by seeing such signs, we attend to them, and consciousness resolves the problem (Duncan & Humphreys, 1989; Marcel, 1983).

Many theorists of consciousness suggest that it serves an adaptive, evolutionary purpose. Its role in survival is to place the really hard problems in life on center stage and to subject them to scrutiny, so as to be able to respond in a flexible way to the issues those problems raise (Baars & McGovern, 1994; Ornstein, 1986; 1991; Rozin, 1976). Consciousness, in other words, is the part of the self that operates so that when your mental models fail and you need to revise them, you can bring your attention, caring, and thought together to converge on the issue and come up with a better way of operating.

But the core essence of consciousness for Pinker (and others) is **sentience**. Sentience refers to the internal, subjective experience: That feeling of what it is like to be someone (Pinker, 1997). This feeling of consciousness includes an awareness of a rich field of sensation coupled with a direct sense of personal ownership of that field, in the midst of which is the spotlight of attention. A person who is conscious and attentive also may sense that he can do something about what he attends to: If he is focused on an ant crawling up his leg, for example, he can choose to let the ant continue, flick it off, or to kill it.

Consciousness links things together in a rich field of sensation; it integrates together sounds, sights, and ideas, so that we see a tree blowing in the wind rather than fragments of sensations. Moreover, consciousness moves from idea to idea, sometimes rushing forward from thought to thought, sometimes bending in an unexpected direction, and at other times slowing down; William James compared its meanderings to a stream (James, 1892; Singer, 1975). Consciousness also integrates is a feeling of self-hood. There is something warm and personal about our own stream of consciousness, and something ultimately impersonal about the streams of consciousness of others. Our own stream of consciousness provides us with our own private eyes on ourselves and the world. It is comfortable, cozy, and ours alone. True, when we go to sleep it goes away, but when we wake up, it always returns to us rather than to someone else (James, 1892).

Scientific Accounting for the Feeling of Consciousness

Consider the following thought experiment. You are seated in a chamber while your brain is being scanned. The experimenter presents you with cards of different colors. Each time she shows you a blue-colored card, a particular part of your brain, which is imaged on the computer monitor, lights up. That, the experimenter says, pointing to the illuminated part of your brain on the monitor, is your consciousness of the color blue. "But no," you say, "that is just a part of my brain being activated when my eyes register blue, it does not convey my conscious feeling of blue!" (Flanagan, 2002).

Where does this feeling of conscious subjective sentience come from? How can this internal subject "blueness" be explained? For the subjective realist, it comes from being hooked up to his own neurons. Subjective realism provides a philosophical integration of the objective scientific understanding of consciousness as it exists thus far, and the subjective experience of consciousness. From the perspective of **subjective realism**, all mental events—including subjective states—are caused by some set of physical events. At the same time, many objectively real objects in the world also have a subjective feeling to them (Flanagan, 2002, p. 89).

Water would be H_20 whether a person was there to witness it or not; it objectively exists. The wetness of water, however, also has a subjective feel that can only be realized by experiencing it through being "hooked up" to the human nervous system, and touching water through it. Subjective realism states that people have certain subjective feelings—including consciousness—that reflect what it is like to be hooked up to a human nervous system operating in a particular fashion, such as being awake, alert, and perceiving something (Flanagan, 2002, p. 89). Someday science may develop a better language for how the subjective experience of blue emerges from being hooked up to the nervous system. For now, say the subjective realists, this is the best that can be said (Flanagan, 2002, p. 87).

Is Consciousness of Recent Origin?

It is not entirely clear when the concept of consciousness first emerged in the West. Early biblical and Greek writings appear to ignore the concept of consciousness. The fact that early records have so few mentions of consciousness has led some scholars to question whether or not consciousness, as we currently understand and perceive it, is of relatively recent origin in the evolution of the human mind. Julian Jaynes (1976) suggested the radical hypothesis that people were not fully conscious in the modern sense of the word, until consciousness evolved some time between the eighth and second centuries B.C.E.. Before that, there was little sense of identity, and people often mistook their inner voices for other people, or even Gods. He traces the emergence of consciousness in various literatures. For example, Amos is one of the earliest books—of Biblical literature—dated back to the 8th century B.C.E. (Jaynes, 1976, p. 295). The book of Amos includes no mention of a mind, or of thinking or thoughts, or of feeling, or of understanding. Amos describes himself as minimally as possible, a shepherd, a "gatherer of sycamore fruit." Nor, in a sense, does Amos even speak. He pronounces, and after each pronouncement, announces, "Thus speaks the Lord!" (Jaynes, 1976, p. 296). For example, Amaziah, the priest of Bethel, reported that Amos was raising a conspiracy against Israel. Amaziah tells Amos directly to leave the land: "…Get out, you seer! Go back to the land of Judah." In response, Amos answers in the third person, saying he is acting on the basis of another's commands:

> …I was neither a prophet nor a prophet's son, but I was a shepherd, and I also took care of sycamore-fig trees. But the Lord took me from tending the flock and said to me, 'Go, prophesy to my people Israel.' Now then, hear the word of the LORD.' (Amos 7:10-12)

There is little sense of personal awareness in the above passage and others like it. By contrast, the book of Ecclesiastes has been dated from the second century, B.C.E.. Here we see personality in all of its introspective grandeur. The author of Ecclesiastes wants to share his knowledge, and teach it to others (Kushner, 1986, p. 36). He says:

> I thought to myself, "Look, I have grown and increased in wisdom more than anyone who has ruled over Jerusalem before me; I have experienced much of wisdom and knowledge." Then I applied myself to the understanding of wisdom, and also of madness and folly, but I learned that this, too, is a chasing after the wind. For with much wisdom comes much sorrow; the more knowledge, the more grief.

> I thought in my heart, "Come now, I will test you with pleasure to find out what is good." But that also proved to be meaningless… I wanted to see what was worthwhile for men to do under heaven during the few days of their lives. [Ecclesiastes 2:1-3]

The contrast between the 8th Century B. C. E. Amos and the 2nd century Ecclesiastes could not be more striking. Here, finally, is a modern-seeming personality talking to us. This same transition to consciousness appears in the literary works of the ancient Greeks, and other peoples of the Middle East, the Mediterranean, and elsewhere (e.g., Jaynes, 1976, p. 74).

Since Jaynes' time, others have reported a waxing and waning of the sense of self. For example, some social psychologists have suggested that peoples' identities were so fixed in the Middle Ages that self-definition and self-conception was minimized. Identity became an important problem only with the onset of more modern social mobility, which encouraged people to make decisions for their own social welfare (Baumeister, 1987).

The Brain and Consciousness

"Neural transmissions just seem like the wrong kind of materials with which to bring consciousness into the world." – Colin McGinn (1950)

A number of theories have been proposed as to how the brain generates conscious awareness. The bicameral theory of mind is one such idea. The **bicameral mind** refers to the fact that speech production and reception are split across the right and left hemispheres of the brain. It envisions a mind based on two working areas of the brain that may only sometimes be in communication with each other. Wernicke's area is a left-hemisphere structure responsible for understanding the meaning of speech. Some believe there evolved a parallel area in the right hemisphere that was responsible for hearing interior voices and understanding them. Jaynes, who proposed this theory, believes that sometime after 800 B.C.E., people began to understand that voices from the right hemisphere were their own thinking processes "talking to them." Before that, however, they had hallucinated the voices of gods. It was this interior talking that evolved into present-day consciousness (Jaynes, 1979, Chapter 5). Although Jayne's tracing of the change in perspective in literature is provocative, relatively little attention has been afforded his brain theory. Rather, contemporary psycho-biologists have developed their own ideas.

Crick & Koch (1995), for example, have suggested that in looking for consciousness, scientists should identify areas of the brain that only operate when the organism is awake and alert. And because consciousness integrates material, we should look for synchronized neural firing from many parts of the brain. A number of neuropsychologists have suggested such holistic patterns for consciousness (e.g., Pribram, 1978). Kosslyn & Koenig (1992) use a simple and resonant metaphor, describing consciousness as a chord being struck by all the individual brain activities (individual notes) sounding at a given moment.

Brain scanning techniques have allowed for a few pieces of information about the brain and consciousness. First, the brain must be active for subjective reports of consciousness to be present. This is important because it establishes a brain-consciousness link. Second, areas of the cortex need to be active for consciousness, particularly the frontal lobes. Beyond that, the support system for consciousness seems to involve much of nervous system, including, potentially, the limbic system, certain areas of the visual cortex, and even nerves from the skin, joints, and gut. This is not an integrated answer yet, but advances in this area are occurring so quickly that much more may be known in a few years (Carter, 2002, pp. 105-106; Gazzaniga & Heatherton, 2003, p. 269).

Consciousness involves more than just watching, of course; it also appears to exert will (Pinker, 1997, p. 135).

Does the Self Possess Free Will?

Our consciousness feels heightened when we are making a difficult personal decision. To be sure, we make "decisions" every day that are not conscious. We may put on our socks without thinking, and turn toward the doorway to go outside with little conscious reflection at all. Important decisions, however, often require conscious attention. William James described several types of decisions, roughly according to the degree that **will** is involved. Will is the self-conscious exertion of mental effort to perform an act (James, 1892, pp. 429-433).

In easy decisions requiring little will, we may recognize that one alternative is simply much better than the other for fairly obvious reasons. Choosing a job we have the skills for, will pay well, will gain us respect, and that is convenient to travel to, requires little consideration. In a second kind of decision (according to James) outside pressures are present and we don't much mind, and go with whatever is desired. For example, if our friend strongly prefers that we wear the striped shirt rather than the solid, well…why not?

In another of James' decision types, however, the person's will is strongly experienced. In this type of decision, the alternatives are kept firmly in mind as we consider the possible outcomes. We recognize that we are having difficulty deciding, perhaps because we know that making the decision will require a price-to-pay, although "it may be better for the long run." James writes (p. 433):

> …it is a desolate and acrid sort of act, an entrance into a lonesome moral
> wilderness…here both alternatives are steadily held in view, and in the very act of
> murdering the vanquished possibility the chooser realizes how much in that instant he is
> making himself lose…the sense of inward effort with which the act is
> accompanied…makes of it an altogether peculiar sort of mental phenomenon.

James (1892) acknowledged that the existence of free will could not be proven, but the subjective experience of free will, he noted, certainly existed in those difficult decisions.

The Debate Over Free Will versus Determinism

"Good resolutions are useless attempts to interfere with scientific laws. Their origin is pure vanity. Their result is absolutely nil." – Oscar Wilde (1854-1900)

The idea of **free will** in its purest form, says that there exists a part of mental life that is itself a "prime mover" that is entirely unconstrained and can choose whatever seems best to itself (Flanagan, 2002, p. 103). The free will concept was stated clearly by the philosopher Descartes (1596-1650), who argued that there existed, in each person, a soul that belonged to a spiritual rather than material world, and that could cause the person to do things. This soul and its free will were independent of any pressures that the body (including the brain) might place on it. The will existed, instead, on a spiritual level (Descartes, 1641/1968, Fourth Meditation, p 137).

The concept of **determinism** is often contrasted with the idea of free will. Strict determinism is the belief that everything in the universe is caused by something—or some set of things—that came before it. It too had religious origins. John Calvin was a 16th-century French theologian who believed that God is eternal and he chose each human being's fate before the creation of the world. So, some Calvinists were saved and some not— from before the Universe began rather than by their own good deeds. Calvinists, it is often said, monitor their own behavior quite closely to find out what God had decided earlier about their eternal fate.

The debate went on. Jacobus Arminius, a 16th-century Dutch theologian, argued with Calvin's doctrine, proposing that people exercised **free will** and could determine their own salvation, if they were sufficiently faithful to Christianity and its teachings.

Scientists in general and personality psychologists in particular are similarly split over free will versus determinism. Most scientists profess to believe in determinism, probably because it initially appeared more scientifically supportable. Both Sigmund Freud, the founder of psychodynamic theory, and Carl Rogers, an eminent humanistic psychologist, professed strict determinism (Freud, 1920/1943, p. 27; Rogers, 1957/1989, pp. 417-418). On the other hand, Henry Murray, who studied motives, not only believed in free will, but viewed those scientists who wished to deny it as dangerously imperiling the future of humanity. The idea that one can "pull oneself up by the bootstraps" or "exercise independent judgment," or "better oneself"—these traditional values and more depend on the idea that people exercise some free will and are their own causal agents. Murray opined that his colleagues who believed in strict determinism made:

> …no provisions for creativity, no admitted margins of freedom…no fitting recognitions of the power of ideals, no bases for selfless action, no ground at all for any hope that the human race can save itself from the fatality that now confronts it. (Murray, 1962, p. 53).

Finally, in a manner calculated to spin philosophers in their graves, Abraham Maslow, a humanistic psychologist, viewed free will as an individual differences variable that some people possessed and others did not (Maslow, 1970, pp. 161-162).

Although the physical and biological sciences may have appeared to rely on strict determinism early in the 20th century, by mid-century, matters were not so clear. In physics, Heisenberg's Uncertainty Principle states that you cannot measure a subatomic particle accurately enough to know both its position and velocity at the same time: They are, effectively, undetermined (Hawking, 1998). Biophysicists have suggested that there is a kind of "trickle up" of indeterminacy from the subatomic level to the level of consciousness and free will.

In one version of this theory, activities at the synaptic gap may be influenced by subatomic influences because the gaps are so small. Energies created by thoughts may influence the synaptic gap given that "these potentials can be influenced by infinitesimal amounts of energy on the order of quantum events." (Pelletier, 1985, p. 134).

Although the above mystery is intriguing, it may not provide a very satisfying answer as to whether free will exists, and if so, how it can be free. Perhaps we have to live with William James' assertion that for now, at least, "The fact is that the question of free-will is insoluble on strictly psychological grounds…" (James, 1892, p. 458).

With no easy solution to the free will—determinism debate in sight, some philosophers of psychology, and psychologists, have suggested it is posed in the wrong terms. These theorists suggest a switch to a more modest problem that is both closer to what the average person means by free will, and easier to address as both a philosophical and empirical problem. Free will, as Descartes and others described it, was a prime mover of the person uninfluenced by either learning or genes—but that is a rather naïve statement of what people most people believe when they speak about free will. What most people mean by free will is a much more limited form of free action. Free will versus determinism is replaced, in this approach, by a distinction between voluntary versus involuntary action. Voluntary action, it is argued, still permits us to have the opportunity to improve ourselves and our world, and to experience the sense of accomplishment and self-respect such improvements will bring. At the same time, it is consistent with a scientific (e.g., deterministic) outlook (Flanagan, 2002, p. 103).

Freedom from the Free Will Debate

According to this position, most people do not mean "free will"—in Descartes' sense—when they say they believe in free will. Most people don't claim to be original causes of events, uninfluenced by anything in their history or their genes. Rather, people who claim to have free will believe in the possibility of voluntary action, and along with it, self-control, self-expression, individuality, and that a person can rationally deliberate and be morally accountable. These qualities collectively are probably more accurately called something like "voluntary action" rather than free will. A more meaningful distinction can be drawn between voluntary and involuntary action (Flanagan, 2002, pp. 143-144).

Voluntary Cause and Control

A voluntary movement can be said to take place when a person causes it. (Note, unlike the case of free will, the person causing the voluntary action may be prompted to do so from past cues). If we watch the balls on a billiard table, for example, we say that one ball caused another to move. People generally identify a cause of a movement when three qualities are present: the cause precedes the movement, the cause is consistent with the movement, and the cause occurs in the absence of some competing explanation (Mischotte, 1963). We noticed the first ball strike the second before the second moved—that is—the first ball's hit of the second preceded its movement. We noticed that balls hitting one another often move, and we noticed no other events that would cause the second ball to move (e.g., no strong person lifted one end of the billiard table). So, if one billiard ball hits a second ball, and that one begins to roll, we say the first billiard ball caused the second to move. This same experience of cause and effect—looking at what happens first, then second, etc.—is often read into the voluntary actions a person takes (Presson & Benassi, 1996).

To illustrate this point, Wegner and colleagues (1999) created ambiguous situations in which participants believed they had voluntarily "willed" something—caused it—to happen. Before describing the experiment, it helps to remember that an **experimental confederate** is someone who appears to be a regular participant in an experiment, but who is actually allied with the experimenter and follows the experimenter's instructions.

In one of Wegner's studies, a research participant and confederate together controlled the action of a cursor on a computer screen. To do so, both students sat across from one another, holding on to respective sides of a floating board that controlled the computer mouse. As they moved the board together on the desk, the cursor would move across the screen in response to the board. Various objects were pictured on the computer screen such as swans, dinosaurs, monkeys, and the like.

For a given trial, the real participant and confederate were told to allow the cursor to come to rest every 30 seconds or so on an object on the screen. The real participant heard background music, and at a given point, the name of an object on the computer screen was repeated over the headphones. The real participant probably assumed in most cases that the confederate was hearing exactly the same thing. In fact, however, the confederate was moving the board (or allowing the real participant to move the board) directly in response to pre-recorded instructions left by the experimenter and played back on the headphones. During some trials, the confederate allowed the real participant to stop the board and cursor it controlled. During other trials, the confederate controlled the board, often so that the cursor stopped at the picture of an object the participant had heard named on the tape.

As soon as the board came to rest, the real participants rated how much they had controlled where the cursor stopped, from "I intended to make the stop" (rated as 100) to "I allowed the stop to happen" (rated at 0). As you have probably guessed by now, participants consistently believed they had caused the stop when it had actually been the confederate—following recorded instructions—who stopped the cursor. When the object's name was read over the headphones just a few seconds before the forced stop, the participants had an even stronger (and mistaken) sense of control. From such experiments, Wegner concludes that, "the experience of will is the way our minds portray their operation to us, then, not their actual operation." The real causes of behavior, he argues, and others have shown, are often unconscious and automatic (e.g., Bargh, 1997; 1999; Wegner & Wheatley, 1999, p. 490).

If Wegner et al.'s studies don't make you think twice about your experience of voluntary behavior, consider the mind-boggling finding that people's voluntary actions often begin before they are conscious of them. That is, people begin a movement before they are conscious that they are going to voluntarily make it. Libet (1985) took advantage of the finding that the brain exhibits a slow negative shift in electrical potential near the scalp about a second or more before the person emits a voluntary motor movement (Kornhuber & Deecke, 1965). Libet set up an experiment in which he started a clock and asked participants to notice when they became aware of deciding to move their finger. As it turned out, their brains emitted a negative electrical shift first, indicating that the move was about to take place. Only 300-400 milliseconds after that did participants became aware of deciding to move their finger. That finding and others like it indicate that the brain moves a finger before the individual is conscious of "willing" it. The participants may have thought that they had willed the finger movement. In fact, however, the movement began automatically a few milliseconds before they became aware of the thought! The above findings open up the possibility that a lot more is controlling voluntary action than the conscious self.

Are There Alternatives to the Conscious Self?

Agencies

The self, then, is conscious, and yet that consciousness is neither unitary nor always accurate, particularly when voluntary self-control is being monitored. The self may overestimate the voluntary control it can exercise. If the self is not in control, then what is? Most commonly, non-conscious brain processes or environmental cues bring about such behaviors. Simple motives can direct the individual toward some aim and away from others, with or without awareness. Such simpler parts exert more-or-less automatic influences on personality.

There is, however, a second possibility that has often been suggested by personality psychologists. This is the operation of a kind of organized "sub-personality" that knits together various functions and operates in partial autonomy from the rest. This class of personality parts have been called **agencies**—and the self is a special, conscious instance of one (e.g., Mayer, 1995; 1998). Agencies are parts of personality that are organized, central to the operation of personality, and that periodically take control of personality and govern its actions.

The most central feature of agencies is that they are **semi-autonomous** agents—parts of personality that act as if they possess "minds of their own." The agency is, in other words, a hypothetical subpart of personality large enough to include groups of motives, ways of thinking, and goals. An agency can be the "conscious self"—self-consciously deciding whether to study harder or to go to a party. Or an agency may be a set of unconscious impulses, connected together and stealthily revealing alternative intentions.

Some evidence for agencies comes from observations of people with **dissociative disorders.** Dissociative disorders represent a class of psychiatric diagnoses in which the identity seems split into multiple parts, each of which has some control over the totality of the person, but seems to operate on its own. Agencies began with the understanding that the memory system is made up of many associations between ideas. Just as ideas could become associated in memory, so can they become disassociated—that is, separated from one another, if some ideas were extremely painful to think of. If so, then whole aggregations of ideas might stay out of consciousness.

Such disassociated ideas, however, would not necessarily go away. Rather, these ideas could, in some cases, continue to operate within personality (Perry & Laurence, 1984, p. 28). Subconscious agencies are sometimes labeled "automatisms." These operate like a second self, cut off from the first. For example, the French neurologist Jean Janet, a contemporary of Freud, had a patient, Irene, who had been a caretaker of her ailing mother, who then died while under her care. The trauma of her mother's death appeared to split Irene's mind into two states. When she awoke from sleeping after her mother's death, she could not remember that her mother had died and, indeed, behaved as if she was very much alive. In a hypnotic trance, however, she could remember everything that had happened surrounding her mother's death.

Remarking on the mystery of her waking state, she noted:

> I know very well my mother is dead since I have been told so several times, since I see her no more, and since I am in mourning; but I really feel astonished at it. When did she die? (cited in Hilgard, 1977, p. 5)

Janet interpreted this as reflecting a divided, or dissociated, mind.

Alters

Those with **dissociative identity disorders (DID)**—the current term for people with multiple personalities (American Psychiatric Association, 1994)—exhibit more than one identity. Each identity is called an **alter.** An "alter" is a contraction for alternative personality, and these, too, are examples of agencies— albeit unusual ones. People with Dissociative Identity Disorder exhibit different behaviors depending upon which identity (e.g., alter) is in control at the time. Each identity within a person may express distinct facial expressions, speech characteristics, gestures, styles of conversation and attitudes (Miller, 1989; Putnum, 1991; Rifkin et al., 1998). There also is some evidence for differences in brain patterns depending upon which alter is active (Cocker et al., 1994).

When Julie, a single mother who brought her son in for counseling because he was having trouble in school, the therapist saw little unusual about the case. During the sixth week of counseling, however, Julie told the therapist she would like to introduce him to someone. He expected to meet a teacher or friend in the waiting room. Instead, however, Julie closed her eyes, and when she opened them again, spoke in a different voice: that of Jerrie, a gay business woman, who remarked, "I wish Julie would stop smoking." Still later in the session, a third personality, Jenny, emerged.

Once this was out in the open, Julie-Jenny-Jerrie's son, Adam, made great strides. He learned to accept his "two" mothers (Jenny stayed "inside" most the time), noting, "Mother is two people who keep going in and out, but both of them love me." Unfortunately, shortly thereafter, the various alters engaged in a pitched battle with one another, and as a consequence, Julie left town, unable to communicate further with the psychologist. In this case, each alter behaved as if it was acting autonomously (Davis & Osherson, 1977).

Cases of people with Dissociative Identity Disorder are very rare. One key contributing factor to the disorder may be an individual's general tendency toward dissociation, which is reflected not only by the disorder itself, but also by extreme susceptibility to hypnosis (virtually all such patients are hypnotizable), and the presence of an early traumatic experience. Indeed, one model for the disorder is that children undergoing trauma may use self-hypnosis in order to enter into altered states and create alternative identities (Putnam & Carlson, 1998).

The Id, Ego, and Superego as Partly Unconscious Agencies

One of Freud's suggestions was that the normal personality, too, is split among agencies: The id, the ego, and the superego (Freud, 1923).

For Freud, the **id** included animal-like motives and emotions, sensations of wishes, emotion related to those wishes, and non-verbal images. This id, according to Freud, "owns" all the mental energy when the person is born. It draws on our unconscious energies. The **unconscious** is a cauldron of unacceptable but powerful unsocialized impulses—of sexual and aggressive motives (or instincts, as he called them), and related, uncontrolled emotions such as envy, jealousy, desire, and hatred. The id's energy is derived from sexual needs to reproduce and aggressive needs used to protect its survival.

We have already discussed the ego earlier in this chapter. The ego is partly **conscious.** That is, it is the part containing (we would say today) the stream of consciousness, a person is aware of. Large portions of the ego are also, however, unconscious. The ego controls bodily movement, among other functions. The ego thinks rationally and tries to satisfy the id's impulses as best it can, given the constraints of outside reality— and its other master, the **superego.**

The superego grows out of the ego, and is composed of two parts: the ego-ideal, which is what the ego aspires to be, and the conscience, which includes societal rules that govern the ego. Collectively, the superego is responsible for the "shoulds" of personality— what the person should and should not do, should and should not be. The superego developed from learning within the family and identifying with the moral codes of parents (Freud, 1923/1960, p. 26). Some of these ideas are captured in Figure 7-1.

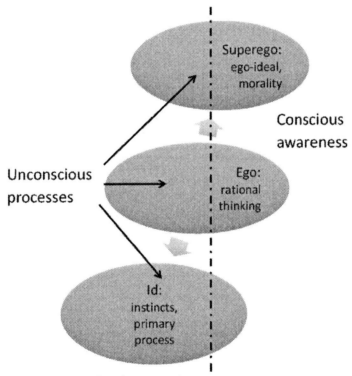

Figure 7-1 Freud's id, ego and superego. Freud viewed the ego as struggling between animal instincts—the "id"— on the one hand (bottom right), and social requirements for moral, idealized qualities—the "superego"— on the other hand (top right). A person's unconscious mental processes (left) complicated the process because an individual's unseen mental life is difficult if not impossible to control. One goal of psychotherapy is to make some of the unconscious accessible to the conscious portions of the ego.

For Freud, each of the entities could variously take over control of personality, and the possibility that some alternative mental structures might do so is worth contemplating in the context of considering the conscious self.

Today, there exist updated divisions of mind that will be examined in the chapter on Structural Organization (Chapter 8).

Are there really agencies? Contemporary psychologists don't find the split-personality metaphor of the id, ego, and superego entirely useful anymore. True, the metaphor of a "split" personality does get across certain ideas of conflict in the mind that are accurate enough. The id, ego, and superego, however, don't seem to be distinctly present and to act as true, organized, global agents as some had thought. Rather the mind is made up of many conflicting parts. That said, it does make sense to divide personality into broad areas of functioning. Certain divisions of mind such as the id, ego, and superego may be somewhat outmoded, but other similar divisions may work fairly well. Some of these will be examined in the next chapter on "How the Parts of Personality Fit Together." Meanwhile, agencies remain one possible way to divide personality—and they may make sense to employ in such cases as dissociative disorders. Their usefulness in describing more common forms of personality is best interpreted as describing distinct areas of function rather than as "sub-personalities." More will be said on this in the next chapter.

How Is the Conscious Self Expressed?

Contents of Consciousness

People vary in the contents of the consciousness they experience, as they vary in other parts of their personalities. Three aspects of the conscious self are examined here: The contents of consciousness, the structured flow of consciousness, and levels of consciousness.

Might there be something we can say about the contents of consciousness itself? The contents of conscious experiences are called **qualia** (singular, **quale**). Qualia are the sounds or sights, thoughts, or urges that pass through our conscious awareness. We all see a banana, but whether we all register it the same way in consciousness is a matter of philosophical debate. The easier question to address is what we are aware of. Hurlburt (2001) gave research participants pagers and asked them to record what they were conscious of at the moment the beepers went off (the beepers were arranged to signal at random intervals. Hurlburt found that people's most common qualia—arising 38% of the time—involved "thinking something" but without any clear words, images, or feelings. Next most common, at 32%, was inner speech—talking to oneself in one's own voice. Sensory awareness—itches, pains, and tickles, for example—was third most common at 27%. Following sensory qualia were emotions and related feelings at 26%, and perceiving remembered and imagined images at 23%. The rest of the qualia most often involved experiences secondary to doing something like reading, watching TV, or cooking.

One likely subject of that inner speech and feelings are current concerns. **Current concerns** are thoughts and feelings related to goals that an individual is seeking, is trying to meet, or is in the process of abandoning. For example, during the summer, a Boston Red Sox fan will have current concerns related to the baseball team's progress and will be interested in everything from the history of the team to its present coaching practices, and of course, the players and opposition teams. Alternatively, a person who wants to get married will attend closely to tips on how to select an eligible partner, how to introduce the question of marriage, and what makes a good marriage. In one study, students were instructed to listen to two narratives, one presented to their right ear and one presented to their left ear, and to flip a switch back and forth to indicate which one they were listening to. Students overwhelmingly chose to listen to narratives that were related to their own current concerns (e.g., the Red Sox), as opposed to someone else's (e.g., marriage; Klinger, 1978).

One form consciousness sometimes takes that has received considerable attention is the daydream. Daydreams appear to be a baseline quality of consciousness; they fill in the gaps not occupied by directed, working thoughts. Daydreams typically have clear beginnings and endings. They are composed of common behaviors the person typically carries out. Although daydreams tell stories that reflect a person's goals, they often lack a disciplined focus: they often disregard the required preconditions and realistic, concrete series of actions needed to reach an objective (Klinger, 1999; Singer, 1966; Varendonck, 1921).

Another form that consciousness sometimes takes is that of the rumination. Ruminations are repetitive thoughts associated with goals that appear to be blocked or otherwise difficult to reach. Ruminations often involve feelings of anger, sadness, and fear, and may reflect a person trying to disengage from a goal. They are often associated with depression—although one notable exception is that people often ruminate when they are falling in love (Lyubomirsky & Nolen-Hoeksema, 1993; Martin & Tesser, 1996).

The Structure of Consciousness and Flow

The contents of consciousness can be diffuse—as in daydreams or ruminations—or structured. A scenario familiar to many adolescents is the sense of boredom and lack of structure they often experience, in which there is little around to challenge them. The teenager often comes back from school, say, drops his or her books in the bedroom, and after getting a snack, heads for the phone or goes out to be with friends. If nothing is going on, the student may sit and listen to the stereo or watch TV. These forms of entertainment are too unchallenging, however, and his or her mind wanders to problems and worries, further sapping mental energy. By this time, if the teenager is tempted to choose a more challenging activity—reading a book or practicing a sport—his or her resolve is unlikely to last long.

Such states invite daydreaming and rumination—the shadowy phantoms that intrude on the unstructured mind. Teenagers are beset by various worries—about their appearance, social life, and future chances. The rumination increases the individual's negativity and further depresses any motivation, in a downward spiral of boredom and depression. At this point, the teen's further choices are limited: more TV or music, or talking to a friend he or she has just spoken to. Worse choices may involve drugs or destructive behavior (Csikszentmihalyi, 1990, pp. 171-172).

One way out of this dilemma is to structure consciousness through a **flow** experience (Csikszentmihalyi, 1990; 1997; Nakamura & Csikszentmihalyi, 2002). Flow states involve an alteration in consciousness that includes the simultaneous concentration on a task with a loss of self-consciousness, the merging of action and awareness, and an accompanying sense of timelessness. Different people will experience flow as they engage in different activities. But given the right person and right level of activity almost any pursuit can create flow.

Consider this example of flow from a dancer who describes how it feels when a performance is going well:

> Your concentration is very complete. Your mind isn't wandering, you are not thinking of something else; you are totally involved in what you are doing... Your energy is flowing very smoothly. You feel relaxed, comfortable, and energetic. (Csikszentmihalyi, 1990, p. 53)

This description of flow comes from the great hurdler, Edwin Moses:

> Your mind has to be absolutely clear. The fact that you have to cope with your opponent, jet lag, different foods, sleeping in hotels, and personal problems has to be erased from consciousness—as if they didn't exist. (Csikszentmihalyi, 1990, p. 59)

A student studying may become engaged and engrossed in the material being learned—and forget that she is studying altogether. In each case notice that when the person is entirely involved in the task the sense of self is in the background. A person's concentration is focused on what is occurring, and the action and the self have merged.

One aspect that makes flow likely to attain is the presence of clear goals or feedback for the task. For a beginner, this may involve working toward a standard laid out by a teacher. For a great artist or thinker, though, the standards may be entirely internal. An experienced painter who is painting, for example, will know after each brush stroke whether it works or not (Csikszentmihalyi, 1990, p. 56). Flow also involves a sense of control.

> A dancer described her flow experience as involving relaxation in the midst of a powerful feeling of control, expansion, and oneness with the world. The dancer felt as though, in that state of oneness, she was prepared and willing to create something of grace and harmony. (Csikszentmihalyi, 1990)

Often, flow will have accompanying it a high sense of organization and coordination. Surgeons often say during a difficult operation that they experience their team as members of a carefully choreographed ballet operating together. That is, rather than a sense of control, per se, there is a feeling of harmony and power (Csikszentmihalyi, 1990, p. 65).

Finally, when a person is in the midst of flow, time is transformed. On the one hand, each moment can be appreciated, and on the other, the entire experience seems to be over in just a moment. A woman who enters flow as she is writing might become so aware of the details of her essay that she proceeds through the paragraphs at just the right pace without feeling rushed. In the end, she may discover that much more time may have passed than she had realized.

How People Attain a Flow State

In the midst of a society that with myriad rules and conventions for how to behave, the individual who has a structured consciousness can behave independently of momentary and even long-term pressures, in order to follow a path that he believes is right. From the above descriptions, it might seem as if flow states just happen unpredictably. But Csikszentmihalyi believes that the entry into flow states is under a person's control. According to Csikszentmihalyi, the flow state will occur when there is a match between an individual's level of skills, and the difficulty of a task that is undertaken. When the individual is doing something too easy, she will feel bored, when she is doing something too hard, she will feel anxious. But when the individual chooses the right level of task difficulty, she will enter into the flow experience. Csikszentmihalyi represents this encounter with a task as illustrated in Figure 7-2.

Csikszentmihalyi (1990, p. 174) recounts the instance of Susan Butcher, a prize-winning Iditarod dog-sled racer. When she is not racing, she lives in isolation in a cabin 25 miles away from the nearest town. Within that isolation, however, she keeps her consciousness structured by setting tasks for herself in the caring of her one hundred and fifty huskies. Most notably, she tries to get to know each dog by name and by its preferences and disposition. Of course, the tasks of everyday living in such isolation keep her engaged as well: In hunting and food gathering, and in keeping the dogs from predators. By setting herself such a routine, Butcher keeps her consciousness structured on manageable tasks and is able to excel and attain flow, and hence, great satisfaction in her chosen pursuits.

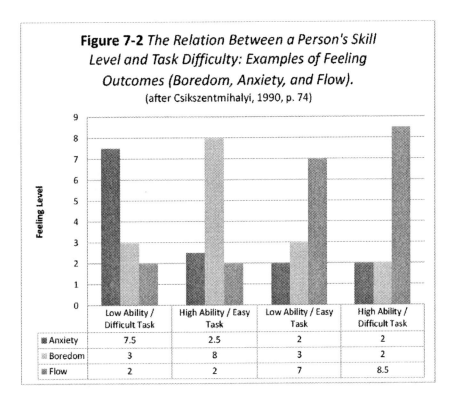

Figure 7-2 *The Relation Between a Person's Skill Level and Task Difficulty: Examples of Feeling Outcomes (Boredom, Anxiety, and Flow).*
(after Csikszentmihalyi, 1990, p. 74)

	Low Ability / Difficult Task	High Ability / Easy Task	Low Ability / Easy Task	High Ability / Difficult Task
Anxiety	7.5	2.5	2	2
Boredom	3	8	3	2
Flow	2	2	7	8.5

Levels of Consciousness

Another aspect of how people differ in consciousness concerns their levels of consciousness. Recall that consciousness is sometimes defined simply as attention or awareness. This might be called direct consciousness (e.g., seeing red). But consciousness also has levels. We can be aware of awareness: A person can think: "I am aware that I see the color red." Reflective consciousness is called higher order consciousness. In fact, some psychologists have argued that this capacity to reflect back on experience is both necessary for consciousness, and explains what consciousness feels like (e.g., Rosenthal, 1993; 2002). These "higher order thoughts" of consciousness can be of multiple orders. "I see red" is zero order, "I am aware I see red," first order, "I am aware I am aware I see red," second order, and so on.

Another use of the "levels of consciousness" metaphor, though, is to refer to developing a higher level of consciousness. Far from reflecting on reflections of awareness, this type of higher consciousness means getting rid of all the layers and layers and focusing instead on a pure experience of consciousness. One way to move in that direction is to take up focused meditation. A person practicing focused meditation clears his mind by focusing his thoughts on a single action or perception, such as a current breath or a mantra—a calming vocal sound he makes such as "oohhmm" as he exhales.

Higher consciousness in this context refers to letting go of extraneous thoughts and distractions so as to experience a state known as pure consciousness, which some practitioners regard as approaching a true understanding of nature and reality (Ornstein, 1986, pp. 191-194). Such ideas of consciousness are often spiritual and dualistic; the practitioner believes she leaves her physical self behind and enters a plane of pure awareness (e.g., Wilbur, 1999). From a solely scientific perspective, however, legitimate interest has been expressed in the sort of brain states, internal phenomena, and behavioral correlates that relate to such higher levels (e.g., Ornstein, 1986).

Studies of Highly Skilled Meditators

Eight highly skilled meditators of the Tibetan Buddhist school agreed to help Newberg, Alevi, and Blaine (2001) understand how the brain changes during meditation. The researchers used Single Photon Emission Computed Tomography (SPECT)—a method that tracks a radioactive substance that tags blood cells as those cells move through the brain. More active brain areas draw more blood toward them. By tracing the tagged blood cells using SPECT, the researchers could see which brain areas were most active.

The meditators began their practice in a candlelit room with incense burning. Each meditator had a piece of string nearby and, by prior arrangement, tugged on it when he or she entered a higher state of consciousness. At that point, a radioactive trace was injected via an earlier implanted intravenous tube, and the meditator was quickly escorted to the brain scan machine.

Compared to a control group, the brains of these expert meditators were emotionally calm. Many structures in their limbic systems—the seat of emotion—were very quiet, including the amygdala and hypothalamic activity. There also was a startling decrease in the parietal lobe activity. The parietal lobe is responsible for the physical model of the self; this suggested that the meditators shut off most sensations from their bodies.

At the same time there was a 20% increase in activity in the meditators' prefrontal cortex—a portion of the brain responsible for the orienting response, or the "What is it?" response of the brain for paying attention to something. In normal consciousness, orientation is constantly changing—we might think about an appointment, driving, a friend, an errand. In concentrative meditation, by contrast, there is prolonged orienting to one object or event (Carter, 2002, pp. 284-288).

Contemporary brain scanning techniques, coupled with meditative practices, can help us understand where in the brain conscious experience comes from. In the case of concentrative meditative experience, the sense of pure consciousness may result from reduced activity in some brain areas, unchanged activity in others, and an increased orienting response of the prefrontal cortex.

Self-Determination Theory

In addition to differences in the expression of consciousness, there are also differences in the expression of will. Self-determination theory is concerned with how much the self acts in accordance with its own desires—voluntary action in a broad sense—versus how much it acts in accordance with everyday outside pressures (Deci & Ryan, 2000; Sheldon & Kasser, 2001). This research takes a page from the humanistic psychology of Abraham Maslow, who, as you will recall, noted that some people had more free will than others.

Generally speaking, a conscious self that acts voluntarily and according to its own needs is considered to operate according to **intrinsic motivation**. Intrinsic motivation involves doing things that are viewed as rewarding to the individual in and of themselves. For example, a person genuinely interested in reporting the news is intrinsically motivated to be a journalist. This might be contrasted with **extrinsic motivation**. Extrinsic motivation describes doing things in order to meet some form of outside expectations or rewards: A young man who attends law school because his parents regard it as a practical and realistic life plan. There exist a number of types of extrinsic motivations, from those entirely due to outside pressures (called the external subtype) to pursuits that are more integrated with one's own needs. For example, a young woman with "identified" extrinsic motivation may be guided by her parents, but she also accepts their ideas as something she believes in as well. Identified extrinsic motivation is often grouped with intrinsic motivation because of their similarities. These and more forms of specific motivation are defined in Figure 7-3.

Intrinsic motivation and identified extrinsic motivation are perceived as volitional, self-chosen, and self-determined. Most other forms of extrinsic motivation are perceived as carried out primarily due to outside pressure of various kinds. Of course, one can also experience **amotivation**: the lack of any motivation at all. People are apt to feel amotivated when they lack any sense of being able to carry out a task successfully.

Amotivation	Extrinsic motivation— External	Extrinsic motivation— Introjected type	Extrinsic Motivation— Identified & Integrated type	Intrinsic Motivation
The individual feels generally unable to carry out a task successfully.	The individual doesn't want to carry out the task, and doesn't believe it to be of importance, but does so to satisfy external demands.	The individual doesn't want to carry out the task, but will do so anyway, in order to satisfy the perceived needs of others.	The individual genuinely wants to please others (identified). The individual has integrated others' perceptions of a tasks' value (integrated).	The individual views a task as rewarding, pleasing, and consistent with his or her goals for its own sake.

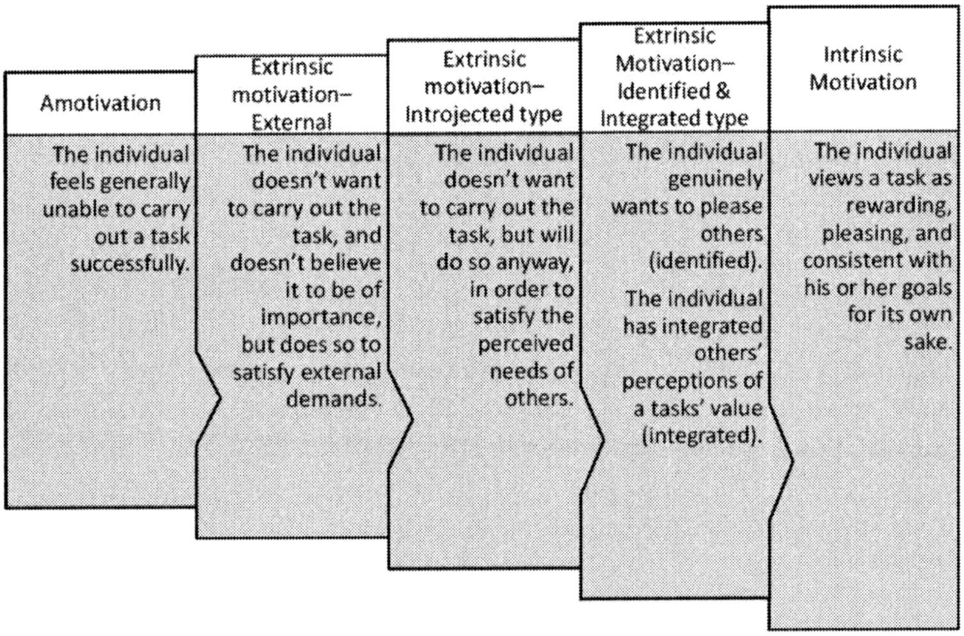

Figure 7-3 *Motivations from Least to Most Self-Determined*
(summarized from Deci and Ryan, 2000, pp. 235-237)

How well a person matches her own voluntary desires to social tasks appears critical to the pleasure, ease, and success with which she proceeds through important life tasks. For example, Miserandino (1996) found that 3rd and 4th grade students were happier, enjoyed school more, and performed better when they were self-motivated, that is, extrinsically identified or intrinsically motivated, than when they experienced other forms of extrinsic motivation. This was the case even after controlling statistically for ability levels among the students. Similarly, college students who are more voluntarily motivated to perform in organic chemistry enjoy the course more and obtain higher grades in it (Black & Deci, 2000). Students with greater self-motivation achieve more progress in school, even controlling for initial achievement levels, and are happier when they attain their goals than those who are at the more extrinsically motivated end of the spectrum (Sheldon & Kasser, 1998; 2001).

Finally, patients in a weight-loss treatment program lost more weight and kept if off better nearly two years later when they were self-motivated, and self-motivated patients more generally are better at following medical regimens (Williams et al., 1996; Williams, Freedman, & Deci, 1998).

Such findings indicate the importance of a sense of voluntary control, and that such voluntary control comes from successfully pairing one's own truly believed needs with the surrounding social environment. The sense of voluntary self-control is important to people, and can amplify their abilities to carry out long-term, demanding requirements. To the extent that the conscious self is responsible for recognizing its own needs, for bringing them into the light of consciousness, and for fitting the self into the environment so that those needs can be met with a sense of self-determination, the conscious self may represent a critical core of personality.

Self-Control: A First Look

The concept of self-determination blends imperceptibly into the concept of self-control—for those with more intrinsic motivation are exercising a form of self-control. There is a considerable research literature on self-control that will be examined later in Chapter 10 on the Dynamics of Self-Control, and also in Chapter 11 on Child Development. Meanwhile, it is worth considering one issue of particular relevance to the expression of self-control here: Is a person's apparent self control a product of the fact that the person already wants to do the right thing, or is it a matter of legitimate "imposed will"? Block and Block (1980) started out studying a concept called "ego control." As the term suggests, the Blocks originally hypothesized that people who possessed ego control had a strong conscious self or ego. Those who lacked ego control lacked it owing to a weak conscious self.

The Blocks found that it made sense to divide the children they studied into under-controlled, flexible, and over-controlled groups. The main determinant of group membership seemed not to be any learned or acquired sense of self-control, so much as the individual's possession of a set of particular motivations. Those who were sensation-seekers and had difficulty maintaining their attention ended up in the under-controlled group. Those who were quite shy and introverted ended up in the over-controlled group. The rest of the sample ended up assigned to the flexible group. From this perspective, the concept of ego control was superfluous—it was all a consequence of a person's motivations and attentional style (e.g., Block, 2002; van Lieshout, 2000).

It is interesting to consider how much the appearance of self-control might be due to some other part of personality. Returning to the example of Gauguin that began this chapter, for example, we might recall the major decisions he made in his life: His decision to devote his life to painting, to leave his family, and to travel to Tahiti, and we might wonder to what degree Gauguin truly made the decisions he claimed to, and to what degree was he compelled by other forces in his personality to do those things.

With the study of the conscious self and its alternatives, it is now possible to draw Part 2 of this book to a close. We examined motives and emotions (Chapter 4), mental models of the self, world, and relationships (Chapter 5), mental abilities including intelligence and creativity (Chapter 6), and finally, conscious and unconscious agencies in this chapter. These are arguably the most important of personality's parts, as understood today. With the proliferation of parts it is important to understand how they fit together and influence one another. That is the topic of Part 3 of the book, on the organization of personality. Chapter 8, the first chapter of Part 3, begins with an examination of how the parts fit together.

Reviewing Chapter 7

This chapter was written to help acquaint you with the role of consciousness in personality, and the issue of free will versus determinism. Those two topics were examined as they relate to parts of personality sometimes referred to as agencies: broad, autonomously acting parts that include the self-as-knower and the ego. Those agencies were described along with some thoughts about how they are expressed.

Questions About "What Is the Conscious Self?"

1. James' Self-as-Knower: The conscious self was an important topic dealt with by William James, among others. What is the nature of the conscious self, as James described it?

2. Freud's Concept of the Ego: Freud proposed the existence of three agencies that described personality—the id, ego, and superego. Of these, the ego is examined in some detail here. How is the

ego similar, and how is it different, from James' concept of the Conscious Self, particularly in terms of how much is conscious?

3. <u>The Dialogical Self</u>: The dialogical self is a recent view of the conscious self in which the consciousness moves from enlivening not only one's own self, but also representations of other internal characters. This is said to occur as a person holds imaginary conversations with others. How is the dialogical self different from the conscious self, and what does the notion of the dialogical self add to the conscious self?

Questions About "What Does It Mean for the Self To Be Conscious?"

4. <u>Consciousness Defined</u>: How has consciousness been defined? What are some central attributes of consciousness?

5. <u>Scientific Accounting for the Feeling of Consciousness</u>: What is subjective realism? How does it distinguish between consciousness as an objective quality and as a subjective quality?

6. <u>Is Consciousness of Recent Origin</u>: Julian Jaynes suggested a radical hypothesis: That consciousness has been recently evolved. To when does he date the appearance of consciousness? How were people different before consciousness evolved?

7. <u>The Brain and Consciousness</u>: Has consciousness been localized in the brain? If so, which part of the brain contains consciousness? If not, what explanations have been offered for how consciousness emerges?

Questions About "Does the Self Possess Free Will?"

8. <u>The Appearance of Will</u>: The will is a power that we exert over ourselves to try to control or ensure that we behave in a particular way. What sorts of decisions did William James say most reflected the exercise of will?

9. <u>The Free Will—Determinism Debate</u>: Is there a free will? Those who believe there isn't are called Determinists. Religious determinism can be found in some religions; Calvinism is an example in the Protestant tradition. Such determinism can also be found in psychology. Both Sigmund Freud and B. F. Skinner were determinists. What does free will mean?

10. <u>Freedom from the Free Will—Determinism Debate</u>: How is the discussion about voluntary versus automatic behavior different from free will versus determinism?

11. <u>Voluntary Cause and Control</u>: A number of experimental studies suggest that people believe they are exercising free will when, in fact, they are not. Can you describe such a study? Does that prove the determinist position?

Questions About "Are There Alternatives to the Conscious Self?"

12. <u>Agencies</u>: Consciousness itself is sometimes described as an agency. Although some agencies are conscious, others are unconscious. What are some qualities of agencies?

13. <u>Agencies are Semi-Autonomous</u>: Agencies are part of personality that are semi-autonomous from the other parts either in that they are self-regulating, or that they otherwise are the origin of some influence over the rest of personality. What do self-regulating and semi-autonomous mean?

14. <u>Alters:</u> Multiple personalities present a fascinating instance of the agency at the extreme. Here are actual full-blown personalities alternating within a single individual. Each personality is doing its own thing: One may even trick another personality or hijack the body someplace another inner personality doesn't want to be. What are the alternative personalities called, and why are they considered agencies?

15. <u>The Unconscious, Id, and Superego:</u> Early in his career, Freud divided the mind into the conscious, preconscious, and unconscious. Later in his career, Freud divided the mind into the id, ego, and superego. Are the unconscious, id, and superego, unconscious agencies? What characteristics of them did you use to decide the issue?

Questions About "How Is the Conscious Self Expressed?"

16. <u>The Stream of Consciousness:</u> The various ideas and associations a person has over a day together form the individual's stream of consciousness. What does the stream of consciousness contain?

17. <u>Levels of Consciousness:</u> What is meant by levels of consciousness? What levels of consciousness have been proposed?

18. <u>The Structure of Consciousness and Flow:</u> Flow experience results from an interaction between a person's skills, and the challenges provided by a task at hand. The Flow experience has a number of characteristics associated with it, including a quicker passage of time and an intense involvement. What other characteristics are there? What is it about the skills and tasks that bring flow about?

Chapter 7 Glossary

Terms in Order of Appearance:

Self-as-Knower: According to William James, the conscious awareness that is a person's innermost identity. It watches with consciousness and exerts will where useful.

Ego: That portion of the mind including a conscious sense of self and capable of rational thought and self-control. Although originally a psychodynamic concept, the term is now used in a number of theoretical orientations.

Dialogical Self: A type of consciousness that switches between a person's model of himself and that same individual's models of other people. As the dialogical self switches from a model of oneself to a model of another person, it animates the given model, bringing first the self to life, and then animating the model of the other person as if she were there, talking or acting.

Self-Awareness: A type of awareness in which the topic, or subject, of awareness is awareness itself; that is, reflective awareness.

Access to Information: In the study of consciousness, the state in which conscious awareness can obtain information, retrieve it, or attend to it, as opposed to being blocked off from information.

Sentience: In the study of consciousness, the state of being someone, of possessing internal, subjective experience.

Subjective Realism: A school of philosophy according to which the subjective experience of consciousness is real, and is generated by the physical and mental organism that experiences consciousness.

Bicameral Mind: A descriptor of the human mind, bicameral refers to the fact that the mind is dependent upon the right and left hemispheres of the brain, which do things in different ways and may not be fully integrated, even in the recent past. In the early bicameral mind, according to Julian Jaynes, before about

300 B.C.E., people did not realize that one part of the brain (speech production) can talk internally to the other (speech reception). As such, this internal speech was misinterpreted as coming from sources outside the individual such as Gods and Apparitions.

Will: That part of the mind that exerts conscious, intentional control over thoughts and actions.

Free Will: The idea that people can exercise self-control in a fashion at least partly independent from any causal influences, and stemming from their own independent judgment.

Determinism: The belief that all action in the universe, including human action, has already been set in motion at the beginning of time, with each event caused by the events that have come before, and, as consequence, that all human behavior is preordained.

Experimental Confederate (or simply, Confederate): A research assistant who impersonates a research participant in front of other research participants, while actually following predetermined instructions of the experimenter.

Agencies: Central parts of the mind distinguished by the fact that they are self-regulating, partly autonomous, and exert influences on the rest of personality.

Semi-Autonomous: Operating partly on their own; partly independently of other influences.

Dissociative Disorders: A group of psychiatric disorders characterized by sudden alterations in identity and its history. Portions of identity may be lost and then regained, or many identities may arise.

Dissociative Identity Disorder (DID): This is a contemporary psychiatric diagnosis for what used to be called Multiple Personality Disorder. In it, a person may alternate among two or more personalities (or identities) over time, with no true central personality.

Alter: A contraction of "alternative personality"—the personalities that appear in Dissociative Identity Disorder.

Id: An older psychodynamic concept referring to a collection of animal instincts, desires, and motives, all of which operate in the mind.

Unconscious: That portion of the mind outside of a person's awareness. Social-cognitive theory emphasizes that it is evolutionarily adaptive for many processes to be outside of awareness. Psychodynamic theory emphasizes that some motivational and emotional processes are painful and threatening, and are purposively avoided by consciousness.

Conscious: Awareness; reflective observing of the inner mind (see text for further discussion).

Superego: A portion of the mind that grows out of the ego and contains both an ideal self and the conscience.

Qualia (*sing.* Quale): Elements, or an element, of consciousness—individual thoughts, feelings, and urges, or images, tastes, and sounds.

Current Concerns: The goals, plans and objectives a person is thinking about carrying out.

Flow: A conscious state in which a person is highly involved in a task, such that time passes quickly, distractions recede, and the person is enjoyably engaged.

Intrinsic Motivation: A type of motivation in which the process of carrying out an activity is rewarding to an individual in and of itself, aside from any outside reward.

Extrinsic Motivation: A type of motivation in which a person's activities are carried out in order to obtain an outside reward such as social recognition or money.

Amotivation: The lack of any type of motivation to carry out activities or tasks.

PERSONALITY PSYCHOLOGY: PART 3

PART 3: PERSONALITY ORGANIZATION builds on our understanding of personality's parts by asking how those parts are organized. Personality possesses structure: The parts that make it up can be organized into larger parts and, ultimately, into broad classes of parts. Personality also is subject to dynamics: chains of causal influences from one part to another. Some dynamics motivate the person to take action in the environment. Other dynamics relate to self-control. Personality Organization concerns both the major structures and dynamics of our minds, how they can be identified within a person, and how they vary from individual to individual.

Chapter 8: How the Parts of Personality Fit Together

A central task of personality is to integrate the many parts of the psychological system and examine how they work together. The many parts of personality include specific motives, emotions, mental models, mental abilities, and the conscious self. These parts were examined in the chapters leading up to this one. Now it is time to begin our look at the organization of personality as a whole.

A first look at personality organization often begins with a consideration of personality's structure. The structure of personality refers to how personality is divided into relatively stable areas, and also concerns how the parts of personality are assigned to each of those areas. Structure tells us how the parts of personality carry out action as pieces of the whole.

Previewing the Chapter's Central Questions

•**What Is Personality Structure?** Personality structure refers to the relatively enduring aspects of personality: for example, areas of function that operate over the long term. Dividing personality into structural areas helps psychologists examine the whole system and its specific parts, together.

•**How Are Personality Traits Structured?** Some approaches to personality structure focus on organizing personality traits. Many traits can be arranged in hierarchies in which "big" or "super" traits organize smaller traits that make them up.

•**What Are Structural Models of Awareness and Why Do They Matter?** Another way to look at personality structure is to consider which parts of personality have channels of communication to conscious awareness, and which parts exist in non-conscious states outside of awareness.

•**What Are the Key Functions of Personality?** A further way to divide personality is according to its different functional areas such as motivation, emotion, and cognition. There are other functional areas as well.

•**What Are the Structural Connections Between Personality and the Environment?** Some further structural divisions specialize in how to connect a person's internal processes to the social environment. Collectively, any of these structural divisions help connect various areas of personality together, and some of them help connect personality to its surrounding environment.

•**What Can Structures Do?** Psychologists use structural models of personality to help them carry out their research. In particular, these models are of help in identifying and organizing personality traits and other variables for study.

What Is Personality Structure?

Personality Structure Described

Personality structure refers to the relatively enduring, stable areas that are inside personality. Psychologists of all theoretical approaches have been concerned with structure (e.g., Block, 1995, p. 188; Cervone, 2005; Mayer, 2005; Rapaport, 1967, p. 803; Sanford, 1970, p. 45).

For the psychodynamic theorist David Rapaport they were the "abiding [continuing] patterns in the flux of processes…" For the trait theorist, structure can take on a specifically mathematical meaning, referring to the "pattern of…a relatively small number of factors that represent the basic dimensions of personality." For the mid-20th-century integrator of personality theories, Nevitt Sanford, structure was the "organization or patterning" of personality's elements (McCrae & Costa, 1997, p. 509; Rapaport 1967, p. 803; Sanford, 1970, p. 46).

The term "structure," is often contrasted with the concept of personality dynamics. Structure speaks of the relatively enduring long-term qualities of the personality system, whereas personality dynamics speak of the relatively rapid, active processes and change within the personality system. All of these perspectives on structure share in common the idea that it consists of the "relations among parts [of personality] that are relatively static and unchanging" (Mayer, 1998, p. 130).

To further clarify the nature of personality structure, consider an analogy to a visible structure—the structure of a city. Imagine taking a flight by hot air balloon over, say, Boston, Massachusetts. A balloon ride is slow enough to allow us time to appreciate the change in perspective that takes place from looking at individual parts of the city to its more global structure. Say we lift off from near the "Frog Pond," a concrete water basin surrounded by parkland. The pond is located in the center of downtown Boston, and is used for sunning in the summer and skating in the winter.

Once our balloon is inflated we are ready to go aloft. As we begin our ascent, we initially see individual people who helped launch us, the individual trees, walkways, the Frog Pond wading pool, and other park fixtures. All these can be thought of as individual parts that make up the city. As we travel further upward, the trees and lawn merge into the greenery of the Boston Common—the historical downtown park of which the Frog Pond is a part. As we rise higher, we take in surrounding parts of the city: streets and cars, office buildings, hotels, and the church spires that characterize this part of New England.

At this level above the ground and beyond, the people, trees, streets, and buildings become too numerous to keep in mind all at once. This problem of viewpoint is similar to the one we face when considering the individual parts of personality—as we step back and try to take in a view of the entire personality system, the parts grow numerous and it helps to consider them from a higher level.

Floating above Boston toward the Atlantic, we will be inclined to shift our view of the city to a higher level. We will make out a new sense of order in what we are seeing as we rise higher into the air. We begin to notice broader lines of demarcation and new patterns on the ground. The greenery of the Boston Common are distinct from a group of older buildings on the hill beneath us—the Beacon Hill neighborhood—marked at its center by the large golden dome of the statehouse

Past that to our left is Storrow Drive running parallel to the Charles River, and on its far banks slightly behind us, Cambridge—the home of Harvard University and the Massachusetts Institute of Technology. The tall buildings to our right and in front of us mark the financial district, which extends down to the Fort Point Channel. As we continue eastward, we will come upon Boston Harbor itself, and the Atlantic Ocean. Thus, individual people, buildings, and roadways give way to a broader sense of the urban and geographical areas of Boston—the parks, neighborhoods, and geography—the visible structure of the city (Gleason, 1985, pp. vi, 7, 17).

Although, we cannot fly over personality and see it as we can Boston, the human personality, too, has its boundaries, its regions, and its areas. As the analogy to a city suggests, one reason we are interested in personality structure is that it provides a way of dividing and organizing—obtaining an overview—of the system.

Why Is Personality Structure Important?

As we have learned, personality has a lot of parts. Personality textbooks such as this one typically mention about 400 common parts (Mayer, 1995). There are hundreds more that psychologists study at a more advanced level. Structural divisions of personality provide a global organization and overview of those parts so that psychologists can view them in meaningful groups rather than always be preoccupied with each one in detail. For example, rather than discuss every single emotion, we can talk of the emotion system.

To see how this operates in practice, consider the personality of one young adult I'll call Larry Mitchell Creighton. Let's say we divide his personality into the areas of motives, emotions, and cognition—a structural division called the "trilogy of mind" we will encounter later in this chapter.

Creighton is motivated in a number of areas. At the age of 12 he began bodybuilding to protect himself from schoolyard bullies, won a lot of fights, and developed a reputation as a tough guy. He is now a tall, large, strong individual. Like most people, in other words, he is motivated to defend himself. He enjoys "a couple of beers," "shooting bull," and riding his Harley-Davidson motorcycle. This suggests he is sociable and (because of the motorcycle) may be motivated to seek thrills and excitement. During the 1980s and 1990s he lived in a cabin on Long Island with his Harley-Davidson motorcycle and cat, and, at the time, worked as a bouncer in a nightclub, earning six thousand dollars per year. His relatively low earnings suggest he might not be motivated to earn money, but other possible explanations also exist (for example, he might enjoy the work a great deal, or be helping a friend who owns the club). He also organized a non-profit organization and is involved in writing a book called "Design for a Universe" (Quain, 2002). He likes to teach himself things. In other words, he appears to be curious and intellectually motivated.

He expresses few emotions with others (Quain, 2002; Sager, 1999). To the extent he does express feelings, the feelings appear to include a mix of happiness and enjoyment, but also some skepticism, doubt, and boredom. His mother told him his father died of a heart attack before he was born—but he says he sometimes doubts his mother was telling the truth. He says he often feels bored when listening to normal conversation (Quain, 2002). He found college boring and dropped out, in part because he felt that the faculty and administrators he met were unsympathetic toward him and the poverty he faced. During one point in his life, he said he maintained no respect toward academics and called them "acadummies." Others say he has a "bit of a chip on his shoulder" (Sager, 1999, p. 145). Part of his emotional distance may be reflected in his philosophical character. He notes, for example, that there are many people in the world, and many of them just get bad breaks, and he identifies with them based on his own experiences.

At this point, you might conclude that Larry Creighton is a fairly ordinary person who has suffered some disadvantages in life. Before you draw too quick a picture of Creighton, though, it is important to continue the overview of all the structural areas of his personality. In the area of intelligence, for example, Larry's IQ has been assessed at 195 (compared to the average college student's IQ of 120, or faculty member's IQ of 130 to 140). That puts him somewhere in the area of Leonardo da Vinci, Ludwig Wittgenstein, and Rene Descartes. He skipped kindergarten through second grade. When he worked on a ranch as a youth, he brought books with him by Bertrand Russell and Albert Einstein to read while he waited for the irrigation ditches to drain. He taught himself advanced math, physics, philosophy, Latin, and Greek. He is now married and helps run Mega-East society, a non-profit organization for the support of the "severely gifted." Most recently, he has begun publication of his theory in academic journals—highly unusual for someone who has dropped out of college. Moreover, his theory has been treated with considerable respect.

The structural overview of Creighton's personality—superficial though it is—shows how examining multiple parts together is an important complement to viewing parts in isolation. If you only knew the motivational and emotional side of Creighton's personality, you might view him as a relatively unexceptional individual. If you only knew of his intelligence, you might imagine him as a highly cerebral individual. Only when a more global (higher-level) perspective is employed from which to view all the parts, is it possible to more fully appreciate the individual who encompasses these qualities. The point of a structural approach is that by considering a few key areas together rather than in isolation we can better describe, predict, and change personality (Lubinski, 2000).

Multiple Depictions of Personality Structures

A little reflection will suggest that there is nearly always more than one good way to divide a complex system, and there exist multiple ways of dividing personality on a structural basis. To make this clearer, again consider the city of Boston and the multiple possibilities for dividing it up. An economist might divide the city according to its economic sectors, including its banking and financial services, its role as a seaport, its high-tech sectors, medical services sector, and its educational institutions. A real estate agent would divide it by neighborhood, examining Allston, Back Bay, and Beacon Hill, through Mattapan and the North End, to Roslindale and West Roxbury. A geologist, by contrast, would divide the city by its scenic landscape, including its urban areas, parks, waterfront, and islands, by its surface deposits, and its bedrock geology, including granite and volcanic types, among others.

Similarly, the different theoretical perspectives on personality psychology call for different kinds of structural divisions of the system. John Digman and others trait psychologists have equated the concept of personality structure to a group of large, important, relatively enduring traits (e.g., Diener, Smith, & Fujita, 1995; Digman, 1990). Such structural models of traits often refer to "super traits" or "big traits," and later in this chapter we'll encounter structural trait models such as the "Big Three" (traits), and the "Big Five." Other trait theorists emphasize personality types that are based on combinations of trait dimensions (Weinberger, 1998, p. 1065).

Psychodynamic theorists are interested in consciousness and self-awareness and as a consequence they emphasize what is conscious or not. The distinction between conscious and unconscious reflects another way that personality structures can be divided into a series of areas or parts—according to channels of communication with consciousness (Rapaport, 1960; 1967). Probably the most common way personality is divided is according to its major functions such as those involving motivation, emotion, and cognition. Other important divisions tell us the relation of personality and its social behavior to the outside world (Mischel & Shoda, 1995). Finally, systems-oriented psychologists may look at ways of employing the different structural divisions in an integrated fashion (Mayer, 2001).

Personality Structure Provides Organization

> "Viewing…structures, the psychic traveler felt he was in possession of superior maps of the mind and better able to navigate than his ancestors."
> — Eugene Mahon

Although there is more than one good way to divide up personality, not all such divisions are equally good. Four criteria in particular can help separate useful personality divisions from less useful ones. These criteria promote personality structures that are economical, useful, and scientifically valid (Mayer, 2001).

The first criterion is that a good structural model should divide personality into a few large, well-chosen areas (see Table 8-1). Using fewer than three divisions could threaten to oversimplify personality; using more than seven would tend to undermine one of the points of a structural division, which is to employ a small number of areas.

The second criterion is that each division of personality should possess an adequate scientific basis. That is, each area of personality should be reasonably recognized as occurring in every healthy personality. Describing an "emotions" area of personality, or a trait structure related to "sociability" or "extraversion" (as in the Big Five) both have sound scientific bases: The phenomena exist, can be readily produced, and plainly have important effects. By contrast, describing an area that receives telepathic (e.g., paranormal) communication would be much more controversial given the ongoing debate as to whether such phenomena in fact exist, and if they do, how to reliably produce such effects (e.g., Bem & Honorton, 1994; Milton & Wiseman, 1999; Storm & Ertel, 2001).

Table 8-1: Criteria for Good Structural Divisions of Personality*

Criteria	Rationale
Appropriateness of the Size of the Set	Personality is most desirably divided into between three and ten parts. If the divisions are fewer than three, they may lack sufficient detail; if the divisions are greater than ten, they may begin to blend into individual parts of personality.
Adequate Empirical Basis	Each division should describe a scientifically plausible division of personality that is found in most or all personalities.
Distinctiveness	The divisions should describe areas of personality that are distinctly different from one another.
Comprehensiveness	The divisions should comprehensively contain all the parts of personality.

*From Mayer, 2001, Table 1.

The third criterion is that the divisions of mind create distinct areas. If we divide the mind into motivation, emotion, and cognition—as is done in the trilogy of mind—it is necessary to be able to explain how one area differs from the other. For example, basic motivations are often said to signal psychophysiological needs, and this distinguishes them from basic emotions, which signal aspects of changing relationships. A hypothetical division that separated an emotional area from a mood area would be less compelling because these phenomena are more closely interconnected, although they can be distinguished (moods outlast emotions).

Fourth, a structural division of personality must be comprehensive in the sense that it covers the most important parts of personality. For example, a set that failed to include motives or failed to account for unconscious areas would be problematic. Even so, a structural model can be useful. For example, the first types of structure we will examine are structures for organizing traits. Although these are undeniably important, they have been criticized exactly because they provide only a partial coverage of the personality system and omit such important personality structures as the self and a conscience (Loevinger, 1994).

How Are Personality Traits Structured?

The Hierarchical Organization of Traits

What if a global picture of personality could be provided by just a few key traits? If that were the case, then just taking one or two quick personality tests would provide an individual with a rich source of self-knowledge he could use to explain his past and to guide himself in the future. Identifying such key divisions is the aspiration of psychologists who try to divide personality into a few large traits.

Psychologists who study trait structure generally agree that traits can be usefully represented in the form of **hierarchical structures of traits**, which consist of several levels. At the lowest, most specific level of a trait hierarchy are individual test items such as "Are you an anxious person?" and "Do you consider yourself sociable?" Next, factor analysis is applied to those groups of items, and broader factors representing a second level of traits are extracted. For example, factor analysis might join together the three following items "Are you an anxious person?" "Do people consider you nervous?" and "Do you have many fears?" to form a factor representing Anxiety. The same factor analysis might group together other items into factors such as Emotional Sensitivity (e.g., "Are you sensitive to others' remarks about you?") and Moodiness (e.g., "Are you moody?"). Those mid-level traits (factors) may themselves be factor analyzed along with others. The result of such a second factor analysis usually results in obtaining a group of **big (or super) traits**. Big or super traits are broad traits such as Neuroticism that encompass the more specific traits. For example, Neuroticism is composed of mid-level traits including Anxiety, Emotional Sensitivity, and Moodiness.

A second example of such a big or super trait is that of Extraversion. Its measurement begins at the individual item level with questions such as "Do you prefer parties to reading?" "Do you often search for thrills?" and "Are you a lively person?" Factor analyses of such items yield mid-level traits such as Sociability, Sensation-Seeking, and Liveliness, and a factor analysis of these yields Extraversion itself. These relationships can be portrayed in tree-like diagrams in which the largest factor structures are on top and the sub-factors that make them up are on the bottom. Figure 8-1 shows the division of extroversion into subtraits such as Sociability, Sensation-Seeking, and Liveliness.

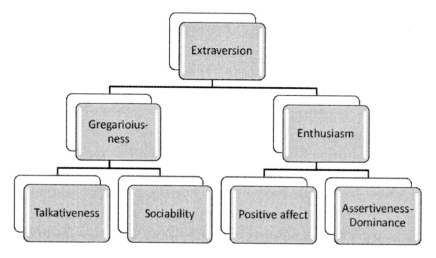

Figure 8-1 *How Extraversion, a "Big" Trait, Divides into the Narrower Traits that are a Part of It.* A division similar to this one has been proposed based on factor analyses (e.g. Young, Quilty & Peterson, 2007).

You may recall from the chapter on intelligence that intelligences, too, were represented as a hierarchy that began with individual mental abilities, included a middle level of specific intelligences such as verbal and perceptual-organizational intelligences, and concluded with general intelligence at the top. This is yet another example of the hierarchical nature of traits. "Trait structure," in the sense just described, refers to this hierarchical structure. The hierarchical structure, in turn, is based on the correlation of test items, the mid-level trait factors identified through factor analysis, and the big or super factors, identified through a second round of factor analysis. The use of the term "structure" to refer to this statistical pattern of relationships is a usage with which virtually all psychologists would agree.

There exists, however, a second sense in which the term trait structure is used that is more controversial. The second way in which trait structure is used is, essentially, synonymous with personality structure. In this sense, each trait is viewed as a bio-psycho-behavioral system that, in combination with other traits, describes much of personality (e.g., McCrae & Costa, 1999). In this sense, Neuroticism refers not only to a correlated pattern of psychological test items, but also to a psycho-neurological structure in the brain that leads to behavioral regularities. Viewed in this "strong" way, the structure of traits becomes synonymous with the structure of personality itself (e.g., Digman, 1990). On the other hand, many psychologists are reluctant to consider neuroticism as a structure per se. Rather, they say, Neuroticism is best thought of as a description, or operating characteristic, of the emotion system (e.g., Averill, 1992; Block, 1995; Mayer, 2001).

Whichever viewpoint you subscribe to, a great deal of research has been conducted over the past 50 years to understand the structure of traits. It is only a slight simplification to say that the march of progress concerning traits over the past 50 years has been almost entirely in one direction: More and more big traits are being found. We begin our coverage of trait structure with the Big Two and Big Three, move to the Big Five, and then briefly consider a Big Six and Big Seven. As we do this you may want to ask yourself, "Is this set of traits enough to describe my whole personality, or is another set needed?"

The Big Two and the Big Three

Sometimes, important scientific ideas emerge from scientific debates. This was the case for the discovery of the hierarchical arrangement of personality traits. Hans Eysenck had proposed a two-dimensional model of personality traits made up of Extraversion-Introversion and Neuroticism (Emotionality)-Stability—as you may recall from Chapter 4 on Motivation and Emotion. Raymond Cattell, another trait psychologist, challenged Eysenck by creating a test with very similar items that contained 16 factors of personality rather than 2. Many of Cattell's suggested traits appeared specific relative to Eysenck's. For example, whereas Eysenck wrote of a broad dimension of Neuroticism-Emotional Stability that included (on the Neurotic end) anxiety, sensitivity, and mood swings, Cattell described narrower traits such as "Reactive," which involved feeling a lack of control over one's life, and "Apprehensive," which included worry and self-doubt; in all, he wrote of 16 primary traits, along with several others (Cattell, 1965, pp. 95-97; IPAT, 1991).

Eysenck and Cattell debated whether a 2- or 16-factor depiction of personality traits was best. The debate was quite frustrating for those who witnessed it—leading two well-known textbook writers to wonder if factor analysis "…is so objective and rational, why is it that those who know most about it are least agreed as to just how the process should go?" (Hall & Lindzey, 1959, pp. 416-417).

Ultimately Eysenck and colleagues demonstrated that when Cattell's 16 factors were treated as items on a test and factor analyzed, they yielded a higher level of traits, which corresponded reasonably well to Eysenck's two dimensions. These became known as the "big factors" or "superfactors" of today. Thus was born the hierarchical structure of traits (e.g., Adcock, Adcock, & Walkey; Cattell, 1956; Eysenck, 1972).

Eysenck's Two-Factor model of Neuroticism-Stability and Extraversion-Introversion thus became a "**Big Two**" model. It was, however, shortly followed by a "**Big Three**" model, in which Eysenck suggested a new broad supertrait he called "Psychoticism." Psychoticism referred to a tendency toward being solitary, uncaring toward people, and troublesome. In some individuals, this may be joined with insensitivity, inhumanity, and cruelty. People high in psychoticism experience alterations in consciousness and suffer many of the symptoms of people with mental disorders, including eccentricity, paranoia, and isolation. Unlike those with mental disorders, however, they do not appear to be at any higher risk for losing contact with reality (Chapman, Chapman, & Kwapil, 1994; Eysenck & Eysenck, 1975, p. 5).

Eysenck's system was not the only Big Three, however. Auke Tellegen and his colleagues' Multidimensional Personality Questionnaire (e.g., Patrick, Curtin, & Tellegen, 2002) provided a second version of a set of three supertraits. The big three of this scale are Negative Affect (similar to Neuroticism), Positive Affect, and Control. Tellegen's Big Three can be conceived of as centering upon emotion and emotion-related self-control. This forms the core of infant and child temperament and is very useful in developmental studies (see Chapter 11).

The Big Five

More popular than any Big Three, however, is a competing solution known as the **Big Five Model**—a group of five traits. The powerful advantage of the Big Five over its earlier competitors is that it employs a unique procedure for how to select items on a test. This procedure is defined by the **lexical hypothesis**. The lexical hypothesis states that the most important personality concepts can be found in people's everyday language. Identifying the personality traits that naturally occur in language should therefore direct psychologists to the most important traits that make up personality structure (Saucier & Goldberg, 2001, pp. 2-5). In practice, this means collecting and analyzing trait adjectives from dictionaries—words like "shy," "emotional," "prompt," and "cultured." By contrast, the earlier 2- and 3-factor tests of Hans Eysenck and 16 factors of Raymond Cattell were based on test items written and selected by the researchers themselves.

To examine the traits embedded in English, Allport, and Odbert (1936) listed approximately 4,500 trait adjectives related to personality from an unabridged dictionary. Cattell (1948) examined their list, and, using factor analysis, suggested that there might exist about 35 bipolar dimensions represented by them. Shortly thereafter, Fiske (1949) reanalyzed some of Cattell's work and suggested that five factors might describe the themes encoded in the language. Others agreed and this Big Five model consisting of a five-factor solution became the preferred one (Digman, 1990; Goldberg, 1993; John et al., 1988).

Although five factors are often treated as the preferred solution, the exact naming of the factors has been a matter of some controversy, as pointed out by John Digman (1990, pp. 422-424). For our purposes, however, a basic description is possible. Briefly, the factors include Neuroticism, Extraversion, Openness, Agreeableness, and Conscientiousness. The first two factors should be familiar because they are essentially Eysenck's Emotionality-Stability and Introversion-Extraversion factors. These, along with the remaining three factors, are listed in Table 8-2. After each dimension is a brief description of what it is expected to measure. In addition to this are "facets"—smaller scales that occupy the mid-level of the hierarchy. The exact facet scales tend to vary from one Big Five model to another (see Costa & McCrae, 1985, for an example).

The widespread use of the Big Five trait approach has meant that results from many personality studies can be compared more easily because the researchers compared the same traits to see how they predict a given criterion (e.g., job success). The use of the Big Five and similar big sets has led to other interesting research as well. For example, Paunonen (1998) compared the use of big traits versus the more specific traits that make them up to see which level of the trait hierarchy would best predict such outcomes as students' grade point averages, how many dates they went on over a month, whether they smoked, and (among the students who drove) how many speeding tickets they had received. The result? The specific traits were often superior to using the broader, big traits. The drawback? There are more traits to contend with and to understand.

Table 8-2: "Big" Personality Factors, Descriptions, and Set Memberships*

Name	Description	In Sets*
Neuroticism-Emotional Stability (or Emotionality-Stability)	Neuroticism-stability reflects a high degree of (frequently) negative emotion on the neurotic end, and a generally stable, pleasant disposition on the other. This dimension can be broken down into narrower traits including anxiety, hostility, and depression, along with vulnerability, neediness, and self-consciousness.	●Eysenck's three ●Big five ●Big six
Extraversion– Introversion	Extraversion-introversion reflects a motivation for and enjoyment of social contact on the extraversion side, and a motivation for and enjoyment of quietude and solitude on the introversion side. Narrower traits that make up extraversion include liveliness, talkativeness, assertiveness, activity, sensation-seeking, and positive emotionality.	●Eysenck's three ●Big five ●Big six
Openness-Closedness (or Cultured-Uncultured)	Openness involves tolerance and flexibility of thought on one end, and a closed rigidity on the other. Narrower traits include fantasy-proneness (daydreaming, etc.), intellectual interests (intellect), and artistic interests (culturedness).	●Big five ●Big six
Agreeableness-Disagreeableness (or Friendliness-Unfriendliness)	People high on the friendliness end tend to be trusting and straightforward, modest, and compliant. Those on the disagreeable end would be suspicious, oppositional, self-aggrandizing, or hostile. The narrower traits involved are warmth, compliance and trust.	●Big five ●Big six
Conscientiousness-Carelessness	Conscientious characters are responsible, orderly, and dutiful; they perform with competence and value achievement. Narrower traits include organization, persistence, and control.	●Big five ●Big six
Honesty/humility-Dishonesty/arrogance	Honest characters are straightforward. People on the dishonest end are pretending and calculating; this dimension also captures humility versus pompous qualities.	●Big six

*The sets referred to are Eysenck's three superfactors, the Big Five, and the Big Six (HEXACO) model. See the sections on big traits for more detail.

Each of the Big Five personality traits can lead to fairly evaluative statements about people: Disagreeable, Careless, and Neurotic, for example (cf. Hare, 1952, p. 111). So what happens if you make the scales more descriptive and less evaluative? Saucier, Ostendorf, & Peabody (2001) created dimensions that were more neutral by substituting terms such as "bold versus cautious" for the more evaluative "courageous versus cowardly." Rather than five factors, they found just two fairly neutral dimensions. The first is a Tight-Loose dimension, and contrasts *orderly, organized,* and *economical* with *social, happy-go-lucky,* and *impulsive.* The second is an Assertive-Unassertive dimension, and contrasts *confident, forceful,* and *aggressive,* with *uncompetitive, unaggressive,* and *naïve.* Interestingly, when people fill out more neutral—less evaluative—ratings, there may be higher inter-rater agreement as to what a person is like.

The Big Six and Other Considerations

But wait a minute…If there is a Big Five, couldn't there be a Big Six, or a Big Seven as well? In fact, some psychologists prefer to study six rather than five traits—a "big six" called the HEXACO model. The HEXACO acronym uses the letters E, X, A, C, and O to stand for the Big Five dimensions of personality, where "E" stands for emotionality (negative affect or neuroticism), "X" stands for extraversion, and the "A," "C," and "O" represent agreeableness, conscientiousness, and openness, just as in the Big Five. The new sixth dimension—H—stands for "humility/honesty." Its opposite pole is arrogance/dishonesty (Ashton et al., 2004). People high in humility are more honest, self-effacing, and sincere than others; those at the other end are more boastful, pompous, and dishonest than others.

There may be more traits beyond even these six. To examine this possibility, researchers examined adjective clusters appearing in the English language that were not already part of the Big Five (Paunonen & Jackson, 2000; Saucier and Goldberg, 1998). Among the potential big factors beyond the first five are: Religious-Nonreligious, Deceptive-Honest, Sexy-Nonsexual, Thrifty-Spendthrift, Conservative-Radical, Masculine-Feminine, Conceited-Humble, and Humorous-Serious (Paunonen & Jackson, 2000).

Is the structure of traits the same thing as the structure of personality? There is considerable controversy about this in the field. Some say a good group of traits can define personality structure. Many others, however, believe that the structure of traits, although essential to understanding personality, is something less than the structure of the whole personality itself. Structural models of traits do not cover interior selves and worlds, or the conscious self. For that reason, some psychologists have denied that they represent personality structure at all (e.g., Block, 1995). There is little question, though, that they at least represent one important approach to personality structure. Before making up your own mind as to whether the trait structures are enough to describe a person, it is helpful to examine some alternatives.

Big Traits: Do They Cross Species?

When measures of the Big Five are examined across species, some traits seem near universal—although they are expressed differently from species to species. Extraversion in the monkey involves playful social contact such as "pulling limbs," "grasping and poking" and "gymnastics" play together; extraversion in the pig, by comparison, involves frequent vocalizations, nose contacts, and location near other pigs in the pen (Gosling & John, 1999). Judges agree with one another and indicate that monkeys show reliable individual differences in their extraversion—as do pigs—over time and situations (Capitanio, 1999).

Extraversion, Neuroticism, and Agreeableness (or close variants) can be found in pigs, dogs, rhesus monkeys, donkeys, and many other animal species—where such behaviors are fairly consistent over time (Svartberg et al., 2005). Even the octopus appears to vary on a trait reasonably close to extraversion, although it seems to miss out on neuroticism and agreeableness. Introverted humans like to stay home, read a book, and avoid contact with others to unwind. The introverted octopus similarly prefers to stay in its protective underwater den during feedings and is more likely than the extroverted octopus to hide itself by changing color or releasing ink into the water (Gosling & John, 1999, p. 70).

Gosling & John (1999, p. 70) argue that in addition to Extraversion, Neuroticism, and Agreeableness, Openness can be found in all forms of monkeys in the form of curiosity and playfulness, including the

Rhesus and Vervet, as well as in the Chimpanzee. According to these authors, you will not find conscientiousness anywhere other than in humans and chimpanzees. Although dogs can learn obedience, their behavior is rated as closer to learning ability and agreeableness than to conscientiousness itself. Chimpanzees, on the other hand, are sometimes judged to be truly dependable or not. The finding that at least some traits are recognizable across species suggests that traits evolved as behavioral strategies, and that they hold adaptive implications for the animals that have them.

What Are Structural Models of Awareness and Why Do They Matter?

Rationale for Structural Models of Awareness

Recall that any complex system, such as the mind, can be divided in more than one way. This holds true for most complex systems. A city, for example, can be divided into electoral districts, or into geological formations, and there will be little resemblance between the two models, although each is useful for its given purpose. Traits provide only one such division. We should not be surprised that there are other divisions useful for other purposes.

Structural models of awareness focus on the distinction between consciousness and unconsciousness. These models divide the contents of the mind according to what a person is and is not aware of. The given purpose of awareness models is to describe self-knowledge and its limits by understanding the flow of information in the mind; specifically, the flow of information into awareness. Structural models of awareness tell us what a person can and cannot know about him- or herself. For example, if people have conscious access to their emotions (e.g., their feelings), but they don't know why they behave the way they do, then asking a person about his or her emotions should be very informative, whereas asking questions about why the person did what he or she did will yield less reliable information.

Western philosophers often argue that if a person lacks good self-knowledge and doesn't know the limits of her own self-awareness, she may be more likely to engage in foolish or reckless behavior. In Plato's ancient Greek meditation on self-knowledge, *Phaedrus*, Socrates exclaims that he cares only about knowing himself, every other pursuit being laughable if his self-knowledge is lacking (Griswold, 1986, p. 2).

The possibilities that self-knowledge might be far more limited than had been acknowledged in classical philosophy became clearer in the 18th and 19th centuries. During that time, more and more evidence accumulated that important parts of the mind might be unconscious. A particularly striking example of this was the "post-hypnotic suggestion." Here, a physician hypnotized a patient and suggested he or she perform some behavior upon awakening. After awakening from the hypnotic trance, the person often performed the act with no recollection of the suggestion. The increasing recognition of placebo cures in medicine—in which a harmless agent was presented to a patient as a cure—and showed a discernable curative effect, was another example of how the mind could apparently fool itself (Ellenberger, 1981).

Structural models that divided consciousness from the unconscious were proposed by Sigmund Freud in Germany and Pierre Janet in France. Their models used terms such as the "preconscious," the "unconscious," and the "subconscious" to describe areas that were not fully connected to conscious awareness (Perry & Laurence, 1984). Conscious awareness, and the unconscious regions of the mind that have been mapped out since the times of Freud and Janet, will be examined next (e.g., Kihlstrom, 1990; Bargh, 1997).

Consciousness and How Ideas Become Conscious

Structural models that separate the conscious from the unconscious typically treat consciousness as synonymous with awareness. In such models, **consciousness** simply refers to those things that are in our attentional spotlight and that we can describe. Freud likened consciousness to an internal sense organ, an inner eye, as it were. People can be asked to report what they are conscious of, and they are often willing to provide as accurate an answer as they can. The question, therefore, becomes what can and what cannot enter consciousness.

Closely related to consciousness is the concept of memories—materials that could become conscious—or not. Freud suggested that there existed a class of mental thoughts that included all those materials in memory that could readily become conscious if needed—such as our name, the sum of five plus five, or the meaning of the word "entertainment." In contemporary cognitive terms, Freud's idea is approximated by **declarative memory**. Declarative memory refers to information retrievable from memory that can be readily brought to mind (Davis, 2001; Eichenbaum, 1997; Ross, 2003). Freud referred to this same aspect of memory as the **preconscious**.

One model of declarative memory is that it consists of associations among concepts. A given concept is then retrieved (becomes conscious) as it is activated. Activation refers to a level of mental energy—perhaps rate of neural firing—associated with a concept at a given moment. When activation rises over a threshold, a concept is retrieved (i.e., becomes conscious). For example, if you wanted to remember the name of a red bird featured in a song, you might try thinking of the color red, and of bird names, to retrieve the name of the type of bird one you are seeking. Thinking of the color red, and of bird names, would activate key areas in your memory. For example, the concept "red" might spread activation to fire trucks, apples, and that elusive bird's name. The concept of "birds' names" might spread activation to pigeons, ostriches, and those elusive birds. When the two sources of activation intersect along such chains of association, the target concept itself—that red, red *something*—is further suffused with mental energy—raising the likelihood, finally, *robin* will come to mind (Collins & Loftus, 1975). So concepts in declarative memory that are below the activation threshold are not conscious, but they may become conscious with the correct retrieval strategy.

Contrasting with consciousness and declarative memory are a number of **unconscious** areas—consisting of those mental processes that have no communication with consciousness. A few of these are illustrated in Figure 8-2.

The "No-Access" Unconscious, or Unconscious Proper

There is good reason to have an unconscious. If we were consciously aware of everything our minds did, we would be constantly distracted—and then we would have trouble concentrating on the really important things of life (like personality psychology). Our consciousness is better put to use focusing on things of interest to us: our goals and values, and how to attain them. Perhaps for that reason, our mind seems to have evolved so that large areas of its activities are sealed off from consciousness and cannot disturb, or even communicate, with it. This sealed-off region goes by several names, including the **no access unconscious** (which we shall use here) and the **unconscious proper** (Dennett, 1978, p. 150; Kihlstrom, 1990, p. 457). The no-access unconscious refers to all mental activities that simply lack any communication channel to consciousness.

The descriptor, "no access," comes from an essay by Daniel Dennett in which he draws an analogy to the operating system of a computer that reads the time from a separate clock in the computer hardware and displays the time on the corner of the screen for the user to see. The operating system displays the time without knowing how the clock works or what "time" is or how it is calculated. Similarly, for Dennett, our minds "display" to us pictures of the surrounding world, but we do not consciously track how the brain composes them—and we are unaware of how the brain composes them.

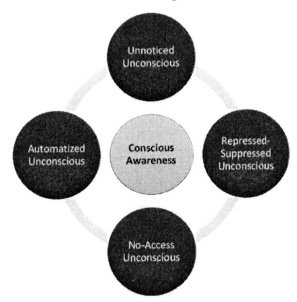

Figure 8-2 *Consciousness Coexists with a Variety of Non-Conscious Mental Processes.* Freud pointed out that we cannot control what we are unaware of in ourselves. Since his time, psychologists have defined various kinds of non-conscious mental activity.

To some extent, parts of the mind form their own separate compartments, and those compartments often have little communication with one another (Fodor, 1985). This idea can be illustrated with the well-known Müller-Lyer illusion shown here in Figure 8-3. We see two lines. It looks as if the bottom line is longer. But they are, in fact, the same length (Müller-Lyer, 1889). No matter how many times we see the image of these two lines (and I suppose you have seen it before), one line looks longer than the other. We can study this illusion, delving in to the principles of depth perception that are believed to bring it about, and yet the illusion will remain. In essence, the perceptual mechanisms for creating the illusion are compartmentalized. We have no conscious access to them, we cannot educate them, and we can't stop them from doing what they are doing. Nor can we understand what they are doing simply through "looking into our own minds" (Fodor, 1988; Nisbett & Wilson, 1977).

The Implicit or Automatic Unconscious

A particular type of no-access unconscious is that which takes place automatically. The term **implicit** or **automatic unconscious** refers to cognitive processes that operate independently of consciousness and yet consistently direct a person's thoughts, judgments, and behaviors according to non-conscious rules and tricks (Bargh & Chartrand, 1999). One example of this involves the **false fame effect** (Jacoby, Woloshyn, and Kelley, 1989).

The false fame effect occurs when people misinterpret their familiarity with a name, as suggesting that the name belongs to a famous person. For example, is "John Digman" famous? If you have been reading along, you have encountered his name several times because of his research with the Big Five personality traits. By most definitions he has made important scientific contributions, but he is not famous. If his name seemed famous, that familiarity may be why.

Figure 8-3: The Müller-Lyer Illusion

This visual illusion (like others) illustrates how one part of the mind can operate in partial independence of another. Even though people know the lines are the same length, one still looks longer.

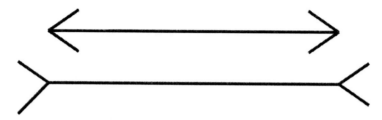

In laboratory studies of the false fame effect, participants first read through a list of names. A day later, the participants are asked to review a new list of names and identify who in the list is famous. The list they see includes some names from the day before, some new names, and some names of genuinely famous people. Participants readily identify the non-famous names they had seen before as famous, along with the names of actually famous people.

This effect is both automatic and hard to make go away. When the experimenter tells participants that no name on the original list is famous, and asks participants to identify any name they recalled from the initial list, the false fame effect still occurs (Jacoby et al. 1989). In one dramatic study, the first list of names was presented to surgery patients while they were under general anesthesia. The patients then exhibited the false fame effect when tested during their recoveries (Jelicic et al., 1992). In the next chapter, we will see further examples of how simple exposure to ideas can promote certain actions taking place, all outside of conscious recognition (e.g., Bargh and Chartrand, 1999).

The Unnoticed Unconscious

Yet another type of unconscious process is the **unnoticed unconscious**. The unnoticed unconscious consists of influences that go on in our mind that we could potentially know about if we paid attention to them, but that we often don't notice or understand (Bowers, 1984). For example, most shoppers prefer merchandise that appears to their right (but don't know this). Nisbett and Wilson (1977) asked shoppers to select the best pair of nylon stockings from among four identical pairs. People in the study preferred the right-most pair of identical stockings more often than the others. When the experimenters asked the consumers why they chose the rightmost pair, most replied that the fabric was smoother, or that the stocking seemed better made. When the experimenters asked shoppers if they simply exhibited a right-side preference, participants often looked at them as if they were crazy.

This sort of unconscious process is of particular significance because a person can be educated to understand it and to work around it if it is causing problems. But some among those who are directed to pay attention to the cause of their behavior may still miss the point. Bowers (1984, p. 245) conducted a study in which he socially reinforced students for choosing either a landscape or a portrait painting (depending upon the condition). During the first twenty experimental trials, the participants' baseline preferences of landscapes or portraits were assessed. In each trial, a participant viewed two postcards—one with a portrait painting and one with a landscape painting—and chose which one he or she preferred. During the next seventy trials, students in the experimental group were reinforced for choosing a class of paintings (e.g., portraits or landscapes) opposite to that of their initial preference. Students in the control group were reinforced for staying with their initial preferences. The experimenter smiled and said "good" after the desired choice so as to provide social reinforcement.

Although the reinforcer changed participant's preferences in the experimental group, many of them failed to notice its influence on their behavior—or even denied it was possible. For example, one young woman had initially preferred portraits and was reinforced to prefer landscapes. After the reinforcement phase, Bowers asked the young woman about her awareness of what was going on:

> Experimenter: Did you notice whether I said anything during the course of the experiment?
>
> Subject: You said "good" whenever I picked landscapes.
>
> Experimenter: Do you think your tendency to pick landscapes was influenced by my reinforcement of them?
>
> Subject: Of course not! I picked landscapes because I liked them better than the portraits. Besides, you only said "good" after I made my choice, so what you said couldn't possibly have influenced my selection of pictures. (Bowers, 1986, p. 245)

The woman failed to recognize that she was being reinforced for choosing landscapes as a general class of painting. Rather, she believed she received a smile for the choice of individual landscape paintings and that this had no bearing on her future choices. As a consequence, she failed to appreciate what was actually controlling her behavior even after it was pointed out to her. She suffered from unconsciousness due to the inability to notice and, in this case, an inability to understand.

The Dynamic Unconscious

By the **dynamic unconscious** is meant an unconscious in which mental contents are purposively banished from consciousness because the ideas contained are too threatening for the individual to face. This unconscious, as elaborated by Sigmund Freud, holds many ideas that could be conscious but are conscious no longer. Consciousness has, in some fashion, turned away or moved its spotlight of attention in such a way as to avoid this threatening content. The dynamic unconscious is constructed through the action of defense mechanisms. **Defense mechanisms** are ways that consciousness has of defending itself from dangerous, painful thoughts. For this to occur, the threatening material must be quickly moved out of consciousness and forgotten before it can be recognized. Nonetheless, the banished material continues to exert an influence over conscious choices.

The discussion of defense and underlying motives is covered in detail in Chapter 10 on the dynamics of self-control. For now, one small example of how unconscious fear can change our reasoning will suffice. People exert considerable effort to keep thoughts of their own deaths out of consciousness (Solomon, Greenberg, & Pyszczynski, 1991).

Undergraduates in one condition of an experiment were asked to write an essay about their own deaths. Members of a comparison condition wrote about what dental pain felt like. In a second phase of the study, students read an essay that either argued that human beings were quite different than animals, or quite similar to animals. Those who had earlier written about their own deaths (relative to those who wrote about dental pain) far preferred the essay that argued humans and animals were quite different from one another (Goldenberg et al., 2001, Study 2).

The study results were explained in this way: Animals are a reminder of death threat in that they are often live short, seemingly meaningless lives, and are frequently killed to be eaten, or are run over, or otherwise die unfortunate deaths (Becker, 1973). People who had participated in thinking about their own deaths were less willing than others to imagine themselves as similar to animals because they didn't want to further heighten their death concerns. The essay that drew the human-animal connection was therefore regarded as problematic.

What Are the Key Functions of Personality?

We have examined two different divisions of personality to this point. First, trait models divide personality into a hierarchy of traits. Second, awareness-based models divide personality according to what is conscious, and various areas of the unconscious. A third way of dividing personality is according to the functional areas that carry out the different tasks of personality. **Functional models** divide personality into different parts based on the tasks those parts carry out. For example, dividing personality into motivational and cognitive areas would represent a functional area division. The motivation area ensures that the individual meets his or her biological needs. The cognitive area, by contrast, is more concerned with logic and thinking. Dividing personality according to its functions can help identify a comprehensive set of personality areas; these models are therefore helpful for making a statement about what personality does.

The Id, Ego, and Superego as a Functional Model

Freud employed several divisions of the mind. One we have examined already was a division of mind by levels-of-awareness into a conscious, preconscious (declarative memory), and unconscious area. Later in his career, Freud employed a functional division; he referred to the three areas as the **id**, **ego**, and **superego** (also see Chapter 7). Freud believed the three areas were ordered according to their evolutionary complexity.

The id's work was to ensure the fulfillment of the organism's animal instincts and needs by communicating those needs to the rest of personality. The id was first to develop and contained an unconscious collection of sexual and aggressive urges common to lower animals such as the need to mate and to protect its territory. It operated according to primary, associationistic, imagistic processes common to those same lower animals.

The ego's work was to compromise between a human being's animal needs and the requirements of social reality. The ego contained portions of the mind that could think rationally. It allowed for reality contact and sensible behavior in the outside world, and ultimately for the intellectual processes unique to human beings.

The superego grew out of the ego and had as its purpose ensuring that the individual complied with the demands of society. It contained the learned commands and influences of society, which a person employed to formulate an ideal self and a conscience.

Freud's division was a good one for its time. At the same time, some of the ways it was elaborated are now contradicted by contemporary research (Mayer, 2001). For example, Freud believed that, analogous to evolutionary development, each person's id developed first, and ego functions were added only later. That was a reasonable hypothesis in 1920, but extensive experimental studies since that time indicate that infants engage in sophisticated perceptual understanding, some rational problem solving, and some rule-governed social behavior from the outset.

Another aspect of the id-ego-superego division is that it splits the associational, imagistic, qualities of the id from the rationality of the ego. Today, associational thinking is viewed as an integrated part of much rational thought. Rational thought, in turn, is viewed as less reliably logical than Freud and others of his time supposed it to be. So, Freud's division can still be applied but other divisions may provide better models of the mind (e.g., Epstein et al., 1996).

The Trilogy and Quaternity of Mind

A Trilogy of Mind

Probably the most continuously employed functional model is the **trilogy of mind** (Hilgard, 1988; Mayer, 2001). The trilogy of mind refers to a division of mind into areas of Motivation (or conation), Affect (emotion), and Cognition. The original trilogy of mind model was introduced during the European Enlightenment by Mendelsohn (1755). The trilogy of mind was developed further within a movement called **faculty psychology**. In this case, faculty refers to a mental faculty—that is, a mental capacity or quality. Two eminent Scottish psychologists elaborated the areas of the trilogy of mind by enumerating the individual capacities of the motivation area, the emotion area, and the cognitive area (Reid, 1785; Stewart, 1833). The system has since reappeared in the thinking of a variety of philosophers and psychologists (Hilgard, 1980).

Table 8-3: The Trilogy of Mind

Topic	Motivation	Emotion	Cognition
What Is Its Function?	Directs organism to carry out basic acts so as to satisfy survival and reproductive needs	Organizes a limited number of basic responses to relationships quickly and adaptively	Capacity to acquire, store, and reason with information
How Is It Initiated?	In response to internal bodily states	In response to changing relationships	In response to internal or external issues
What Is its Temporal Course?	Precede action; rise and fall rhythmically	Time course determined in part by specific feeling(s)	No set time line
What Information Does It Provide?	Specific as to what is lacking and what must be done	Identifies events that must be addressed; not specific as to how	Specific or general depending upon problem
In What Area of the Brain Might It be Located?	Limbic system, especially the hypothalamus	Limbic system, especially the amygdala and hypothalamus	Association and cerebral cortex

cf. Mayer, Chabot, & Carlsmith (1998).

There is common agreement now as to what each area denotes. According to one contemporary summary, each functional area evolved to process different stimuli, in different ways, in different areas of the brain (see Table 8-3, first 3 columns; Mayer, Chabot, & Carlsmith, 1998). Motivation directs the organism to carry out basic acts so as to satisfy survival. It arises in response to bodily states, precedes action, is very specific about what is needed, and seems related to multiple areas of the limbic system. Emotion, by contrast, organizes response patterns that may occur in reaction to changes in relationships. Emotions identify interpersonal events that must be addressed, and are related to the amygdala and hypothalamic brain areas. Cognition concerns the capacity to acquire, store, and reason with knowledge. It arises in response to a broad variety of issues and is rather flexible in responding to problems. Its brain locus is the association cortex and cerebral cortex.

Some recently have suggested turning the trilogy of mind into a **quaternity of mind**. The quaternity of mind refers to a modification of the trilogy in which consciousness is added as a fourth functional area (Mayer, Chabot, & Carlsmith, 1988). Consciousness arises when responses to novel or unusually intense events are called for, and it is plastic and creative in how it addresses issues (Ornstein, 1991). A variety of areas of the brain have been hypothesized to be associated with consciousness. When consciousness is added to the trilogy, the trilogy appears more complete in covering mental functions, as well as more comprehensive in organizing the traits of personality (Mayer, 2001).

A Brain to Match?

One reason that the trilogy of mind model may be so useful is its correspondence to a division of the brain called the "**Triune Brain**" (MacLean, 1977; 1993). The idea of the triune brain is that the brain underwent three evolutionary bursts of development. Each burst of development resulted in three rather different sets of neurological structures (see Figure 8-4).

The Reptilian Brain

The first evolutionary burst occurred as animals left the sea for life on land and the brain's evolutionary development accommodated the behavior of reptiles. The newly enlarged **reptilian brain** helped reptiles defend territory on land, secure food, and reproduce; all qualities associated with basic motivations. This earliest-evolved portion of the brain today forms its innermost core.

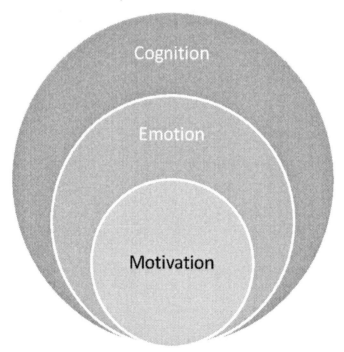

Figure 8-4 *The Trilogy of Mind*

If you follow the spinal cord into the head, the pons marks the entry of nerve signals from the body to the beginning of the reptilian brain. The reptilian brain consists of several structures. Peripherally, there exist inputs from the nose—the olfactory bulb and tubercule, and other sense organs (the optic chiasma). More centrally located are the pons, the amygdala, and the cerebellum. Reptilian brains also possess some aspects of the thalamus and hypothalamus associated with feeding and sexual behavior, as well as other reward and punishment experiences (Zuckerman, 1991, pp. 159-164).

The Paleo-Mammalian Brain

The second evolutionary burst occurred as mammal evolved from reptiles. Mammals differ from reptiles in giving live birth to and rearing their young (as opposed to laying eggs and leaving them). Rearing the young and forming social groups requires more socio-emotional coordination than was necessary for the egg-laying, earlier-evolved reptiles. This required a new second layer of brain structures: A **paleo-mammalian brain** shared in common by cats and dogs, sheep, cows, and most other mammals. The paleo-mammalian brain supports the increased emotional and social complexities and requirements of mammalian life.

The paleo-mammalian brain is located around the reptilian brain, and, in addition to the thalamus and hypothalamus, which it shares with the reptilian brain, consists of such other structures as the hippocampus, the corpus callosum, the cingulate gyrus, and the hippocampal gyrus of the temporal lobe. Together with the reptilian brain, this newer brain is sometimes said to form the limbic system, which is responsible for socio-emotional learning and responding. In addition, it includes the corpus callosum, a structure that permits communication the between right and left hemispheres, and which may contribute to the integration of thought and feeling (Halpern, 1997, p. 1094).

The Neo-Mammalian Brain

Finally, a third, most sophisticated area of brain called the **neo-mammalian brain** developed among primates. The reason for the substantial brain expansion over and above the old-mammalian brain is not fully understood. The most plausible explanation is that a growing capacity for pre-language communication and language itself provided an extraordinary evolutionary advantage to those who possessed it, and brought along with it the opportunity to better use flexible thinking (Deacon, 1997; Jerison, 2000).

The neo-mammalian brain surrounds the paleo-mammalian brain. It consists of a thick outer layer of tissue called the *cerebral cortex* that is wrapped around the earlier-evolved brain structures. The cerebral cortex consists of massive inter-associations of neurons with the general function of planning, thinking, judging, communicating, and performing other sophisticated information-processing tasks. The neo-mammalian brain is divided into two hemispheres, right and left; each hemisphere can be divided further into four lobes: the frontal, parietal, occipital, and temporal.

The frontal lobes (one in each hemisphere) appear important for mental synthesis, coordination, and control (Zuckerman, 1991, pp. 148-149). The back area of the frontal lobe contains the *primary motor cortex*. Running parallel across from it in the front-most area of the parietal lobe is the adjoining *somatosensory cortex*. Together, these structures are sometimes called the **body homunculus**. That is where Freud placed the developing ego, incidentally, so that it could control the person's actions according to its own rational judgments (Freud, 1923, p. 16). The temporal and occipital lobes are located further back and lower down in the brain.

Summary of MacLean's Tri-Partite Division of the Brain

One of the points here is that the trilogy of mind model corresponds to some degree to the three-fold division of the triune brain, where motivation corresponds to the reptilian brain, emotion to the old-mammalian, and cognition to the neo-mammalian (Mayer, Chabot, & Carlmsith, 1998). MacLean stressed that each of the three brains had its own means of operation and its own distinct design, and were not fully integrated. For example, the more emotional, lower limbic system in the paleo-mammalian mind might not fully understand or appreciate the cerebral cortex's impressive thought and judgment (Bailey, 1987). That said, it also is true that the brain is far more interconnected than the MacLean model might suggest (Issacson, 1982). For example, some specific brain functions such as language integrate the three functions of motivation, emotion, and cognition (Zuckerman, 1992). Nonetheless, the MacLean structural model remains a useful introduction to envisioning how the brain works.

> "It is the personality structure of an individual that, energized by motivations, dynamically organizes perceptions, cognitions, and behaviors so as to achieve certain 'system' goals." – Jack Block (1924-2010)

Integration in the Systems Set

With the development of criteria for good structural divisions of the mind, and the collection of earlier models such as the trilogy of mind and Freud's divisions, the opportunity arose to see if some more complete structural divisions of personality were possible. The systems set is one such model, illustrated in Figure 8-5.

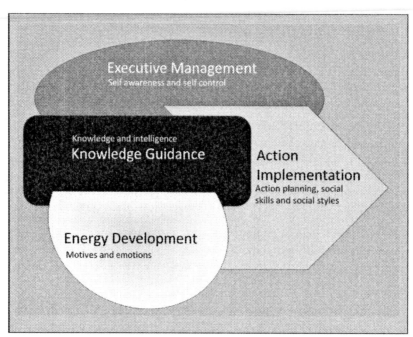

Figure 8-5 *The Systems Set Division of Personality*
The Systems Set begins with a comprehensive picture of the individual's major psychological systems divided into four areas: energy development, knowledge guidance, action implementation, and looking over them, executive management. Functions that are more internal are to the left; those more external, to the right. Systems that are more molecular are toward the bottom, those that are more molar are toward the top.

The **systems set** is a structural division that marks out four general areas of personality functions. Briefly, *energy development* includes motives and emotions (lower left). These can be distinguished from more cognitive-oriented systems devoted to *knowledge guidance* that include intelligence, mental abilities, and models of the self and world (middle left). *Action implementation* includes plans to implement behavior using preferred social styles and the social roles a person performs (right side). Finally, *executive management* includes self-awareness and self-regulation (top).

In the systems set, self-awareness has access to some parts of personality but not to others—that determines what is conscious and unconscious. Some parts of the mind are simply unconnected with self-awareness, such as portions of the visual system responsible for optical illusions. Defense mechanisms block additional contents out of consciousness if they are too threatening. A structural model such as this one also can organize personality traits according to areas—into motivational traits, traits of intelligence, and traits of socio-behavioral expressions such as extraversion (Mayer, 2003).

What Are the Boundaries Between Structural Areas Like?

If multiple areas of the mind exist, are there also boundaries between them? For example, if there is an emotion area and a cognitive area, is there some line, gradient, or neutral zone between them? Similarly, could there be a line, gradient, or neutral zone between conscious and non-conscious areas? Ernest Hartmann and his colleagues have examined whether some people have thin boundaries and others have thick boundaries between their areas of mental functioning (Hartmann, Harrison, & Zborowski, 2001).

In Hartmann's terms, a person with very thick boundaries is someone who can easily keep matters in focus and block out distractions. The person is aware of either thinking or feeling, but would not do both at the same time. The individual is awake when awake, and asleep when asleep, and experiences few in-between states. The individual has a very clear sense of boundaries, identity, and group identity as well ("I am a Baltimore Orioles fan and will always be one."). Many matters are black and white for this individual.

A person with very thin boundaries, by comparison, often has a blend of sensory experiences (called synesthesia). The individual may see images in response to musical sounds or hear notes in response to tastes. The individual may respond to inputs from many different sources at once, and can be easily overwhelmed and confused by too much input. The thin-boundary person is often aware of feeling and thinking at the same time ("I always feel when I think.") and often experiences half-asleep, half-awake states. Thin-boundary people may blend together different ages when thinking about themselves, seeing their inner child as adults, for example, and often think in shades of grey.

Hartmann and colleagues have developed "The Boundary Questionnaire" (BQ) to assess people's boundaries. People with thin boundaries endorse items such as, "When I awake in the morning, I am not sure whether I am really awake for a few minutes," "At times I have felt as if I were coming apart," and "Sometimes I don't know whether I am thinking or feeling." By comparison, people with thick boundaries endorse items such as "I keep my desk and work table neat and well organized," "I like heavy, solid clothing," and "A good relationship is one in which everything is clearly defined and worked out."

The Boundary Questionnaire is empirically related both to Tellegen's Absorption Scale (which predicts hypnotic susceptibility) and to the Big Five Scale of Openness, with which it correlates $r = .73$. Thick boundary people refer to themselves as solid and reliable, and to thin scorers as flaky and far out. On the other hand, thin boundary people refer to themselves as exciting and innovative and refer to thick boundary people as dull, rigid, and unimaginative.

High scorers on the BQ include art students, music students, models, adults with nightmares, frequent dream recallers, "lucid dreamers," people with unusual mystical experiences, and those with personality disorders in the odd and eccentric cluster (e.g., Schizoid and Schizotypal). Low scorers (those with thick boundaries) include naval officers, salespersons, lawyers, persons suffering from alexithymia (e.g., lack of emotional insight), and patients with sleep apnea.

Physiological recordings of brain activities indicate that those with thick boundaries have more clear-cut states of waking, NREM, and REM sleep. Those with thin boundaries have more blurred sleep physiology. For example, Phasic Integrating Potentials—a sign of REM sleep—occur far more often outside of REM sleep for thin boundary than for thick boundary people. Similarly, musicians, who score as having thinner boundaries than other groups, have more massive connections between their left and right hemispheres than average (e.g., larger corpus callosums; Schlaug et al., 1995).

What Are the Structural Connections Between Personality and the Environment?

The last group of structural organizations we will examine connect personality to its surroundings. We know that personality influences how the individual survives and thrives in its surrounding world; **connective structural models** provide a framework for examining how personality is connected to the outside world. The first structural division is a specific one designed to highlight how personality makes sense of the environment and responds to it.

Structures of Social Interaction

Social-cognitive psychologists are interested in understanding how personality operates in the real world, and how it makes sense of the social situations it encounters as it navigates its way through life. These models further concern how an individual behaves differently in different situations: quiet in a library, cheering at a football game, and lining up in a post office. Social cognitive psychologists have been particularly interested in such relationships (e.g., Kammrath, Mendoza-Denton, & Mischel, 2005; Mischel & Shoda, 1995; Cervone, 2005).

For example, Walter Mischel and Yuichi Shoda have created a model of mental structures responsible for acting in the environment, called the **Cognitive-Affective Personality System (CAPS)**. This model structurally divides the personality system into five parts (Mischel and Shoda, 1995). These are illustrated in Table 8-4.

The first structures, *encodings*, refer to the mental models people employ to understand the outside situations they face. Encodings consist of the perceptual meanings people assign to the events and behaviors they observe. Imagine a sixth-grader is walking down a school hallway. Just then, a bigger child who often bullies other children turns the corner and walks toward him. The bully contorts his face as he passes by the child. The sixth-grader may encode the bully's face in several ways. He might guess that the bully is goofing around—pretending he is in mock-pain for some reason, or he might guess that the bully is making fun of him by contorting his face. These encodings will determine how the sixth-grader will react.

Expectancies and beliefs, the second set of structures, concern what the person expects and believes of the world around him. An individual who believes the world is an unsafe place and that many people don't like him or her is more likely to perceive personal threats and insults in surrounding people. A child with such expectancies is likely to encode the larger child as making fun of him.

The third structure, *affects*, include emotions and other feelings (such as sleepiness or alertness) with which a person responds to the encodings and expectancies surrounding them. A happy child seeing the bigger child contorting his face may find it amusing and even laugh aloud. An anxious child may become frightened at what the larger child may do.

The first three structural areas, (1) encodings, (2) expectancies and beliefs, and (3) affects, tell us how the person interprets the surrounding world and how he feels about it. The fourth structures, *goals and values*, direct what the person does with that understanding and feeling. If the person's goal is safety, he or she may attempt to avoid a larger child who behaves like a bully. If the child's goal is to impress others, however, a bully who is not too big and strong may serve as a perfect opportunity for a conversation, and even a challenge to a fight.

Table 8-4: Mischel & Shoda's Cognitive-Affective Units in Personality*

Cognitive-Affective Units	Description
Encodings	Categories into which people, situations, and events are sorted
Expectancies & Beliefs	Outcomes that a person expects are possible in a given situation
Affects	Emotions and related feelings in response to people, situations, and their outcomes
Goals & Values	Desirable outcomes the person hopes to achieve; and undesirable outcomes the person hopes to avoid
Self-Regulatory Plans	What the person hopes to do, based on a sense of his or her own competencies and beliefs about events, to bring about desired goals

*Adapted from Mischel & Shoda (1995, Table 1, p. 253).

Finally, we act in ways that are determined in part by the fifth kind of unit, *competencies and self-regulations*. If we are competent at poking friendly humor at others, a comment about the bully's contorted face might bring a laugh to everyone—the aggressive child included. A child would be ill advised to try the same thing if his humor is more on the insulting side, and his capacities to run and/or fight are not so strong.

These units operate in parallel with one another, sending messages through the system and collectively sorting out what a situation means and how to respond to it: Is that a bully? Is he attacking me? Do I have a good joke on hand? Will it work? How fast can I run if it doesn't? Understanding the status of each unit of a structural type can help predict how the person will behave in a given situation (Mischel & Shoda, 1995, pp. 253-254). The Mischel-Shoda model is useful for understanding the structures involved in coping with situations. Situations, however, are just one part of surrounding personal environment.

Using Structural Dimensions to Fill in Personality

The systems framework used to organize this book includes a more general structural model that connects personality to situations and to a broader **life space** (the area around personality). The framework's structural model is based on the idea that most personality theorists use a common structural language to describe how personality works and interacts with other systems.

First (you may recall from Chapter 1), personality is organized from smaller units beginning with smaller neuropsychological parts, and ranging up to larger, molar units such as the individual's major psychological subsystems—motives, emotions, and mental models. That is, personality and its parts exist along a molecular-molar dimension. Second, most theories of personality share in common a view that personality is internal to the person and interacts with an external world. That is, it exists along an internal-external dimension (Mayer, 1995a).

Those two dimensions—a molecular-molar dimension, and an internal-external one—can be used to develop a diagram of personality and its relation to the outside environment. That two-dimensional portrayal was shown in Chapter 1 and is reproduced here in greater detail in Figure 8-6 (Mayer, 2005). Recall that the vertical dimension represents molecular versus molar systems, and the horizontal dimension separates the internal from the external.

Personality and its major systems (see Figure 8-6, for example) are to the middle left. The interactive situation is at the psychological level, but to the right—outside the person. To be sure, it has an objective, physical reality—sound, movement, people—but what goes on in the situation is understood at the psychological level. Both personality and the situation emerge from smaller systems; in the case of personality, it emerges from brain and other biological processes. The situation emerges from its components: its setting, props, and elements—rocks, wood, flesh, and blood. The incorporative systems (on top) include the person, the interactive environment, and other smaller systems that make them up.

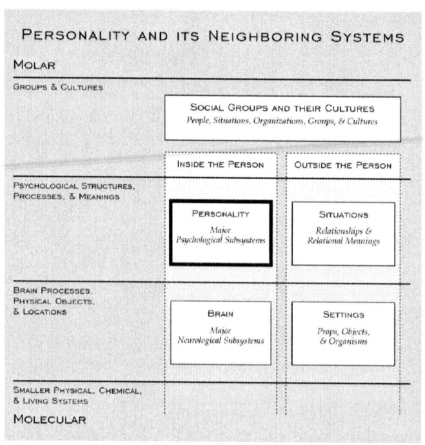

Figure 8-6 *Personality and Its Neighboring Systems*

The structural model of personality and its surroundings shown here elaborates one of the first views of personality provided in this textbook. Here, personality is shown at a psychological level, within the mind. The outside situation is at the same psychological level. To be sure, the external situation is physical and objective, but it takes its meanings from the way it is understood by the individual. Below the psychological level are the person's brain and biological systems (within the person) and the social setting (outside). Above personality and the situation are the incorporative, social environments.

Figure 8-6 shows one possible unified structural model, therefore, of the various internal regions of personality and the external life space with which it interacts. Other models are possible, of course, that will emphasize other aspects of personality. The model shown here was chosen for its generality.

What Can Structures Do?

Revisiting the Organization of Traits

Structures matter for everything from organizing traits, to relating personality to the environment, to ensuring that a given individual's personality is viewed in a balanced fashion.

To begin with, consider the issue of organizing traits. Earlier in this chapter, various trait-based structures of personality were examined such as the Big Two, the Big Three, and the Big Five and beyond. Functional divisions of mind, such as the trilogy of mind, the id, ego, and superego, and the systems set, also can be used to organize traits. In this case, traits are arranged not by the correlations among them (as in the Big Five), but rather, according to the functions of personality to which they are related.

For example, using the trilogy of mind model, psychologists have divided traits into motivational, emotional, and cognitive types, depending upon the area of personality function they describe (again, regardless of their correlations with one another; e.g., Buss & Finn, 1987; Mayer, 1995). Motivational traits include the need for achievement, sensation seeking, and nurturance. Emotion traits include neuroticism and positive affect. Cognitive traits include intelligence and creativity—those that describe our cognition. When researchers use the systems set, a more comprehensive classification of traits is possible. Raters are able to classify more than 80% of all traits using the system set classification. Some examples are illustrated in Table 8-5 (Mayer, 2003).

Table 8-5: Using the Systems Set to Organize Traits*

The Four Areas of the Systems Set			
Energy Development *An interweaving of motivation and emotion*	**Knowledge Guidance** *Acquired models and the intelligence that acts on them*	**Executive Management** *Conscious awareness, self-control, and voluntary behavior*	**Action Implementation** *Planning that connects the person to outside acts*
Traits Related to Each System Set Area			
n Achievement *n* Affiliation Neuroticism-Stability Friendliness-Hostility	Creativity Intelligences: *Verbal, Spatial, Personal, etc.* Locus of control	Self-Consciousness Absorption Will power	Athletic Non-Conforming Artistic Machiavellianism

*Adapted from Mayer (2003).

Now consider how personality is positioned relative to the structure of a person's outer world—the life space that surrounds each of us: our underlying biology, our setting, the situations we face, and the groups we belong to.

Traits of the Life Space

A person's surrounding life space, too, has a structure and has "traits." For example, researchers can ask questions about a person's surrounding environment. They ask college students to fill out surveys containing more than a thousand questions that ask about each area of their individual lives: biological, situational setting, interactions, and group memberships (Bracket, Mayer, & Warner, 2004; Mayer, Carlmsith,

& Chabot, 1998). The questions about a person's setting ask how many shoes, political posters, shot glasses, umbrellas, and jars of vitamins a person owns. Interaction questions include how many times a person has spoken with family members or watched a video over the past week.

When the items from such surveys are factor analyzed, some very interesting dimensions emerge. First is a cared-for, positive, social orientation that involves lots of healthy social interactions. Another dimension is a sports dimension that involves participating in a lot sports activities, rooting for teams, and owning sports equipment. A third commonly found dimension involves a drug culture environment that includes owning, taking, and perhaps abusing alcohol and drugs. Yet another life-space dimension involves being highly interested and involved in the arts, and still another involves being involved in solitary intellectual pursuits. You probably can identify friends and others who would score high on one or another of these dimensions. As life space dimensions become increasingly worked out, one project will be to see which personality traits go together with which "traits" of the life space (Bracket, Mayer, & Warner, 2004; Mayer, Carlmsith, & Chabot, 1998).

Structure and the Description of the Person

Another point of structurally dividing personality is to ensure that psychologists provide a relatively complete overview of an individual's mental functioning. For example, using the trilogy of mind ensures an examination of an individual's motivation, emotion, and cognition. Using the systems set reminds us to consider many aspects of a person: her motives and emotions (energy development) intelligence and knowledge (knowledge guidance), social skills (action implementation), and the executive consciousness that overlooks the rest. By considering the broader picture of a person we are unlikely to get caught up in any of her individual flaws (or positive qualities) and lose the overall sense of who she is. Rather, we can begin to see how her mental qualities work together to create a functioning whole.

From Structures to Dynamics

The models covered in this chapter describe the trait-structures, awareness-structures, and function-based structures into which personality and its surroundings can be divided. Each of these structural models helps us understand the relatively stable aspects of personality organization.

In addition to organizing the parts of personality, structure also describes the context in which personality dynamics operate. **Personality dynamics**—the way one part of personality influences another—take place across the various areas of personality. For example, one chain of dynamics extends from the innermost working areas of personality—beginning with its motivational urges—and extends outward toward social action in the life space. This chain of dynamics could be said to begin motivationally, be amplified emotionally, and thought about cognitively. Finally, it goes on to be expressed in the outer world. This chain of dynamics will be examined in Chapter 9, coming up next.

Reviewing Chapter 8

The purpose of this chapter is to acquaint you with the notion of personality structure, why it is important, and some of the major structures that have been proposed for personality psychology. Basically, structure is important because it provides a relatively stable organizational scheme for defining parts of personality (which exist within a given structure or area of personality) and dynamics of personality, which cross structures.

It is possible to have more than one good structural system to describe personality. The majority of this chapter is aimed at introducing different structures that stem from different perspectives: Those based on traits, on levels of awareness, on functions, and on connecting personality to the outside world.

Questions About "What Is Personality Structure?"

1. <u>Personality Structure Described:</u> What is personality structure and what does it let us do? What are some similarities between personality structure and the structure of a city?

2. <u>Uses of Personality Structure:</u> Several reasons are given for the importance of understanding personality structure. How can they help us understand the many parts of personality? How can they help us make sure we have a comprehensive picture of an individual when studying a specific case?

3. <u>Multiple Personality Structures:</u> The chapter outlines several valid types of personality structure. Personality, like other complex systems, can be divided in more than one way, and more than one division can be valid, even when they are quite unlike one another. Do you know the criteria for valid or good structural divisions?

Questions About "How are Personality Traits Structured?"

4. <u>The Big Two and the Big Three:</u> What were Eysenck's 2 factors, or Raymond Cattell's 16 factors of personality and how do they relate? What is a Superfactor or Big Factor. What are the Big Three?

5. <u>The Big Five:</u> What is the lexical hypothesis, and how did it lead to the Big Five personality traits. What are the Big Five personality traits? *Suggestion*: the mnemonic, "OCEAN," can be helpful for learning the five factors: O=openness, C=conscientiousness…, can you fill in the rest? What argument could you provide that the Big Five personality traits are better than, say, the Big 2 or Big 3.

6. <u>The Big Six:</u> Although many psychologists are happy with the Big Five model of personality trait structures, others would like to add in more dimensions. Why would they like to do so, and what are some suggestions of additional dimensions they would like to add?

Questions About "What Are Structural Models of Awareness and Why Do They Matter?"

7. <u>Rationale for Structural Models of Awareness:</u> Among the first structural models of personality was Freud's division of the mind into conscious and unconscious processes. Why have structural models that divide the consciousness from the unconscious been so interesting to psychologists?

8. <u>The No-Access Unconscious (or Unconscious Proper):</u> Most mental processing takes place in the no-access unconscious. For example, when we perceive depth, and visual illusions, or mentally construct any image, it occurs unconsciously. What are the defining characteristics of this no-access unconscious?

9. <u>The Implicit or Automatic Unconscious:</u> The implicit or automatic unconscious refers to memory events that often take place under the threshold of awareness, in the no-access unconscious. It is often demonstrated with the use of memory priming—that is, showing stimuli and then covering them up. Can you describe an experimental demonstration of the operation of the implicit, automatic unconscious?

10. <u>The Unnoticed Unconscious:</u> Many mental functions would be accessible to us if only we noticed them. Can you give an example of an experimental phenomenon that illustrates that people don't notice what is actually influencing their behavior?

11. <u>The Dynamic Unconscious:</u> Freud's idea was that some material resides outside of awareness because it is too threatening to enter into consciousness. These motives and associated ideas nonetheless can influence our thinking, and may be exhibited through dreams and errors in behavior, including slips of the tongue. Can you give an example of a study that demonstrates the action of the dynamic unconscious?

Questions About "What Are the Key Functions of Personality?"

12. <u>The Id, Ego, and Superego:</u> What work areas of personality did Freud's id, ego, and superego describe?

13. <u>The Trilogy and Quaternity of Mind:</u> Long before modern psychology, many philosophers and "faculty psychologists" had begun to divide the mind into its basic functional areas. The trilogy-of-mind refers to three functions; can you name them? When consciousness is added in as a fourth area, the quaternity-of-mind is formed.

14. <u>A Brain to Match:</u> Some brain scientists have suggested a rough division of the brain according to its evolution into the reptilian brain, paleo- (or old) mammalian brain, and neo-mammalian brain? The neo-mammalian brain corresponds to cognition. What functions of the trilogy do the reptilian and old-mammalian brain correspond to? What evolutionary pressures prompted the development of the old-mammalian brain?

15. <u>The Systems Set:</u> As structural divisions are better understood, along with the criteria they must meet, it becomes more readily apparent how personality might be divided. One such new division is the systems set. Can you name its four areas?

Questions About "What Are the Structural Connections Between Personality and the Environment?"

16. <u>Structures of Social Interaction:</u> The social-cognitive perspective of the mind is directly interested in relating personality to its acts in the outside world. Such psychologists divide the mind into areas particularly important to predicting such outside action. For example, a person's expectancies of reward are very important to what they do. What other divisions do social-cognitive psychologists employ?

17. <u>Using Structural Divisions to Fill In Personality:</u> As we saw in Chapter 1, two dimensions: The molecular-molar, and internal-external, can be used to arrange personality amidst its surrounding system. These dimensions can also be employed to organize parts of personality. What parts are most molecular to personality? What parts are more molar?

18. <u>Extending Personality to the Life Space:</u> Just as personality has a structure, so does the environment surrounding it. When people are asked questions about their environment, what sorts of dimensions of the surrounding environment are obtained?

Questions About "What Can Structures Do?"

19. <u>Organizing Traits by Processing Area:</u> Psychologists have sought to organize traits according to the part of the trilogy (or quaternity) of mind they describe. Can you give an example of a trait that would describe each of the three areas? What are the similarities and differences of this approach to the trait structures that are found from factor analysis (hint: factor analysis is based on the correlation among traits).

Chapter 8 Glossary

Terms in Order of Appearance:

Personality structure: Personality structure refers to the relatively enduring, distinct major areas of the personality system, and their interrelations and interconnections. These different areas of personality can be distinguished according to their different contents, functions, or other characteristics.

Hierarchical Structure of Traits: This is a structural conception or theory about traits in which there are said to be big traits or super traits that can be divided into a larger number of lower-level, specific traits.

Big or Super Traits: These are very general, broad, thematic expressions of mental life that are relatively consistent within the individual, and that can be subdivided into more specific traits.

Big Two Super Traits: This is a specific hierarchical structural model of traits, proposed by Hans Eysenck, in which two traits, Extraversion-Introversion and Neuroticism-Stability, are divisible into more specific traits. Collectively, the two super traits and their subdivisions are said to describe much of personality.

Big Three Super Traits: This is a later modification of the Big Two Super Trait model by Eysenck (see glossary/text) in which a third super trait, Psychoticism-Tender Mindedness, was added.

Big Five Model: This is a hierarchical structural model of traits, developed by a number of researchers, in which five broad traits are used to describe personality. The five are: Neuroticism-Stability, Extraversion-Introversion, Openness-Closedness, Agreeableness-Disagreeableness, and Conscientiousness-Carelessness.

Lexical Hypothesis: The hypothesis that the most important personality traits are those that can be found in the language people use to describe one another.

Consciousness: A subjective experience of awareness, and the capacity to reflect on that awareness.

Declarative Memory or Preconscious: Declarative memory includes all the information in memory that could be consciously retrieved if necessary. The preconscious was Freud's earlier term for this aspect of memory.

Unconscious: A part of the mind that cannot or does not readily enter awareness.

No-Access Unconscious or Unconscious Proper: Portions of neural activity which take place with no connection to consciousness, such as the firing of individual nerve pathways or the elementary processing of psychological information.

Implicit (or Automatic) Unconscious: A type of unconscious bias or process that can be determined from experimental measures of memory but which the person is unaware of.

False Fame Effect: An effect in which familiarity with a name leads a person to falsely believe the name is of a famous person.

Unnoticed unconscious: A type of unconscious process that consists of influences that could be known if the person paid attention or if the person was taught about the influence, but that goes unnoticed for many or most people.

Dynamic Unconscious: Material that is made unconscious, through the redirection of attention, because the material is too painful or unpleasant to think about or feel.

Defense Mechanisms: Mental processes that divert attention from painful or unpleasant things to think about. Defense mechanisms help keep material dynamically unconscious.

Functional Models: Divisions of personality based on the idea that different parts of the system carry out different forms of work (e.g., meeting needs [motivation] versus problem-solving and cognition).

Id: Latin for the "it." One part of Freud's later, structural division of mind (the other parts are the ego and superego). The id contains sexual and aggressive instincts, and wishes and fantasies related to those instincts.

Ego: Latin for the "self," a part of Freud's 1923 structural division of mind that involves rational thought and the control of the person's actions in the world.

Superego: Latin for "above the self," the superego is a part of Freud's 1923 structural division of the mind that involves internalized social rules of conduct and a sense of the ideal one would like to become.

Trilogy of Mind: This structural model of personality divides the system into three different functional areas: conation (motivation), affect (emotion), and cognition (thought).

Faculty Psychology: An 18th-century movement, predating modern personality psychology, to divide the mind into separate intellectual functions, called faculties, that include such broad areas as motivation, emotion, and cognition. Each functional area is, in turn, divided into more specific functions. For example, cognition is subdivided into specific faculties of memory, judgment, evaluation, and the like.

Quaternity of Mind: An expanded version of the trilogy of mind that adds consciousness to the traditional areas of motivation, emotion, and cognition.

Triune Brain: A structural model of the human brain that divides its physical areas according to whether the structures resemble those found in reptiles, or whether the brain structures evolved at a later time and resemble those of early mammals, or of more recently evolved mammals.

Reptilian Brain: The oldest part of the brain and the part of the "Triune Brain" structural model that includes such early-evolved, inner structures of the brain as the amygdala and the cerebellum, and portions of the thalamus and hypothalamus.

Paleo (Old-) Mammalian Brain: A recently evolved portion of the brain, shared in common among smaller mammals, and part of the "Triune Brain;" it includes limbic system structures such as the thalamus and hypothalamus, hippocampus, corpus callosum, and the hippocampal gyrus of the temporal lobe.

Neo (New-) Mammalian Brain: The newest-evolved portion of the brain, shared in common among primates and including the thick outer layer of the cerebral cortex.

Body Homunculus: A band of areas in the cerebral cortex, where each area corresponds to a part of the body, in order, such as toes, foot, lower leg, and so forth.

Systems Set: A work-area structural model of personality that emphasizes four areas: the energy lattice (motivation and emotion), the knowledge works (mental models and intelligence), the social actor (procedural knowledge for behavior), and the executive consciousness (self-awareness and control).

Connective Structural Models: Connective structural models are those that illustrate the relationship between personality and its surrounding environment.

Cognitive-Affective Personality System (CAPS): A structural division of personality proposed by Walter Mischel and his colleagues, which divides personality into cognitive structures such as expectancies and beliefs, and into affects (emotions).

Life Space: The systems, including biological underpinnings, social settings, interactive situations, and group memberships, which surround the individual and in which the individual operates.

Personality Dynamics: Most generally speaking, the influence of one part of personality on another.

Chapter 9: Dynamics of Action

Personality dynamics concern the interaction of personality's parts, and how those interactions are expressed in a person's environment. These dynamics take place against the background of the relatively stable processing areas of personality—its structural organization, which was discussed in the last chapter. For example, the dynamic interplay of motivation with other systems such as the emotions system, can bring about dramatic changes and re-directions within the personality system. Such dynamics guide how personality is expressed in the environment, and how personality is affected by the environment in return.

Previewing the Chapter's Central Questions

• **What Are Dynamics of Action?** Personality dynamics are introduced and defined as chains of mental events that range from the small and local to those that occur across much of personality.

• **Which Needs Will Begin Action?** A person has many needs at a given time. We'll examine the competition among needs, including how one need can serve another, and what happens when needs conflict.

• **How Does Action Develop in the Mind?** As needs develop, we often have feelings and thoughts about them—those feelings and thoughts may increase (or decrease) the likelihood we express our desires. The likelihood of a plan being translated into action can be expressed as a function as our thoughts about the plan. Sometimes actions are only partially expressed: one example is a slip of the tongue.

• **How Are Acts Performed?** When we intend to do something, we're ready to express our plan in the broader world. At that moment, our private personality works through communication channels—speech, movement, and other signals—to operate in the social world. The sometimes double-nature of our acts are considered—they may signal more than one motive. To express ourselves well, we also engage in the stagecraft of self-presentation. And, of course, we need to take our social situation into account.

What Are Dynamics of Action?

Personality Dynamics and Personality Structure

Personality dynamics concern the influence of one part or area of personality on another, as well as the mutual interaction between personality and its surroundings. The subject matter of personality is inherently dynamic (Vallacher, Read, & Nowak, 2002). You may have noticed earlier that Freud called his theory "Psychodynamic Theory." This might seem strange. He could have called it "Unconscious Theory," or "Theory of the Id, Ego, and Superego." Social-cognitive psychologists like to speak of dynamics as well, and trait psychologists sometimes speak of "dynamic" traits. So, what then is so important to these psychologists as to lead to their emphasis on dynamics? A beginning answer to that question can be obtained by considering what the term "dynamics" refers to in this context more generally.

To understand the term "dynamics," it is worth drawing an analogy to the dynamics of a city. Recall that we drew such an analogy between personality structure and city structure in Chapter 8. Whereas city structures involved the relatively stable areas of the city—its neighborhoods, parks, and waterways, city dynamics concern the "movement" or "moving parts" of the city. As with structures, many of the dynamics of a city are visible. This is particularly true of its daily rhythms: We can see children head off for school, and people going to work in the morning; traffic circulating (or stuck) on roads, trains and mass transit in operation. We can see children return home from school in the afternoon, and those who commute return in the evening. When the weather permits, we can see public concerts and festivals in the parks. Throughout the day, we can see some results of the activities carried out by the city's citizens: People are fed, clothed, cared for, and they meet one another, plan activities, and build things.

Note that all this dynamic activity will potentially influence the city's structure. If the people are prosperous and well organized, they will build more homes, rebuild decaying parts of the city, and create prosperous new areas while preserving and enhancing the natural environment. The city may gradually expand by bringing more people, housing, business, and enterprise within its influence, while preserving its rivers, lakes, and parks. If the people are not prosperous, though, the city may fall into disrepair. Poorer sections, tent cities, and other impoverished areas may arise, and neighborhoods (structure) may decay and ultimately become abandoned. Dynamics, in other words, represent the action and change in a city. Dynamics determine what the system does and whether it prospers.

Dynamics as Critical Chains of Events

Personality dynamics, like city dynamics, concern movements, interactions, and changes—but within a person's psychology. Personality dynamics refers to a variety of phenomena concerning influences of motives on emotions, emotions on thoughts, self-regulation, and social action. These movements render such dynamics absolutely critical to understanding how personality works and how it changes.

Loosely speaking, the sort of personality dynamics examined in this chapter involve a chain of events that begin with an urge or a desire in one part of personality, which then may be channeled into goals, and ultimately may be carried out successfully. This progression from urge to expression is by no means assured. The exact dynamic that emerges will depend on the nature of the personality an individual possesses. Even given a goal, urges are sometimes turned back, unexpressed. At other times, they are defeated by external obstacles. It is also true, however, that on occasion when an urge finds the right goal in the right environment, a person's energy can be released like an explosion.

For example, Homer H. Hickam, Jr. was born in Coalwood, a rural coal-mining town in West Virginia. His father was a manager at the mine who wanted his son to follow in his footsteps. Homer Jr. was 11 years old in 1957, when the Soviet Union launched Sputnik, the first human-launched satellite. As it turned out, the Russian rocket, which threatened American technological esteem, passed right over southern West Virginia, and Homer and his neighbors went out to watch (Hickam, 1998, pp. 30-32).

Homer Jr. organized his friends so as to launch a rocket themselves—something Homer didn't have much of an idea of how to do. When he announced his plans at the dinner table, his mother told him not to blow himself up, his father ignored him, and his brother snickered (Hickam, 1998, p. 34). At Homer's instigation, he and his friends took the powder out of twelve fire crackers, loaded them into the body of a small plastic flashlight, added a fuse, and fit the whole apparatus into the body of a plastic model airplane.

The night of the launch, Homer and his friends attached the rocket to his mother's beloved rose garden fence, lit the fuse, and stood back. In a moment, there arose a considerable explosion that launched a sizeable portion of the fence into the air and set the still earth-bound portion of the fence on fire. Fortunately, the young boys survived unscathed (Hickam, 1998, pp. 39-40).

When Homer's parents rushed to the screen door to see what happened, Homer expected to be severely scolded by his mother. Instead, she came out, sat beside him, and asked, "Sonny, do you think you could build a real rocket?" He replied, "No ma'am...I don't know how." "I know you don't know how," his mother responded, "I'm asking you if you put your mind to it, could you do it?" If he remained in the coal-town, she said, his future would be a dangerous and difficult one working in the mines. Rather, she badly wanted him to get out of Coalwood and go to college. To do that, however, he needed to demonstrate to his father he could succeed at something practical on his own. "Show him you can do something!" she challenged. "Build a rocket!" (Hickam, 1998, pp. 44-45).

Homer's somewhat disorganized, dreamy urge—a still unfocused interest and competitiveness—had led to something beyond casual play with firecrackers. His mother recognized the potential seriousness behind her son's act, and helped him galvanize that urge. From there, he enlisted the help of more scientifically minded friends, machinists at the mine, and other townspeople and supporters. His project led to ever-larger and more successful rocket launches, regional fame, and finally, a dreamed-of career with the National Aeronautics and Space Administration.

The transition of an urge through to its outward expression in successful behavior represents the form of a personality dynamic that will be examined in this chapter. First, though, we need to consider the nature of a dynamic in greater detail. We can better understand dynamics if we contrast micro-, meso-, and macrodynamics, examine how they change, and consider the existence of a special group of traits termed dynamic traits.

Dynamic Traits and Micro Dynamics

Earlier in the book we defined a **personality dynamic** as occurring when one part of personality influenced another. But this can happen on a relatively micro or small scale, or on a larger scale. As it turns out, we have already discussed many such small-scale, or **micro-level dynamics**. Micro-dynamics are causal connections that extend from one smaller, specific part of personality to another. Examples of micro-dynamics include how guilt might interfere with love, or how spatial intelligence might influence reading a map, or how a given script of social interaction might govern how a person understands the world.

One kind of micro-dynamic is especially germane to global chains of action discussed in this chapter. Those are **dynamic traits**. Dynamic traits represent tendencies toward certain classes of needs and goals. These traits possess a particular capacity to propel a person, to initiate dynamics throughout an individual's personality. Raymond Cattell (1965, pp. 28, 165) defined dynamic traits as those concerned with "why and how [the person] is moved to do what he does…[and] the incentives to which he has learned to respond." The needs for achievement, power, and affiliation all are examples of dynamic traits (see Chapter 4). Another example might be a trait related to how motives are expressed, such as reflectiveness-impulsiveness—which concerns the degree to which a person thinks over his or her actions before carrying them out. Similarly, those who study animal behavior frequently employ the term "dynamic trait" to refer to mating and other behaviors that relate one animal to another—for example, to summarize how a bird moves its feathers so as to attract mates (e.g., Rosenthal, Evans, & Miller, 1996).

"But wait a minute!" you might wonder, "Aren't all traits dynamic? Don't introversion and intelligence and emotionality all speak to how dynamic actions are carried out?" To some extent you would be right. There is no absolute boundary between traits that are dynamic and those that are not. Psychologists such as Cattell distinguished the dynamic traits from emotion-related traits (which he called temperament traits) and traits of mental ability such as intelligence. The basis for this is one of degree: Dynamic (i.e., motivational) traits are directly related to personal, self-directed action. Emotional or ability traits modify or refine how the actions are carried out (Cattell, 1965, pp. 28, 165).

Mid-level (Meso-) and Macro-Level Dynamics

As dynamic traits propel personality they exert their influence on many different systems at one time. Dynamics that cross several systems are called mid-level or **meso-level dynamics**. **Meso-dynamics** are dynamics that are larger in reach than micro-dynamics, while less grand than the far-reaching macro-dynamics of action or self-control. An example of such a meso-level dynamic is the **causal attribution**. Causal attributions concern an individual's beliefs about what determines events in the world. For example, if you think everything in the world is due to your own behavior, you develop a strong sense of control over the world. Another person may see the same kinds of events occur but attribute them to the situation, to chance, or to fate (Weiner & Graham, 1999).

People who attribute events to their own stable, global, qualities have a higher sense of responsibility than others, but are also considered more prone to pessimism and depression (e.g., Abramson, Alloy, & Metalsky, 1995; Peterson, 1991). So, this mid-level dynamic—how a person attributes causes—can influence the sorts of actions a person engages in, as well as his or her mood. Some contemporary dynamic theorists have tried to build computer models of portions of the personality system involving such dynamic interactions (Read & Miller, 2002; Vallacher et al., 2002).

Macro-level personality dynamics concern mental events that cross, or centrally effect, the entire personality system. The dynamics of action—the topic of this chapter—provide an example of a macro-dynamic that spans all of personality. For action to occur, it must begin someplace in the mind, be thought about (or not), cross from the mind to some external expression of the person (that is, be translated into behavior) and somehow influence the world. This chapter follows that chain of events from beginning to end.

Dynamics and Their Change

An important aspect of dynamics, and one thing that makes them so interesting, is that they can bring about change. Dynamic change occurs through learning, with experience, with education, and sometimes with counseling and psychotherapy. For example, Freud's psychotherapy began with the idea that dynamic changes could cure neurotics of their symptoms. In particular, Freud was interested in making unconscious processes conscious, and in learning about oneself in general (Paniagua, 2001; Weiner, 1975, pp. 40-44). Since Freud's time, therapies have continued their focus on dynamic change. All share the idea that strategic alterations in the parts of personality and how they dynamically interact can lead to change.

Consider the relationship between mental models and depression. People who dynamically respond to situations with persistently critical and negative interpretations of themselves are said to possess depressive schema (Segal, 1988). Such individuals are at greater risk for depression. If the depression lifts as a consequence of pharmacological (i.e., drug) therapy or simply due to the passage of time, the individual will still be at risk because the depressive schemas remain (e.g., Hedlund & Rude, 1995; Wenzlaff, Rude, & West, 2002).

For that reason psychotherapists often help depression-prone people to learn new more positive viewpoints. The therapist helps the client identify his irrational, exaggerated negative views of himself and others, and then encourages him to change his perspective by relearning habitual ways of thinking. Clients who gradually replace their of depressive schemas with more positive ones experience long-term improvements in their well-being and better resistance to future depressions (Segal, Gear, & Williams, 1999).

The contribution of dynamics to personal action and change make them crucial to understand. This chapter takes us step by step through a dynamic of action: From a motivated urge to its emotional and cognitive reverberations, to its translation into behavior, and finally, its social expression.

Which Needs Will Begin Action?

Urges, Needs, and Presses

People are often in motion, carrying out actions, expressing themselves. Many of these actions begin with a set of **urges**. These urges may express one or more bodily needs: to eat, drink, or sleep. They may include biosocial urges such as the needs for affiliation or for achievement. Each **need** is defined as a mental dynamic that guides personality so as to transform a lack of satisfaction into satisfaction. Needs often are focused such that they have specific aims (Murray, 1938). For example, the need for achievement might be represented in the aim of studying enough to get an A on a test. The urges may be triggered by the moment, or as a consequence of longer-term planning.

Needs also respond to environmental **presses** (Murray, 1938). An environmental press involves the incentives and disincentives of the surrounding situation, which can elicit some motives and suppress others. The environmental presses on a college student will often support studying, and be different from the presses faced by a high school friend who works locally as a carpenter, or an older sibling who is married with children. But, at some point, an action sequence is begun around one or more urges, or even the hint of urges.

Needs and Their Relative Strengths

Murray's Model

For Henry Murray, an early 20th century personality psychologist, control of personality moved around from need to need. He suggested it was useful to monitor an individual's **regnant process**. Regnant has the same Latin root, *regnans*, as reign and ruler, and refers to governing. The regnant process—typically a particular need—exerts control over personality at a given point in time (Murray & Kluckhohn, 1956). Needs can be in conflict, however, and the question of which one is in control is a matter of how those needs interact. What follows are some observations Murray had of how motives or needs influence one another (Murray, 1953, pp. 85-87; 1951, p. 452).

Murray started with the idea that every person experienced a hierarchy of needs in which certain needs were more important, or prepotent, relative to others. A **prepotent need** is one that would take over the control of personality—become regnant—most quickly if it is not satisfied at a certain level. Basic needs such as pain avoidance and hunger are prepotent over others. If a person is famished, he must be fed before other needs take on importance. Or, as Bertolt Brecht put it in his *Threepenny Opera*: "First feed our stomachs, then talk politics."

Determinant Needs and Subsidiary Needs

Determinant needs are those basic needs that can motivate a person to do other seemingly less important things. **Subsidiary needs** arise when a goal must be pursued to fulfill the determinant need. That is, the most determinant need sets the agenda; the other need is subsidiary to it. For example, a child might have a determinant need of being loved by his or her parents, and that might lead to a subsidiary to study hard so as to please them. Such a situation is illustrated in a study by Dowson & McInerney (2001), who interviewed 86 middle school children, to find out why they wanted to achieve in school.

The interviews included questions such as, "Do you want to do well in school?" and "What reasons do you have for wanting to do well at school?" The researchers found that being together with friends was often a determinant need, and working hard and studying was a subsidiary need that helped the students remain with their friends who were performing well. As one student put it, "Me and my friends try to get the teacher to let us work together, but then we have to show her that we're doing the work, or she won't let us be together next time."

For another group of students, a desire to nurture others (or to look good oneself) was determinant; working hard was again subsidiary. These children felt concerned when they saw others having trouble, and good about themselves if they could help. They said things like, "If I know my work well, then I can help my friends if they need it. I like to help when I can" and "If my friends don't understand what they have to do, they ask me what to do because they know I like to help them." (Dowson & McInerney, 2001, p. 37).

Freud would have been unsurprised by the students' comments, perhaps asking, "Why would any child be interested in school learning for its own sake?" Freud believed, as did Murray, that people have basic needs for survival and reproduction and these shape more complex social behavior. For Freud, every person enters into an implicit contract with society: Each individual learns, works, and upholds civilized values; in exchange, society provides people with safety, the opportunity to socialize and the chance to engage in productive work (Freud, 1930). Freud would interpret studying with others as means of developing companionship and preparing to carry out productive work in the future.

Even if intellectual work begins for other reasons, some early theorists believed it could become **functionally autonomous**. Functionally autonomous motives take on an independent role of their own (Allport, 1968). Since Freud's time, however, other motivational theorists have been happy to accept intellectual interest as an innate motive in itself. For example, it may have evolved by leading people to learn more about their environment, others around them, and their culture, which would itself enhance chances of survival (e.g., De Waal, 2001, p. 24).

In the survey discussed above, the children didn't always want to study, of course. The young students sometimes felt bored, lazy, and angry. They made remarks such as: "I don't like subjects that are too hard. I'd rather be somewhere else," and "...most of the time, I just try to do as little as possible" (Dowson & McInerney, 2001, p. 38). When a desire to achieve collides with a desire to do as little as possible, the result is called a need or goal conflict.

Needs and Need Conflicts

Each individual experiences a wide number of needs—many of which can come into conflict. For example, every person has both the need to be alone and to socialize. In such cases, the prepotent—or neediest—need typically wins out. Those people who have higher needs to socialize than to be alone will act sociable. Those who have higher needs to be alone than to socialize will remain solitary. Still, the conflict between the social and the solitary will be present to some degree in each person.

What effect do conflicts between needs have on the individual? Emmons and King (1988; 1989) reasoned that such conflicts would exert a negative overall influence on a person's emotional life. Emmons and King had previously studied **personal strivings** (see Chapter 4). Personal strivings are tasks a person is trying to carry out over the short- or medium-term in the course of meeting longer-term goals. Examples of personal strivings include the tasks of "appearing attractive," "seeking new and exciting experiences," and "avoiding being noticed by others." They proposed a model in which conflicts among needs would interfere with attaining certain goals. This, in turn, would cause an individual to dwell on missing their goals, returning their thoughts repeatedly to the problem—a state called rumination. The added stress would cause the person negative emotions and poorer health.

Emmons and King asked people to list their personal strivings (the average person in their study lists about 15), and then to identify any potential conflicts among them. The authors identified two different kinds of conflicts. The first is a **conflictual striving**—based on the direct conflict between one striving and another (cf. Heilizer, 1964). To identify conflictual striving, a given participant examines all pairs of their strivings and indicates those that are in conflict. For example, "to appear more intelligent than I am," is often rated as in conflict with "to always present myself in an honest light." (Emmons & King, 1988, p. 1042). Another conflicting pair was "to keep my relationships on a 50-50 basis" and "to dominate, control, and manipulate people and situations." A person's overall goal-conflict rating was the average of the conflict ratings they gave each striving pair.

The second kind of conflict—called **ambivalent striving**—involves a striving that has its own conflict intrinsic in it. Meeting certain goals, for example, can simply create conflict by themselves. On top of the list of such ambivalent strivings (as rated by students in the same study) were: "to be all things to all people," "to be honest," and "to avoid being aggressive if I feel I've been wronged." (Emmons & King, 1988, p. 1042).

Emmons and King correlated the level of a person's conflictual and ambivalent striving with such criteria as the individual's well-being, the number of physical symptoms they experienced, and even the number of the trips they made to the student health service and the severity of the diagnosis for a medical problem they experienced after they arrived there.

Students with goal conflicts of any type reported thinking about them (ruminating) more and experiencing more stress on account of those thoughts. They had more negative feelings and a reduced sense of well-being. Those goal-conflicted people also reported more physical symptoms than others, and, more than a year later they reported more often to the student health service and were diagnosed with more severe health problems (Emmons & King, 1988, Study 3). Goal conflicts may be especially problematic for those who optimistically hope they can meet conflicting goals. Such naïve optimists appear susceptible to greater immune system dysfunction than those who accept they cannot achieve all their desires (Segerstrom (2001).

Need Fusion

Finally, in fortunate cases, a person may experience **need fusion**. Need fusion occurs when a person's diverse needs are combined together to work toward a single aim. For example, a person's decision to go to college may fuse a variety of needs: the need to be curious, through the opportunity to learn; the need for achievement, through mastering a subject area; the need for status, through obtaining a college degree; and the need for affiliation, through the opportunity to make new friends. When a goal is a good one, it creates a powerful positive motivation as the person's energy is fused and directed toward a single aim that will help him or her meet many needs together.

How Does Action Develop in the Mind?

Motivation, Emotion, and Mood-Congruent Thought

Mood Congruency and Feedback to Motivation

If motives guide and direct people toward goals, how are those guides then elaborated in thoughts and feelings? Chapter 4 described how sometimes emotions can amplify or suppress motivation. As motives arise, they are often accompanied by emotional reactions. For example, a need for control may be accompanied by anger, which may lead a person to try to control others with threats. A desire to nurture someone may be accompanied by happiness, which will amplify the helping (see Chapter 4). These accompanying emotions, in turn, trigger mood-related thoughts.

From one cognitive perspective, memory is viewed as a network of nodes and their connections (Bower, 1981; Collins & Loftus, 1975). The nodes represent concepts, and the connections between the nodes represent the associations that exist between the concepts. Thus, the proposition "Jane wants to go to the circus" would be represented as a series of associations among the nodes *Jane*, the verb, *to go*, and the place she went, the *circus*. Gordon Bower (1981) has suggested that in this memory network, there exist special nodes that represent moods such as *happiness, anger*, and *sadness*. The proposition that "Jane wants to go to the circus" might be associated with happiness because the circus brings to mind happy thoughts for many people. When a person became happy, the "happy" node in memory would become activated—suffused with mental energy (e.g., the firing rate of a neuron). That energy would then spread out from the "happy" concept node to related concepts such as circus, and the person would be primed to remember that Jane liked the circus, rather than a more neutral or negative thought such as that "Jane wants to avoid the dangerous part of town." Should a person enter a sad mood, however, the sadness would be more likely to activate Jane's desire to avoid the dangerous part of town, perhaps—rather than the circus.

That is, there is a connection between moods and thoughts related to them. This is often referred to as a **mood-congruent cognition effect**. The "mood-congruence" of mood-congruent cognition refers to a match between the emotional quality of a person's mood and of his or her ideas. Thus, if a person is sad and thinking about war, the mood and the thoughts are mood-congruent because they are both unpleasant. Similarly, if a person is happy and thinking about winning the lottery, her mood and cognitions are congruent because they are both pleasant. However, a sad person who thinks about good weather is thinking in a mood-incongruent fashion.

Mood-congruent cognition has been studied a number of ways. **Mood-congruent judgment** refers more specifically to the tendency of judgment to shift congruently with mood. In a landmark study, Isen, Clark, Shalker, & Karp (1978) examined mood-congruent judgment in a local shopping mall. They stationed a first researcher at the beginning of an L-shaped portion of a shopping mall corridor, where she distributed small gifts of combs (to women) and pads of paper (to men) as the shoppers passed by. A pilot study had indicated such gifts made shoppers happy. The "interviewer" was around the corner, in the perpendicular section of the "L" where she could not see the gift giver at work. A third researcher was strategically placed in the bend of the "L" where she could see the other two, and could record which shoppers had received the positive-mood induction. By the time shoppers turned the corner of the "L" they had stashed their gifts away. The interviewer, unaware of which subjects were happier, stopped shoppers and asked them a series of questions concerning repairs to their vacuum cleaners, dishwashers, and so forth. The consumers who received the positive mood induction recalled more positive features of their vacuum cleaners, dishwashers, and other appliances than did other consumers.

It isn't necessary to manipulate people's mood to find the effect. In one study, five hundred residents of the state of New Hampshire, randomly selected from the phone book, were contacted for a telephone survey. Embedded in the survey were mood-congruent judgment questions (e.g., "What is the likelihood the economy of New Hampshire will improve in the next five years?"). At the end of the survey, which included many other questions concerning regional water quality, the state Department of Transportation, and statewide political figures, respondents were asked their mood. As predicted by the mood-congruent judgment hypothesis, the respondents' moods correlated with the positivity of their judgments in the survey (Mayer, Gaschke, Gomberg-Kaufman, & Blainey, 1992).

To determine whether such natural changes were really due to a mood effect, fraternity and sorority students were studied over a four-week period. Over that time, there was clear evidence that the individual Greek-house members' moods and judgments shifted together, with greater changes taking place over longer periods of time (Mayer & Hanson, 1995). The findings concerning mood-congruency are quite extensive and cover many other such findings (Forgas, 2001). There are also similar findings concerning people who suffer from mood disorders. The causal direction can go either way. That is, bad thoughts can, in turn, enhance bad moods and lower motivation (e.g., Beck, 1967; Seligman, 1975).

The mind reverberates, in other words, around the particular urge or need. For example, a student deciding whether to study or take a break from studying will have many parts of her mind engaged in making that decision. This may be largely unconscious, or there may be an internal conversation about it. Either way, the striving to study brings up both feelings and thoughts that will contribute to the expression of any action.

From Thought to Action

"Think before you act." — Pythagoras (580-500 B.C.E.)

Automatic Action

As needs and their associated emotions and thoughts are elaborated, how are they turned into action? We can talk about automatic tendencies toward action and considered action. Let's begin with automatic action tendencies. Carpenter (1874) popularized the notion of **ideomotor action**—the idea that simply thinking of an act will increase its likelihood of occurring (Bargh & Chartrand, 1999). Many have argued that ideas lead directly to action, and indeed there is consistent evidence for that proposition. The ideas need not be at the center of attention or even related to the task at hand.

It is somewhat provocative to understand that ideas that do not seem particularly important, or are far from the center of attention, can influence action. In one study, participants were told that they would be involved in two unrelated experiments. First, they were asked to solve word puzzles that included a number of neutral words, along with several experimentally manipulated target words. In the politeness condition, the target words were *respect*, *considerate*, and *polite*; in the rudeness condition, they were *rude*, *impolite*, and *obnoxious* (Bargh, Chen, & Burrows, 1996).

After solving the word puzzles, participants were instructed to interrupt a conversation the experimenter was holding, so as to ask for the second experimental task. There actually was no second experiment. Rather, the measure of interest was how rude or polite the participant would be when interrupting the experimenter. Raters blind to the hypotheses judged that participants exposed to the rude words were far ruder than participants exposed to the politeness words (Bargh, Chen, & Burrows, 1996). Similarly, Carver et al. (1983) first exposed participants to aggressive words in a manner that led them to believe it was irrelevant to the main study. They then found that, in a second experiment, the participants exposed to the aggressive words gave longer electric shocks to learners.

Expectancies and the Likelihood of Action

The healthy individual expresses only some motives and urges. Some urges are insufficiently strong to merit expression. Even strong urges, however, may be held back due to social constraints. Sexual and aggressive ideas in particular might be held back from expression even when they preoccupy the individual. Only a disturbed individual freely expresses a need to tell off his boss, or to rub up against someone for a sexual thrill. Healthy people keep a good number of their motives and urges strictly to themselves.

Assuming an action is socially acceptable, how do we decide whether to carry it out? Social cognitive theorists such as Julian Rotter developed motivational formulae to try to predict the likelihood someone would carry out an action. For Rotter (1954), action was a product of the **expectancy of reward** and its **reward value**. The expectancy of a reward concerned how likely a person's actions would be in securing the reward. For example, if there was no likelihood of getting the reward no matter what a person did, the expectancy would be zero. If, on the other hand, hard work would get a person the reward two out of three times, then the expectancy would be 2/3 or .67. The second part of the equation, the reward value, concerns how rewarding the individual would find attaiting the desired goal. Some goals are relatively unrewarding, such as avoiding a parking ticket, and would have a low value (e.g., .1) whereas others are highly rewarding, such as meeting the love of your life, and would have a high value (e.g., .98).

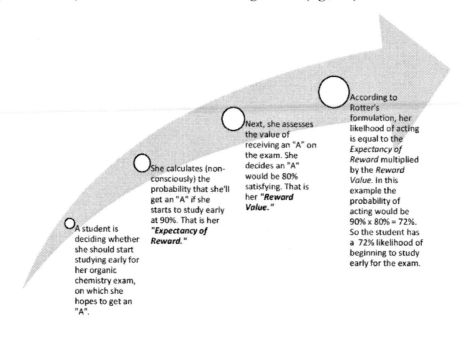

Figure 9-1 *An Example of Rotter's Formula for Action* (From Rotter, 1954)

To illustrate the reward expectancy and reward value concepts together, consider the scenario depicted in Figure 9-1. A student was hoping to go to medical school and had enrolled in a course on organic chemistry. To predict if she would study early and intensively for her midterm, we would want to know her expectation of a reward (an "A" in the course), on the one hand, and how important it was to her to get the "A" on the other. Let's say the student believes with a 90% likelihood that if she studies enough, she could get an "A." Even so, she may still not work hard if her desire to go to medical school is only lukewarm, at 40% on a "satisfaction" scale that runs from 1 to 100%. We could calculate the likelihood of studying hard as a 90% expectancy of getting an "A" multiplied by her 40% reward value, leading to a 36% likelihood of studying hard. If medical school seemed more desirable (e.g., an 80% on the 1 to 100% scale), her likelihood of hard work would rise to 72% (e.g., 90% times 80%). Although people are not always quite this rational, there is experimental evidence that they do behave somewhat according to these logical rules (Champagne & Pervin, 1987; Eccles & Wigfield, 2002).

What happens to motives and urges that don't make the cut? Say the student is in love with someone but the probability of gaining the loved one's attention is near zero? In such cases, the motivations and urges associated with the aim are turned back from behavioral expression. In Freud's terms, the idea undergoes **regression**—it backs away from behavioral action, and reenters the motivational, emotional, and planning sphere, where it may continue to be elaborated unconsciously, or in daydreams or art works, at night in dreamy wishes, or in other mental manifestations of unfilled hopes and aspirations (Freud, 1900/1960, p. 541, e.g., Fig. 3). In Freud's early psychoanalytic theory, art works and writings, as well as dreams, were the consequences of unfulfilled wishes. As Freud (1962) put it—perhaps somewhat overstating the case— "Happy people never make fantasies, only unsatisfied ones do." Singer (1965, pp. 90-97), however, makes the important point that although fantasies may indeed serve drive-reducing functions, they also arise for other reasons, for example, as a means of distraction or, for that matter, out of a creative desire to muse over different possibilities.

Partial Expressions and Slips of the Tongue

Finally, urges that "don't make the cut" may be partially or half expressed—sometimes in an embarrassing fashion. This often happens in **parapraxes**—mistaken behaviors that reveal hidden intentions. A common and heavily studied type of parapraxis is the slip of the tongue, or Freudian slip. For Freud, highly activated urges—sometimes hidden in the unconscious—might be mistakenly expressed when conscious self-control was weak, perhaps due to fatigue or stress. Freud referred to the unintended exposure of such urges as part of the "psychopathology of everyday life." Describing a German parliamentary session that was sure to become heated and factious, Freud recounted how the President of the Lower House had, "…with his first words <u>closed</u> the sitting instead of opening it." Freud observed:

> …we feel inclined, in view of our knowledge of the circumstances in which the slip of the tongue occurred, to recognize that the parapraxis had a sense. The President expected nothing good of the sitting and would have been glad if he could have brought it to an immediate end…Or, once more, we are told that a lady who was well-known for her energy remarked on one occasion: 'My husband asked his doctor what diet he ought to follow; but the doctor told him he had no need to diet: he could eat and drink *what I want*.' Here again the slip of the tongue has an unmistakable other side to it: it was giving expression to a consistently planned programme. (Freud, 1920, p. 35; italics added)

See Table 9-1 for more contemporary examples of slips. But are slips of the tongue really caused by underlying urges that ought not to be expressed? Research evidence supports the case. In one study, for example, male participants were asked to take two letter strings such as "od" and "ong" and insert the letter "l" before the first one and "n" before the second, and read them aloud. Thus, if a participant saw the strings: "od ong," "est in," and "ice egs," he was to say aloud, "lod nong, lest nin, and lice negs." Such a task is designed to produce involuntary slips of the tongue such as "nod long" for "lod nong" and "nice legs" for "lice negs."

One group of men were administered the experiment under neutral conditions. In the other, the male participants were administered the experiment by an attractive woman in a short skirt. According to Freud, the presence of the woman could generate sexual ideas among the men that they would try to repress during the experiment. Indeed, the males who interacted with the short-skirted woman experimenter more frequently substituted "nice legs" for "lice negs" than in the other condition—and expressed considerable embarrassment when they did so. Similar findings have been found for the production of sexual innuendos (Motley, Camden, & Baars, 1983), but there also have been difficulties in replication so this effect is not fully understood as of yet (Baars et al., 1992). We might further ask: What are the ways that the inside of personality gets expressed?

Table 9-1: Two Real-Life Examples of Freudian Slips

	Example 1	*Example 2*
The Context	Two colleagues were setting up a meeting. The second colleague was going through a divorce at the time.	The rather stern principal of a public high school in New England was giving his address to the graduating students and their parents at the end of the school year.
The Slip	*First colleague:* We could do it February 14th...Oh, I don't know if that would work for you, it's a holiday. *Second colleague*: Oh yes good, that's on Veteran's Day, oh no, *Valentine's* Day.	Here is what he said near the very end: "And to the graduating class, I wish you much future sex..., [correcting himself as the audience roared], future *success*."
The Interpretation	The second colleague viewed himself as a veteran of a marriage that had become a war. He welcomed an appointment on a day that would honor him as a veteran (and take his mind off relationships).	Freud said it all.

How Are Acts Performed?

The Communication Channels

The Motor Cortex

Recall that the brain has an area for motor control called the primary motor cortex. Located across the surface of the rearmost portion of the frontal lobe, its motor areas are arranged in sequences that mirror, in part, the arrangement of the external body. One such sequence, for example, extends from toes, foot, leg and knee, up through the eye, nose, face, lips, and tongue. Because it is arranged somewhat like the body itself, it is sometimes referred to as the **motor homunculus** (a homunculus is a little person).

That motor homunculus provides access to the individual's outward expressions of personality. Control of the motor homunculus is sometimes referred to as **access to motility** (or access to movement). Through the motor cortex, the personality system directs motor, vascular, and other organs and can express itself through a diverse set of communication channels (Ekman, 1986). What began as urges, and developed into intentions can be expressed, through the motor cortex, as social acts (Rosenbaum, 2005).

Human Communication Channels Considered

A person's communications and other acts are of many sorts, and involve language, emotional signals, and other nonverbal cues (Buck, 1984). Verbal communications use the vocal cords, mouth, lips, and tongue, and are sometimes accompanied by various physical gestures of the face, head, and hands (see Table 9-2). Some aspects of language and communication appear to have co-evolved with discrete facial expressions. For example, each basic emotion has coupled to it a set of basic, often involuntary, facial expressions—such as sadness, anger, and genuine happiness, and mirth (see Chapter 4). In addition, there exist voluntary or controlled facial expressions including a "social smile," that is, a smile we produce on command when we greet others—even when we may not be feeling happy.

Table 9-2: Language-Related Communication Channels Through the Body

I. Contributions of the vocal cords, mouth, tongue, and lips

Words	People's greatest and most unique quality of communication involves the words they compose and speak. We can communicate in any number of verbal forms from one-word utterances, to sonnets, to songs, to various types of oratory.
Language Flow	There is a flow of words in addition to the words themselves: The flow concerns whether the words are interrupted or not, cover one another, are fragmentary, or flow in a well-planned, well-fashioned stream.
Voice expression	The voice also changes as means of expression; sometimes loud, sometimes soft, sometimes rising with anxiety or falling with calmness.

II. Contributions of the head and hands

Emblems	Non-verbal gestures called emblems are very precise movements that have an approximate or definite meaning to everyone in a given culture. Examples of emblems include vertical head nods to mean "yes," lateral head shakes for "no," and shrugs for "it doesn't matter," and the hand-to-ear "can you speak up?" signal.
Illustrators	Illustrators primarily involve movements of the hands to clarify and emphasize speech, although sometimes raised eyebrows and other parts of the face may be employed. Examples of illustrators are moving the hands to indicate how small or big something is, or to indicate the points of arguments, and similar indications. In comparison to emblems, illustrators do not possess clear meaning apart from speech.

III. Other contributions of the hands to communication

Sign language	We use our hands specifically in the service of speech in the cases of baseball signals (and similar coded conversations) and, more broadly, many people speak and read sign language.
Keyboarding	Hands may express verbal language through typing and musical language by playing a musical keyboard.

Language is often modified or amplified through specific bodily movements. **Emblems** are fairly precise gestures that have specific meanings in our culture, such as when someone shakes her head up and down to mean "yes," or side to side to mean "no." Another emblem: a man who cups his hand to his ear to mean "can you speak up?" **Illustrators** involve movements of the hands or other body parts to provide emphasis or other modifications of our speech, as when a fisherman spreads his hands to indicate exactly how big a fish he is speaking of. Unlike emblems, illustrators take on their meaning from the context. A small child may use the same gesture of holding her hands apart in order to ask for a hug (Ekman & Friesen, 1969). In literate cultures, language also is expressed through writing with the hands, and, with the advent of pianos, typewriters, and computers, through keyboarding (Rosenbaum, 1991). The whole body itself can be a communication device. Through posture, a person may express social dominance, reticence, extreme unease through rigidity, and the like. For example, a person's erect posture may indicate social confidence and dominance, whereas a bowed posture may convey socially lowered status and submissiveness. In Japan, people can indicate social status through exchanges of bowing, in which the degree to which someone bows indicates her assessment of her social status relative to the other person. Some bodily organs of communication, such as our skin, are not entirely under our control. We may sweat when experiencing social discomfort or blush when we feel embarrassed. We may break out in acne or a rash over the course of a difficult week.

We can use **locomotion** to express our reactions to someone or some idea, moving closer to them to indicate greater intimacy, or leaving a room to indicate a desire for greater privacy. Of course, the body and hands also are involved in complex tool use. We use our whole bodies to help move yard debris in a wheelbarrow. Our hands are involved in everything from the use of eating utensils at a meal to a computer keyboard at work. In such contexts, hands can communicate everything from anger and disgust (throwing down one's silverware) to the poetic subtleties of meaning in an e-mail poem.

Table 9-3: Other Communication Channels Through the Body

I. Social communication with the whole body

Whole body posture	The nature of a person's overall posture can indicate aspects of their social status and intended action. For example, a stooped posture may indicate social submissiveness.
Locomotion	Similarly, moving toward someone can indicate interest or aggression; moving away can indicate termination of a relationship, rejection, or fear.

II. Emotion-related expression through the face

Involuntary facial expressions	A variety of automatic facial expresses are connected with emotions. Many of these are universal across human beings, and include joy, fear, anger, sadness, and disgust. These expressions are also quite close to those made by other primates.
Voluntary facial expressions	In addition, people learn to create voluntary facial expressions that mimic the automatic ones (to smile on command), or to alter facial expressions (to mask anger). These are voluntary facial expressions.

III. Other emotional expression

Sweating	A person who sweats when others are feeling cool may communicate discomfort or stress.
Blushing	Some people who become embarrassed may find blood runs to their face and that they blush.

Conscious and Automatic Forms of Action

As motives and their elaborations travel from the inner mind to the outer world, the activities they unleash often communicate a meaning—and sometimes more than one. Moreover, external behaviors can be conscious or be unconscious, just like the thoughts that control them. Human behavior can be conducted in an "unconscious" fashion because it often exists in automatized form. **Automatized actions** are those we perform over and over again until they are so automatic we need no longer pay attention to them. For example, when you first learned to tie your shoelaces, it required considerable concentration—and some luck—to carry out correctly. Nowadays, however, you probably don't pay much attention to tying your laces. You may remember how hard it was to first learn to ride a two-wheel bicycle, whereas now it is second nature. You may even listen to the radio or exchange pleasantries with your roommate such that the activity is at the periphery of awareness, if in awareness at all.

Once behavior becomes automatized, it is possible to carry it out with hardly noticing it. Sometimes this is regrettable, as when a busy person eats her lunch at her desk while working and hardly tastes it. Powerful examples of automatized behavior can take place as well. For example, a graduate student was being videotaped when she was severely criticized by her advisor. On the video, one hand rested on her knee, its middle finger extended in an obscene gesture toward her advisor. Fortunately, her advisor didn't notice.

When asked about her hand gesture by the video-maker, she was utterly unaware of having done it (Ekman, 1992).

Latent versus Manifest Content

Earlier in this chapter, we examined the fact that motives often conflicted with one another. Sometimes that conflict can be carried through into the public expressions of intentions. A person's single expressive act can convey two or more meanings, presumably both intended by the individual. Psychodynamic psychologists have worked out a language for separating out two meanings of the same message, distinguishing between the messages' **manifest** and **latent content**. **Manifest content** refers to what the words or actions of a particular communication are directly about. **Latent content** refers to a second, rather different meaning that accompanies the first and that is equally conveyed by the words. The difference between manifest and latent content can be illustrated with a joke told by the comedian Groucho Marx. Marx was interviewing a contestant on a serialized, live-broadcast television show when he improvised the following:

> Groucho: How are you?
>
> Man: Fine.
>
> Groucho: Well, tell me, are you married?
>
> Man: Yes; I've been married for nine years.
>
> Groucho: Gee, that's swell! Do you have any kids?
>
> Man: Yes, nine already and the tenth is on the way.
>
> Groucho: Wait a minute! Ten kids in nine years?!
>
> Man: (sheepishly) Well, I happen to love my wife very much.
>
> Groucho: Well, I love my cigar too, but I take it out of my mouth once in a while.
> (Reprinted in Erdelyi, 1984, p. 93)

In this case, Groucho's comment is, at the manifest level, about his cigar. The joke, however, takes place at a latent level: the cigar's representation of something else. Latent messages can be powerful. Most television viewers probably got the joke. A few of them even called in to complain: so much so, that Groucho's show was temporarily removed from the air.

Identifying Manifest and Latent Content in Real Events

A divergence between manifest and latent content may take place in more serious contexts as well. The manifest content may communicate a socially acceptable message, whereas the latent content may express a communication that is more undesirable or threatening. Erdelyi (1984, pp. 98-101) reported the case of a close friend who, after completing a brilliant year working at a prestigious university, had traveled abroad, and inexplicably returned home troubled and changed: anxious, experimenting with drugs, and drinking heavily. Soon thereafter, he lost a prestigious job and ended up working as a clerk.

Around that time, Erdelyi telephoned his friend to ask how he was. In response, the man answered, "*I have done it! I have flipped!*" Erdelyi asked him anxiously what was wrong. He replied, "*Right in front of my apartment. The sidewalk was a sheet of ice* [it was winter]. *I flipped full circle and broke my leg… My whole leg is in a cast.*" Erdelyi wondered whether there was a second latent conversation taking place. His friend went on to say that at first he had minimized the problem but that he was "*only now coming to realize how ill* [he] *truly was.*" He then began to talk about a visit to the United States by his brother, and that he would be unable to meet him.

Raising his voice, he described how his mother and he had fought over whether he could pick up his brother at the airport. He bitterly said his brother could take care of himself and concluded that, *"By God, [I have a broken leg and am] in no condition to go meeting anybody"* at an airport (Erdelyi, 1984, pp. 98-101).

Several weeks later, Erdelyi asked his friend whether there might have been a second meaning to the statement that he had "finally flipped," beyond that of turning over on the ice. Yet, his friend denied it, or was unaware of it (Erdelyi, 1985, p. 102). In real-life conversations such as this (as opposed to laboratory-induced slips of the tongue, say), there is often no way to know for sure what has happened. Our experimental methods allow us only to know that such double meanings often arise. The exact moments when such double meanings actually take place are not always as clear as they are in Groucho Marx's joke.

Stagecraft and Self-Presentation

Tracing the dynamics of action makes clear that there exist a boundary between the private personality that lies within and the visible expression of personality outside (Henriques, 2003; Singer, 1984). The fact that personality processes are private allows a person to control and modify public expressions of that personality. It allows the person to engage in calculated self-presentation—the stagecraft of social life. This presentation may be for innocent reasons of entertainment and, perhaps, a bit of self-aggrandizement, or it may involve intentional deception designed to smooth social occasions—or calculated to bring about more nefarious ends.

The Emergence of Acting

Historians suggest that social acting may have begun before recorded history, perhaps around campfires when people recounted stories of their exploits, and realized it was easier to show than to tell. One person might narrate the action of the hunt, for example, by saying, "I held the rock and threw it just like this..." it would be impossible to mimic the action perfectly, and so there would be small deviations from the way it happened. Under such circumstances, it would be easy to falsify on the side of embellishing one's own stature (Duerr, 1962, pp. 5-7).

Documents indicate that ancient priests also engaged in a form of amateur acting as they narrated the creation and similar other religious stories for their congregations. In ancient Greece, the first professional actor took to the stage in about 534 B.C.E. His name was Thespis, and he wrote four plays. For each play, he donned a mask and portrayed a character other than himself. By so doing, he "invented" the actor. And this new creation, acting things out, very much appealed to the people who came to see him. Incidentally, early actors were called *hypocrites* in Greek, which meant, "answerers." From the same word we get "hypocrite"—someone who pretends to be virtuous while not being so.

Whereas Greek plays were so carefully crafted that the actors seemed nearly superfluous, the theater that spread to Rome required actors to more powerfully reach out and manipulate the audience. It was said that the Roman actors were able to preserve many inferior plays by enacting them in a lively, captivating way. Masks gave way to a direct view of the human actor's face (Duerr, 1962, p. 44).

Two broad approaches to acting are often taught. In first, actors are taught to imagine a role to the fullest and to "get into the head" of the character they will portray. The great champion of this approach was Constantin Stanislavski (1948), who wrote *An Actor Prepares*. In it, he recommended such techniques as empathizing with the tragedies faced by the character one is playing so as to cry on stage. If that didn't work, he suggested that the actor recall a sad memory of her own to substitute for the character's memory. The major alternative to Stanislavski's techniques is called theatricalism. Theatricalism teaches actors how to move and act on a stage. An actor who can move his face so that it perfectly emulates sadness, and who can manipulate his muscles in such a way as to appear to cry while, with a sleight of hand, dropping tears down his cheeks from an eye-dropper, can also draw in an audience. Some theatrical professionals believe that the best acting combines the psychological and the theatrical. Too much theatricality can bring a false, as-if quality to life. Too much psychological fit to the character can ignore the requirements of the role.

When people portray social roles, they also act. A young man getting ready to ask a young woman on a date may rehearse his lines until they sound smooth and confident. Or, a person may rehearse asking for a raise at work. Students may rehearse the more important presentations they prepare for classes. There is a considerable stagecraft of everyday life (Goffman, 1959/2002, p. 131). Researchers have developed measures of the overall capacity to portray social roles—and, unsurprisingly, people vary in how well they can enact various roles. Social acting appears to consist of six discrete dimensions or factors: (a) the ability to imitate, (b) to become involved in fantasy, (c) to remember others' mannerisms, (d) to fake convincingly, (e) to play unusual roles, and (f) to tell stories (Fletcher & Averill, 1984).

> "I figured I needed a gimmick, so I dreamed up the drawl, the squint, and a way of moving which meant to suggest that I wasn't looking for trouble but would just as soon throw a bottle at your head as not." – John Wayne (1907-1979), on acting in the movies

Symbolic Interactionism and Social Alignment

People act to maintain interpersonal interactions in a smooth and mutually understood way. **Symbolic interactionism** is a branch of American sociology that attends to the self and its presentation in everyday life. It consists of several core ideas. First, individuals often think of themselves in the "third person," as it were—as an objective being, in terms of their individual reputations or membership in a group. Second, individuals have the capacity to act in situations. Third, the way individuals are identified and act in situations can be analyzed according to the symbolic meanings they express (Hewitt, 2003, Chapter 2).

Symbolic interactionism—and much social psychology—is concerned with the stagecraft of everyday life—the acts they use to present themselves to the world. For example, **disclaimers** are verbal devices people use to decrease the negative implications of something they are about to do. Examples of common disclaimers are, "I'm not prejudiced but I do believe…", or "I'm no psychologist but…", and "I don't mean this as a threat but…" (Stokes & Hewitt, 1976). People who use disclaimers can influence how others view them, making themselves seem less negative despite the concerns their comments raise for the listener (Shapiro & Bies, 1994).

Our **accounts** are the excuses or justifications we provide for our behavior; accounts smooth our social functioning so that our problematic behavior can be shelved and our interactions with another person continued. A person who uses justifications accepts responsibility but denies that the act was wrong or injurious (e.g., "I was late but it really didn't cause a problem," Scott & Lyman, 1968). When a person employs an excuse, she acknowledges her act was wrong, but denies responsibility for her conduct. Excuses are a common form of interaction between students and professors. Anonymous surveys reveal that students fabricate nearly half of the excuses they tell provide in class that involve personal illness, family emergencies, alarm clock failures, and papers left in the dorm. Students invest considerable staging and enactment to make their claims seem plausible, experiencing increased nervousness and reduced happiness thereafter (Caron, Whitbourne, & Halgin, 1992).

Another social technique known as **altercasting** involves presenting another person in a somewhat different manner than she is accustomed to. Politicians often altercast when they refer to their opponents as "tax and spend liberals" or "knee jerk conservatives." At an everyday level, people may altercast that someone is a more intimate friend than she really is, perhaps to obtain information or a special favor from her (e.g., Weinstein & Deutschberger, 1963).

The ways we express ourselves can be crucial to our success. Camp counselors, teachers, waiters, and police officers all understand the importance of acting the role of authority to carry out their jobs. One teacher privately acknowledged:

> You can't ever let them [students] get the upper hand on you or you're through. So I start out tough. The first day I get a new class in, I let them know who's boss…then you can ease up as you go along. If you start out easy-going, when you try to get tough, they'll just look at you and laugh. (Goffman, 1959/2002, p. 134)

Or consider the skills involved in waiting tables. A waitress:

> …may find that a new customer has seated himself before she could clear off the dirty dishes and change the cloth. He is now leaning on the table studying the menu. She greets him, says, "May I change the cover, please?" and, without waiting for an answer, takes his menu away from him so that he moves back from the table, and she goes about her work. The relationship is handled politely but firmly, and there is never any question as to who is in charge. (Whyte, 1946, pp. 132-133)

Sometimes society casts us in a role against our will—according to our ethnicity, gender, or religion. Robin Kelley, a sociologist of West-Indies/African heritage, recounted being thrust into a role that had nothing to do with who he was. One moment he was home, patiently cajoling his four-year-old daughter to put her toys away. He felt so ineffectual that he finally announced, "Okay, I'm going to tell Mommy!" From this mild-mannered role at home, he went out to buy theater tickets and, because he was late, ran through the lobby to the ticket counter.

The young woman who was selling tickets misinterpreted the young man running toward her as signaling the beginning of a robbery. Fortunately, she recognized her error almost immediately, became very embarrassed, and apologized to him. As he ruefully noted, members of minority groups, and particularly American men of African ancestry have mistakenly been arrested or much worse under similar circumstances. The contrasting dramas indicate the power of roles: On the home stage Kelley had trouble intimidating his four-year-old daughter; cast by society in a different role, he had trouble innocently buying a movie ticket (Kelley, 1995, pp. 356-357).

Social Deception and the Dark Triad of Personality

Certain people among us falsely enact roles with an eye to taking advantage of our trust. Paulhus and Williams (2002) described a dark triad of qualities that afflict some individuals: narcissism, Machiavellianism, and psychopathy. **Narcissism** refers to a combination of grandiosity and the willingness to exploit others. **Psychopathy** refers to low anxiety, low empathy, and reckless disregard for others. The **Machiavellian Personality**, after the Italian diplomat, Niccolo Machiavelli, involves the intentional manipulation and deception of others.

People with one of these qualities are likely to share heightened levels of them all. Still there are differences. Among the three, Machiavellians are more likely to plagiarize essays; narcissists are most likely to self-enhance and to punish other who threaten them; and psychopaths are most likely to bully others (Furnham, Richards & Paulhus, 2013).

Christie and Geis (1970) first described the Machiavellian personality. To measure it, they ask people to agree or disagree with test items like: "People who get ahead in the world often use a combination of deception and connection," and "It makes sense to tell people what they really want to hear to get them to do something."

Buss & Craik (1985, Table 3, p. 942) found that at least some college students regularly carry out Machiavellian acts, agreeing with test items such as "I made a friend in order to obtain a favor" (see Table 9-4).

Table 9-4: Are You Machiavellian? Calculating Acts Students Report Performing*

An Act that Represents "Calculating" Social Behavior (also known as "Machiavellianism")	Percent doing this past three months
I made a friend in order to obtain a favor.	12%
I asked "innocent" questions intending to use the information against someone.	13%
I pretended I was hurt to get someone to do me a favor.	17%
I tricked a friend into giving me personal information.	12%
I flattered a person in order to get ahead.	25%
I pretended to be sick at work, knowing I would not be there the next day.	12%
I made others feel guilty to get what I wanted.	29%

*Data regarding the seven most calculating Machiavellian acts, adapted from Buss & Craik (1985, Tables 1 and 3).

Low scorers employ a more cooperative strategy based on reciprocity ("you scratch my back; I'll scratch yours"). Many people carry out a Machiavellian act at least occasionally: a sample of 93 married couples indicated that between 25 and 29% of them admitted to performing a calculating act at one time or another in their marriage (e.g., "I flattered a person in order to get ahead," "I made others feel guilty to get what I wanted." (See Table 9-3; from Buss & Craik, 1985, Table 3, p. 942). It is nonetheless true that the vast majority of people are generally honest in their behavior most of the time. Most people prefer the rewards of honest cooperation, and prefer social respect and mutuality (e.g., Dubner & Levitt, 2004; Fiske, 1991).

People consistently high in Machiavellianism report more often than others that they engage in behaviors such as: "I made a friend in order to obtain a favor," and "I asked 'innocent' questions, intending to use the information against someone," (Buss & Craik, 1985, p. 940). In experimental settings where their social behavior is carefully evaluated, people high in Machiavellianism are better liars than others, telling more convincing lies, making closer eye contact, and sticking to their story more consistently (Exline et al., 1970). Another study found that high Machiavellians generally fare best in loosely structured organizations that are only minimally constrained by rules (cutthroat stockbrokerages and automobile dealerships—perhaps similar in some respects to the emerging Italian city states of the Renaissance that Machiavelli lived amidst). They fare less well in more highly structured organizations (Wilson, Near, & Miller, 1996).

The Urge and the Situation

We are taught how to present ourselves from an early age. Parents begin to define different situations for their young children by asking them to use a quieter voice, to blow their noses, wash their hands, be kind to their siblings, and the like (Thomas, 2003, p. 81). In this tug of war between the individual and the situation, who is more powerful, on average—the person or the situation? As discussed in Chapter 3 (in the section on social cognition), the typical prediction from a personality trait—such as a motive—to a single behavior is about $r = .40$ across many psychological studies. The typical correlation between various situations and behaviors are at a similar level; that is, about $r = .40$ (Bowers, 1973; Funder & Ozer, 1983). So, the individual's personality is in a constant give-and-take with the social situation in determining what will transpire.

A closing example illustrates how personal urges and the environment can interact: A student is studying for an exam in her dorm-room. She expects that with another two hours of studying, she could get an "A," and that would make her very proud.

Just then, the sweet scent of tomato sauce, cheese, and garlic reaches her—a pizza was just delivered to a dorm room down the hall. The idea of joining her friends (need for affiliation) and eating command her attention, rearranging her priorities (the "press" of the situation).

She realizes that she wants to go out to eat with someone but she is low on cash. In a Machiavellian moment, she invites a particularly well-off dorm-mate to go out for a pizza break with her. True, she isn't quite as fond of this dorm-mate as she is of some other students in the residence hall, but her acquaintance is generous and might pay for part of the meal.

Will she return to studying later? Perhaps not if dinner goes well and she becomes engaged in an interesting conversation. Certainly, however, her expectancies about studying and her hopes for an A incline her to return to work. She might well remember her goals and head back to her room in time to study. The dynamics of how she exerts such self-guidance in the face of situational pressures are examined in the next chapter.

Reviewing Chapter 9

The purpose of this chapter is to introduce you the idea of personality dynamics—streams of mental action that cross parts of the mind. In addition, some attention is provided to the issue that some action dynamics are conscious, whereas others are not.

The dynamic path specifically under consideration in this chapter begins with motivational urges, and ends with the stagecraft of personal expression. Along the way, motives are filtered through the emotion system, and then emotions influence the possibility of behavior. Behavior itself is not necessarily a direct expression of motives and emotions, but rather may represent deception and false beliefs.

Questions About "What Are Dynamics of Action?"

1. Dynamics Traits and Local Dynamics: Motivational traits are typically labeled as dynamic. Why is this?

2. Mid-Level and Global Dynamics: What are mid-level and global dynamics, and how do they differ from local dynamics. What kind of dynamics are the dynamics of action described in this chapter?

3. Dynamics and their Change: How are dynamics different than traits? If you can change a person's dynamic functioning, can you change what they do?

Questions About "Which Needs Will Begin Action?"

4. Needs and Their Potency: Which needs are most important? What happens if one need is stronger than another?

5. <u>Determinant Needs and Subsidiary Needs:</u> According to Freud, the major determinant needs were sex and aggression. What would this mean in regard to subsidiary needs? Can you define determinant and subsidiary needs?

6. <u>Need Conflicts:</u> Two sorts of conflicts arise around needs. One kind of conflict involves the case when two needs lead a person in different directions. What is the other kind of need conflict? When a person experiences many need conflicts, what can be expected in regard to the individual's well being?

7. <u>Need Fusion:</u> Need fusion arises when a single aim satisfies many needs. How would this relate to need conflicts and the relation between determinant and subsidiary needs?

Questions About "How Does Action Develop in the Mind?"

8. <u>Motivation, Emotion, and Mood-Congruent Thought:</u> Happy liveliness can work to enhance a person's overall motivation, whereas depression can be a global de-motivator, undermining a person's energy and interest in doing things. Mood can also influence motivation-related thoughts through the mood-congruent cognition effects—influencing both memory and judgment. Can you give advantages of each effect?

9. <u>Expectancies and the Likelihood of Action:</u> Julian Rotter introduced the idea of expectancies and the likelihood of action. In Rotter's conception, expectancies interacted with a second aspect of motivation to determine a person's actions. Can you name the second aspect? How did expectancies and that other aspect of motivation combine to predict a person's motivation?

10. <u>Partial Expressions and Slips of the Tongue:</u> Not all motives are ready for action, and some ideas and urges are turned back rather than expressed. What happens to these turned-back ideas? Sometimes the ideas may be expressed accidentally through slips of the tongue. Why are these called Freudian slips, and is there any research evidence to support their occurrence?

Questions About "How Are Acts Performed?"

11. <u>The Communication Channels:</u> Communication begins at the motor cortex. Where is the motor cortex and what is it like? People communicate through language and physical acts. What are some physical channels such as facial expressions through which people express themselves?

12. <u>Conscious and Automatic Forms of Action:</u> Some behavior can be automatic, such as when acts are performed repeatedly. Why might it be adaptive for such repeated behaviors to become non-conscious?

13. <u>Latent versus Manifest Content:</u> Communication can be complex, and carry multiple meanings. One simple approach to deciphering it is to distinguish between a communication's simple, direct, obvious meaning, and its underlying meaning. Sometimes this is referred to as a communication's manifest versus latent content. Do you know which is which?

14. <u>Stagecraft and Self-Presentation:</u> People manage their self-presentation so as to have desired influences on others; sometimes, however, their impact may be out of their control. Can you provide an example of an intentional and unintended aspect of self-presentation?

15. <u>Symbolic Interactionism:</u> Symbolic interactionism is a school of social psychology that focuses on the symbolic analysis of interpersonal communication. In symbolic interactionism, a person attempts to conform his or her behavior to particular roles he or she desires. To maintain such roles, the individual may employ disclaimers, accounts, and altercasting. Can you define these and provide examples of each?

Chapter 9 Glossary

Terms in Order of Appearance:

Personality Dynamic: A motivated chain of inter-related psychological events that cross a set of major mental areas to bring about an outcome. Personality dynamics are potentially reversible or modifiable.

Micro-Level Dynamics: A smaller personality dynamic that involves one part of personality influencing another.

Dynamic Traits: A class of long-term stable mental patterns related to motives, including such examples as *n* achievement, sensation-seeking, and the like.

Meso-Level Dynamics: A dynamic that crosses two or three major functional areas of personality.

Causal Attributions: Models of the self and world that are especially focused on what causes a particular behavior, event, or situation. Some people tend to see the world as caused by themselves, others tend to see the world as caused by other people or situations.

Macro-Level Personality Dynamics: A larger dynamic that crosses all or almost all the many major functional areas or parts of personality.

Urge: The conscious psychological awareness of a need.

Need: A need refers to a state of tension within the individual that can be satisfied by a specific goal such as eating or being sociable.

Press: Aspects of the environment that elicit needs in a person.

Regnant Process: A process that is directing or ruling personality at a given point in time.

Prepotent Need: A need that would take over the actions of personality—that is, become a regnant process—more quickly than other needs, that is, a very important need.

Determinant Needs: Basic needs which may cause the establishment of secondary needs, as when a person's desire to be intimate with another person creates a need to behave well toward others as a means to impress the individual.

Subsidiary Needs: A state of needs in which one need serves another, as when a person tries to do well in school (need for achievement) so as to attain the ultimate goal of impressing others (need for esteem).

Functionally Autonomous: The state of a need or motive, which, although originally caused by a biological urge, has taken on an independent life of its own.

Personal Strivings: Specific activities a person is currently attempting to carry out so as to meet long-term plans and goals.

Conflictual Striving: A personal striving or plan that meets one set of goals while frustrating another set of goals. This might happen, for example, when a person who is working hard in school so as to satisfy her needs to achieve simultaneously thwarts her needs to have fun.

Ambivalent Striving: A personal striving that involves a goal that is, itself, fraught with problems. For example, striving to be honest, although very desirable, entails many costs.

Need Fusion: A state or condition of several distinct needs that occurs when a person engages in an action or objective that satisfies all the needs simultaneously.

Mood-Congruent Cognition Effect: Mood congruent cognition is an effect in which ideas or concepts that match a mood in tone (e.g., pleasant thoughts; happy moods) seem more memorable, plausible, reasonable, and/or likely, than ideas or concepts that mismatch the individual's mood.

Mood-Congruent Judgment: A special case of the mood-congruent cognition effect concerning judgments of plausibility or likelihood. For example, in a happy mood, good weather seems more likely.

Ideomotor Action: A scientific label for the concept that simply thinking of a physical movement brings it about or increases the likelihood of bringing it about.

Expectancy of Reward: The belief a person holds as to how likely it is he or she will or can succeed at gaining a particular, sought-after objective.

Reward Value: The assessment a person makes of how desirable or pleasurable a particular objective or goal is.

Regression (of an Idea): The state of an idea or desire to act, when that desire is blocked from action. In such a case, the idea returns to the mind and where it must be dealt with. It may, for example, be expressed through an emotional fantasy.

Parapraxes: Mistaken behaviors or slips of the tongue that reveal something about a person's hidden motivations.

Motor Homunculus: A part of the brain, located on the surface of the rearmost area of the frontal lobe that controls the movement of the body. The areas of this surface region are arrayed in sequences that mirror, in part, the arrangement of the external body.

Access to Motility: The capacity of a portion of the brain or mind to control and direct the individual's external movement, activity, and language.

Emblems: Fairly precise gestures that have specific meanings in one's culture, such as shaking the head up and down to mean "yes," or side to side to mean "no."

Illustrators: Movements of the hands or other body parts to supplement the meanings of speech, as when a person holds his hands close together to illustrate how small a child is.

Locomotion: Movement of the body or parts of the body for purposes of going someplace.

Automatized Actions: Physical movements that a person has performed over and over again until they are so over-learned that the individual pays little or no attention to them. Example: leaning right and left to keep one's balance on a bicycle.

Manifest Content: The relatively direct and obvious meaning a communication; compare to "latent content."

Latent Content: Meanings of a communication that are symbolic, secondary, or conveyed indirectly, but that still can be understood by a careful observer.

Symbolic Interactionism: A sociological perspective on social behavior that concentrates on how people represent themselves and each other in society.

Disclaimers: Statements people make to request a pardon or otherwise reduce the negativity of something they are about to say that they recognize may not meet the social ideals or expectations of the listener.

Accounts: Excuses or rationalizations people give of why they did or did not do something they should have or were expected to have done.

Altercasting: The attempt to make other people look a certain way; for example, drawing attention to qualities that may make them seem more courageous or cowardly than otherwise.

Narcissism: A mental condition characterized by grandiosity, self-love, and the willingness to exploit others. At the extreme, narcissism is considered a personality disorder.

Psychopathy: A mental condition of low anxiety, low empathy, and reckless disregard for others that is often associated with mental disorders and criminal behavior.

Machiavellian Personality: A quality of the individual to be motivated and calculating so as to intentionally manipulate social situations for gain and power.

Chapter 10: Dynamics of Self-Control

Does a person exert conscious self-control over his or her personality? Is it necessary? The conscious self provides a vantage point from which to pull together the various parts of personality and to direct the system in a well-considered manner. For that reason, people seek feedback as to what they are doing, and ways to improve their lives. At the same time, however, some self-control takes place at a non-conscious level. Some people have wondered whether the self might be improved, for example, by the effortful repetition of positive thoughts. Meanwhile, feedback can become painful at times and a person's mechanisms of defense may block worrisome messages—but how does this work? Self-control is an intricate operation. Wouldn't the lack of self-control, however, be even more problematic?

Previewing the Chapter's Central Questions

- **What Are Dynamics of Self-Control?** Dynamics of self-control concern the ways we guide our own behavior. These dynamics of self-guidance are compared with the dynamics of action, and the significance of self-control is considered. The section also examines the sorts of goals people set for themselves.

- **How Does Self-Control Occur?** For self-control to occur, the individual must have some kind of dynamic self-representation—that is, a sense of what we are doing at a given time. One important way of obtaining this information is through feedback. We examine feedback loops, the role of feedback in self-control, and the idea of feedback loops as a structure for describing personality dynamics.

- **Is Self-Control Always Conscious?** Although a lot of self-control is conscious, some self-control takes place outside of awareness. Psychologists sometimes use hypnosis as an experimental procedure to explore conscious and non-conscious self-control.

- **How Do We Deal With the Pain of Falling Short?** When we receive feedback about how we are doing, we sometimes encounter critical remarks that make us feel bad. Our personality system often makes use of defense mechanisms so as to cope with that painful feedback.

- **How Is Self-Control (or its Absence) Expressed?** The concluding section recounts some studies of people with higher versus lower levels of self-control.

What Are Dynamics of Self-Control?

How Dynamics of Self-Control Are Distinctive

This chapter focuses on a class of dynamics essential for the operation of personality: the dynamics of self-control. Many dynamics of self-control begin with the part of personality variously called the **conscious self**, **conscious executive**, or **ego**. These terms refer to that part of us which is aware; our innermost consciousness, that part of our self that seems most clearly aligned with our innermost core. The self-awareness of our own desires and their possible positive and negative ramifications motivate us to try to exert control over ourselves: to pick one thing to do, and reject another.

Sometimes a conscious executive is in control (or at least, it seems that way; Wegner, 2002). Although much of self-control and its influences are perceived as originating with the conscious self, some dynamics of control originate outside of awareness, in automatic personal self-regulation and control. In these instances, we might speak more generally of personal control. Personal control may involve various automatic feedback loops that take place outside of awareness, as well as other, intentionally guided control that is lacking in conscious awareness as well, despite the fact that it takes place at a high level of the system and, perhaps, *could be* conscious. Both self-control and more general, non-conscious personal control will be examined in this chapter.

In the last chapter, the dynamics of action were described as beginning with an urge, and extending to how the urge is felt and thought about, and ultimately expressed in the outer world. The self control we are most concerned with here takes place in the context of gaining self-understanding and then using it to exert control over that chain of action, as well as over other processes such as our feelings and thoughts.

Katherine Graham, publisher of the *Washington Post* for three decades, exhibited considerable self-control in both her private and public lives (Graham, 1997, p. 611). She was a teenager when her father bought the then-bankrupt newspaper. While working at the paper, she met Phil Graham, a young lawyer in Washington, DC. They fell in love, married, and had four children. Katherine managed the household and gradually reduced her work at the *Post*, as her father and her husband continued to build the newspaper, which her husband took over in 1947. At the ages of 33 and 31, she and her husband became the newspapers' owners (Graham, 1997, p. 182).

Graham's husband developed psychiatric symptoms during this time: He began to treat her in a condescending, mean-spirited fashion. In the fall of 1957, he became deeply depressed; this was followed by cycles of bipolar disorder, from depression to mania and back again. During this time, he took a reporter as a mistress, publicly humiliating Katherine. Although estranged and hurt, she continued to care for her husband, and threw a party with her mother to show that she was unbowed even in her difficult circumstances (Graham, 1997, p. 324; Halberstam, 1979).

As her husband's illness worsened, Katherine wondered who would run the newspaper—until a close friend remarked, "Don't be silly, dear. You can do it." (Graham, 1997, p. 319). When Graham's husband committed suicide, she did indeed take over the company, writing:

> I naively thought the whole business would just go on as it had while I learned by listening. I didn't realize that nothing stands still—issues arise every day…and they start coming at you. I didn't understand the immensity of what lay before me…and how many anxious hours and days I would spend for a long, long time. Nor did I realize how much I was eventually going to enjoy it all. (Graham, 1997, p. 340)

Her self-guidance created a network of caring friends around her. With their help, and her own talents and commitment—"I felt I *had* to make it work"—and some luck, she guided herself and the paper forward (Graham, 1997, p. 343). She was attentive to feedback about the paper, and actively addressed some of its problems such as its below-standard editorial quality (Graham, 1997, p. 379). Her self-image gradually shifted. She stopped comparing herself to her late husband; gradually she exerted her own form of self-control—and control over the paper, realizing, "…I could only do the job in whatever way *I* could do it" (Graham, 1997, p. 341). Ultimately, she built the Washington Post Company into a Fortune 500 company, and the *Washington Post* itself into an international newspaper. By doing so, she fulfilled her father's and her husband's dreams, as well as her own passionate devotion to the paper, which her father had viewed as a public trust (Graham, 1997, pp. 620-621; Halberstam, 1979).

The Need for Self-Control

Personality With and Without Control

We exert self-control to fulfill our needs—everything from nourishment and safety to aspirations for power. Part of our skill at self-control involves recognizing which of our goals go together, which conflict, and prioritizing them as best we can. This chapter focuses on how self-control takes place.

If we fail to control ourselves—if our personalities become destabilized, and we can no longer self-govern, our personality system degenerates into a disorganized collection of functions. The consequences of a lack of self-control are seen most vividly among the most severe cases of mental illness. Those who have lost their capacity for self-monitoring and control engage in erratic behavior, are irrational and self-destructive, and in the extremes of untreated mental illness, may stay in bed day after day, or shout at themselves, without a plan to follow. People with poor self-control also end up in courts and prisons: Some crime results when individuals simply cannot or will not control their impulses and, instead, rob or assault others out of their own poorly restrained greed or anger.

Fortunately, most healthy human beings, as well as the majority of those suffering from various mental disorders, maintain large areas of successful self-control. Dynamic self-control organizes personality so as to handle its urges in productive ways, ensuring personality's coherent functioning and promoting its long-term growth (a topic we'll examine in greater detail in the forthcoming chapters on development).

Aims of Self-Control

Self-control is intimately related to the goals people set for themselves. If people had no goals, they wouldn't need to behave in any particular way. But people pursue goals they regard as important. Roberts and Robins (2000) surveyed people as to their aims in life and found that above all else people sought satisfying marriages and other relationships, rating such goals as 4.8 in importance on a 5-point scale. People next wished to live a purpose-driven life (4.6 on the scale). They also sought a good career (4.5) and hoped to have a variety of fun experiences (4.3 on the scale). Living in an aesthetically pleasing area ranked surprisingly highly (4.0). People were somewhat less interested in other kinds of goals. Promoting social welfare was a step down (3.7) and political influence, religious goals, and supporting the arts were not terribly engaging for most people (rated 2.8, 2.7 and 2.5).

Table 10-1: Life Goals Rated as Important by U.S. 12th Graders*

	1981		1991		2001	
	Male	Female	Male	Female	Male	Female
Being successful in my line of work	58%	57%	60%	64%	59%	66%
Having a good marriage and family life	71%	82%	71%	83%	72%	83%
Having lots of money	24%	13%	37%	19%	33%	19%
Making a contribution to society	19%	17%	20%	22%	21%	22%
Working to correct social and economic inequalities	9%	10%	11%	13%	10%	10%
Being a leader in my community	8%	7%	12%	10%	15%	14%

*US. Department of Health and Human Services, 2002, pp. 193-194.

Not everyone ranks these goals in the same fashion and values shift over time, if only gradually. A study by the *U.S. Department of Health and Human Services* indicated that among 12th graders the importance of becoming a community leader rose from about 7.5% to 14.5% in importance between 1981 and 2001. For the most part, the ranking of values in that survey is consistent with the findings by Roberts and Robins (2000), with having a good marriage the most important of all.

Roberts and Robins also found that people's personality traits correlate with their goals. Extroverts find goals involving pleasure (e.g., fun, exciting life) and a good career are much more important than less extroverted people do. People scoring high in openness, on the other hand, put a greater emphasis on aesthetic goals. Those high in neuroticism value goals concerning the welfare of others.

How Does Self-Control Occur?

The Self in Control

One defining characteristic of self-control is that it integrates a sense of oneself into plans for action. For example, say a person is aware she wants to be alone. To exert self-control is to say something on the order of, "I prefer to be alone, and therefore I am going to decline this invitation," or even, "I prefer to be alone. In this case, however, I am going to make an effort to enjoy this party because I know it is important to my friends." Another, different example, might be the thought, "I am not a vindictive person and therefore I am going to forgive this error." All these statements of self-control begin with a conscious sense of the self, and the knowledge of what that self is like. This section therefore begins with a consideration of the conscious self and its qualities.

The Problem of the Egotistical Ego

If accurate self-knowledge can contribute to effective self-control, one of the issues involved is obtaining accurate self-knowledge. One of the central obstacles to this is the very nature of the conscious self in the first place. This conscious self—oftentimes referred to as the conscious ego—is, well, egocentric. The ego is naturally and normally narcissistic and self-centered in that the world revolves around its own perspective.

Greenwald (1980) characterized the typical conscious self as a **totalitarian ego**. By totalitarian ego, Greenwald meant that a person's conscious self typically behaves like a dictator, in a self-preserving and often self-aggrandizing fashion. For example, the ego is naturally **egocentric**. Egocentrism means that the ego is at the center of things. In some sense this is true for all of us. Each person sees the world through his or her own eyes, and in particular, with him or herself as at the center of that world. After all, how else can the person honestly perceive matters? The cognitive psychologist Donald Norman agrees, using an example of some of his own recollections:

> My memory for the University of Toronto campus in Canada...cannot be separated from my memory of my last visit to Toronto. Trying to recall how ones goes to the Psychology Department automatically recreates the last visit there—the snow, the heavy traffic, the various people I met, and the restaurants at which I ate. (Norman, 1976, p. 189, cited in Greenwald, 1980)

Because we remember so much in relation to ourselves, it is inevitable that our perception of events is self-centered. Because memory is so much a part of who we are, the ego cannot help but be egocentric in this regard.

Our thinking has built into it certain biases that often favor the conscious self and its role. **Beneffectance** refers to the tendency to take credit for the good things in our lives and to avoid responsibility for the bad. In regard to the good, athletes on sports teams tend to overestimate their effort, abilities and other contributions to team wins (e.g., Greenberg, Pyszczynski, & Solomon, 1982; Mullen & Riordan, 1988). In regard to the bad, those in automobile accidents, for example, tend to deny their responsibility. Consider these actual descriptions people reported to their insurance companies:

> As I approached the intersection, a sign suddenly appeared in a place where a stop sign had never appeared before. I was unable to stop in time to avoid an accident.

Here's a second:

> The telephone pole was approaching. I was attempting to swerve out of its way when it struck my front end. (*San Francisco Examiner and Chronicle*, April 22, 1979, p. 35, cited in Greenwald, 1980, p. 605)

People often also suffer from a **confirmation bias** in which they seek to confirm ideas they already hold—often by ignoring contrary information (Nickerson, 1998). For example, if people believe someone they are about to interview is an introvert, they are likely to ask questions that are biased toward the introvert hypothesis (e.g., "Do you like to read books?") in order to confirm their beliefs (Snyder & Swann, 1978). Another example involves attitude research. People consistently tend to accept arguments that agree with their prior opinions and reject those that disagree with them (Sherif & Hovland, 1961).

The ego appears to be engineered to be a bit out-of-touch with its own fallibility. Some psychologists believe this is adaptive because it encourages the ego to keep going even when matters are tough (Taylor & Brown, 1988; 1994). This does not, however, tell the entire story. If the ego were totally self-centered and utterly out of contact with others' viewpoints, it would not be an effective self-manager. One way the ego has of better responding to the outside world is by learning from feedback.

Feedback and the Feedback Loop

People's self-control is based at least in part on receiving accurate information about themselves and how they are doing. Accurate information about the self can be regarded as **feedback**. The children's game "hot and cold" nicely illustrates how feedback guides our action. In the game, a child searches for a hidden object as other players watch. The other players, who know where the object has been hidden, call out "hot" or "cold" as the person gets closer or further from the goal. The feedback from other players lets the child know how close he is from the goal and, in the case of "cool" or "ice cold," for example, to try another direction. As the child gets nearer the hiding place, the audience calls out "warmer" and "hot" and even "sizzling" when the child is very close. The child's search is governed and directed by feedback.

A central building block of control in the hot-and-cold game is the **feedback loop**. A feedback loop involves a cycle that includes acting, receiving information about the success or failure of the act, and then acting again. The concept of a feedback loop comes from the field of **cybernetics**. In 1949, Norbert Weiner, a philosopher who studied many subjects including biology, physics and mathematics, founded the field of cybernetics (Weiner, 1949). From Weiner's perspective, any self-governing machine (or person) relies on information to guide its behavior. For example, if you want to pick up a cup of coffee and drink from it, your eyes need to scan your environment for the coffee container and your hands are guided by your eyes. Wiener's idea was that the flow of communication between your eyes and hands can be analyzed. Information is "input," through the eyes, and as the information is processed, your motor system makes incremental movements of your hand toward the coffee cup. Each movement, in turn, is an output that "feeds back" to the visual system so as to fulfill the plan of drinking the coffee. Cybernetic theory drew together terms such as "input," "output," and "feedback" and gave them their modern meanings. The concept of a feedback loop, which is a primary component of cybernetic theory, is relevant to our self-control.

The **negative feedback loop** in particular is key to how we control ourselves. The loop is called "negative" because it attempts to eliminate (negate) any discrepancy between a standard and an outcome. The hot-and-cold game can be analyzed in terms of a negative feedback loop. In it, the person tries to minimize the discrepancy between where he is searching and the object of his search. The standard is, ultimately, to have zero distance between one's hand and the object sought. So, the person plans a move, moves, and receives feedback from other players as to whether the direction was right. The person, in essence, "inputs" the feedback to a **comparator**. The comparator is so called because it compares the feedback—"hot" or "cold"—in this case, with the aim—"hot" or some variation of it. If the person hears "ice cold," a change in direction is called for. "Hot" encourages the person to proceed. That is how the loop works: The person is aiming in a direction and receives more or less continuous feedback as to how to orient himself. In this way, the person almost always finds the object. The principles of the hot-and-cold game are very fundamental and underlie many of our behaviors.

Personal Control as a Hierarchy of Feedback Loops

Some psychologists have viewed personality as consisting of a hierarchy of levels, with feedback loops at each level (e.g., Powers, 1973). At the more molecular level of the nervous system are feedback loops governing the autonomic nervous system including heart rate and respiration.

At a somewhat higher level are simple negative feedback loops employed in motor control (e.g., Powers, 1973; Rosenbaum, 1990; Wiener, 1948). For example, if you are standing on the deck of a boat, and the boat is swaying, you must adjust your legs constantly so as to remain in an upright, standing position. The feedback loop takes as its standard "standing up straight." As the boat tilts to the right, the comparator checks your position (you are tilting to the right) with the goal of standing up straight. Information about balance comes from neural circuits in the inner ear. Action is initiated to maintain yourself upright: You automatically bend your left leg to lower the left side of yourself and extend your right leg so as to raise your right. When the comparator sees that your position meets the standard, the action ceases. As the boat moves back toward center, however, the comparator now notes you are listing to the left. To compensate you now begin to reverse your leg movements.

William T. Powers suggested that the middle-level of personality consists of feedback loops concerning simple goal-directed sequences of behavior such as finding our eyeglasses, buying some milk, and conducting certain aspects of interpersonal relationships (Powers, 1973, pp. 151-160). As an example, let's say you are trying to impress your cousin. To do so, you might e-mail her a story about a recent time you hit a home run in a baseball game and embellish it, describing your heroic levels of practice the week before the game and the pressure of the competition when you were at bat, so that it is very impressive. The sequence of psychological events and acts is illustrated in Figure 10-1. In actuality, of course, your story might not have the desired effect of impressing your cousin, but it would be the best you could do in the situation without any feedback.

Powers believed that it was far more typical to conduct such a social exchange with some considerable feedback. Consider the same situation with your cousin, but this time you are in the same room. As you begin to tell the story, your cousin reacts by emitting approving or disapproving facial expressions and you witness those reactions. If she likes your story (or appears to) you continue. If she expresses boredom or displeasure, however, you change your story, and then re-enter the loop. Of course, if she decides you are conceited, or laughs at you for trying to impress her, you will need to change loops altogether. This response is depicted in Figure 10-2.

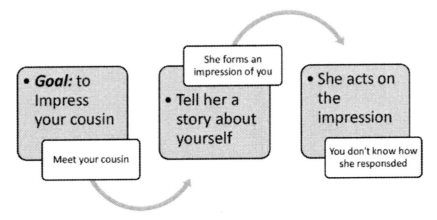

Figure 10-1 A Simple Method for Impressing Your Cousin The flow chart
shows a procedure for impressing your cousin in the absence of feedback.

Here, we have presented the feedback loop as a computer-like diagram. It is worth noting that neurons have the capacity to form negative feedback sequences, and people constantly behave in ways that are sensitive to feedback (Carver & Scheier, 1981; 1998; Powers, 1973a; Powers, 1973b, pp. 27-34).

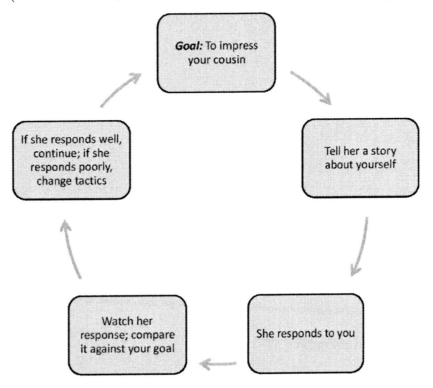

Figure 10-2 *A Feedback Loop for Impressing your Cousin* The diagram depicts
a feedback loop in which you start trying to impress your cousin by telling a story. Feedback
from your cousin (see "External Events") can then be used to continue the story or change it.

The highest levels of feedback control begin with heuristics and brief intentions such as, "I'll help her," or "Honesty is the best policy" (Powers, 1973, p. 168), and range up to the most general principles of control involving moral, factual, and abstract principles such as being loyal to a country, or adhering to the principles of democracy and free elections. The point of feedback at this level is for the person to maintain his or her behavior in line with these abstract principles (Powers, 1973, pp. 171-173).

Levels of Action and Behavioral Identification

People control themselves at different levels: from low-level physical control to high-level personal goals. A person out on a boat engages in low-level physical control to maintain his balance as the boat rocks. As the deck rocks with the water, he must adjust his posture to stay vertical. At higher levels, people attempt to meet their needs in the situations they face. Vallacher and Wegner (1987) became interested in what level of control was most common for a person and why. They found people preferred to describe their actions at a higher more conceptual level. For example, when asked to describe what they were doing after a dinner at a friend's house, most people would prefer to reply, "helping a friend by washing the dishes," rather than "moving a sponge across the plate." That said, people do tend to employ concrete sensory-motor descriptions under some circumstances. The sponge-across-the-plate kind of response is preferred when tasks are unfamiliar and complex, when people believe they are doing poorly, or when their performance is disrupted (e.g., Vallacher & Wegner, 1987).

The Behavioral Identification Form (BIF; Vallacher & Wegner, 1989) measures the level at which people think about carrying out a sample of behaviors. The BIF consists of a number of behaviors such as "Attending class," and "Getting a job," and asks the test-taker how they would identify the activity. For example, "Attending class," can be identified as a specific task such as "Hearing the lecture," or at a higher level as "Getting an education."

High scorers on the test see their actions in relation to their causes and effects, their social meanings, and the goals they satisfy. Low scorers on the test perceive the world primarily at the level of detail and view their actions as carrying out mechanical activities. High scores are related to more proficiency at such tasks, and a wide range of task activity, including diverse hobbies and activities. Low scores on the BIF are correlated with individual reports of difficulty with carrying out tasks; low-scoring individuals also experience failure more often as they carry out activities.

Perhaps because high scores on the BIF reflect an individual's ability to plan and understand their own actions, the high BIF scorer is more reflective and less impulsive than the low BIF scorer. Along those lines, in a sample of juvenile detainees, those with higher BIF scores were less likely to have a record of criminal offenses; lower scorers had higher offense records. Finally, the high BIF scorer may have a more developed self-concept than others, and may understand him or herself more often in relation to consistent traits and a consistent self-concept (Vallacher & Wegner, 1989, p. 666). These kinds of findings suggest that there may be something very useful in the concept of the hierarchical control concept.

Kelly's Circumspection-Preemption-Control (C-P-C) Cycle

People's global self-control differs from the control of a mechanical feedback loop in several ways. For one, people's personalities are composed of many parts that are not always pulling in the same direction: feelings may conflict with thoughts, and thoughts may conflict with each other. In such a context, a person's choices and decision-making will be more complex than a smoothly functioning machine.

The psychologist George Kelly (1955a) characterized the human decision-making loop as involving a **Circumspection-Preemption-Control cycle**, or *C-P-C* cycle. The *C-P-C* cycle is a kind of feedback loop in a human context. Based on their mental models (that Kelly referred to as a "construct system"), they tried to make decisions about themselves and the outside world.

In the *C-P-C* Cycle, a person's circumspection involves looking at himself and deciding how he could make the best choice for himself. For example, a college student who is trying to decide on a career would try to match her own interests and aptitudes to the careers she was considering—to search for a satisfactory fit.

At the *P*, or preemption, point of the *C-P-C* cycle, the individual seeks to narrow down the alternatives to just a few, and then to choose before important opportunities are lost. Perhaps the student reaches her senior year and it is time to apply for jobs. At this point, she must no longer wait or hope for other possibilities, but rather must preempt the process and choose what realistically is before her.

This brings the individual to the final *C* (control or choice) part of the cycle. The individual must choose one course of action and take it. Presumably the correct choice will help her get closer to her goals. But a person can exit the cycle too quickly—deciding without checking on what's best for herself. Alternatively, she can get stuck in the loop prolonging her circumspection while opportunities fade away (Leong & Chervinko, 1996; Kelly, 1955a, pp. 514-517; cf. Lounsbury et al., 2005). Little research work has been done on the *C-P-C* cycle although it seems compatible with research work and it is intuitively compelling.

The Search for—and Effect of—Feedback

Seeking Feedback

How ever people perceive their actions, they often seek feedback to guide them—and respond to feedback that matters are going well—or not. For example, people are used to counteracting the effects of pain by taking over-the-counter pain relievers such as aspirin and similar products. As the pain rises, they take the pain-reliever to reduce the pain. As the pain declines, they stop taking the medicine.

When a person adjusts her pain medication according to her symptoms, she is in a feedback loop: a discrepancy—pain—requires action; no pain, no action. To react accordingly feels natural—and that familiar pattern can work against us if we have a disease without easy-to-detect symptoms. The real symptoms of high blood pressure—emotional distress, dry mouth, and sleep disturbance—are only loosely tied to the disease and are sporadic. Unfortunately, many people who suffer from high blood pressure take their medication only when the real or imagined symptoms are present. Instead, they would be better off taking their medication constantly because the high blood pressure is there all the time. The absence of good feedback is, in this case, potentially quite lethal (Baumann & Leventhal, 1985; Meyer, Leventhal, & Gutmann, 1985).

So people characteristically do seek and employ feedback, a process sometimes called **self-monitoring**. Self-monitoring is a process of collecting feedback about the self. Carver and Scheier (1981; 1998) have suggested that people who employ self-directed attention use feedback more extensively to better adhere to their personal standards than do others. In Carver and Scheier's experiments, self-consciousness is heightened by placing participants in front of a mirror or a video camera. When people see themselves or know that others will see them under such conditions, it encourages them to think about themselves, to become self-conscious, and to attend to feedback.

In one experimental study of self-monitoring, students were asked about their attitudes concerning the use of punishment as a tool in education. Afterward, they were placed in the role of a teacher to see if they behaved in accord with their attitudes (Carver, 1975). In the teacher role, participants were asked to teach another participant (actually a confederate of the experimenter) a word list, and to use mild electrical shock as a punishment for incorrect answers if they thought it might speed the learning.

Some students were randomly assigned to a mirror condition, in which they saw their reflections as they filled out the survey on educational practices and when they entered the role of the teacher; others were in a no-mirror condition. When participants were tested in front of a mirror (thereby inducing self-focus), their behavior agreed with their earlier-recorded attitudes about punishment in education. That is, those who believed punishment could be of value administered more shocks; those who believed punishment was out-of-place in an educational environment administered fewer shocks. By contrast, students tested without the mirror showed no correspondence between their attitudes and behaviors. This suggested that, when self-monitoring, people do indeed employ feedback loops to create consistency between their attitudes and behavior. People who score higher on scales of self-monitoring also show a closer match between their attitudes and behaviors than do others (Fenigstein, Scheier, & Buss, 1975).

Rigging the (Feedback) System

People often alter the feedback they receive to suit their purposes. They may, for example, seek to confirm their biases—that their decisions were correct and good—while ignoring evidence to the contrary. Sometimes, however, people focus on negative feedback so as to enhance their performance.

Norem and colleagues have studied **defensive pessimism**. When facing a challenge, defensive pessimists initially feel anxious and out-of-control and as if they are going to do poorly—despite evidence to the contrary. For example, a defensive pessimist facing an upcoming exam may think, "I'll do very badly at this one." These individuals endorse items such as, "I generally go into academic situations with low expectations, even though I know things usually turn out alright." (Norem & Illingworth, 1993, p. 825). Only the top 25% scorers on such scales are classified as defensive pessimists.

In essence, such individuals are "rigging" their feedback, pretending that all signs point to a poor outcome. Such a pretense solves two problems: first, it makes the defensive pessimist feel calmer by giving them permission to fail, but paradoxically, it also motivates them, because they believe that only by studying really hard can they avoid failure. As it turns out, defensive pessimists perform just as well as optimists on exams as well as on a broad variety of other tasks. In addition, defensive pessimists will perform worse if they are made less anxious or try to use other strategies (Norem & Illingworth, 1993).

Exiting the Feedback System

Of course, sometimes people don't always want feedback, and when they don't, they may engage in a variety of activities to avoid it, such as getting drunk. Alcohol appears to act by reducing self-awareness in those who drink. As self-awareness is lowered, people pay less attention to their standards of behavior, goals, and beliefs (Denton & Krebs, 1990; Hull, 1981; Hull & Rielly, 1986). For that reason, when people get drunk they often behave in an evermore disorganized fashion, participating in activities they would never take part in if sober, saying things they may later regret, and generally taking risks they would not otherwise take.

Bottom-Up Control?

If personal control takes place at multiple levels, is there a particular level that exerts control over the others? Freud believed control over personality is exerted from the bottom up—that is from biological urges and energy; rather than from the top down. To get an idea of what Freud meant, you might imagine yourself with no bodily desires and no social needs. What would you do? How would you behave? Why would you bother to behave?

> "A man without self-control is like a city broken into and left without walls." – Proverbs 25-28

Using the id to represent biological urges and the ego to refer to higher logical levels of control, Freud noted that the ego:

> ...in its relation to the id...is like a man on horseback, who has to hold in check the superior strength of the horse...The analogy may be carried a little further. Often a rider, if he is not to be parted from his horse, is obliged to guide it where it wants to go; so in the same way the ego is in the habit of transforming the id's will into action as if it were its own. (Freud, 1923/1960, p. 15)

Thus, our biological drives and needs determine our direction contingent upon our capacities. Freud says, in essence, look to the biological urges to find out where the person's trajectory in life will go.

Dynamic Self Control

In all these examples, the self-view is a dynamic, changing entity. The person perceives his or her self as closer or farther from goals, and behaves so as to better attain those goals. Sometimes, self-perception may shift from lower level tasks such as how to perform a task (e.g., impress a friend), to higher-level aims, such as establishing a relationship and getting married. Sometimes, people may rig the system by viewing themselves as less prepared than they really are—so as to help motivate themselves. These shifts in self-perception and self-evaluation create a picture of dynamic self-concept—one that varies to suit a particular purpose (Markus & Wurf, 1987).

> "The man of thought who will not act is ineffective; the man of action who will not think is dangerous." – Richard M. Nixon (1913-1994)

Is Self-Control Always Conscious?

Automatic Control and Dissociation

The limitations of the conscious self are considerable. Working memory can handle only about seven chunks of information at a given moment. Attention can be directed toward one or two matters at a time. Conscious self-control, in other words, is a highly limited resource. We have already encountered the idea of a hierarchy of feedback loops that control personality. Surely, however, not all those feedback loops involve the self or consciousness.

For these reasons, it useful to think more broadly of **personal control**. Personal control involves the regulatory mechanisms of personality generally, some of which involve conscious self-control, and other portions of which involve non-conscious control more generally. It isn't surprising that personal control will commonly be carried out at automatic or subconscious levels as well as at conscious levels. In fact, self-control may be more efficient when behaviors that can be carried out automatically are shifted outside of conscious control, with some monitoring so as to be able to return them to consciousness if necessary.

When thoughts and action programs are separated from consciousness temporarily, they are referred to as **dissociated**. Dissociated thoughts can be considered as divided off from consciousness. For instance, when a person performs two activities simultaneously, thoughts related to one activity may be conscious, while the unattended-to thoughts are unconscious (Hilgard, 1977; 1994).

Many people experience a kind of dissociation called highway hypnosis. Perhaps you have driven down a highway and then have begun to pay attention to the radio or to a conversation, and, suddenly, you arrive where you were going without much recollection of how you got there. Plainly, some part of you was driving while your own awareness was diverted elsewhere. In essence, the thought processes involved in driving can become divided from consciousness. Some people can barely remember details of their ride home (Lahey, 1989).

Tired college students preparing for examinations will often find themselves reading an assignment, turning the pages at the approximate rate at which they read, and suddenly realize they had no idea what they had seen for the past 2 or 3 pages (and sometimes more). Once again we may ask, "Who was reading?" (or at least "Who was turning the pages?") It may turn out that the answer was the subconscious part of the personality. (Don't rely on this subconscious part to get the exam questions right, though!)

Dissociation and the Unconscious

When certain portions of consciousness are divided off, or dissociated from the rest, the divided-off mental processes are said to be subconscious (Hilgard, 1994; James, 1892). The idea of divided or dissociated unconscious was first suggested by the French neurologist Jean Janet, a contemporary of Freud. Janet believed that thoughts become conscious through their associations with prior thoughts. If so, then other ideas might also stay out of consciousness because they had become dissociated from conscious concepts. Sometimes this is just for mental efficiency—such as highway hypnosis. At other times, however, ideas may be dissociated because they are threatening or painful.

Such disassociated ideas, however, would not simply go away. Rather, they would continue to exert influence as an "automatism" (Perry & Laurence, 1984, p. 28). The subconscious automatism was not "lower" than conscious; it was more like a second person, cut off from the first. The automatism—the closely inter-associated idea—acted independently of the person, but with some control over the person's beliefs, thoughts, and actions.

Hilgard's (1977) theory of **neo-dissociationism** preserves much of Janet's original conception, but updates the conceptions to fit a more recent cognitive psychology. In Hilgard's (1974) approach, cognitive barriers are dynamically erected by an individual in his or her perceptual/memory associations, so as to block out certain thoughts. For example, if a person feels pain and dissociates it, he does so by erecting a second thought that "I feel no pain," and buffers the feelings of painful sensation with a dynamic barrier, formed by inattention to the pain. In this model, a person dissociating from pain attends to anything but the painful sensation and inserts into his consciousness the idea "I am feeling no pain." Together, these result in analgesia—the experience of markedly reduced pain such as what occurs with painkillers or when under hypnosis.

Individual Differences in Dissociation

Not everyone seems equally able or likely to dissociate ideas in consciousness. A trait related to dissociation is whether or not an individual experiences something called conscious **absorption**. The trait of absorption describes a person's ability to become lost in a stream of consciousness so intensely as to lose track of everything else. Paradoxically, absorption in one's own train of thoughts appears to be related to dissociation in general. The more intense one's conscious focus, it appears, the more may go on outside of consciousness, unattended to and unseen. For example, the correlation between absorption and the capacity to be hypnotized is about $r = .35$, a moderate relationship (Weitzenhoffer & Hilgard, 1962).

The Classic Suggestion Effect

Some people can "feel" or witness dissociation even as it is happening; this occurs in the classic suggestion effect. The **classic suggestion effect** occurs when someone suggests that you do something or feel something, and a part of you follows the suggestion but without the participation of the conscious self. For example, a person might be told to hold out his arms in front of him and feel how heavy his right hand feels. Some people will indeed feel their right hand is very heavy—and that the verbal suggestion itself caused this new feeling. For some people, that responsiveness to the suggestion seems to occur outside of their own conscious choice. Responsiveness to the classic suggestion effect is often used as a screening device to identify people more likely to enter a hypnotic state, with which it correlates about $r = .35$ (Bowers, 1982).

The Dissociative Experiences Scale indicates that there may exist two types of dissociation. One type, which is fairly common among healthy people, involves absorption and involvement in imagination and imagery. This is measured by items such as (does this describe you?): "Some people can get so involved in watching TV or a movie that they lose track of what is going on around them." People experience more dramatic dissociations as well. Some survey respondents have agreed they have shared these experiences: "Some people have the experience of finding new things among their belongings that they do not remember buying," and "Some people have the experience of finding themselves in a place and having no idea how they got there" (Waller, Putnam, & Carlson, 1996).

Severe dissociation is sometimes associated with trauma. A case of historical importance to the field concerned soldiers who were caught in an intense aerial bombardment during World War I (one of the first in military history). Although they returned physically unharmed, they reported having lost their sight. In this case, the physicians hypothesized that what they had seen was so horrible that they created a mental barrier against seeing. The use of hypnotherapy restored the sight of several soldiers (see Redlich & Bingham, 1960).

Evidence from Case Studies

A number of case studies of dissociated mental ideas exist. An everyday case of dissociation concerns Elizabeth (the name is changed), a first-year graduate student in a psychology program (Erdelyi, 1984). Whenever Elizabeth became angry, she would break out in a peculiar rash that included pink blotches that turned to dark spots of red and scarlet in response to her anger. Her rash, in other words, was an external signal that indicated her emotional condition. When her verbal reports contradicted such signals, unconscious dissociations were likely to be present.

Elizabeth had been making poor progress in the psychology laboratory in which she worked. One day a new graduate student joined the group. After Elizabeth had presented some of her recent work, he adopted an overbearing superior attitude, and soundly criticized her work. During this, her rash appeared, and the professor put an end to the meeting. After the student left, the professor urged her not to be too angry. She responded, "But I wasn't angry!" The professor, overcome by his curiosity, said: "But Elizabeth, you have your famous rash all over your face and neck; you look like a pink leopard!"

Her answer: "You are putting me on!" With a hint of annoyance, she reached into her pocketbook, took out her compact, and looked at herself. She started shaking her head and giggled in embarrassment. A normal blush lit up the pale rest of her face. "That's amazing," she said, "I was completely unaware of it." (Erdelyi, 1984, pp.75-76).

Non-Consciousness Personal Control: The Model of Hypnosis

To study non-conscious forms of personal control, psychologists have used the model of the hypnotic trance. Hypnosis provides an experimental condition in which a researcher can control portions of a person's mental processes, apart from the individual's consciousness. As a research tool, the hypnotic induction is valuable for suggesting possibilities of how non-conscious urges and commands can control the individual, apart from consciousness.

One limitation of the use of hypnosis to understand mental control is that it may not be generalizable to everyone; only some people can be hypnotized. The individual differences in dissociation and in hypnotic ability are profound. About a third of all people are relatively unaffected by hypnosis. The other two thirds are increasingly susceptible to its influence, up to a small group called **hypnotic virtuosos** who are able to enter into deep hypnotic states with ease, and to carry out profoundly difficult mental dissociations and alterations of consciousness once in the state (Hilgard, 1965).

A Brief History of Hypnosis

Franz Anton Mesmer (1734-1815) is often credited as the first hypnotist. Mesmer grew up in a rural, densely forested part of Austrian countryside and completed a medically approved dissertation in Vienna.

At that time in Europe, word was spreading about magnetism—a new and fascinating force. Mesmer was interested in whether magnetism could influence people. At that time, most magnets were in the universities, many of which were administered by Jesuits, clergy of the Catholic Church particularly responsible for education. In 1774, Mesmer borrowed his first magnet from a Jesuit astronomer with the unlikely name of Maximilian Hell.

Mesmer brought it home to treat a woman who was employed part-time in his household and who had numerous physical complaints. As he waived the magnet over her body and suggested its forces would work on her, she felt "surging sensations" which Mesmer believed indicated that fluids were moving through her. After the treatment, her complaints went away. Over a series of further experiments, Mesmer discovered the original iron magnet was not necessary. Believing he himself had become magnetized, he began to refer to himself as possessing "Animal Magnetism."

Mesmer moved to Paris where he set up a practice curing the ills of wealthy and noble patients, using the power of his personal magnetism. He often dressed in black cloaks, wore a sorcerer-like hat and waved a wand that he believed carried magnetic forces.

In the tumultuous times just before the French Revolution, Mesmer raised suspicions of the authorities. In 1784, the King of France appointed a number of august scientists to investigate his practice. The committee concluded that psychological forces were in play, or as they put it: "imagination without magnetism produces convulsions, and…magnetism without imagination produces nothing." (cited in Bowers, 1976, p. 8)

Some scientists saw the potential of this new psychological phenomenon. Around 1850, a French physician named Braid coined the term hypnosis, which more accurately reflected that magnetism was not involved in the process. In 1885, the eminent French neurologist Jean Charcot, who was then at the peak of his professional career, began to use hypnosis with his patients. Charcot's name finally brought hypnosis some respectability. And scientists continued to subject it to study.

Studying Hypnosis Today

Today, hypnotic ability is measured with scales such as the Stanford Scale of Hypnotic Susceptibility, Version C. It employs a graded set of mental challenges that a person attempts while under hypnosis—such as imagining a bothersome insect where there is none. Only a few people can perform them all (Kurtz & Strube, 1996; Weitzenhoffer & Hilgard, 1959; Weitzenhoffer & Hilgard, 1962). Advances in understanding have laid the groundwork for a potential new generation of hypnotic scales as well (e.g., Kirsch, 1997; Kirsch & Lynn, 1995; Lynn & Rhue, 1988; Woody, 1997).

Characteristics of the Hypnotic State

One interpretation of hypnosis is that an individual's conscious self-control is temporarily disabled, and that a part of the personality comes under the control of the hypnotist. In old movies, hypnotists induced a trance by saying, "you are under my control…you will hear only my voice, you will do as I say…." This is not a very good hypnotic induction. Actually, it would be so anxiety provoking to many people as to keep them quite alert. But it does get across the idea of dissociation: that a part of our aware self is split off from our own control and enters the sphere of someone else's commands.

Indeed, a primary characteristic of hypnotic states is the suppression of one's own planning and self-direction (Hilgard, 1965). A person who suppresses his planning temporarily puts aside his own goals and plans and follows the guidance of someone else (see Table 10-2 for an overview of this and the other characteristics). In one study, hypnotized students were given instructions to attend a holiday party going on in the building, and to pretend they were not hypnotized (Hilgard, 1965). Experimental observers followed each hypnotized student to study what he or she did, and for the participant's own safety.

At first, the hypnotized individuals behaved like everyone else at the party, chatting and helping themselves to the food. After a while, however, the hypnotized party-goers became a bit glassy eyed, and many of them, after some time, found themselves a comfortable chair in which to relax, and stared blankly out into space. They remained there until finally rescued by the experimenters. Under hypnosis, the hypnotized participants seemed to have lost their own line of conscious intentions, at least temporarily. Incidentally, you may wonder what might have happened if the participants had been left in their seats indefinitely. The vast majority of hypnotic participants would have awoken on their own after a time. (A few exceptional participants might not awaken until obtaining the proper attention.)

Perhaps related to this dissociation is the redistribution of attention. The person can (under instruction) block out awareness of certain parts of the environment. For example, a hypnotized person may not see someone else who is in the room with them, or the hypnotized person may feel no pain, if so instructed. "Make a stroke on paper or blackboard, and tell the subject it is not there…" remarked William James, with some amazement:

> …and he will see nothing but the clean paper or the board. Next, he not looking, surround the original stroke with other strokes exactly like it and ask him what he sees. He will point out one by one all the new strokes and omit the original one every time, no matter how numerous the new strokes may be, or in what order they are.
>
> Obviously, then, he is not blind to the kind of stroke in the least…and paradoxical as it may seem to say so, he must distinguish it with great accuracy from others like it, in order to remain blind to it… (James, 1890, II, 607-08)

Also while under hypnosis, people will accept realities that they wouldn't accept when awake. The hypnotic state involves the enhanced availability of visual and emotional memories. With less conscious monitoring, there is also the greater chance for more poorly directed behavior—and maybe more creative, associative thinking. For example, people under hypnosis exhibit increased suggestibility—the tendency to accept others' ideas under hypnosis. A simple suggestion, such as, "Your right arm is getting stiff," may result in hypnotized people being unable to move their right arms. Needless to say, such a suggestion would have little effect on most people under normal circumstances.

Table 10-2: Seven Characteristics of a Hypnotic State*

Characteristic	Description
Suppression of Planning	The hypnotic participant gives up control of planning to the hypnotist or other party.
Redistribution of Attention	The hypnotized person attends to certain parts of the environment and can screen out other parts.
Enhanced Availability of Visual and Emotional Memories	People in a hypnotic trance often recall experiences from the past in a more emotionally and visually intense manner than outside the trance.
Reduction in Reality Testing	Highly hypnotizable people are prepared to imagine and accept alternative realities such as imaginary beings or creatures.
Increased Suggestibility	Once in a hypnotic trance, people respond to suggestions such as "Your arm is getting stiff," or "There is a fly on your nose."
Role Behavior	Hypnotized individuals can readily act out unaccustomed or forgotten roles, such as an adult becoming her ten-year-old self.
Spontaneous Amnesia	Some people may forget some or all of the hypnotic session afterward without being instructed to do so.

*Summarized from Hilgard (1965).

The hypnotic trance involves a marked reduction in reality testing. For example, if instructed to do so, a hypnotized individual may believe that there is a third person in the room with him when there are only two, and the hypnotized participant may even see the imaginary person as if he or she were really there. In fact, there is always the possibility that people will add imagined events to what they recall under hypnosis—the reason the American Psychological Association cautions against employing hypnosis when the police interview witnesses to a crime. (e.g., Scheflin, Spiegel, & Spiegel, 1998)

A most relevant and striking aspect of the trance in regard to non-conscious personal control is the post-hypnotic suggestion. For this, the hypnotist asks the participant to carry out a task—such as opening a window upon a signal (e.g., when the clock chimes the hour). The participant is also told he or she will remember nothing about the suggestion. The participant is then awakened, and will carry out the task of opening the window at the prescribed time, with no apparent knowledge of why he or she did it. Actually, the person will typically supply an incorrect explanation—such as that the room was stuffy. This has led some psychologists to argue, on the basis of the hypnotic model, that complex chains of behavior can and do take place in otherwise normal individuals without their awareness. And that moreover the individual will provide a false reason for doing so afterward.

Causes of Hypnotic Susceptibility

What leads a person to behave in a hypnotically susceptible way? There is some evidence that hypnotizability may be genetic (Morgan, 1973). Jean Hilgard (1979) concluded that hypnotic ability also arises in childhood among individuals who find pathways into the altered state. Some of the central pathways to hypnotic ability include the childhood experience of fantasy involvement in reading, drama, creative artwork, and related activities such as religious imagination, among others.

In the case of reading, for example, hypnotizable adults reported that as children they didn't simply read, but rather entered in a new fantasy world. Upon putting down a book, a hypnotizable person might imagine herself talking or playing with the characters in the book for several days thereafter, as if they had become real people, in a real world of their own. Recent research has suggested that hypnotic susceptibility may also be related to everything from intense attachments to pets to certain milder aspects of schizophrenic-spectrum disorders (Brown & Katcher, 2001; Graham, 2001).

Positive Affirmations

Hypnosis provides a dramatic example of shifting self-control to an automatized state. Can we also improve ourselves by making some helpful thoughts automatic? In the early 1900s, a French physician, Coué, suggested that people repeat to themselves over and over, "*Tous les jours à tous points de vue, je vais de mieux en mieux*," or, in English, "Every day in every way, I am getting better and better." Coué argued that substantial repetition of this formula—20 times upon waking up, going to bed, and several times during the day, if possible, would provide an automatic positive self-concept for people that could be helpful.

If Coué's phrases sound vague and simplistic to you, he argued that there was a sophisticated reason for it: People would be less inclined to automatically argue against it precisely because the statement was general. For example, a woman might repeat that she was a good friend to others; Coué argued that affirmation was too specific and she might end up dwelling on exceptions to the statement and lose any confidence its truth. Coué's therefore crated his phrase to illicit as few specific rational objections as possible. Of course, Coué was not the only one to suggest this. Yogananda Paramahansa, among the first California gurus, introduced such self-affirmations in the 1930s (Paulhus, 1993, p. 375).

Coué's method became the rage in France, and crossed the English Channel where it was similarly popular (in English form) in London. For some reason, the idea fared a bit less well in America, where one might imagine its optimistic message would be popular.

Arguing from the standpoint of contemporary psychology, Paulhus suggests that an automatic self-concept is important because attentional processes are limited. The automatic self-concept fills in the gaps when a person is focusing on other matters. In a series of studies Paulhus and his colleagues found that when people are distracted by white noise or through heightened exam anxiety, their self-descriptions become more globally positive and less believable and accurate. They conclude that honest trait descriptions require attentional capacity (Paulhus & Lower, 1987; Paulhus & Linn, 1987, cited in Paulhus, 1993).

Consistent with the above, Paulhus and his colleagues have found that repetition of general positive statements about the self do change the self-concept. First, participants make optimally positive statements about themselves. Later, they are asked to endorse self-descriptive traits flashed on a computer screen under two conditions: An honesty condition in which they are asked to be as accurate as possible, and then, secondly, a speeded condition in which they are asked to respond as quickly as they can. Results indicate that, particularly in the speeded condition, the repetition of positive statements biases their self-image positively—for up to 24-hour periods (the longest they have investigated thus far). More generally, Epton and colleagues have found that self-affirmation induced by reflecting upon our personal qualities and relationships can support our flexibility and ability to change in response to health threats (Epton et al., 2015).

How Do We Deal With the Pain of Falling Short?

"Nothing is as easy as deceiving yourself, for what you wish you readily believe." – Demosthenes (384-322 B.C.E.)

Falling Short and Mental Defense

No matter how much we can control ourselves, we are never adequate in relation to every possible yardstick. As human beings, we all share desires that cannot be met and social shortcomings, and we fall short of moral commandments that few human beings are good enough to meet all the time. As if all that were not enough, we must contend with the fear of death, a death that greets everyone at the end no matter how well we act. We can—and do—try, try again. And yet, we don't always make it. People often employ defense mechanisms to block out the pain that such thoughts inevitably raise.

One way that individuals maintain their self-esteem is through the action of such **defense mechanisms**. In Freud's original formulation, defense mechanisms protected consciousness from psychic pain caused by ideas related to threatening sexual and aggressive desires. These defenses were later systematized by the psychoanalyst Anna Freud (1937), Freud's daughter. Today, defense mechanisms are understood to protect the conscious self from threats to self-esteem and psychic pain more generally (Fenichel, 1945). The defenses do this by blocking out or modifying any information that would seriously threaten the individual's sense of security (e.g., Baumeister, Dale, & Sommer, 1998; Cooper, 1998).

Suppression

You are probably aware of having said something to yourself like, "I'm just not going to worry about this now," or "I need to distract myself from this problem." This is called **suppression**. Suppression involves the conscious blocking out of awareness of unpleasant thoughts (Wegner, 1989). For example, surveys indicate that when individuals feel an unpleasant emotion, they often urge themselves: "don't think about it," "fight the feeling," and "pretend everything is okay" (Mayer, Salovey, Gomberg-Kaufman, & Blainey, 1991; Mayer, Stevens, Bryan, & Nishikawa, 1992).

In a series of experiments, Wegner (1989) had people try <u>not</u> to think about something. Participants in an experimental group were instructed to try not to think about a white bear for three minutes—to block any thought of white bears out of their mind. Whenever a white bear came into their mind, they signaled the mental intrusion by pressing a button, and then continued to attempt to block out the white bear thought. A comparison group spent three minutes actively thinking of white bears. Later, when members of each group were asked to think about anything they pleased, the group that had blocked out white bears thought a lot more about white bears than did members of the control group. When we suppress ideas they tend to return.

Suppressed feelings sometimes emerge as well. A patient, "Mary," had been hospitalized for depression when she sought a weekend pass to go home and visit her family. In reality, she was quite unhappy and had every intention of killing herself on the way home. She lied to her psychiatrist and the treatment team so successfully, however, that she received the pass. Fortunately, she had second thoughts about suicide before going home, and confessed them to the psychiatrist.

As it had turned out, the session with the psychiatrist had been videotaped. Was anything on the videotape that might reveal Mary's true feelings? While searching through the tape of Mary's conversation with the psychiatrist, Paul Ekman and his colleagues found a number of partial physical expressions such as shrugs related to depression. Moreover, as Ekman put it:

> …using slow-motion repeated replay, we saw a complete sadness facial expression, but
> it was there only for an instant, quickly followed by a smiling appearance. (Ekman,
> 1985, Telling Lies, pp. 130-131)

These were **micro-expressions**. A micro-expression is a complete, full-faced, emotional expression that takes place in a highly compressed period of time—in about 40 milliseconds, and that is invisible to the naked eye. Pure micro expressions are fairly rare, but other emotions are suppressed all the time. Squelched expressions—expressions covered up by another one—frequently happen in social interactions. We might momentarily glare at someone because we are angry, and then cover it quickly with a smile (Ekman, 1985, p. 131).

Repression

It is not a giant leap from suppression to **repression**. Repression involves the motivated non-perception or forgetting of unpleasant material. For example, a student who doesn't want to study for examinations might forget about an upcoming exam entirely. It may begin as a suppression—a conscious ignoring of the idea, but then the suppression itself may become automatized and both the feared exam, and his attempt to forget about it may gradually sink below consciousness altogether. Most defense mechanisms typically use repression, either alone, or in combination with other mental processes.

Weinberger, Schwartz, and Davison (1979) studied repression in a group of male college students who were told that they would be receiving a painful electrical shock. The experimenters monitored the students' fear in two ways. First, they measured well-accepted physiological indicators of fear including blood pressure and heart rate. Second, they asked the students if they were afraid. Most men responded to the threat of the shocks physiologically with increased heart rate and blood pressure, suggesting a fear reaction. Most also reported being afraid. There existed a few men, however, who were "physiologically" afraid (e.g., increased heart rate), but reported being entirely calm. This last group was labeled "repressors," because they apparently repressed their feelings. Subsequent studies have clarified that such individuals are doing more than impression management, and appear to lack access to internal experiences (Weinberger & Davidson, 1994). Weinberger et al. speculated that these men had learned early to please themselves and others by displaying little or no negative feeling. Interestingly, a decade of follow-up studies has suggested that such repressors show unusually high levels of health problems (Weinberger, 1995).

It is worth mentioning that some repression may be automatic, and may never involve conscious awareness at all. Collins, McLeod, & Jacoby (1992) conducted experiments in which they asked participants two different kinds of questions—neutral and threatening—that were masked by a louder background noise. An example of a neutral question was, "Is Albany the capital of New York State?"; a threatening question asked was, "Would it be upsetting if your parents stopped supporting you?"

The questions themselves were played at a level below the threshold of reliable hearing, and the participants' job was to judge the loudness of the background noise. The sentences and background noise were carefully controlled for clarity and loudness. Participants in the experiment judged background noise as much noisier when the threatening sentences played. This suggests that part of their minds were blocking out what other parts found fearful to hear—as Freud described repression. Additional studies indicated that this perception of loudness was non-consciously controlled, and that participants could not overcome it (Jacoby et al., 1988).

Specific Defense Mechanisms

Anna Freud suggested that there existed a developmental hierarchy of specific defense mechanisms—an idea investigated and supported by contemporary researchers (e.g., Cramer, 1991; Vaillant, 1981). Each of the defense mechanisms can be viewed as a dynamic of self-control specifically designed to avoid personal pain. The earliest developing defense is denial.

Denial

Denial is a normal form of mental defense for children between the years of 3 and 6 years old, but its use decreases thereafter. That makes it among the earliest forms of defense that children learn to use. Denial can be defined as the outright rejection of something that is clearly true. For example, a small child might wave her hands and, while doing so, spill her glass of milk onto the floor. Her father might observe, "Oh, you spilled your milk because you were waving your arms." A child using denial will innocently respond, "*I didn't do it.*" If asked *who* did it, the child is likely to shrug as if ignorant, or make up a story—"My teddy bear!"

Healthy adults employ denial only in times of extreme stress. Adults who lose a loved one might momentarily experience denial, but the use of denial becomes less frequent with age. Still, it can persist as a personality pattern. For example, students believe that tests are less valid and fair when they do poorly on them than well (e.g., Pyszczynski, Greenberg, & Holt, 1985; Schlenker, Weigold, & Hallum, 1990), particularly when their self-esteem is unstable (Kernis, Cornell, Sun, Berry, & Harlow, 1993). In addition, young adults who score high on projective measures of denial are more irresponsible, unpredictable, and rebellious; they are also less able to see the heart of a problem, and less straightforward in their communications (Cramer, 2002).

Projection

The mental defense of **projection** involves a confusion between one's own characteristics, and the characteristics of another person (or people). Projection can be defined as denying a negative quality in oneself and yet falsely identifying it in others. So, for example, a businessman who spends much of his time cheating others might view most other businesspeople as cheats. Such projection is sometimes used to explain bigotry in which a person's own negative impulses—say laziness—are seen as the characteristics of other ethnic or religious groups. Over time, a person who projects negative qualities on others will have higher than usual self-esteem, but also increased anxiety, perhaps because disconfirming evidence of her beliefs become harder to block out (Cramer & Tracy, 2005).

The most robust experimental finding related to projection is that people tend to see others as more like themselves than they really are (Ross, Greene, & House, 1977). This effect, called the **false consensus effect**, also occurs more frequently in those with higher self-esteem (Crocker, Alloy, & Kayne, 1988). Still, the research evidence is less complete when it comes to finding evidence that the person then represses his or her own bad qualities (Baumeister, et al., 1998).

Rationalization

Rationalization is a commonly used defense in which a person finds some false reason for doing (or not doing) something so as to cover up the real reason. For example, a person who is afraid of going on a date because she is painfully shy and ashamed of her body, may find all sorts of reasons not to go on the date that have nothing to do with the real reason: "I have to prepare for an exam," "I don't have any clean clothes,"—and of course, "I'm not feeling well." In any single instance, these reasons may make sense. But if a person always finds a different excuse to avoid the same activity it becomes clearer over time that rationalization is being used. Kunda (1990) developed a theory of motivated reasoning, in which she finds that people do what they feel like, and find a reason for it afterward. For example, a person may like a member of a different ethnic group he meets. If so, he will recall a positive stereotype of the ethnic group to support the feeling (Kunda & Sinclair, 1999); if he doesn't like the person, he will recall negative stereotypes (cf. Tsang, 2002).

Reaction Formation

The defense of **reaction formation** begins with a person denying an unwanted trait in him- or herself, and then acting in ways that are opposite to the covered-up characteristic so as to hide it. For example, a woman might really feel superiority and hatred toward others, but might try to cover it up from both herself and others by claiming to love them. For example, European-American, non-prejudiced, participants in a research study were told (depending upon their experimental condition) that their test results indicated they were racist. Such participants later gave a panhandler of African American heritage more money than they gave a similar European American pan-handler, relative to others in a control condition (Dutton & Lake, 1973). In another study, male participants who exhibited higher blood flow to the genital area (indicating sexual responsiveness) while watching a videotape of homosexual intercourse expressed the most homophobia on several attitude measures (Adams, Wright, & Lohr, 1996).

There also are striking examples of cases where an individual's hidden personal characteristics finally break through. Jim Bakker, with his wife Tammy, developed Please the Lord (PTL) Ministries, an evangelical religious empire with a budget in the hundreds of millions of dollars. The couple joined an elite group of evangelists on national television, and based their mission on preaching love, purity, and wholesomeness before God. In 1987, while preaching on television, however, Bakker also was committing adultery with a church secretary and using ministry money to buy her silence. More significantly to the United States government, he had fraudulently oversold at least $158 million dollars' worth of lodging-partnerships to the members of his ministry—which amounted to the largest consumer mail fraud in the United States at that time (Tidwell, 1993).

So, Bakker was at the same time preaching the importance of moral behavior, while engaging in fraudulent behavior himself. Moreover, Bakker was judged personally responsible for these and other transgressions to the degree necessary for him to be found guilty of the crime. Awareness is not an all-or-nothing matter, however. To the extent that Bakker's role as a minister helped him avoid paying attention to his own impulses toward deception and their consequences, we might conclude that the processes of reaction formation were at play.

Sublimation

Sublimation is among the healthiest of defenses. Here, the individual represses an unacceptable desire, but then finds a constructive social role that will let that desire express itself. For example, by choosing to become a painter or sculptor, a person can satisfy various sexual impulses in a socially approved way. Spreading paints, or molding clay provide tactile experiences that can be similar to those involved in physical contact with a sexual partner. Moreover, artists often take human figures as their models, and this opportunity to look carefully at others' bodies is another way in which a sexual drive can be partially satisfied. Similarly, people who choose to become butchers, police officers, or surgeons may be sublimating an aggressive drive, and by doing so, turning their desire to act aggressively to the service of the community.

In a survey of research on defense mechanisms, Baumeister, Dale, & Sommer (1998) were unable to find research in the psychological literature that they considered relevant to the defense of sublimation. This raises the question of whether there is no evidence for the defense, or whether, because the defense is so much a part of healthy functioning, it has been ignored. Sublimation, then, is an understudied topic at present.

How Is Self-Control (or Its Absence) Expressed?

The Search for Self-Control

Self-control can direct a search for a better life. People control themselves in difficult circumstances, delay gratification, and make difficult but correct decisions to obtain gains in the long term. Early studies of mental control often divided people who were strong-willed and could control their impulses from those who were relatively weak-willed, and who were subject to the pressures of everyday life with little capacity to plan or adhere to those plans (Klausner, 1965; Wegner & Pennebaker, 1993). In the early 1920s though, the eminent educator, Dewey (1922) argued that the will could be educated and improved.

A cottage industry of self-help books has long existed, which coaches people about how to increase their self-control (Dornbush, 1965). At the same time, there has been little research to refer to on the matter, so most such popular works were speculative. More recently, psychologists have begun to examine the processes of self-control with an eye to what its outcomes might be, and how to improve self-control (Wegner & Pennebaker, 1993). Some fascinating findings already have emerged, including that self-control demands considerable effort and cost. For example, the control of thoughts elicits heightened physiological activity (e.g., Wegner, et al., 1990; Gross & Levenson, 1997). Exerting self-control can also interfere with other cognitive activity, because a person can only think (or not think) about a few things at once (Gilbert, 1991; Wegner & Pennebaker, 1993).

The varieties of self-control mean that the different ways in which it is expressed are potentially infinite. Here we will examine just a few examples of this important new research area.

Control versus Impulsiveness

In a now classic series of studies, Mischel and Ebbesen (1970) studied children's self-control. To do so, they first developed a method in which preschool children would be willing to wait in a room by themselves for at least a short time without becoming upset. The experimenter and child played a game together in which the experimenter left the room and the child could immediately call the experimenter back by a simple signal. When summoned, the experimenter quickly darted back inside the room. This step was practiced thoroughly, until the child felt secure that her or his signal would be answered.

Figure 10-3: Waiting Time as a Function of the Presence of Reward
(After Mischel & Ebbesen, 1970)

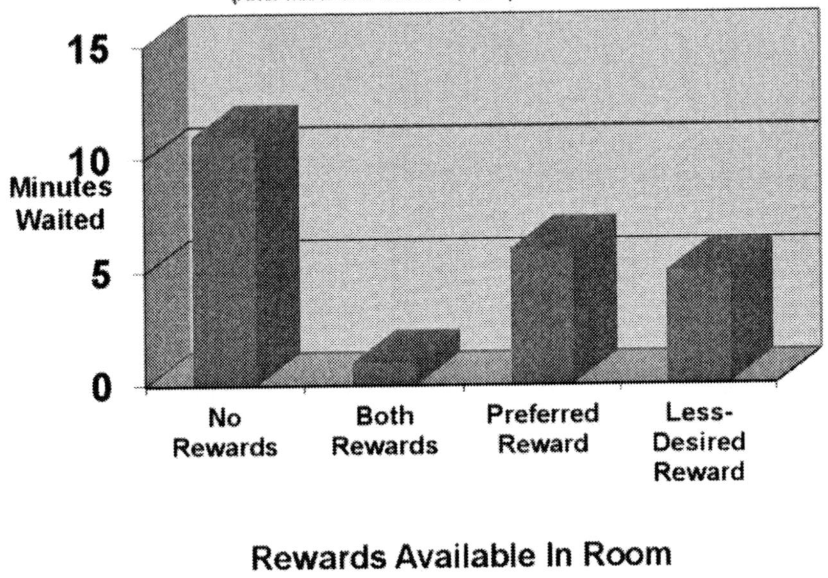

Rewards Available In Room

Next, the child was shown two food treats, one of which the child was known to prefer from pre-testing, and a second, less-preferred treat. Children were told that the experimenter was going to leave. If the child signaled for the experimenter, he or she could have the less-preferred treat right away. If the child could wait for the experimenter to return "by himself," however, he or she would get the preferred treat. That is, the longer they waited, the greater the reward. There were four conditions: One in which neither of the treats were visible, one in which both rewards were visible, one in which only the less-preferred (immediate) treat could be seen, and one in which only the most-preferred (delayed) treat could be seen. Generally speaking, children waited far longer when no treat was present, and least well when both treats were present, as shown in Figure 10-3. The children most successful at waiting created highly inventive strategies—they did nearly anything and everything to distract themselves. Rather than sit and stare at the less-preferred treat, some children covered their eyes with their hands, or rested their heads in their hands. Some children invented elaborate tapping games with their hands and feet to create a rhythm to distract themselves. Some talked animatedly to themselves, others sang songs aloud. When all else failed, a few tried to go to sleep—and one child successfully did fall asleep during the wait! All these preschoolers surely deserved the treats they ultimately received.

Implications of Self-Control

As we will see in the coming chapters on personality development, individual differences in being able to wait—to postpone gratification—are highly predictive of life outcomes over time. The children in the

Mischel study, for example, were followed up as adolescents. Those who were more controlled as preschoolers were described when they were adolescents by their parents (on California Q-Sorts) as more verbally fluent, better able to concentrate, good planners, and competent and skillful. Those who had had difficulty waiting, on the other hand, were described as easily rattled, and as going to pieces under stress (Mischel, Shoda, & Peake, 1988, Table 2).

Similarly, Smith (1967) rated a number of students on their impulsiveness prior to their entry to college. The higher the impulsiveness of the student, the lower the college GPA; with a substantial correlation of $r = -.47$. Similarly, Kipnis (1971) found that students with self-reported impulsivity had lower average grade point averages than did comparable students who were not impulsive. This effect held true only for high SAT students, suggesting either that higher SAT students knew better when they were impulsive, or that impulsiveness interferes more strongly with those high in intellectual ability. Bio-psychologists have begun to trace the chemical roots of such impulsivity (Cools et al., 2005).

Increasing research also studies the best ways to exert self-control. The research is sufficiently recent that few conclusions can be drawn from it at present. One compelling conclusion, however, is that self-control is a limited resource, and if we try to exert self-control in too many areas at once the energy for self-control will become depleted (Muraven & Baumeister, 2000). Another finding is that the best form of self-control to employ may vary from challenge to challenge. For example, breaking certain habits is sometimes more easily done when changing one's circumstances—such as moving, or transferring to a different college (Wood, Tam, & Witt, 2005). A person might need to draw on a different strategy, though, to control her overeating or to change her negative thoughts.

Self-control is critically important to us in everyday life, and also has implications for our futures. We will revisit this topic in the next chapters on personality development, where further evidence of the importance of personal self-control on future outcomes will be presented.

Reviewing Chapter 10

The purpose of this chapter is to examine how the conscious executive (the self) intervenes and controls the rest of personality—and the difficulties it has in doing so. We begin with an examination of why control is necessary. The conscious executive is by its nature somewhat egocentric. It governs the person and sees things its own way. It also seeks feedback, however, and acts on the basis of that feedback. It engages in feedback loops in an attempt to meet its goals. It may also be described as employing a circumspection-preemption-control (CPC) cycle.

Self-control is often distributed in the sense that some of it is automatic and unconscious. Conscious control can be divided or dissociated experimentally and studied through the use of hypnosis.

Mechanisms of defense form one way in which the executive consciousness prevents uncomfortable ideas and feelings from reaching consciousness. Sigmund Freud and his daughter, Anna Freud, provided good descriptions of these. Is there any evidence for them? Experimental evidence comes from studying hypnosis, facial expressions, and cognitive psychology.

Studies examining self-control show that individual differences in such control are already evident in children and have important consequences for later behavior.

The following questions should help you test your knowledge about this chapter.

Questions About "What Are Dynamics of Self-Control?"

1. <u>How Dynamics of Self-Control Are Distinctive, and the Need for Self Control:</u> The dynamics of self-control begin with a sense of wanting to do something and carrying through on it. What kinds of activities are enhanced by self-control? Can you describe what personality is like when the individual loses self-control?

2. <u>Aims of Self Control:</u> When peoples' goals are studied in surveys, certain goals appear again and again, and some of them are more important than others. For example, relationship goals are consistently among the most important in people's estimations. What other goals are of importance? Do those high in extraversion order their goals differently than those high in neuroticism?

Questions About "How Does Self-Control Occur?"

3. <u>The Problem of the Egotistical Ego:</u> From some standpoints, it is altogether normal to see the world in an egotistical fashion. People's memories, for example, naturally revolve around themselves as actors. Greenwald described the ego as experiencing three biases or qualities so as to maintain its positive self-regard; can you identify them and provide examples of each?

4. <u>Feedback and the Feedback Loop:</u> Norbert Weiner, the founder of cybernetics, identified negative feedback loops as a central part of the self-control of systems. Can you identify the parts of a feedback loop? How can feedback loops be applied to self-control in personality?

5. <u>The Search for—and Effect of—Feedback:</u> Do people actually seek feedback? There is a psychological dimension called "self-monitoring." People high in self-monitoring do seem more prone to seeking feedback. Can self-monitoring be induced? If so, how?

6. <u>Self-Control as a Hierarchy of Feedback Loops:</u> How did Powers apply feedback loops to personality? What would be an example of a feedback loop at the motor level, the mid-level of personality, and at the highest levels of plans and goals?

7. <u>Levels of Action and Behavioral Identification:</u> Wegner and Vallacher examined how people conceive of their own acts. Sometimes they view them as relatively basic, and at other times as involving higher levels of planning. What difference, if any, does this make?

8. <u>Bottom-Up Control:</u> Freud suggested that lower levels of control are in charge, and higher levels often follow along. What part of personality was most in control, according to Freud? Does this make sense to you?

9. <u>Kelly's Circumspection-Preemption-Control Cycle:</u> In Kelly's CPC cycle, people begin looking at a decision by circumspecting—that is, by connecting their own characteristics, values, and goals to the various possible alternatives. At some point they narrow down alternatives and exert control to make a decision. How do people get stuck in the CPC cycle—and what happens if they exit it too quickly?

Questions About "Is Self-Control Always Conscious?"

10. <u>Automatic Self-Control and Dissociation:</u> Consciousness is limited, and for that reason, much control must be unconscious. What is dissociation?

11. <u>Dissociation and the Unconscious:</u> Janet suggested that, in dissociation, people dis-associate ideas from their consciousness. Then, those ideas might take on a life of their own. How did Hilgard apply his revised theory of dissociation (neo-dissociation theory) to pain control?

12. <u>Divided Consciousness and Hypnosis:</u> People dissociate in everyday life, and some people seem very responsive to suggestions. Can you give some examples of each?

13. <u>The Characteristics of the Hypnotic State:</u> Hilgard enumerated several characteristics of people in hypnotic states, these ranged from the suppression of planning to enhanced role-taking. What were some of the other characteristics?

14. <u>Individual Differences in Dissociation:</u> Some people dissociate rather frequently, and are higher in hypnotic suggestibility. According to studies by Jean Hilgard, these individuals found "paths" into hypnosis at an early age. Can you identify some of the paths?

15. <u>Positive Affirmations:</u> Positive affirmations involve repeating general, simple, positive things about oneself over and over. Why are the affirmations repeated, and why have some argued that it is best for them to be simple and general? Are there any research findings that show such affirmations work?

Questions About "How Do We Deal With the Pain of Falling Short?"

16. <u>Suppression:</u> One way people have of maintaining their positive self-regard is to avoid thinking of negative events or problems. What sorts of suppression do people use when experiencing a bad mood? What happens when people do successfully suppress material? (hint: Do the suppressed thoughts come back?)

17. <u>Repression:</u> Repression involves the forgetting of unsetting material. How is the same and how is it different from suppression? What research evidence exists that repression takes place? For example, how do studies of listening to threatening comments and the noise that masks them provide evidence for the concept?

18. <u>Specific Defenses:</u> Specific defenses are sometimes said to form a rough developmental hierarchy from most primitive to most advanced. Can you state the most primitive of the specific defenses? If children employ that defense, does that mean they are having psychological problems? What is some of the evidence for and against projection? Can you name the remaining specific defenses covered here and say something about them?

Questions About "How Is Self-Control (or Its Absence) Expressed?"

19. <u>Control versus Impulsiveness:</u> Research often looks at those who can exert conscious self-control versus those who seem overcome by impulsiveness. A classic study was conducted on children's ability to delay gratification. Who conducted the study and what strategies did the children use to get a valued treat?

20. <u>Learning Conscious Self-Control:</u> The study of children's delay of gratification found that when they distracted themselves they were able to delay their gratification best. Is that always the case? For example, when adults think of food, does that increase their eating? What sorts of strategies are useful in pain relief?

Chapter 10 Glossary

Terms in Order of Appearance:

Conscious Self, Conscious Executive, or Ego: The conscious, aware part of the self. *Note:* The "ego" was also used by Sigmund Freud as part of the id/ego/superego division of the mind. Freud's ego was defined differently than it is here.

Totalitarian Ego: Anthony Greenwald's characterization of the ego as an entity that carefully controls information so as to promote its own positive image.

Egocentric: The quality of constructing mental models with one's own interests and perspective at their center.

Beneffectance: In Greenwald's theory of the totalitarian ego, taking credit for causing good outcomes to happen while avoiding accepting blame for bad outcomes.

Confirmation Bias: The tendency of people to search for information that supports their point of view in preference to challenging information.

Feedback: Information about how close an agent (a person or machine) is to reaching a desired outcome. In personality psychology: information about how close a person is to attaining his goal.

Feedback Loop: A mechanism for controlling the action of a system that involves feedback as to whether or not it is meeting its goals.

Cybernetics: A field of study that focuses on communication and control in systems, particularly in relation to the system's self-governance.

Negative Feedback Loop: A mechanism for controlling the action of a system in which the discrepancy between a goal and its attainment is reduced (negated) through feedback.

Comparator: A portion of a feedback loop that judges the difference between the current state of affairs and the desired goal.

Circumspection-Preemption-Control (C-P-C) cycle: A mental process described by the social-cognitive psychologist George Kelly, in which a person thinks about a problem (circumspects), decides enough time has been spent on it (preemption), and makes a decision about how to act (control).

Self-Monitoring: A state within a person, or a long-term trait, that describes a condition in which the individual closely observes his or her own mental processes or behaviors.

Defensive Pessimism: An adaptive type of pessimism in which a person imagines bad outcomes so as to motivate her- or himself toward higher achievement.

Personal Control: High-level control exerted by the personality system in general, some of which involve conscious self-control, and other portions of which involve unconscious mechanisms.

Dissociated: A state in which concepts that are naturally associated in memory are divided off from one another, in a process called dissociation, and the ideas then operate independently of the ideas to which they had been related previously.

Neo-Dissociationism: A theory proposed by Ernest Hilgard in the 1970s to re-explain earlier ideas of dissociation and automatism—which dated from the 1890s—in more contemporary psychological language.

Absorption: A personality trait reflecting the tendency or capacity to become so focused on an idea, action, or other stimulus as to lose track of what is going on around oneself; the trait is related to both hypnotic susceptibility and to flow.

Classic Suggestion Effect: An introspective feeling that one has involuntarily responded to a direction, such as hearing the direction to move one's head, and then having it move without willing it to do so.

Hypnotic Virtuoso: A hypnotic participant who is especially able to enter into the trance state and is especially talented at carrying out mental tasks under hypnosis.

Defense Mechanisms: Mental processes that are in place to protect the conscious self (ego) from psychic pain.

Suppression: A defense mechanism that involves the conscious blocking out or expelling thoughts that one wishes to avoid thinking about.

Micro-Expressions: Full facial expressions of basic emotions that occur in roughly a quarter of a second or less and then disappear.

Repression: The unconscious forgetting or blocking out of unpleasant or threatening ideas that one wishes to avoid thinking about.

Denial: A defense mechanism in which the individual maintains a claim in the face of obvious information to the contrary.

Projection: A defense mechanism in which the individual sees his or her own unpleasant attributes in another person while being unable to see them in him- or herself.

False Consensus Effect: A research finding that people often believe more others agree with them than is actually the case.

Rationalization: A defense mechanism in which a person employs a plausible but false reason for explaining her or his behavior, which covers up a real but more unpleasant or threatening reason.

Reaction Formation: A defense mechanism in which someone acts in ways opposite to their real inclinations in order to hide them, e.g., is intentionally generous in order to mask feelings of stinginess.

Sublimation: A defense mechanism in which a person directs a potentially socially-undesirable need into a productive social behavior.

PERSONALITY PSYCHOLOGY: PART 4

PART 4: PERSONALITY DEVELOPMENT continues and concludes the exploration of the personality system. How stable is personality over the life span: Is it relatively unchanging, or does it proceed through stages? What parts of personality are with us at birth? What parts develop later as a consequence of family and other influences? Personality Development examines the challenges of personality in childhood, such as gender development and identity development. The section continues with an examination of adult development including issues of personality and both love and work. The section concludes with an examination of the optimal development of personality later in life.

Chapter 11: Personality Development in Childhood and Adolescence

How does personality begin? Do infants possess a sense of self? Personality development concerns the changes that personality undergoes over time. Infants vary from one another in their reactions, behaviors, and attachments to others. Family influences such as parenting style and family size may all have impact on the growing child. The child must also navigate the social world: forming friendships and developing a sense of what he or she can do. By adolescence, the young person is often attempting to establish an identity: a sense of who he or she is. These changes in personality from infancy forward are the departure point for the study of personality development.

Previewing the Chapter's Central Questions

- **What Is Personality Development?** Personality development concerns the growth and change of personality over the life span. Research in personality development has its own special methods of cross-sectional and longitudinal designs. Personality can be viewed as developing according to stages or as developing more or less continuously.

- **Do Infants Have a Personality?** What kind of personality might an infant have? What are its limits? The section on infancy examines such issues as an infant's underlying physiological responsiveness (called temperament) and attachment to others.

- **How Does the Young Child's Personality Develop?** Early childhood is shaped in part by genetics, and by environmental influences such as the child's parents and their style of parenting, and the individual's birth order, gender, and family size.

- **What Are the Challenges of Middle Childhood?** Personality in middle childhood is also influenced by— and influences—friends and peers.

- **What Are Adolescents Doing?** The final section of this chapter focuses on adolescent development. It examines the psychological aspects of puberty, and looks at the formation of identity and its influence on personality.

What Is Personality Development?

Questions of Personality Development

Each individual's development is the result of a wide range of unique influences—genes, parental practices, the social environment, and the individual's own reactions to these. Each individual's life is an "experiment of one" in the sense that influences are applied to a person's life in a way that can never be duplicated for anyone else. Most children are reared in a good environment, but some children face more challenges than others.

In her memoir, the writer Joelle Fraser describes her early upbringing in the counterculture of the 1960s. Her memoir is a carefully researched document based on her mother's diaries, her interviews with friends and relatives, and her own recollections. She took turns living with her mother's family on the Oregon coast, with her mother in the San Francisco Bay area, and with her father in Hawaii. Her father and mother had separated during her first year.

As an infant, Joelle lived in a commune-like environment, sometimes in disheveled apartments, sometimes in houseboats so rickety that their floors would become covered with water at high tide. She experienced the 1960s drug culture as a toddler, taking hits of joints along with her parents' friends, and drinking beer from a straw and wine from a plastic cup. Thereafter, her father's drinking intensified and she was surrounded by her mother's boyfriends and husbands. She writes: "Any man, every man, could be my father…I was loved. I had no bedtime. I fell asleep on laps and couches and on piles of coats, and sometimes a dog or another kid slept beside me. I was never alone." (Fraser, 2002, p. 20)

As she grew, her mother took various partners and husbands and she, in turn, experienced a series of fathers:

> My fathers, in chronological order: Ken, Michael, Mac, Tom, Brad, and Steve. That's how I keep track—I put them in order… Some fathers let me jump on the bed; others watched to make sure I made it properly. The older I got, the smarter I felt. I believed I was superior to the new man, that I knew something he didn't. I placed bets…on how long the guy would stick around. (Fraser, 2002, pp. 96-97)

She also developed an ability to withstand and thrive despite the fairly unique challenges she faced. She describes her capacity to cope in these words: "…by sixteen I'd become very good at taking reality and turning it just slightly so that it was seen at another, more pleasant angle—like a kaleidoscope. I could do this as long as I had to…" (Fraser, 2002, p. 89). Describing a particularly difficult visit with her first (biological) father, who had just taken a lover not much older than herself, she noted, "That is how I got through those few days, by shifting the truth in my mind, by seeing what I wanted to see" (Fraser, 2002, p. 89). Fraser's father died of liver failure, and she reread his one novel, trying to understand him better. She grew up to become reconciled with her now more stable mother. She became acclaimed as a memoirist and successful essayist.

People who are able to withstand difficult upbringings possess a characteristic that psychologists call **resilience**. Resilience is the capacity to survive and thrive in response to tough circumstances (Rutter, 2000; Werner & Smith, 2002). Yet, like many of us, Frasier wonders about the effects of her early upbringing on who she is today. For example, she wonders if she keeps a greater distance from others because of it: "It became natural by the fourth or fifth father to withdraw a bit, keep my distance. This was wise because of the new rules and habits to adapt to" (Fraser, 2002, p. 89). Resilience appears to be more common than was once believed (Bonanno, Papa, & O'Neill, 2001).

Because each of us is a "case of one," understanding causes and effects in individual growth patterns is challenging and cannot necessarily be answered in a given instance. By examining and tracking the regularities in personality development across many people, however, consistent patterns can be identified and understood with greater certainty. Understanding these regularities in growth and development is what the science of personality development is about.

More formally, **personality development** refers to how the parts of personality and their organization grow and change throughout the life span. The study of personality development, like personality psychology more generally, emphasizes personality's major parts and their configurations. The developmental perspective focuses on how those major parts and their organization develop and change over time. For example, psychologists who study personality development examine broad trends in motivational and emotional responsiveness, called personality **temperament**, which many believe to be the building blocks of traits. For example, Joelle Fraser described her child-self as quiet and self-controlled (Fraser, 2002, p. 5). Such characteristics may be important in a person's ultimate capacity to thrive.

Another way that developmental psychologists have examined personality growth is by dividing people into different groups based on their **personality types** or **forms** (Mayer, 1999). Throughout this book, we have examined dozens of parts and dynamics of personality. To observe the development of each of these different parts and dynamics individually would require an entire second book at least. To simplify the research process, experts in personality development (as well as those in personality psychology more generally) have attempted instead to group people according to their different types of personalities (Caspi & Roberts, 1999). As we proceed in this chapter, some of those groupings will be examined.

To understand personality development, psychologists must take into account numerous influences on the system. They may study biological influences such as temperament, social setting concerns such as birth order and family size, social interactions such as friendship, and larger groups such as parents and peer groups. For example, in Fraser's case, she was influenced by the unique time period and culture in which she grew up—the 1960s counterculture of hippies, as well as by a special family configuration of one mother but many fathers in succession, as well as by her unique constellation of friends and siblings. Figure 11-1 diagrams some of those influences in the by-now familiar systems framework structural model (e.g., Chapters 1, 2, and 8).

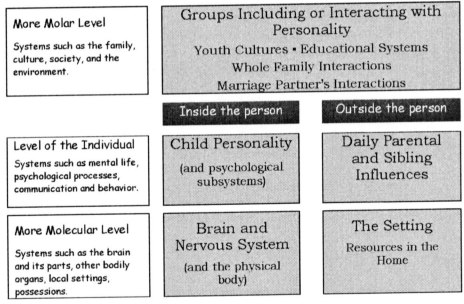

Figure 11-1 *Personality Arranged Among its Developmental Influences* (after Mayer, 1998 & Peterson & Rollins, 1987, Figure 3, p. 497)

Dividing the Life Span

Another central point about personality development concerns the specific research approaches that are employed in the field. The single most distinguishing feature of research in personality development is that time is central to the research question. Time is reflected in such studies by intervals between testing, or by examining people at different ages, or in different grade-levels in school, or during different historical periods. Whatever the way that time is involved, its importance distinguishes developmental research from other personality research in which measures are taken closely together in time of people who are roughly the same age.

Table 11-1: Erikson's Stages of Development from Infancy to Adolescence

The Stage	Description
I. Trust vs. Mistrust (Infancy)	As the infant explores the world for the first time, parents provide a secure environment that promotes the infant's sense of confidence and security. If parents fail to support the exploring infant, the infant may feel insecure and distrustful of the environment.
II. Autonomy vs. Shame (Toddler-hood—early childhood)	The young child takes on responsibility for the first time. She learns she can successfully control bodily functions (e.g., learning to use the toilet) and social conduct. Alternatively, she develops an uncomfortable sense of being watched and judged negatively; at times she wishes to disappear.
III. Initiative vs. Guilt (Early childhood)	The young child develops goals and plans in the family (e.g., to entertain others, or diminish a sibling's influence). The child succeeds with some plans while being mindful of social responsibilities, or, preoccupied with his shortcomings, he fails to live up to social rules.
IV. Industry vs. Inferiority (Middle/Late childhood)	The child learns and develops skills for acting in the world including a sense of industry and accomplishment—of competing successfully in the world beyond the family. Problems arise if the child compares herself to others and develops a sense of inferiority—an inability to carry out the tasks and jobs that are required by society.
V. Identity vs. Role Diffusion (Adolescence / Youth)	With rapid sexual and physical maturation, the adolescent now looks much different, both to him- or herself and to others. The adolescent explores new identities, often trying out social, occupational, political, and ethnic groups. Other youths are unable to develop an identity and feel confused as to who they are.
VI. Intimacy vs. Isolation (Young adulthood)	The young adult seeks intimacy and love with a partner. Members of the relationship couple are able to discuss their roles and plans with each other as well as their relationship, and to balance their needs against the pressures of society. Alternatively, individuals avoid contact and exist alone and in isolation from potential partners, even if in a partnership. Sometimes the individual partners, but lives in isolation from the partner.
VII. Generativity vs. Stagnation (Middle adulthood)	The healthy adult works to create a new, hopefully better future for the world. The adult forms a new family and/or adds to society through labor, research, teaching, arts, and commerce. But some individuals are stagnant, repeating their existence on a day-by-day basis with little giving, struggling in an ordeal to get by.
VIII. Ego Integrity vs. Despair (Maturity)	The individual develops a love of the world that transcends her individual ego and extends to others in history, the present time, and future generations; she recognizes her life as joining biography with history. Alternatively, the individual fears death, realizes the impossibility of starting over, and rejects her life.

Developmental psychologists often divide the life span into time periods and discuss each time period in turn. Sometimes such psychologists will speak of **developmental stages**—relatively fixed phases or units of development into which a person's growth can be divided. For example, Erik Erikson famously divided the human life span into eight "ages" or stages. There is probably no single best way of dividing personality development into stages. Moreover, some people might pass through a set of stages in a different order than others. That said, however, Erikson's outline provides a useful first overview of personality development.

Erikson's first five stages track the individual from infancy to adolescence. During each developmental period, a child's personality develops in ways that create a foundation for the future. In stage I, *trust versus mistrust*, most infants learn to trust their parents, other significant people, and their surroundings. In stage II, *autonomy versus shame*, toddlers develop a sense of independence—of being able to carry out activities on their own. In stage III, *initiative versus guilt*, young children begin to carry out their own plans and goals as they take on family and social responsibilities. By stage IV, *industry versus inferiority*, the now middle-school students receive feedback as to their abilities at school and possess a growing sense of their ability to accomplish things well. In the transitional stage to adulthood (V), young people enter adolescence and establish a sense of identity: of who they are and how they relate to the world. This chapter will study personality from infancy to adolescence—a growth period that corresponds to these five stages. A synopsis of all of Erikson's eight stages of personality is shown in Table 11-1. Chapter 12, on adult development, will cover the portion of the life span relevant to Erikson's last three stages: the search for intimacy, for generativity, and for integrity.

Research Designs in Developmental Studies

Psychologists study people's development across time using one of two basic approaches. **Cross-sectional research designs** are those in which children (or adults) of two or more different ages are examined at a single point in time so as to compare and contrast their personality characteristics. For example, preschoolers and 5th graders might be compared according to their understanding of friendship. Such a design tells us about relative differences in development at different ages. By contrast, **longitudinal research designs** follow the same people across a period of time—sometimes over a few years or even decades—examining the growth and maturation of the individuals within the group. Both methods are of substantial importance and value. Generally speaking, however, the longitudinal design is considered the gold standard in developmental research because it provides a researcher both with a view of differences across age groups, and also with an understanding of how individuals within the longitudinal sample develop over time (Block & Block, 1980). Needless to say, longitudinal research is challenging, difficult, and requires great patience. Nonetheless, a great deal of it has been carried out, and this and Chapter 12 on adult personality development are the richer for it. We can begin our studies of personality development with the infant personality.

Do Infants Have a Personality?

The Infant's Challenge

"Babies are such a nice way to start people." – Don Herald (1889-1966)

Does a newborn possess a personality? At the outset of this book, personality was described as the developing organization of the important parts of a person's psychology. But does the infant's mind possess enough organization—or even parts—to constitute a personality? William James, the founder of American psychology, described the infant's new world as "…one great blooming buzzing confusion" (James, 1890/1950, p. 488). If James was correct and the infant's mind were literally all confusion, the infant could legitimately be said to have no personality. Rather, the infant might be in a state of preparation for personality, or, perhaps, pre-personality.

Since James wrote that, however, we have learned that the newborn brain and mind already possess substantial organization. At a minimum, that mind is prepared for social contact. For example, newborn infants studied in the laboratory presented with sets of faces and abstract patterns will gaze nearly twice as long at the face-like image than at similar non-face images (Umilta, Simion, & Valenza, 1996). Infants also prefer to look at objects that are about 8-12 inches away—the approximate distance of the nursing infant's eyes to its mother's eyes (Maurer & Maurer, 1988).

Between six and ten weeks, the infant reliably produces a broad grin called the **social smile**, accompanied by cooing, both of which encourage parental care in return (Sroufe & Waters, 1976). Brief facial expressions of anger arise during the first two months and can be elicited toward the end of the first year in response to frustrations, such as removing a sucking object from an infant's mouth; these brief angry responses increase in consistency in response to frustration over the first two years of life (Stenberg & Campos, 1990). By about eight months, the now crawling infant develops stranger anxiety. When the infant sees an unfamiliar face, he or she becomes distressed and seeks a familiar adult (Kagan, 1984). To be sure, much of what the infant does involves eating and sleeping. Yet, personality—in the form of preparedness for social interaction—is developing right from the beginning. Increasingly through this developmental time, the infant interacts with others, explores, and learns.

There is little evidence of much sense of self during the first year. Put a six-month-old in front of a mirror, for example, and the infant will reach and touch the image in the mirror as if it belonged to another child. Once the child has reached between 15 and 18 months, however, the image in the mirror is recognized. How do researchers know? When researchers covertly put rouge on the nose of the six-month-old, it goes unnoticed in the mirror. The 15- to 18-month-old, however, will reach toward his or her own nose: There is both something expected about his own face by that age, and recognition of it in the mirror (Buttersworth, 1992; Gallup & Suarez, 1986). Such self-recognition requires considerable cognitive capacity. Across species, chimpanzees and orangutans are the only other animals that can do this. Reflecting the cognitive demands involved even for humans, infants who suffer from Down Syndrome and its accompanying mental retardation are able to accomplish the same task, but take until they are 3 or 4 years of age to do so (Mans, Cicchetti, & Sroufe, 1978).

To be sure, the two-year-old, toddler-eyed view of the world is a limited view in many respects. For months, the infant may not recognize that parts of its body are its own. More generally, when the infant loses sight of an object, it may believe that object has ceased to exist and stop looking for it. Is it also confused, then, about the continued disappearance and reappearance of its mother? The psychoanalyst Melanie Klein (1935/1975) suggested that the infant may imagine multiple mothers, some good, some bad, and some in between. Some have suggested that these multiple images of the mother may provide a developmental basis for the adult phenomenon of splitting, in which a person alternately idealizes and devalues a loved partner. In some forms of psychopathology this split image can become so extreme that it's as if the person is interacting with multiple partners (e.g., Siegel & Spellman, 2002). What keeps severe splitting out of most relationships, it is said, is that most healthy children later develop an integrated picture of the multiple images of the mother. It seems equally reasonable to suppose, however, that the infant simply accepts appearances and disappearances of the mother as normal without specially inquiring into their meaning beyond the temporary loss of security.

The infant must operate within a context in which there are frustrations, fears, failures to meet its needs, and, hopefully, lots of hugs, smiles, and kisses, to smooth the way toward a promising future. The early psychoanalyst Erik Erikson believed that if the parents understood the infant, could meet its needs well enough, and kindly encouraged the infant to explore, then the infant would most likely end up with a sense of security. If, on the other hand, the parents neglected the infant and his or her emotional needs, then the infant would end up insecure in its environment.

Whereas secure infants will learn about the world around them and begin to form connections to the parents and others, the insecure infant will be more bound to the parent and less able to explore. Emerging parts of the personality will determine the nature of those interactions, explorations, and learning.

Infant Temperament

Temperament refers to the basic motivational and emotional building blocks that make up personality traits (as described earlier in this chapter). Temperament is often described according to a range of customary responses emitted by the developing infant. It may involve a child's activity level, physiological responsiveness, tempo, and emotional reactivity. There is a belief that the basic temperamental styles exhibited by the newborn will gradually differentiate into recognizable adult personality traits (Finch & Graziano, 2001). For example, the infant who responds to a toy with agitated motor movements and begins to cry may be less happy and more shy growing up than an infant who exhibits a different pattern (Kagan, 2003). Temperament researchers attend to a variety of cues as to an infant's growing personality (Mebert, 1991).

Three examples of temperament research can help illustrate some of the questions addressed in this area. The first instance involves the work of the physicians Thomas, Chess, and Birch (1970), who were interested in the challenges that parents faced with their children. Thomas and his colleagues suggested that infants varied along nine behavioral dimensions, including activity level, rhythmicity, distractibility, and adaptability. The nine characteristics shown in Table 11-2 formed the core of their measurement approach. This research has often been said to have begun modern temperament research.

Table 11-2: Three Temperament Styles*

Temperament	The Child's Characteristics
The Easy Child	This kind of child is somewhat moderately high in activity, very regular in eating and sleeping, and approachable. The child is mild or moderate in her reactions, and typically positive in mood. This kind of child is relatively easy to parent, and when mistakes are made, the child can adjust readily.
The Slow to Warm Up Child	This kind of child is typically low to moderate in activity, and varies in rhythmicity of his eating and sleeping cycles. The child is mildly reactive, and slightly negative in mood. The child is somewhat easy to handle, but somewhat lacking in warmth in relationships.
The Difficult Child	This child is variable in activity, very irregular in eating and sleeping cycles, and tends to withdraw. The child is intensely emotionally reactive, and negative in mood. He or she presents many issues for her parents and requires skillful handling and patience from the start.

*Summarized from Thomas & Chess (1970).

After examining such behavioral dimensions the researchers created a classification of children into "easy," "slow to warm up," and "difficult." Table 11-2 also shows those three designations. For example, the easy children are very regular in their rhythms, very adaptable, and mildly reactive and positive in their moods. The difficult children are described as irregular in their rhythms, slowly adaptable, and intensely reactive and negative in their moods.

Thomas et al. (1970) took ratings of 141 children, drawn from 85 upper middle-class families of businesspeople and professionals, and followed those children from birth, for over a decade. About 65% of the children could be classified into these three groups of easy, slow to warm up, and difficult. The remainder could not be reliably classified in that way. The researchers found considerable consistency as temperament gave way to personality traits—particularly when the temperament was extreme. For example, the case of

Donald provides a possible example of a difficult child, due to his "extremely high activity level" from birth onward:

> At three months, his parents reported, he wriggled and moved about a great deal while asleep in his crib. At six months he "swam like a fish" while being bathed. At 12 months he still squirmed constantly while he was being dressed or washed. At 15 months he was "very fast and busy"; his parents found themselves "always chasing after him." At two years he was "constantly in motion, jumping and climbing." At three he would "climb like a monkey and run like an unleashed puppy." In kindergarten his teacher reported humorously that he would "hang from the walls and climb on the ceiling." By the time he was seven Donald was encountering difficulty in school because he was unable to sit still long enough to learn anything and disturbed the other children by moving rapidly about the classroom. (Thomas, Chess, & Birch, 1970, p. 104)

Such observations were important because they marked a first modern recognition of the importance of infant differences in responsiveness. These infants will be revisited later in this chapter.

A second example of temperament research reveals the rewards of an in-depth examination of infant responsiveness in temperament. Jerome Kagan, Nancy Snidman, and their colleagues (e.g., Kagan & Snidman, 1991) studied a number of children from infancy to middle childhood, taking dozens of physical, psychophysical, and behavioral measures potentially related to a dimension of shyness to uninhibitedness.

In one series of studies, four-month-old infants were put through a series of tasks, such as having the mother look at the child in a soothing way but not speak, looking at novel toy objects that were sometimes fun, but at other times mildly menacing (e.g., a robot face), or listening to nonsense syllables spoken at different volumes. The infants showed reliable individual differences in response to such situations. Some showed increased sucking or kicking in response to threat, and readiness to cry in response to threatening stimuli, whereas others were relatively unresponsive. Coders watched videos of the infants and rated their motoric restlessness and how often they cried. The overall fearfulness (e.g., high fretting and crying) at four months predicted the average number of fear responses at both 9 and 14 months, as they begin to differentiate into shy, average, and uninhibited groups (Kagan & Snidman, 1991). Among Caucasian infants (with whom most of their research was conducted) about 25% fell into the uninhibited, sociable group, about 10% of the group were inhibited, shy, and cautious, and the remainder fell in between. This research is important because it provides experimental observations and measures of infant temperament. Kagan and Snidman's groups of children and their development across time also will be examined later in this chapter.

A third example of temperament research is important because it allows for a connection between temperament measures and adult personality traits. Rothbart and her colleagues (e.g., Rothbart, 1981; Rothbart, Ahadi, & Evans, 2000; Rothbart & Mauro, 1990) examined three broad dimensions of temperament that they refer to as surgency, negative affect, and affiliation. The first dimension, surgency, describes infants with high activity level, smiling and laughing, high-intensity pleasure, and a willingness to approach others. The second dimension, negative affect, includes distress in response to limits, fearfulness, sadness, and high reactivity to stimuli. The third dimension, affiliation, involves calm orienting (attention) toward others, calmness, soothability, and cuddliness. We also will examine how these dimensions map on the Big Five personality traits later in this chapter. First, however, it is worth examining some other personality characteristics that arise in the infant and toddler.

Attachment Patterns

Infants and young children hold their parents close for comfort; when their parents aren't available, they may seek soft cuddly toys, blankets, and other objects to which they have become attached. There may be a direct bond between the way the infants cuddle with their parent(s) and the way infants comfort themselves with blankets and teddy bears. Soft cuddly toys are particularly important in the West, where babies often sleep in a separate room from their parents at night; such cuddly toys are less common in the East, where infants and their parents often sleep in the same room (Hong & Townes, 1976; Morelli et al., 1992).

This drive for comfort from parents and from other objects of attachment is a fundamental one in human beings and in other primate species. In the 1970s, University of Wisconsin psychologist Harry Harlow had been following the standard practice of separating baby chimps early from their mothers for reasons of experimental control and sanitation. He noticed that these same separated chimps became closely attached to their blankets, perhaps, he reasoned, because they missed their mothers. Other scientists were skeptical. Many behaviorists of the day contended we were attached to our parents primarily because they fed us and cared for us, rather than due to any independent emotional bond.

To test which was the case, Harlow created two surrogate mothers: one made of terrycloth and the other made of wire. The wire mother had a milk bottle inside it, with a feeding tube that extended to the outside. When presented with the choice, infant monkeys clung to the terrycloth mothers, and, when they were hungry, reached their mouths awkwardly over to the bottles in the wire mothers so as to feed. They also returned to those terrycloth mothers when they became anxious. Harlow's work contradicted a common behavioral notion of the time, that the parental bond was a consequence of association between parents and feeding. Other evidence contradicting the behavioral view included that many children become closely attached to their fathers and other close relatives who hadn't regularly fed them.

World War II saw a number of separations between children and their parents. The well being of infants in orphanages also became a matter of concern. Various studies suggested that infants without steady caretakers to whom they could attach were at a developmental disadvantage (e.g., Skodak & Skeels, 1949; Spitz, 1946). Even when children are with their parents, poor attachment bonds can impact their development. Although controversial, some researchers maintain that some instances of "failure to thrive" babies—infants who stop growing during infancy due to a reduced intake of food—are a consequence of poor parent-child attachment, including neglect and abuse (e.g., Ward, Lee, & Lipper, 2000). (A large group these infants, who are diagnosed with "Feeding Disorder in Infancy," have been identified with gastro-intestinal problems.)

John Bowlby (1958; 1988) examined orphans in England during and after World War II. He developed **attachment theory**, a theory about the existence of an **attachment system** in each person that is responsible for modulating the important relationship bonds the individual has with others around them (Bowlby, 1988). Bowlby suggested that the impaired development of children in orphanages, and in similar conditions, was due to the lack of a close emotional bond between the infant and the caretaker.

According to attachment theory, newborns begin developing characteristic relationships with their mothers or other significant caretaker almost immediately. Each infant has an "attachment system" that is programmed by these early relationships and has as its goal the establishment of a secure relationship with a caretaker. In order to become secure, the infant must have interactions with individuals who will care for it sufficiently. These relationships with (relatively) powerful primary caretakers are called **attachment patterns**.

But not everyone develops the same patterns, and Bowlby found that infants in orphanages faced particularly challenging circumstances in which to develop healthy attachments.

Attachment theory might have remained only a theory had it not been for a classic series of studies by Mary Ainsworth and her colleagues (Ainsworth et al., 1978). To identify attachment patterns, Ainsworth and her colleagues took recordings of infant-mother interactions in the home. From those naturalistic observations they then created a small drama called the **strange situation**, which infants could undergo in a laboratory setting. Mother-child behavior at home and in the laboratory were similar (Bretherton & Waters, 1985, p. 15). The patterns of attachment Ainsworth and her colleagues observed in the first year are still largely present at the age of 6, and may be somewhat stable through adulthood (Bretherton & Waters, 1985, p. 19; Hazan & Shaver, 1994). Ainsworth divided those attachments patterns into three types that a person might develop: secure attachment, anxious-avoidant, and anxious-resistant (Bowlby, 1988).

To understand the three patterns, it first helps to consider the strange situation in a bit more detail. Basically, it consists of a standard set of interaction episodes the infant experiences. First, an infant is placed in a playroom with its mother. After some time, a stranger enters the room and the mother leaves. Eventually, the mother returns. During these stages, researchers observe the interaction between mother and child, focusing specifically on how the child responds to the reunion with its mother.

Secure attachment in the infant-mother pair has a distinctive and desirable quality. The mother consistently attends to the infant and responds to its feelings accurately and sympathetically. In addition, the mother attends to the infant's play and encourages it when it has difficulty. In the laboratory, such infants appear to tolerate their mothers' absence better than others do. And, when the mother returns, she and her child greet each another warmly and directly. More generally, secure attachment refers to a relationship pattern in which the individual feels that other people are comforting, important, and dependable.

Anxious-resistant attachment in the infant-mother pairs presents a mixed picture. Although the mothers here sometimes attend to their infants, they do not do so with consistency. Their infants, upon separation, are less able to tolerate being by themselves. They appear unsure about how they will next be treated by their mother. As a result, when the mother returns, the infants are very tentative about approaching her. It is as if they know they may be rejected. The quality of their attachment to their mothers is therefore fundamentally different from that of the more securely attached infants. More generally, anxious-resistant attachment refers to a relationship pattern in which the individual views others as important, but not always comforting, and somewhat unpredictable rather than dependable.

In **anxious-avoidant attachment** in the mother-infant pairs, the mothers seem uninterested in their infants and seem to rebuff them consistently. As a consequence, the infant doesn't seek out the caretaker, but rather seems to expect rejection. More generally, the anxious-avoidant attachment pattern describes an infant or growing person who perceives caretakers to be rejecting and non-nurturing. Anxious-avoidant-attached individuals attempt to deny the importance of others and avoid them; at the same time, the lack of a dependable other may render them anxious about those contacts with others that they do form.

A child's attachment pattern can develop independently of her temperament. In one study, for example, 100 temperamentally difficult infants were randomly assigned to two conditions. In the experimental condition, mothers were taught how to respond to their infants needs in an empathic, responsive fashion. In the control condition, mothers received no such training. By the end of their first year of life, two-thirds of the infants with trained mothers were securely attached; compared to less than one-third of the control group infants; moreover, differences between the groups were still observed at age 3 ½ (Van den Boom, 1995).

How Does the Young Child's Personality Develop?

The Young Child's Self-Concept

Beyond toddlerhood, during the period from roughly 2 ½ to 5 years of age, the young child faces a new set of demands—and her personality and mental capacities will emerge in more powerful forms to address them. Freud characterized the young child as involved in a series of give-and-take interactions with the parent. The most central of these interactions involve issues of parental control versus self-control surrounding toilet training (Freud, 1905, pp. 186-187). Similarly, the psychoanalyst Erik Erikson believed children become more responsible for their actions during this time. Among a child's growing responsibilities are the ability to control his own bodily functions, and also to control his own feelings and actions more generally, so as to develop a sense of autonomy and self-control. For Erikson, the young child develops a sense of autonomy as he becomes able to exert self-control and to exercise restraint independent of parental urgings. When self-control fails, shame may emerge in response to being watched and judged unsuccessfully.

Profound cognitive changes also take place between the ages of 3 and 4 that help to bring about an explicit sense of a continuous self. For one, children are able to develop permanent memories of life events for the first time. Events before about age 3 are part of what Freud called "infantile amnesia." The young child cannot remember what he or she was thinking or doing at an earlier age. For example, preschoolers at a daycare center were quickly ushered from the building after a fire-alarm was sounded in response to a burning popcorn maker. Seven years later, those who had been 4 or 5 years of age could recall the fire alarm and what caused it. Those who were 3 years old at the time, however, could not remember the cause of the alarm and often mistakenly recalled being outside when the alarm rang (Pillemer, Picariello, & Pruett, 1995). Toddler-eyed memories may simply be too different from more mature thinking to understand: An older child who tries to retrieve earlier recollections may become confused as to their meaning. From this perspective, asking a 4-year-old to recall early events is like expecting a new-generation computer to read from an obsolete memory storage system (Loftus & Kaufman, 1992).

With a growing command of language and memory the child is able to describe him- or herself in some considerable detail. One child recounted:

> I'm 3 years old and I live in a big house with my mother and father and my brother, Jason, and my sister, Lisa. I have blue eyes and a kitty that is orange and a television in my own room. I know all of my ABC's, listen: A, B, C, D, E, F, G, H, I, J, K, L, M, N, O, P, Q, R, S, T, U, V, W, X, Y, Z. I can run real fast. I like pizza and I have a nice teacher at preschool. I can count up to 100, want to hear me? I love my dog Skipper. I can climb to the top of the jungle gym, I'm not scared! I'm never scared! I'm always happy. I have brown hair and I go to preschool. I'm really strong. I can lift this chair, watch me!" (Harter, 1999, p. 37)

Self-Control as a Part of Temperament

Recall that some temperament researchers describe infants in terms of their surgency (positive affect), negative affect, and social affiliation (cuddliness). Consistent with the idea that early childhood is a time in which self-control is important, parents now begin to regularly notice and reflect on their children's self-control as a new dimension of temperament (Goldsmith 1996; Rothbart & Putnam, 2002). By early childhood, self-control becomes central to coping with the child—and surpasses even affiliation (cuddliness) in its importance (Rothbart & Putnam, 2002). From the parent's perspective, the young child who is able to be calmed and soothed, and who can respond to parental control by augmenting it with self-control, is an easier child to cope with than a child who is non-responsive to social demands.

Parents and the Family Context

> "Children have never been very good at listening to their elders, but they have never failed to imitate them." – James Baldwin (1924-1987)

The family, and parents in particular, continue to exert their influence on the young child. Their influence is, in part, a function of the family structure in which the child lives. A 2009 United States Census Bureau Survey indicated the wide variety of living arrangements that U.S. children experience. Sixty-nine percent live with both parents, 24% with their mothers only, 4% with their fathers only, and 3% live in some other arrangement including with a grandparent or with no parent (Kreider & Ellis, 2011). A child's living configuration, especially the impact of divorce and other parental loss, can influence a child considerably.

Styles of Parenting

As the infant grows the parent(s)' roles come into play as they set examples and control the child's behavior and environment. But what is it, exactly, that parents do? In a series of pioneering studies, Diana Baumrind (1971; 1973) observed preschool children at home with their parents, at school in interaction with their mothers, and at school on their own. Baumrind distinguished between two fundamental dimensions of parenting: **Nurturance** and **Control**. Nurturance concerned the degree to which the parents supported, cared for, and provided love and caring for the child. Control concerned the degree to which the parents influenced the child, from dictating what the child must do, to allowing the child total freedom. Depending upon whether parents were low on both dimensions, high on them both, or high on one or the other, four parental types can be identified, as shown in Table 11-3 (Maccoby & Martin, 1983).

Table 11-3: Styles of Parenting*

		Level of Nurturance	
		Responsive, Child Centered	**Rejecting, Parent Centered**
Level of Control	**Demanding, High on Control**	Authoritative	Authoritarian
	Undemanding, Low on Control	Permissive	Uninvolved

*Adapted from Maccoby & Martin (1983, Figure 2).

Authoritative parents are both nurturing and controlling. These parents express care for their young children while at the same time guiding their behavior through gentle discipline and rule-setting. As their children grow, they guide through setting examples, reasoning, and continued setting of limits. **Authoritarian parents** are also controlling, but tend to exercise control through setting rules and enforcing them through discipline. These parents employ relatively little explanation or justification of their goals, and are lower in nurturance more generally. **Permissive (or Indulgent) parents** are highly nurturing, caring and loving, but generally fail to set limits or exercise control over their children. Finally, **Uninvolved (or Neglectful) parents** neither express caring for their children nor set limits or exercise discipline.

Parenting styles emerge as an interaction between parents and children, with the parenting influencing the child and vice versa. Certain types of parenting and types of children generally appear to go together. In general terms, authoritarian parents use more aggression and violence for control. In turn, they raise children who themselves are more violent, have poorer peer relations, and who are at risk for being bullied (Pettit et al., 1996). Children of authoritarian parents also suffer from lower self-esteem, less empathy for others, and poorer adjustment to school (e.g., Krevans & Gibbs, 1996). On average, children of permissive parents are similar to those of authoritarian parents in the sense of a relative lack of social responsibility and independence (Baumrind, 1973).

The authoritative parent, by contrast, is more likely to raise children who are relatively friendly with peers and cooperative with adults. Such children tend to be more self-controlled, independent, and more achievement-motivated (Baumrind, 1973). As children of authoritative parents reach adolescence, they exhibit greater academic performance, more pro-social behavior, and less involvement with substance abuse than others (Radziszewska et al., 1996).

Perhaps the most problematic parenting style of all is the uninvolved or neglectful parent (Maccoby & Martin, 1983). These individuals seem uninvolved with their role as parents and emotionally distant from their children. As their children grow, these parents tend to neglect them—having few conversations with their children, ignoring their activities, and knowing little about what is going on in their lives. Their children seem to be at greater risk of lower self-esteem, lower levels of some cognitive capacities, and of higher levels of aggression, maladjustment, and drug abuse (Steinberg et al., 1994; Weiss & Schwartz, 1996).

Parents and the Limits of Their Influence

Parenting research is intriguing and elegant, and no one doubts parents' contributions to their children or that some parents create particularly helpful conditions in which children grow well. At the same time, there often are limits to what parents do to influence their children's personalities.

Harris (1995; 1998) argued that friends, peer groups, and schools are far more important to a child's development than are parental practices. For example, the children of immigrants adopt the language and ways of the dominant culture although the parents may have recreated the language and culture of their country of origin at home. Harris suggests, in fact, that if parents only knew how little influence they had, middle-class parents wouldn't delay having children until they were ready, but would rather hand them over to a nanny, a daycare center, or even a boarding school (Gladwell, 1998).

Evidence backs up the importance of genetics and other biological influences on many different aspects of personality, some of which were described in Chapter 3. One key source of information about the influence of genes comes from the Minnesota Study of Twins Reared Apart (Segal, 1999). Separating twins at birth (or shortly thereafter) strikes most people as unfair and unkind—if not tragic. The twins in the Minnesota studies were mostly separated at birth in the 1950s and 1960s to hide the then-serious stigma of their illegitimate births. Others were separated due to the death or divorce of parents, or because the adoption agency was unable to find suitable parents who could adopt two children at once. A few cases even involved "switching" at birth (Segal, 1999, p. 116).

When the "Jim twins," were separated, Jim Springer's adoptive parents were told by the adoption agency that his twin had died at birth. When he was 39, he contacted the adoption agency to find out more about his background and was surprised to learn that his twin was still alive. He called his twin and they were reunited several weeks later.

When the "Jim twins" were brought to Minnesota for study, their remarkable similarities stretched people's imaginations about what genetics might account for in our personalities. Both Jims had dogs named "Toy" as a child. The twins each married a Linda, divorced them, and then married a Betty. One twin had a son named James Allen; the other had a son named James Alen. Both visited the same three-block stretch of a Florida beach for vacation, each one driving a blue Chevrolet. Both worked part-time as sheriffs, smoked Salems, and enjoyed Miller Lite beer. Both bit their fingernails, suffered from the same type of headache, and spread love-notes to their wives around the house. They did, however, have different hairstyles, and express their thoughts rather differently; one twin had divorced a second time (Segal, 1999, p. 118). The late John Stroud, a British social service official, developed a unique specialty of reuniting twins, and reunited the famous "Giggle Twins," Barbara Herbert and Daphne Goodship. Each twin sets off prolonged laughter in the other and those outside the pair often cannot understand why (Segal, 1999, pp. 127-128).

Parents and the Transmission of Culture

Whatever parenting style they employ, parents are agents of cultural transmission. They communicate to their children what the culture is, the role of parents within it, and what is expected of the child. In many Western cultures, children are encouraged to be independent and autonomous. In many Eastern cultures, children are more encouraged to be part of the family and larger social groups. Such teachings influence both how children perceive and act in social situations.

Liechtman, Wang, and their colleagues found some important differences between parental speech in Asian collectivist societies such as China and Korea, and more individualistic countries such as the United States (Han, Leichtman, & Wang, 1998; Wang & Leichtman, 2000; Wang, Leichtman, & Davies, 2000).

Chinese mothers, when compared to Americans, made more comments and asked more questions regarding moral standards, social norms, and behavioral expectations (Mom: "Tell Mom, when a Mom takes her child to cross the street, where should they look?" Child: "Look to their left and right. Look at the zebra lines.") American mothers, on the other hand, made more comments about personal needs and preferences, judgments or opinions (Mom: "Is there anything else about camping that you really liked?" Child: "Swimming.")

Mirroring the mothers' talk, Chinese children spoke more about social standards whereas American children spoke more about independence (Wang, Leichtman, & Davies, 2000, p. 170).

The increased connection of the child's self-concept to the community in collectivist cultures is illustrated in the stories 6-year-old children from both cultures told about getting lost in a store. Both stories end with the children reuniting with their parents, but in ways that differ markedly in their sense of interdependence and autonomy. The American girl's story began with her getting lost and playing happily in the toy department of a store. It concludes with her leaving the store:

> And then the little girl, she had a map in her pocket and she took it out and she found her way home. And she walked inside and there was nobody there and she decided to stay anyway. And then her Mommy came home. And then they had dinner and they went to sleep. (Wang & Leichtman, 2000, p. 1340)

The Chinese girl's describes the same moment of discovering she is lost in somewhat different terms, with her crying, and then being discovered:

> …an uncle policeman came and asked, "Little girl, what happened with you?" The little girl said, "My Mom and I got lost from each other." The policeman said, "What's the telephone number of your house?" She said, "Our number is 2929335876." Then the uncle policeman made a call. Five minutes later a taxi came. Mom said, "Where were you just now? Why didn't you follow mom?" The little girl felt very ashamed, said,

"Sorry, Mom, I'll follow you next time." They thanked the uncle policeman, and they went home. (Wang & Leichtman, 2000, p. 1340)

Similar research suggests that character formation probably diverges across cultures in substantial ways at a very young age. As cultures themselves change, so do the teachings that are conveyed by parents. For example, mother-child interactions within Native American cultures have changed as Western-style education has been introduced to those cultures, reflecting how cultural influences in regard to schooling in turn affect home life (Chavajay & Rogoff, 2002).

Family Size and Birth Order

Family Size

Another aspect of the family context is the number of siblings a child has, and the birth order of a child. Does family size or birth order influence personality and later attainment? Sociologists have long noted that the larger the number of siblings, the lower the academic attainment of the children in a family, on average. In larger families, each child has available a smaller fraction of the overall family resources. As a consequence, parents may more often be forced into non-optimal parental styles such as taking authoritarian, permissive, or neglectful approaches, because of the greater demands on their time (Steelman et al., 2002). Children in such families perform with a very slightly lower level of cognitive ability. Larger families in which there is greater spacing between siblings show less of the negative impact of family size. When the intervals between children are spaced out, the parents may benefit from taking rests in-between, and the later-born children may benefit from the greater financial resources of the family at that time (Kidwell, 1981; Powell & Steelman, 1995).

Birth Order

Beyond number of siblings, there may be further effects of birth order (and being an only child) on personality. In the 1800s, Sir Francis Galton, an individual-differences researcher with special interests in intelligence, argued for the relative eminence of the first-born. The psychoanalytically oriented Alfred Adler (1931) mused about the first-born's hostility over being "dethroned" by later-borns, and suggested that the middle child was psychologically healthiest. Yet, reliable findings in these areas have been hard to come by, and the matter pretty much rested there until the end of the 20th century (Ersnt & Angst, 1983; Rodgers, 2001).

Then, Frank Sulloway (1996) advanced a sophisticated new theory that appeared to explain at least some psychological data. In Sulloway's view, siblings compete among one another for limited resources in the family. To do so, each individual must find a niche for him- or herself. In this struggle, first-borns are at an advantage relative to later-borns as they are already known to their parents, have had access to resources first, and are larger and stronger than their newborn siblings. Sulloway points out that in some animal species, parents and first-borns may team up and punish, or even kill, later-borns as a means of preserving their precious resources (Sulloway, 1996, pp. 60-65).

In human families, first-born children, because they are on the scene earliest, often identify more closely with their parents than with other siblings. As a consequence, such first-borns may be more comfortable with parental power relative to later children. As they grow, this comfort may lead them to become more conservative, to uphold society as it stands, and favor the status quo. Sulloway regards only children as similar to first-borns in this regard. Later-borns, on the other hand, question authority, and are open to alternative ideas and power structures. In Sulloway's terms, such later-borns are "born to rebel."

Sulloway was a historian of psychology who looked to history for evidence of his hypotheses. For example, Sulloway identified scientists who were contemporaries of Charles Darwin and who had responded to Darwin's then-controversial theory of evolution by taking a side for or against it. He then asked professional historians who had studied those scientists, but were blind to Sulloway's hypotheses, to rate the scientists' support of Darwin's theory. Those scientists who argued for the scientific status quo and against Darwin's hypothesis were almost exclusively first-born. Those who rebelled against the scientific status quo and supported Darwin were nearly exclusively later-borns (Sulloway, 1996, p. 31).

In another analysis, Sulloway looked at 83 scientist siblings—brothers, sisters, or brothers and sisters—who were both on record responding to an innovative scientific theory. The first-born members of the pairs supported innovations at a rate of 50%, whereas the later-borns supported innovation at a rate closer to 85% (Sulloway, 1996, p. 51).

Not everyone has found relations between birth order and rebellious social attitudes, suggesting that Sulloway's findings may hold true for a specific historical period (e.g., Freese, Powell, & Steelman, 1999). On the other hand, supportive evidence is found in the personality characteristics of contemporary siblings. Paulhus, Trapnell, & Chen (1999) examined the children in 1,022 families, and compared the first- to later-born children within each family. Note that this research design eliminates differences between families in socio-economic status, ethnicity, and other variables. As Sulloway's theory predicted, first-borns were consistently nominated as more achieving and conscientious than later-borns, whereas later-borns were identified as more rebellious, liberal, and agreeable than first-borns. Another study found that whereas first-borns tend to prefer products that others say are good, later-borns preferred more innovative newer products (Saad, Gill, & Nataraajan, 2005).

The Gendered World

Another influence on development is the child's **sex** and the cultural expectations as to how a person of that sex will behave. A person's sex denotes the genetically designated reproductive role the human being can carry out, and the biological characteristics associated with that role. A **gender role** defines the characteristic behaviors a person is expected to perform in relation to his or her sex. Some aspects of the gender role may be relatively easy for the growing child to fit into, and other aspects of the role may be more difficult depending upon the individual's personality system.

Sexual development diverges for the male and female fetus at about 9 weeks after conception, when the ovaries and testes differentiate (Moore & Persaud, 1993). Upon birth, most infant girls and boys are identifiable as of one or the other sex, although there exist much rarer genetically or chemically caused ambiguous sexes as well (Bender & Berch, 1987; Money & Lehne, 1999). The sexual development of the fetus into an infant girl or boy, or with intersex anatomy, will have continued influence on the individual's personality throughout life. Some of those influences will be due to different levels of sexual hormones and other sex-linked characteristics. Other influences will be due to social understandings of gender.

Children in 30 nations completed a survey about gender roles to study their understanding across cultures. In the survey, children read about various people, and their job was to assign the person a sex. For example, one item read, "One of these people is emotional. They cry when something good happens as well as when everything goes wrong. Which is the emotional person?" The child was then asked to point to a male or female figure to indicate their belief (Williams & Best, 1982, p. 33).

By five years of age, most children show some evidence of knowing the gender roles in their culture (Best et al., 1977; Williams & Best, 1982). By this time, children generally play with toys and choose television programs preferred by members of their same sex (Luecke-Aleksa et al., 1995; Martin, Eisenbud, & Rose, 1995). Moreover, social play is segregated by sex for most children and will stay so through adulthood (Maccoby, 1990).

To jump forward momentarily to middle childhood, by 8 years of age, 50 to 90% of children in most cultures identified gender-based stereotypes reliably. Fifty percent viewed men as less orderly than women and 90% viewed men as stronger and more aggressive. Seventy-five percent or more of 8-year-olds across nations saw women as more affectionate, gentle, emotional, and dependent than men. But children of different nations did vary in how they viewed some attributes. U.S. and Brazilian children viewed men as fairly independent relative to women; German children were less convinced and Japanese children saw women as slightly more independent.

By 8 years of age, on average, boys and girls understand how they are expected to behave according to their sex and are often involved in gender-exclusive friendships. This influence continues until puberty, when sexual maturation introduces new changes in the relation between the sexes.

What Are the Challenges of Middle Childhood?

Middle-Childhood's Challenges and Self-Concept

In middle childhood, the growing person is dealing with the academic environment of school and the surrounding social world, and starting to more seriously think about adult relationships and occupations. Some of the child's tasks involve maintaining social relations and personal industry in school. If social relations fail, the child may become victim of others; if industry fails, the child may begin to develop feelings of inferiority. The self-conception continues to grow in complexity and sophistication. One fourth-grade girl described herself as follows:

> …I'm pretty popular, at least with the girls. That's because I'm nice to people and
> helpful and can keep secrets…I try to control my temper, but when I don't, I'm
> ashamed of myself. I'm usually happy when I'm with my friends, but I get sad if there is
> no one to do things with. At school, I'm feeling pretty smart in certain subjects like
> Language Arts and Social Studies. I got A's in these subjects…But I'm feeling pretty
> dumb in Math and Science…Even though I'm not doing well in those subjects, I still
> like myself as a person, because Math and Science just aren't that important to me…I
> also like myself because I know my parents like me and so do other kids. That helps you
> like yourself." (Harter, 1999, p. 48)

From Temperament to Traits

The Persistence of Temperament

Early temperament continues to exert influence on the child in middle childhood. Recall Chess, Thomas, and their colleagues' first modern study of temperament. They had divided a sample of 141 infants into three groups based on whether they were easy, slow to warm up, or difficult. By the time the children were in middle childhood, 70% of the difficult children had developed behavioral problems that called for psychiatric attention, whereas only 18% of the easy children did so. For easy children nearly any parental style worked well. Greater efforts at parenting, however, had been necessary to cope with the more difficult children. Thomas et al. observed that in the hands of more expert parents, the difficult children had been successfully guided toward psychological health.

A more nuanced understanding of the transition from underlying temperament to visible traits is provided by the research program of Jerome Kagan and his colleagues on shy children. Recall that those researchers had sorted 9- and 14-month-old infants and toddlers into groups of shy, normal, and uninhibited groups. The idea that biology underlies temperament was supported by the finding that, by middle childhood, certain physical differences were associated with the temperamental ones. As one example, in this mostly Caucasian sample, one child in four of the shy (high-reactive) children were small in size and had blue eyes, compared with only one in 20 in the disinhibited group (Kagan, 2003).

In Kagan's research, 11-year-olds who had been classified as high-reactive (shy) or low-reactive (e.g., uninhibited) at 4 months of age were retested at 11 years of age. The high-reactive (shy) infants continued to exhibit higher-than-usual emotional activation in brain responsiveness as measured by greater EEG activation in certain brain locations, and brain stem responsiveness (Fox, 1992; McManis et al., 2002). Although this was the case, a small number of the high-reactive 11-year-olds exhibited no evidence of being shy or subdued. Although these 11-year-olds remained more physiologically reactive, they no longer exhibited the trait of shyness or negative affect (Kagan, 2003, p. 10). Kagan has speculated that parental coaching, coupled with other favorable environmental influences, permitted these children to compensate for their initially higher reactivity so as to become more sociable than they might otherwise have been.

Temperament-Trait Correlations

The multiple features of infant temperament appear gradually to become organized into the growing child's traits. By preschool and middle childhood, children are able to complete personality scales on their own (and observers can also do this). By middle childhood, parents often perceive their children in part in terms of the Big Five personality traits: Neuroticism, Extraversion, Openness, Agreeableness, and Conscientiousness (e.g., Kohnstamm et al., 1988; 1998). Earlier dimensions of temperament such as the threesome of surgency, negative affect, and self-control, studied by Rothbart and her colleagues, can be related to the Big Five (Rothbart, Ahadi, & Evans, 2000).

Temperaments are the building blocks from which from which traits emerge (Caspi, Roberts, & Shiner, 2005). Dimensions of temperament do not always map directly onto the Big Five, but they predispose a person toward certain traits. For example, surgency—a tendency toward energetic and active feeling states—is a building block of Extraversion, correlating significantly with it. Similarly, negative affect—anxiety, depression, and frustration—correlates with Neuroticism. Self-control—which manifests itself as "effortful attention"—relates to Conscientiousness. A fourth temperament dimension, termed "Orienting sensitivity," involves sensitivity to low-level distractions, and daydreaming. That dimension correlates with the Big Five trait of Openness. These relations are fairly substantial, in the range from $r = .40$ to $.60$ (Rothbart, Ahadi, & Evans, 2000).

Overcontrolled, Undercontrolled, and Flexible Children

As researchers study people's lives over time, they may change the measures they use to study personality from one year to the next: that allows them to introduce new tests that are developed or to test new hypotheses. Using different tests across time creates methodological complications for interpreting how the children who are being studied may have changed.

Jack and Jeanne Block developed one good solution to this problem for one 20th-century longitudinal study. The Blocks asked trained psychologists to go through all the data and—after forming as accurate an impression of the child as possible—to evaluate each child on the **California Q-Sort**. The Q-Sort procedure involves sorting 100 statements concerning the child into 11 piles depending upon how well each statement described them. For example, if "Gets along well with others," was highly descriptive of the child, it would be placed in the "most descriptive" pile; if "tends to avoid others" failed to describe the child, it would be placed in a pile for less descriptive statements. The Q-sort provides an integrative language into which trained psychologists can interpret findings from diverse measures.

The Blocks found that, when they applied statistical techniques to the California Q-Sort, their evaluators tended to perceive the children along two dimensions: **ego strength** and **ego control**. Ego strength referred to the relative positivity of an individual's emotion system. Children high in ego strength experienced positive affect and extraversion; children low in ego strength were anxious, depressed and angry, and introverted. Ego control, on the other hand, referred to the strength of control an individual exerted over himself. At the under-controlled end, children and youth are impulsive, substance abusing, sexually promiscuous, and overtly risk-taking. At the over-controlled end, they may become obsessive, rigid, and joyless. In between, a person's self-control is viewed as flexible (Block, 2002, p. 9).

Children tend to fall into three groups defined especially along the ego control dimension. Some children are under-controlled on the ego control dimension. They act out, behaving impulsively and angrily with their peers. Other children are over-controlled. They are shy, and overly cautious to the point of fearfulness. A third "just right" group are characterized by flexible control and more positive affect on the whole (Eisenberg et al., 2000; Caspi, 2000).

For example, Caspi and others (2000) analyzed data from the Dunedin (New Zealand) longitudinal study. The sample consists of 1,037 individuals studied since 1972-1973—91% of all those born in the city over those years. Based on a mathematical analysis, the researchers labeled about 40% of the sample as "well adjusted," because they were emotionally stable in the face of new situations, possessed self-confidence, and were capable of self-control when it was demanded of them. The second, "under-controlled" type, about 10% of the sample, were emotionally reactive, negative, distractible, impulsive, and restless. The third, "inhibited" type, another 10% of the sample, included children who were socially shy and easily upset by strangers. Their study revealed two further groups: A confident, impulsive group that is eager to explore but not negativistic accounted for about 2% of the sample. Finally, a reserved but not cautious or withdrawn group made up 1.5% of the sample (Robins et al., 1998).

Friendship Patterns

By middle childhood, there is a great difference in the sorts of friendships different children maintain. Some children are well accepted, and others are rejected by nearly everyone. For example, in one classroom, a child had written a note that was being passing up and down the school room, and read, "If you hate Graham, sign here." The note had been signed by virtually all the children in the class—and was headed to Graham's desk when the teacher intercepted it! (Asher and Rose, 1997, p. 196).

Differences in social skills—and how they impact friendships—are vividly illustrated by watching a child trying to join others who are already at play. Some children do this very well; others lack the necessary skills. Black and Hazen (1990) asked children in a private setting whom they most and least liked to play with in their preschool-room. On the basis of that interview, children in the classroom were divided into "liked," "disliked," "low-impact" (neither liked nor disliked), and "mixed" (liked by some; disliked by others) groups. The children themselves were then divided into groups of three. Two children of each group were taken to a play area where they started playing, and the third child was introduced 10 minutes later. How would the third child try to enter the dyad of children already playing?

Children who enter the social situation successfully often express their willingness to join those already at play, agreeing to do what they are doing. For example, when one of the two already-playing children told an entry child, "We're being witches here, and I am the mean witch," a child with a good entry strategy replied, "Oh, hello witches, I am a witch, too." A poor entry strategy, on the other hand, would be to make an irrelevant comment such as, "My mom is taking me to get shoes today." Each entry-child's speech behavior was coded on a number of dimensions. Disliked children, relative to liked children, failed to direct their comments clearly to one or another dyad nearly twice as much as did liked children. The disliked children made irrelevant comments nearly three times as often.

Those who foster friendship gain valuable support. Even very young children will express concerns or fears in their play, and may find comfort in the caring of others. For example, in the following passage 4 ½-year-old Naomi, who is playing with a dinosaur, comforts her 3 ½-year-old best friend, Eric, who is playing with a skeleton:

Naomi: I'm your friend the dinosaur.

Eric: Oh, hi dinosaur. You know, no one likes me.

Naomi: But I like you. I'm your friend.

Eric: But none of my other friends like me...They don't like my skeleton suit. It's really just me. They think I'm a dumb-dumb.

Naomi: I know what. He's a good skeleton.

Eric: I am not a dumb-dumb and that's so.

Naomi: I'm not calling you a dumb-dumb. I'm calling you a friendly skeleton. (Asher & Rose, 1997, p. 202)

By middle school, third and fifth graders can speak clearly about friendships, noting the highs, such as, "Me and Lamar makes each other laugh and we play kick soccer," and intimacy, such as, "Yesterday me and Diana talked about how our parents got a divorce and how the world is going to end," and mutual responsibility, as in, "My friend is really nice. Once my nose was bleeding about a gallon every thirty minutes and he helped me" (Parker & Asher, 1993, pp. 270-271).

Both early attachment patterns and current relationships with parents can predict the quality of friendships among those in middle childhood. Ten-year-old children in 49 families and their parents were interviewed as part of the Northern German Longitudinal Study (Grossman et al., 1985). Secure attachment measured during infancy correlated with positive parent-child communication at age 10. Both infant attachment and current parent-child communication predicted the quality of the child's friendships at age 10 (Freitag et al., 1996).

A child's own traits may also promote or impede friendship. Lower use of both verbal and physical aggression is associated both with better adjustment—as assessed by teachers' ratings of their students—and with better friendships. Teachers' ratings of their students' agreeableness also predicted less use of aggression and better friends—but for girls only. Self-rated agreeableness is unrelated to such qualities perhaps because children of that age may be unable to judge their own agreeableness (Jensen-Campbell & Graziano, 2001, p. 343).

Victimization and Friendship

Friendship is crucial to adjustment. An extreme example of how friendship can help a person is in the context of bullying. The type of child most likely to be bullied is characterized by submissive or non-assertive social behavior. This submissive style appears to be a consequence, perhaps, of temperament, maternal over-protectiveness, and general negativity in the home (Olweus, 1993; Schwartz et al., 1993). The second type of child at risk for bullying consists of aggressive victims whose angry responses may tend to provoke abusers. These victims often experience early home environments that include exposure to violence in the forms of spousal abuse, child abuse, or both (Schwartz et al., 1997).

Data analyses were conducted to examine the role of friendship in preventing bullying in two separate longitudinal studies: The Child Development Project, a multi-site study of children's social development and adjustment, and Fast Track, a multi-site study of schools in four geographic regions in the United States. Results from both longitudinal studies indicated that strong friendships reduced or prevented bullying for both at-risk boys and girls, and for both passive and aggressive-type victimized children (Schwartz et al., 2000).

What Are Adolescents Doing?

Puberty and the Changing Self-Concept

Having developed some experience in the world of relationships and skills, the child enters the world of adolescence. (In this chapter, we move along far more quickly than real life!) Adolescence begins as a series of physical changes that occur with **puberty**, a time during which the child undergoes rapid sexual maturation and achieves the capacity to reproduce. These events include a growth spurt in the skeleton, and the maturation of the primary sexual organs. In boys, testes and penis mature, and secondary sex characteristics mature as well: Their facial hair grows, their shoulders broaden, and childhood fat tissue changes to muscle. In girls, the vagina, uterus, and ovaries mature and **menarche**, the first menstrual period, occurs. Girls assume a more rounded appearance, and their breasts mature (Brooks-Gunn & Reiter, 1990).

With rapid sexual and physical maturation, the child now looks much different, and often feels that all eyes are on her or him. The youth now becomes preoccupied with this outward appearance, and how to reconcile it with how he or she feels on the inside. At the same time, a new sense of identity must be worked out. The young person may carry out a series of experiments in identification. These include a search for things and people with which to identify or fall in love. These "fallings in love" may be with peer groups and with broader ideologies ranging from politics, to religion, to ethnic groups. In the social realm, the young person will feel yearnings and love toward other youths. From an adult vantage point, the love has not yet deepened to mature caring, but it seems overwhelmingly strong to the person feeling it (Erikson, 1963).

During this stage, the adolescent will begin to think about his or her fit with the world, and try to experiment with some available social roles. These may start with the various groups to be found in school, but will set the stage for decisions about occupational, familial, political, religious, and ethnic identifications later on. Some psychologists believe that to successfully traverse this stage, the individual must begin to understand the range of possibilities open to him or her in each of these areas (Erikson, 1963; Marcia et al., 1993). Much adolescent exploration is healthy and provides important learning experiences. At other times, however, such explorations can become potentially risky and self-destructive. For example, some personality characteristics put the exploring young person at risk for the abuse of drugs.

Some self-consciousness and self-exploration is illustrated in this self-description by a young woman in middle adolescence (15 years old):

What am I like as a person? I'm complicated! With my really *close* friends, I am very tolerant...but I can get pretty obnoxious and intolerant if I don't like how they're acting…At school, I'm serious, even studious every now and then, but on the other hand, I'm a goof-off too, because if you're *too* studious, you won't be popular…which means I don't do all that well in terms of my grades. But that causes problems at home…my parents…get pretty annoyed with me…I can switch so fast from being cheerful with my friends, then coming home and feeling anxious, and then getting frustrated and sarcastic with my parents. Which one is the *real* me? I have the same question when I'm around boys…I'll be a real extrovert, fun-loving and even flirtatious… Then I get self-conscious and embarrassed and become radically introverted, and I don't know who I really am! So I think a lot about who is the real me… (from Harter, 1999, pp. 67-68)

The next section examines some of the identity issues surrounding sex and gender; then adolescent identity is examined more broadly.

Sexual and Sex-Role Development

With puberty comes a renewed focus on sex and gender in the growing person's self-concept. The sexes diverge dramatically in their desires regarding their sexual activity. Both women and men struggle with thoughts of sex, yet men experience the struggle more intensely. For example, male college students in the Netherlands more strongly agreed with such items as, "My desire for sex disturbs my daily life," "I think about sex more than I would like," and "My sexual behavior sometimes makes me not live up to my responsibilities" relative to women (Vanwesenbeeck, Bekker, & van Lenning, 1998).

Peer groups exert increasing influence over the adolescents' behaviors. Men's peer groups often encourage them to experiment with and try sex. Men have far more positive attitudes toward casual sex, desiring upwards of 18 sexual partners during their lives, compared with an average ideal of four or five sexual partners reported by women (Buss & Schmitt, 1993; Oliver & Hyde, 1993). One survey of college students in California indicated greater extremes: that women ideally wished to have two or three sex partners over a lifetime; whereas men hoped for 64 (Miller & Fishkin, 1997).

At this age, women discuss their sexual behavior with their peers with some regularity. Women's peer groups, however, are different than men's. They are concerned with what their friends think of their sexual activity and try to restrain one another's sexual activity. For example, a group of college women friends may make a pact before going on spring break to refrain from sexual activity—and to help one another do so (Maticka-Tyndale, Herold, & Mewhinney, 1998).

Sex Differences in Traits

There exist specific but important differences between men and women in the motivational, emotional, and cognitive domains. In regard to aggression, men score more highly on aggression, relative to women on various measures including projective tests such as the Thematic Apperception Test (TAT), observer-ratings, and self-judgments (Hyde, 1986). Men are also far more aggressive behaviorally and commit far more violent crime than women; men are responsible for 90% of the homicides worldwide; women, only 10% (Daly & Wilson, 1988). The largest difference on the Big Five inventory for women and men is on the friendliness-unfriendliness dimension (which reflects aggression).

Adult women are more susceptible to depression than men. The two sexes start out with equal rates of depression in childhood. After puberty, however, the rates of depression in women relative to men rise to two or three times as high. These higher rates of depression relative to men occur in many different cultures and nations (Huyenga & Huyenga, 1993).

In regard to motivation more specifically, there is a pronounced difference between men and women on a dimension sometimes referred to as "people versus things." Women (relative to men) far prefer to be involved with other people, and conversely men (relative to women) far prefer to be involved with things. Interest in people manifests itself as interest in social planning, being with others, discussing relationships, and forming intimate connections with others. Interest in things concerns interests in objects such as chemicals, motors, gadgets, and computers, among many others. "Thing interest" includes understanding how things work, how they can be built, how to fix them, and how to use them. The people-versus-thing dimension is important to occupational choice, as many occupations such as management and human services place an emphasis on working with people, whereas other occupations such as engineering and the physical sciences place an emphasis on working with things (Lippa, 1998).

In the 1970s and 1980s, something similar to this people-versus-thing dimension was measured by scales that went under the names of **masculinity** and **femininity**. **Masculinity** referred to a person's correspondence to a uniquely male character. **Femininity** referred to a person's correspondence to a uniquely female character. In those earlier scales, masculinity was largely defined as interest in objects or things, and heightened assertiveness. Femininity was measured as interest in people. **Androgyny** was defined as having a more flexible character and being attracted to both masculine and feminine interests. The idea was that androgyny would be the healthiest style because it was the most flexible (Bem, 1974; Spence, Helmreich, & Stapp, 1974). According to Bem, the most problematic style was the undifferentiated role; these individuals exhibited characteristics of neither type. A schematic of that arrangement is indicated in Figure 11-2.

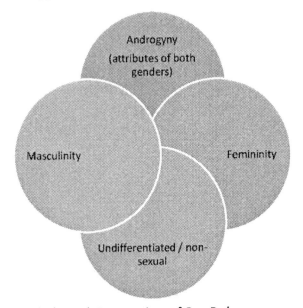

Figure 11-2 *Bem's (1974) Conception of Sex Roles* Sandra Bem suggested that people high in both masculinity and femininity expressed a special sex-role quality called androgyny.

Although Bem's theory remains of interest, the scales she developed to measure sex roles have been criticized for measuring qualities other than sex-roles themselves (for example, an interest in things versus an interest in people). For that reason, other measures have been introduced.

To understand sexual character more closely, Six and Eckes (1991) examined gender stereotypes for men and women. The stereotyped groups they uncovered may more closely approach what we mean by masculinity and femininity than have alternative approaches—but they are stereotypes, reflecting social attitudes that not everyone will be happy with. For men, the groups included: first, men who were soft, quiet, philanthropic or alternative, and gay. Next were "career men," "managers and bureaucrats." The third group was labeled "middle-class egotists." The fourth included "playboys" and "lady-killers," and the fifth and last group were "macho and cool."

The women's first cluster included "confident, intellectual, left-leaning feminists." The second cluster included "conforming, maternal housewives." The third cluster included (what they referred to as) "sexual vamps and tarts." Smaller groups included "nasty pieces of work" and a group that combined "spoiled young girls" and "society ladies."

The sexes don't come off terribly well in this research—few among us would like to be typed in most of those ways—but it may capture real albeit critical perceptions of sex roles around us. Masculinity and femininity remain rich areas for continued study, and the picture of these important dimensions will be clarified (and perhaps defined more positively) in the future.

Establishing Identity in Adolescence

Identity refers to who one is, the groups one belongs to, and the beliefs that guide one's life. The growing person needs to establish an identity so as to help navigate her many life choices. The psychological and physical growth spurts of adolescence directly encourage acute self-observation. Coupled with the looming decisions an adolescent faces concerning her education and occupational futures, the establishment of identity becomes a central task. People who successfully create an identity will be able to proceed forward in their lives guided by a sense of who they are.

Adolescents who are unable to assemble such an identity as suffer from an **identity crisis**. The term originated with Erik H. Erikson, the psychodynamic psychologist whose rich description of this stage emerged in part from his own experiences. Erikson himself had dropped out of school in his adolescence and drifted across the beaches of southern Europe, trying on the identity of a bohemian artist. He reflects that he was in the throes of a serious psychological crisis, occupying the borderland between anxious depression and loss of reality (Erikson, 1975, p. 26). Although in psychic pain, Erikson was involved in a valuable psychological process: **identity exploration**.

Identity exploration involves a young person's conscious self-exploration and self-understanding so as to form an identity. **Identity commitment**, in contrast, involves whether the individual could commit to one of the identities that were explored—to say, "I am this," and not something else. These two dimensions were employed by Marcia (e.g., 1964; 1966), who used them to divide adolescents into one of four possible identity-status categories. An **identity status** refers to the outcome of an identity-seeking process (Marcia, 2002).

At the lowest level was the individual with **identity diffusion status**. This individual has not yet conducted any self-exploration, and has made no commitments to an identity of one sort or another. At as nearly a low level is the individual with **foreclosure status**. This person has appeared to make a commitment but has done so with no self-exploration. Such a foreclosed adolescent often has agreed to carry out plans set for him or her by parents or other authority figures. This commitment is not viewed as mature, however, because it does not factor in any self-understanding achieved apart from the viewpoints of those others. The student whose father wants her to be a doctor and never questions the goal would be said to be in a foreclosed status. Marcia's identity status conception is depicted in Table 11-4.

Table 11-4: Overview of Marcia's Four Types of Identity Status

		Commitment to a Life Plan	
		Uncommitted	**Committed**
Self-Exploration	**High Self-Exploration**	**Moratorium** The person has an unformed identity, but by exploring himself, he may form a clear identity in the future.	**Achievement** The person commits to a given identity following an exploration of many possibilities.
	Low Self-Exploration	**Diffusion** The person neither explores herself nor seems to commit to any personal definition.	**Foreclosure** The person commits strongly to an identity based on others' opinions, without much (or any) self-exploration leading up to it.

Adapted from Marcia (1966).

Marcia discussed a psychotherapy patient named "Linda" who grew up in a rural town in northeastern Canada. Her mother was a homemaker, and her father was an alcoholic railway worker who somehow always provided her with money to buy nice clothes. Her mother wanted her to attend nursing school, and Linda enrolled, but was uninterested and ended up dropping out. She then tried fashion design at two other institutions, but found herself unable to persist in the programs. During this time, Linda could be described as possessing a diffused identity status. A diffused identity status refers to the absence of a coherent sense of whom one is in relation to the worlds of relationships and work. She neither explored identities on her own nor made a commitment to anyone else's vision of her.

Over the next years of her life, though, Linda's willing explorations marked the beginnings of a gradual transition to a higher level of identity status: **moratorium status**. The moratorium status reflects a person who is interested and engaged in self-exploration but is not yet ready to make a commitment. Linda spent the next decade of her life trying different life roles, but not staying with many of them for too long.

In Linda's case, it took many years of further development (she was in her early 40s) before she reached an **achieved identity status**. The achieved identity status reflects the individual who has engaged in self-exploration and does understand what he or she wants to do. At that time she enrolled in college, where she ended up doing quite well, in contrast to her earlier experiences, and was also able to relate in more mature ways in her relationships (Marcia, 1999, pp. 23-24).

In our multicultural society, one aspect of identity formation involves how an individual integrates a sense of ethnic, religious, or racial identity into the broader picture of self-hood. An 18-year-old female student described this recognition of her identity and ethnicity:

> When my family first migrated here, our parents separated us from the majority culture largely because they knew so little about it. Physical appearance for us was always a barrier, too. Our mother strictly forbade us girls ever to date a "European boy," and with us living at home, she was easily able to do this. But last year I left home for university…I was curious to discover what I was doing here, and who I really

was…Questions like, "Where am I going?" and "Who will I become?" are still unanswered…I think feeling comfortable with my ethnic identity is a prerequisite to discovering my personal identity. (Kroger, 2000, p. 126)

Many researchers would agree that coming to terms with one's ethnic identity is a crucial aspect of forming a total personal identity. Growing up as an ethnic minority (as a plurality of people do) complicates identity formation by providing a set of possible identities different from those of the mainstream culture (Phinney, 1989; Phinney & Rosenthal, 1992). Somewhat parallel to Marcia's identity statuses, ethnic minority youth often progress through stages in which they first identify with the majority culture, then discover their own ethnicity, then immerse themselves in that ethnic culture, and finally, internalize or integrate their own sense of ethnic identity with their own broader, personal identity (Cross, 1987). Bicultural identity also has come in for some analysis. Here, key variables include the degree to which the two cultures are perceived as overlapping or not, and the degree to which they are perceived as in harmony or in conflict (Benet-Martinez & Haritatos, 2005).

To classify an individual into one of Marcia's identity statuses, researchers use either clinical interviews or personality scales. Both approaches ask the adolescent about various areas of his or her life. For example, such areas as occupation, religion, politics, dating, sex roles, and recreation may be examined. From such information, an individual is coded according to the degree of identity exploration and identity commitment the individual has expressed (Grotevant & Adams, 1984; Adams, Shea, & Fitch, 1979; Marcia, 1966). From these two dimensions, participants are classified as belonging to one of the four identity statuses. Agreement between the clinical interview and self report tests is moderately good—classifying 50% of the people in the same category—or up to 80% using specially selected and trained raters (Berzonsky & Adams, 1999, p. 566).

Studies of adolescents and young adults in high school and college show that many individuals do follow a progression roughly from diffused identity states, to brief periods of foreclosure and moratorium, to an achieved identity. There are also, however, many who do not change at all, some who follow a different order toward identity achievement, and a substantial minority who appear to regress from moratorium, say, to foreclosure or diffuseness (Bezonsky & Adams, 1999; van Hoof, 1999, pp. 530-531; Waterman, 1999).

Several factors influence the development of identity status. For example, adolescents who exhibit less defensive patterns on the Thematic Apperception Test were better able to advance toward identity achievement relative to more defensive students (Cramer, 1998). College students enrolled in academic departments that emphasize an expanding awareness of social issues such as national and world events may more readily attain a secure identity, compared to students in departments that placed lower emphasis on such expanding awareness (Adams & Fitch, 1983). Students with supportive peers are more likely to question who they are and, in turn, are more likely to achieve a sense of identity (Berzonsky & Adams, 1999, p. 583).

Another series of findings suggest that people who go through identity exploration—that is, who are classified either as in moratorium or identity achievement statuses—have richer and more differentiated self-concepts than those whose identities are foreclosed. Those who have reached identity achievement status appear better able to compare themselves with others in an integrated fashion; those who have not often described themselves along numerous, unintegrated dimensions (e.g., Berzonsky and Neimeyer, 1988). Students asked to create photo essays of themselves create richer, more integrative and individualistic descriptions when they are higher in self-exploration (Dollinger & Dollinger, 1997).

The not unreasonable assumption behind the identity formation research is that self-exploration and the establishment of an achieved identity status will provide a secure foundation for further growth and development. As fascinating as this research line is, it is particularly unfortunate that little is known about the outcome of identity formation later in life. One notable exception to this is a longitudinal study by Josselson (1996), who found that among 30 women, those classified as identity achievers in their senior year of college were able to move ahead with their lives in their 30s and 40s in a more a clear and deliberate fashion than the other groups, and with a sense of meaning concerning what they were doing. Although they encountered obstacles and dead ends in their lives, they were better able to continue in the face of such setbacks.

Concluding Notes

With the establishment of identity in adolescence, we come to a close of our consideration of personality development in childhood and adolescence. The stage has now been set for the growth of the individual's personality, and the development of the individual's life in adulthood. That will be the subject of Chapter 12 on adult development.

Reviewing Chapter 11

The learning goals of this chapter are to help you begin to understand how personality grows to meet the challenges of the individual. The chapter opens with a brief consideration of developmental stages and research approaches. The focus on childhood examined influences of infant temperament on later development, and also the influence of birth order. The chapter concluded with an examination of identity formation in adolescence.

Questions About "What Is Personality Development?"

1. Internal and External Influences on Personality: Each individual is born into a different time and place—an "experiment of one." Infants can develop well—sometimes even under demanding circumstances. What do psychologists call the quality that enables them to do so?

2. Developmental Research Defined: A key element of developmental studies is that they include time as a central feature of their study. In thinking about development over the life span, it is often convenient to divide growth into stages. What are Erikson's stages from birth through adolescence? How is time included in developmental research; what is the difference between longitudinal and cross-sectional research design?

Questions About "Do Infants Have a Personality?"

3. The Infant's Challenge: The newborn infant already has some organized perception of the surrounding environment. Can you distinguish a few examples of what is *not* a "blooming, buzzing, confusion" in the infant's mind?

4. Infant Temperament: Temperamental qualities are described as the building blocks of traits. What were some of the original dimensions of temperament studied by Chess, Thomas, and their colleagues? How were these simplified by later researchers?

5. Infant Attachment: Infants develop models of other people in their lives. The models for intimate relationships are sometimes called attachment patterns. What are the major attachment patterns?

Questions About "How Does the Young Child's Personality Develop?"

6. The Young Child's Self Concept: What are the young child's challenges? Does the young child have a sense of self? How is this different from the infant's sense of self?

7. <u>Self Control as a Part of Temperament:</u> What sorts of activities during young childhood reveal levels of self-control? Why is this important to parents and how is it reflected in temperament?

8. <u>Parents and the Family Context:</u> The growing child is dependent upon and greatly influenced by parents and the family constellation. Two dimensions of parenting are nurturance and control. How do these combine to form parenting styles? Children from larger families often obtain less education; what variable can eliminate that negative effect? Sulloway studied historical acceptance of scientific and political revolutions. What characteristics distinguished first- from later-born children?

9. <u>The Gendered World:</u> Girls and boys learn about their culturally assigned gender roles as they grow. How similar are some of the perceived differences between males and females across cultures? Is there something different about the case of Japan?

Questions About "What Are the Challenges of Middle Childhood?"

10. <u>Middle Childhood's Challenges:</u> What are the tasks faced by the growing person in middle childhood?

11. <u>From Temperament to Traits:</u> Features of temperament are thought to underlie traits. In middle childhood, children can begin to fill out personality questionnaires. How would you characterize the relationship between temperament and traits such as the Big Five?

12. <u>Over-Controlled, Under-Controlled, and Flexible Children:</u> Under-controlled children have difficulties with controlling their impulses; over-controlled children are often shy. Some children change groups over time; why might this be?

13. <u>Friendship Patterns:</u> Children have a very accurate understanding of the importance of friendship to support, intimacy, and having fun. At the same time, not all children benefit from friendship. Who is likely to be bullied in childhood; who is likely to bully? How can the existence of a friend affect bullying?

Questions About "What Are Adolescents Doing?"

14. <u>Puberty and the Changing Self-Concept:</u> Puberty represents the stage in which children mature sexually. During this time, they often feel as if all eyes are on them, and they become particularly self-conscious. What are some of the tasks of adolescence?

15. <u>Sexual and Sex-Role Development:</u> What are some of the differences that arise between girls, boys, and their peer groups at this time?

16. <u>Establishing Identity in Adolescence:</u> Identity is often said to involve the exploration of possible roles for the self, coupled with making a commitment to one particular role. These two dimensions— exploration and commitment—have been said to describe four types of identity status. What is identity status and what are the four statuses that might arise? How does ethnic identity factor in?

Chapter 11 Glossary

Terms in Order of Appearance

Resilience: The capacity of the individual child or adult to grow healthily and thrive in the context of negative social or environmental circumstances.

Personality Development: A sub-field of psychology concerned with how the parts of personality and their organization develop and change over time.

Temperament: Bio-behavioral elements of the individual, such as tempo, activity level, and positive emotions that form building blocks of later traits and behavior.

Personality Types or Forms: A personality type (or form) represents a constellation of mental features such as traits or dynamics that occurs with enough frequency to form a category. Members of the group are different in their mental qualities from members of other groups.

Developmental Stages: Periods of growth, arranged in a sequence, in which each period can be distinguished from the next according to a set of criteria.

Cross-Sectional Research Design: An approach to developmental research in which people of two or more different ages are compared so as to assess the influence of age on mental functioning.

Longitudinal Research Design: An approach to developmental research in which people are followed across time to see how they change or stay the same.

Social Smile: A broad smile produced by 6-month-old infants. Evolutionary psychologists believe the smile evolved to encourage parental attention.

Attachment Theory: A theory proposed by John Bowlby that there exists a special a special mental system in infants responsible for establishing secure relationships with a caretaker, and that continues to exert control over relationships as the individual matures.

Attachment System: The system responsible for establishing an infant's secure relationship with a caretaker, which continues to exert control over relationships as the individual matures.

Attachment Pattern: A distinctive relationship an infant can form with its mother or other primary caretaker.

Strange Situation: An experimental situation in which attachment patterns are measured. A mother sits in a playroom and the infant is evaluated according to how far s/he will separate from her. The mother leaves briefly, a stranger comes in and leaves, and the other returns. All the while, the infant's reactions are monitored.

Secure Attachment: A relationship in which an individual has a reliable bond with another person that allows for safe separation and independence, coupled with comfortable, welcomed returns to the caretaker.

Anxious-Resistant Attachment: A relationship in which an individual has an uncertain or nervous bond with another person that limits independence and is coupled with somewhat fretful, yet welcomed returns to the caretaker.

Anxious-Avoidant Attachment: A relationship in which an individual has an uncertain or nervous bond with another person that limits independence and is coupled with somewhat ambivalent, uncertain return to the caretaker.

Nurturance: One of two dimensions of parenting proposed by Baumrind; Nurturance concerns providing emotional support and caring for children.

Control: One of two dimensions of parenting proposed by Baumrind; Control concerns governing a child's behavior and ensuring that it is personally and socially responsible.

Authoritative Parenting: An approach to raising children in which the caretaker exercises control over the child in a nurturing fashion, for example, by establishing and enforcing rules for the child's benefit while also explaining the purpose of such rules.

Authoritarian Parenting: An approach to raising children in which the caretaker exercises control over the child, but with little explanation for the reasons why control is exerted, and with little concern for the child's needs or feelings.

Permissive (or Indulgent) Parenting: An approach to raising children in which the caretaker treats the child in a nurturing, caring, fashion, but without providing much structure and without enforcing important rules.

Uninvolved (or Neglectful) Parenting: An approach to raising children in which the caretaker is relatively unconcerned with a child, and neither monitors or enforces any rules concerning the child or the child's behavior, and fails to nurture the child.

Sex: The genetically designated reproductive role a person is biologically assigned.

Gender role: The social behaviors and actions a person is expected to carry out in relation to his or her sex.

California Q-Sort: A measurement technique in which a trained psychologist integrates case and/or test material about a person and then arranges 100 descriptions about an individual into 11 piles, according to those that best describe the individual to those that least describe the individual.

Ego Strength: A trait describing the relatively stable, positive qualities of a person's ego-system: his or her thoughts, feelings, and goal-directed behaviors.

Ego Control: A trait describing the relative capacity of an individual to respond flexibly to the environment in a fashion that is neither over-controlled nor under-controlled.

Puberty: A period of sexual maturation during which a child achieves the capacity to reproduce.

Menarche: In girls, the time, often between 11 and 13 years of age, during which the ovary, uterus, and vagina mature and the first menstrual period occurs.

Masculinity: Traits or other qualities typically associated with being male.

Femininity: Traits or other qualities typically associated with being female.

Androgyny: The quality of possessing traits or other qualities associated both with being male and with being female.

Identity: Identity refers to the model one creates of who one is in one's life. The term often suggests a specifically social emphasis, concerning in particular how one fits into or plans to fit into the surrounding world.

Identity Crisis: A stage or period of time during which a person experiences frustration, concern, and worry about who he or she is in the social world and seeks to better understand how to fit in with the world.

Identity Exploration: A process during which an individual explores different identities, searching for the one that best fits his or her own being and outlook.

Identity Commitment: A process by which an individual gradually entrusts him or herself to a particular social self-concept for fitting into society and the world more generally.

Identity Status: A classification of how a person views his occupational and social roles, based on whether the person has sufficiently explored those roles and committed to one.

Identity Diffusion Status: An identity status in which a young person fails to develop a coherent model of who he is; rather, the individual will employ a series of partial or contradictory models of his social and occupational roles.

Foreclosure Status: An identity status that arises when a young person commits to social and occupational roles without having explored alternatives.

Moratorium Status: An identity status that involves postponing making a commitment to a social and occupational role until one has completed further exploration.

Achieved Identity Status: The highest level of identity status in which a person has adequately explored social and occupational roles available and committed to one that fairly represents her or his desires, needs, values, and goals.

Chapter 12: Personality Development in Adulthood

Does a child's personality extend into adulthood? Will the emerging adult have a chance to change his or her personality? Adult development involves both consistency and change. The growing individual faces new life tasks, including, for many, finding a partner and choosing a career. Accomplishing these tasks means we take seriously the qualities of our own personalities—our preferences, styles, skills, and desires. How does our personality influence the kind of relationships we choose? Will our personality match the demands of a specific occupation? What is the optimal personality like?

Previewing the Chapter's Central Questions

•**What Is the Nature of Adult Development?** Adult development addresses the consistency and changes in personality from young adulthood to the final stages of life. The continuity of personality from childhood to early adulthood is examined, and some of the challenges of adulthood are described in this first section.

•**What Are Young Adults Like?** One of the major tasks of the young adult is to find intimacy by choosing a mate and creating a positive and intimate relationship with that partner; different people go about accomplishing these goals differently. A second task is to match our interests and abilities to an occupation that we're happy with, and to develop our skills at work.

•**How Does the Individual Traverse Middle Adulthood?** With relationships and careers begun, the mid-life adult often has the freedom to focus on maintaining important relationships and achieving success in an occupation. The ways in which personality contributes to such processes, and also to physical health, are examined. In addition, personality change is considered with an eye to who changes and who stays the same.

•**Where Is Personality Headed in the Concluding Parts of Life?** Personality develops up to the end of the life. The last stages of life often involve making meaning, developing a sense of one's life, and coming to terms with one's death.

What Is the Nature of Adult Development?

Questions of Adult Development

Mohandis Karamchand Gandhi (1869-1948) was born in Porbandar, Kathiawar, in India, to a merchant family. He was an unremarkable student, leaving behind no brilliant record as a scholar or as an athlete, yet, in a premonition of the future, his teachers often gave him good certificates of character (Gandhi, 1942, p. 284). India was then a British colony, and as a young man Gandhi traveled to England to study law after his father's death. It was in England that he was first exposed to religious writings, including the Hindu scripture, *The Bhagavad-Gita*, as well those from other religious traditions. These caught his attention and initiated the religious pursuits that would occupy him throughout his life.

After completing his legal training, Gandhi traveled to South Africa to establish a law practice there. He personally experienced the discrimination leveled against the Indian population of that nation. In response, he put his spirituality into practice, experimenting with methods of political influence through editorial writing and non-cooperation with the South African authorities. At the request of his fellow Indian citizens, he remained in the country to fight discrimination rather than return to India as he had planned. Like many adults, Gandhi began to employ his own psychological gifts—his spiritual and his political skills—in an attempt to make a better world. This process of using our assets to care for the next generation is what the psychologist Erik Erikson referred to as generativity (for more about his theory, see "Dividing the Life Span" in Chapter 11).

In 1914, at 45 years of age, Gandhi returned to India. There he staged a series of peaceful political struggles so as to foster the well being of Indian workers. He respected both sides of a confrontation, and frequently left good will behind him after engaging in a conflict. His opponents in these negotiations often felt relief when he shifted his focus to other political matters, for he was a formidable adversary. After Gandhi's successes on behalf of Indian workers, he set his sights on promoting Indian independence from Great Britain.

Gandhi used the term "self rule," or *swaraj*, to refer to Indian independence. *Swaraj* has two meanings. Politically, it denoted India's liberation from England. Its second meaning, however, was no less significant and referred to an individual's spiritual self-management. *Swaraj* in this sense refers to freedom from illusion and ignorance. *The Bhagavad-Gita* saw the liberated individual as someone who acts without craving and without possessiveness, and who can find peace in awareness of the infinite spirit. For Gandhi and his followers, *swaraj* represented not only a political movement but a personal journey to self-knowledge and mastery (Dalton, 1993, p. 2). Self-awareness is sought by many adults in various secular and religious traditions.

Gandhi was a charismatic leader at a time of many significant 20th-century charismatic leaders. He became known as Mahatma Gandhi (Mahatma is an honorific referring to a particularly wise teacher). No individual can be a role model to all, of course, given the extent to which people differ from one another. In Gandhi's case, his spirituality and non-violence led to his making choices that most people—even those who respected him—would choose not to emulate (Erikson, 1969, p. 417). He had made a commitment to celibacy and poverty, whereas most adults will seek marriage and a successful career. His leadership sometimes failed, his empathy did not extend in all directions, and, toward the end of his life, his personal behavior raised questions of sexual propriety (Dutton, 1993, p. 136; Erikson, 1969, pp. 404-406). Nonetheless, he helped usher in Indian political independence coupled with peace and democracy. Moreover, he expressed a commitment to love, non-violence, and a caring for excluded groups that was rare for his time and for our own. These are objectives to which many aspire but only a few attain so fully.

Psychologists have described Gandhi's greatness as having been achieved through the very highest levels of moral thought (Simonton, 1994, pp. 262-264), through generativity and caring for the next generation (Erikson, 1965), and as a potent expression of both the personal and social intelligences (Gardner, 1993, pp. 239, 252). Others have simply remarked that he could love well beyond the capabilities of most (Rokeach, 1960, p. 392). The fact that he was far from perfect also represents an inescapable feature of adult development.

Why do some people develop such greatness? Or, more prosaically, how can any of us become a better version of ourselves? Although the study of personality development cannot answer the question directly, it does speak to the challenges we face and the pathways to greater psychological health.

The Transition to Adulthood

The issue of developing well as an adult is an important one, especially so given the length that adulthood can now extend. Longevity nearly doubled between 1850 and 1995 from, on average, 40 years to

77 years. The added years increase the importance of adulthood as a time of life (Stillion & McDowell, 2001-2002). People who expect to live longer also have a greater sense of control over their lives (e.g., Lewis, Ross, & Mirwosky, 1999; Mirowsky, 1997). Contemporary young people will have more time to express their personalities in adulthood—and to be subject to the troubles and rewards that their personal qualities may help bring about.

There exists an extraordinarily broad range of adult choices. An individual could be single, married, divorced, or widowed; be employed in an office, at home, or unemployed; be sedentary or fit; have a large family or none. Although social factors play a crucial role in one's future, the individual, too, exerts an influence on how his life events unfold.

Personality development at the threshold of adulthood follows on what has come before. Emerging adults build their occupational and social progress on the identities they defined during their adolescence. People use their still-developing identities to help guide them choose a life partner and an occupation (Mayer, 2014). Of Erikson's eight stages of development, three pertained directly to adulthood: The individual finds a partner and experiences intimacy (intimacy versus isolation), experiences a sense of generativity by contributing to society (generativity versus stagnation), and experiences a sense of integrity through seeing the meaning in her life (integrity versus despair).

Stage models alternative to Erikson's offer further insights into this period. Levinson (1976) studied the life stages of 40 men from different occupations and social strata in depth. He divided early adult life into a series of stages that began with an early transition into adulthood between the ages of 17 and 22, and then marked off the decades of the 20s, 30s, and 40s. His stages continued through the years from 40 to 65 and later. An overview of his system is in Table 12-1. Levinson described each period of development with considerable richness. For example, the "Age 30 transition," he said, represents a time during which adult life becomes "more restrictive, serious, and 'for real.'" (Levinson, 1977, p. 104). In response, men often feel pressured to initiate changes in their lives before it is too late. For some, the transition is relatively smooth, involving a reaffirmation of what has come before; they may make only modest changes to an already fairly well-developed adulthood. Other men who made missteps in their earlier life choices—picking the wrong career or friends—now face a time of reckoning. For the larger majority of men, significant changes appear necessary. A few men would experience life as intolerable, and yet the means to attain a better life might be difficult to figure out or beyond reach. Still other men find themselves in a low point unlike any they have experienced during their preceding decades and must choose an altogether new path.

During the Age 30 transition, marital difficulties and divorce seemed more common among the men studied than at other times. There were often shifts in occupation: Some men settled down from a time of trying out many jobs; others chose new careers. Men sought psychotherapy with a higher frequency. As troubled as this time was for some men, making adjustments in their lives at age 30 was a wise choice because it was still early enough to make a fresh start. As time goes on, such readjustments become more difficult, according to the theory.

Temperament and Traits: From Childhood Through Adulthood

Some adult qualities seem predictable from childhood. In regard to temperament and traits, 3-year-olds who had an emotionally negative temperament—prone to distress and impulsivity—were more likely to be aggressive, conflict-prone, and poorly controlled as 21-year-olds (Newman et al., 1997). Moreover, such undercontrolled young adults develop into less self-controlled middle-aged adults as well.

Table 12-1: Levinson's Stages of Adult Men's Lives*

Stage	Brief Description
17-22: The Early Adult Transition	During this transitional stage, emerging adults question their place in the world and try out their initial choices for adult living. To accomplish this, they must end many pre-adulthood relationships and begin early adult ones.
22-28: First Adult Life Structure	During this first stage of adulthood, the individual tries to connect the most valued parts of himself to adult society. To do so, he makes initial choices regarding what occupation to enter, in love, in relationships, and regarding values and lifestyle. He then lives with those choices for extended periods of time.
28-33: The Age 30 Transition	The Age 30 Transition represents a time during which adult life becomes more constrained, serious, and "for real."
32-40: Settling Down	The Settling Down stage represents a time for the person to continue the newly revised life structure formed over the several years leading up to it, during the Age 30 transition. During this Settling time, the person hopes to climb the occupational ladder, establish his niche, and work at "making it" in terms of his valued goals.
40-45: Mid-Life Transition	Much like the Age 30 Transition, the Mid-Life Transition is a potentially tumultuous time of reflection and re-evaluation, this time centered on questions such as: "What have I done with my life?" and "What has happened to my childhood dreams?" In Levinson's sample, most men again experienced a considerable struggle during this time. At its conclusion, some men were able to reattach to the people in their lives and the work environments around them, others made new choices, and still others entered into a decline.
40-65: Middle Adulthood	The stage from 40 to 65 reflected the outgrowth of the stages that came before. Although there remained time for further re-evaluation and change during these years, the bases of one's life had by now been established. During these and later stages, life unfolded based on one's earlier choices and other life circumstances.

*Adapted from various sources including Levinson (1977).

Traits: Set Like Plaster?

During adulthood, an individual's traits are relatively stable. For example, people generally maintain their relative standings on the Big Five personality dimensions throughout adulthood (e.g., Siegler, George, & Okun, 1979; Douglas & Arenberg, 1978; Costa et al., 1986; Costa & McCrae, 1988). At the same time, the average level of traits shifts over the life span. For example, between the ages of 20 and 80, Neuroticism, Extraversion, and Openness can be expected to decline roughly one half of a standard deviation in the population. Agreeableness and Conscientiousness, on the other hand, either stay stable, or rise slightly (Costa & McCrae, 2002). These changes can be detected in the relatively brief four-year span of college. For example, 270 college students who were followed across their college years exhibited the expected decline in Extraversion and Neuroticism, as well as the expected rise in Agreeableness and Conscientiousness. Perhaps in response to the educational process, however, openness rose slightly for these students during college, in contrast to its gradual decline in adulthood (Robins et al., 2001).

Models of the Self and World

Another area of continuity concerns the person's mental models of the self and world. The development of the self, which is so central to the young child's personal identity, remains a lens through which the adult sees the world. Young adults, like adolescents, possess considerable self-consciousness, and overemphasize the degree to which others notice them. In one experiment, college students at Cornell University were asked to wear a slightly embarrassing tee-shirt into a room of their normally dressed peers. The tee-shirt had a picture of a pop-singer on it who was considered to reflect generally poor musical taste at the time (Barry Manilow). Those wearing the tee-shirts imagined that about half of the students in the room would notice their Manilow tee-shirts when in fact only about a quarter did (Gilovich & Savitsky, 1996).

By early adulthood the self has integrated within it a long line of significant personal memories, personal traits, and formulations of identity (Pillemer, 2000; 2001; Singer & Salovey, 1993; Singer & Bluck, 2001). For example, Thorne and Klohnen (1990) studied 95 ethnically diverse 23-year-olds who had been followed since they were 3 years old (Block & Block, 1980). These investigators asked the then-23-year-olds to recall 10 specific memories that were personally important or represented problematic encounters from their childhoods.

The researchers found continuities between undercontrolled behavior in childhood and the adult's personally important memories of childhood. One of their participants, Edith Fay (a pseudonym), was consistently identified as undercontrolled through the years by various interviewers. Now, as a 23-year-old, she recalled five early memories—all about failing to receive help. Her memories included being left to cry after her older sister stuck her with a pin while diapering her, and her father's telling her to go to sleep without her favorite teddy bear after it had fallen on the floor, rather than helping her retrieve it (Thorne & Klohnen, 1993, p. 248). Her difficulties in life now had become a part of her life story and broader identity.

The environment that a person experiences or creates for him- or herself also may exert control on personality and cause it to change. Ongoing family conflict can make first-year adjustment to college more challenging (e.g., Feenstra, Banyard, Rines, & Hopkins, 2001). Looking ahead a bit, the emerging adult can exert some control over the environment in regard to marital choice. For example, Caspi and Herbener (1990) divided married couples into those who had married others most similar to themselves, and those who had married people relatively different from themselves. Personality was assessed according to the California Q-Sort, which, recall, is a list of statements arranged according to the degree that they apply to the individual. The researchers found that those who married people most similar to themselves appeared to choose similar situations to each other, expected to change each other less, and as a consequence, possessed personalities that remained relatively unchanged across adulthood. By comparison, those who married people more different from themselves changed more over the 11-year period than others.

What Are Young Adults Like?

The Tasks of Young Adulthood

Developmental psychologists generally recognize a period that marks a transition to adulthood, termed the Early Adult Transition or, Emerging Adulthood (Arnett, 2000; Levinson, 1977). This period involves a sort of rehearsal for later life in which one begins to put into practice one's plans for adulthood. During this period, occupations are chosen, adult relationships are commenced (or continued), and the young person begins "climbing the steps" of a ladder toward greater accomplishments. During this period, the young person typically tries to keep some options open, because he or she is neither certain about the career or the relationships that are best. There is great diversity of possible living arrangements and life pursuits during the beginnings of the stage, relative to many other times of life (Arnett, 2000). As time goes on, however, the young person gradually increases his or her commitments. The tale is told that Sigmund Freud was once asked what he thought a normal person should be able to do well. He replied, quite briefly, "to love and to work" —and those are indeed central tasks of this time as well as of later adulthood ("Lieben und arbeiten"; Erikson, 1963, pp. 164-165).

Finding a Desirable Partner

In Search of Intimacy

In terms of personal relationships, both men and women share the desire to marry someone who is kind and understanding, and who has an exciting personality. Beyond that, however, lie some interesting sex differences. In survey research crossing dozens of cultures, men tend to favor physical appearance attributes more than do women, whereas women seek men with financial status and ambition that may lead to their higher status.

Such differences have both evolutionary and social explanations—which at times appear not so different. The general idea is that, in seeking physical attractiveness, men have developed the notion that physical attractiveness in a mate is likely to correspond to health and fertility. In seeking financial resources in men, women have developed the idea that, since men in many cultures exert more control over money, if they want good resources, that is an important part of choosing a spouse. Some psychologists believe that such ideas may be developed as a way of maximizing opportunities for survival and reproduction; others argue that the culture simply taught these ideas apart from their possible evolutionary advantages (Buss & Barnes, 1986).

These attitudes filter into how a person presents him- or herself to the opposite sex. Consider the personal advertisements men and women place in newspapers and circulars, so as to meet one another. Women's ads more often describe their physical attributes, emphasizing their own attractiveness; on average, they seek men older than themselves. Men's ads more often stress their financial resources and occupational status; they seek women younger than themselves (Kenrick & Keefe, 1992).

Another sex difference is that young men report preferring far more sexual partners than women (see Chapter 11). To see whether this preference operated in actual behavior, Clark and Hatfield (1989) studied male or female students who were walking alone across campus during the day. When they spotted a student, they sent an attractive individual of the other sex to the student walking alone. This person—called an experimental confederate—was actually working with the experimenter but hid this information. The confederate addressed the student, saying, "I've been noticing you around campus. I find you very attractive." Depending upon the randomly selected condition, the confederate then went on to ask one of three questions: "Would you go out with me tonight?", "Would you come over to my apartment tonight?", or "Would you go to bed with me tonight?"

In the three separate times this study was conducted, in 1978, 1982, and 1990, the results were much the same. Both men and women were willing to go on a date with the confederate at least 50% of the time (men, 60 to 70%; women, 50%). This makes some sense because of the developmental need during this time to find a partner. On the other hand, men were far more willing to go to an apartment with a woman than the other way around (50% to 70% for men versus 1% to 10% for women, across studies). Most dramatically, about 70% of the men expressed willingness to go to bed with the women after a three-sentence invitation; among women, not one accepted the invitation over three studies over three decades. Women typically responded, "You've got to be kidding!" or "What's wrong with you?" Men, on the other hand, felt a need to make excuses if they *didn't* accept the invitation to go to bed. This sex difference has been explained both in terms of the evolutionary pressures for women to exert greater care over their choice of partner, as well as social considerations of the proper standards of behavior, their reputations, and concerns over their safety (Clark, 1990).

Strategies to Attract Partners

In their everyday lives, men and women use a variety of strategies to meet one another. In the 1980s, Buss surveyed 107 newlywed couples (214 people): all the "just married" couples in a single U.S. county over the course of a year, and asked both the men and women what they had done to attract their present spouse (Buss, 1988, Study 2). The typical man admitted he had lifted weights, flexed his muscles, bought expensive electronics, and mentioned both his high status at work and his expectation of earning a lot of money to his potential partner. He also gave encouraging glances and brought the woman to a nice restaurant for dinner. The average women, by comparison, acknowledged that she wore facial makeup (and in some instances learned how to do so), shaved her legs, wore jewelry, and spent more than an hour making her appearance pleasant. She was also more likely than usual to wear attractive outfits and to diet ahead of time. Once coupled with her prospective partner, she had been inclined to make him an article of clothing and was likely to express sympathy to him when he confided his troubles.

Despite such differences, men and women tend to value many of the same character traits in their prospective mates. Both men and women value a "good sense of humor," a partner who is "sympathetic to their troubles," and who is well-mannered, helpful, and spends time with them. Another area valued by both men and women is appearance ("showered daily," "wore attractive outfits") and health more generally, including staying physically fit (Buss, 1988, Tables 5 and 6).

The Role of General Physiological Arousal

General physiological arousal heightens sexual attraction to a potential sexual partner. For example, male participants in one study sat next to a very attractive female participant—actually, an experimental confederate—in a laboratory. The identified experimenter told the pair of young people that they would be receiving either mild or painful shocks. The young male participant and female confederate were then told to go into separate rooms to complete a questionnaire, during which the shock equipment would be readied. First, though, the attractive woman stood up, stepped directly in front of the man and searched for a pencil in her coat, so as to attract the young man's attention. On average, men who were expecting to receive stronger shocks reported on their questionnaires that they were more attracted to the woman than those expecting milder shocks (Dutton & Aron, 1974, Experiment 3). In other studies, women who have just gone through a very upsetting experience also find an attractive man more romantically appealing than in other circumstances. The effects are found even when experimenters point out the arousing nature of the threat, so that participants know they are aroused by something other than someone else's attractiveness (Allen et al., 1989).

There exist powerful individual differences in sexuality as well. Recall from Chapter 4 that Shafer (2001) had developed a scale of sexuality that included self-descriptors such as alluring, sexy, seductive, ravenous, and lusty. These and other sexual terms are distinct enough from the Big Five traits to have been proposed as different dimensions, although some argue that they might fall into a Big-Five-like pattern (e.g., Schmitt & Buss, 2000). People who score high on such sexuality scales are more likely to be single, have higher interest in dating, date for longer periods of time, and more readily get over their last relationship to start dating again (Shafer, 2001). So, higher levels of sexuality may well predict having more partners and a more active dating life in early adulthood.

Falling in Love

The degree to which someone is attracted to another may also be determined by their preferred romantic style. Several models have been proposed to describe individual differences in romance and love. Perhaps the most common distinction among such theories is between **passionate love** and **companionate love**. Passionate love involves intense arousal and longing for joining with another. It feels powerful, full of desire, and difficult to ignore on a moment-by-moment basis. By contrast, companionate love refers to the caring and desire we feel for another person with whom our lives intertwine. It emphasizes tenderness, intimacy, and concern (Berscheid & Walster, 1983; Hatfield, 1988). Beyond that, classifications of love include **possessive love**, in which a partner wants to bind together and control the other; **altruistic love**, in which a person is willing to suffer and sacrifice to protect the other; and **erotic love**, in which there is a great deal of physical and sexual excitement (e.g., Hendrick, & Hendrick, 1986; Sternberg, 1987; 1997). Exactly what causes people to fall in love is, you will not be surprised to hear, not yet not entirely understood.

Similarity in Mate Selection

Two competing hypotheses concerning choosing a partner are the **assortative mating** hypothesis: that a person chooses someone similar to herself, and the **complimentary selection** hypothesis: that opposites attract. As it turns out, people fairly clearly engage in assortative mating, choosing others who are like themselves. A number of mechanisms contribute to the preference for a similar partner: Freud (1927) observed that parents serve as a child's first love, and that later romantic attraction was triggered by finding characteristics in a new person in common with one's parents. Evolutionary biologists added that finding someone like our parents (and ourselves) promotes the survival of our genes better than finding someone dissimilar (e.g., Epstein & Guttman, 1984). Beyond that, our opposite-sex parent may influence such selection more strongly in heterosexual unions, although both parents may exert such influences (Daly & Wilson, 1990; Epstein & Guttman, 1984; Geher, 2003; Jedlicka, 1984).

Empirical findings support matches both to oneself and to one's parents (Geher, 2003). Five hundred undergraduates, their romantic partners, and their parents all described themselves on the Big Five personality traits. The prediction from the parent to the chosen partner persisted even after the student's own self-rated profile (which resembled both the parent and the romantic partner) was statistically controlled for.

Despite the overall evidence for assortative mating, there are some intriguing exceptions. Under strict assurances of confidentiality, Lykken and Tellegen (1993) asked identical twins whether they were attracted to their co-twin's spouse. They found that identical twins were no more attracted to their twin's spouse than were fraternal (dizygotic) twins. Indeed, many twins disliked their co-twin's spouse. Nor were those who married an identical twin particularly attracted to the co-twin. The raised the recurring question of whether people who are similar simply spend more time together, for example, because people attending the same college are likely to be somewhat similar in skills, or because people who share the same religion may meet one another while worshipping. If various social contexts bring together similar people, romantic love might operate in such contexts as a rather random phenomenon—and it would seem as if assortative mating was taking place.

How similar are the members of a couple? Modestly so: Across pairs of couples, physical size and shape correlate between $r = .10$ and $.30$, physical attractiveness is higher at $r = .52$ (Murstein, 1972; Plomin, DeFries, & Roberts, 1977; White, 1980). IQ and educational attainment correlate between $r = .35$ and $.46$ (Bouchard & McGue, 1981; Plomin et al., 1977). The coefficients for self-reported personality traits range from about $r = .15$ to $.35$. The similarity for religious belief may range as high as $r = .60$ (Buss, 1984; Caspi, Herbener, & Ozer, 1992; Lykken & Tellegen, 1993).

In Search of Good Work

Just as young people search for partners who are similar to themselves, they also seek jobs that match their interests and skills. Every occupation, like every person, has its own character. One widely employed classification of occupations divides them into six broad categories: **Realistic**, **Investigative**, **Artistic**, **Social**, **Enterprising**, and **Conventional occupations**—described by the acronym RIASEC (Holland, 1997). Realistic occupations include farmers, surveyors, mechanics, and carpenters, who must respond to the definite requirements of the land, of raw materials, and of manufactured objects. Investigative occupations include biologists, chemists, and anthropologists, who undertake scientific research. Artistic occupations include writers, actors, art directors, and interior decorators, who must employ creativity and shape communication.

These occupations can be arranged in a hexagram to portray relationships among them (see Figure 12-1). Those types that are opposite one another have little overlap in interests or traits. For example, the realism of the mechanic or carpenter shares relatively little overlap with the social occupations, including social workers, teachers, therapists, and clergy, who enjoy working with people.

On the other hand, occupations next to each other are more closely related, such as the enterprising and conventional. Enterprising occupations include salespeople, politicians, and television reporters, who share in common their interest in influencing others. Conventional occupations include bookkeepers, accountants, and industrial engineers, who enjoy working in an organized way with words and numbers.

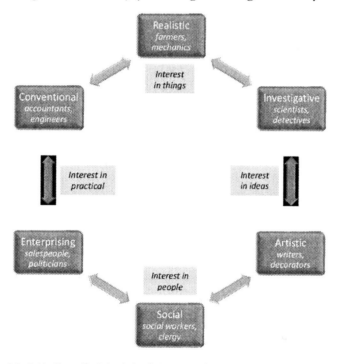

Figure 12-1 *Holland's Model of Occupational Interests*
In Holland's model, occupations that are most similar are next to each other in the diagram; occupations least alike are opposite one another.

People often try to align their interests to an occupation, just as they seek someone similar to themselves in a romantic pairing. Many of the occupational interest tests designed today are intended to help match a person to others with similar interests. The basic assumption here is that if a person has interests and abilities that are called upon to perform the job, then the person will be relatively happy in the job. For example, 345 paying-and-receiving bank tellers were studied at a major bank from the time they were hired to a follow-up four months later. Expected satisfaction with their job was an excellent predictor of actual job satisfaction four months later, at *r* = *.67* (Gottfredson & Holland, 1989).

Next, each of the beginning tellers' test profiles on vocational interest survey was compared to the ideal profile of the profession. Bank tellers tend to score high on the conventional, enterprising, and social scales of occupational inventories relative to other scales (e.g., Holland, 1987). After statistically controlling for satisfaction, the interest-to-occupation match predicted job satisfaction and involvement, with an *r* = .36. So, matching exists, and is important. It does, however, operate secondarily to an individual's general sense of satisfaction (Gottfredson & Holland, 1990).

Occupations contribute to the individual's sense of meaning and purpose in life. They provide economic support for the individual, her family and their descendants, and to society more generally.

How Does the Individual Traverse Middle Adulthood?

"Mathematicians tell the following joke: A certain individual had a personality that was so negative, that when he walked into a party, people would ask, 'who left?'" – Recounted by Paul Hoffman (b. 1956)

Some people experience middle adulthood as a time of calm progress in their family and occupational spheres. Others are less satisfied and may confront the need for major change. For many individuals, the ages of 30, 40, and 50 are considered landmark ages in that they refer to the end of an old decade and beginning of a new one. As people traverse such landmark years, they are often prompted to consider how things have gone and might be expected to go in the future. Many people experience love and growth at home, and experience promotions and other signs of appreciation at work (Levinson, 1978).

Other people will lead less enviable lives. Some will obviously fail, being denied promotion or advancement, or losing jobs regularly. They will experience marital discord and risk divorce. Others, although maintaining the outward trappings of success, will suffer inwardly because they failed to adequately connect their interests to their activities earlier on; they now fail to feel their part, as it were, and experience a sense of alienation from their lives (Levinson, 1978). Some may try to stay the course while others find continuing up the ladder to be intolerable, and attempt to break out. This may be successful sometimes, but it is purchased at a high cost, for it often takes 8 to 10 years to re-stabilize in another setting: Young adults who try to change their life course must not only break out from their present occupation or relationship, but also break into a new career and a new relationships. There efforts will often be at a disadvantage relative to others who have gotten there years earlier. In this section we will examine success in marriage, at work, in health—and mid-course corrections.

Staying Married

Success in marriage involves both being satisfied with one's relationship and avoiding divorce. Divorce has been a regularly studied outcome as it provides a reasonably certain indication of a failed marriage. A number of factors predict marital satisfaction and divorce, including factors related to society, personality, and development. Among the social factors contributing to divorce, economic hardship looms large (Conger et al., 1990). A number of studies indicate that divorce rates rise during times of economic turbulence and dislocation such as occurred, for example, during the great depression in the 1930s and the lesser economic pressures of the 1980s in the United States (Bakke, 1940; Elder, 1974; Dooley & Catalano, 1988). Mounting economic pressures on families generally bring budgetary concerns into focus, creating a sense of frustration, irritability, and anger in the couple (Liker & Elder, 1983). In regard to parental influences, having nurturing, involved parents leads to greater social competence and relationship satisfaction—even after controlling statistically for the influence of personality traits (Donnellan, Larsen-Rife, & Conger, 2005). But what are the traits related to marriage and divorce?

Kelly and Conley (1987) followed 300 couples from their engagement in the 1930s through their lives at age 68. The personality of the members of the couples were rated by acquaintances on a number of personality dimensions at the time of their engagement. The authors found that three variables were predictive of marital satisfaction and continued stability of the marriage: The emotional calmness of the husband, the emotional calmness of the wife, and the lack of impulsivity in the husband. The researchers found that early-life ratings on impulsivity were related to the likelihood the husband would have an extra-marital affair—one of the major listed causes of divorce in the sample. Indeed, impulsivity in the husband and negative emotionality in the husband and wife together accounted for nearly 50% of the variance in whether the couple would be among the roughly 1 in 6 who divorced in the study—a very high rate of prediction.

Other studies have obtained similar findings for negative emotion (Eysenck, 1980), and for poor self-control (e.g., Loeb, 1966). Still other personality factors—like extraversion—appear to enhance the social opportunities for promiscuity (Bentler & Newcomb, 1978; Eysenck, 1980; Kelly & Conley, 1987). Twin studies, too, have found some evidence for a genetic basis of mental life that leads to divorce, with estimates ranging from 25 to 50% contributions of personality to divorce (McGue & Lykken, 1992).

In a study of nearly 2000 couples, Jockin, McGue, and Lykken (1996) found that a number of personality traits are related to maintaining a marriage. They employed the traits measured by the Multidimensional Personality Questionnaire. At the broadest level, these included positive affect, negative affect, and control (see Table 12-2). The researchers found that negative emotionality predicted a greater likelihood of divorce, whereas more positive emotionality *also* predicts divorce. The reasons for negative emotionality are fairly clear—such emotions trigger frustration, hostility, and anger in the couple over time. A partner with highly positive emotions may be more willing than others to consider alternative partners. A third superordinate factor, personal constraint (the reverse of impulsiveness), is related more highly to maintaining a marriage.

These general patterns are elucidated more clearly at the level of more specific traits that their test also measures. Among those specific factors, traits such as social potency contributed to higher likelihoods of divorce. Social potency involves forcefulness, decisiveness, dominance, and leading—which are likely to attract other potential partners and, perhaps, make dissatisfied partners even more unhappy. Alienation, a feeling of being mistreated or victimized, also predicts divorce. Absorption—that is, a certain capacity to become lost in thought, to be hypnotizable, and to exhibit absentmindedness, also negatively impacts a marriage. Reactivity to stress—for husbands only—increases the likelihood of divorce as well.

Among factors that maintain a marriage, a higher desire for control—among wives only, serves as a positive factor. In addition, as a desire for traditionalism rises in either or both spouses, the marriage is more likely to be maintained. The same is true for a desire to avoid personal harm. Members of a couple who are self-protective are more likely to maintain their union.

How important are these effects? The predictions account for about 14% of the variance of marriage maintenance in women and 8% in men, or about a quarter of the variance in divorce risk for a couple, which is substantial when considering other social, economic, and chance factors (Jockin, McGue, & Lykken, 1996, p. 296).

Finally, in keeping with our developmental perspective, it is worth noting the effect of divorce on the next generation. The children of divorce are known to suffer relative to children of intact marriages (Amato,

& Keith, 1991; Hetherington, Bridges & Insabella, 1998). Is that due to a genetic predisposition toward troubled traits on the part of children, or due to the negative impact of the divorce itself? A novel answer to this question was provided by O'Connor et al. (2000), who studied the biological and adopted children of parents who divorced. Those researchers found that all children reacted to divorce with elevated psychological problems, including increased substance abuse. This was true even though the adopted children shared little genetic relation to their parents. On the other hand, the biological children of divorced parents— but not the adopted children—exhibited lower achievement and poorer social skills, suggesting that lower mental skills in the parents led both to a greater likelihood of divorce and produced a negative genetic impact on their biological children's academic and social skills. These are average, relative effects for the children of divorce; even given such findings, many of the children can be expected to go on to thrive in the future.

Table 12-2: Correlations of Personality Traits With Staying Married*

Measures		Men	Women
Higher Order Scales	Positive emotion	-.07*	-.15**
	Negative emotion	-.13**	-.12**
	Constraint	.11**	.15**
Primary Scales	Well-being	.06*	.04*
	Social potency	-.14**	-.20**
	Achievement	-.03	-.16*
	Social closeness	.02	.05*
	Reactivity to stress	-.10**	.04
	Alienation	-.08**	-.02
	Control	.05	.11**
	Harm avoidance	.07*	.12**
	Traditionalism	.20**	.24**
	Absorption	-.11**	-.17**

*Adapted from report of results in Jockin, McGue, & Lykken (1996, p. 293).

Finding Occupational Success

General Factors

Career success can be measured in relation to two general criteria: a person's subjective sense of satisfaction and achievement, and more objective measures of the individual's level of responsibility, prestige, and salary. Personality influences each of these areas. By far the most pervasive findings are that general intelligence and conscientiousness lead to greater objective success across occupations (Barrick & Mount, 1991; Judge et al., 1999; Ree, 1991). For example, the overall effect for conscientiousness on objective success is about $r = .17$ (Barrick & Mount, 1991). Conscientious workers are rewarded with higher salaries, particularly those beginning on their career paths. Emotionally stable workers also earn more (Nyhus & Pons, 2005).

Judge et al. (1999) studied occupational success by analyzing data from three longitudinal studies, involving 354 individuals. By following a single group over time, the investigators controlled for the economic and historical factors that often add variation to cross-sectional studies and lead to the underestimation of personality's effects. In Judge and colleagues' sample, general mental ability contributed to objective career success with a correlation slightly above $r = .50$. The Big-Five factor of Conscientiousness predicted objective success at $r = .40$. Figure 12-2 shows the relationships of several further personality attributes and ultimate career success in middle age. The contributions to subjective career success (e.g., career satisfaction) were similar, but with Conscientiousness and Intelligence reversed in importance. Next after these two influences, Emotional Stability (that is, low Neuroticism) contributes considerably to the picture, followed by Openness. The Judge et al. findings also indicate that job satisfaction and objective qualities of one's job are somewhat related.

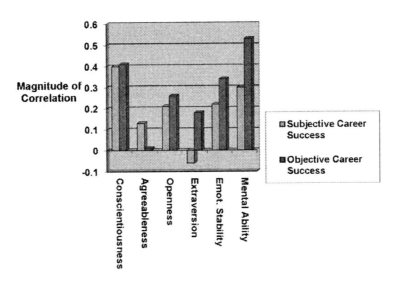

Figure 12-2: Personality Attributes and their Correlations with Career Success
(Based on Judge et al., 1999)

Personality Attributes

Positivity and Job Satisfaction Over the Life Span

A second longitudinal study of careers placed more emphasis on studying motivation- and emotion-related traits and their influences. The sample was the approximately 1037 children born during the year beginning April 1, 1972 in Dunedin, New Zealand (Roberts, Caspi, & Moffitt, 2003). For this study, the participants' personalities were assessed at the age of 18, and then their occupational status and personality were examined again eight years later at the age of 26.

The four broad traits studied included (a) negative affect, including aggression, alienation, and stress reactions, (b) positive communitarian emotions, including well-being and social closeness, (c) positive agentic emotions, including the need for achievement and social potency, and (d) personal constraint, including traditionalism and harm avoidance. Negative affect predicted lower occupational attainment, lower pay, and less work satisfaction. Positive, communitarian emotions, positive active emotions, and personal constraint each individually predicted higher occupational and financial attainment.

Interestingly, young people with negative affect who nonetheless managed to obtain higher status occupations at age 18 became more positive and self-controlled at age 26—approaching in satisfaction those who were already more positive. There appears, therefore, to be a mutually positive interaction between positive communitarian traits and high status positions (Roberts, Caspi, & Moffit, 2003).

Having a Temper

Undercontrolled childhood personality—especially evidenced by severe temper tantrums—may still exert problematic influences later in life. Caspi, Elder, and Bem (1987) obtained developmental data on a number of men and women over a 40-year period. Many of the children in the study had been rated by their mothers on their temper tantrums at the ages of 8, 9, and 11. The researchers formed two groups: The first contained about 40 percent of the boys, and 30 percent of the girls who had been rated as having particularly frequent and severe temper tantrums. The comparison group consisted of their calmer peers.

In the military (which 70% of the boys had entered), those with explosive tempers as children had achieved lower rank, on average, than their calmer peers. As they neared 50, there were clear occupational differences between this temper tantrum group and the other children. The boys who had experienced explosive temper tantrums as children were less occupationally successful than the other boys. This appeared related to their shifting jobs more frequently and their longer periods of unemployment. In fact, those from a middle-class upbringing had been downwardly mobile and could now no longer be distinguished from their working-class counterparts. Finally, the men in the explosive temper group were divorced at nearly double the rate of their calmer peers (40 versus 22%).

Biological underpinnings may affect success in some occupations. Dabbs (1992) was interested in the paradoxical effects of testosterone on male status. Within animals, testosterone is associated with aggression that serves to achieve status (Svare, 1983). Among contemporary men, however, aggression is not highly prized, and greater aggressiveness may be problematic. Dabbs found that among more than 4,000 men who were tested in the armed services, those with the highest levels of testoterone later were more likely to be unemployed or in industrial occupations such as welders, ironworkers, and miners. Those with lower testosterone were more likely to work as professionals and managers (farmers were also a lower testosterone group). Among women, however, testosterone may increase the likelihood of attaining career status. For example, women with high testosterone were more likely to become professional or technical workers relative to clerical workers or homemakers (Purifoy & Koopmans, 1979).

The Positivity Factor Further Considered

Positive emotionality is particularly important in areas that involve selling an idea or concept, or in selling oneself—as in an election. Indeed, one of the most important psychological variables in winning elections seems to be the optimism of the candidates who are running. The optimist holds the advantage. An extreme example of this was the Eisenhower--Stevenson presidential election of 1952. In Eisenhower's acceptance of the nomination, he announced, "Ladies and gentlemen, you have summoned me on behalf of millions of your fellow Americans to lead a great crusade—for freedom in America and freedom in the world." His opponent, Adlai Stevenson, by contrast, expressed considerable conflict over his own nomination: "That my heart has been troubled, that I have not sought the nomination, that I could not seek it in good conscience, that I would not seek it in honest self-appraisal, is not to say I value it the less." (Simonton, 1994, p. 253). Eisenhower won. Candidates who employ an optimistic style in their campaigning won in 18 of 22 presidential elections from 1900 to 1984. Another domain in which optimism is important is athletics, where the belief one has about being able to win is related to winning (Simonton, 1994, p. 253).

Toward Greatness

If you want to be more successful in a field, one especially key factor appears to be effort. The **Lotka-Price Law** (Price, 1963; 1986, Chapter 3) states that, given k people active in discipline, the square root of k identifies the number of people responsible for half the contributions. For example, there are about 250 classical composers whose music is still played actively. These range from the well-known, such as Mozart and Beethoven, to the relatively obscure, such as Busoni, Dukas, and Ponchielli. The square root of 250 is 15.8 = 16. By the Lotka-Price Law, we split the 250 classical composers into two groups: 16 top composers and the remaining 234 composers. The top ten among these 16 include Mozart, Beethoven, Bach, Wagner,

Brahms, Schubert, Handel, Tchaikovsky, Verdi, and Haydn. These and the remaining top 16 top composers account for 50% of all pieces played and recorded. The remaining 234 account for the rest (Moles, 1958/1966, pp. 28-29).

In psychology, Sigmund Freud's bibliography lists 330 articles and books. Among inventors, Thomas Edison obtained 1,093 patents—still the record at the United States Patent Office (Simonton, 1994, p. 139). Effort may be the key to membership in the top group. Even in the 18th century, Sir Joshua Reynolds' lectures to art students emphasized the idea that well-directed, hard work would suffice for a great career. Those who lacked natural genius could make up for it through hard work; natural genius would benefit even more with such work (Reynolds, 1769-90/1966, p. 37). As important as effort is, recent research reminds us that the aptitude to carry out a given line of work may be more important than Sir Reynolds apparently hoped (Hambrick et al., 2014).

Type A personality describes people who are extremely competitive and hostile, work extremely hard and urgently, and have little time for their families—or anyone else. Mothers with high expectations of their children tend to have more Type A adult children. Type A students exhibit better academic success than Type B students and later in life exhibit higher career success (Mathews, Glass, Rosenman, & Bortner, 1977; Mathews, Helmreich, Beane, & Lucker, G. 1980). Type A behavioral research also includes attempts to link the pattern to heart disease.

Although great accomplishments are more common earlier than later in adulthood, many accomplishments are brought about by those who have started late but persevered. Table 12-3 illustrates how some people continue to accomplish great ends into their 70s, 80s, and 90s.

Personality and Health

> Asked in his 90s what his doctor thought of his cigar smoking, the comedian George Burns replied, "My doctor's dead." – George Burns (1896-1996)

A substantial body of research has focused on the relationship between personality and health. The brief treatment here can only hint at the richness of research in this area.

Many people believe that a positive disposition, good moods, and optimism will lead to good health. Sloan (2011) has developed an intellectual history of this thinking-your-way-healthy approach, tracing it from the belief that unconscious repressed hostile impulses caused ulcers to more contemporary works like Byrne's 2006 *The Secret*, which argues that you can think your way to health.

There are two pieces of widely acknowledged circumstantial evidence that support the relationship between good moods and health. First, people in happier moods tend to report fewer medical symptoms than people who are crankier and more irritable. Research findings bear this out (e.g., Diener & Chan, 2011). Second, people who are ill are often in bad moods.

But there isn't much *causal* evidence that bad moods cause bad health. People who are sick are also often unhappy. In fact, a variety of illnesses and injuries from mild concussions to some viral infections all cause irritability, sleep loss, and concentration difficulties, so the causal relation is unclear (Friedman & Kern, 2014, p. 718). Indeed, psychotherapy or simple suggestions to cheer up can improve people's motivation to live well in the face of disease, but there is no evidence that it will stop the progression of cancer or cardiovascular disease (Coyne & Tennan, 2010; Thombs et al., 2013).

The clearest evidence of personality's contributions to health is the relationship between people's psychological traits and their longevity (Friedman & Kern, 2014). It's reasonably likely that someone who dies was in relatively poor health before their demise, whereas people who live longer are in relatively better health. There are three well-substantiated relationships between personality and longevity.

First, depression is known to reduce longevity—so much so that the American Heart Association recommends screening all heart patients for depression. It's less clear, however, whether the general state of depression itself causes the reduction in life span, or whether a more specific attribute of depression is responsible for the reduced longevity. A French study indicated that hostility rather than depression is the key life-reducing factor. Hostility is a known risk factor for suicide, homicide, accidents and unhealthy behavior (Lemogne et al., 2010).

The two clearest and largest influences on longevity are not happiness or sadness, in fact, but intelligence and conscientiousness (Friedman & Kern, 2014; Roberts et al., 2007). Why do higher conscientiousness and intelligence have these effects? No one knows for sure, but there are some compelling explanations for the effect. People who are intelligent are more likely to rise in socio-economic status over time, allowing them access to better health care. Intelligence may also be an indicator of good overall health (because ill health often reduces mental capacity). Conscientious people are more likely to be more dutiful and regular in following health recommendations. They are also more careful about avoiding risky behaviors. Extraversion also shows some predictive validity in relation to longevity—but, as noted above, it is unclear whether this is due to sicker people lacking energy.

In the shorter term, coping with stress—or failing to do so—also impacts health. People who are stressed are more susceptible to transient illnesses such as colds, and the depressed may give up—and die— sooner, upon contracting a chronic or fatal disease (e.g., Burton et al., 1986; Carney, Rich, & Freedland, 1988; Frasure-Smith, Lesperance, & Talajic, 1993; Salovey, Rothman, Detweiler, & Steward, 2000). Positive emotionality may buffer the influence of negative emotionality (Salovey et al., 2000).

Individual differences in the ability to cope can be learned and represent a stable individual-differences-variable in people—and sometimes in animals as well—that may reduce illness and its effects (e.g., Drugan, et al., 1989; Snyder, 1995). Successful coping can increase the release of natural tranquilizers in the brain and mitigate other harmful health effects (Drugan et al., 1994; Snyder, 1995). Learning to control stress appears to be a promising means of enhancing health in the context of chronic medical conditions (e.g., Tennen, Affleck, Armeli, & Carni, 2000).

Who Adjusts Course?

As has become clear, many people enjoy considerable social and occupational success, good heath, and general satisfaction in middle adulthood; many others, however, will be less fortunate. This means, too, that while some people will stay on the same course, others will feel the need for change. There are many reasons a person may choose to change. Block (1971) studied changers and non-changers among children growing up in the Berkeley, California area, who were part of the Berkeley Guidance and Oakland Growth Studies. His focus was on individuals whose personalities remained stable over a 15-year span from adolescence to adulthood, versus those who changed over the same period. Personality was assessed with the California Q-Sort. Recall that the technique employs about 100 statements about a person, which are ranked from most to least applicable to a person. Q-Sorts were completed at adolescence and at adulthood.

Block found that stable individuals of both sexes were more intellectually, emotionally, and socially successful as adolescents than the changers, and also better adjusted. It seems as if consistent individuals stay the same in part because they have good ego-control, and that permits them to traverse society's requirements in productive ways.

Table 12-3: Accomplishments of the Famous at Older Ages*	
Name	The Accomplishment
James Earl Carter at 70	U.S. President. After presidency brokered four-month ceasefire between Bosnian Muslims and Serbs and secured pledges to resume peace negotiations.
Cecil B. DeMille at 74	Produced and directed *The 10 Commandments.*
Nelson Mandela at 75	After release from life sentence in prison, won presidential election against F. W. de Klerk in South Africa, and led nation to a new peaceful era.
John H. Glenn, Jr. at 77	First American to orbit the earth, later, a U.S. Senator. Then, blasted off as payload specialist on the space shuttle *Discovery.*
Betty Friedan at 79	At age 42 wrote *The Feminine Mystique*, which helped launch the women's movement. Recently wrote a memoir entitled *Life so far.*
Giuseppe Verdi at 79	Wrote the opera *Falstaff.*
Akira Kurosawa at 80	Director of many well-known films, including *Dreams.*
Benjamin Franklin at 81	Helped to draft the United States Declaration of Independence.
Agatha Christie at 84	Prolific mystery novelist and playwright. Wrote the novel, *Curtain* one year before death.
Vladimir Horowitz at 85	Concert pianist who continued performing in concert until his death.
Duncan MacLean at 90	Athlete who ran 200 meters in 40 seconds.
Frank Lloyd Wright at 91	Architect who designed and completed the Guggenheim Museum.

*From Papalia et al. (2002, pp. 223-224); Wallechinsky & Wallace (1995).

In contrast, changers change for a variety of reasons (Caspi & Bem, 1990, p. 557). Some changers may appear to change more simply because they were more immature to begin with, and their change was a reflection of undergoing more maturation than the rest of the (presumably more mature) sample. That is, they may have needed more time to build up a better-controlled, better-adjusted personality.

A second reason people may change is the pressure of social norms. Many of the changers in the Block study had personalities that, according to various measures, were rather unpleasant to be around. It seems likely that those around such unpleasant individuals put pressure on them over time to change in a more socially desirable direction. On the other hand, that cannot explain all the change, because many changers remained rather unpleasant, if different, as adults.

A third reason people may appear to change is that, although they are mostly the same, society views them differently. For example, some women who changed in Block's study became adults between 1945 and 1960, when they were rated by others around them as rebellious and poorly adjusted. The women's movement intervened in the late 1960s, and by later adulthood these women were considered better adjusted, although still unconventional and rebellious. It is quite possible that these rebels may have been better adjusted later because society had changed the definition of a well-adjusted woman. Indeed, it seems likely that these women were the ones who participated in the women's movement and changed how society treated women.

Helson's Typology of Growth

People continue to grow psychologically, whether they stay on a consistent path or make changes in their lives. Two dimensions along which this growth may occur are in peoples' **Adaptive Functioning** and in their **Personal Growth** (Helson & Wink, 1987). Adaptive functioning concerns the sense of working well on practical, pragmatic aspects of life, with a focus on achieving in life. Personal growth involves a more internal development that may occur apart from social norms of success and failure.

People can be classified into four groups according to whether they are above or below average in the pursuit of adaptive functioning and personal growth (Ryff, 1989). That leads to four groups: **Achiever**, **Conserver**, **Seeker**, or **Depleted**, illustrated in Table 12-4.

Helson and Srivastava (2001) studied 111 graduates of Mills College, a private women's college in Oakland, California, from the classes of 1958 and 1960. The women were divided into the four groups based on the results of psychological testing employing the Ryff well-being scale. Most of the women were Caucasian, reflecting the ethnic makeup of the college at the time, most had fathers who were professionals and mothers who were homemakers.

Table 12-4: Groups Varying in Personal Growth and Environmental Mastery

		Environmental Mastery	
		High	**Low**
Personal Growth	**High**	Achievers	Seekers
	Low	Conservers	Depleteds

Adapted from Helson & Srivastava (2001).

Achievers want it all: They want to be high in both the visible signs of success and in inward psychological growth. Conservers, on the other hand, are happy to have the visible signs of success without necessarily seeking personal growth. Seekers desire high personal growth, but do not necessarily seek high mastery of the environment. Finally, Depleteds have stopped searching for growth of any type and are drifting along.

The four groups were examined on a variety of measures including the California Q-Sort, measures of maturity, emotionality, and social and intellectual competence. Figure 12-3 shows some of the findings. Achievers are satisfied with their jobs and unconventional in their social adjustment. Conservers are high in life satisfaction although they are conventional and less creative at work. Seekers have average life and job satisfaction but are highly creative at work. The Depleted group's most noticeable characteristic is their dramatically low life satisfaction—far lower than any other group.

Helson and Srivastava also presented examples of several women who characterized the membership of each of the four groups. A few highlights from three of their lives are shown in Table 12-5.

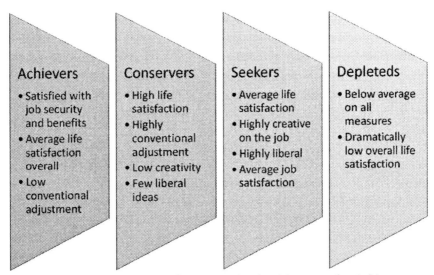

Figure 12-3 *Levels of Life Satisfaction and Other Measures for Achiever, Conserver, Seeker, and Depleted Personality Groups* Interpretation of z-scores from Helson & Srivastava (2001, Table 5, p. 1005).

Table 12-5: Life Course Examples of a Conserver, Seeker, and Achiever*

Cathy: Conserver	Sarah: Seeker	Andrea: Achiever
*Married young to man approved by family *Supported his career problems by going to work in people-oriented job *Quit after 20 years of high competence because people were disrespectful to her *Much sought out by church & community groups	*Described by interviewer as unusually perceptive, but with tendency to disengage abruptly *Dropped out of graduate school when unexpectedly became pregnant *Worked at becoming more sociable *In helping profession, where must work around bureaucracy *Hopes to write great American novel	*Did not want to marry or have children *Went straight to professional school from college *Continued career progress but began to drink heavily *Overcame problem with great determination at age 40 *Married a charming and successful man, created good relations with his children *Retired, and had second career as volunteer

*Drawn from Helson & Srivastava (2001, pp. 1006-1007).

Where Is Personality Headed in the Concluding Parts of Life?

The last developmental period to examine extends roughly from late middle age to the end of life. Increasingly, thanks to modern medicine and healthier lifestyles, this can itself be a long period during which a person may begin a new career, get married or remarried, and enjoy many activities. To treat it as a single stage is, therefore, more of a necessity dictated by keeping this book at a reasonable length, than a true reflection of what these years can mean.

That said, a person in later adulthood is apt to reflect on himself and what he has accomplished: He asks what became of his childhood dreams, what he has contributed to the world, and what he has received in return. Some individuals arrive at good answers to their questions—answers that promote their enthusiasm and hope. Still others look back with a more mixed sense of their progress: They may feel committed to some old choices, but need to need to make changes other areas of the lives to go on well. Yet another group has by now become so defeated and overwhelmed that its members see few opportunities to go on in a satisfied way (Levinson, 1978).

Many of the individual and social choices that a person has made earlier in her life may continue to affect the aging individual. This period is one that is often marked by loss of others—of relatives and friends one's own age and those older and younger as well. Those who have established good coping skills, personal senses of well-being, and more positive social support networks will be able to face such losses with greater equanimity than others (e.g., Bonanno, Wortman, & Lehman, 2002; Wallace, Bisconti, & Bergeman, 2002). For example, in a prospective study of the elderly, those who were more psychologically healthy in the sense of experiencing positive affect and higher well-being before the loss of a spouse recovered from the loss more quickly. Interestingly, those who were in difficult marriages before the loss of the spouse also improved after the loss. Others, however, who showed poor adjustment before the loss continued in that state afterward (Bonanno, Wortman, & Lehman, 2002).

Optimal Personality and Values

If we believe that the individual can become better—or even enter into an optimal state, what would that state be like? What would the now mature person like to look back on during these concluding years? Throughout the ages, philosophers and theologians have recommended ways for people to develop their personalities. In the present time, too, psychologists have made various suggestions. Today's psychological recommendations are, of course, every bit as value-laden as were those of the earlier philosophers and theologians. Most people accept and seek some shared values in their lives, however. They believe in such values as truth, beauty, respect for others, love, and mercy—and they would not entertain recommendations for a good life that did not take such values into account.

Good Functioning

The functional perspective views an individual as psychologically healthy if he or she is able to perform basic tasks necessary to a productive life. That is, a person should possess certain personality characteristics—emotional stability, the capacity for at least average coping, freedom from too much egocentrism—that are basics for good interpersonal relations. The **Diagnostic and Statistical Manual of the American Psychiatric Association (DSM)** is the reference work that assigns legal psychiatric diagnoses in the United States. According to the DSM, unhealthy individuals typically suffer from "dysfunction in social or occupational functioning." (American Psychiatric Association, 2013). Presumably, by contrast, healthy people are able to function in both social and work spheres: to love and to work, as Freud put it. This view of personal mental health as freedom from illness may seem rather minimalist. On the other hand, one of the advantages of this kind of approach is that, so long as one is free from a disorder, a person can be any sort of a positive person he or she wants to be.

Idealized (and Devalued) Views

Another set of positions concerning the healthy individual are those expressed in the folk conceptions. Folk conceptions may involve such ideas as "always courageous" or "always rational" or "always generous." Such conduct, however, isn't very likely—and may not always be desirable. Most people do engage in repeated mistakes of one type or another or have weaknesses in one area or another. As one investigator of very healthy individuals put it, "…we could not use perfection as a basis for selection, since no subject was perfect." (Maslow, 1970, p. 151). Take the example of "thinking rationally." On the one hand, much of our educational folk-wisdom says that a good person must reason carefully through problems. On the other hand, research in cognition and other areas of psychology tells us persuasively that people often think heuristically—that is, according to tricks and simplifications—rather than rationally. With the assistance of education and training, it seems reasonable to expect a healthy person to think rationally in certain circumstances when she or he desires to, but to expect consistent rational thought of anyone would be unrealistic.

Adding Strengths: Positive Psychology

Rather than examine the mere absence of psychopathology or meeting unrealistic goals, some psychologists have sought to identify specific positive strengths that a person can develop and have created a new field called **positive psychology**. Positive psychology is a term for the study of the positive aspects of human nature. Members of the movement pursue a taxonomy of human strengths, and an understanding of how to enhance those strengths and what those strengths lead to (e.g., Seligman & Csikszentmihalyi, 2001).

We have examined a number of these positive attributes throughout this textbook—positive affect, optimism, self-control, for example—and there are indeed positive things to say about each. One of the issues, however, is the sheer number of positive possibilities. For example, a recent handbook of positive psychology included over 55 chapters—with 43 chapters devoted to specific individual positive strengths. These included authenticity, benefit finding, compassion, creativity, flow, gratitude, goal-setting, hope, humility…and so on through uniqueness-seeking and wisdom (e.g., Snyder & Lopez, 2002, pp. xii-xiii). A few examples of these strengths are described in Table 12-6.

Perhaps we should simply be thankful there exist so many human strengths. The number of strengths does raise the question, however, of which strengths we should focus on. In fact, if we examine a particular strength in greater detail, we may discover it can sometimes be a weakness.

Strengths in Context

For example, a central positive trait in this pantheon of strengths is optimism (e.g., Norem & Chang, 2001; Peterson & Seligman, 1987; Scheier & Carver, 1985). Certainly people with an optimistic attitude will do well facing many circumstances: trying to make a sale, win an election, and persevere in the face of illness. Yet other psychologists are concerned that positive psychology—and Americans in general—create a "tyranny of positivity" in which positive qualities are recklessly elevated to levels of admiration they do not deserve and anything negative is uninvited (Held, 2002, pp. 966, 974). The reflexive labeling of optimism as a strength may be misguided unless one knows something about the type of optimism, the individual's personality, and the sorts of challenges a person faces. For example, among coronary heart patients, optimism considered as a whole has no effect on exercise. Only after researchers distinguish between optimism as realistic hope versus as naïve unrealistic beliefs are instructive effects obtained. Naïve optimists are already optimistic about their future health. For that reason, they have *less* motivation to engage in an exercise program (Davidson & Prkachin, 1997; Epstein & Meier, 1989). Naïve optimists endanger their own health with their relaxed attitudes; only realistic optimists are likely to exercise—which will enhance their likelihood of survival.

In other circumstances, something that looks like a drawback may serve as a strength in some personalities. We saw in Chapter 10, for example, that defensive pessimists calm themselves—and improve their performance—by beginning with the expectation that they will perform poorly at a task.

Table 12-6: Eight of the Many Strengths Studied by Positive Psychologists

Strength	Description
Subjective Well-Being	A person's positive emotional and intellectual evaluation that he or she is experiencing a good life, that that he or she is likable, and that the life he or she lives is satisfying (Diener, Lucas, & Oishi, 2002, p. 63).
Resilience	A person's capacity to adjust and adapt positively in the face of significant challenges, bad luck, and risk (Masten & Reed, 2002, p. 74).
Flow	A person's complete and total absorption in life projects and the things one does (Nakamura & Csikszentmihalyi, 2002, p. 89).
Creativity	A person's independent, nonconformist perspective, coupled with wide interests and openness to new experiences, and cognitive flexibility (Simonton, 2002, p. 192).
Authenticity	A competent sense of knowing and being oneself that stabilizes one's sense of self in social interactions (Swann & Pelham, 2002, p. 366).
Humility	A person's ability to accurately assess his or her strengths and weaknesses, to acknowledge his or her limitations in social contexts, and to de-emphasize her or his own self in social settings (Tangney, 2002, p. 411).
Empathy and Altruism	Empathy is an emotional response directed at another person, which leads one to want to help the other. Altruism leads to actions that benefit the other (Batson, et al., 2002, p. 485).
Morality	A true concern with the well-being of others leading to the development of principles of good behavior and one's identification with moral groups (Schulman, 2002, pp. 499-450).

Optimal Types

The idea that we must deal with strengths and weakness in context has given rise to the notion that a more powerful way to understand positive people is to understand them as a complete type so as to take into account the interaction of strengths and weaknesses within the individual. Abraham Maslow sought to understand very healthy individuals. This was a considerable innovation in the 1950s when he began his work, for at that time, psychology was heavily focused on the pathological and disease models of personality.

Maslow first tried to study healthy people by combing literature and drama for examples, but could find few fictional characters who seemed healthy enough. In contrast, various descriptions of psychological health in folk wisdom appeared too demanding for real people to follow. He next examined his students, but found that they were too young to be considered fully developed. For these reasons, he ended up studying a diverse group of people including a number selected from among personal acquaintances and friends, and a number from among public and historical figures (Maslow, 1954/1970, Chapter 11).

Among the public and historical figures he found were Abraham Lincoln in his later years, Thomas Jefferson, Albert Einstein, Eleanor Roosevelt, Jane Addams, William James, and Baruch Spinoza. He also included 16 younger people who "seemed to be developing" in the direction of self-actualization, including G.W. Carver, Eugene V. Debs, Albert Schweitzer, and Goethe. Maslow labeled these individuals **self-actualized**. By this Maslow meant that these individuals had managed to develop their own inner selves in a true and healthy fashion. Maslow concluded that these especially healthy individuals possessed certain core characteristics in common. These characteristics are listed in Table 12-7.

Table 12-7: Maslow's View of the Self-Actualized Person*

Characteristic	Further Description
A. Efficient Reality Perception	Intimate and accurate contact with reality
B. Acceptance	Acceptance of even those things many find unacceptable
C. Spontaneity	Ability to do things at the spur of the moment, have fun
D. Problem Centering	Center lives around important tasks to be solved
E. Detachment	Deal well with solitude, view things independently of what others believe
F. Autonomy	Independent of others around them
G. Freshness Of Appreciation	Can appreciate simple beauties as if they had never seen them before
H. Peak Experiences	Experience intense, mystical moments of appreciation for the world
I. Gemeinschaftsgefühl	Interested in helping the world
J. Special Relationships	Have relationships so intimate that they are like those among children
K. Democratic Character	Appreciate others for who they are (their personalities) not what they are (race, religion, etc.)
L. Means-Ends	Value both means and ends to a problem
M. Unhostile Sense Of Humor	Sense of humor is philosophical rather than involving putting others down
N. Creativity	Creative in all areas of life, including social relations
O. A Few Faults	May be too trusting or tolerant of others, or seem harsh when they decide others do not warrant their attentions

*Summary drawn from Maslow (1970, Chapter 11).

According to Maslow, the self-actualized individual is governed most of all by an intense appreciation of and connection to reality. These individuals correctly and accurately perceive and understand many aspects of the human condition—including the painful ones. They are better able to distinguish between people who are real versus those who present false selves. They are also better able to distinguish real from phony or exploitative feeling in the arts and music.

Reality, of course, can often be painful and uncertain. The self-actualized person can accept the unpleasant motivations of people, the realities of nature, and their own limitations. When they themselves have done something wrong, they seek to do better next time, and, if necessary, to make amends, rather than succumbing to crippling guilt or shame. They also accept aspects of themselves, such as sexual needs or lusts, as part of being human. Such individuals are therefore low in defensiveness and artificiality. Their lack of defensiveness, in turn, allows them to frequently feel spontaneous. Although they often appear to follow social rules, they follow them so as to not offend others rather than out of a genuine conviction. These individuals are centered on a particular problem or life task that they try to fulfill. For example, the great 20th-century physicist Albert Einstein was singularly focused on understanding the laws of the universe. When he was offered a highly expensive psychotherapy at no cost—so as to reveal the workings of his mind for the scientific community, he respectfully declined, noting that he was so committed to his pursuits in physics that he had never much thought about himself.

Because such individuals see things so much more clearly than those around them, they have a sense of being apart from others. Fortunately, they are well able to tolerate being alone. What stops their autonomous pursuits from becoming unpleasant is their ability to continuously perceive things with freshness. In nature, every sunset is as lovely as the first they saw, every moon as awe-inspiring. They have a particularly intense relationship with sexual experience, which may feel almost like a religious experience to them.

Often, in fact, their internal conscious experience becomes so intense and disorganized that they feel themselves merge with a sort of cosmic consciousness. In this **peak experience**, they feel one with all of life. Like most people who experience this feeling, it may last for just a little while. But perhaps because of the self-actualized individual's lack of defensiveness, they may enter into peak experiences as many as five or six times a day—as opposed to, perhaps, once every few months or few years for the average person.

Self-actualized people can be identified in part by their philosophical, unhostile sense of humor and their creativity. Hostile humor includes insult humor and violent humor and puts oneself or another person down. **Philosophical humor**, on the other hand, draws attention to some oddity of being human, without putting it down. The comedian Steven Wright often draws humor from such oddities in brief observations delivered in a very plain tone, as in, "A lot of people are afraid of heights. Not me—I'm afraid of widths," and, "I have a large seashell collection, which I keep scattered on beaches all over the world," and "I bought some batteries but they weren't included so I had to buy them again" (recounted in Brown, 1998, pp. 144, 255). Jerry Seinfeld is philosophical, as well as he observes and comments on human nature:

> Candy is the only reason you want to live when you're a kid. And you have your favorite candies that you love. Kids actually believe they can distinguish between twenty-one versions of pure sugar. When I was kid, I could taste the difference between different color M&M's. I thought the red was heartier, more of a main course M&M. And the light brown was a mellower, kind of after-dinner M. (Jerry Seinfeld, quoted in Brown, 1998, p. 39)

To the above is also added a capacity for creativity, along with a sense of **Gemeinschaftsgefühl** (social feeling). These individuals have a strong identification and sympathy with humanity that leads them to care for and try to help others.

If the above seems too good to be true, Maslow listed a few faults of the self-actualized as well. These individuals may often seem aloof and even cold because they are not interested in daily conversation or party-going. In addition, they can be ruthless if they find someone isn't living up to important standards. One self-actualized person quickly cut himself off from a business partner who he found out was dishonest. He refused to have any further contact with the man, even though the two had known each other for many years.

Carol Gilligan's Critique

Maslow examined self-actualized women and men. But he stressed autonomy almost to the exclusion of interconnectedness. Carol Gilligan has enriched depictions of healthy individuals with an eye to the unique ways that women attain psychological health. As she puts it, "…women bring to the life cycle a different point of view and order human experience in terms of different priorities" (Gilligan, 1982, p. 22). Gilligan studied healthy professional women and found that they more often described themselves in terms of relationships than did men. For example, a doctor in training recounted:

> …I see myself in a nurturing role, maybe not right now, but…as a physician, as a mother…It's hard for me to think of myself without thinking about other people around me that I'm giving to. (Gilligan, 1982, pp. 158-159)

Another woman described her hard-working and responsible professional life, and then went on to recount that:

> …The other very important aspect of my life is my husband and trying to make his life easier and trying to help him out. (Gilligan, 1982, pp. 158-159)

Such remarks and commentaries help Gilligan illustrate the point that for both women and men, self-actualization may involve autonomy at times, but also interconnectedness and intimate relations with others.

A Final Life Review

Erik Erikson brings his discussion of the various ages of a human being to a close with a discussion of the final passage of personality development: The stage of ego-integrity versus ego despair. Despair can be a consequence of a person's bad decisions, or, sometimes, a consequence of good decisions that have been thwarted by an impervious or hostile environment. A person with past regrets, who has not come to terms with them, tends to have lower well-being at this time of life (Torges, Stewart, & Miner-Rubino, 2005).

The more vibrant, hopeful end of life, however, involves something Erikson called ego-integrity. The person with ego-integrity has mostly come to terms with his or her regrets, and goes far beyond this: He or she possesses a deep acceptance of life. The individual's personal integrity permits a transcendence of the self that reaches out to all humanity. Although this end stage is full of self-respect and self-love, it is no longer as self-centered as before:

> It is a post-narcissistic love of the human ego—not of the self—as an experience which conveys some world order and spiritual sense, no matter how dearly paid for. It is the acceptance of one's one and only life cycle as something that had to be and that, by necessity, permitted of no substitutions: it thus means a new, a different love of one's parents. It is a comradeship with the ordering ways of distant times and different pursuits…the possessor of integrity is ready to defend the dignity of his own life style…he knows that an individual life is the accidental coincidence of but one life cycle with but one segment of history; and that for him all human integrity stands or falls with the one style of integrity of which he partakes…In such final consolidation, death loses its sting. (Erikson, 1950/1963, p. 168)

Reviewing Chapter 12

Chapter 12 takes you through a person's development from young adulthood to the end of life. First considered is the legacy of childhood on the life of the developing young adult. Many attributes, particularly traits and the degree to which a person is undercontrolled, controlled, or overcontrolled, carry over into adult life, although there is room for change. During young and middle adulthood, the growing person attempts to find intimacy in relationships, and ultimately a stable home life. The person also seeks out a good occupational fit, and, ultimately, work success. Such searches may continue into later adulthood, or begin anew.

At the same time, later adulthood is a time for reflection and renewed meaning-making in one's life. Throughout the life span, many individuals aim toward a healthier or optimal version of themselves. This involves freeing themselves of psychopathology to the greatest extent possible, adding strengths, and creating an overall personality that is the best possible for the individual.

Questions About "What Is the Nature of Adult Development?"

1. <u>Questions of Adult Development and the Transition to Adulthood:</u> Mahatma Gandhi represents one image of adult development. In what ways is his life typical, in what ways is it exceptional? According to Erikson and others, what are the main issues faced by the young adult? The extended life span influences adult personality development by making it more critical. How does increased longevity influence a person's sense of control?

2. <u>The Child Parent to the Adult:</u> A great deal of personality growth and development has taken place in childhood, including the coalescence of temperament into traits, and the development of substantial models of the self and the world. What would this lead you to expect about childhood bases of personality?

3. <u>Childhood Influences on Temperament and Traits; Models of the Self and World:</u> Given that childhood personality carries over to adulthood, in specific, what can you say about the influence of childhood personality traits on adulthood? What about mental models developed in childhood?

4. <u>The Stability of Traits:</u> Findings in the middle 1970s indicated that personality traits are relatively set for the individual by young adulthood. There are, however, individual changes, as well as group changes in the overall level of traits. How do the Big Five personality traits, for example, change over adulthood?

Questions About "What Are Young Adults Like?"

5. <u>In Search of Intimacy:</u> One of the tasks of young adulthood is to find a partner with whom to be intimate. What are some of the ways young adults do this? How are men's and women's strategies for impressing their potential partners the same or different? To whom are they attracted?

6. <u>In Search of Good Work:</u> Another task of young adulthood is finding a good occupation. What are some of the criteria people use for finding a good job? What variables contribute to occupational satisfaction?

Questions About "How Does the Individual Traverse Middle Adulthood?"

7. <u>Finding Occupational Success:</u> Some people find more occupational success than others. What are some of the personality variables that lead to success across occupations? How does positivity enter into job success? What is necessary for high levels of achievement?

8. <u>Staying Married:</u> For those people who have been able to partner, the task of middle adulthood is to maintain the relationship. Here, too, personality traits and other variables can contribute. What are some of the personality traits that tend to preserve marriages; which traits might place marriages in danger?

9. <u>Personality and Health:</u> It turns out that although people with high negative affect (e.g., Neuroticism) complain more about their health, there are few objective health differences between such individuals and more positive people. Personality traits do, however, enter into the health equation. What findings in particular stand out?

10. <u>Helson's Typology of Change:</u> People who have trouble early in their lives are more inclined to change than others. Helson argued that there were two dimensions, of Personal Mastery and Personal Growth. What four groups of changers does that theory create?

Questions About "Where Is Personality Headed in the Concluding Parts of Life?"

11. <u>Good Functioning:</u> One approach to psychological health is to identify what is required for good functioning. Do you know how Freud referred to the capacity to function well? It also means being free of mental illness.

12. <u>Adding Strengths; Strengths in Context:</u> Another approach to psychological health is to identify a number of potential strengths personality can take on, for example, acceptance, caring, compassion, and optimism have all been identified as strengths. Are there other such strengths you can identify? When is optimism not a strength? When is its opposite—pessimism—a strength?

13. <u>Optimal Types; Optimal Types in Context:</u> Maslow suggested that the self-actualized person represented an optimal type. This individual had excellent reality perception, acceptance of the reality of the world, and freshness of perception. What other attributes did the self-actualized individual possess? What did Carol Gilligan believe was an alternative strength to Maslow's idea of autonomy?

Chapter 12 Glossary

Terms in Order of Appearance

Passionate Love: A strong feeling for a potential or actual life partner involving intense arousal and longing for joining with the other.

Companionate Love: A caring and desire for another person with whom our lives intertwine. It emphasizes intimacy and concern for the other.

Assortative Mating: The tendency to find a mate who is similar to oneself on one or more dimensions.

Complimentary Selection: The tendency to find a mate who is different from oneself on one or more dimensions.

Realistic Occupations: Those jobs or careers dealing with work that must respond to definite requirements of land or objects (e.g., farming, mechanic).

Investigative Occupations: Those jobs or careers involving the investigation of information, or exploration of new ideas or possibilities.

Artistic Occupations: Those jobs or careers stressing communication, creativity, art, and entertainment.

Social Occupations: Those jobs or careers involving working with people, including social workers, managers, and therapists.

Enterprising Occupations: Those jobs or careers involving the influence of others, including salespeople, politicians, and entrepreneurs.

Conventional Occupations: Those jobs or careers involving work with numbers and letters, including secretaries, bookkeepers, accountants, and engineers.

Lotka-Price Law: A law of productivity of the members of a given field that states that the square root of the total will account for half the productivity.

Type A Personality: A personality type that emphasizes time pressure, competitiveness, achievement striving, impatience, and hostility, and that has been related to heart disease and high professional attainment.

Adaptive Functioning: The degree to which one can solve the practical, pragmatic problems of life.

Personal Growth: The degree to which one can attain inner understanding and wisdom apart from the social norms of success and failure.

Achievers: An adult developmental group described by interest in both practical attainments and personal improvement.

Conservers: An adult developmental group described by interest in practical attainment.

Seekers: An adult developmental group described by interest in personal and spiritual self-development.

Depleteds: An adult developmental group that is no longer seeking further goals in life.

Diagnostic and Statistical Manual (DSM): A manual of psychiatric diagnoses published by the American Psychiatric Association and providing the descriptions of mental disorders recognized by law in the United States.

Positive Psychology: A scientific movement to identify the positive strengths in individual's personalities.

Self-Actualized: The state of a person who is able to develop his or her innermost self in a healthy fashion that represents, expresses, and satisfies his or her true needs and characteristics.

Peak Experience: An altered state of consciousness in which one's awareness appears to merge with a cosmic consciousness, and an individual feels at one with the surrounding environment or universe.

Philosophical Humor: A type of humor employed by the self-actualized that gently pokes fun at the oddities and commonalities of the human experience.

Gemeinschaftsgefühl: An attitude of caring concern for the rest of humanity that leads to a desire to help others in one's life projects. Considered to be a quality of the self-actualized person.

REFERENCES

Abramson, L. Y., Alloy, L. B., & Metalsky, G. 1995). Hopelessness depression. In G. Buchanan & M. Seligman (Eds.). *Explanatory style (pp. 113-134).* Hillsdale, NJ: Erlbaum.

Adams, G. R., & Fitch, S. A. (1983). Psychological environments of university departments: Effects on college students' identity status and ego-stage development. *Journal of Personality and Social Psychology, 44,* 1266-1275.

Adams, G. R., Shea, J., & Fitch, S. A. (1979). Toward the development of an objective assessment of ego-identity status. *Journal of Youth and Adolescence, 8,* 223-237.

Adams, H. E., Wright, L. W., & Lohr, B. A. (1996). Is homophobia associated with homosexual arousal? *Journal of Abnormal Psychology, 105,* 440-445.

Adcock, N. V., Adcock, C. J., & Walkey, F. H. (1974). Basic dimensions of personality. *International Review of Applied Psychology, 23,* 131-137.

Adler, A. (1930). Individual psychology. In C. Murchison (Ed.). *Psychologies of 1930 (pp. 395-405).* Worcester, MA: Clark University Press.

Adler, A. (1958). *What life should mean to you.* New York: G.P. Putnam's Sons. [Original work published 1931].

Aiken, L. R. (2003). Psychological testing and assessment (11th ed.). Boston: Allyn & Bacon.

Ainsworth, M. D. S. (1989). Attachments beyond infancy. *American Psychologist, 44,* 709-716.

Ainsworth, M. D. S., Blehar, M. C., Waters, E., & Wall, S. (1978). *Patterns of attachment: A psychological study of the strange situation.* Hillsdale, NJ: Lawrence Erlbaum.

Alderfer, C. P. (1969). An empirical test of a new theory of human needs. *Organizational Behavior & Human Performance, 4,* 142-175.

Alderfer, C. (1972). *Existence, relatedness, & growth.* New York: Free Press.

Alexander, F. (1942). *Our age of unreason.* Philadelphia: Lippencott.

Allen, J. B.; Kenrick, D. T.; Linder, D. E. (1989). Arousal and attraction: A response-facilitation alternative to misattribution and negative-reinforcement models. *Journal of Personality and Social Psychology, 57,* 261-270.

Allen, M. J. & Yen, W. M. (1979). Introduction to measurement theory. Monterey, CA: BrooksCole Publishing.

Allport, G.W. (1937). *Personality: A psychological interpretation.* New York: Holt, Rinehart, & Winston.

Allport, G. W. (1968). *The person in psychology: Selected essays by Gordon W. Allport.* Boston: Beacon Press.

Allport, G.W., & Odbert, H.S. (1936). Trait names: A psycho-lexical study. *Psychological Monographs, 47.* No. 211.

Allport, G. W., & Vernon, P. E. (1931). A test for personal values. *Journal of Abnormal and Social Psychology, 26,* 231-248.

Almada, S. G., Zonderman, A. B., Shekelle, R. B., Dyer, A. R., Daviglus, M. L., Costa, P. T., & Stamler, J. (1991). Neuroticism and cynicism and risk of death in middle-aged men: The Western Electric Study. *Psychosomatic Medicine, 53,* 165-175.

Amabile, T. M. (1996). *Creativity in context.* Boulder, CO: Westview.

Amato, P. R., & Keith, B. (1991). Parental divorce and the well-being of children: A meta-analysis. *Psychological Bulletin, 110,* 26-46.

American Psychiatric Association (2013) Diagnostic and Statistical Manual of Mental Disorders, 5th Edition: DSM-5.

Ammerman, R. T., Lynch, K. G., Donovan, J. E., Martin, C. S., & Maisto, S. A. (2001). Constructive thinking in adolescents with substance abuse disorders. *Psychology of Addictive Behaviors, 15,* 89-96.

Andersen, S.M., & Cole, S.W. (1990). "Do I know you?" The role of significant others in general social perception. *Journal of Personality and Social Psychology, 59,* 384-399.

Anderson, C. A. (1983). Imagination and expectation: The effect of imagining behavioral scripts on personal influences. *Journal of Personality & Social Psychology, 45,* 293-305.

Anderson, D. D., Rosenfeld, P., & Cruikschank, L. (1994). An exercise for explicating and critiquing students' implicit personality theories. *Teaching of Psychology, 21,* 174-177.

Anderson, J. R. (1980). Cognitive psychology and its implications. San Francisco: Freeman.

Andreasen, N. C., Flaum, M., Swayze, V. W., & O'Leary, D. S. (1993). Intelligence and brain structure in normal individuals. *American Journal of Psychiatry, 150,* 130-134.

Anshel, M. H., Williams, L. R. T., & Williams, S. M. (2000). Coping style following acute stress in competitive sport. *Journal of Social Psychology, 140,* 751-773.

Argyle, M. (1987). *The psychology of happiness.* New York: Methuen.

Arnett, J. J. (2000). Emerging Adulthood. A theory of development from the late teens through the twenties. *American Psychologist, 55,* 469-480.

Aronoff, J. (1967). *Psychological needs and cultural systems: A case study.* Princeton, NJ: Van Nostrand.

Aronson, J, Lustina, M. J. Good, C. (1999). When White men can't do math: Necessary and sufficient factors in stereotype threat. *Journal of Experimental Social Psychology, 35,* 29-46.

Arnheim, R. (1974). *Art and visual perception: A psychology of the creative eye (The New Version).* Berkeley, CA: The University of California Press.

Asher, S. R., & Rose, A. J. (1997). Promoting children's social-emotional adjustment with peers. In P. Salovey, & D. J. Sluyter (Eds.). *Emotional development and emotional intelligence.* New York: Basic Books.

Ashton, M. C., Jackson, D. N., Helmes, E., & Paunonen, S. V. (1998). *Joint factor analysis of the Personality Research Form and the Jackson Personality Inventory: Comparisons with the Big Five, 32,* 243-250.

Atwater, L. E. (1992). Beyond cognitive ability: Improving the prediction of performance. *Journal of Business and Psychology, 7,* 27-44.

Averill, J. R. (1992). The structural bases of emotional behavior: A metatheoretical analysis. *Review of Personality and Social Psychology, 13,* 1-24.

Averill, J. R., Ekman, P., Panksepp, J., Scherer, K. R., Schweder, R. A., Davidson, R. J. (1994). Are there *basic emotions?* In P. Ekman & R. J. Davison (Eds.). *The nature of emotion: Fundamental questions.* New York: Oxford University Press.

Averill, J. R., & Thomas-Knowles, C. (1991). Emotional creativity. In K. T. Strongman (Ed.). *International review of studies on emotion (Vol 1, pp. 269-299).* London: Wiley.

Ax, A.F. (1953). The physiological differentiation between fear and anger in humans. *Psychosomatic Medicine, 15*, 433-442.

Baars, B. J. & McGovern, K. (1994). Consciousness. *Encyclopaedia of Human Behavior, 1*, 687-699.

Bacon, Francis (2001). *The advancement of learning.* G. W. Kitchin (Ed.). Philadelphia, PA: Paul Dry Books. [Original work published 1861].

Bailey, K. G. (1987). *Human paleopsychology applications to aggression.* Hillsdale, NJ: Erlbaum.

Bakke, E. W. (1940). *Citizens without work.* New Haven, CT: Yale University Press.

Bajema, C.J. (1968). A note on the interrelations among intellectual ability, educational attainment, and occupational achievement: A follow-up study of a male Kalamazoo public school population. *Sociology of education, 41*, 317-319.

Balmary, M. (1979). Psychoanalyzing psychoanalysis: Freud and the hidden fault of the father. Baltimore: Johns Hopkins Press.

Banaji, M.R., & Greenwald, A.G. (1994). Implicit attitudes and unconscious prejudice. In M.P. Zanna & J.M. Olson (Eds.). *Psychology of prejudice: The Ontario Symposium on Personality and Social Psychology, 7*, 55-76. Hillsdale, NJ: Lawrence Erlbaum Associates.

Bandura, A. (1977). *Social learning theory.* Englewood Cliffs, NJ: Prentice Hall.

Bandura, A. (1978). The self system in reciprocal determinism. *American Psychologist, 33*, 344-358.

Bandura, A. (1984). Representing personal determinants in causal structures. *Psychological Review, 91*, 508-511.

Bandura, A. (1986). *Social foundations of thought and action.* Englewood Cliffs, NJ: Prentice-Hall.

Bandura, A. (1999). Self-efficacy: Toward a unifying theory of behavioral change. In R. F. Baumeister (Ed.) *The self in social psychology: Key readings in social psychology (pp. 285-298).* Philadelphia, PA: Psychology Press.

Bandura, A. & Walters, R. H. (1963). *Social learning and personality development.* New York: Holt, Rinehart, & Winston.

Bargh, J. A. (1997). The automaticity of everyday life. In R. S. Wyer, Jr. (Ed.). *Advances in social cognition (Vol 10, pp. 1-61).* Mahwah, NJ: Erlbaum.

Bargh, J. A. & Chartrand, T. L. (1999). The unbearable automaticity of being. *American Psychologist, 54*, 462-479.

Bargh, J., Chen, M., & Burrows, L. (1996). Automaticity of social behavior: Direct effects of trait construct and stereotype activation on action. *Journal of Personality and Social Psychology, 71*, 230-244.

Barrick, M. R., & Mount, M. K. (1991). The Big Five personality dimensions and job performance: A meta-analysis. *Personnel Psychology, 44*, 1-26.

Bartlett, F.C. (1932). *Remembering: An experimental and social study.* Cambridge: Cambridge University Press.

Baruss, I. (1986-7) Metanalysis of definitions of consciousness. *Imagination, Cognition, and Personality, 6*, 321-329].

Bates, T. C., Eysenck, H. J. (1993). Intelligence, inspection time, and decision time. Intelligence, 17, 523-531.

Bateson, G. (1975). Logical categories of learning and communication. In *Steps to an Ecology of Mind.* New York: Ballentine.

Batson, C. D., Ahmad, N., Lishner, D. A., & Tsang, J-A. (2002). Empathy and altruism. In C. R. Snyder & S. J. Lopez, *Handbook of Positive Psychology (pp. 485-498).* New York: Oxford University Press.

Baumann, L. J., & Leventhal, H. (1985). "I can tell when my blood pressure is up, can't I?" *Healthy Psychology, 4*, 203-218.

Baumeister, R. F. (1987). How the self became a historical problem: A psychological review of historical research. *Journal of Personality and Social Psychology, 52,* 163-176.

Baumeister, R. F. (1997). *Evil: Inside human violence and cruelty.* New York: W. H. Freeman and Company.

Baumeister, R. F., & Tice, D. (1994). Editorial. *Dialogue: Society for Personality and Social Psychology, 9, p. 10.*

Baumeister, R. F., Dale, K., & Sommer, K. L. (1998). Freudian defense mechanisms and empirical findings in modern social psychology: Reaction formation, projection, displacement, undoing, isolation, sublimation, and denial. *Journal of Personality, 66*, 1081-1124.

Baumrind, D. (1971). Current patterns of parental authority. *Developmental Psychology Monographs, 4*(1, Pt. 2).

Baumrind, D. (1973). The development of instrumental competence through socialization. In A. D. Pick (Ed.). *Minnesota Symposia on Child Development (Vol. 7).* Minneapolis: University of Minnesota Press.

Beattie, M. (1987). *Codependent no more.* San Francisco: Harper and Row.

Bechger, T. M., Maris, G., Verstralen, H. H., Beguin, A. A. (2003). Using classical test theory in combination with item response theory. *Applied Psychological Measurement, 27*, 319-334.

Beck, A. T. (1967). *Depression: Clinical experimental and theoretical aspects.* New York: Harper & Row.

Becker, E. (1973). *The denial of death.* New York: Free Press.

Bekoff, M., & Goodall, J. (2002). *Minding animals: Awareness, emotions, and heart.* Oxford, UK: Oxford University Press.

Bell, R. A. (1985). Conversational involvement and loneliness. *Communication Monographs, 52*, 217-235.

Bem, D. J., Honorton, C. (1994). Does psi exist? Replicable evidence for an anomalous process of information transfer. Psychological Bulletin, 115, 4-18.

Bem, S. L. (1974). The measurement of psychological androgyny. *Journal of Clinical and Consulting Psychology, 42*, 153-162.

Benassi, V. A., & Fernald, P. S. (1993). Preparing tomorrow's psychologists for careers in academe. *Teaching of Psychology, 20,* 149-155.

Benet-Martínez, V. & Haritatos, J. (2005). Bicultural Identity Integration (BII): Components and Psychosocial Antecedents. *Journal of Personality, 73*, 1015-1050.

Bender, B. G. & Berch, D. B. (1987). Sex chromosome abnormalities: Studies of genetic influences on behavior. *Integrative Psychiatry, 5*, 171-176.

Benedict, R. (1959). *Patterns of Culture.* Boston: Houghton Mifflin.

Bennett, G. K., Seashore, H. G., & Wesman, A. G. (1989). *Differential Aptitude Test (DAT) – Form W (Personnel).* San Antonio, TX: The Psychological Corporation.

Bentler, P. M. (2000). EQS-6 Structural equation program manual. Encino, CA: Multivariate software.

Bentler, P. M., & Newcomb, M. D. (1978). Longitudinal study of marital success and failure. *Journal of Consulting and Clinical Psychology, 46,* 1053-1070.

Berne, E. (1957). Ego states in psychotherapy. *American Journal of Psychotherapy, 11,* 293-309.

Berscheid, E., & Walster, E. (1974). *Interpersonal attraction.* Reading, MA: Addison-Wesley.

Bergeman, C. S., Chipuer, H. M., Plomin, R., Pedersen, N.L., McClearn, G. E., Nesselroade, J.R., Costa, P., Jr., & McCrae, R. R. (1989). Genetic and environmental effects on openness to experience, agreeableness, and conscientiousness: An adoption/twin study. *Journal of Personality, 61,* 159-179.

Berkowitz, L. (1989). Frustration-aggression hypothesis: Examination and reformulation. *Psychological Bulletin, 108,* 59-73.

Berzonsky, M. D., & Adams, G. R. (1999). Reevaluating the identity status paradigm: Still useful after 35 years. Developmental Review, 19, 557-590.

Berzonsky, M. D., & Neimeyer, G. I. (1988). Identity status and personal construct systems. Journal of Adolescence, 11, 195-204.

Berzonsky, M. D., Rice, K. G., & Neimeyer, G. J. (1990). Identity status and self-construct systems: Process X structure interactions. Journal of Adolescence, 13, 251-263.

Best, D. L., Williams, J. E., Cloud, J. M., Davis, S. W., Robertson, L. S., Edwards, J. R., Giles, H., & Fowles, J. (1977). Development of sex-trait stereotypes among young children in the United States, England, and Ireland. *Child Development, 48,* 1375-1384.

Beutler, L. E., Crago, M., & Arezmendi, T. G. (1986). Research on therapist variables in psychotherapy. In S. L. Garfield, & A. R. Bergen (Eds.). *Handbook of psychotherapy and behavior change (3rd ed.).* New York: Wiley.

Bigler, E. D., Johnson, S. C., & Blatter, D. D. (1999). Head trauma and intellectual status: Relation to quantitative magnetic resonance imaging findings. *Applied Neuropsychology, 6,* 217-225.

Birren, J.E., & Morrison, D.F. (1961). Analysis of the WAIS subtests in relation to age and education. *Journal of Gerontology, 16,* 363-369.

Black, A. E., & Deci, E. L. (2000). The effects of student self-regulation and instructor autonomy support on learning in a college-level natural science course: A self-determination theory perspective. *Science Education, 84,* 740-756.

Black, B., & Hazen, N. L. (1990). Social status and patterns of communication in acquainted and unacquainted preschool children. *Developmental Psychology, 26,* 379-387.

Black, J. (2000). Police testing and police selection: Utility of the 'Big Five.' *New Zealand Journal of Psychology, 29,* 2-9.

Blackman, M. C., & Funder, D. C. (1998). The effect of information on consensus and accuracy in personality judgment. *Journal of Experimental Social Psychology, 34,* 164-181.

Blais, M. (1995). *In these girls, hope is a muscle.* New York: The Atlantic Monthly Press.

Block, J. (1971). *Lives through time.* Berkeley, CA: Bancroft.

Block, J. (1995). A contrarian view of the five-factor approach to personality description. Psychological Bulletin, 117, 187-215.

Block, J. (2002). Personality as an affect-processing system. Mahwah, NJ: Lawrence Erlbaum Associates.

Block, J. H., & Block, J. (1980). The role of ego-control and ego-resiliency in the organization of behavior. In W. A. Collins (Ed.). *Development of cognition, affect, and social relations: The Minnesota symposia on child psychology, (Vol. 13; pp. 40-101).* Hillsdale, NJ: Erlbaum.

Block, N. (1995). On a confusion about the function of consciousness. Behavioral and Brain Sciences, 18, 227-287.

Blum, D. (2002). Love at Goon Park. Harry Harlow and the science of affection. Cambridge, MA: Perseus Books Group.

Boesky, D. (1994). Dialogue on the Brenner Paper Between Charles Brenner, M.D., & Dale Boesky, M. D. *Journal of Clinical Psychoanalysis, 3,* 509-540.

Bonanno, G. A., Papa, A., & O'Neill, K. (2002). Loss and human resilience. *Applied and Preventive Psychology, 10,* 193-206.

Bonanno, G. A., Wortman, C, B., Lehman, D. R. (2002). Resilience to loss and chronic grief: A prospective study from preloss to 18-months postloss. Journal of Personality & Social Psychology, 83, 1150-1164

Bondanella, P. (1998). *The films of Federico Fellini.* Cambridge, UK: Cambridge University Press.

Bong, M. (1999). Comparison between self-concept and self-efficacy in academic motivation research. *Educational Psychologist, 34,* 139-153.

Bonwell, C. G., & Eisen, J. A. (1991). *Active learning: Creating excitement in the classroom.* ERIC Clearinghouse on Higher Education. Washington, DC.

Bouchard, T. J., & McGue, M. (1981). Family studies of intelligence: A review. *Science, 212,* 1055-1059.

Boushka, B. (2000). Do ask; do tell: Gay Conservative Lashes Back: Individualism, Identity, Personal Rights, Responsibility and Community in a Libertaria. New York: iUniverse.

Bower, G. H. (1981). Mood and memory. *American Psychologist, 36,* 129-148.

Bowers, K.S. (1976). *Hypnosis for the seriously curious.* New York: W.W. Norton.

Bowers, K. S. (1973). Situationism in psychology: An analysis and critique. *Psychological Review, 80,* 307-336.

Bowers, K.S. (1984). On being unconsciously influenced and informed. In K.S. Bowers & Meichenbaum, D. (Eds.) *The Unconscious Reconsidered (Pp. 227-272).* New York: Wiley.

Bowers, P. (1982). The classic suggestion effect: Relationships with scales of hypnotizability, effortless experiencing, and imagery vividness. *International Journal of Clinical and Experimental Hypnosis, 30,* 270-279.

Bowlby, J. (1958). The nature of the child's tie to his mother. *International Journal of Psychoanalysis, 39,* 350-373.

Bowlby, J. (1988). *A secure base: Parent-child attachment and healthy human development.* New York: Basic Books/Harper Collins.

Bowman, M. L. (1989). Testing individual differences in ancient China. *American Psychologist, 44,* 576-578.

Boyce, D. A. (2002) The correlation of emotional intelligence, academic success, and cognitive ability in master's level physical therapy students. [Abstract]. Dissertation Abstracts International: Section B: The Sciences & Engineering, 62(12-B), 5677.

Brackett, M. A., & Mayer, J. D. (2003). Convergent, discriminant, and incremental validity of competing measures of emotional intelligence. *Personality and Social Psychology Bulletin, 29,* 1147-1158.

Brackett, M. A., Mayer, J. D., Warner, R. M. (2004). Emotional intelligence and its relation to everyday behavior. *Personality and Individual Differences, 36,* 1387-1402.

Bradburn, N.M. & Berlew, D. E. (1961). Need for achievement and English economic growth. *Economic Development and Cultural Change, 10,* 8-20.

Bradway, K.P., & Robinson, N.M. (1961). Significant IQ changes in twenty-five years: A follow-up. *Journal of Educational Psychology, 52,* 74-79.

Bradway, K.P., Thompson, C.W., & Cravens, R.B. (1958). Preschool IQ's after twenty-five years. *Journal of Educational Psychology, 49,* 278-281.

Brennan, K. A., Clark, C. L., & Shaver, P. R. (1998). Self-report measurement of close relationships. In J. A. Simpson & W. S. Rholes (Eds.). *Attachment theory and close relationships (pp. 46-76).* New York: Guilford Press.

Bretherton, I.,. & Waters, E. (1985). Attachment theory: Retrospect and Prospect. In I. Bretherton & E. Waters (Eds.) *Growing Points of Attachment Theory and Research/ Monographs of the Society for Reseach in Child Development, 50*(1-2) [Serial no. 209].

Brigham, C. C (1930). Intelligence tests of immigrant groups. *Psychological Review, 37,* 158-165.

Brod, J. H. (1997). Creativity and schizotypy. In G. S. Claridge (Ed.). Schizotypy: Implications for illness and health (pp. 276-298). Oxford: Oxford University Press.

Brooks-Gunn, J., & Reiter, E. O. (1990). The role of pubertal processes. In S. S. Feldman & G. R. Elliott (Eds.). *At the threshold.* Cambrdge, MA: Harvard University Press.

Brown, J. (1998). *Joke Soup.* Kansas City: Andrews McMeel Publishing.

Brown, R. T. (1989). Creativity: What are we to measure? In J. A. Glover, R. R. Ronning, & C. R. Reynolds (Eds.). *Handbook of creativity (pp. 3-32).* New York: Plenum Press.

Brown, S., & Katcher, A. H. (2001). Pet attachment and dissociation. *Society and Animals, 9,* 25-41.

Bruner, J. S., & Taguiri, R. (1954). The perception of people. In G. Lindzey (Ed.). Handbook of social psychology (pp. 634-654). Cambridge, MA: Addison-Wesley.

Bruner, J. S. (1986). (1986). *Actual minds, possible worlds.* Cambridge, MA: Harvard University Press.

Bruner, J. S. (1990). *Acts of meaning.* Cambridge, MA: Harvard University Press.

Buck, R. (1984). *The communication of emotion.* New York: Guilford Press.

Burger, J. (1990). *Personality, 2nd ed.* Belmont, CA: Wadsworth.

Burnstein, E., Crandall, C., & Kitayama, S. (1994). Some neo-Darwinian decision rules for altruism: Weighing cues for inclusive fitness as a function of the biological importance of the decision. *Journal of Personality and Social Psychology, 67(5),* 773-789.

Burton, H. J., Kline, S. A., Lindsay, R. M., & Heidenheim, A. P. (1986). The relationship of depression to survival in chronic renal failure. *Psychosomatic Medicine, 48,* 261-269.

Bushman, B. (2002). Does venting anger feed or extinguish the flame? Catharsis, rumination, distraction, anger and aggressive responding. *Personality and Social Psychology Bulletin, 28,* 724-731.

Buske-Kirschbaum, A., Kirschbaum, C., Stierle, H., Jabaij, L., & Hellhammer, D. (1994). Conditioned manipulation of natural killer (NK) cells in humans using a discriminative learning protocol. *Biological Psychology, 38,* 143-155.

Buss, A.H., & Durkee, A. (1957). An inventory for assessing different kinds of hostility. *Journal of Consulting Psychology, 21,* 343-349.

Buss, A. H., & Finn, S. E. (1987). Classification of personality traits. *Journal of Personality and Social Psychology, 52,* 432-444.

Buss, D. M. (1984). Marital assortment for personality dispositions: Assessment with three different data systems. *Behavior Genetics, 14,* 111-123.

Buss, D. M. (1988a). The evolution of human intrasexual competition: Tactics of mate attraction. *Journal of Personality and Social Psychology, 54,* 616-628.

Buss, D. M. (1988b). Love acts: The evolutionary biology of love. In R. J. Sternberg & M. L. Barnes (Eds.). *The psychology of love (pp. 100-108).* New Haven: Yale University Press.

Buss, D. M. (1988c). Biography. *American Psychologist, 44,* 636-637.

Buss, D. M. (1989). Sex differences in human mate preferences: Evolutionary hypotheses tested in 37 cultures. *Behavioral and Brain Sciences, 12,* 1-49.

Buss, D. M. (1991). Evolutionary personality psychology. *Annual Review of Psychology, 42,* 459-492.

Buss, D. M., & Barnes, M. L. (1986). Preferences in human mate selection. Journal of Personality and Social Psychology, 50, 559-570.

Buss, D. M., & Craik, K. H. (1985). Why *Not* Measure that trait? Alternative criteria for identifying important dispositions. *Journal of Personality and Social Psychology, 48,* 934-946.

Buss, D. M., Larsen, R. J., Westen, D., & Semmelroth, J. (1992). Sex differences in jealousy: Evolution, physiology, and psychology. Psychological Science, 3, 251-255. [Reprinted in H. S. Friedman, & M. W. Schustack (Eds). Readings in personality: Classic theories and modern research. (pp. 93-100). Boston, MA: Allyn & Bacon].

Buss, D. M, & Schmitt, D. P. (1993). Sexual strategies theory: An evolutionary perspective on human mating. *Psychological Review, 100,* 204-232.

Butcher, J. N. (1995). Clinical personality assessment: An overview. In *Clinical personality assessment: Practical approaches.* New York: Oxford University Press.

Buttersworth, G. (1992). Origins of self-perception in infancy. *Psychological Inquiry, 3,* 103-111.

Buunk, B., Angleitner, A., Oubaid, V., & Buss, D. M. (1996). Sexual and cultural differences in jealousy: Tests from the Netherlands, Germany, and the United States. *Psychological Science, 7,* 359-363.

Cacioppo, J. T., Gardner, W. L., & Berntson, G. G. (1999). The affect system has parallel and integrative processing components: Form follows function. *Journal of Personality and Social Psychology, 76,* 839-855.

Campbell, J. (1949). *The hero with a thousand faces.* New York: Bollingen Foundation.

Campbell, J. (1972). *Myths to live by.* New York: Viking.

Cantor, N. (1986). Biography. *American Psychologist, 41*, 366-367.

Cantor, N., & Kihlstrom, J. F. (1987). Personality and social intelligence. Englewood Cliffs, NJ: Prentice Hall.

Cantor, N., & Mischel, W. (1977). Traits as prototypes: Effects on recognition memory. *Journal of Personality and Social Psychology, 35*, 38-48.

Capitanio, J. P. (1999). Personality dimensions in adult male rhesus macaques: Prediction of behaviors across time and situation. *American Journal of Primatology, 47*, 299-320.

Capitanio, J. P., Widaman, K. F. (2005). Confirmatory factor analysis of personality structure in adult male rhesus monkeys (Macaca mulatta). *American Journal of Primatology, 65*, 289-294.

Carnegie, D. (1936/1998). *How to win friends and influence people.* New York: Pocket books.

Carney, R. M., Rich, M. W., & Freedland, K. E. (1988). Major depressive disorder predicts cardiac events in patients with coronary-artery disease. *Psychosomatic Medicine, 50*, 627-633.

Caron, M. D., Whitbourne, S. K., & Halgin, R. P. (1992). Fraudulent excuse making among college students. *Teaching of Psychology, 19*, 90-93.

Carpenter, W. B. (1874). *Principles of mental physiology.* New York: Appleton.

Carroll, J. B. (1993). *Human cognitive abilities: A survey of factor-analytic studies.* New York: Cambridge University Press.

Carter, R. (2002). *Exploring consciousness.* Berkeley, CA: University of California Press.

Carver, C. S. (1975). Physical aggression as a function of objective self-awareness and attitudes toward punishment. *Journal of Experimental Social Psychology, 11*, 510-519.

Carver, C. S., Ganellen, R. J., Froming, W. J., & Chambers, W. (1983). Modeling: An analysis in terms of category accessibility. *Journal of Experimental Social Psychology, 19*, 403-421.

Carver, C. S., & Scheier, M. F. (1981). *Attention and self-regulaiton: A control theory approach to human behavior.* New York: Springer-Verlag.

Carver, C. S., & Scheier, M. F. (1998). *On the self-regulation of behavior.* New York: Cambridge University Press.

Carver, C. S. & Scheier, M. F. (2000). *Perspectives on personality (4th ed).* Boston, MA: Allyn & Bacon.

Carter, T. J. (1998). Psychological factors associated with anabolic steroid use in male body builders. *Dissertation Abstracts International: Section B: The Sciences & Engineering, Vol 58 (8-B),* pp. 4439 [Abstract].

Caspi, A. (2000). The child is father of the man: Personality continuities from childhood to adulthood. *Journal of Personality and Social Psychology, 78*, 158-172.

Caspi, A., & Bem, D.J. (1990). Personality continuity and change across the life course. In In L. Pervin (ed.). *Handbook of Personality Theory and Research (Pp. 549-575).* New York: Guilford.

Caspi, A., Elder, G. H., & Bem, D. J. (1987). Moving against the world: Life-course patterns of explosive children. *Developmental Psychology, 23*, 308-313.

Caspi, A., & Roberts, B. W. (1999). Personality continuity and change across the life course. In L. A. Pervin & O. P. John (Eds.). *Handbook of Personality: Theory and Research (pp. 300-326).* New York: Guilford.

Caspi, A., Roberts, B. W., & Shiner, R. L. (2005). Personality development: Stability and change. *Annual Review of Psychology, 56*, 453-484.

Cattell, R.B. (1947). Confirmation and clarification of primary personality factors. *Psychometrika, 12*, 197-220.

Cattell, R. B. (1956). Second-order personality factors in the questionnaire realm. Journal of Consulting Psychology, 20, 411-418.

Cattell, R.B. (1963). The theory of fluid and crystalized intelligence: A critical experiment. *Journal of Educational Psychology, 54*, 1-22.

Cattell, R. B. (1965). The scientific analysis of personality. Chicago: Aldine Publishing Company.

Cattell, R. B. (1971). *Abilities: Their structure, growth, and action.* Boston: Houghton Mifflin.

Cattell, R. B. (1969). *16PF (Form C, 1969 Edition R)* Champaign, IL: Institute for Personality and Ability Testing (IPAT).

Cattell, R. B., & Butcher, H. J. (1968). *The prediction of achievement and creativity.* Indianapolis, IN: Bobbs-Merrill.

Cattell, R.B., Horn, J., & Butcher, H.J. (1962). The dynamic structure of attitudes in adults: A description of some established factors and of their measurement by the motivational analysis test. *British Journal of Psychology, 53*, 57-69.

Casey, M. B., Pezaris, E., Benbow, C. P., & Nuttall, R. (1995). The influence of spatial ability on gender differences in mathematics college entrance test scores across diverse samples. *Developmental Psychology, 31*, 697-705.

Caspi, A., & Herbener, E. S. (1990). Continuity and change: Assortative mating and the consistency of personality in adulthood. *Journal of Personality and Social Psychology, 58*, 250-258.

Caspi, A., Herbener, E. S., & Ozer, D. J. (1992). Shared experiences and the similarities of personalities: A longitudinal study of married couples. *Journal of Personality and Social Psychology, 62*, 281-291.

Caspi, A., & Moffitt, T.E. (1992). When do individual differences matter? A paradoxical theory of personality coherence. *Psychological Inquiry.*

Caughey, J. L. (1980). Personality identity and social organization. *Ethos, 8*, 173-203. [Selections reproduced with permission in D. C. Funder and D. J. Ozer, *Pieces of the personality puzzle (pp. 378-382).* New York: W. W. Norton.

Cattell, R.B. (1966). *The scientific analysis of personality.* Chicago: Aldine Publishing Company.

Ceci, S. J. (1996). *On intelligence.* Cambridge, MA: Cambridge University Press.

Cerf, C., & Navasky, V. (1998). *The experts speak: The definitive compendium of authoritative misinformation.* New York: Villard.

Cervone, D. (2004). The architecture of personality. *Psychological Review, 111*, 183-204.

Cervone, D. (2005). Personality architecture: within-person structures and processes. *Annual Review of Psychology, 56*, 423-452.

Cervone, D., Shadel, W. G., Jencius, S. (2001). A social-cognitive theory of personality assessment. *Personality and Social Psychology Review, 5*, 33-51.

Champagne, B., & Pervin, L. A. (1987). The relation of perceived situation similarity to perceived behavior similarity:

Implicatiosn for social learning theory. *European Journal of Personality, 1,* 79-92.

Chapin, F. S. (1968). *The social insight test.* Palo Alto, CA: Consulting Psychologists Press.

Chapman, J. P., Chapman, L. J., & Kwapil, T. R. (1994). Does the Eysenck Psychoticism Scale predict psychosis? A ten year longitudinal study. *Personality and Individual Differences, 17,* 369-375.

Chapman, M. (1997). French embrace common sense on surgeons with AIDS virus. *Human Events, 53,* 6.

Chavajay, P., & Rogoff, B. (2002). Schooling and traditional collaborative social organization of problem solving by Mayan mothers and children. *Developmental Psychology, 38,* 55-66.

Cheeseman Day, J., & Neuberger, E. C. (2002). The big payoff: Educational attainment and synthetic estimates of work-life earnings. U.S. Bureau of the Census, Special Reports [P23-210], Washington, DC: U.S. Government Printing Office.

Christiansen, N. D., Wolcott-Burnam, S., Janovics, J. E., Burns, G. N., & Quirk, S. W. (2005). The Good Judge Revisited: Individual Differences in the Accuracy of Personality Judgments. *Human Performance, 18*(2), 123-149. doi:10.1207/s15327043hup1802_2

Christie, R., & Geis, F. L. (1970). *Studies in Machiavellianism.* New York: Academic Press.

Claridge, G. S., Canter, S., & Hume, W. I. (1973). *Personality differences and biological variations: A study of twins.* Oxford, England: Pergamon.

Clark, R. D. & Hatfield, E. (1989). Gender differences in receptivity to sexual offers. *Journal of Psychology and Human Sexuality, 2,* 39-55.

Clark, R. D. (1990). The impact of AIDS on gender differences in willingness to engage in casual sex. *Journal of Applied Social Psychology, 20,* 771-782.

Cloninger, S. C. (2000). *Theories of personality (3rd Ed.).* Upper Saddle River, NJ: Prentice Hall.

Cobb, C., & Mayer, J. D. (2000). Emotional intelligence: What the research says. *Educational Leadership, 58,* 14-18.

Cocker, K. L., Edwards, G. A., Anderson, J. W., & Meares, R. A. (1994). Electrophysiological changes under hypnosis in multiple personality disorder: A two-case exploratory study. *Australian Journal of Clinical and Experimental Hypnosis, 22,* 165-176.

Coetsee, A. S. J. (1933). The comprehension of spatial relations (among primary school children) by the elaboration of two-dimensional visual stimuli. *South African Journal of Psychology & Education, 1.2,* 25-33.

Cohen, D., & Strayer, J. (1996). Empathy in conduct-disordered and comparison youth. *Developmental Psychology, 32,* 988-998.

Cohen, S., Tyrrell, D. A., Smith, A. P. (1991). Psychological stress and susceptibility to the common cold. New England Journal of Medicine, 325, 606-612.

Cohen, S, Frank, E., Doyle, W. J. (1998). Types of stressors that increase susceptibility to the common cold in healthy adults. Health Psychology, 17, 214-223.

Cohler, B. J. (1982). Personal narrative and the life course. In P. Baltes & O. G. Brim, (Eds.). *Life span development and behavior.* (Vol. 4, pp. 205-241). New York: Academic Press.

Cohn, E. S., White, S. O., & Sanders, J. (2000). Distributive and procedural justice in seven nations. *Law & Human Behavior, 24,* 553-579.

Collins, A. M., & Loftus, E. F. (1975). A spreading-activation theory of semantic processing. *Psychological Review, 82,* 407-428.

Collins, J.C., McLeod, D., & Jacoby, L.L. (1992). *When a hush falls over the room: An indirect measure of emotionality.* Unpublished manuscript.

Collins, N. L., & Read, S. J. (1990). Adult attachment, working models, and relationship quality in dating couples. *Journal of Personality and Social Psychology 58,* 644-663.

Combs, A. W. (1947). A comparative study of motivation as revealed in Thematic Apperception stories and autobiographies. *Journal of Clinical Psychology, 3,* 65-75.

Conger, R. D., Elder, G. H., Lorenz, F. O., Conger, K. J., Simons, R. L., Huck, S., & Melby, J. N. (1990). Linking economic hardship to marital quality and instability. *Journal of Marriage and the Family, 52,* 643-656.

Conry, R., & Plant, W. T. (1965). WAIS and group test predictions of an academic success criterion: high school and college. *Educational and Psychological Measurement, 25,* 493-500.

Cooley, C. H. (1902). *Human nature and the social order.* New York: Scribner.

Cools, R., Blackwell, A., Clark, L., Menzies, L., Cox, S., & Robbins, T. (2005). Tryptophan depletion disrupts the motivational guidance of goal-directed behavior as a function of trait impulsivity. *Neuropsychopharmacology,* 30, 1362-1373.

Cooper, L. A., & Shepard, R. N. (1984). Turning something over in the mind. *Scientific American, 251,* 106-114.

Cooper, S. H. (1998). Changing notions of defense within psychoanalytic theory. *Journal of Personality, 66,* 947-964.

Coopersmith, S. (1967). The antecedents of self-esteem. San Francisco: W. H. Freeman.

Coopersmith, S. (1975). Self-concept, race, and education. In C. K. Verna & C. Bagley (Eds.), *Race and education across cultures.* London: Heinemann.

Cortés, J. B. (1960). The achievement motive in the Spanish economy between the 13th and 18th centuries. *Economic Development and Cultural Change, 9,* 144-163.

Cortina, J. M., Doherty, M. L., Schmitt, N., Kaufman, G., & Smith, R. G. (1992). The "Big Five" personality factors in the IPI and MMPI: Predictors of police performance. *Personnel Psychology, 45,* 119-140.

Costa, P.T., Jr., & McCrae, R. R. (1980). Influence of extraversion and neuroticism on subjective well-being: happy and unhappy people. *Journal of Personality and Social Psychology, 38,* 668-78.

Costa, P.T., Jr., & McCrae, R.R. (1985). *Revised NEO Personality Inventory (NEO PI-R) and NEO Five-Factor Inventory (NEO-FFI): Professional manual.* Odessa, FL: Psychological Assessment Resources, Inc.

Costa, P. T., Jr., & McCrae, R. R. (1988). Personality in adulthood: A six-year longitudinal study of self-reports and spouse ratings on the NEO Personality Inventory. *Journal of Personality and Social Psychology, 54,* 853-863.

Costa, P. T., Jr., & McCrae, R. R. (2002). Looking Backward: Changes in the mean levels of personality traits from 80 to 12. In D. Cervone & W. Mischel, (Eds.) *Advances in Personality Science (219-237)*. New York: Guilford.

Costa, P. T., Jr., McCrae, R. R., Zonderman, A. B., Barbano, H. E., Lebowitz, B., & Larson, D. M. (1986). Cross-sectional studies of personality in a national sample: 2. Stability in neuroticism, extraversion, and openness. *Psychology and Aging, 1,* 144-149.

Cox, C.M. (1926). *Genetic studies of genius: Volume II: The early mental traits of three hundred geniuses*. Stanford, CA: Stanford University Press.

Coyne, J. C., & Tennen, H. (2010). Positive psychology in cancer care: Bad science, exaggerated claims, and unproven medicine. *Annual Behavioral Medicine, 39,* 16–26.

Craik, K. H. (1993). The 1937 Allport and Stagner texts in personality psychology. In K. H. Craik, R. Hogan, & R. N. Wolfe (Eds.) *Fifty years of personality psychology (pp. 3-20)*. Plenum: New York.

Craik, K. H. (1998). Personality systems concepts and their implications. *Psychological Inquiry, 9,* 145-148.

Cramer, P. (1991). The development of defense mechanisms: Theory, research, and assessment. New York: Springer-Verlag.

Cramer, P. (1998). Freshman to senior year: A follow-up study of identity, narcissism, and defense mechanisms. *Journal of Research in Personality, 32,* 156-172.

Cramer, P. (2002). Defense mechanisms, behavior, and affect in young adulthood. *Journal of Personality, 70,* 103-126.

Cramer, P. & Tracy, A. (2005). The pathway from child personality to adult adjustment: The road is not straight. *Journal of Research in Personality, 39,* 369-374.

Crick, F., & Koch, C. (1995). Are we aware of neural activity in primary visual cortext? *Nature, 375,* 121-123.

Crocker, J., Alloy, L. B., & Kayne, N. T. (1988). Attributional style, depression, and perceptions of consensus for events. *Journal of Personality and Social Psychology, 54,* 540-546.

Cronbach, L. J. (1960). Essentials of psychological testing (2nd ed.). New York: Harper & Row.

Cronbach, L. J., Rajaratnam, N., & Gleser, G. C. (1965). Theory of generalizeability: A liberalization of reliability theory. *The British Journal of Statistical Psychology, 16,* 137-163.

Cronbach, L.J., & Meehl, P.E. (1955). Construct validity in psychological tests. *Psychological Bulletin, 52,* 281-302.

Cross, W. E. (1987). A two-factor theory of Black identity: Implications for the study of identity development in minority children. In J. S. Phinney & M. J. Rotheram (Eds.), *Children's ethnic socialization*. Newbury Park, CA: Sage.

Crowell, J. A., Treboux, D., Gao, Y., Fyffe, C., Pan, H., & Waters, E. (2002). Assessing secure base behavior in adulthood: Development of a measure, links to adult attachment representations, and relations to couples' communication and reports of relationships. *Developmental Psychology, 38,* 679-693.

Csikszentmihalyi, M. (1990). *Flow: The psychology of optimal experience*. New York: Harper Collins.

Csikszentmihalyi, M. (1997). *Finding flow: The psychology of engagement with everyday life*. New York: Basic Books.

Dabbs, J. M. (1992). Testosterone and occupational achievement. *Social Forces, 70,* 813-824.

Dabbs, J. M., Jr., Carr, T. S., Frady, R. L., & Riad, J. K. (1995). Testosterone, crime, and misbehavior among 692 male prison inmates. *Personality and Individual Differences, 18,* 627-633.

Dahlstrom, W.G., Welsh, G.S., & Dahlstrom, L.E. (1972). *An MMPI handbook*. Minneapolis: University of Minnesota Press.

Daly, M., & Wilson, M. (1988). *Homocide*. New York: Aldine de Gruyter.

Daly, M. & Wilson, M. (1990). Is parent-offspring conflict sex-linked? Freudian and Darwinian models. *Journal of Personality, 58,* 163-189.

Dalton, D. (1993). *Mahatma Gandhi: Nonviolent power in action*. New York: Columbia University Press.

Darley, J. M., & Latane, B. (1968). Bystander intervention in emergencies. Diffusion of responsibility. *Journal of Personality and Social Psychology, 27,* 100-108.

Darwin, C. (1873). The expression of the emotions in man and animals. New York: D. Appleton and Company.

Darwin, C. (1965). The expression of the emotions in man and animals. Chicago: The University of Chicago Press. pp 194-165.

Davidson, K., & Prkachin, K. (1997). Optimism and unrealistic optimism have an interacting impact on health-promoting behavior and knowledge changes. *Personality and Social Psychology Bulletin, 23,* 617-625.

Davies, M., Stankov, L., & Roberts, R. D. (1998). Emotional intelligence: In search of an elusive construct. *Journal of Personality and Social Psychology, 75,* 989-1015.

Davidson, R. J., & Tomarken, A. J. (1989). Laterality and emotion: An electrophysiological approach. In F. Boller & J. Grafman (Eds.), *Handbook of Neurology (pp. 419-441)*. Amsterdam: Elsevier.

Davis, P. H., & Osherson, A. (1977). The current treatment of a multiple-personality woman and her son. *American Journal of Psychotherapy, 31,* 504-515.

David, T. J. (2001). Revising psychoanalytic interpretations of the past: An examination of declarative and non-declarative memory processes. *International Journal of Psychoanalysis, 82,* 449-462.

Day, A. L., & Carroll, S. A. (2004). Using an ability-based measure of emotional intelligence to predict individual performance, group performance, and group citizenship behaviours. *Personality and Individual Differences, 36,* 1443-1458.

Dayan, K., Kasten, R., & Fox, S. (2002). Entry-level police candidate assessment center: An efficient tool or a hammer to kill a fly? *Personnel Psychology, 55,* 827-849.

De St. Aubin, E. (1996). Personality ideology polarity: Its emotional foundation and its manifestation in individual value systems, religiosity, political orientation, and assumptions concerning human nature. *Journal of Personality and Social Psychology, 71,* 152-165.

De Raad, B., & Kokkonen, M. (2000). Traits and emotions: A review of their structure and management. *European Journal of Personality, 14,* 477-496.

De Waal, F. (2001). *The ape and the sushi master: Cultural reflections of a primatologist*. New York: Basic Books.

DeYoung, C. G. (2011) Intelligence and personality. In R. J. Sternberg & S. B. Kaufman (Eds.) *The Cambridge handbook of intelligence (pp. 711-737).* New York: Cambridge University Press.

Deacon, T. W. (1997). *The symbolic species: The co-evolution of language and the brain.* New York: W. W. Norton.

Deci, E. L. & Ryan, R. M. (2000). The "what" and "why" of goal pursuits: Human needs and the self-determination of behavior. *Psychological Inquiry, 11,* 227-268.

Dennett, D.C. (1978). *Brainstorms.* Cambridge, MA: MIT Press.

Denton, K. & Krebs, D. (1990). From the scene to the crime: The effect of alcohol and social context on moral judgment. Journal of Personality & Social Psychology, 59, 242-248.

Depue, . R. A., Luciana, M., Arbisi, P., Collins, P., & Leon, A. (1994). Dopamine and the structure of personality: Relation of agonist-induced dopamine activity to positive emotionality. *Journal of Personality and Social Psychology, 67,* 485-498.

DeRivera, J. (1977). A structural theory of the emotions. *Psychological Issues, 40,* 9-179.

Descartes (1641/1968). *Discourse on Method and the Meditations.* New York: Penguin Books.

de Silva, P., Rachman, S., Seligman, M. E. (1977). Prepared phobias and obsessions: Therapeutic outcome. Behaviour Research & Therapy, 15, 65-77.

Deutsch, A. (1983). Psychiatric perspectives on an eastern-style cult. In D.A. Halperin (ed.) *Psychodynamic perspectives on religion, sect, and cult (pp. 113-129).* Boston: Joh, n Wright PSG Inc.

Dewey, J. (1922/1892). Human nature and conduct. New York: Holt.

Dewey, J. (1887/1967). Psychology. In *John Dewey: The early works. 1882-1898, Vol 2: 1887.* Carbondale: Southern Illinois University Press. (Original work published 1887).

Diener, E., & Chan, M. (2011). Happy people live longer: Subjective well-being contributes to health and longevity. *Applied Psychology: Health Well-Being, 3,* 1–43.

Diener, E., & Diener, C. (1996). Most people are happy. *Psychological Science, 7,* 181-185.

Dieier, E. & Emmons, R. A. (1984). The independence of positive and negative affect. *Journal of Personality and Social Psychology, 47,* 1105-1117.

Diener, E., Lucas, R. E., & Oishi, S. (2002). Subjective well-being: The science of happiness and life satisfaction. In C. R. Snyder & S. J. Lopez, *Handbook of Positive Psychology (pp. 63-73).* New York: Oxford University Press.

Diener, E., & Seligman, M. E. P. (2002). Very happy people. *Psychological Science, 13,* 81-83.

Diener, E., Smith, H., & Fujita, F. (1995). The personality structure of affect. *Journal of Personality and Social Psychology, 69,* 130-141.

Digman, J.M. (1990). Personality structure: Emergence of the five-factor model. *Annual Review of Psychology, 41,* 417-440.

Cambridge handbook of intelligence (pp. 711-737). New York: Cambridge University Press.

Ditzfeld, C. E. & Showers, C. J. (2014). Self-structure and emotional experience. *Cognition and Emotion, 28,* 596-621.

Dodge, K., & Frame, C. (1982). Social cognitive biases and deficits in aggressive boys. *Child Development, 53,* 629-635.

Dollard, J., Doob, J., Miller, N., Mowrer, O., & Sears, R. (1939). *Frustration and aggression.* New Haven, CT: Yale University Press.

Dollard, J., & Miller, N. (1950). *Personality and psychotherapy.* New York: McGraw Hill.

Dollinger, S. J., & Dollinger, S. M. C. (1997). Individuality and identity exploration: An autophotographic study. Journal of Research in Personality, 31, 337-354.

Dooley, D., & Catalano, R. (Eds.) (1988). Special issue on: Psychological effects of unemployment. Journal of Social Issues, 44, 1-191.

Donnellan, M. B., Larsen-Rife, D., & Conger, R. D. (2005). Personality, family history, and competence in early adult romantic relationships. Journal of Personality and Social Psychology, 88, 562-576.

Dornbusch, S. M. (1965). Popular psychology: A content analysis of contemporary inspirational nonreligious books. In S. Z. Klausner (Ed.). The question for self-control (pp. 126-140). New York: Free Press.

Douglas, K., & Arenberg, D. (1978). Age changes, cohort differences, and cultural change on the Guilford-Zimmerman Temperament Survey. Journal of Gerontology, 33, 737-747.

Dowson, M., & McInerney, D. M. (2001). Psychological parameters of students' social and work avoidance goals: A qualitative investigation. *Journal of Educational Psychology, 93,* 35-42.

Doyle, K. O., Jr. (1974). Theory and practice of ability testing in ancient Greece. *Journal of the History of the Behavioral Sciences, 10,* 202-212.

Drugan, R. C., Basile, A. S., Ha, J-H., Ferland, R. J. (1994). The protective effects of stress control may be mediated by increased brain levels of benzodiazepine receptor agonists. *Brain Research, 661,* 127-136.

Drugan, R. C., Skolnick, P., Paul, S. M., & Crawley, J. N. (1989). A pretest procedure reliably predicts performance in two animal models of inescapable stress. *Pharmacology Biochemistry and Behavior 33,* 649-654.

Dubner, S. J., & Levitt, S. D. (June 6, 2004). What the Bagel Man Saw. *New York Times Magazine, 153,* 62-66.

Duerr, E. (1962). *The length and depth of acting.* New York: Holt, Rinehart, & Winston.

Duncan, J. & Humphries, G. W. (1989). Visual search and stimulus similarity. *Psychological Review, 96,* 433-548.

Dunn, A. J. (1989). Psychoneuroimmunology for the psychoneuroendocrinologist: A review of animal studies of nervous system--immune system interactions. *Psychoneuroendocrinology, 14,* 251-274.

Dunning, D. (2005). *Self-insight: Roadblocks and detours on the path to knowing thyself.* New York, NY: Psychology Press.

Dutton, D. G., & Lake, R. A. (1973). Threat of prejudice and reverse discrimination in interracial situations. *Journal of Personality and Social Psychology, 28,* 94-100.

Dutton, D. G., & Aron, A. P. (1974). Some evidence for heightened sexual attraction under conditions of high anxiety. *Journal of Personality and Social Psychology, 30,* 510-517.

Dutton, D. G., & Aron, A. (1989). Romantic attraction and generalized liking for others who are sources of conflict-based arousal. *Canadian Journal of Behavioral Science, 21,* 246-257.

Dyer, M.G. (1983). The role of affect in narratives. *Cognitive Science,* xx, 211-242.

Eccles, J. C. (1953). *The neurophysiological basis of mind: the principles of neurophysiology.* Oxford, England: Clarendon press.

Eccles, J. S., & Wigfield, A. (2002). Motivational beliefs, values, and goals. *Annual Review of Psychology, 53,* 109-132.

Edwards, A.L. (1942). The retention of affective experiences -- A criticism and restatement of the problem. *Psychological Review, 49,* 43-53.

Edwards, A.L. (1957). *Manual for the Edwards Personal Preference Schedule.* New York: The Psychological Corporation, 1957.

Edwards, A.L., Abbott, R.D., & Klockars, A.J. (1972). A factor analysis of the EPPS and PRF personality inventories. *Educational and Psychological Measurement, 32,* 23-29.

Edwards, A.L., & Abbott, R.D. (1973). Relationships among the Edwards Personality Inventory Scales, the Edwards Personality Preference Schedule, and the Personality Research Form Scales. *Journal of Consulting and Clinical Psychology, 30,* 27-32.

Eich, E. (1995). Searching for mood dependent memory. *Psychological Science, 6,* 67-75.

Eichenbaum, H. (1997). Declarative memory: Insights from cognitive neurobiology. *Annual Review of Psychology, 48,* 47-572.

Eisenberg, N., Cumberland, A., & Spinrad, T. L. (in press). Parental socialization of emotion. *Psychological Inquiry.*

Eisenberg, N., Fabes, R. A., Guthrie, I. K., & Reiser, M. (2000). Dispositional emotionality and regulation: Their role in predicting quality of social functioning. *Journal of Personality and Social Psychology, 71,* 136-157.

Eisenberg, N., Fabes, R.A., Schaller, M., Miller, P. A., Carlo, G., Poulin, R., Shea, C., & Shell, R. (1991). Personality and socialization correlates of vicarious emotional responding. *Journal of Personality and Social Psychology, 61,* 459-471.

Eisenberg, N., Schaller, M., Fabes, R. A., Bustamante, D., Mathy, R., Shell, R., & Rhodes, K. (1988). The differentiation of personal distress and sympathy in children and adults. *Developmental Psychology, 24,* 766-775.

Ekman, P. (1973). Cross-cultural studies of facial expression. In P. Ekman (Ed.) Darwin and Facial Expression. And also from Ekman, P. (1973). Introduction (in the same book).

Ekman, P. (1984). Expression and the nature of emotion. In Scherer, K. R., & Ekman, P. *Approaches to emotion.* Hillsdale, NJ: Lawrence Erlbaum Associates.

Ekman, P. (1985). *Telling lies: Clues to deceit in the marketplace, politics, and marriage.* New York: W. W. Norton.

Ekman, P. (1999). Facial expressions. In T. Dalgleish & M. Power (Eds.) *Handbook of Cognition and Emotion (pp. 301-320).* New York: John Wiley & Sons.

Ekman, P., & Friesen, W. V. (1969). The repertoire of nonverbal behavior. Categories, origins, usage, and coding. *Semiotica, 1,* 49-98.

Ekman, P., & Friesen, W. V. (1975). *Unmasking the face.* Englewood Cliffs: NJ: Prentice-Hall.

Ekman, P., Friesen, W. V., & Ellsworth, P. (1972). *Emotion in the Human Face: Guidelines for Research and an Integration of Findings.* New York: Pergamon Press.

Elder, G. H. (1974). *Children of the great depression: Social change in life experiences.* Chicago: University of Chicago Press.

Elfenbein, H. A. (2013). Nonverbal dialects and accents in facial expressions of emotion. *Emotion Review, 5,* 90-96.

Ellenberger, H. F. (1981). *The discovery of the unconscious: The history and evolution of dynamic psychiatry.* New York: Basic Books.

Elliott, A. (1994). *Psychoanalytic theory: An introduction.* Cambridge: Blackwell.

Emde, R. N., & Sorce, J. E. (1983). The rewards of infancy: Emotional availability and social referencing. In J. D. Call, E. Galenson, & R. Tyson (Eds.). *Frontiers of infant psychiatry (Vol 1). (pp. 17-30).* New York: Basic Books.

Emihovich, C., & Lima, E. S. (1995). The many facets of Vygotsky: A cultural historical voice from the future. Anthropology & Education Quarterly, 26, 375-383.

Emmons, R.A. (1985). Personal strivings: An approach to personality and subjective well-being. *Journal of Personality and Social Psychology, 51,* 1058-1068. Emmons, R. A. (1998). A systems framework or systems frameworks? *Psychological Inquiry, 9,* 148-150.

Emmons, R. A. (2000). Spirituality and intelligence: Problems and prospects. International Journal for the Psychology of Religion, 10, 57-64.

Emmons, R. A., & King, L. A. (1988). Conflict among personal strivings: Immediate and long-term implications for psychological and physical well-being. *Journal of Personality and Social Psychology, 54,* 1040-1048.

Emmons, R. A., & King, L A., (1989). Personal striving differentiation and affective reactivity. *Journal of Personality and Social Psychology, 56,* 478-484.

Epstein, E. & Guttman, R. (1984). Mate selection in man: Evidence, theory, and outcome. *Social Biology, 31,* 243-278.

Epstein, S. (1973). The self-concept revisited, or a theory of a theory. *American Psychologist, 28,* 404-416.

Epstein, S. (1979). The stability of behavior: I. On predicting most of the people much of the time. *Journal of Personality and Social Psychology, 37,* 1097-1126.

Epstein, S. (1997). This I have learned from over 40 years of personality research. *Journal of Personality, 65,* 3-32.

Epstein, S. (1998). Constructive thinking: The key to emotional intelligence. Westport, CT: Praeger.

Epstein, S., & Meier, P. (1989). Constructive thinking: A broad coping variable with specific components. *Journal of Personality and Social Psychology, 57,* 332-350.

Epstein, S., & O'Brien, E.J. (1985). The person-situation debate in historical and current perspective. *Psychological Bulletin, 98,* 513-537.

Epstein, S., Pacini, R., Denes-Raj, V., Heier, H. (1996). Individual differences in intuitive-experiential and analytical-rational thinking styles. *Journal of Personality and Social Psychology, 71,* 390-405.

Epton, T., Harris, P. R., Kane, R., van Koningsbruggen, G. M. & Paschal, S. (2015). The impact of self-affirmation on health-behavior change: A meta-analysis. *Health Psychology, 34,* 187-196.

Erdelyi, M.H. (1984). *Psychoanalysis: Freud's cognitive psychology.* New York: W.H. Freeman and Company.

Erikson, E.H. (1958). The nature of clinical evidence. *Daedalus,* pp. 55-65.

Erikson, E.H. (1963). *Childhood and society (2nd ed.)* New York: W.W. Norton & Company.

Erikson, E. H. (1965). Psychoanalysis and ongoing history: Problems of identity, hatred, and nonviolence. *The American Journal of Psychiatry, 122,* 241-250.

Erikson, E. H. (1969). *Gandhi's Truth.* New York: Norton.

Erikson, E. H. (1975). *Life history and the historical moment.* New York: W. W. Norton & Company.

Ernst, C., & Angst, J. (1983). *Birth order: Its influence on personality.* Berlin: Springer-Verlag.

Exline, R. V., Thiabaut, J., Hickey, C. B., & Gumpart, P. (1970). Visual interactions in relation to expectations, and situational preferences: Personality influences on the decision to participate in volunteer helping behaviors. *Journal of Personality, 67,* 470-503.

Eysenck, H. J. (1967). *The biological basis of personality.* Springfield, IL: Charles C. Thomas.

Eysenck, H. J. (1972). Primaries or second-order factors: A critical consideration of Cattell's 16 PF Battery. British Journal of Social & Clinical Psychology, 11, 265-269.

Eysenck, H. J. (1980). Personality, marital satisfaction, and divorce. Psychological Reports, 47, 1235-1238.

Eysenck, H.J. (1982). *A model of intelligence.* New York: Springer.

Eysenck, H.J. (1990). Biological dimensions of personality. In L.A. Pervin (Ed.) *Handbook of Personality* (pp. 244-270). New York: Guilford.

Eysenck, H.J., & Eysenck, S.B.G. (1968). *Manual: Eysenck Personality Inventory: Manual.* San Diego, CA: Educational and Testing Service [EDITS].

Eysenck, H. J., & Eysenck, S. B. G. (1975). *Manual: Eysenck Personality Questionnaire.* San Diego, CA: EDITS/Educational and Industrial Testing Service.

Eysenck, H. J. & Gudjonsson, G. (1989). *Causes and cures of delinquency.* New York: Plenum Press.

Eysenck, H.J., & Kamin, L. (1981). *The intelligence controversy.* New York: Wiley.

Eysenck, S. B. G., & Eysenck, H. J. (1963). The validity of questionnaire and rating assessments of extraversion and neuroticism, and their factorial stability. *British Journal of Psychology, 54,* 51-62.

Faber, M. A. & Mayer, J. D. (2009). Resonance to archetypes in media: There's some accounting for taste. *Journal of Research in Personality, 43,* 307-322.

Fagan, J.F. (1992). Intelligence: A theoretical viewpoint. *Current Directions in Psychological Science, 1,* 82-86.

Fancher, R.E. (1985). *The intelligence men: Makers of the IQ controversy.* New York: W.W. Norton.

Faulkner, W. (1929/1956). *The sound and the fury.* New York: Random House.

Feenstra, J. S., Banyard, V. L., Rines, E., & Hopkins, K. R. (2001). First-year students' adaptation to college: The role of family variables and individual coping. *Journal of College Student Development, 42,* 106-113.

Fenichel, O. (1945). *The psychoanalytic theory of neurosis.* New York: Norton.

Fenigstein, A., Scheier, F. M., & Buss, A. H. (1975). Public and private self-consciousness: Assessment and theory. *Journal of Consulting and Clinical Psychology, 43,* 522-527.

Fields, J. (2001). Living arrangements of Children. *Current Population Reports.* Washington, DC: U.S. Census Bureau.

Fieve, R.R. (1975). Mood swing. New York: Morrow.

Finch, J. F., & Graziano, W. G. (2001). Predicting depression from temperament, personality, and patterns of social relations. *Journal of Personality, 69,* 27-54.

Fischer, J. E., Mohanty, A., Herrington, J. D., Koven, N. S., Miller, G. A., & Heller, W. (2004). Neuropsychological evidence for dimensional schizotypy: Implications for creativity and psychopathology. *Journal of Research in Personality, 38,* 24-31.

Fiske, A. P. (1991). The cultural relativity of selfish individualism: Anthropological evidence that humans are inherently sociable. In M. S. Clark (Ed.) *Prosocial behavior (pp. 176-214).* Thousand Oaks, CA, US: Sage Publications.

Fiske, D.W. (1949). Consistency of the factorial structures of personality ratings from different sources. *Journal of Abnormal and Social Psychology, 44,* 107-112.

Flanagan, O. J. (2002). The problem of the soul: two visions of mind and how to reconcile them. New York: Basic Books.

Flashman, L. A., Andreasen, N. C., Flaum, M., & Swayze, V. W. (1998). Intelligence and regional brain volumes in normal controls. *Intelligence, 25,* 149-160.

Fletcher, K. E., & Averill, J. R. (1984). A scale for the measurement of role-playing ability. *Journal of Research in Personality, 18,* 131-149.

Fodor, J.A. (1985). Precis of "The Modularity of Mind". *The Behavioral and Brain Sciences, 8,* 1-42.

Folkman, S., & Lazarus, R. S. (1980). An analysis of coping in a middle-aged community sample. Journal of Health & Social Behavior, 21, 219-239.

Folkman, S., & Lazarus, R. S. (1985). If it changes it must be a process: Study of emotion and coping during three stages of a college examination. *Journal of Personality and Social Psychology, 48,* 150-170.

Folkman, S., Lazarus, R. S., Dunkel-Schetter, C., DeLongis, A., & Gruen, R. J. (1986). *Journal of Personality and Social Psychology, 50,* 992-1003.

Foos, P. W. (2001). A self-reference exercise for teaching life expectancy. *Teaching of Psychology, 28,* 199-201.

Forgas, J. P. (Ed.) (2001). Handbook of affect and social cognition. Mahway, NJ: Lawrence Erlbaum Associates.

Formica, S. (1998). *Description of the socio-emotional life space: Life qualities and activities related to emotional intelligence.* Unpublished honors thesis, University of New Hampshire, Durham, NH.

Fowles,D. C. (1987). Application of a behavioral theory of motivation to the concepts of anxiety and impulsivity. *Journal of Research in Personality, 21,* 417-435.

Fowles, D. C. (1994). A motivational theory of psychopathology. In W. Spaulding (Ed.), *Nebraska Symposium on Motivation: Integrated Views of Motivation, Cognition, and Emotion* (Vol. 41, pp. 181-238). Lincoln: University of Nebraska Press.

Fox, N. A. (1991). If it's not left, it's right. *American Psychologist, 46,* 863-872.

Fox, N. A., Henderson, H. A., Marshall, P. J., Nichols, K. E., Ghera, M. M. (2005) Behavioral inhibition: Linking biology and behavior within a developmental framework. *Annual Review of Psychology, 56,* 235-262,

Frank, L. K. (1939). Projective methods for the study of personality. *Journal of Personality, 8*, 343-389.

Frank, L. R. (2001). *Quotationary*. New York: Random House.

Fraser, J. (2003). *The territory of men: A memoir*. New York: Random House.

Fraser, S. (1995). *The bell curve wars*. Basic Books.

Frasure-Smith, N., Lesperance, F., & Talajic, M. (1993). Depression following myocardial infarction: Impact on six-month survival. *JAMA: Journal of the American Medical Association, 270*, 1819-1825.

Fredrickson, B. L. (2002). Positive emotions. In C. R. Snyder, & S. J. Lopez (Eds.), *Handbook of positive psychology*. New York: Oxford University Press.

Freese, J., Powell, B., & Steelman, L. C. (1999). Rebel without a cause or effect: birth order and social attitudes. *American Sociological Review, 64*, 207-231.

Freitag, M. K., Belsky, J., Grossmann, K., Grossmann, K. E., & Scheuerer-Englisch, H. (1996). Continuity in parent-child relationships from infancy to middle childhood and relations with friendship competence. *Child Development, 67*, 1437-1454.

Freud, A. (1937/1966). *The Ego and the Mechanisms of Defense (Revised Edition)*. New York: International Universities Press, Inc. [C. Baines (Trans.); Original work published 1937].

Freud, S. (1900/1960). *The interpretation of dreams*. J. Strachey (Ed.). New York: Basic Books.

Freud, S. (1905/1953). Three contributions to the theory of sex: II. Infantile sexuality. In *The standard edition of the complete psychological works of Sigmund Freud (Vol. VII)*. London: Hogarth.

Freud, S. (1912/1958). The dynamics of transference. In J. Strachey (Ed. and Trans.), *The standard edition of the complete psychological works of Sigmund Freud* (Vol. 12, pp. 99-108). London: Hogarth Press (Original work published 1912).

Freud, S. (1913/1989). The Theme of the Three Caskets. In P. Gay (Ed.). *The Freud Reader (pp. 514-522)*. New York: W. W. Norton. [Original work published 1913].

Freud, S. (1914/1958). Remembering, repeating, and working through. *The standard edition of the complete psychological works of Sigmund Freud*, Vol XII. London: Hogarth, pp. 145-156. [Original work published 1914].

Freud, S. (1915/1963a). The unconscious. In P. Rieff (Ed.) & C.M. Baines (Trans.), *General psychological theory: Papers on metapsychology* (pp. 83-103). New York: Macmillan. [Original work published 1915].

Freud, S. (1917/1966). *Introductory lectures on psychoanalysis*. J. Strachey, (Ed.). New York: W.W. Norton.

Freud, S. (1920/1943). *A general introduction to psychoanalysis*. (J. Riviere, Trans.). Garden City, NY: Garden City Publishing Company.

Freud, S. (1920/1966). *Introductory lectures on Psychoanalysis*. (J. Strachey (Trans. & Ed.) New York: W. W. Norton.

Freud, S. (1923/1960). *The ego and the id*. J. Riviere (Trans.), J. Strachey (Ed.). New York: W. W. Norton.

Freud, S. (1927). Some psychological consequences of the anatomical distinction between the sexes. In J. Strachey (Ed. and Trans.), *The standard edition of the complete psychological works of Sigmund Freud (Vol. 8) (pp. 133-142)*. London: Hogarth Press.

Freud, S. (1930/1961). *Civilization and its discontents*. (J. Strachey, Trans.). New York: W. W. Norton. [Original work published 1930].

Freud, S. (1933/1965). *New Introductory Lectures on Psychoanalysis*. J. Strachey (Trans.). New York: W. W. Norton. (Original work published 1933).

Freud, S. (1937/1964). Analysis terminable and interminable. *The standard edition of the complete psychological works of Sigmund Freud*, Vol. XXIII. London: Hogarth, pp. 216-253. [Original work published 1937].

Freud, S. (1937/1964). Analysis terminable and interminable. In J. Strachey (Ed. and Trans.), *The standard edition of the complete psychological works of Sigmund Freud* (Vol. 23, pp. 209-253). London: Hogarth Press. (Original work published 1937).

Freud, S. (1962). Creative writers and daydreaming. In J. Strachey (ed.), *The standard edition of the complete psychological works of Sigmund Freud*. London: Hogarth, Vol. IX.

Friedman, H. S., & Kern, M. L. (2014). Personality, well-being, and health. *Annual Review Of Psychology, 65*, 719-742. doi:10.1146/annurev-psych-010213-115123

Friedman, M., & Rosenman, R. H. (1959). Association of a specific overt behavior pattern with increases in blood cholesterol, blood clotting time, incidence of arcus senilis and clinical coronary artery disesase. *JAMA, Journal of the American Medical Association, 169*, 1286-1296.

Friedman, H. S., & Schustack, M. W. (2003). *Personality: Classic theories and modern research*. Boston: Allyn & Bacon.

Funder, D. C. (1995). On the accuracy of personality judgment: A realistic approach. *Psychological Review, 102*, 652-670.

Funder, D. C. (1999). *Personality judgment: A realistic approach to person perception*. San Diego, CA: Academic Press.

Funder, D. C. (1998). Why does personality theory exist? *Psychological Inquiry, 9*, 150-152.

Funder, D. C. (2000). Personality. *Annual Review of Psychology, 52*, 172-221.

Funder, D. C. (2001). *The Personality Puzzle* (2nd ed.). New York: W. W. Norton.

Funder, D. (2004). *The personality puzzle* (3rd ed.). New York: Norton.

Funder, D. C. & Colvin, C. R. (1988). Friends and strangers: Acquaintanceship, agreement, and the accuracy of personality judgment. *Journal of Personality and Social Psychology, 55*, 149-158.

Funder, D. C. & Colvin, C. R. (1991). Explorations in behavioral consistency: Properties of persons, situations, and behaviors. *Journal of Personality and Social Psychology, 60*, 773-794.

Funder, D. C., & Dobroth K. M. (1987). Differences between traits: Properties associated with inter-judge agreement. *Journal of Personality and Social Psychology, 52*, 409-418.

Funder, D. C. & Ozer, D. J. (1983). Behavior as a function of the situation. *Journal of Personality and Social Psychology, 44*, 107-112.

Furnham, A., Richards, S. C., & Paulhus, D. L. (2013). The dark triad of personality: A 10 year review. *Social and Personality Compass, 7*, 199-216.

Ghandi, Mohandas (Karamchand) (1942). In M. Block (Ed.), E. M. Trow (Managing Ed.) Current Biography 1942. New York: H. W. Wilson Company.

Gale Research (1988). 'Marilyn Vos Savant." *Newsmakers, Issue Cumulation.* Reproduced in *Biography Resource Center.* Farmington Hills, MI: The Gale Group, 2003; http://www.galenet.com/servlet/BioRc.

Gallup, G. G. & Suarez, S. D. (1986). Self awareness and the emergence of mind in humans and other primates. In J. Suls & A. G. Greenwald (Eds.). *Psychological perspectives on the self (Vol. 3).* Hillsdale, NJ: Erlbaum.

Galvin, J. (February/March, 2002). Poet's Sample: Emily Wilson. *Boston Review.* Boston, MA.

Garb, H. N., Wood, J. M., Lilienfeld, S., & Nezworski, M. T. (2003). Effective use of projective techniques in clinical practice: Let the data help with selection and interpretation. *Professional Psychology: Research and Practice, 33,* 454-463.

Gardner, H. (1983). *Frames of mind.* New York: Basic Books.

Gardner, H. (1993). *Frames of Mind: The Theory of Multiple Intelligences (10th Anniversary Edition.* New York: Basic Books.

Gardner, H. (2000). A case against spiritual intelligence. *International Journal for the Psychology of Religion, 10,* 27-34.

Gartstein, M. A., & Rothbart, M. K. (2003). Infant behavior questionnaire – revised: A fine-grained approach to assessment of temperament in infancy.

Garza, D. L., & Feltz, D. L. (1998). Effects of selected mental practice on performance, self-efficacy, and competition confidence of figure skaters. *The Sports Psychologist, 12,* 1-15.

Gasking, D. A. T. (1946). Types of questions. *Melbourne University Magazine,* pp. 4-6.

Gauguin, Paul. (1998). Entry in *The New Encyclopaedia Britannica (Vol. 5; pp. 147-148).* Chicago: Encyclopaedia Britannica, Inc.

Gay, P. (1988). *Freud: A life for our times.* New York: Norton.

Gazzaniga, M. S., & Heatherton, T. F. (2003). *Psychological science.* New York: Psychological Science.

Geher, G. (2003). Perceived and actual characteristics of parents and partners: A test of a Freudian model of mate selection. In N. J. Pallone (Ed.) *Love, romance, sexual interaction (pp. 75-102).* New Brunswick, NJ (USA): Transaction Publishers.

Geher, G., Warner, R. M., & Brown, A. S. (2001). Predictive validity of the Emotional Accuracy Research Scale. Intelligence, 29, 373-388.

Giancola, P. R., Shoal, G. D., Mezzich, A. C. (2001). Constructive thinking, executive functioning, antisocial behavior, and drug use involvement in adolescent females with a substance use disorder. *Experimental and Clinical Psychopharmacology, 9,* 215-227.

Gilbert, D. T. (1991). How mental systems believe. *American Psychologist, 46,* 107-119.

Gill, M., & Hoffman, I (1982a). Analysis of transference: Studies of nine audio-recorded psychoanalytic sessions. *Psychological Issues, Monograph 54,* 1-229.

Gill, M., & Hoffman, I. (1982b). A method for studying the analysis of aspects of the patient's experience of the relationship in psychoanalysis and psychotherapy. *Journal of the American Psychoanalytic Association, 25,* 471-490.

Gilligan, C. (1982). *In a different voice.* Cambridge, MA: Harvard University Press.

Gilovich, T., & Savitsky, K. (1999). The spotlight effect and the illusion of transparency: Egocentric assessments of how we are seen by others. *Current Directions in Psychological Science, 8,* 165-168.

Gladwell, M. (1998, August 17). Do parents matter? *The New Yorker,* 55-64.

Gleason, D. K. (1985). *Over Boston: Aerial photographs by David King Gleason.* Louisiana State University Press: Baton Rouge and London.

Gleick, J. (1987). *Chaos: Making a new science.* New York: Wiley.

Goddard, H. H. (1917). Mental tests and immigrants. *Journal of Delinquency, 2,* 243-277.

Godfrey, D. K., Jones, E. E., & Lord, C. G. (1986). Self-promotion is not ingratiating. *Journal of Personality and Social Psychology, 50,* 106-115.

Goffman, E. (1959/2003). The presentation of self. In J. A. Holstein & J. F. Gubrium (Eds.). *Inner lives and social worlds (pp. 130-139).* New York: Oxford University Press. [Original work published 1959].

Goldberg, C. (1983). Courage and fanaticism: The charismatic leader and modern religious cults. In D.A. Halperin (ed.) *Psychodynamic perspectives on religion, sect, and cult (pp. 163-185).* Boston: John Wright PSG Inc.

Goldberg, L. R. (1990). An alternative "description of personality": The Big-Five factor structure. *Journal of Personality and Social Psychology, 59,* 1216-1229.

Goldberg, L. R. (1993). The structure of phenotypic personality traits. *American Psychologist, 48,* 26-34.

Goldberg, L. R., & Rosolack, T. K. (1994). The Big Five factor structure as an integrative framework: An empirical comparison with Eysenck's P-E-N model. In C. F. Halverson, G. A. Kohnstamm & R. P. Martin (Eds.), *The developing structure of temperament and personality from infancy to adulthood* (pp. 7-35). Hillsdale, NJ: Lawrence Erlbaum Associates.

Goldenberg, J. L., Pyszczynski, T., Greenberg, J., Solomon, S., Kluck, B., & Cornwell, R. (2001). I am *not* an animal: Mortality salience, disgust, and the denial of human creatureliness. *Journal of Experimental Psychology: General, 130,* 427-235.

Gollwitzer, P. M. (1999). Implementation intentions: Strong effects of simple plans. *American Psychologist, 54,* 493-503.

Goodenough, F. L. (1949). *Mental testing: Its history, principles, and applications.* New York: Rinehart.

Gorsuch, R. L. (1983). *Factor analysis (2nd ed.).* Hillsdale, NJ: Lawrence Erlbaum.

Gosling, S. D., Ko, Sei Jin, Mannarelli, T., Morris, M. E. (2002). A room with a cue: Personality judgments based on offices and bedrooms. *Journal of Personality and Social Psychology, 82,* 379-398.

Gosling, S. D., & John, O. P. (1999). Personality dimension in nonhuman animals: A cross-species review. *Current Directions in Psychological Science, 8,* 69-75.

Gottfredson, G. D. & Holland, J. L. (1990). A longitudinal test of the influence of congruence: Job satisfaction, competency utilization, and counterproductive behavior. *Journal of Counseling Psychology, 27,* 389-398.

Gottfredson, G. D., & Holland, J. L. (1989). *Dictionary of Holland Occupational Codes (2nd Ed.).* Odessa, FL: Psychological Assessement Resources

Gottfredson, L. S. (2003). Dissecting practical intelligence theory: Its claims and evidence. *Intelligence, 31,* 343-397.

Gottman, J. M., Katz, L. F., & Hooven, C., (1996). Parental meta-emotion philosophy and the emotional life of families: Theoretical models and preliminary data. *Journal of Family Psychology, 10,* 243-268.

Gottman, J. M., & Silver, N. (1999). *The seven principles for making marriage work.* New York: Three Rivers Press.

Gough, M.G., McKee, & Yandell, R.J. (1955). Adjective check list analyses of a number of selected psychometric and assessment variables. OFficer Education Research Laboratory, Technical Memorandum, OERL-TM-55. [Cited in Dahlstrom, Welsh, & Dahlstrom, 1972].

Gould, D., Dieffenbach, K., Moffett, A. (2002) Psychological characteristics and their development in Olympic champions. Journal of Applied Sport Psychology, Vol 14, 72-204.

Gould, S.J. (1981). *The mismeasure of man.* New York: W.W. Norton.

Gould, S. J. (1991). Exaptation: A crucial tool for an evolutionary psychology. *Journal of Social Issues, 47,* 43-65. [Reprinted in Friedman, H. S., & M. W. Schustack, *Readings in personality: Classic theories and modern research.* Boston: Allyn and Bacon.

Graham, J.R. (1990). *MMPI-2: Assessing personality and psychopathology.* New York: Oxford University Press.

Gray, J. A. (1987a). Perspectives on anxiety and impulsivity: A commentary. *Journal of Research in Personality, 21,* 493-509.

Gray, J.A. (1987). The neuropsychology of emotion and personality. In S.M. Stahl, S.D. Iversen, & E.C. Goodman (Eds.), *Cognitive Neurochemistry (pp. 171-190).* Oxford: Oxford University Press.

Green, D. P., Salovey, P., & Truax, K. (1999). Static, dynamic, and causative bipolarity of affect. *Journal of Personality and Social Psychology, 76,* 856-867.

Greenberg, G. (1994). *The self on the shelf: Recovery books and the good life.* Albany, NY: State University of New York Press.

Greenberg, J., Pyszczynski, T. A.; Solomon, S. (1982). The self-serving attributional bias: Beyond self-presentation. Journal of Experimental Social Psychology, 18, 56-67.

Greenbie, M. B. (1932). *Personality and the divers methods by which some men and here and there a woman have achieved it.* New York: The Macmillan Company.

Greenlaw, L. (1999). *The hungry ocean: A swordboat captain's journey.* New York: Hyperion.

Greenwald, A. (1980). The totalitarian ego. *American Psychologist, 35,* 603-618.

Greenwald, A. G., Klinger, M. R., & Schuh, E. S. (1995). Activation by marginally perceptible ("subliminal") stimuli: Dissociation of unconscious from conscious cognition. *Journal of Experimental Psychology: General, 124,* 22-42.

Grigorienko, E. L. (2002). In search of the genetic engram of personality. In D. Cervone & W. Mischel (Eds.), *Advances in personality science (pp. 29-82).* New York: Guilford Press.

Grippo, A. J. & Johnson, A. K. (2002). Biological mechanisms in the relationship between depression and heart disease. *Neuroscience and Biobehavioral Reviews, 26,* 941-962.

Griswold, C. L. (1986). *Self-knowledge in Plato's Phaedrus.* New Haven: Yale University Press.

Gross, J. J., & Levenson, R W. (1997). Hiding feelings: The acute effects of inhibiting negative and positive emotion. *Journal of Abnormal Psychology, 106,* 95-103.

Gross, J. J., Sutton, S. K., & Ketelaar, T. (1998). Relations between affect and personality: Support for the affect-level and affective reactivity views. *Personality and Social Psychology Bulletin, 24,* 279-288.

Grossmann, K., Grossmann, K. E., Spangler, G., Suess, G., & Unzner, L. (1985). Maternal sensitivity and newborns' orientation responses as related to quality of attachment in northern Germany. In I. Bretherton, & E. Waters (Eds.), Groring points in attachment theory and research (pp. 233-257). *Monographs of the Society for Research in Child Development, 50,* (1-2, Serioal No. 209).

Grotevant, H. D. & Adams, G. R. (1984). Development of an objective measure to assess ego identity in adolescence: Validation and replication. *Journal of Youth and Adolescence, 10,* 419-438.

Grunbaum, A. (1986). Precis of *The foundations of psychoanalysis: A philosophical critique. Behavioral and Brain Sciences, 9,* 217-284.

Guilford, J.P. (1959). *Personality.* New York: McGraw Hill.

Guilford, J. P. (1967). *The nature of human intelligence.* New York: McGraw-Hill.

Gustafsson, J-E. (2001). Schooling and intelligence: Effects of track of study on level and profile of cognitive abilities. Paper presented to the 3rd Annual Spearman Conference. Sydney, Australia.

Hagerty, M. R. (1999). Testing Maslow's hierarchy of needs: National quality-of-life across time. *Social Indicators Research, 46,* 249-271.

Haier, R. J., Siegel, B. V., Nuechterlein, K. H., Hazlett, E., Wu, J. C., Pack, J., Browning, H. L., & Buchsbaum, M. S. (1988). Cortical glucose metabolic rate correlates of abstract reasoning and attention studied with positron emission tomography. *Intelligence, 12,* 199-217.

Haier, M. S., Siegel, B., Tanc, C., Abel, L., & Buchsbaum, M. S. (1992). Intelligence and changes in regional cerebral glucose metabolic rate following learning. *Intelligence, 16,* 415-426.

Halberstam, D. (1979). *The powers that be.* New York: Knopf.

Hall, C. S., & Lindzey, G. L. (1957). Theories of Personality. New York: John Wiley & Sons.

Hall, C. S., & Lindzey, G. L. (1978). *Theories of Personality (3rd ed.).* New York: John Wiley & Sons.

Hall, M. H. (1977). A conversation with Abraham Maslow. In R. E. Schell (Ed.). *Readings in developmental psychology today.* New York: CRM Books [Original interview published in 1968 in *Psychology Today*].

Halpern, D. (1997). Sex differences in intelligence. *American Psychologist, 52,* 1091-1102.

Hamblin, C. L. (1967). "Questions" in Edwards, P. (Editor and Chief), *The encyclopedia of philosophy (Vol 7) (pp. 49-53).* New York: Macmillan Publishing Company & the Free Press.

Hambrick, D. Z., Oswald, F. L., Attmann, E. M., Meinz, E. J., Gobet, F., Fernand, C. (2014). Deliberate practice: Is that all it takes to become an expert?. *Intelligence, 45,* 34-45.

Hamilton, R. J. (1985). A framework for the evaluation of the effectiveness of adjunct questions and objectives. *Review of Educational Research, 55,* 47-85.

Hamilton, W. D. (1964). The evolution of social behavior. *Journal of Theoretical Biology, 7,* 1-52.

Hampden-Turner, C. (1981). *Maps of the mind.* New York: MacMillan.

Han, J. J., Leichtman, M. D., & Wang, Q. (1998). Autobiographical memory in Korean, Chinese, and American children. *Developmental Psychology, 34,*

Hare, B. & Wrangham, R. (2002). Integrating two evolutionary models for the study of social cognition. In M. Bekoff, C. Allen, & G. Burghardt (Eds.). *The cognitive animal: Empirical and theoretical perspectives on animal cognition (pp. 363-369).* Cambridge, MA: MIT Press.

Hare, R. M. (1952). *The language of morals.* Oxford, England: Clarendon.

Hargrave, G. E., & Hiatt, D. (1989). Use of the California Psychological Inventory in law enforcement officer selection. *Journal of Personality Assessment, 53,* 267-277.

Harnqvist, K. (1968). Relative change in intelligence from 13 to 18. *Scandinavian Journal of Psychology, 9,* 50-82.

Harrell, T.W., & Harrell, M.S. (1945). Army General Classification Tests scores for civilian occupations. *Educational and psychological measurement, 5,* 229-239.

Harris, J. R. (1995). Where is the child's environment? A group socialization theory of development. *Psychological Review, 102,* 458-489.

Harris, J. R. (1998). *The nurture assumption: Why children turn out the way they do.* New York: Free Press.

Harter, S. (1999). *The construction of the self: A developmental perspective.* New York: Guilford Press.

Hartmann, E. L. (1973). *The functions of sleep.* New Haven, CT: Yale University Press.

Hartmann, E., Harrison, R., & Zborowski, M. (2001). Boundaries in the mind: Past research and future directions. *North American Journal of Psychology, 3,* 347-368.

Haselton, M. G., & Funder, D. (2006). The evolution of accuracy and bias in social judgment. In M. Schaller, D. T. Kenrick, & J. A. Simpson (Eds.), *Evolution and social psychology* (pp. 15-37). New York: Psychology Press.

Haslam, N., & Baron, J. (1994). Intelligence, personality, and prudence. In Ruzgis & R.J. Sternberg (Eds.), *Intelligence and Personality* (pp. 32-58). New York: Cambridge University Press.

Haslam, N (1994). Categories of social relationship. *Cognition, 53,* 59-90.

Hatfield, E. (1988). Passionate and companionate love. In R. Sternberg & M. L. Barnes (Eds.), *The psychology of love.* New Haven: Yale University Press.

Hathaway, S.R., & Meehl, P.E. (1952). Adjective check list correlates of MMPI scores. Unpublished materials. [Cited in Dahlstrom, Welsh, & Dahlstrom, 1972].

Hattie, J., & Cooksey, R. W. (1984). Procedures for assessing the validities of tests using the "known-groups" method. *Applied Psychological Measurement, 8,* 295-305.

Hawking, S. W. (1998). *A brief history of time.* New York: Bantam Books.

Hazan, C., & Shaver, P. R. (1987). Romantic love conceptualized as an attachment process. *Journal of Personality and Social Psychology, 52,* 511-524.

Hazan, C., & Shaver, P. R. (1994). Attachment as an organizational framework for research on close relationships. Psychological Inquiry, 5, 1-22.

Hecht, J. (2002). When did dogs become our best friends? *New Scientist, 176,* p. 16.

Heckhausen, H. (1969). *The anatomy of achievement motivation.* New York: Academic Press.

Hedlund, S., & Rude, S. S. (1995). Evidence of latent depressive schemas in formerly depressed individuals. *Journal of Abnormal Psychology, 104,* 517-525.

Heider, K. (1991). *Grand valley Dani: Peaceful warriors (2nd ed.)* Fort Worth, TX: Holt, Rinehart, & Winston.

Heilizer, F. (1964). Conjunctive and disjunctive conflict: A theory of need conflict. *Journal of Abnormal and Social Psychology, 68,* 21-37.

Held, B. S. (2002). The tyranny of the positive attitude in America: Observation and speculation. *Journal of Clinical Psychology, 58,* 965-992.

Helson, R. & Srivastava, S. (2001). Three paths of adult development: Conservers, seekers, and achievers. *Journal of Personality and Social Psychology, 80,* 995-1100.

Helson, R., & Wink, P. (1987). Two conceptions of maturity examined in the findings of a longitudinal study. *Journal of Personality and Social Psychology, 53,* 531-541.

Hendrick, C., & Hendrick, S. (1986). A theory and method of love. *Journal of Personality and Social Psychology, 50,* 392-402.

Hendrick, C., & Hendrick, S. S. (2003). Romantic love: Measuring cupid's arrow. In S. J. Lopez & C. R. Snyder (Eds.). Positive psychological assessment: A handbook of models and measures (pp. 235-249). Washington, DC: American Psychological Association, 2003.

Henriques, G. (2003). The tree of knowledge system and the theoretical unification of psychology. *Review of General Psychology, 7,* 150-182.

Hermans, H. J. M., Kempen, H. J. G., & van Loon, R. J. P. (1992). The dialogical self: Beyond individualism and rationalism. *American Psychologist, 47,* 23-33.

Herrnstein, R.J. (1971). I.Q. *Atlantic Monthly, 228,* 43-64.

Herrnstein, R.J. (1973). *IQ in the meritocracy.* Boston: Little, Brown, & Company.

Heschel, A. J. (1965). *Who is man?* Stanford University Press.

Hess, T. M., Pullen, S. M., McGee, K. A. (1996). Acquisition of prototype-based information about social groups in adulthood. *Psychology and Aging,* 11, 179-190. Hesse, E. (1999). The adult attachment interview: Historical and current perspectives. J. Cassidy & P. R. Shaver (Eds.), *Handbook of attachment: Theory, research, and clinical applications (pp. 395-433).* New York: Guilford.

Hetherington, E. M., Bridges, M., & Insabella, G. M. (1998). What matters? What does not? Five perspectives on the association between marital transitions and children's adjustment. *American Psychologist, 53,* 167-184.

Heyns, R. W., Veroff, J., & Atkinson, J. W. (1992). A scoring manual for the affiliative motive. In In C. P. Smith (Ed.), *Motivation and personality: Handbook of thematic content analysis (pp. 211-223).* New York: Cambridge.

Hewitt, J. P. (2003). *Self and society (9th Ed.).* Boston: Allyn & Bacon.

Hibbard, S. (2003). A critique of Lilienfeld et al.'s (2000) "The scientific status of projective techniques." *Journal of Personality Assessment, 80,* 260-271.

Hickam, H. H. (1998). *Rocket boys: A memoir.* Delacorte Press.

Higgins, C. A., & Judge, T. A. (2004). The effect of applicant influence tactics on recruiter perceptions of fit and hiring recommendations: A field study. *Journal of Applied Psychology, 89,* 622-632.

Higgins, E.T. (1987). Self-discrepancy theory: A theory relating self and affect. *Psychological Review, 94,* 319-340.

Higgins, E. T., Shah, J., & Friedman, R. (1997). Emotional responses to goal attainment: Strength of regulatory focus as moderator. *Journal of Personality and Social Psychology, 72,* 515-525.

Hilgard, E.R. (1965). *Hypnotic susceptibility.* New York: Harcourt, Brace, & World.

Hilgard, E. R. (1973). A neodissociation interpretation of pain reduction in hypnosis. *Psychological Review, 80,* 403-419.

Hilgard, E. R. (1974). Toward a neo-dissociation theory: Multiple cognitive controls in human functioning. *Perspectives in Biology and Medicine, 17,* 301-316.

Hilgard, E.R. (1977). *Divided consciousness: Multiple controls in human thought and action.* New York: Wiley.

Hilgard, J.R. (1979). *Personality and hypnosis: A study of imaginative involvement (2nd Ed.).* Chicago: University of Chicago Press.

Hilgard, E.R. (1980). The trilogy of mind: Cognition, affection, and conation. *Journal of the History of the Behavioral Sciences, 16,* 107-117.

Hilgard, E. R. (1994). Neodissociation theory. In S. J. Lynn & J. Rhue (Ed). Dissociation: Clinical and theoretical perspectives (32-51). New York: Guilford.

Hoffman, E. (1999). The right to be human. New York: McGraw Hill.

Hoffman, P. (1998). *The man who loved only numbers.* New York: Hyperion.

Hogan, R. (1998). What is personality psychology? *Psychological Inquiry, 9,* 152-153.

Hogan, R. (1983). A socioanalytic theory of personality. In M.M. Page (Ed.), *Personality, current theory and research. Nebraska symposium on motivation 1982 (pp. 55-90).* Lincoln, NE: University of Nebraska Press.

Holland, J. L. (1985). *Professional manual for the Self-Directed Search.* Odessa, FL: Psychological Assessment Resources.

Holland, J. L. (1987). *Manual supplement for the Self-Directed Search.* Odessa, FL: Psychological Assessment Resources.

Holland, J. L. (1997). *Making vocational choices: A theory of vocational personalities and work environments (3rd edition).* Odessa, FL: Psychological Assessment Resources.

Holland, J. L., Whitney, D. R., Cole, N. S., & Richards, J. M. (April, 1969). An empirical occupational classification derived from a theory of personality and intended for practice and research. *ACT Research Report 29,* 1-22. Iowa City, IA: American College Testing Program.

Holmes, D.S. (1974). Investigations of repression: Differential recall of material experimentally or naturally associated with ego threat. *Psychological Bulletin, 81,* 632-651.

Holmes, D.S., & Shallow, J.R. (1969). Reduced recall after ego threat: Repression or response competition? *Journal of Personality and Social Psychology, 13,* 145-152.

Home, J. A., & Osberg, O. (1976). A self-assessment questionnaire to determine morningness-eveningness in human circadian rhyhms. *International Journal of Chronobiology, 4,* 97-110.

Hong, K. & Townes, B. (1976). Infant's attachment to inanimate objects. *Journal of the Academy of Child Psychiatry, 15,* 49-61.

Horner, M. S. (1972). Toward an understanding of achievement-related conflicts in women. *Journal of Social Issues, 28,* 157-176.

Horner, M. S. (1992). The motive to avoid success. In C. P. Smith (Ed.). Motivation and personality: *Handbook of thematic content analysis.* Cambridge, England: Cambridge University Press.

Horney, K. (1945). *Our inner conflicts: A constructive theory of neurosis.* New York: W.W. Norton.

Hovey, H.B. (1953). MMPI profiles and personality characteristics. *Journal of Consulting Psychology, 17,* 142-146.

Hoyenga, K. B., & Hoyenga, K. T. (1993). *Gender-related differences: Origins and outcomes.* Boston: Allyn & Bacon.

Hull, J. G. & Reilly, N. P. (1986). Information processing approach to alcohol use and its consequences. In R. E. Ingram (Ed) Information processing approaches to clinical psychology (pp. 151-167). San Diego, CA: Academic Press, Inc,..

Hull, J. G. & Slone, L. B. (2004) Alcohol and self-regulation. In Baumeister, R. F. & Vohs, K. D. (Eds.) Handbook of self-regulation: Research, theory, and applications (pp. 466-491). New York: Guilford Press.

Hunt, N. (1967). *The world of Nigel Hunt: The Diary of a Mongoloid Youth.* New York: Garrett Publications.

Hurlburt, R., Koch, M., & Heavey, C. L. (2001). Descriptive experience sampling demonstrates the connection of thinking to externally observable behavior. *Cognitive Therapy and Research, 26,* 117-134.

Hurley, J. R. (1955). The Iowa Picture Interpretation Test: A multiple-choice variation for the TAT. *Journal of Consulting Psychology, 19,* 372-376.

Husen, T. (1951). The influence of schooling upon IQ. *Theoria, 17,* 61-88.

Huston, H. L., Rosen, D. H., & Smith, S. M. (1999). Evolutionary memory. In D. Rosen, & M. Luebbert (Eds.). *The evolution of the psyche (pp. 139-149).* Westport, CT: Praeger.

Hyde, J. S. (1986). Gender differences in aggression. In J. S. Hyde & M. C. Linn (Eds.). *The psychology of gender: Advances through meta-analysis.* Baltimore: Johns Hopkins University Press.

Isaacson, R. L. (1982). *The limbic system (2nd ed.).* New York: Plenum.

IPAT Staff (1991). *Administrator's manual for the Sixteen Personality Factor Questionnaire.* Champaign, IL: Institute for Personality and Ability Testing.

Isen, A. M., Shalker, T. E., Clark, M., Karp, L. (1978). Affect, accessibility of material in memory, and behavior: A cognitive loop? *Journal of Personality and Social Psychology, 36,* 1-12.

Ivcevic, Z., Brackett, M. A., & Mayer, J. D. (2007). Emotional intelligence and emotional creativity. *Journal Of Personality, 75*(2), 199-235. doi:10.1111/j.1467-6494.2007.00437.x

Ivcevic, Z., Mayer, J. D., & Brackett, M. A. (2003). Exploration personality the natural way: An inquiry into open-ended self-descriptions. *Imagination, Cognition, and Personality, 22,* 211-238.

Izard, C. E. (1992). Basic emotions, relations among emotions, and emotion-cognition relations. *Psychological Review, 99,* 561-565.

Izard, C. E., Libero, D. Z., Putnam, P., & Haynes, O. M. (1993). Stability of emotion experiences and their relations to traits of personality. *Journal of Personality and Social Psychology, 64,* 847-860.

Jackendoff, R. (1987). *Consciousness and the computational mind.* Cambridge, MA: MIT Press.

Jackson, D. N. (1974). *Personality Research Form Manual.* Goshen, NY: Research Psychologists Press.

Jackson, F. (1982). Epiphenomenal Qualia. *Philosophical Quarterly, 32,* 127-136.

Jacoby, L.L., Allan, L.G., Collins, J.C., & Larwill, L.K. (1988). Memory influences subjective experience: Noise judgments. *Journal of Experimental Psychology: Learning, Memory, and Cognition, 14,* 240-247.

Jacobs, W.J., & Nadel, L. (1985). Stress-induced recovery of fears and phobias. *Psychological Review, 92,* 512-531.

Jacoby, L.L., Lindsay, S., & Toth, J.P. (1992). Unconscious influences revealed: Attention, awareness, and control. *American Psychologist, 47,* 802-809.

Jacoby, L.L., Woloshyn, V., & Kelley, C.M. (1989). Becoming famous without being recognized: Unconscious influences of memory produced by dividing attention. *Journal of Experimental Psychology: General, 118,* 115-125.

James, W. (1890/1950). *The principles of psychology (Vol. 1).* New York: Henry Holt.

James, W. (1892). *Psychology.* New York: Henry Holt.

James, W. (1920). *Psychology: The briefer course.* New York: Holt.

Jamieson, G. A. (2001). Hypnotic susceptibility is positively related to a subset of schizotypy items. *Contemporary Hypnosis, 18,* 32-37.

Jamison, K. R. (1993). *Touched with fire: Manic-depressive illness and the artistic temperament.* New York: Free Press.

Jamison, K. R. (1996). In J. Schildkraut, O. Aurora (Eds). *Depression and the spiritual in modern art: Homage to Miro (pp. 15-32).* Oxford, England: John Wiley & Sons.

Jang, K. L., McCrae, R. R., Angleitner, A., Riemann, R., & Livesley, W. J. (1998). Heritability of facet-level traits in a cross-cultural twin sample: Support for a hierarchical model of personality. *Journal of Personality and Social Psychology, 74,* 1556-1565.

Jaynes, J. (1976). *The origin of consciousness in the breakdown of the bicameral mind.* Boston: Houghton Mifflin Company.

Jelicic, M., De Roode, A., Bovill, J.G., & Bonke, B. (1992). Unconscious learning established under anaesthesia. *Anaesthesia, 47,* 835-837.

Jelicic, M.; Bonke, B., De Roode, A. (1993). Implicit learning during anesthesia. In: P. S. Sebel, B. Bonke, & E. Winograd (Eds) Memory and awareness in anesthesia: III (pp. 81-84). New York: Prentice Hall Professional Technical Reference

Jemmott, J. B. III, Hellman, C., McClelland, D. C., Locke, S. E., Kraus, L., Williams, R. M., & Valeri, C. R. (1990). Motivational syndromes associated with natural killer cell activity. *Journal of Behavioral Medicine, 13,* 53-73.

Jencks, C. (1972). *Inequality: A reassessment of the effect of family and schooling in America.* New York: Basic Books.

Jensen, A. (1980). *Bias in mental testing.* New York: Free Press.

Jensen, A. (1987). Psychometric *g* as a focus of concerted research effort. *Intelligence, 11,* 193-198.

Jensen-Campbell, L. A., & Graziano, W. G. (2001). Agreeableness as a moderator of conflict. *Journal of Personality, 69,* 324362.

Jerison, H. J. (2000). The evolution of intelligence. In R. J. Sternberg (Ed.), *Handbook of intelligence* (pp. 216-244). Cambridge: Cambridge University Press.

Jedlicka, D. (1984). Indirect parental influence on mate choice: A test of the psychoanalytic theory. *Journal of Marriage and the Family, 46,* 65-70.

Jensen, A. & Johnson, F.W. (1994). Race and sex differences in head size and IQ. *Intelligence, 18,* 341.

Joachim, K. (1996). The politics of self esteem. *American Educational Research Journal, 33,* 3-22.

Jockin, V., McGue, M., & Lykken, D. (1996). Personality and divorce: A genetic analysis. *Journal of Personality and Social Psychology, 71,* 288-299.

John, O.P., Angleitner, A., & Ostendorf, F. (1988). The lexical approach to personality: A historical review of trait taxonomic research. *European Journal of Personality, 2,* 171-205.

Johnson, W.G., Wildman, H.E., Downey, C., & Bell, S. (1980). Personality: Trends in theory and research. *Social Behavior and Personality, 8,* 209-211.

Jones, A., & Crandall, R. (1986). Validation of a short index of self-actualization. *Personality and Social Psychology Bulletin, 12,* 63-73.

Jones, K., & Day, J. D. (1997). Discrimination of two aspects of cognitive-social intelligence from academic intelligence. *Journal of Educational Psychology, 89,* 486-497.

Jopling, D A. (2000). *Self knowledge and the self.* New York: Routledge.

Jöreskog, K. G., & Sörbom, D. (1999). LISREL8.30: User's reference guide. Chicago: Scientific Software.

Josselson, R. (1995). Narrative and psychological understanding. *Psychiatry, 58,* 330-343.

Josselson, R. (1996). *Revising herself: The story of women's identity from college to midlife.* New York: Oxford University Press.

Judge, T. A. (2001). A rose by any other name: Are self-esteem, generalized self-efficacy, neuroticism, and locus of control indicators of a common construct? In B W. Roberts, R. Hogan (Eds.). *Personality psychology in the workplace: Decade of Behavior (pp. 93-118).* Washington, DC: American Psychological Association.

Judge, T. A., Higgins, C. A., Thoresen, C. J., & Barrick, M. R. (1999). The big five personality traits, general mental ability, and career success across the life span. *Personnel Psychology, 52,* 621-652.

Jung, C. (1934/1953). The relations between the ego and the unconscious. Reprinted in C. G. Jung (1953). *Two essays on analytical psychology (pp. 131-253).* R. F. C. (Trans.). Cleveland, OH: World Publishing. [Original work published 1934].

Jung, C. (1953). *Two essays on analytical psychology*. Cleveland, OH: World Publishing.

Jung, C. (1968). *Analytical psychology: Its theory and practice; The Tavistock Lectures*. [With a foreword by E. A. Bennet]. New York: Random House

Kagan, J. (1984). *The nature of the child*. New York: Basic Books.

Kagan, J. & Snidman, N (1991). Infant predictors of inhibited and uninhibited profiles. *Psychological Science, 2,* 40-44.

Kagan, J. (2003). Biology, context, and developmental inquiry. *Annual Review of Psychology, 54,* 1-23.

Kamin, L. (1974). *The science and politics of I.Q.* New York: Erlbaum Associates.

Kaminer, W. (1992). *I'm dysfunctional, you're dysfunctional: The recovery movement and other self-help fashions*. Reading, MA: Addison-Wesley Publishing Company.

Kammrath, L. K., Mendoza-Denton, R., Mischel, W. (2005). Incorporating If ... Then ... Personality Signatures in Person Perception: Beyond the Person-Situation Dichotomy. *Journal of Personality and Social Psychology, 88,* 605-618.

Kamphaus, R. W., Benson, J., Hutchison, S., & Platt, L. O. (1994). Identification of factor models for the WISC-III. *Educational and Psychological Measurement, 54,* 174-186.

Karlsson, J. L. (1984). Creative intelligence in relatives of mental patients. *Hereditas, 100,* 83-86.

Karni, A., Meyer, G., Adams, M., Turner, R., & Ungerleider, L. G. (1994). The acquisition and retention of a motor skill: A functional MRI study of long-term motor cortex plasticity. *Abstracts of the Society for Neuroscience, 20,* 1291.

Kelley, R. D. G. (2003). Confessions of a nice Negro, or why I shaved my head. In J. A. Holstein & J. F. Gubrium (Eds.). *Inner lives and social worlds (pp. 356-361)*. New York: Oxford University Press. [Original work published 1995].

Kelly, E. L., & Conley, J. J. (1987). Personality and compatibility: A prospective analysis of marital stability and marital satisfaction. *Journal of Personality and social Psychology, 52,* 27-40.

Kelly, G. A. (1955a). *The psychology of personal constructs. Volume One: A theory of personality*. New York: W. W. Norton.

Kelly, G. A. (1955b). *The psychology of personal constructs: Volume Two: Clinical diagnosis and psychotherapy*. New York: W. W. Norton & Company.

Kenny, D. A., Albright, L., & Malloy, T. E., & Kashy, D. A. (1994). Consensus in Interpersonal Perception: Acquaintance and the Big Five. *Psychological Bulletin, 116,* 245-258.

Kenrick, D. T., & Keefe, R. C. (1992). Age preferences in mates reflect sex differences in reproductive strategies. *Behavioral and Brain Sciences, 15,* 75-91.

Kernis, M. H., Cornell, D. P., Sun, C-R., Berry, A., & Harlow, T. (1993). There's more to self-esteem than whether it's high or low: The importance of stability of self-esteem. *Journal of Personality and Social Psychology, 65,* 1190-1204.

Keys, A., Brozek, J., Henschel, A., Mickelsen, O., & Taylor, H. L. (1950). The biology of human starvation. Minneapolis, MN: University of Minnesota Press.

Kidwell, J. S. (1981). Number of siblings, sibling spacing, sex, and birth order: their effects on perceived parent-child relationships. *Journal of Marriage and Family, 78,* 763-766.

Kipnis, D. (1971). *Character structure and impulsiveness*. New York: Academic Press.

Kinsey, A. C., Pomeroy, W. B., & Martin, C. E. (1948). *Sexual behavior in the human male*. Philadelphia: Saunders.

Kinsey, A. C., Pomeroy, W. B., Martin, C. E., & Gebhard, P. H. (1953). *Sexual behavior in the human female*. Philadelphia: Saunders.

Kihlstrom, J.F. (1990). The psychological unconscious. In L.A. Pervin (Ed.), *Handbook of Personality* (pp. 445-464). New York: Guilford.

Kihlstrom, J. F. & Cantor, N. (2000). Social intelligence. In. R. J. Sternberg (Ed.). *Handbook of intelligence (359-379)*. Cambridge, UK: Cambridge University Press.

Kirsch, I. (1997). Suggestibility or hypnosis: What do our scales really measure? *International Journal of Clinical and Experimental Hypnosis, 45,* 212-225.

Kirsch, I. & Lynn, S. J. (1995). The altered state of hypnosis: Changes in the theoretical landscape. *American Psychologist, 50,* 846-858.

Klausner, S. Z. (1965). *The quest for self-control*. New York: Free Press.

Klein, M. (1935/1975). A contribution to the psychogenesis of manic-depressive states. In R. E. Money-Kyrle (Ed.). *The writings of Melanie Klein (Vol 1, 262-289)*. New York: The Free Press.

Kleinmuntz, B. (1982). *Personality and psychological assessment*. New York: St. Martin's Press.

Klinger, E. (1978). Modes of normal conscious flow. In K. S. Pope & J. L. Singer (Eds.). *The stream of consciousness: Scientific investigations into the flow of human experience (pp. 225-258)*. New York: Plenum.

Klinger, E. (1999). Thought flow: Properties and mechanisms underlying shifts in content. In J. A. Singer & P. Salovey. *At play in the fields of consciousness: Essays in honor of Jerome L. Singer*. Mahwah, NJ: Lawrence Erlbaum Associates.

Kluckhohn, C. K. M., & Murray, H. A. (1953). Personality formation: The determinants. In C. K. M. Kluckhorn, H. A. Murray, & D. Schneider (Eds.), *Personality in nature, culture, and society (pp. 53-67)*. New York: Knopf.

Knafo, D., Jaffe, Y. (1984). Sexual fantasizing in males and females. Journal of Research in Personality, 18, 451-462.

Kobasa, S.C.O. (1985). Personality and health: Specifying and strengthening the conceptual links. In P. Shaver (Ed.) *Review of Personality and Social Psychology, 6,* 291-311. Beverly Hills: Sage.

Kochanska, G., Murray, K. T., and Harlan, E. T. (2000). Effortful control in early childhood: Continuity and change, antecedents, and implications for social development. *Developmental Psychology, 36,* 220-232.

Koestner, R. & McClelland, D. C. (1992). The affiliation motive. In In C. P. Smith (Ed.), *Motivation and personality: Handbook of thematic content analysis (pp. 205-210)*. New York: Cambridge.

Kohnstamm, G., Halverson, C. F., Mervielde, I., & Havill, V. L. (1998). *Parental descriptions of child personality: Antecedents of the Big Five?* Mahwah, NJ: Lawrence Erlbaum Associates.

Kolar, D. W., Funder, D. C., & Colvin, C. R. (1996). Comparing the accuracy of personality judgments by the self and knowledgeable others. *Journal of Personality, 64,* 311-317.

Kosslyn, S.M. (1992). *Wet mind*. New York: Macmillan.

Kosslyn, S. M., & Koenig, O. (1992). *Wet mind: The new cognitive neuroscience*. New York: Free Press.

Krakauer, J. (1999). *Into thin air (with a new afterword)*. New York: Anchor Books.

Krevans, J. & Gibbs, J. C. (1996). Parents' use of inductive discipline: Relations to children's empathy and prosocial behavior. *Child Development, 67*, 3263-3277.

Kroger, J. (2000). *Identity development: Adolescence through adulthood*. Newbury Park, CA: Sage.

Kubie, L. S. (1939). The experimental induction of neurotic reactions in man. *Yale Journal of Biology and Medicine, 11*, 541-545.

Kunda, Z. (1990). The case for motivated reasoning. *Psychological Bulletin, 108*, 480-498.

Kunda, Z. & Sinclair, L. (1999). Motivated reasoning with stereotypes: Activation, application, and inhibition. *Psychological Inquiry, 10*, 12-22.

Kurtz, R. M., & Strube, M. J. (1996). Multiple susceptibility testing: Is it helpful? *American Journal of Clinical Hypnosis, 38*, 172-184.

Kushner, H. (1986). *When all you've ever wanted isn't enough*. New York: Pocket Books.

Kushner, L. *God was in this place and I, i did not know*. Woodstock, VT: Jewish Lights Publishing.

Kyllonen, P. C., Lohman, D. F., & Woltz, D. J. (1984). Componential modeling of alternative strategies for performing spatial tasks. *Journal of Educational Psychology, 76*, 1325-1345.

La Coste-Messelière, 1950: La Coste-Messelière, P. (1950). The treasures of Delphi. Paris: Éditions du Chêne.

Lafferty, P., Beutler, L. E., & Crago, M. (1989). Differences between more and less effective psychotherapists: A study of select therapist variables. *Journal of Consulting & Clinical Psychology, 57*, 76-80.

Lahey, B.B. (1989). *Psychology: An Introduction (3rd Edition)*. Dubuque, Iowa: Wm. C. Brown Publishers.

Lam, L.T., Kirby, S. L. (2002). Is emotional intelligence an advantage? An exploration of the impact of emotional and general intelligence on individual performance. Journal of Social Psychology, 142, 133-143.

Landy, F. J. (1986). Stamp collecting versus science: Validation as hypothesis testing. American Psychologist, 41, 1183-1192.

Lang. J. W. B. (2014). A dynamic Thurstonian item response theory of motive expression in the picture story exercise: Solving the internal consistency paradox of the PSE. Psychological Review, Vol 121(3), Jul, 2014. pp. 481-500.

Lang, A. J., Craske, M. G., Brown, M., & Ghaneian, A. (2001). Fear-related state dependent memory. Cognition and Emotion, 15, 695-703.

Lapsley, D. K. & Lasky, B. (2001). Prototypic moral character. *Identity: An International Journal of Theory and Research, 1*, 345-363.

Larkin, J. H., McDermott, J., Simon, D. P., & Simon, H. A. (1980). Expert and novice performance in sovling physics problems. *Science, 208*, 1335-1342.

Larsen, R. J., & Buss, D. M. (2002). *Personality psychology: Domains of knowledge about human nature*. Boston: McGraw Hill.

Larsen, R.J., & Kasimatis, M. (1990). Individual differences in the entrainment of mood to the weekly calendar. *Journal of Personality and Social Psychology, 58*, 164-171.

Laszlo, E. (1975). The meaning and significance of general system theory. *Behavioral Science, 20*, 9-24.

Laumann, E. O., Gagnon, J. H., Michael, R. T., & Michaels, S. (1994). *The social organization of sexuality: Sexual practices in the United States*. Chicago: University of Chicago Press.

Lawrence, J. (May, 2000). What's your fitness personality? *Vegetarian Times*, pp. 64-72.

Leary, M. R. (2004a). Editorial: What is the self? A plea for clarity. *Self and Identity, 3*, 1-3.

Leary, M. R. (July/August, 2004b). Get over yourself! *Psychology Today*, 62-65.

Lee, J-E., Wong, C. M. T., Day, J. D., Maxwell, S. E., & Thorpe, P. (2000). Social and academic intelligence: A multi-trait-multimethod study of their crystallized and fluid characteristics. *Personality and Individual Differences, 29*, 539-553.

Lee, K., & Ashton, M. C. (2004). Psychometric properties of the HEXACO personality inventory. *Multivariate Behavioral Research, 39*, 329-358.

Lei, H. & Skinner, H. A. (1982). What difference does language make: Structural analysis of the personality research form. *Multivariate Behavioral Research, 17*, 33-46.

Leo, J. (April 2, 1990). The trouble with self-esteem. *U.S. News and World Report, 108*, 16.

Leong, F. T. L., & Chervinko, S. (1996). Construct validity of career indecision: Negative personality traits as predictors of career indecision. *Journal of Career Assessment, 4*, 315-329.

Lerner, B. (1980). The war on testing: David, Goliath, & Gallup. *Public Interest, 60*, 119-147.

Lerner, B. (1981). Representative democracy, "men of zeal," and testing legislation. *American Psychologist, 36*, 270-275.

Lemogne, C., Nabi, H., Zins, M., Courdier, S., Ducimetière, P., Goldberg, M., & Consoli, S. M. (2010). Hostility may explain the association between depressive mood and mortality: Evidence from the French GAZEL cohort study. *Psychotherapy and Psychosomatics., 79*, 164–71.

Lewin, K. (1935). *A dynamic theory of personality: Selected Papers*. D. K. Adams & K. E. Zener (trans.). New York: McGraw-Hill.

Lewis, C. S. (1970). *The discarded image*. Cambridge: Cambridge University Press.

Lewis, S. K., Ross, C. E., & Mirowsky, J. (1999). Establishing a sense of personal control in the transition to adulthood. *Social Forces, 77*, 1573-1599.

Levenson, R. W., Ekman, P, & Heider, K. (1992). Emotion and autonomic nervous system activity in the Minangkabau of West Sumatra. Journal of Personality and Social Psychology, 62, 972-988.

Levenson, R., & Ruef, A. (1992). Empathy: A physiological substrate. *Journal of Personality and Social Psychology, 63*,

Levinson, D. J. (1977). The mid-life transition: A period in adult psychosocial development. *Psychiatry, 40*, 99-112.

Levy, L. H. (1970). *Conceptions of personality*. New York: Random House.

Lewicki, P. (1984). Self-schemata and social information processing. *Journal of Personality and Social Psychology, 47*, 1177-1190.

Lewis, C.S. (1970). *The Discarded image*. Cambridge, England: Cambridge University Press.

Lewis, M. (2000). The emergence of human emotions. In M. Lewis & J. M. Haviland-Jones, *Handbook of Emotions (2ⁿᵈ Ed)*. *(pp.265-280)*. New York: Guilford Press.

Libet, B. (1985). Unconscious cerebral initiative and the role of conscious will in voluntary action. *Behavioral and Brain Sciences, 8*, 529-566.

Liker, J. K., & Elder, G. H. (1983). Economic hardship and marital relations in the 1930's. *American Sociological Review, 48*, 342-359.

Lippa, R. (1998). Gender-related individual differences and the structure of vocational interests: The importance of the people-things dimension. *Journal of Personality and Social Psychology, 74*, 996-1009.

Little. B. R. (2005). Personality science and personal projects: six impossible things before breakfast. *Journal of Research and Personality, 39*, 4-21.

Littwin, S. (1986). *The postponed generation: Why America's grown-up kids are growing up later*. New York: William Morrow and Company.

Loeb, J. (1966). The personality factor in divorce. *Journal of Consulting Psychology, 30*, 562.

Loehlin, J. C. (2002). Group differences in intelligence. R. J. Sternberg (Ed.). *Handbook of Intelligence*, Cambridge, UK: Cambridge University Press.

Loevinger, J. (1967). Objective tests as instruments of psychological theory. In D. N. Jackson, & S. Messick (Eds.). *Problems in human assessment (pp. 78-123)*. New York: McGraw-Hill. (Reprinted from *Psychological Reports, 1957, Monograph Supplement 9*.).

Loevinger, J. (1994). Has psychology lost its conscience? *Journal of Personality Assessment, 62*, 2-8.

Loftus, E. F., & Kaufman, L. (1992). Why do traumatic experiences sometimes produce good memory (flashbulbs) and sometimes no memory (repression)? In E. Winograd & U. Neisser (Eds.), *Affect and accuracy in recall: Studies of "flashbulb" memories*. New York: Cambridge University Press.

Lohman, D. F. (2000). Complex information processing and intelligence. In R. J. Sternberg (Ed.). *Handbook of Intelligence (pp. 285-340)*, Cambridge, UK: Cambridge University Press.

Lohman, D. F. & Kyllonen, P. C. (1983). Individual differences in solution strategy on spatial tasks. In R. F. Dillon & R. Schmeck (Eds.), *Individual differences in cognition* (Vol. 1, pp. 105-135). *New York: Academic Press*.

Lounsbury, J.W., Hutchens, & T., Loveland, J.M. (2005). An investigation of big five personality traits and career decidedness among early and middle adolescents. *Journal of Career Assessment, 13*, 25-39.

Lopes, P. N., Brackett, M. A., Nezlak, J. B., Schutz, A., Sellin, I., & Salovey, P. (2004). Emotional intelligence and social interaction. *Personality and Social Psychology Bulletin, 30*, 1018-1034

Lopes, P. N., Salovey, P., Coté, S., & Beers, M. (2005). Emotion regulation abilities and the quality of social interaction. *Emotion, 5*, 113-118.

Lubinski, D. (2000). Scientific and social significance of assessing individual differences: "Sinking shafts at a few critical points." Annual Review of Psychology, 51, 405-444.

Lubinski, D, Webb, R. M., Morelock, M. J. (2001). Top 1 in 10,000: A 10-year follow-up of the profoundly gifted. *Journal of Applied Psychology, 86*, 718-729.

Luborsky, L., Crits-Christoph, P., & Mellon, J. (1986). Advent of objective measures of the transference concept. *Journal of Consulting and Clinical Psychology, 54*, 39-47.

Luborsky, L., & Crits-Christoph (1988). Measures of psychoanalytic concepts -- The last decade of research from 'the Penn Studies'. *International Journal of Psychoanalysis, 69*, 75-85.

Luecke-Aleksa, D., Anderson, D. R., Collins, P. A., & Schmitt, K. L. (1995). Gender constancy and television viewing. *Developmental Psychology, 31*, 773-780.

Luria, A. R. (1932). *The nature of human conflicts, or Emotion, conflict and will, an objective study of disorganization and control of human behavior*. W. Horsley Gantt (trans.). New York: Liveright Publications.

Lyubomirsky (2008). *The how of happiness*. New York: Penguin.

Lyubomirsky, S., & Nolen-Hoeksema, S (1993). Self-perpetuating properties of dysphoric rumination. *Journal of Personality and Social Psychology, 65*, 339-349.

Lykken, D. T., & Tellegen, A. (1993). Is human mating adventitious or the result of lawful choice? A twin study of mate selection. *Journal of Personality and Social Psychology, 65*, 56-68.

Lynn, S. J., & Rhue, J. W. (1988). Fantasy proneness: Hypnosis, developmental antecedents, and psychopathology. *American Psychologist, 43*, 35-44.

Maccoby, E. E. (1 990). Gender and relationships: A developmental account. *American Psychologist, 45*, 513-520.

Maccoby, E. E., & Martin, J. A. (1983). Socialization in the context of the family: Parent-child interaction. In E. M. Hetherington (Ed.), *Handbook of child psychology: Vol. IV. Socialization, personality, and social development*. New York: Wiley.

MacLean, P. D. (1977). The triune brain in conflict. Psychotherapy & Psychosomatics, 28 (1-sup-4), 207-220.

MacLean, P. D. (1993). On the evolution of three mentalities. In J. B. Ashbrook, (Ed); Brain, culture, & the human spirit: Essays from an emergent evolutionary perspective (pp. 15-44). Lanham, MD: University Press of America.

Maddi, S. R. (1972). *Personality theories: A comparative analysis*. Homewood, IL: The Dorsey Press.

Maddi, S. R. (1993). The continuing relevance of personality theory. In K. H. Craik, R. Hogan, & R. N. Wolfe (Eds) *Fifty years of personality psychology (pp. 85-101)*. New York: Plenum Press.

Mans, L., Cicchetti, D., & Sroufe, L. A. (1978). Mirror reactions of Down's syndrome infants and toddlers: Cognitive underpinnings of self-recognition. *Child Development, 49*, 1247-1250.

Marcel, A. J. (1983). Conscious and unconscious perception: An approach to the relation between phenomenal experience and perceptual processes. *Cognitive Psychology, 15*, 238-300.

Marcia, J. E. (1964). Determination and validation of ego identity status. Unpublished doctoral dissertation. Ohio State University: Columbus, Ohio.

Marcia, J. E. (1966). Development and validation of ego identity status. *Journal of Personality and Social Psychology, 3*, 551-558.

Marcia, J. E., Waterman, A. S., Matteson, D. R., Archer, S. L., & Orlofsky, J. L. (1993). *Ego identity: A handbook for psychosocial research.* New York: Springer-Verlag.

Marcia, J. E. (2002). Identity and psychosocial development in adulthood. *Identity: An International Journal of Theory and Research, 2,* 7-28.

Marinoff, L. (1999). *Plato not Prozac!* New York: HarperCollins Publishers.

Markus, H. (1977). Self-schemata and processing information about the self. *Journal of Personality and Social Psychology, 35,* 63-78.

Markus, H., & Kitayama, S. (1991). Culture and self: Implications for cognition, emotion, and motivation. *Psychological Review, 98,* 224-253.

Markus, H., & Nurius, P. (1986). Possible Selves. *American Psychologist, 41,* 954-969.

Markus, H., & Wurf, E. (1987). The dynamic self-concept: A social psychological perspective. *Annual Review of Psychology, 38,* 299-337.

Marsella, A. J., Dubanoski, J., Hamada, W. C., & Morse, H. (2000). The measurement of personality across cultures: Historical, conceptual, and methodological considerations. *American Behavioral Scientist, 44,* 41-62.

Marsh, H. W. (1993). Relations between global and specific domains of self: The importance of individual importance, certainty and ideals. *Journal of Personality and Social Psychology, 65,* 975-992.

Marsland, K. W., & Likavec, S. C. (2003, June). *Maternal emotional intelligence, infant attachment and child socio-emotional competence.* Poster presented at the annual meeting of the American Psychological Society, Atlanta, GA.

Martin, C. L., Eisenbud, L., & Rose, H. (1995). Children's gender-based reasoning about toys. *Child Development, 66,* 1453-1471.

Martin, L. L., & Tesser, A. (1996). Some ruminative thoughts. In R. S. Wyer, Jr. (Ed.). *Advances in social cognition (Vol 9, pp. 1-48).* Hillsdale, NJ: Lawrence Erlbaum Associates.

Maruyama, G. M. (1998). *Basics of structural equation modeling.* Thousand Oaks, CA: Sage.

Mascaro, N., & Rosen, D. H. (2005). Existential meaning's role in the enhancement of hope and prevention of depressive symptoms. *Journal of Personality, 73,* 985-114.

Maslow, A. H. (1943). A theory of human motivation. *Psychological Review, 50,* 370-396.

Maslow, A.H. (1970). *Motivation and Personality (2nd Ed.).* New York: Harper and Row.

Masten, A. S., & Reed, M-G. J. (2002). Resilience in development. In C. R. Snyder & S. J. Lopez, *Handbook of Positive Psychology (pp. 74-88).* New York: Oxford University Press.

Masters, W. H. & Johnson, V. E. (1966). *Human sexual response.* Boston: Little, Brown.

Matarazzo, J.D. (1972). *Wechsler's measurement and appraisal of adult intelligence (5th and enlarged edition).* New York: Oxford University Press.

Matarazzo, J. D., & Herman, D. O. (1984). Relationship of education and IQ in the WAIS-R standardization sample. *Journal of Consulting and Clinical Psychology, 52,* 631-634.

Matarazzo, J. D. (1992). Biological and physiological correlates of intelligence. *Intelligence, 16,* 257-258.

Matthews, G., Zeidner, M., & Roberst, R. D. (2002). *Emotional intelligence: Science and myth.* Cambridge, MA: MIT Press.

Matheny, A. P. (1989). Children's behavioral inhibition over age and across situations: Genetic similarity for a trait during change. *Journal of Personality, 57,* 215-235.

Mathews, K. A. (1988). CHD and Type A behavior: Update on and alternative to the Booth-Kewley and Friedman quantitative review. *Psychological Bulletin, 104,* 373-380.

Mathews, K. A, Glass, D. C., Rosenman, R. H., & Bortner, R. W. (1977). Competitive drive, pattern A, and coronary heart disease: A further analysis of some data from the Western Collaborative Group Study. *Journal of Chronic Disease, 30,* 489-498.

Mathews, K. A., Helmreich, R. L., Beane, W. E., & Lucker, G. W. (1980). Pattern A, achievement striving, and scientific merit: Does pattern A help or hinder? *Journal of Personality and Social Psychology, 39,* 962-967.

Maticka-Tyndale, E., Harold, E. S., & Mewhinney, D. (1998). Casual sex on spring break: Intensions and behaviors of Canadian students. *Journal of Sex Research, 35,* 254-264.

Maurer, D. & Maurer, C. (1988). The world of the newborn. New York: Basic Books.

Mayer, J. D. (1993-1994). A System-Topics Framework for the study of personality. *Imagination, Cognition, and Personality, 13,* 99-123.

Mayer, J. D. (1994). A System-Topics Alternative. Dialogue: Society for Personality and Social Psychology, 9, 7.

Mayer, J. D. (1995a). The System-Topics Framework and the location of systems and boundaries within and around personality. *Journal of Personality, 63,* 459-493.

Mayer, J. D. (1995b). A framework for the classification of personality components. *Journal of Personality, 63,* 819-877.

Mayer, J. D. (1998). A Systems Framework for the Field of Personality Psychology. *Psychological Inquiry, 9,* 118-144.

Mayer, J. D. (1998). The systems framework: Reception, improvement, and implementation. *Psychological Inquiry, 9,* 169-179.

Mayer, J. D. (1998). A framework for the study of individual differences in personality formations. In J.A. Singer & P. Salovey (Eds.), *At play in the fields of consciousness (pp. 143-173).* Mahwah, NJ: Lawrence Erlbaum.

Mayer, J. D. (2000). Spirituality intelligence or spiritual consciousness? *International Journal for the Psychology of Religion, 10,* 47-56.

Mayer, J. D. (2001a). Primary divisions of personality and their scientific contributions: From the trilogy-of-mind to the systems set. *Journal for the Theory of Social Behaviour, 31,* 449-477.

Mayer, J. D. (2001b). A Field Guide to Emotional Intelligence. In J. Ciarrochi, J. P. Forgas, & J. D. Mayer (Eds.) *Emotional intelligence and everday life (pp.3-24).* New York: Psychology Press.

Mayer, J. D. (2003). Structural divisions of personality and the classification of traits. *Review of General Psychology, 7,* 381-401.

Mayer, J. D. (2004). A classification system for the data of personality psychology and adjoining fields. *Review of General Psychology, 8*, 208-219.

Mayer, J. D. (2005). A tale of two visions: Can a new view of personality help organize psychology? American Psychologist, 60, 294-307.

Mayer, J. D. (2007). The big questions of personality psychology: Defining common pursuits of the discipline. *Imagination, Cognition, and Personality, 27*, 83-103.

Mayer, J. D. (2008). Personal intelligence. *Imagination, Cognition, and Personality, 27*, 209-232.

Mayer, J. D. (2009). Personal intelligence expressed: A theoretical analysis. *Review of General Psychology, 13*, 46-58.

Mayer, J. D. (2014). *Personal intelligence: The power of personality and how it shapes our lives*. New York: Scientific American / Farrar, Straus & Giroux.

Mayer, J. D., & Allen, J. L. (2013). A personality framework for the unification of psychology. *Review of General Psychology, 17*, 196-202.

Mayer, J.D., & Bower, G.H. (1986). Learning and memory for personality prototypes. *Journal of Personality and Social Psychology, 51*, 473-492.

Mayer, J. D. & Carlsmith, K. M. (1997). Eminence rankings of personality psychologists as a reflection of the field. *Personality and Social Psychology Bulletin, 23*, 707-716.

Mayer, J. D., & Carlsmith, K. M. (1998). The Systems Framework Web Site. [www.princeton.edu/personality_framework; or *www.unh.edu/personality_framework*].

Mayer, J. D., Carlsmith, K.M., & Chabot, H.F. (1998). Describing the person's external environment: Conceptualizing and measuring the Life Space. *Journal of Research in Personality, 32*, 253-296.

Mayer, J.D., Caruso, D. R., & Salovey, P. (2015). Emotional intelligence today and tomorrow. *Emotion Review*.

Mayer, J.D., Caruso, D.R., Zigler, E., & Dreyden, J.I. (1989). Intelligence and intelligence-related personality traits. *Intelligence, 13*, 119-133.

Mayer, J.D., Chabot, H.F., & Carlsmith, K.M. (1997). Conation, affect, and cognition in personality. In G. Matthews (Ed.). *Cognitive science perspectives on personality and emotion*. Oxford: Elsevier.

Mayer, J. D., DiPaolo, M. T., & Salovey, P. (1990). Perceiving affective content in ambiguous visual stimuli: A component of emotional intelligence. *Journal of Personality Assessment, 54*, 772-781.

Mayer, J.D., & Gaschke, Y. (1988). The experience and meta-experience of mood. *Journal of Personality and Social Psychology, 55*, 102-111.

Mayer, J.D., & Hanson, E. (1995). Mood-congruent judgment over time. *Personality and Social Psychology Bulletin, 21*, 237-244.

Mayer, J.D., Gaschke, Y., Braverman, D.L., & Evans, T. (1992). Mood-congruent judgment is a general effect. *Journal of Personality and Social Psychology, 63*, 119-132.

Mayer, J. D., & Geher, G. (1996). Emotional intelligence and the identification of emotion. *Intelligence, 22*, 89-113.

Mayer, J. D., & Lang, J. L. (2011). A three dimensional view of personality: A commentary on Sheldon, Cheng, and Hilpert's "Understanding well-being and optimal functioning: Applying the multilevel personality in context model" *Psychological Inquiry, 22*, 36-39.

Mayer, J. D., McCormick, L. J., & Strong, S. E. (1995). Mood-congruent recall and natural mood: New evidence. *Personality and Social Psychology Bulletin, 21*, 736-746.

Mayer, J. D., & Mitchell, D. C. (1998). Intelligence as a subsystem of personality: From Spearman's *g* to contemporary models of hot-processing. In W. Tomic & J. Kingma (Eds). *Advances in cognition and educational practice (Volume 5: Conceptual issues in research in intelligence) (pp. 43-75)*. Greenwich, CT: JAI Press.

Mayer, J. D., Panter, A. T., & Caruso, D. R. (2012). Does personal intelligence exist? Evidence from a new ability-based measure. *Journal of Personality Assessment, 94*, 124-140.

Mayer, J. D., Perkins, D. M., Caruso, D. R., & Salovey, P. (2000). Emotional intelligence and giftedness. *Roeper Review, 23*, 131-137.

Mayer, J.D., Rapp, H.C., & Williams, L. (1993). Individual differences in behavioral prediction: The acquisition of personal-action schemata. *Personality and Social Psychology Bulletin, 19*, 443-451.

Mayer, J. D., & Salovey, P. (1993). The intelligence of emotional intelligence. *Intelligence, 17*(4), 433-442.

Mayer, J. D. & Salovey, P. (1997). What is emotional intelligence? In P. Salovey & D. Sluyter (Eds). *Emotional Development and Emotional Intelligence: Implications for Educators (pp. 3-31)*. New York: Basic Books.

Mayer, J.D., Salovey, P., & Caruso, D. R. (2000). Models of emotional intelligence. In R. Sternberg (Ed.). *Handbook of Human Intelligence (2nd ed.)* New York: Cambridge.

Mayer, J. D., Salovey, P., & Caruso, D. R. (2002). *Mayer-Salovey-Caruso Emotional Intelligence Test (MSCEIT) Users Manual*. Toronto, ON: Multi-Health Systems.

Mayer, J. D., Salovey, P. & Caruso, D. R. (2008). Emotional intelligence: New ability or eclectic traits? *American Psychologist, 63*, 503-517.

Mayer, J. D., Salovey, P., Caruso, D. R., & Sitarenios, G. (2003). Measuring emotional intelligence with the MSCEIT V2.0. *Emotion, 3*, 97-105.

Mayer, J.D., Salovey, P., Gomberg-Kaufman, M., & Blainey, K. (1991). A broader conception of mood experience. *Journal of Personality and Social Psychology, 60*, 100-111.

Mayer, J. D., & Stevens, A. A. (1994). An emerging understanding of the reflective (meta-) experience of mood. *Journal of Research in Personality, 28*, 351-373.

Mazlish, B. (1973). In *search of Nixon: A psychohistorical inquiry*. New York: Penguin Books.

McAdams, D. P. (1992a). The intimacy motive. In C. P. Smith (Ed.), *Motivation and personality: Handbook of thematic content analysis (pp. 224-228)*. New York: Cambridge.

McAdams, D. P. (1992b). The intimacy motivation scoring system. In C. P. Smith (Ed.), *Motivation and personality: Handbook of thematic content analysis (pp. 229-253)*. New York: Cambridge.

McAdams, D. P. (1993). *The stories we live by: Personal myths and the making of the self*. New York: William Morrow.

McAdams, D. P. (1995). What do we know when we know a person? *Journal of Personality, 63*, 365-396.

McAdams, D. P. (1998). Trick or treat: Classifying concepts and accounting for human individuality. *Psychological Inquiry, 9,* 154-158.

McAdams, D. P. (2001). The psychology of life stories. *Review of General Psychology, 5,* 100-122.

McAdams, D. P. (1996). Personality, modernity, and the storied self: A contemporary framework for studying persons. *Psychological Inquiry, 7,* 295-321.

McAdams, D. P., Diamond, A., de St. Aubin, E., & Mansfield, E. (1997). Stories of commitment: The psychosocial construction of generative lives. *Journal of Personality and Social Psychology, 72,* 678-694.

McAdams, D. P., & Bowman, P. J. (2001). Narrating life's turning points: Redemption and contamination.. In D. P. McAdams & Josselson, R. (Ed.) *Turns in the road: Narrative studies of lives in transition (pp. 3-34).* Washington, DC: American Psychological Association.

McAdams, D.P., Reynolds, J., Lewis, M., Patten, A. H., & Bowman, P. J. (2001). When bad things turn good and good things turn bad: Sequences of redemption and contamination in life narrative and their relation to psychosocial adaptation in midlife adults and in students. *Personality and Social Psychology Bulletin, 27,* 474-485.

McAdams, D. P.; West, S. G. (1997). Personality psychology and the case study. Introduction. *Journal of Personality, 65,* 757-783.

McBain, D. A. (1995). Empathy and the salesperson: A multidimensional perspective. *Psychology and Marketing, 12,* 349-370.

McCallum, M. & Piper, W. E. (1997). *Psychological mindedness: A contemporary understanding.* Mahwah, NJ, US: Lawrence Erlbaum Associates, Publishers.

McClelland, D.C. (1958). The use of measures of human motivation in the study of society. In J. W. Atkinson (Ed.) *Motives in fantasy, action and soceity* (pp. 518-552). Princeton, NJ: Van Nostrand.

McClelland, D. C. & Koessstner, R. (1992). The achievement motive. In C. P. Smith (Ed.), *Motivation and personality: Handbook of thematic content analysis (pp. 143-152).* New York: Cambridge.

McClelland, D. C. (1961/1976). *The achieving society.* Princeton, NJ: Van Nostrand.

McClelland, D. C., Koestner, R., & Weinberger, J. (1992). How do self-attributed and implicit motives differ? In C. P. Smith (Ed.), *Motivation and personality: Handbook of thematic content analysis (pp. 49-72).* New York: Cambridge.

McClelland, D. C., Atkinson, J. W., Clark, R. A., & Lowell, E. L. (1992). A scoring manual for the achievement motive. In C. P. Smith (Ed.), *Motivation and personality: Handbook of thematic content analysis (pp. 153-178).* New York: Cambridge.

McClelland, D. C., & Koestner, R. (1992). The achievement motive. In C. P. Smith (Ed.), *Motivation and personality: Handbook of thematic content analysis (pp. 143-152).* New York: Cambridge.

McCrae, R. R. (1998). An empirically based alternative framework. *Psychological Inquiry, 9,* 158-160.

McCrae, R. R., & Costa, P. T. (1990). *Personality in adulthood.* New York: Guilford.

McCrae, R. R., & Costa, P. T. (1997). Personality trait structure as a human universal. *American Psychologist, 52,* 509-516.

McCrae, R. R., & Costa, P. T. (1999). A Five-Factor Theory of Personality. In L. A. Pervin & O. P. John (Eds.). *Handbook of personality (2nd ed.) (pp. 139-153).* New York: Guilford.

McEwen, B. S. (1991). Sex differences in the brain: What they are and how they arise. *In:* M. T. Notman, & C. C. Nadelson (Eds.) *Women and men: New perspectives on gender differences (pp. 35-41).* Washington, DC, US: American Psychiatric Association.

McGue, M., Bouchard, T. J., Iacono, W. G., & Lykken, D. T. (1993). Behavioral genetics of cognitive ability: A life-span perspective. In R. Plomin & G. e. McClearn (Eds.). *Nature, nurture, and psychology.* Washington, DC: American Psychological Association.

McGue, M., & Lykken, D. T. (1992). Genetic influence on risk of divorce. *Psychological Science, 6,* 368-373.

McGuire, W. (1984). Search for the self: Going beyond self-esteem and the reactive self. In R. A. Tucker, J. Aronoff, & A. J. Rabin. *Personality and the prediction of behavior (pp. 73-120).* Orlando, FL: Academic Press.

McManis, M. H., Kagan, J., & Snidman, N. C., Woodward, S. A. (2002). EEG asymmetry, pwer, and temperament in children. *Developmental Psychology, 41,* 169-177.

Mead, G. H. (1934). *Mind, self, and society.* Chicago, IL: University of Chicago Press.

Mead, M. (1939). From the South Seas: Studies of adolescence and sex in primitive societies. New York: Morrow.

Mebert, C. J. (1991). Dimensions of subjectivity in parents' ratings of infant temperament. *Child Development, 62,* 352-361.

Mednick, S. A. (1962). The associative basis of the creative process. *Psychological Review, 69,* 220-232.

Meehl, P. E. (1975). Hedonic capacity: Some conjectures. *Bulletin of the Menninger Clinic, 39,* 295-307.

Mendelsohn, G. A. (1993). It's time to put theories of personality in their place, or, Allport and Stagner got it right, why can't we? In K. H. Craik, R. Hogan, & R. N. Wolfe (Eds). *Fifty years of personality psychology (pp. 103-129).* New York: Plenum Press.

Menninger, K. A. (1930). *The human mind.* Literary Guild of America.

Meyer, B. & Pilkonis, P. A. (2001). Attachment style. *Psychotherapy: Theory, Research, Practice, Training, 38,* 466-472.

Meyer, D., Leventhal, H., & Guttman, M. (1985). Common-sense models of illness: The example of hypertension. *Health Psychology, 4,* 115-135.

Meyer, G. J., Finn, S. E., Eyde, L. D., Kay, G. G., Moreland, K. L., Dies, R. R., Eisman, E. J., Kubiszyn, T. W., & Read, G. M. (2001). Psychological testing and psychological assessment: A review of evidence and issues. *American Psychologist, 56,* 128-156.

Michotte, A. (1963). The perception of causality. (T. R. Miles & E. Miles, Trans.). New York: Basic Books.

Miech, R., Essex, M. J. & Goldsmith, H. H. (2001). Socioeconomic status and the adjustment to school: The role of self-regulation during early childhood. *Sociology of Education, 74,* 102-120.

Miller, L. C., & Fishkin, S. A. (1997). On the dynamics of human bonding and reproductive success: Seeking windows on the adapted-for human-environmental interface. In J. Simpson & D. Kenrick (Eds.), *Evolutionary Social Psychology (pp. 197-235)*. Mahwah, NJ: Erlbaum.

Miller, S. D. (1989). Optical differences in cases of multiple personality disorder. *The Journal of Nervous and Mental Disease, 177*, 480-486.

Miller, T. Q., Turner, C. W., Tindale, R. S., Posovac, E. J., & Dugoni, B. (1991). Reasons for the trend toward null findings in research on Type A behavior. *Psychological Bulletin, 119*, 322-348.

Miller, W. R., & Taylor, C. A. (1980). Relative effectiveness of bibliotherapy, individual and group self-control training in the treatment of problem drinkers. *Addictive Behavior, 5*, 13-24.

Mills, J., & Clark, M. S. (1982). Exchange and communal relationships. In L. Wheeler (Ed.). *Review of personality and social psychology (Vol. 3, pp. 121-144)*. Beverly Hills, CA: Sage.

Milton, J., & Wiseman, R. (1999). Does psi exist? Lack of replication of an anomalous process of information transfer. Psychological Bulletin, 125, 387-391.

Mineka, S., Davidson, M., Cook, M., & Keir, R. (1984). Observational conditioning of snake fears in rhesus monkeys. *Journal of Abnormal Psychology, 93*, 355-372.

Mirowsky, J. (1997). Age, subjective life expectancy, and the sense of control: The horizon hypothesis. *Journals of Gerontology: Series B: Psychological Sciences and Social Sciences, 52B*, S125-S134.

Mischel, W. (1968). *Personality and assessment*. New York: Wiley.

Mischel, W. (1973). Toward a cognitive social learning reconceptualization of personality. *Psychological Review, 80*, 252-283.

Mischel, W. (1990). Personality dispositions revisted and revised. In L. Pervin (ed.), *Handbook of Personality Theory and Research (Pp. 111-134)*. New York: Guilford.

Mischel, W. (1998). *Introduction to personality*. New York: Wiley.

Mischel, W. & Ebbesen, E. B. (1970). Attention in delay of gratification. *Journal of Personality and Social Psychology, 3*, 45-53.

Mischel, W. & Shoda, Y. (1995). A cognitive-affective system theory of personality: Reconceptualizing situations, dispositions, dynamics, and invariance in personality structure. *Psychological Review, 102*, 246-268.

Mischel, W., Shoda, Y., & Peake, P. K. (1988). The nature of adolescent competencies predicted by preschool delay of gratification. *Journal of Personality and Social Psychology, 54*, 687-696.

Miserandino, M. (1996). Children who do well in school: Individual differences in perceived competence and autonomy in above average children. *Journal of Educational Psychology, 88*, 203-214.

Moles, A. (1958/1966). Information theory and esthetic perception. University of Illinois Press. [Original work published 1958; J. E. Cohen, Trans. English Edition].

Money, J., & Lehne, G. K. (1999). Gender Identity disorders. In R. T. Ammerman, M. Hersen, C. G. Last (Eds). Handbook of prescriptive treatments for children and adolescents (2nd ed.) (pp. 214-228). Boston: Allyn & Bacon.

Mongar, T. (1976). A cybernetic model of personality structure: A theoretical proposal. *Psychology: A Journal of Human Behavior, 13*, 33-48.

Monte, C. F. (1999). *Beneath the mask: An introduction to theories of personality (6th Ed)*. New York: Harcourt Brace College Publishers.

Mook, D. G. (1996). *Motivation: The organization of action (2nd ed.)*. New York: Norton.

Moore, K. L., & Persaud, T. V. N. (1993). *Before we are born (4th ed)*. Philadelphia: W. B. Saunders Co..

Moran, R. A. (1993). Never confuse a memo with reality and other business lessons too simple not to know. New York: HarperCollins.

Moravec, H. (2000). Shaper of things to come. *Discover, 21*, 32ff.

Morelli, G., Rogoff, B., Oppenheim, D., & Goldsmith, D. (1992). Cultural variation in infants' sleeping arrangements: Questions of independence. *Developmental Psychology, 28*, 604-613.

Morgan, A. H. (1973). The heritability of hypnotic susceptibility in twins. *Journal of Abnormal Psychology, 82*, 55-61.

Morgan, D.M. (1989). *The voyage of the* American Promise. Boston: Houghton Mifflin.

Morgan, W. G. (1995). Origin and history of the Thematic Apperception Test images. *Journal of Personality Assessment, 65*, 237-254.

Morokoff, P. J. (1985). Effects of sex guilt, repression, sexual "arousability," and sexual experience on female sexual arousal during erotica and fantasy. *Journal of Personality and Social Psychology*, 49, 177-187.

Morris, T. W., & Levinson, E. M. (1995). Relationship between intelligence and occupational adjustment and functioning: A literature review. *Journal of Counseling & Development, 73*, 503-514.

Morrison, D.F. (1976). *Multivariate statistical methods (2nd ed.)* New

York: McGraw Hill.

Moss, F. A., & Hunt, T. (1927). Are you socially intelligent? *Scientific American, 137*, 108-110.

Motley, M.T., Camden, C.T., & Baars, B.J. (1983). Covert formulation and editing of anomalies in speech production: Evidence from experimentally elicited slips of the tongue. *Journal of Verbal Learning and Verbal Behavior, 21*, 578-594.

Motley, M.T., Camden, C.T., & Baars, B.J. (1983). Polysemantic lexical access: Evidence from laboratory-induced double entendres. *Communication Monographs, 50*, 193-205.

Mroczek, D. K. (2001). Age and emotion in adulthood. *Current Directions in Psychological Science, 10*, 87-90.

Mroczek, D. K. & Kolarz, C. M. (1998). The effect of age on positive and negative affect: A developmental perspective on happiness. *Journal of Personality and Social Psychology, 75*, 1333-1349.

Mullen, B., & Riordan, C. A. (1988). Self-serving attributions for performance in naturalistic settings: A meta-analytic review. Journal of Applied Social Psychology, 18, 3-22.

Müller-Lyer, F. C. (1889). Optische Urteilstäuschungen Dubois-Reymonds Archive für Anatomie und Physiologie, Supplement,-263.[Deception of visual judgment].

Muraven, M., Baumeister, R. F. (2000). Self-regulation and depletion of limited resources: Does self-control resemble a muscle? Psychological Bulletin, 126, 247-259.

Murchison, C. (Ed.) (1930). *Psychologies of 1930*. Worcester, MA: Clark University press.

Murphy, K. R., & DeShon, R. (2000). Progress in psychometrics: Can industrial and organizational psychology catch up? Personnel Psychology, 53, 913-924.

Murray, H.A. (1938). *Explorations in Personality*. New York: Oxford University Press.

Murray, H. A. (1951). Toward a classification of interaction. In T. Parsons & E. A. Shils (Eds.), *Toward a general theory of action (pp. 434-464)*. Cambridge: Harvard University Press.

Murray, H. (1962). The Personality and career of Satan. *The Journal of Social Issues*, October, 1962. Also in Bakan's *the Duality of Human Existence*.

Murray, H. A., & Kluckhohn, C. (1956). Outline of a conception of personality. In C. Kluckhohn, H. A. Murray, & D. M. Schneider, *Personality in nature, society, and culture (pp. 3-49)*. New York: Alfred A. Knopf.

Murstein, B. I. (1972). Physical attractiveness and marital choice. *Journal of Personality and Social Psychology, 22*, 8-12.

Myers, D. G. (2000). The funds, friends, and faith of happy people. *American Psychologist, 56*, 56-67.

Myers, D. G., & Diener, E (1995). Who is happy? *Psychological Science, 6*, 10-19.

Nakamura, J., & Csikszentmihalyi, M. (2002). The concept of flow. In C. R. Snyder & S. J. Lopez, *Handbook of Positive Psychology (pp. 89-105)*. New York: Oxford University Press.

Nasby, W., & Read, N. W. (1997). 7. The hero's return. *Journal of Personality, 65*, 1013-1042.

Natsoulas, T. (1986-87). The six basic concepts of consciousness and William James' stream of thought. *Imagination, Cognition, and Personality, 6*, 289-319.

Newberg, A., Alavi, A. Baime, M., Pourdehnad M; Santanna J; d'Aquili E. (2001). The measurement of regional cerebral blood flow during the complex cognitive task of meditation: A preliminary SPECT study. Psychiatry Research: Neuroimaging, 106, 113-122.

Newman, D. L., Caspi, A., Moffitt, T. E., & Silva, P. A. (1997). Antecedents of adult interpersonal functioning: Effects of individual differences in age-3 temperament. Developmental Psychology, 33, 206-217.

Nickerson, C. (June 13, 1999). Literary star revisits dark side. *The Boston Sunday Globe*, pp. A4-A5.

Nickerson, R. S. (1998). Confirmation bias: A ubiquitous phenomenon in many guises. Review of General Psychology, 2, 175-220.

Nisbett, R. E. (1980). The trait construct in lay and professional psychology. In L. Festinger (Ed.). *Retrospectives on social psychology*. New York: Oxford University Press.

Nisbett, R.E. & Wilson, T.C. (1977). Telling more than we can know: Verbal reports on mental processes. *Psychological Review, 84*, 231-259.

Nissel, A. (2001). *The broke diaries*. New York: Villard Books.

Nixon, R. M. (1978). *RN: The memoirs of Richard Nixon*. New York: Grosset & Dunlap.

Nixon, R. M. (1990). *In the arena: A memoir of victory, defeat, and renewal*. New York: Simon & Schuster.

Norem, J. K., & Chang, E. C. (2002). The positive psychology of negative thinking. *Journal of Clinical Psychology, 58*, 993-1001.

Norem, J. K., & Illingworth, S. (1993). Strategy-dependent effects of reflecting on self and tasks: Some implications of optimism and defensive pessimism. *Journal of Personality and Social Pyshchology, 65*, 822-835.

Novick, M. R. (1966). The axioms and principal results of classical test theory. *Journal of Mathematical Psychology, 3*, 1-18.

Nowlis, V. (1965). Research with the Mood Adjective Checklist. In S. S. Tomkins & C. E. Izard (Eds.), *Affect, cognition, and personality (pp. 98-128)*. New York: Springer.

Nyhus, E.K., & Pons, E. (2005). The effects of personality on earnings. *Journal of Economic Psychology, 26*, 363-384.

O'Connor, T. G., Caspi, A., DeFries, J. C., & Plomin, R. (2000). Are associations between parental divorce and children's adjustment genetically mediated? An adoption study. *Developmental Psychology, 36*, 429-437.

Oliner, S.P., & Oliner, P.M. (1988). *The altruistic personality: Rescuers of Jews in Nazi Europe*. New York: Free Press.

Oliver, M. B., & Hyde, J. S. (1993). Gender differences in sexuality: A meta-analysis. *Psychological Bulletin, 114*, 29-51.

Olweus, D. (1993). Victimization by peers: Antecedents and long-term outcomes. In K. H. Rubin & J. B. Asendopf (Eds.). *Social withdrawal, inhibition, and shyness in childhood (pp. 315-341)*. Hillsdale, NJ: Erlbaum.

Orlinsky, D. E., & Howard, K. I. (1986). Process and outcome in psychotherapy. In S. L. Garfield, & A. E. Bergin (Eds.), *Handbook of psychotherapy and behavior change (3rd ed.) (pp. 311-381)*. New York: Wiley.

Ornstein, R. (1986). *The psychology of consciousness (Rev. ed.)*. New York: Penguin Books.

Ornstein, R. (1991). *The evolution of consciousness*. New York: Simon & Schuster.

Ortony, A., Clore, G.L., & Collins, A. (1988). *The cognitive structure of emotions*. Cambridge: Cambridge University Press.

Ortony, A., & Turner, T. J. (1990). What's *basic* about *basic* emotions? *Psychological Review, 97*, 315-331.

O'Sullivan, M., & Guilford, J. P. (1976). Four factor tests of social intelligence: Manual of instructions and interpretations. Orange, CA: Sheridan Psychological Services.

Oxenstierna, G., Edman, G., Iselius, L., Oreland, L., Ross, S. B., & Sedvall, G. (1986). Concentrations of monoamine metabolites in the cerebrospinal fluid of twins and unrelated individuals: A genetic study. *Journal of Psychiatric Research, 20*, 19-20.

Oyserman, D. & Markus, H. R. (1990). Possible selves and delinquency. *Journal of Personality and Social Psychology, 59*, 112-125.

Oyserman, D. & Saltz, E. (1993). Competence, delinquency, and attempts to attain possible selves. *Journal of Personality and Social Psychology, 65*, 360-374.

Pajares, F. (1996). Self-efficacy beliefs in academic settings. *Review of Educational Research, 66*, 543-578.

Paniagua, C. (2001). The attraction of topographical technique. *International Journal of Psychoanalysis, 82*, 671-684.

Papalia, D. E., Camp, C., & Feldman, R. D. (2002). *Adult development and aging.* New York: Mcgraw-Hill.

Park, A. (Feburary, 11th, 2002). Three U.S. stars. One Gold medal. Get ready for spit city: Not long ago, Sarah Hughes idolized Michelle Kwan. Now she and Sasha Cohen will challenge Kwan's Olympic glory. *Time, 159,* p. 44.

Parker, J. G. & Asher, S. R. (1993). Beyond group acceptance: Friendship adjustment and friendship quality as distinct dimensions of children's peer adjustment. In D. Perlman & W. H. Jones (Eds.), *Advances in personal relationships (Vol 4) (pp. 261-294).* London: Kingsley.

Parkinson, B., & Manstead, A. S. R. (1992). Appraisal as a cause of emotion. *Review of Personality and Social Psychology, 13,* 122-149.

Parrott, G. W. (1993). Beyond hedonism: Motives for inhibiting good moods and for maintaining bad moods. In D. M. Wegner & J. W. Pennebaker (Eds.), *Handbook of Mental Control (pp. 278-305).* Englewood Cliffs, NJ: Prentice-Hall, Inc.

Patrick, C. J., Curtin, J. J., & Tellegen, A. (2002). Development and validation of a brief form of the Multidimensional Personality Questionnaire. *Psychological Assessment, 14,* 150-163.

Pavlov, I. P. (1906). The scientific investigation of the psychical faculties or processes in the higher animals. *Science, 24,* 613-619.

Paulhus, D. L. (1993). Bypassing the will: The automatization of affirmations. In D. M. Wegner & J. Pennebaker, *Handbook of Mental Control (pp. 573-587).* Upper Saddle River, NJ: Prentice Hall.

Paulhus, D. L., Lysy, D. C. & Yik, M. S. M (1998). Self-report measures of intelligence: Are they useful as proxy IQ tests? Journal of Personality, 66, 525-554.

Paulhus, D. L. & Nadine, B. M. (1992). The effect of acquaintanceship on the validity of personality impressions: A longitudinal study. *Journal of Personality and Social Psychology, 63,* 816-824.

Paulhus, D. L., Trapnell, P. D., & Chen, D. (1999). Birth order effects on personality and achievement within families. *Psychological Science, 10,* 482-488.

Paulhus, D. L. & Williams, K. M. (2002). The dark triad of personality: Narcissism, Machiavellianism and psychopathy. *Journal of Research in Personality, 36,* 556-563.

Paunonen, S. V. (1998). Hierarchical organization of personality and prediction of behavior. *Journal of Personality and Social Psychology, 74,* 538-556.

Paunonen, S. V., & Jackson, D. N. (2000). What is beyond the Big Five? Plenty! *Journal of Personality, 68,* 822-835.

Pedersen, N. P., Plomin, R., McClearn, G. E., & Friberg, L. T. (1988). Neuroticism, extraversion, and related traits in adult twins reared apart and reared together. *Journal of Personality and Social Psychology, 55,* 950-957.

Pelletier, K.R. (1985). *Toward a science of consciousness.* Berkeley, CA: Celestial Arts.

Pennington, B. F., Filipek, P. A., Lefly, D., Chhabildas, N., Kennedy, D. N., Simon, J. K., Filley, C. M., Galaburda, A., DeFries, J. C. (2000). A twin MRI study of size variations in the human brain. *Journal of Cognitive Neuroscience, 12,* 223-232.

Perry, B. (February, 2001a). *Big questions* Real answers. *Scholastic Choices, 16,* p. 30.

Perry, B. (March, 2001b). *Big questions* Real answers. *Scholastic Choices, 16,* p. 30.

Perry, B. (April, 2001c). *Big questions* Real answers. *Scholastic Choices, 16,* p. 30.

Perry, C., & Laurence, J-R. (1984). Mental processing outside of awareness: The contributions of Freud and Janet. In K. S. Bowers & D. Meichenbaum (Eds.). *The unconscious reconsidered (pp. 9-48).* New York: John Wiley & Sons.

Pervin, L. A. (1990). *Handbook of Personality: Theory and research.* New York: Guilford.

Pervin, L. A. (2003). *The Science of Personality (2nd edition).* Oxford: Oxford University Press.

Perry, C. & Laurence, J-R. (1984). Mental processing outside of awareness: The contributions of Freud and Janet. In K.S. Bowers & D. Meichenbaum (eds.). *The Unconscious Reconsidered* (pp. 9-48). New York: John Wiley & Sons.

Pervin, L. A. (1990). *Handbook of Personality: Theory and Research.* New York: The Guilford Press.

Pervin, L.A. (1990). A brief history of modern personality theory. In L.A. Pervin (ed.), *Handbook of personality theory and research.* New York: Guilford.

Pervin, L. A. & John, O. P. (Eds.) (1999). *Handbook of personality: Theory and research.* New York: Guilford Press.

Peterson, C. (1991). The meaning and measurement of explanatory style. *Psychological Inquiry, 2,* 1-10.

Peterson, C. A. (1997). Tests in Print, IV. *Journal of Personality Assessment, 68,* 475-477.

Peterson, B.E. & Stewart, A.J. (1993). Generativity and social motives in young adults. *Journal of Personality and Social Psychology, 65,* 186-198.

Peterson, C. A., & Seligman, M. E. (1987). Explanatory style and illness. *Journal of Personality, 55,* 237-265.

Peterson, G. W. & Rollins, B. C. (1987). Parent-Child Socialization. In M. B. Sussman, & S. K. Steinmetz (Eds.). *Handbook of marriage and the family.* New York: Plenum Press.

Phelps, M. E., & Mazziotta, J. C. (1985). Positron emission tomography: Human brain function and biochemistry. *Science, 228,* 799-809.

Phinney, J. S. (1989). Stages of ethnic identity development in minority group adolescents. *Journal of Early Adolescence, 9,* 34-49.

Phinney, J. S., & Rosenthal, D. A. (1992). Ethnic identity in adolescence: Process, context, and outcome. In G. R. Adams, T. P. Gullotta, & R. Montemayor, R. (Eds.). *Advances in Adolescent Development (Adolescent identity formation), 4,* 145-172. Newbury Park, CA: Sage.

Pietikainen, P. (1998). Archetypes as symbolic forms. *Journal of Analytical Psychology, 43,* 325-343

Pillemer, D. B., Picariello, M. L., & Pruett, J. C. (1994). Very long-term memories of a salient preschool event. *Applied Cognitive Psychology, 8,* 95-106.

Pillemer, D. B. (2000). *Momentous events, vivid memories.* Cambridge, MA: Harvard University Press.

Pillemer, D. B. (2001). Momentous events and the life story. *Review of General Psychology, 5,* 123-134.

Pinker, S. (1997). *How the mind works.* New York: Norton.

Plomin, R. (1990). *Nature and nurture.* Pacific Grove, CA: Brooks/Cole.

Plomin, R., DeFries, J. C., & Roberts, M. K. (1977). Assortive mating by unwed biological parents of adopted children. *Science, 196,* 449-450.

Plutchik, R. (1980). *Emotion: A psychoevolutionary synthesis.* New York: Harper & Row.

Plutchik, R. (1991). Emotions and evolution. In K.T. Strongman (Ed.). *International Review of Studies on Emotion (Vol 1) (pp. 37-58).* New York: Wiley.

Plutchik, R. (1984). Emotions: A general psychoevolutionary theory. K.R. Scherer & P. Ekman (Eds.), *Approaches to emotion (pp. 197-219).* Hillsdale, New Jersey: Lawrence Erlbaum.

Pohl, F. & Moravec, H. (1993). Souls in silicon. *Omni, 16,* 66-71.

Polivy, J. (1976). Perception of calories and regulation of intake in restrained and unrestrained subjects. *Addictive Behaviors, 1,* 237-243.

Polivy, J. & Herman, C. P., Hackett, R., & Kuleshnyk, I. (1986). The effects of self-attention and public attention on eating in restrained and unrestrained subjects. *Journal of Personality and Social Psychology, 50,* 1253-1260.

Poulton, R., Waldie, K.E., Menzies, R. G., Craske, M. G., & Silva, P. A. (2001). Failure to overcome 'innate' fear. A developmental test of the non-associative model of fear acquisition. *Behavioural Research Therapy, 35,* 413-421.

Powell, A., & Royce, J. R. (1981). An overview of a multifactor-system theory of personality and individual differences: I. The factor and system models and the hierarchical factor structure of individuality. *Journal of Personality and Social Psychology, 41,* 818-829.

Powell, B. & Sttelman, L. C. (1995). Feeling the pinch: Child spacing and constrains on parental economic investments in children. *Social Forces, 73,* 1465-1486.

Powers, W. T. (1973a). Feedback: Beyond behaviorism. *Science, 179,* 351-356.

Powers, W. T. (1973b). *Behavior: The control of perception.* Chicago, IL: Aldine Publishing.

Presson, P. K., & Benassi, V. A. (1996). Illusion of control: A meta-analytic review. *Journal of Social Behavior and Personality, 11,* 493-510.

Pribram, K. H. (1978). Consciousness: A scientific approach. Journal of Indian Psychology, 1, 95-118.

Pribram, K. H. & Meade, S. D. (1999). Conscious awareness: Processing in the synaptodendritic web. New Ideas in Psychology, 17, 205-214.

Price, D. J. (1963). *Little science, big science.* New York: Columbia University Press.

Price, D. J. (1986). *Little science, big science…and beyond.* New York: Columbia University Press.

Prince, M. (1973). *The unconscious (2nd ed.).* New York: Arno Press. [Original work, 1921].

Prochaska, J. O., & Norcross, J. C. (1999). *Systems of psychotherapy (4th ed.).* Brooks/Cole Publishing.

Purifoy, F. E., & Koopmans, L. H. (1979). Androstenedione, testosterone, and free testosterone concentration in women of various occupations. *Social Biology, 26,* 179-188.

Putnam, F. W. (1991). Recent research on multiple personality disorder. *Psychiatric Clinics of North America, 14,* 489-502.

Putnam, F. W., & Carlson, E. B. (1998). Hypnosis, dissociation, and trauma: Myths, metaphors, and mechanisms. In J. D.

Bremmer & C. R. Marmar (Eds.), *Trauma, memory, and dissociation (pp. 27-55).* Washington, DC: American Psychiatric Press.

Pyszczynski, T., Greenberg, J., & Holt, K. (1985). Maintaining consistency between self-serving beliefs and available data: A bias in information processing. *Personality and Social Psychology Bulletin, 11,* 179-190.

Quain, J. R. (January 21, 2002). Wise guy. *Popular Science,* 000-000.

Radziszewska, B., Richardson, J. L., Dent, C. W., & Flay, B. R. (1996). Parenting style and adolescent depressive symptoms, smoking, and academic achievement: Ethnic, gender, and SES differences. *Journal of Behavioral Medicine, 19,* 289-305.

Rapaport, D. (1960). The structure of psychoanalytic theory: A systematizing attempt (Monograph 6). *Psychological Issues, 2,* 1-158.

Rapaport, D. (1967). The points of view and assumptions of metapsychology. In M M. Gill (Ed.). *The collected papers of David Rapaport (pp.795-811).* New York: Basic Books.

Rapetti, R. (1996). Gauguin, Paul. In J. Turner (Ed.), *The Dictionary of art (pp. 187-196).* London: Macmillan Publishers Lmt..

Raykov, T., & Marcoulides, G. A. (2000). A first course in structural equation modeling. Mahwah, NJ: Lawrence Erlbaum Associates.

Redlich, F., & Bingham, J. (1960). *The inside story: Psychiatry and everyday life.* New York: Vintage Books.

Ree, M.J., & Earles, J.A. (1992). Intelligence is the best predictor of job performance. *Current Directions in Psychological Science, 1,* 86-89.

Read, S. J., & Miller, L. C. (2002). Virtual personalities: A neural network model of personality. *Personality and Social Psychology Review, 6,* 357-369.

Reed, T.E., & Jensen, A.R. (1991). Arm nerve conduction velocity (NCV), reaction time, and intelligence. *Intelligence, 15,* 33-47.

Reid, T. (1971). (Facsimile reproduction) *Essays on the intellectual powers of man.* Scolar Press (Original work published 1785, Menston, England). Reimer, A. (2001). *Hughes.* Sydney: Duffy & Snellgrove.

Reynolds, C.R., Chastain, R.L., Kaufman, A.S., & McLean, J.E. (1987). Demographic characteristics and IQ among adults: Analysis of the WAIS-R standardization sample as a function of the stratification variables. *Journal of School Psychology, 25,* 323-342.

Reynolds, J. (1966). Discourses on art. New York: Collier. [Original work published 1769-1790].

Richards, R., Kinney, D. K., Lunde, I., Benet, M., & Merzel, A. P. C. (1988). *Journal of Abnormal Psychology, 97,* 281-288.

Richters, J. E., & Cicchetti, D. (1993). Mark Twain meets *DSM-IIIR.* Conduct disorder, development, and the concept of harmful dysfunction. *Development and Psychopathology, 5,* 5-29.

Rifkin, A., Ghisalbert D., Dimatou, S., Jin, C., & Sethi, M. (1998). Dissociative identity disorder in psychiatric inpatients. *American Journal of Psychiatry, 155,* 144-145.

Roback, A. A. (1928). *The psychology of character; With a survey of temperament.* New York: Harcourt, Brace, & Company.

Roberts, B. W., Caspi, A., & Moffitt, T. E. (2003). Work experiences and personality development in young adulthood. *Journal of Personality and Social Psychology, 84,* 582-593.

Roberts, B. W., & Robins, R. W. (2000). Broad dispositions, broad aspirations: The intersection of personality traits and major life goals. *Personality and Social Psychology Bulletin, 26,* 1284-1296.

Roberts, B. W., Kuncelm, N. R., Shiner, R., Caspi, A., & Goldberg, L. R. (2007). The power of personality: The comparative validity of personality traits, socioeconomic status, and cognitive ability for predicting important life outcomes. *Perspectives on Psychological Science, 2*(4), 313-345.

Robins, R. W., Fraley, R. C., Roberts, B. W., & Trzesniewski, K. H. (2001). A longitudinal study of personality change in young adulthood. *Journal of Personality, 69,* 617-640.

Robins, R. W., John, O. P., Caspi, A., Moffitt, T. E., & Stouthamer-Loeber, M. (1996). Resilient, overcontrolled, and undercontrolled boys: Three replicable personality types. *Journal of Personality and Social Psychology, 70,* 157-171.

Robins, R. W., John, O. P., & Caspi, A. (198). The typological approach to studying personality. In R. B. Cairns, L. R. Bergman, & J. Kagan (Eds.). *Methods and models for studying the individual (pp. 135-157).* Thousand Oaks, CA: Sage.

Robinson, D. N. (1995). *An intellectual history of psychology (3rd ed.).* Madison: University of Wisconsin Press.

Robinson, J. P., Shaver, P. R., Wrightsman, L. S. (1991). *Measures of personality and social psychological attitudes.* San Diego, CA: Academic Press.

Rodgers, J. L. (2001). What causes birth order-intelligence patterns. *American Psychologist, 56,* 505-510.

Rogers, C.R. (1951). *Client-centered therapy.* Boston: Houghton Mifflin.

Rogers, C. R. (1959). A theory of therapy, personality, and interpersonal relationships, as developed in the client-centered framework. In S. Koch (Ed.), *Psychology: A study of a science: Vol. 3: Formulations of the person and the social context (pp. 185-256).* New York: McGraw-Hill.

Rokeach, M. (1960). *The open and closed mind.* New York: Basic Books.

Rokeach, M. (1973). *The nature of human values.* New York: The Free Press.

Rorer, L.G. (1990). Personality assessment: A conceptual survey. In L.A. Pervin (ed.). *Handbook of Personality Theory and Research* (pp. 693-720). New York: Guilford

Rosch, E., Mervis, C.B., Gray, W., Johnson, D., & Boyes-Braem, P. (1976). Basic objects in natural categories. *Cognitive Psychology, 8,* 382-439.Roseman, I.J. (1984). Cognitive determinants of emotions: A structural theory. In P. Shaver (Ed.), *Review of personality and social psychology: Vol. 5. Emotions, relationships, and health* (pp. 11-36). Beverly Hills, CA: Sage.

Roseman, I. J., & Smith, C. A. (2001). Appraisal theory: Overview, assumptions, varieties, controversies. In K. R. Scherer. A. Schorr, T. Johnstone (Eds.). *Appraisal theories in emotion: Theory, methods, research. (pp. 3-19).* London: Oxford University Press.

Rosen, D. H., Smith, S. M., Huston, H. L., & Gonzalez, G. (1991). Empirical study of associations between symbols and their meanings: Evidence of collective unconscious (archetypal) memory. *Journal of Analytical Psychology, 36,* 211-228.

Rosenbaum, D. A. (1991). *Human motor control.* New York: Academic Press.

Rosenbaum, D. A. (2005). The Cinderella of psychology: The neglect of motor control in the science of mental life and behavior. *American Psychologist, 60,* 308-317.

Rosenberg, A. (2000). *Philosophy of science: A contemporary introduction.* New York: Routledge.

Rosenberg, M. (1965). *Society and the adolescent self-image.* Princeton, NJ: Princeton University Press.

Rosenthal, D. (1993). Higher-order thoughts and the appendage theory of consciousness. Philosophical Psychology, 6, 155-166.

Rosenthal, D. (2002). The higher-order thought model of consciousness. In R. Carter (Auth. & Ed.). Exploring Consciousness (pp. 45-47). Berkeley, CA: University of California Press.

Rosenthal, G. G., Evans, C. S., & Miller, W. L. (1996). Female preference for dynamic traits in the green swordtail, Xiphophorus helleri. Animal Behavior, 51, 811-820.

Rosenzweig, S. (1941). Need-persistive and ego defensive reactions to frustration as demonstrated by an experiment on repression. *Psychological Review, 48,* 347-349.

Ross, A.O. (1987). *Personality: The Scientific Study of Complex Behavior.* New York: Holt, Rinehart, & Winston.

Ross, J. M. (2003). Preconscious defence analysis, memory, and structural change. *International Journal of Psychoanalysis, 84,* 59-76.

Ross, L., Greene, D., & House, P. (1977). The "false consensus effect": An egocentric bias in social perception and attribution processes. *Journal of Experimental and Social Psychology, 13,* 279-301.

Rothbart, M. K. (1981). Measurement of temperament in infancy. *Child Development, 52,* 569-578.

Rothbart, M. K., Ahadi, S. A., & Evans, D. E. (2000). Temperament and personality: Origins and outcomes. *Journal of Personality and Social Psychology, 73,* 122-135.

Rothbart, M. K. & Mauro, J. A. (1990). Questionnaire approaches to the study of infant temperament. In J. W. Fagen and J. Colombo (eds.), *Individual differences in infancy: reliability, stability, and prediction (411-429).* Hillsdale, NJ: Erlbaum.

Rothbart, M. K., & Putnam, S. P. (2002). Temperament and socialization. In Pulkkinen, L. & Caspi, A. *Paths to successful development: Personality in the life course (pp. 19-45).* Cambridge: Cambridge University Press.

Rotter, J. B. (1954). *Social learning and clinical psychology.* New York: Prentice Hall.

Rotter, J. B. (1990). Internal versus external control of reinforcement: A case history of a variable. American Psychologist, 45, 489-493.

Rozin, P. (1976). The evolution of intelligence and access to the cognitive unconscious. In J. M. Sprague & A. A. Epstein (Eds.). *Progress in psychobiology and physiological psychology (pp. 245-280).* New York: Academic Press.

Rubin, M. M. (1999). *Emotional intelligence and its role in mitigating aggression: A correlational study of the relationship between emotional intelligence and aggression in urban adolescents.* Unpublished dissertation, Immaculata College, Immaculata, Pennsylvania.

Ruble, T. L. (1983). Sex stereotypes: Issues of changes in the 1970's. *Sex Roles, 9,* 397-402.

Runco, M. A. (1986). Predicting children's creative performance. *Psychological Reports, 59,* 1247-1254.

Rushton, J.P., & Ankney, C. D. (1996). Brain size and cognitive ability: Correlations with age, sex, social class, and race. *Psychonomic Bulletin & Review, 3,* 21-36.

Russell, J. A. (1999). On the bipolarity of positive and negative affect. *Psychological Bulletin, 125,* 3-30.

Russell, J. A., & Barrett, L. F. (1999). Core affect, prototypical emotional episodes, and other things called emotion: Dissecting the elephant. *Journal of Personality and Social Psychology, 76,* 805-819.

Russell, J. A., Weiss, A. & Mendelsohn, G. A. (1989). Affect Grid: A single-item scale of pleasure and arousal. Journal of Personality & Social Psychology, 57, 493-502.

Rutter, M. (2000). Resilience reconsidered: Conceptual considerations, empirical findings, and policy implications. In J. P. Shonkoff & J. S. Meisels (Eds). *Handbook of early child intervention (2ⁿᵈ edition) (pp. 651-682).* New York: Cambridge University Press.

Rychlak, J. F. (1981). *Introduction to Personality and Psychotherapy (2ⁿᵈ ed.).* Boston: Houghton Mifflin Company.

Ryff, C. D. (1989). Happiness is everything, or is it? Explorations on the meaning of psychological well-being. *Journal of Personality and Social Psychology, 57,* 1069-1081.

Ryle, G. (1949). *The concept of mind.* New York: Barnes & Noble.

Saad, G., Gill, T., & Nataraajan, R. (2005). Are laterborns more innovative and nonconforming consumers than firstborns? A Darwinian perspective. *Journal of Business Research, 58,* 902-909.

Saarni, C. (2000). The social context of emotional development. In M. Lewis & J. M. Haviland-Jones, *Handbook of Emotions (2ⁿᵈ Ed). (pp. 306-332).* New York: Guilford Press.

Sager, M. (November, 1999). The smartest man in America. *Esquire, 132* 145-148, 184, 186.

Salovey, P., & Mayer, J.D. (1990). Emotional intelligence. *Imagination, Cognition, and Personality, 9,* 185-211.

Salovey, P., Mayer, J. D., Goldman, S., Turvey, C., & Palfai, T. P. (1995). Emotional attention, clarity, and repair: Exploring emotional intelligence using the trait meta-mood scale. In Pennebaker, J. W. (Ed.) *Emotion, disclosure, and health (pp. 125-154).* Washington, DC: American Psychological Association.

Salovey, P., Mayer, J.D., & Rosenhan, D.L. (1991). Mood and helping: Mood as a motivator of helping and helping as a regulator of mood. In M.S. Clark, (Ed.) *Prosocial behavior/ Review of Personality and Social Psychology, 12,* 215-237.

Salovey, P., Rothman, A. J., Detweiler, J. B., & Steward, W. T. (2000). Emotional states and physical health. *American Psychologist, 55,* 110-121.

Sampson, E. E. (1989). The challenge of social change for psychology: Globalization and psychology's theory of the person. *American Psychologist, 44,* 914-921.

Sanford, N. (1963). Personality: Its place in psychology. In S. Koch (Ed.). *Psychology: A study of a science* (Vol. 5, pp. 488-592). New York: McGraw-Hill.

Sanford, N. (1970). *Issues in personality psychology.* San Francisco: Jossey-Bass.

Sattler, J. M. (1992). Assessment of children: WISC-III and SPPSI-R supplement. San Diego: Author.

Saucier, G. (1992). Benchmarks: Integrating affective and interpersonal circles with the Big-Five personality factors. *Journal of Personality and Social Psychology, 62,* 1025-1035.

Saucier, G. & Goldberg, L. R. (1998). What is beyond the Big Five? *Journal of Personality, 66,* 495-524.

Saucier, G., & Goldberg, L. R. (2001). Lexical studies of indigenous personality factors: Premises, products, and prospects. *Journal of Personality, 69,* 847-879.

Saucier, G., Ostendorf, F., & Peabody, D. (2001). The non-evaluative circumplex of personality adjectives. *Journal of Personality, 69,* 537-582.

Scarr, S. (1981). *Race, social class, and individual differences in I.Q..* Hillsdale, NJ: Erlbaum.

Schank, R., & Abelson, R. (1977). *Scripts, plans, goals and Understanding.* Hillsdale, NJ: Lawrence Erlbaum.

Scheflin, A. W., Spiegel, H., & Spiegel, D. (1998). Forensic uses of hypnosis. In A. K. Hess & Weiner, I. B. (Eds.), *The handbook of forensic psychology (2ⁿᵈ ed).* New York: Wiley.

Scheier, M. F., & Carver, C. S. (1985). Optimism, coping, and health: Assessment and implications of generalized outcome expectancies. *Health Psychology, 4,* 219-247.

Scherer, K. R. Schorr, A., & Johnstone, T. (Eds.) (2001). *Appraisal theories in emotion: Theory, methods, research.* London: Oxford University Press.

Schlaug, G., Jaencke, L., Huang, Y. Staiger, J. F., et al. (1995). Increased corpus callosum size in musicians. *Neuropsychologia, 33,* 1047-1055.

Schlenker, B. R., Weigold, M. F., & Hallam, J. R. (1990). Self-serving attributions in social context: Effects of self-esteem and social pressure. *Journal of Personality and Social Psychology, 58,* 855-863.

Schmitt, D. P., & Buss, D. M. (2000). Sexual dimensions of person description: Beyond or subsumed by the Big Five? *Journal of Research in Personality, 34,* 141-177.

Schneider, W. J., & Newman, D. A. (2015). Intelligence is multidimensional: Theoretical review and implications of specific cognitive abilities. *Human Resource Management Review, 25*(1), 12-27.

Schopenhauer, A. (1819/1966). World as will and representation. E. F. J. Payne (Trans.). New York: Dover. [Original translation published 1958; Original work published 1819].

Schretlen, D., Pearson, G. D., Anthony, J. C., Aylward, E. H., Augustine, A. M., Davis, A., & Barta, P. (2000). Elucidating the contributions of processing speed, executive ability, and frontal lobe volume to normal age-related differences in fluid intelligence. *Journal of the International Neuropsychological Society, 6,* 52-61.

Schulman, M. (2002). How we become moral. In C. R. Snyder & S. J. Lopez, *Handbook of Positive Psychology (pp. 499-512).* New York: Oxford University Press.

Schultheiss, Oliver C.; Yankova, Diana; Dirilikvo, Benjamin; Schad, Daniel J.; Are implicit and explicit motive measures statistically Independent? A fair and balanced **test** using the

Picture Story Exercise and a cue- and response-matched questionnaire measure. Journal of Personality Assessment, Vol 91(1), Jan, 2009. pp.72-81.

Schultz, D. P., & Schulz, S. E. (2001). *Theories of personality.* Belmont, CA: Wadsworth.

Schultz, L. H., Barr, D. J., & Selman, R. L. (2001). The value of a developmental approach to evaluating character development programees: an outcome study of *Facing History and Ourselves. Journal of Moral Education, 30,* 3-27.

Schutte, N. S., Malouff, J. M., Simunek, M. (2002). Characteristic emotional intelligence and emotional well-being. Cognition & Emotion, 16, 769-785.

Schwartz. D., Dodge, K. A., & Coie, J. D. (1993). The emergence of chronic peer victimization in boys' play groups. *Child Development, 64,* 1755-1772.

Scwartz, D., Dodge, K. A., Pettit, G. S., & Bates, J. E. (1997). The early socialization of aggressive victims of bullying. *Child development, 68,* 665-675.

Schwartz, D., Dodge, K. A., Pettit, G. S., & Bates, J. E. (2000). Friendship as a moderating factor in the pathway between early harsh home environment and later victimization in the peer group. *Developmental Psychology, 36,* 646-662.

Schwartz, G.E., Weinberger, D.A., & Singer, J.A. (1981). Cardiovascular differentiation of happiness, sadness, anger, and fear following imagery and exercise. *Psychosomatic Medicine, 43,* 343-364.

Scott, M., & Lyman, S. M. (1968). Accounts. *The American Sociological Review, 33,* 46-62.

Seabrook, J. (1999). Letter from the Skywalker Ranch: Is the force still with us? In Kline, S. (Ed.). *George Lucas Interviews.* Jackson, MI: University of Mississippi Press. [Original Published in the *New Yorker,* January 6th, 1997, pp. 40-53].

Sears, R. R. (1950). Personality. *Annual Review of Psychology, 1,* 105-118.

Sears, R. R. (1959). Personality theory: The next forty years. *Monographs of the Society for Research in Child Development, 24,* (Serial No. 74: 37-50).

Segal, N. L. (2000). *Entwined lives: Twins and what they tell us about human behavior.* New York: Dutton/Penguin.

Segal, Z. V. (1988). Appraisal of self-schema in cognitive models of depression. *Psychological Bulletin, 103,* 147-162.

Segal, Z. V., Gemar, M., & Williams, S. (1999). Differential cognitive response to a mood challenge following successful cognitive therapy or pharmacotherapy for unipolar depression. *Journal of Abnormal Psychology, 108,* 3-10.

Segerstrom, S. C. (2001). Optimism, goal conflict, and stressor-related immune change. *Journal of Behavioral Medicine, 24,* 441-467

Segerstrom, S. C. (2005). Optimism and immunity: Do positive thoughts always lead to positive effects? *Brain, Behavior and Immunity, 19,* 195-200.

Seligman, M. E. P. (1975). *Helplessness: On depression, development, and death.* San Francisco: Freeman.

Seligman, M. E. P., Csikszentmihalyi, M. (2000). Positive psychology: An introduction. *American Psychologist, 55,* 5-14.

Seligman, M. E. P., & Csikszentmihalyi, M. (2001). Reply to comments. *American Psychologist, 56,* 89-90.

Seligman, M. E. P.; Steen, T. A., Park, N., Peterson, C. (2005). Positive Psychology Progress: Empirical Validation of Interventions. *American Psychologist, 60,* 410-421.

Seltzer, R., & Glass, W. (1991). International politics and judging in Olympic skating events: 1968-1988. *Journal of Sport Behavior, 14,* 189-200.

Shafer, A. B. (2001). The big five and sexuality trait terms as predictors of relationships and sex. *Journal of Research in Personality 35,* 313-338.

Shapiro, D. L., & Bies, R. J. (1994). Threats, bluffs, and disclaimers in negotiations. *Organizational Behavior & Human Decision Processes, 60,* 14-35.

Sharp, S.E. (1899). Individual psychology: A study in psychological method. *The American Journal of Psychology, 10,* 329-391.

Shea, D. L., Lubinski, D., Benbow, C. P. (2001). Importance of assessing spatial ability in intellectually talented young adolescents: A 20-year longitudinal study. *Journal of Educational Psychology, 93,* 604-614.

Sheldon, K. M., & Kasser, T. (1998). Pursuing personal goals: Skills enable progress but not all progress is beneficial. *Personality and Social Psychology Bulletin, 24,* 1319-1331.

Sheldon, K. M., & Kasser, T. (2001). Goals, congruence, and positive well-being: New empirical support for the humanistic theories. *Journal of Humanistic Psychology, 41,* 30-50.

Sheldon, K. (2011). Consilience within the biopsychological system. *Psychological Inquiry, 22,* 52-65.

Sheldon, W. H., & Stevens, S. S. (1940). *The varieties of human physique.* New York: Harper.

Sheldon, W. H., & Stevens, S. S. (1942). *The varieties of temperament.* New York: Harper.

Shepard, R. N., & Metzler, J. (1971). Mental rotation of three-dimensional objects. *Science, 171,* 701-703.

Sherif, M., & Hovland, C.I. (1961). *Social judgment.* New Haven: Yale University Press.

Shill, M. A., & Lumley, M. A. (2000). The Psychological Mindedness Scale: Factor structure, convergent validity and gender in a non-psychiatric sample. *Psychology and Psychotherapy: Theory, Research and Practice, 75,* 131-150.

Shoda, Y., & Leetiernan, S. (2002). What remains invariant? Finding order within a person's thoughts, feelings, and behaviors across situations. In D. Cervone & W. Mischel (Eds.). *Advances in personality science (pp. 241-270).* New York: Guilford.

Shoda, Y., Mischel, W., & Wright, J.C. (1994). Intraindividual stability in the organization and patterning of behavior: Incorporating psychological situations into the idiographic analysis of personality. *Journal of Personality and Social Psychology, 67(4),* 674-687.

Shostrom, E. L. (1964). An inventory for the measurement of self-actualization. *Educational and Psychological Measurement, 24,* 207-217.

Showers, C. J. (2002). Integration and compartmentalization: A model of self-structure and self-change. In D. Cervone, & W. Mischel (Eds.). *Advances in personality science (pp. 271-291).* New York: Guilford.

Shweder, R. A. (1975). How relevant is an individual difference theory of personality? *Journal of Personality Psychology, 43,* 455-484.

Shweder, R. A., & D'Andrade, R. G. (1979). Accurate reflection or systematic distortion? A reply to Block, Weiss, & Thorne. *Journal of Personality and Social Psychology, 37,* 1075-1084.

Siegel, J. P., & Spellman, M. E. (2002). The dyadic splitting scale. *The American Journal of Family Therapy, 30,* 117-124.

Siegler, I.C., George, L. K., & Okun, M. A. (1979). Cross-sequential analysis of adult personality. *Developmental Psychology, 15,* 350-351.

Simonton, D. K. (1994). *Greatness: Who makes history and why.* New York: Guilford.

Simonton, D. (1986). Presidential personality: Biographical use of the gough Adjective Check List. *Journal of Personality and Social Psychology, 51,* 149-160.

Simonton, D. (1988). Presidential style: Personality, biography, and performance. *Journal of Personality and Social Psychology, 55,* 928-936.

Simonton, D. K. (1997). Creative productivity: A predictive and explanatory model of career trajectories and landmarks. *Psychological Review, 104,* 66-89.

Simonton, D. K. (2002). Creativity. In C. R. Snyder & S. J. Lopez, *Handbook of Positive Psychology (pp. 189-201).* New York: Oxford University Press.

Singer, J.A. (1984). The private personality. *Personality and Social Psychology Bulletin, 10,* 7-30.

Singer, J. A. (1997). Message in a bottle: Stories of men and addiction. New York: Free Press.

Singer, J. A. (1998). Applying a Systems Framework to self-defining memories. *Psychological Inquiry, 9,* 161-164.

Singer, J. A, & Bluck, S. (2001). New perspectives on autobiographical memory: The integration of narrative processing and autobiographical reasoning. *Review of General Psychology, 5,* 91-99.

Singer, J. A., Salovey, P. (1993). *The remembered self: Emotion and memory in personality.* New York: Free Press.

Singer, J. L. (1966). *Daydreaming: An introduction to the experimental study of inner experience.* New York: Random House.

Singer, J. L. (1975). Navigating the stream of consciousness: Research in daydreaming and related inner experience. American Psychologist, 30, 727-738.

Singer, J. L. (1984). The private personality. *Personality and Social Psychology, 10,* 7-30.

Six, B., & Eckes, T. (1991). A closer look at the complex structure of gender stereotypes. *Sex Roles, 24,* 64.

Skodak, M. & Skeels, H. M. (1949). A final follow-up of one hundred adopted children. *Journal of Genetic Psychology, 75,* 85-125.

Slabbinck, H., De Houwer, J., Van Kenhove, P. (2013). Convergent, discriminant, and incremental validity of the Pictorial Attitude Implicit Association Test and the Picture Story Exercise as measures of the implicit power motive. *European Journal of Personality, 27*(1), 30-38.

Smith, G. M. (1967). Usefulness of peer ratings of personality in educational research. *Educational and psychological measurement, 27,* 967-984.

Smith, C.A. & Ellsworth, P.C. (1985). Patterns of cognitive appraisal in emotion. *Journal of Personality and Social Psychology, 48,* 813-838.

Smith, M. L., & Glass G. V. (1977). Meta-analysis of psychotherapy outcome studies. *American Psychologist, 32,* 752-760.

Smith, M. L., Glass, G. V., & Miller, T. I. (1980). *The benefits of psychotherapy.* Baltimore: Johns Hopkins University Press.

Smith, R. (September, 2002). Cosmo quiz: Are you open to change? *Cosmopolitan, 234,* 236.

Snow, R. (1995). Foreword. In D. H. Saklofske & M. Zeidner (Eds.), *International handbook of personality and intelligence (pp. 11-15).* New York: Plenum.

Snyder, C. R. (1995). Coping: The psychology of what works. New York: Oxford University Press.

Snyder, C.R. & Lopez, S.J. (Eds.) (2002), *The handbook of positive psychology (pp. 159-171).* New York: Oxford University Press.

Snyder, M. & Swann, W.B. (1978). Hypothesis-testing processes in social interaction. *Journal of Personality and Social Psychology, 36,* 1202-1212.

Snyderman, M., & Rothman, S. (1987). Survey of expert opinion on intelligence and aptitude testing. *American Psychologist, 42,* 137-144.

Solomon, S., Greenberg, J., & Pyszczynski, T. (1991). A terror-management theory of social behavior: The psychological functions of self-esteem and cultural worldviews. In M. P. Zanna (Ed.), *Advances in experimental social psychology (pp. 91-159).* San Diego: Academic Press.

Sorce, J. F. & Emde, R. N. (1981). Mother's presence is not enough: Effect of emotional availability on infant exploration. Developmental Psychology, 17, 737-745.

Sorce, J. F., Emde, R. N., Campos, J. J., & Klinnert, M. D. (1985). Maternal emotional signaling: Its effect on the visual cliff behavior of 1-year-olds. Developmental Psychology, 21, 195-200.

Spearman, C. (1904). General intelligence determined and measured.

American Journal of Psychology, 15, 201-293.

Spence, J. T., Helmreich, R., & Stapp, J. (1974). The Personal Attributes Questionnaire: A measure of sex-role stereotypes and masculinity and femininity. *Journal Supplement Abstract Service Catalog of Selected Documents in Psychology, 4,* 42 (No. 617).

Solomon, R.L., & Corbit, J.D. (1974). An opponent-process theory of motivation: I. Temporal dynamics of affect. *Psychological Review, 81,* 119-145.

Sontag, L.W., Baker, C.T., & Nelson, V.L. (1958). Mental growth and personality development: A longitudinal study. *Monographs of the Society for Research in Child Development, 23*(2, Serial No. 68).

Spaeth, E. B. (1999). What a lawyer needs to learn. In R. J. Sternberg, & J. A. Horvath (Eds.). *Tacit knowledge in professional practice: Researcher and professional perspectives (21-36).* Mahwah, NJ: Lawrence Erlbaum Associates.

Spearman, C. (1927). The abilities of man. New York: Macmillan.

Spielberger, C. D., & DeNike, L. D. (1966). Descriptie behaviorism versus cognitive theory in verbal operant conditioning. *Psychological Review, 73,* 306-326.

Spiller, H. A., Hale, J. R., De Boer, J. Z. (2002). The Delphic oracle: A multidisciplinary defense of the gaseous vent theory. *Clinical Toxicology, 40,* 189-196.

Spinoza, 0000. *Ethics.*

Spitz, R. (1946). Anaclitic depression. *Psychoanalytic Study of the Child, 2,* 313-342.

Stagner, R. (1937). Psychology of personality. New York: McGraw-Hill.

Stanislavsky, K. (1948). *An actor prepares.* New York: Theatre Arts Books. [E. R. Hapgood, Trans].

Statman, D. (Ed.). *Moral luck.* Albany, NY: State University of New York Press.

Steele, C. M. (1998). Stereotyping and its threat are real. American Psychologist, 53, 680-681.

Steele, C. M. & Aronson, J. (1995). Stereotype threat and the intellectual test performance of African Americans. Journal of Personality & Social Psychology, 69, 797-811.

Steelman, L. C., Powell, B., Werum, R., & Carter, S. (2002). Reconsidering the effects of sibling configuration: Recent advances and challenges. Annual Review of Sociology, 28, 243-269.

Steinberg, L. Lamborn, S. D., Darling, N., Mounts, N. S., & Dornbush, S. (1994). Over-time changes in adjustment and competence among adolescents from authoritative, authoritarian, indulgent, and neglectful families. Child Development, 65, 754-770.

Steinsaltz, A. (1987). Soul Searchng. In A. A. Cohen & P. Mendes-Flohr (1987). *Contemporary Jewish Religious Thought (pp. 897-902).* New York: The Free Press.

Stern, D. (1987). *The interpersonal world of the infant.* New York: Basic Books.

Stern, W. (1914). *The psychological methods of intelligence testing.* G. M. Whipple (Trans.). Baltimore, MD: Warwick and York.

Sternberg, C. R.; Campos, J. J. (1990). The development of anger expressions in infancy. In N. L. Stein, & B. Leventhal (Eds) Psychological and biological approaches to emotion (pp. 247-282).

Sternberg, R. J. (1981). Intelligence and non-entrenchment. *Journal of Educational Psychology, 73,* 1-16.

Sternberg, R. J. (1986). A triangular theory of love. Psychological Review, 93, 119-135.

Sternberg, R. J. (1987). Liking versus loving: A comparative evaluation of theories. Psychological Bulletin, 102, 331-345

Sternberg, R. J. (1997). Construct validation of a triangular love scale. European Journal of Social Psychology, 27, 313-335.

Sternberg, R. J. (1997). The concept of intelligence and its role in lifelong learning and success. American Psychologist, 52, 1030-1037.

Sternberg, R. J. (2003). Our research program validating the triarchic theory of successful intelligence: Reply to Gottfredson.. Intelligence, 31, 399-413.

Sternberg, R. J. (2003). A broad view of intelligence: The theory of successful intelligence. *Consulting Psychology Journal: Practice & Research, 55,* 39-154.

Sternberg, R. J., Forsythe, G. B., Helund, J., Horvath, J. A., Wagner, R. I., Williams, W. M., Snook, S. A., & Grigorenko, E. L. (2000). *Practical intelligence in everyday life.* New York: Cambridge University Press.

Sternberg, R. J., & Grigorenko, E. (2001). *Unified psychology, 56,* 1069-1079.

Sternberg, R. J. & Horvath, J. A. (Eds) (1999). *Tacit knowledge in professional practice: Researcher and practitioner perspectives.* Mahwah, NJ, US: Lawrence Erlbaum Associates, Publishers.

Sternberg, R. J., & O'Hara, L. A. (2000). Intelligence and creativity. In R. J. Sternberg (Ed.). *Handbook of intelligence (pp. 611-630).* Cambridge, UK: Cambridge University Press.

Sternberg, R. J., & Ruzgis, P. (Eds.) (1994). *Personality and intelligence.* Cambridge, UK: Cambridge University Press.

Stevens, A. (2000). Jungian analysis and evolutionary psychotherapy: An integrative approach. In P. Gilbert & K. G. Bailey (Eds.). *Genes on the couch: Explorations in evolutionary psychotherapy.* New York: Brunner-Routledge.

Stevens, R. (1983). *Erik Erikson: An introduction.* Milton Keynes: The Open University Press.

Stevenson, L., & Haberman, D. L. (1998). *Ten theories of human nature.* Oxford: Oxford University Press.

Stewart, D. (1833/1963). Elements of the philosophy of the human mind. Facsimile reprint by University Microfilms International, Ann Arbor, MI. (Original work published 1833, Cambridge: James Munroe).

Stewart, N. (1947). A.G.C.T. scores of army personnel grouped by occupation. *Occupation, 26,* 5-41.

Stifter, C. A., & Moyer, D. (1991). The regulation of positive affect: Gaze aversion activity during mother-infant interaction. *Infant Behavior and Development, 14,* 111-123.

Stillion, J. M., & McDowell, E. E. (2001-2002). The early demise of the "Stronger" sex: Gender-related causes of sex differences in longevity. *Omega, 44,* 301-318.

Stokes, R., & Hewitt, J. P. (1976). Aligning actions. *The American Sociological Review, 46,* 838-849.

Stone, W. F., & Schaffner, P. E. (1988). The psychology of politics. New York: Springer-Verlag.

Storm, L., Ertel, S. (2001). Does psi exist? Comments on Milton and Wiseman's (1999) meta-analysis of Ganzfield research. Psychological Bulletin, 127, 424-433.

Strachey, J. (1960). Editor's introduction. In Freud, S. (1960). *The ego and the id (pp. ix-xvii).* New York: W.W. Norton.

Styron, W. (1990). *Darkness visible.* New York: Random House.

Sulloway, F. J. (1996). *Born to rebel: Birth order, family dynamics, and creative lives.* New York: Pantheon Books.

Swann, W. B., & Pelham, B. W. (2002). The truth about illusions: Authenticity and positivity in social relationships. In C. R. Snyder & S. J. Lopez, *Handbook of Positive Psychology (pp. 366-381).* New York: Oxford University Press.

Swann, W. B., & Seyle, C. (2005). Personality psychology's comeback and its emerging symbiosis with social psychology. *Personality and Social Psychology Bulletin, 31,* 155-165.

Swift, , E. M. (March 4, 2002). Head turner: Skating with utter confidence and uninhibited joy, Sarah Hughes soared from fourth place to gold and became the new queen of the ice. *Sports Illustrated, 96,* 48ff.

Svare, B. B. (1983). *Hormones and aggressive behavior.* Plenum.

Tangney, J. P. (2002). Humility. In C. R. Snyder & S. J. Lopez, *Handbook of Positive Psychology (pp. 411-419).* New York: Oxford University Press.

Tart, C. (1972). *Altered states of consciousness.* Garden City, NY: Doubleday.

Taylor, S. E., & Brown, J. D. (1988). Illusion and well-being: A social psychological perspective on mental health.. Psychological Bulletin, 103, 193-210.

Taylor, S. E., & Brown, J. D. (1994). Positive illusions and well-being revisited: Separating fact from fiction. Psychological Bulletin, 116, 21-27.

Tennen, H., & Affleck, G. (1998). Three compulsions of stress and coping research: A Systems Framework cure? *Psychological Inquiry, 9,* 164-168.

Tennen, H., Affleck, G., Armeli, S., & Carney, M. A. (2000). A daily process approach to coping: Linking theory, research, and practice. *American Psychologist, 55,* 626-636.

Terman, L.M. (1917). The intelligence quotient of Francis Galton in childhood. *American Journal of Psychology, 28,* 208-215.

Terman, L.M. (1926). Excerpts from the early writings of young geniuses (Appendix II). In C.M. Cox. *Genetic Studies of Genius Volume II: The early mental traits of three hundred geniuses.* Stanford, CA: Stanford University Press.

Tetlock, P. E., Peterson, R. S., & Berry, J. M. (1993). Flattering and unflattering personality portraits of integratively simple and complex managers. *Journal of Personality and Social Psychology, 64,* 500-511.

Theophrastus (372-287 B.C./1929). Demarcated characters. In Edmunds (ed.), *The characters of Theophrastus* (p. 48-49).

Thomas, A., Chess, S., & Birch, H. G. (1970). The origin of personality. *Scientific American, 223,* 102-109.

Thomas, W. I. (1928/2003). The definition of the situation. In In J. A. Holstein & J. F. Gubrium (Eds.). *Inner lives and social worlds (pp. 80-81).* New York: Oxford University Press. [Original work published 1928].

Thombs, B. D., Roseman, M., Coyne, J. C., de Jonge, P., Delisle, V. C., Arthurs, E., Ziegelstein, R.C. (2013). Does evidence support the American Heart Association's recommendation to screen patients for depression in cardiovascular care? An updated systematic review. *PLoS ONE, 8,* e52654.

Thompson, R. A. (1994). Emotion regulation: A theme in search of definition. *Monographs of the Society for Research in Child Development, 59* (2-3, Serial No. 240, 25-52).

Thorndike, E.L. (1906). *Principles of teaching.* New York: Seiler.

Thorndike, E. L. (1920). Intelligence and its use. *Harper's Magazine, 140,* 227-235.

Thorndike, E. L. (1921). Intelligence and its measurement: A symposium. *Journal of Educational Psychology, 12,* 123-147, 195-216, 271-275.

Thorndike, E. L. & Stein, S. (1937). An evaluation of the attempts to measure social intelligence. *Psychological Bulletin, 34,* 275-285.

Thorndike,R. L., Hagen, E. P., & Sattler, J. P. (1986). *Technical manual for the Stanford-Binet Intelligence Scale, Fourth Edition.* Chicago: Riverside.

Thorne, A., & Klohnen, E. (1993). Interpersonal memories as maps for personality consistency. In D. C. Funder, R. D. Parke, C. Tomlinson-Keasey, & K. Widaman, *Studying lives through time: Personality and development (pp. 223-253).* Washington, DC: American Psychological Association.

Thurstone, L. L. (1924). The nature of intelligence. New York: Harcourt Brace.

Thurstone, L. L. (1938). Primary mental abilities. Chicago: University of Chicago Press.

Tice, D. M. (1992). Self-concept change and self-presentation: The looking glass self is also a magnifying glass. *Journal of Personality and Social Psychology, 63,* 435-451.

Tidwell, G. L. (1993). The anatomy of a fraud. *Fund Raising Management, 24,* 58-65.

Tierney, J. (July 21, 1991). Behind Monty Hall's Doors: Puzzle, debate, and answer? *The New York Times (Section 1; Part 1),* pp. 1ff.

Tomarken, A. J., & Keener, A. D. (1998). Frontal brain asymmetry and depression: A self-regulatory perspective. *Cognition and Emotion, 12,* 387-420.

Tomkins, S. S. (1979). Script theory. In H. E. Howe, Jr., and R. A. Dienstbier (Eds.), *Nebraska Symposium on Motivation, 26,* 201-236. [pp. 201-236; Lincoln, NE: University of Nebraska Press].

Tomkins, S. S. (1983). Left and right: A basic dimension of ideology and personality. In R. W. White (Ed.). *The study of lives (pp. 388-411).* New York: Atherton Press.

Tomkins, S. S. (1984). Affect theory. In K.R. Scherer & P. Ekman, *Approaches to emotion.* Hillsdale, NJ: Lawrence Erlbaum.

Tooby, J., & Cosmides, L. (1990). On the universality of human nature and the uniqueness of the individual: The role of genetics and adaptation. *Journal of Personality, 58,* 17-67.

Torges, C.M., Stewart, A.J., & Miner-Rubino, K. (2005). Personality after the prime of life: men and women coming to terms with regrets. *Journal of Research in Personality, 39,* 148.

Torrance, E. P. (1972). Career patterns and peak creative achievements of high school students twelve years later. *The Gifted Child Quarterly, 16,* 75-88.

Torrance, E. P. (1975). Creativity research in education: Still alive. In I. A. Taylor & J. w. Getzels (Eds.). *Perspectives in creativity (pp.278-296).* Chicago: Aldine.

Torrance, E. P. (1988). The nature of creativity as manifest in its testing. In R. J. Sternberg (Ed.). *The nature of creativity (pp. 43-75).* Cambridge, England: Cambridge University Press.

Totterdell, P. (1999). Mood scores: Mood and performance in professional cricketers. *British Journal of Psychology, 90,* 317-332.

Triandis, H. C. (2001). Individualism-collectivism and personality. *Journal of Personality, 69,* 907-924.

Tsang, J. (2002). Moral rationalization and the integration of situational factors and psychological processes in immoral behavior. *Review of General Psychology, 6,* 25-50.

Tulving, E. (2002). Episodic memory: From mind to brain. Annual Review of Psychology, 53, 1-25.

Tulsky, D., Zhu, J., & Ledbetter, M. F. (Project directors). (1997). *WAIS-III, WMS-III Technical Manual.* San Antonio: Psychological Corporation.

Tulsky, D. S., & Ledbetter, M. F. (2000). Updating to the WAIS-III and WMS-III. Considerations for research and clinical practice. *Psychological Assessment, 12,* 253-262.

Tulving, E. (1972). Episodic and semantic memory. In B. Tulivng and W. Donaldson (Eds.), *Organization and memory.* New York: Academic Press.

Tulving, E. (2002). Episodic memory: From mind to brain. *Annual Review of Psychology, 53,* 1-25.

Twenge, J. M. (2002). Birth cohort, social change, and personality. In D. Cervone & W. Mischel (Eds.) *Advances in personality science*. New York: Guilford Press.

Tyler, L.E. (1965). *The psychology of human differences*. New York: Appleton-Century-Crofts.

Umilta, C., Simion, F., & Valenza, E. (1996). Newborn's preference for faces. *European Psychologist, 1,* 200-205.

U.S. Department of Health and Human Services (2002). *Trends in the well-being of America's Children and Youth.* (http://aspe.hhs.gov/hsp/02trends/index.htm).

Vaillant, G. E. (1971). Theoretical hierarchy of adaptive ego mechanisms. *Archives of General Psychiatry, 24,* 107-118.

Vallacher, R. R., Nowak, A., Froelich, M., & Rockloff, M. (2002). The dynamics of self-evaluation. *Personality and Social Psychology Review, 6,* 370-379.

Vallacher, R. R., Read, S. J., & Nowak, A. (2002). The dynamical perspective in personality and social psychology. *Personality and Social Psychology Review, 6,* 264-273.

Vallacher, R. R., & Wegner, D. M. (1987). What do people think they're doing? Action identification and human behavior. *Psychological Review, 94,* 3-15.

Vallacher, R. R. & Wegner, D. M. (1989). Levels of personal agency: Individual variation in action identification. *Journal of Personality and Social Psychology, 57,* 660-671.

Van den Boom, D. C. (1995). Do first-year intervention effects endure? Follow-up during toddlerhood of a sample of Dutch irritable infants. Child Development, 66, 1798-1816.

Van Lieshout, C. F. M. (2000). Lifespan personality development: Self-organising goal-oriented agents and developmental outcome. International Journal of Behavioral Development, 24, 276-288.

Vandeputte, D. D., Kemper, S., & Hummert, M. L. (1999). Social skills of older people: Conversations in same- and mixed-age dyads. *Discourse Processes, 27,* 1999. pp. 55-76.

Vanwesenbeeck, I., Bekker, M., & van Lenning, A. (1998). Gender attitudes, sexual meanings, and interactional patterns in heterosexual encounters among college students in the Netherlands. *Journal of Sex Research, 35,* 317-327.

Varendonck, J. (1921). The psychology of daydreams. New York: Macmillan.

Veenhoven, R. (1993). *Happiness in nations*. Rotterdam, Netherlands: Risbo.

Veroff, J. (1992). A scoring manual for the power motive. In C. P. Smith (Ed.), *Motivation and personality: Handbook of thematic content analysis (pp. 286-310)*. New York: Cambridge.

Vockell, E. L., Felker, D. W., & Miley, C. H. (1973). Birth order literature: 1967-1972. *Journal of Individual Psychology, 29,* 39-53.

Vogt, D. S., & Randall, C. C. (2005). Assessment of accurate self-knowledge. *Journal of Personality Assessment, 84,* 239-251.

Von Bertalanffy, L. (1975a). Theoretical models in biology. In E. Taschdjian (Ed.). *Perspectives on general systems theory* (pp. 103-114). New York: George Braziller.

Von Bertalanffy, L. (1975b). A biological world view. In E. Taschdjian (Ed.). *Perspectives on general systems theory* (pp. 115-126). New York: George Braziller.

Von Bertalanffy, L. (1975c). New patterns of biological and medical thought. In E. Taschdjian (Ed.). *Perspectives on general systems theory* (pp. 40-52). New York: George Braziller.

Von Hoof, A. (1999). The identity status field re-reviewed: An update of unresolved and neglected issues with a view on some alternative approaches. *Developmental Review, 19,* 497-556.

Von Knorring, L; Moernstad, H.; Forsgren, L. (1986). Saliva secretion rate and saliva composition in relation to extraversion. *Personality & Individual Differences, 7,.* 33-38.

Wagner, R. K. (1987). Tacit knowledge in everyday intelligent behavior. *Journal of Personality and Social Psychology, 52,* 1236-1247.

Wagner, R. K. (2000). Practical intelligence. In R. J. Sternberg (Ed.) *Handbook of intelligence* (pp. 380-395). Cambridge, UK: Cambridge University Press.

Wagner, R. K., & Sternberg, R. J. (1985). Practical intelligence in real-world pursuits: The role of tacit knowledge. *Journal of Personality and Social Psychology, 49,* 436-458.

Wallace, K. A.; Bisconti, T. L., Bergeman, C. S (2001). The mediational effect of hardiness on social support and optimal outcomes in later life. Basic & Applied Social Psychology, 23, 267-279.

Wallach, M., & Kogan, N. (1965). *Modes of thinking in young children*. New York: Holt, Rinehart, & Wilson.

Wallechinsky, D., & Wallace, A. (1995). *The book of lists: The '90's edition*. Boston: Little, Brown and Company.

Waller, N. G., Putnam, F. W., & Carlson, E. B. (1996). Types of dissociation and dissociative types: A taxometric analysis of dissociative experiences. *Psychological Methods, 1,* 300-321.

Wampold, B. E., Minami, T., Baskin, T. W., & Tierney, S. C. (2002). A meta- (re)analysis of the effects of cognitive therapy versus "other therapies" for depression. *Journal of Affective Disorders, 69,* 159-165.

Wanderer, J. J. (1987). Social factors in judges' rankings of competitors in figure skating championships. *Journal of Sport Behavior, 10,* 93-102.

Wang, A. Y. (1997). Making implicit personality theories explicit: A classroom demonstration. *Teaching of Psychology, 24,* 258-261.

Wang, Q., & Leichtman, M. D. (2000). Same beginnings, different stories: A comparison of American and Chinese children's narratives. *Child Development, 71,* 1329-1346.

Wang, Q., Leichtman, M. D., & Davies (2000). Sharing memories and telling stories: American and Chinese mothers and their 3-year-olds. *Memory, 8,* 159-177.

Ward, M. J., Lee, S. S., & Lipper, E. G. (2000). Failure-to-thrive is associated with disorganized infant-mother attachment and unresolved maternal attachment. *Infant Mental Health Journal, 2,* 428-442.

Waterman, A. S. (1999). Identity, the identity statuses, and identity status development: A contemporary statement. *Developmental Review, 19,* 591-621.

Watkins, C. E. (1992). Adlerian-oriented early memory research: What does it tell us? *Journal of Personality Assessment, 59,* 248-263.

Watson, D. (2002). Positive affectivity: The disposition to experience pleasurable emotional states. In C. R. Snyder & S. J. Lopez (Ed.). *Handbook of Positive Psychology (pp. 106-119)*. Oxford: Oxford University Press.

Watson, D., & Tellegen, A. (1985). Toward a consensual structure of mood. *Psychological Bulletin, 98,* 219-235.

Watson, D., Wiese, D., Vaidya, J., & Tellegen, A. (1999). The two general activation systems of affect: Structural findings, evolutionary considerations, and psychological evidence. *Journal of Personality and Social Psychology, 76,* 820-838.

Watts, B. L. (1982). Individual differences in circadian activity rhythms and their effects on roommate relationships. *Journal of Personality, 50,* 374-384.

Watzlawick, P., Beavin, J. H., Jackson, D. D. (1967). *Pragmatics of human communication.* New York: W. W. Norton, Inc.

Wechsler, D. (1950). Cognitive, conative, and non-intellective intelligence. American Psychologist, 5, 78-83.

Wechsler, D (1958). The measurement and appraisal of adult intelligence (4th ed.). Baltimore, MD: Williams & Wilkins.

Wechsler, D. (1975). Intelligence defined and undefined: a relativistic appraisal. *American Psychologist, 30,* 135-139.

Wegner, D. (1989). *White bears and other unwanted thoughts.* New York: Viking.

Wegner, D. M. (2002). *The illusion of conscious will.* Cambridge, MA: MIT Press.

Wegner, D. M. & Pennebaker, J. W. (1993). Changing our minds: An introduction to mental control. In D. M. Wegner & J. W. Pennebaker (Eds.). *Handbook of mental control (pp. 1-12).* Englewood Cliffs, NJ: Prentice-Hall.

Wegner, D. M., Shortt, J. W., Blake, A. W., & Page, M. S. (1990). The suppression of exciting thoughts. *Journal of Personality and Social Psychology, 58,* 409-418.

Wegner, D. M., & Vallacher, R. R. (1977). *Implicit psychology: An introduction to social cognition.* New York: Oxford University Press.

Wegner, D. M. & Wheatley, T. (1999). Apparent mental causation. *American Psychologist, 54,* 480-492.

Wehr, T. A., & Goodwin, F. K. (1981). Biological rhythms and psychiatry. In S. Arieti & H. K. Brodie (Eds.), *American handbook of psychiatry: Advances and new directions (Vol. 7.)* New York: Basic Books.

Weinberger, D. A. (1995). The construct validity of the repressive coping style. In J. L. Singer (Ed); Repression and dissociation: Implications for personality theory, psychopathology, and health (pp. 337-386).

Weinberger, D. A., Schwartz, G. E., & Davidson, R. J. (1979). Low-anxious, high-anxious, and repressive coping styles: Psychometric patterns and behavioral and physiological responses to stress. *Journal of Abnormal Psychology, 88,* 369-380.

Weinberger, D. A., & Davidson, M. N. (1994). Styles of inhibiting emotional expression: Distinguishing repressive coping from impression management. Journal of Personality, 62, 587-613.

Weinberger, D. A. (1998). Defenses, personality structure, and development: integrating psychodynamic theory into a typological approach to personality. Journal of Personality, 66, 1061-1080.

Weiner, B., & Graham, S. (1999). Attribution in personality psychology. In L. A. Pervin, & O. P. John (Eds). *Handbook of personality: Theory and research (605-628).* New York: The Guilford Press.

Weiner, I. B. (1975). *Principles of psychotherapy.* New York: John Wiley & Sons.

Weinstein, E., & Deutschberger, P. (1963). Some dimensions of altercasting. *Sociometry, 26,* 545-566.

Weiskrantz, L. (1986). *Blindsight: A case study and implications.* Oxford, England: Oxford University Press.

Weiss, L. H., & Schwartz, J. C. (1996). The relationship between parenting types and older adolescents' personality, academic achievement, adjustment, and substance abuse. *Child Development, 67,* 2101-2114.

Weissman, A. E., & Ricks, D F. (1966). *Mood and personality.* New York: Holt, Rinehart, & Winston, Inc.

Weissman, M. & Olfson, M. (1995). Depression in women: Implications for health care research. *Science, 269,* 799-801.

Weitzenhoffer, A M. & Hilgard, E. R. (1959). *Stanford Hypnotic Susceptibility Scale, Form C.* Palo Alto, CA: Consulting Psychologists Press.

Weitzenhoffer, A M. & Hilgard, E. R. (1962). *Stanford Hypnotic Susceptibility Scale, Form C.* Palo Alto, CA: Consulting Psychologists Press.

Wenzlaff, R. M., Rude, S. S., & West, L. M. (2002). Cognitive vulnerability to depression: The role of thought suppression and attitude certainty. Cognition and Emotion, 16, 533-548.

Werner, E. E. & Smith, R. S.(2001). *Journeys from childhood to midlife: Risk, resilience, and recovery.* Ithica, NY: Cornell University Press.

Westen, D. (1990). Psychoanalytic approaches to personality. In L. Pervin (ed.). *Handbook of Personality Theory and Research (21-65).* New York: Guilford.

Westen, D. (1991). Social cognition and object relations. Psychological Bulletin, 109, 429-455.

Westen, D. (1992). The cognitive self and the psychoanalytic self: Can we put our selves together? *Psychological Inquiry, 3,* 1-13.

Westen, D. (1998). The scientific legacy of Sigmund Freud: Toward a psychodynamically informed psychological science. *Psychological Bulletin, 124,* 333-371.

Westen, D., & Morrison, K. (2001). A multidimensional meta-analysis of treatments for depression, panic, and generalized anxiety disorder: An empirical examination of the status of empirically supported therapies. *Journal of Consulting and Clinical Psychology, 69,* 875-899.

White, G. L. (1980). Physical attractiveness and courtship progress. *Journal of Personality and Social Psychology, 39,* 660-668.

Whitehead (1929/1978). *Process and reality.* New York: Free Press.

Whyte, W. F. (1946). When workers and customers meet. (Chapter VII) In. W. F. Whyte (Ed.). *Industry and society.* New York: McGraw Hill.

Wicker, F. W., Brown, G., Weihe, J. A., Hagen, A. S., & Reed, J. L. (1993). On reconsidering Maslow: An examination of the deprivation/domination proposition. *Journal of Research in Personality, 27,* 118-133.

Wickett, J. C., Vernon, P. A., & Lee, D. H. (2000). Relationships between factors of intelligence and brain volume. *Personality and Individual Differences, 29,* 1095-1122.

Wiebe, D. J., & Smith, T. W. (1997). Personality and health: Progress and problems in psychosomatics. In R. Hogan, J. Johnson, & S. Briggs (1997). *Handbook of personality psychology.* New York: Academic Press.

Wiedeman, G. H. (1972). Comments on the structural theory of personality. *International Journal of Psychoanalysis, 53,* 307-314.

Wiener, N. *Cybernetics.* New York; John Wiley, 1948.

Wiggins, J. S. (1997). Circumnavigating Dodge Morgan's interpersonal style. *Journal of Persoanlity, 65,* 1069-1086.

Williams, B. (1993). Moral luck. In D. Statman (Ed.). *Moral luck (pp. 35-55).* Albany, NY: State University of New York Press.

Williams, G. C., Freedman, Z., & Deci, E. L. (1998). Supporting autonomy to motivate patients with diabetes for glucose control. *Diabetes Care, 21,* 1644-1651.

Williams, G. C., Grow, V. M., Freedman, Z., Ryan, R. M., & Deci, E. L. (1996). Motivational predictors of weight loss and weight-loss maintenance. *Journal of Personality and Social Psychology, 70,* 115-126.

Williams, J. E., & Best, D. L. (1982). Measuring sex stereotypes: A thirty-nation study. Beverly Hill, CA: Sage Publications.

Wilbur, K. (1999). The spectrum of consciousness. In K. Wilbur (Ed.), *The collected works of Ken Wilbur (Vol. 1, pp. 33-414).* Boston: Shambhala.

Wilson, D. S., Near, D., & Miller, R. R. (1966). Machiavellianism: A synthesis of the evolutionary and psychological literatures. *Psychological Bulletin, 119,* 285-299.

Wilson, E. (2001). *The keep.* Iowa City: University of Iowa Press, 2001.

Wilson, E. H. (1995). The genesis of a humanist manifesto. Amherst, NY: Humanist Press.

Wilson, T. D. & Dunn, E. W. (2004). Self-knowledge: Its limits, value and potential for improvement. *Annual Review of Psychology, 55,* 493-518.

Winter, D. G. (1996). *Personality: Analysis and interpretation of lives.* New York: The McGraw-Hill Companies.

Winter, D.G. (1991). Measuring personality at a distance: Development of an integrated system for scoring motives in running text. *Perspectives in Personality (Vol. 3) (pp. 59-89).* Jessica Kingsley Publishers, Ltd.

Winter, D.G. (1992a). Content analysis of archival materials, personal documents, and everyday verbal materials. In C. P. Smith (Ed.), *Motivation and personality: Handbook of thematic content analysis (pp. 110-125).* New York: Cambridge.

Winter, D.G. (1992b). Power motivation revisted. In C. P. Smith (Ed.), *Motivation and personality: Handbook of thematic content analysis (pp. 301-310).* New York: Cambridge.

Winter, D.G. (1992c). A revised scoring system for the power motive. In C. P. Smith (Ed.), *Motivation and personality: Handbook of thematic content analysis (pp. 311-324).* New York: Cambridge.

Winter, D. G. (2005). Things I've learned about personality from studying political leaders at a distance. *Journal of Personality, 73,* 557-584.

Winter, D. G., & Barenbaum, N. B. (1999). History of modern personality theory and research. In Pervin, L. A., & John, O. P. (Eds.), *Handbook of Personality: Theory and Research (2nd Edition) (pp. 3-27).* New York: Guilford Press.

Winter, D. G., & Carlson, L. (1988). Using motive scores in the psychobiographical study of an individual: The case of Richard Nixon. *Journal of Personality, 56,* 75-103.

Winter, D. G., John, O. P., Stewart, A. J., Klohnen, E. C., Duncan, L. E. (1998). Traits and motives: Toward an integration of two traditions in personality research. *Psychological Review, 105,* 230-250.

Wood, W., Tam, L., & Witt, M. G. (2005). Changing circumstances, disrupting habits. *Journal of Personality and Social Psychology, 88,* 918-933.

Woodhouse, M. B. (1984). *A preface to philosophy (3rd Edition).* Belmont, CA: Wadsworth Publishing.

Woody, E. Z. (1997). Have the hypnotic susceptibility scales outlived their usefulness? *International Journal of Clinical and Experimental Hypnosis, 45,* 226-238.

Wu, K., Lindsted, K.D., & Lee, J.W. (2005). Blood type and the five factors of personality in Asia. Personality & Individual Differences, 38, 797-808.

Wundt, W. (1897). *Outlines of psychology* (C.H. Judd, Trans.). Leipzig: Wilhelm Englemann. (Original work published 1896).

Wylie, R. (1974). *The self-concept.* Lincoln, NE: University of Nebraska Press.

Xu, X., Mellor, D., Xu, Y. Duan, L. (2014). An update of Murrayan needs: A pilot study among American college students. Journal of Humanistic Psychology, Vol 54(1), Jan, 2014. pp. 45-65.

Yik, M. S. M., Russell, J. A.; Barrett, L. F. (1999). Structure of self-reported current affect: Integration and beyond. *Journal of Personality and Social Psychology, 77,* 600-619.

Zeidner, M., & Mathews, G. (2000). Intelligence and personality. In R. J. Sternberg (Ed.). *Handbook of intelligence (pp. 581-610).* Cambridge, UK: Cambridge University Press.

Zevon, M. A., & Tellegen, A. (1982). The structure of mood change: An idiographic/nomothetic analysis. *Journal of Personality and Social Psychology, 43,* 111-122.

Zuckerman, M. (1991). *Psychobiology of personality.* Cambridge: England: Cambridge University Press.